Lecture Notes in Computer Science 8913

Commenced Publication in 1973
Founding and Former Series Editors:
Gerhard Goos, Juris Hartmanis, and Jan van Leeuwen

Rachid Guerraoui   Paolo Romano (Eds.)

Transactional Memory

Foundations, Algorithms, Tools, and Applications

COST Action Euro-TM IC1001

 Springer

Volume Editors

Rachid Guerraoui
EPFL, Lausanne, Switzerland
E-mail: rachid.guerraoui@epfl.ch

Paolo Romano
INESC-ID, Lisboa, Portugal
E-mail: romano@inesc-id.pt

ISSN 0302-9743   e-ISSN 1611-3349
ISBN 978-3-319-14719-2   e-ISBN 978-3-319-14720-8
DOI 10.1007/978-3-319-14720-8
Springer Cham Heidelberg New York Dordrecht London

Library of Congress Control Number: 2014958340

LNCS Sublibrary: SL 1 – Theoretical Computer Science and General Issues

Acknowledgments: Euro-TM is an Action supported by the COST Association that
has gathered researchers from 17 European countries and over 40 institutions. All the
authors of the book have actively participated in the activities of Euro-TM.
The editors are grateful to the COST programme for supporting the Euro-TM initia-
tive (IC1001 - Transactional Memories: Foundations, Algorithms, Tools, and Applications), a forum that was fundamental for the preparation of this book. The editors
also express their gratitude to all authors, for their enthusiastic and meticulous cooperation in the preparation of this book. A special thank goes to Maria Couceiro for
her valuable support with the editing of the book.
This publication is supported by COST.

Typesetting: Camera-ready by author, data conversion by Scientific Publishing Services, Chennai, India

Printed on acid-free paper

Springer is part of Springer Science+Business Media (www.springer.com)

COST Description

COST - European Cooperation in Science and Technology is an intergovernmental framework aimed at facilitating the collaboration and networking of scientists and researchers at European level. It was established in 1971 by 19 member countries and currently includes 35 member countries across Europe, and Israel as a cooperating state.

COST funds pan-European, bottom-up networks of scientists and researchers across all science and technology fields. These networks, called 'COST Actions', promote international coordination of nationally-funded research.

By fostering the networking of researchers at an international level, COST enables break-through scientific developments leading to new concepts and products, thereby contributing to strengthening Europe's research and innovation capacities.

COST's mission focuses in particular on:

- Building capacity by connecting high quality scientific communities throughout Europe and worldwide;
- Providing networking opportunities for early career investigators;
- Increasing the impact of research on policy makers, regulatory bodies and national decision makers as well as the private sector.

Through its inclusiveness policy, COST supports the integration of research communities in less research-intensive countries across Europe, leverages national research investments and addresses societal issues.

Over 45 000 European scientists benefit from their involvement in COST Actions on a yearly basis. This allows the pooling of national research funding and helps countries research communities achieve common goals.

As a precursor of advanced multidisciplinary research, COST anticipates and complements the activities of EU Framework Programmes, constituting a "bridge" towards the scientific communities of emerging countries.

Traditionally, COST draws its budget for networking activities from successive EU RTD Framework Programmes.

COST Association Legal Notice

COST is supported by the EU
Framework Programme
Horizon 2020

To waves and wind,
to the marvel and the fury of elements,
to the search for perfection.

Preface

Parallel programming (PP) used to be an area once confined to a few niches, such as scientific and high-performance computing applications. However, with the proliferation of multicore processors, and the emergence of new, inherently parallel and distributed deployment platforms, such as those provided by cloud computing, parallel programming has definitely become a mainstream concern.

Unfortunately, writing scalable parallel programs using traditional lock-based synchronization primitives is well known to be a hard, time-consuming, and error-prone task, mastered by a minority of programmers only. Thus, to bring parallel programming into the mainstream of software development, we are in urgent need of better programming models.

Building on the abstraction of atomic transactions, and freeing programmers from the complexity of conventional synchronization schemes, transactional memories (TMs) promise to respond exactly to this need, simplifying the development and verification of concurrent programs, enhancing code reliability, and boosting productivity.

Over the last decade, TM has been subject to intense research in computer science and engineering, with hundreds of papers published in prestigious international conferences and journals addressing a wide range of complementary aspects including hardware and operating systems (OSs) support, language integration, as well as algorithms and theoretical foundations. Moreover, even if TMs were first introduced in the context of shared-memory multiprocessors, the abstraction of distributed transactional memory (DTM) has been garnering growing interest of late in the area of cloud computing, due to two main reasons. On the one hand, the increasing reliance of cloud computing platforms on in-memory data management techniques, fostered by the need for maximizing efficiency and supporting real-time data processing of ever-growing volumes of data. On the other hand, the inherent complexity of building large-scale applications on top of the weakly consistent models embraced by the first generation of large-scale NoSQL data stores, which has motivated intensive research on mechanisms aimed to enforce strong consistency semantics in large-scale distributed platforms.

The growing interest in TMs has not only been confined to academic environments. On the industrial side, some of the major players of the software and hardware markets have been up-front in the research and development of prototypal products providing support for TMs. The maturing of research in the field of TM has recently led to hardware TM implementations on several mainstream commercial microprocessors and to the integration of TM support for the world's leading open source compiler.

In such a vast inter-disciplinary domain, the Euro-TM COST Action (IC1001) has served as a catalyzer and a bridge for the various research communities looking at disparate, yet subtly interconnected, aspects of TM. Starting in February 2011 and ending in February 2015, Euro-TM established a Pan-European research network that brought together more than 250 researchers from 17 European countries. Over the last 4 years Euro-TM helped shape the research agenda in the TM area and ensured timely dissemination of research results via thematic workshops; fostered joint publications and research projects; showcased relevant research results in the area in industrial conferences; and educated early-stage researchers via doctoral schools hosting renowned specialists both from industry and academy.

This book emerged from the idea to have Euro-TM experts compile recent results in the TM area in a single and consistent volume. Contributions have been carefully selected and revised to provide a broad coverage of several fundamental issues associated with the design and implementation of TM systems, including their theoretical underpinnings and algorithmic foundations, programming language integration and verification tools, hardware supports, distributed TMs, self-tuning mechanisms, as well as lessons learnt from building complex TM-based applications.

Organization. The book is organized in four sections. The four chapters encompassed by Section 1 address theoretical foundations of TM systems, focusing not only on the definition of safety (Chaps. 1 and 3) and liveness (Chap. 2) guarantees in TM, but also on the problem of designing disjoint-access (i.e., inherently scalable) TM implementations (Chap. 4).

Section 2 covers algorithmic aspects associated with the design of TM systems. First, it illustrates the main algorithmic alternatives in the design space of software (Chap. 5) and hardware (Chap. 6) implementations of TM. Next, it addresses the design and implementation of multi-version TM (Chaps. 7 and 8). Finally, it surveys existing techniques in the literature on TM support for parallel nesting (Chap. 9).

Section 3 deals with the issue of mitigating or even avoiding contention in TM systems, by leveraging on various policies for contention management and transaction scheduling (Chap. 10), as well as techniques that attempt to leverage on semantic knowledge on the code to be executed transactionally (Chap. 11).

Section 4 investigates aspects related to TM and reliability from a twofold perspective: how to leverage on the TM abstraction to simplify exception handling in programming languages (Chap. 12) and mask exceptions at the hardware level (Chap. 13); how to ensure the correctness of TM-based applications by means of automatic verification tools (Chap. 14).

Section 5 addresses the design of DTM platforms. Chapter 15 first provides background on algorithms for replication of transactional systems, by focusing on fully replicated systems (in which each node maintains a full copy of the system state). Chapter 16 considers partially replicated TM systems, analyzing trade-offs between the data-flow and control-flow paradigms. The section is concluded by a survey of existing protocols for DTM systems that adopt the data-flow paradigm.

Finally, Section 6 covers the development of TM-based applications, and on their self-tuning. In more detail, Chap. 17 reports the lessons learnt while developing complex TM-based applications. Chapters 18 and 19 focus instead on self-tuning techniques for TM systems. The former addresses the issue of dynamically adapting the degree of parallelism in shared-memory TM systems. The latter discusses the key challenges associated with the design of self-tuning mechanisms in DTM platforms, surveying existing work in this area.

In summary, the present book provides a unique collection of tutorials, which will allow graduate students in computer science to get familiar with state-of-the-art research in TM and its applications, typically along their road to doctoral studies.

It is noteworthy that this book has only been made possible thanks to the dedication and expertise of our contributing authors, many of whom are from the COST Action Euro-TM. Their effort resulted in a book that is an invaluable tool for researchers active in this emerging domain.

October 2014

Rachid Guerraoui
Paolo Romano

This book may be cited as
COST Action IC1001 (Euro-TM) - "Transactional Memory: Foundations, Algorithms, Tools, and Applications", Editors Rachid Guerraoui and Paolo Romano, ISBN 978-3-319-14719-2, 2015

Table of Contents

Theoretical Foundations

Consistency for Transactional Memory Computing 3
   Panagiota Fatourou, Dmytro Dziuma, and Eleni Kanellou

Liveness in Transactional Memory 32
   Victor Bushkov and Rachid Guerraoui

Safety and Deferred Update in Transactional Memory 50
   Hagit Attiya, Sandeep Hans, Petr Kuznetsov, and Srivatsan Ravi

Disjoint-Access Parallelism in Software Transactional Memory 72
   Hagit Attiya and Panagiota Fatourou

Algorithms

Algorithmic Techniques in STM Design 101
   *Panagiota Fatourou, Mykhailo Iaremko, Eleni Kanellou, and
   Eleftherios Kosmas*

Conflict Detection in Hardware Transactional Memory 127
   *Ricardo Quislant, Eladio Gutierrez, Emilio L. Zapata,
   and Oscar Plata*

Multi-versioning in Transactional Memory 150
   Idit Keidar and Dmitri Perelman

Framework Support for the Efficient Implementation of Multi-version
Algorithms 166
   Ricardo J. Dias, Tiago M. Vale, and João M. Lourenço

Nested Parallelism in Transactional Memory 192
   Ricardo Filipe and João Barreto

Contention Management and Scheduling

Scheduling-Based Contention Management Techniques for Transactional
Memory 213
   Danny Hendler and Adi Suissa-Peleg

Proactive Contention Avoidance 228
   Hillel Avni, Shlomi Dolev, and Eleftherios Kosmas

Transactional Memory and Reliability

Safe Exception Handling with Transactional Memory 245
    Pascal Felber, Christof Fetzer, Vincent Gramoli, Derin Harmanci,
    and Martin Nowack

Transactional Memory for Reliability 268
    Gulay Yalcin and Osman Unsal

Verification Tools for Transactional Programs...................... 283
    Adrian Cristal, Burcu Kulahcioglu Ozkan, Ernie Cohen,
    Gokcen Kestor, Ismail Kuru, Osman Unsal, Serdar Tasiran,
    Suha Orhun Mutluergil, and Tayfun Elmas

Distributed Transactional Memory

Introduction to Transactional Replication 309
    Tadeusz Kobus, Maciej Kokociński, and Paweł T. Wojciechowski

Transaction Execution Models in Partially Replicated Transactional
Memory: The Case for Data-Flow and Control-Flow 341
    Roberto Palmieri, Sebastiano Peluso, and Binoy Ravindran

Directory Protocols for Distributed Transactional Memory 367
    Hagit Attiya, Vincent Gramoli, and Alessia Milani

Applications and Self-tuning

Tuning the Level of Concurrency in Software Transactional Memory:
An Overview of Recent Analytical, Machine Learning and Mixed
Approaches 395
    Diego Rughetti, Pierangelo Di Sanzo, Alessandro Pellegrini,
    Bruno Ciciani, and Francesco Quaglia

Self-tuning in Distributed Transactional Memory..................... 418
    Maria Couceiro, Diego Didona, Luís Rodrigues, and Paolo Romano

Case Study: Using Transactions in Memcached 449
    Michael Spear, Wenjia Ruan, Yujie Liu, and Trilok Vyas

Author Index 469

Theoretical Foundations

Consistency for Transactional Memory Computing

Dmytro Dziuma[2], Panagiota Fatourou[1], and Eleni Kanellou[3]

[1] FORTH ICS & University of Crete, Heraklion (Crete), Greece
faturu@csd.uoc.gr
[2] FORTH ICS, Heraklion (Crete), Greece
dixond@acm.lviv.ua
[3] FORTH ICS, Heraklion (Crete), Greece & University of Rennes 1, Rennes, France
kanellou@ics.forth.gr

Abstract. This chapter provides *formal definitions* for a comprehensive collection of consistency conditions for transactional memory (TM) computing. We express all conditions in a uniform way using a formal framework that we present. For each of the conditions, we provide two versions: one that allows a transaction T to read the value of a data item written by another transaction T' that can be live and not yet commit-pending provided that T' will eventually commit, and a version which allows transactions to read values written only by transactions that have either committed before T starts or are commit-pending. Deriving the first version for a consistency condition was not an easy task but it has the benefit that this version is weaker than the second one and so it results in a wider universe of algorithms which there is no reason to exclude from being considered correct. The formalism for the presented consistency conditions is not based on any unrealistic assumptions, such as that transactional operations are executed atomically or that write operations write distinct values for data items. Making such assumptions facilitates the task of formally expressing the consistency conditions significantly, but results in formal presentations of them that are unrealistic, i.e. that cannot be used to characterize the correctness of most of the executions produced by any reasonable TM algorithm.

1 Introduction

Software Transactional memory (or STM for short) [21,35] is a promising programming paradigm that aims at simplifying parallel programming by using the notion of a transaction. A *transaction* executes a piece of code containing accesses to pieces of data, known as *data items*, which are accessed simultaneously by several threads in a concurrent setting. A transaction may either *commit* and then its updates take effect or *abort* and then its updates are discarded. By using transactions, the naive programmer needs only enhance its sequential code with invocations of special routines (which we call *transactional operations*, or *t-operations* for short) to read or write data items. When a transaction executes all its reads and writes on data items, it tries to commit. From that point on and until its completion, the transaction is *commit-pending*. Once a transaction starts and before its completion, it is *live*.

The STM algorithm provides implementations for t-operations (from base objects) so that all synchronization problems that may arise during the concurrent execution of

R. Guerraoui and P. Romano (Eds.): Transactional Memory, LNCS 8913, pp. 3–31, 2015.

transactions are addressed. The implementation details of the STM algorithm are hidden from the naive programmer whose programming task is therefore highly simplified. STM has been given special attention in the last ten years with hundreds of papers addressing different problems arising in STM computing (see e.g. [20,19] for books addressing different aspects of STM computing).

One of the most fundamental problems of STM computing is to define when an STM algorithm is correct. Most STM consistency conditions [4,18,19,24,15,9,10] originate from existing shared memory or database consistency models. However, in contrast to what happens in shared memory models where correctness has been defined in the granularity of single operations on shared objects, correctness in STM computing is defined in terms of *transactions*, each of which may invoke more than one read or write t-operations on data items. Comparing now to database transactions, the main difficulty when presenting consistency conditions for STM computing is that the execution of a t-operation has duration and is usually overlapping with the execution of other t-operations, whereas in database transactions reads and writes are considered to be atomic. For these reasons, existing consistency conditions for these two settings (shared memory and database concurrent transactions) cannot be applied verbatim to STM algorithms. Formalizing consistency conditions for STM computing requires more effort.

This chapter presents a comprehensive collection of consistency conditions for STM computing. All conditions are expressed in a uniform way using a formal framework that we present in Section 2. This chapter can therefore serve as a survey of *consistency conditions* for STM computing. However, it aspires to be more than this.

For all known STM consistency conditions we provide a new version, called *eager*, in which a transaction T is allowed to read the value of a data item written by another transaction T' that can be live and not yet commit-pending provided that T' will eventually commit (or that T' will commit if T commits). Most STM consistency conditions [4,9,10,18,19,24] presented thus far did not allow a transaction to read values that have been written by transactions that are neither committed nor commit-pending; we call this version of a consistency condition *deferred-update* (or *du* for short). The eager version of a consistency condition is weaker than its deferred-update version, thus resulting in a wider universe of algorithms which should not be excluded from being considered correct. For instance, in a database system, a transaction T may perform a *dirty read*, i.e. T may read a value v for a data item x written by a transaction T' which is still live (and not commit-pending) when T's read of x completes. To ensure the well-known consistency condition from databases, called recoverability [8], one technique described in the database literature [40], is to employ deferred commits and enforce cascading aborts whenever necessary. This is usually achieved by providing sufficient bookkeeping to determine essential orderings of commit and abort events that need to be enforced. In the aforementioned scenario, T has to defer its commit until T' completes its execution, and it necessarily aborts in case T' aborts. If an STM algorithm worked in a similar way, there would be no reason for executions of the algorithm not to be considered correct. However, current consistency conditions, as they are formally expressed, exclude such executions from the set of executions they allow. The eager version of a consistency condition we present here solves this problem.

In [37], Siek and Wojciechowski discuss why well-known STM consistency conditions, like opacity [18], serializability [29], virtual world consistency [24], and the TMS family [15] fail to support early release [30,36]. Early release is a technique introduced for optimizing performance; it allows a transaction to read a value for a data item written by another live transaction that is not commit-pending. Siek and Wojciechowski also discuss in [37] how one can design consistency conditions that support early release. They then use the proposed conditions to characterize the correctness of a distributed STM system they present in [36]. The way the eager versions of the consistency conditions are formulated in this chapter is flexible enough to support early release.

It is remarkable that deriving the eager version of consistency conditions was not an easy task so we consider their presentation as a significant contribution of this chapter. For the derivation of the presented consistency conditions, we do not make any restrictive assumptions, such as that t-operations are executed atomically or that writes write distinct values for data items. Making such assumptions is unrealistically restrictive since all STM algorithms produce executions that do not satisfy these assumptions. Thus, a consistency condition that has been expressed making such an assumption cannot be used to characterize such executions, and thus fail to also characterize whether the STM algorithm itself satisfies the condition. We remark that making such assumptions significantly facilitates the task of formally expressing a consistency condition but the formal presentation of the condition that results is very restrictive since it cannot be used to characterize the correctness of most of the executions produced by any reasonable STM algorithm.

Among the consistency conditions met in STM computing papers are strict serializability [29], serializability [29], opacity [18,19], virtual world consistency [24], TMS1 [15] (and TMS2 [15]), and snapshot isolation [3,13,32,9,10]. Weaker consistency conditions like processor consistency [10], causal serializability [9,10] and weak consistency [10] have also been considered in the STM context when proving impossibility results.

Strict serializability, as well as serializability, are usually presented in an informal way in STM papers which cite the original paper [29] where these conditions have first appeared in the context of database research. Thus, the differences that exist between database and STM transactions have been neglected in STM research. We present formal definitions of these consistency conditions here. Additional consistency conditions originating from the database research are presented in [4]. To present their formalism, the authors of [4] make the restrictive assumption that t-operations are atomic. The presentation of most of the other consistency conditions (e.g. opacity [18,19], virtual world consistency [24], snapshot isolation [3,13,32,9,10] and weaker variants of them [9,10]) is based on the assumption that a read for a data item by a transaction T can read a value written by either a transaction that has committed or is commit-pending when T starts its execution. Finally, the definition of virtual world consistency [24] is based on the assumption that each instance of WRITE writes a distinct value for the data item it accesses (or that the t-operations are executed atomically).

In this chapter, we do not cope with transactions whose code is determined at run time (i.e. after the beginning of the execution of the transaction). For instance, such a transaction could be produced on a web environment by deciding the next t-operations to be invoked by the transaction while executing it. We also do not discuss consistency issues that arise when data items are accessed not only by transactions but also outside the transactional scope (as it is e.g. the case for systems that support *privatization* [1,26,34,25,27,38]).

The rest of this chapter is organized as follows. Section 2 presents the formal framework which is employed in Section 3 to express the studied consistency conditions. Table 1 shows the relationships between consistency conditions.

2   Model

2.1   System

The system is asynchronous with a set of threads executed in it. Each thread is sequential (i.e. it executes a single sequential program) but different threads can be executed concurrently. Threads communicate via shared memory, i.e. by accessing simple shared objects, called base objects, usually provided by the hardware. Formally, a *base object* has a state and supports a set of operations, called *primitives*, to read or update its state. Base objects are usually as simple as read/write or CAS objects. A read/write object O stores a value from some set and supports two atomic primitives read and write; read(O) returns the current value of object O without changing it, and write(O,v) writes the value v into O and returns an acknowledgement. A CAS object O stores a value and supports, in addition to read, the atomic primitive CAS(O,v',v) which checks whether the value of O is v' and, if so, it sets the value of O to v and returns true, otherwise, it returns false and the value of O remains unchanged.

We model each thread as a state machine. A *configuration* describes the system at some point in time, so it provides information about the state of threads and the state of base objects. In an *initial configuration*, threads and base objects are in initial states. A *step* of a thread consists of applying a single primitive on some base object, the response to that primitive, and zero or more local computation performed by the thread; local computation accesses only local variables of the thread, so it may cause the internal state of the thread to change but it does not change the state of any base object. As a step, we will also consider the invocation of a routine or the response to such an invocation; notice that a step of this kind (1) is either the first or the last when executing the routine (more steps may be needed after the invocation of the routine in order for it to respond), and (2) does not change the state of any base object. Each step is executed atomically. An *execution* α is an alternating sequence of configurations and steps starting with an initial configuration. An execution is *legal* if the sequence of steps performed by each thread follows the algorithm for that thread and, for each base object, the responses to the primitives performed on the base object are in accordance with its specification (and the state of the base object at the configuration that the primitive is applied).

2.2   STM Definitions

Transactions and t-Operations. A *transaction* is a piece of sequential code which accesses (reads or writes) pieces of data, called *data items*. A data item may be accessed by several threads simultaneously when a transaction is executed in a concurrent environment. Transactions call specific routines, called READ and WRITE, to read and update, respectively, data items. A transaction may *commit* and then all its updates to data items take effect, or *abort* and then all its updates are discarded.

An STM algorithm uses a collection of base objects to store the state of data items. It also provides an implementation, for each thread, for READ and WRITE (from the base objects). READ receives as argument the data item x to be accessed (and possibly the thread p invoking READ and the transaction T for which p invokes READ) and returns either a value v for x or a special value A_T which identifies that T has to abort. WRITE receives as arguments the data item x to be modified, a value v (and possibly the thread p invoking WRITE and the transaction T for which p invokes WRITE), and returns either an acknowledgment or A_T. The STM algorithm provides implementations for two additional routines, called COMMIT and ABORT, which are called to try to commit or to abort a transaction, respectively. When COMMIT is executed by some transaction T it returns either a special value C_T, which identifies that T has committed, or A_T. ABORT always returns A_T.

We refer to all these routines as *t-operations*. A t-operation starts its execution when the thread executing it issues an *invocation* for it; the t-operation completes its execution when the thread executing it receives a *response*. Thus, the execution of a t-operation op is not atomic, i.e. the thread executing it may perform a sequence of primitives on base objects in order to complete the execution of the t-operation. Moreover, the invocation and the response of op are considered as two separate steps (with each of them being atomic). The invocation and the response of a t-operation are referred to as *events*. We sometimes say that these events are caused by T.

Histories. A *history* is a finite sequence of events. Consider any history H. A transaction T (executed by a thread p) *is in* H or H *contains* T, if there are invocations and responses of t-operations in H issued (or received) by p for T. The *transaction subhistory* of H for T, denoted by $H|T$, is the subsequence of all events in H issued by p for T. We say that a response *res matches* an invocation *inv* of a t-operation op in some history H, if they are both by the same thread p, *res* follows *inv* in H, *res* is a response for op, and there is no other event by p between *inv* and *res* in H. A history H is said to be *well-formed* if, for each transaction T in H, $H|T$ is an alternating sequence of invocations and matching responses, starting with an invocation, such that:

- no events in $H|T$ follow C_T or A_T;
- if T' is any transaction in H executed by the same thread that executes T, either the last event of $H|T$ precedes in H the first event of $H|T'$ or the last event of $H|T'$ precedes in H the first event of $H|T$.

From now on we focus on well-formed histories. Assume that H is such a history. A t-operation is *complete* in H, if there is a response for it in H; otherwise, the t-operation is *pending*. Thus, in H, there are two events for every complete t-operation op, an invocation $inv(op)$ and a matching response $res(op)$; moreover, H contains only one event for each pending t-operation in it, namely its invocation. A transaction T is *committed* in H, if $H|T$ includes C_T; a transaction T is *aborted* in H, if $H|T$ includes A_T. A transaction is *complete* in H, if it is either committed or aborted in H, otherwise

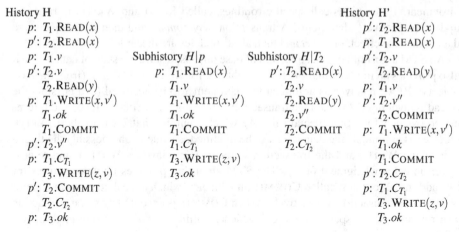

History H

    p: $T_1.\text{READ}(x)$
    p': $T_2.\text{READ}(x)$
    p: $T_1.v$
    p': $T_2.v$
    $T_2.\text{READ}(y)$
    p: $T_1.\text{WRITE}(x,v')$
    $T_1.ok$
    $T_1.\text{COMMIT}$
    p': $T_2.v''$
    p: $T_1.C_{T_1}$
    $T_3.\text{WRITE}(z,v)$
    p': $T_2.\text{COMMIT}$
    $T_2.C_{T_2}$
    p: $T_3.ok$

Subhistory $H|p$

    p: $T_1.\text{READ}(x)$
    $T_1.v$
    $T_1.\text{WRITE}(x,v')$
    $T_1.ok$
    $T_1.\text{COMMIT}$
    $T_1.C_{T_1}$
    $T_3.\text{WRITE}(z,v)$
    $T_3.ok$

Subhistory $H|T_2$

    p': $T_2.\text{READ}(x)$
    $T_2.v$
    $T_2.\text{READ}(y)$
    $T_2.v''$
    $T_2.\text{COMMIT}$
    $T_2.C_{T_2}$

History H'

    p': $T_2.\text{READ}(x)$
    p: $T_1.\text{READ}(x)$
    p': $T_2.v$
    $T_2.\text{READ}(y)$
    p: $T_1.v$
    p': $T_2.v''$
    $T_2.\text{COMMIT}$
    p: $T_1.\text{WRITE}(x,v')$
    $T_1.ok$
    $T_1.\text{COMMIT}$
    p': $T_2.C_{T_2}$
    p: $T_1.C_{T_1}$
    $T_3.\text{WRITE}(z,v)$
    $T_3.ok$

Fig. 1. Examples of histories: A history H, the subhistories $H|p$ and $H|T_2$ of H, and a history H', which is equivalent to H

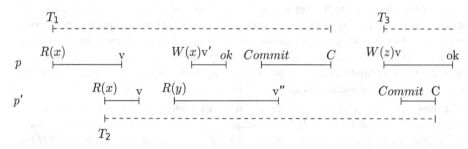

Fig. 2. A schematic representation of H presented in Figure 1. The horizontal axis represents time.

it is *live*. A transaction T is *commit-pending* in H if T is live in H and $H|T$ includes an invocation to COMMIT for T. If $H|T$ contains at least one invocation of WRITE, T is called an *update* transaction; otherwise, T is *read-only*. We denote by $comm(H)$ the subsequence of all events in H issued and received for committed transactions.

For each thread p, we denote by $H|p$ the subsequence of H containing all invocations and responses of t-operations issued or received by p. Two histories H and H' are *equivalent*, if for each thread p, $H|p = H'|p$. Roughly speaking, two histories H and H' are equivalent if they contain the same set of transactions, and each t-operation invoked in H is also invoked in H' and receives the same response in both H and H'. This means that the order of invocation and response events may be different in H' compared to H, although the orders of invocation and response events are the same in $H|p$ and $H'|p$ for each thread p. An example of history equivalence is presented in Figure 1. It shows H as a sequence of invocation and response events, and presents H', which is a history equivalent to H. History H is further illustrated in Figure 2.

We denote by $Complete(H)$ a set of histories that extend H. Specifically, a history H' is in $Complete(H)$ if and only if, all of the following hold:

1. H' is well-formed, H is a prefix of H', and H and H' contain the same set of transactions;
2. for every live transaction[1] T in H:
    (a) if $H|T$ ends with an invocation of COMMIT, H' contains either C_T or A_T;
    (b) if $H|T$ ends with an invocation other than COMMIT, H' contains A_T;
    (c) if $H|T$ ends with a response, H' contains ABORT$_T$ and A_T.

Roughly speaking, each history in $Complete(H)$ is an extension of H where some of the commit-pending transactions in H appear as committed and all other live transactions appear as aborted. We say that H is *complete* if all transactions in H are complete. Each history in $Complete(H)$ is complete.

Given an execution α, the history of α, denoted by H_α, is the subsequence of α consisting of just the invocations and the responses of t-operations. The *execution interval* of a complete transaction T in an execution α is the subsequence of consecutive steps of α starting with the first step executed by any of the t-operations invoked by T and ending with the last such step. The *execution interval* of a transaction T that does not complete in α is the suffix of α starting with the first step executed by any of the t-operations invoked by T. We remark that similar definitions to the ones given on the base of histories, can also be given for executions: We say that a t-operation is complete in some execution α if it is complete in H_α; otherwise it is pending. A transaction T is committed (res. live, commit-pending) in α if it is committed (res. live, commit-pending) in H_α, etc.

Real-Time Order on Transactions and Sequential Histories. Consider a well-formed history H. We define a partial order, called *real time order* and denoted $<_H$, on the set of *transactions* in H, as follows:

- for any two transactions T_1 and T_2 in H, if T_1 is complete in H and the last event of $H|T_1$ precedes the first event of $H|T_2$ in H, then $T_1 <_H T_2$.

Transactions T_1 and T_2 are *concurrent* in H, if neither $T_1 <_H T_2$ nor $T_2 <_H T_1$. Similarly, transactions T_1 and T_2 are *concurrent* in an execution α, if neither $T_1 <_{H_\alpha} T_2$ nor $T_2 <_{H_\alpha} T_1$. We say that a history H (or an execution α) is *sequential* if no two transactions in H (in α) are concurrent.

Legality. Consider a sequential history S and a transaction T in S. We say that T is *legal* in S, if for every invocation inv of READ on each data item x that T performs, whose response is $res \neq A_T$, the following hold:

1. if there is an invocation of WRITE for x by T that precedes inv in S then res is the value argument of the last such invocation,
2. otherwise, if there are no committed transactions preceding T in S which invoke WRITE for x, then res is the initial value for x,

---

[1] We remark that the order in which the live transactions of H are inspected to form H' is immaterial, i.e. all histories that result by processing the live transactions in any possible such order are added to $Complete(H)$.

3. otherwise, *res* is the value argument of the last invocation of WRITE with parameter
   x, by any committed transaction that precedes T in S.

A complete sequential history S is *legal* if every transaction in S is legal.

Real-Time Order on t-operations and Operation-wise Sequential Histories. We define a partial order, called *operation real-time* order and denoted by $<_H^{op}$, on the set of *t-operations* in H, as follows:

- for any two t-operations op_1 and op_2 in H, if H contains a response for op_1 which precedes the invocation of op_2, then $op_1 <_H^{op} op_2$.

Operations op_1 and op_2 are *concurrent* in H, if neither $op_1 <_H^{op} op_2$ nor $op_2 <_H^{op} op_1$. H is *operation-wise sequential* if no two t-operations in H are concurrent.

Let S_{op} be an operation-wise sequential history equivalent to H. Since S_{op} is equivalent to H, S_{op} and H contain the same set of transactions. We say that S_{op} *respects* some relation $<$ on the set of *transactions* in H if the following holds: for any two transactions T_1 and T_2 in S_{op}, if $T_1 < T_2$, then $T_1 <_{S_{op}} T_2$. We say that S_{op} respects some relation $<^{op}$ on the set of *t-operations* in H if the following holds: for any two t-operations op_1 and op_2 in S_{op}, if $op_1 <^{op} op_2$, then $op_1 <_{S_{op}}^{op} op_2$. Notice that a partial order is a relation, so these definitions hold for partial orders as well.

3   TM Consistency

In this section, we present a collection of consistency conditions for STM computing.

3.1   Strict Serializability

Strict serializability was first introduced in [29] as a (strong) consistency condition for executions of concurrent transactions in database systems. Roughly speaking, an execution α is strictly serializable if each complete transaction that does not abort (as well as some of the live transactions) is executed in α like if it was executed serially at some point within its execution interval. A special case of strict serializability where transactions are restricted to consist of a single t-operation applied to a single data item is known as linearizability [22].

In STM computing, strict serializability can be expressed in several different flavors, two of which are discussed below. We start with *eager strict serializability* (or *e-strict serializability* for short).

Definition 1 (e-Strict Serializability). *We say that an execution α is e-strictly serializable if it is possible to do all of the following:*

- *If A is the set of all complete transactions in α that are not aborted, for each transaction $T \in A$, to associate with T a point $*_T$ somewhere between T's first invocation of a t-operation and T's last response of a t-operation in α.*
- *To choose a subset B of the **live** transactions in α and, for each transaction $T \in B$, associate with T a point $*_T$ somewhere after T's first invocation of a t-operation in α.*

For each $T \in A \cup B$, $*_T$ is called the serialization point *of T. Let σ be the sequential execution we get by serially executing (the code of) each transaction $T \in A \cup B$ at the place that its serialization point has been selected in α starting from the initial configuration. The set B and the serialization points of transactions in $A \cup B$ should be selected so that:*

- *for each transaction $T \in A$, the same t-operations, as in α, are invoked by T in σ and the response of each such t-operation in σ is the same as that in α, and*
- *for each transaction $T \in B$, a prefix of the t-operations invoked by T in σ is the same as the sequence of t-operations invoked by T in α and the response of each such t-operation in σ is the same as that in α (if it exists in α).*

An STM algorithm is e-strictly serializable *if each execution it produces is e-strictly serializable.*

If an execution α is e-strictly serializable, there exists a sequential execution σ (and a set B of live transactions in α) that satisfies the properties of Definition 1; we say that σ (and B) *justifies* that α is e-strictly serializable. Notice that since σ is the sequential execution produced by serially executing (the code of) each transaction at its serialization point starting from an initial configuration, σ is a legal execution and each transaction $T \in B$ commits in σ. Moreover, H_σ is a legal history containing only committed transactions.

We continue to provide a stronger version of e-strict serializability in Definition 2, called *deferred-update strict serializability* (or *du-strict serializability* for short), which is based on the definition of *Complete*.

Definition 2 (du-Strict Serializability, expressed in terms of histories). *A history H is du-strictly serializable, if there exist a history $H' \in Complete(H)$ and a history S equivalent to $comm(H')$ such that:*

- *S is a legal sequential history, and*
- *S respects $<_{comm(H')}$.*

An execution α is du-strictly serializable, if H_α is du-strictly serializable. An STM algorithm is du-strictly serializable, if each execution α it produces is du-strictly serializable.

Definition 2 follows the standard technique, employed in STM theory research, of presenting consistency conditions in terms of histories. We remark that this is not straightforward to achieve when defining the e-version of a consistency condition since in the e-version, serialization points can be associated even with live transactions (that are not commit-pending) for which it is unknown which t-operations they would invoke if they were to continue their execution until they complete. For compatibility with Definition 1, we present below, in Definition 3, du-strict serializability in terms of executions.

Definition 3 (du-Strict Serializability, expressed in terms of executions). *We say that an execution α is du-strictly serializable if it is possible to do all of the following:*

- *If A is the set of all complete transactions in α that are not aborted, for each transaction $T \in A$, to associate with T a point $*_T$ somewhere between T's first invocation of a t-operation and T's last response of a t-operation in α.*
- *To choose a subset B of the **commit-pending** transactions in H_α and, for each transaction $T \in B$, associate with T a point $*_T$ somewhere after T's first invocation of a t-operation in α.*

For each $T \in A \cup B$, $*_T$ is called the serialization point of T. Let σ be the sequential execution we get by serially executing (the code of) each transaction $T \in A \cup B$ at the place that its serialization point has been selected in α starting from the initial configuration. The set B and the serialization points of transactions in $A \cup B$ should be selected so that:

- *for each transaction $T \in A \cup B$, the same t-operations, as in α, are invoked by T in σ and the response of each such t-operation (other than COMMIT) in σ is the same as that in α.*

An STM algorithm is du-strictly serializable if each execution it produces is du-strictly serializable.

Lemma 1 argues that Definitions 2 and 3 are equivalent. Its proof is heavily based on the definitions of the concepts employed in Definitions 2 and 3.

Lemma 1. *Definitions 2 and 3 are equivalent in whatever concerns du-strictly serializable executions and STM algorithms.*

Sketch of proof. For the purpose of the proof, we will call an execution (or history) which satisfies the properties of Definition 2, *history-based du-ss*. Similarly, we will call an execution (or a history) which satisfies the properties of Definition 3, *execution-based du-ss*.

1. Consider an execution α which is history-based du-ss. We prove that α is execution-based du-ss.

    Since α is history-based du-ss, Definition 2 implies that H_α is history-based du-ss. Specifically, there exists a history $H' \in Complete(H_\alpha)$ and a history S equivalent to $comm(H')$ such that:

    - S is a legal sequential history, and
    - S respects $<_{comm(H')}$.

    By definition of $Complete(H_\alpha)$, H' is an extension of H_α where some of the commit-pending transactions in H_α appear as committed and all other live transactions appear as aborted. Let B be those commit-pending transactions in H_α that are committed in H', and let A be the set of all complete transactions in α (which are the same as in H_α) that do not abort. By definition of $comm$, $comm(H')$ is the subsequence of all events in H' issued and received for committed transactions, i.e. $comm(H')$ is the subsequence of all events issued or received for transactions in $A \cup B$.

    Since S is equivalent to $comm(H')$, S contains all transactions in $A \cup B$ (and no more transactions), and thus all transactions in S commit. Since S is sequential, it defines a total order on all transactions in $comm(H')$. Since S is equivalent to $comm(H')$ and respects $<_{comm(H')}$, it is possible to do the following: (1) for each transaction $T \in A$, to assign a serialization point for T somewhere between T's first invocation of a t-operation and T's last response of a t-operation in α, and (2) for each transaction $T \in B$, to assign a serialization point for T somewhere after T's first invocation of a t-operation in α, so that the total order defined by the serialization points on transactions in $A \cup B$ to be the same as that defined on transactions by S.

Let σ be the sequential execution, starting from the initial configuration, in which each transaction in S is serially executed, in the order it appears in S. Since S is legal, it is a straightforward induction to prove that, each transaction invokes the same t-operations in σ as in S and for each such invocation inv, inv has the same response in σ as in S. Thus, σ justifies that α is execution-based du-ss.

2. Now consider an execution β which is execution-based du-ss. We prove that β is history-based du-ss.

Let A be the set of complete transactions in β that are not aborted, and let B and σ be the set of commit-pending transactions in β and the sequential execution, respectively, that justify the (execution-based) du-ss property of β. Let H' be an extension of H_β which is constructed as follows: (1) for each commit-pending transaction $T \in B$ we add a C_T response, and (2) for each other live transaction T in β we add an A_T response. Then, $H' \in Complete(H_\beta)$ and $comm(H')$ is the subsequence of H' containing all events issued or received for transactions in $A \cup B$.

Let $S = H_\sigma$. Since σ is the sequential execution produced by serially executing (the code of) each transaction in $A \cup B$ at its serialization point, σ is a legal execution and each transaction $T \in A \cup B$ commits in σ. Thus, S is a legal sequential history which contains all transactions in $A \cup B$ (and no further transactions), and all these transactions commit in S. Since for each transaction $T \in A \cup B$, the same t-operations, as in β (or in H_β), are invoked by T in σ (or in H_σ) and the response of each such t-operation (other than COMMIT) in H_σ is the same as that in H_β, it follows that S is equivalent to $comm(H')$.

Since (1) for each transaction $T \in A$, $*_T$ is placed between T's first invocation of a t-operation and T's last response of a t-operation in β, and (2) for each transaction $T \in B$, $*_T$ is placed somewhere after T's first invocation of a t-operation in β, it follows that $S = H_\sigma$ respects $<_{comm(H')}$. So, H' and S justify that H_β is history-based du-ss. Therefore, β is history-based du-ss.

$\square$

Since a commit-pending transaction is live, it is straightforward to see that Definition 1 provides a weaker version of strict serializability than Definition 3 (or Definition 2). Intuitively, this is so since Definition 1 allows a transaction to read a value for a data item written by another transaction that is not committed or commit-pending in H. (This is allowed only if eventually, all complete transactions that are not aborted, and some of those that are still live can be "serialized" within their execution intervals.) It follows that if an execution is du-strictly serializable, it is also e-strictly serializable. However, the opposite is not true. For instance, let's consider the history H and its prefix

H_1 both shown in Figure 3. H is both e-strictly serializable and du-strictly serializable, whereas H_1 is just e-strictly serializable.

Lemma 2. *If an execution α is du-strictly serializable then α is e-strictly serializable, but not vice versa.*

A set $\mathscr{S}$ of sequences is prefix-closed if, whenever H is in $\mathscr{S}$, every prefix of H is also in $\mathscr{S}$. Recall that the history H shown in Figure 3 is du-strictly serializable but its prefix H_1 is not. Thus, du-serializability is not a prefix-closed property. On the contrary, e-strict serializability is a prefix-closed property. We remark that prefix-closure can be imposed to du-strict serializability in an explicit way, i.e. by directly stating in Definition 2 that each prefix H_p of H must also satisfy the conditions imposed by the definition. This would make Definition 2 stronger.

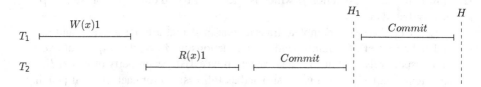

Fig. 3. Example of a history H showing that du-strict serializability is not a prefix-closed property. We remark that H is operation-wise sequential. In all our example histories, we assume that the initial value of each of the employed data items is 0.

3.2 Serializability

As with strict serializability, serializability was first introduced in [29] as a consistency condition for executions of concurrent transactions in database systems. It is weaker than strict serializability in that it does not ensure that the serialization point of each transaction is within its execution interval. Below, we discuss two different flavors of serializability in a way similar to that for strict serializability.

Definition 4 (e-Serializability). *We say that an execution α is e-serializable if it is possible to do all of the following:*

- *If A is the set of all complete transactions in α that are not aborted, for each transaction $T \in A$, to associate with T a point $*_T$ in α.*
- *To choose a subset B of the live transactions in α and, for each transaction $T \in B$, to associate with T a point $*_T$ in α.*

For each $T \in A \cup B$, $*_T$ is called the serialization point of T. Let σ be the sequential execution we get by serially executing (the code of) each transaction $T \in A \cup B$ at the place that its serialization point has been selected in α starting from the initial configuration. The set B and the serialization points of transactions in $A \cup B$ should be selected so that:

- *for each transaction $T \in A$, the same t-operations, as in α, are invoked by T in σ and the response of each such t-operation in σ is the same as that in α, and*

- *for each transaction $T \in B$, a prefix of the t-operations invoked by T in σ is the same as the sequence of t-operations invoked by T in α and the response of each such t-operation in σ is the same as that in α (if it exists in α).*

An STM algorithm is e-serializable if each execution it produces is e-serializable.

We continue to provide a stronger version of serializability in Definition 5, called *deferred-update serializability* (or *du-serializability* for short), which is based on the definition of *Complete*.

Definition 5 (du-Serializability). *A history H is du-serializable, if there exists a history $H' \in Complete(H)$ and a history S equivalent to $comm(H')$ such that:*

- *S is a legal sequential history.*

An execution α is du-serializable, if H_α is du-serializable. An STM algorithm is du-serializable if each execution α it produces is du-serializable.

Notice that S in Definition 5 respects the program order of t-operations executed by the same thread in H. This is implied by the definition of equivalent histories.

We remark that, similarly to the corresponding definitions of strict serializability, Definition 4 provides a weaker version of serializability than Definition 5. This can be easily seen by deriving an execution-based version of Definition 5 (in the spirit of Definition 3) and proving that this version is equivalent to Definition 5 (as proved in Lemma 1 for du-strict serializability).

Lemma 3. *If an execution α is du-serializable then α is e-serializable, but not vice versa.*

The difference between serializability and strict serializability is that strict serializability additionally ensures that the real-time order of transactions is respected by the sequential history defined by the serialization points. Thus, every history/execution that is (du-) e-strictly serializable is also (du-) e-serializable but not vice versa.

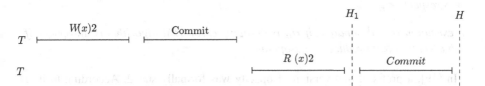

Fig. 4. Example showing that du-serializability is not a prefix-closed property

Lemma 4. *If an execution α is strictly serializable then α is serializable, but not vice versa[2].*

---

[2] When we say that an execution (or an STM algorithm) satisfies a consistency condition without specifying which variant of the condition it satisfies, then the claim holds for both variants of that condition.

It is worth pointing out that e-serializability and du-serializability are not prefix-closed properties. This is so, since it is easy to design a history H which is e-serializable (as well as du-serializable) in which a committed transaction T (executed by some thread p) reads for some data item x a value v and then commits. H also contains a second transaction T' (executed by some thread $p' \neq p$) which starts its execution after T has completed, writes v into x, and commits. Such a history is shown in Figure 4. We remark that H is e-serializable and du-serializable. However, the prefix of H up until C_T is neither e-serializable, nor du-serializable.

We remark that prefix-closure can be imposed to e-serializability (as well as to du-serializability) in an explicit way, as discussed for du-strict serializability above. It is not clear if the versions that would then result will be weaker than the corresponding versions of strict serializability. Imposing prefix closure to the consistency conditions presented in Sections 3.4-3.5 may be too restrictive as well. Thus, we present the non-prefix-closed versions of them given that it is straightforward to derive their prefix-closed versions, in an explicit way.

Several impossibility results [6,11,16] and lower bounds [6] in STM computing have been proved for strict serializability or serializability. Most STM algorithms in the literature (see e.g. [12,39,14,33] for some examples) satisfy some form of serializability.

3.3   Opacity

Opacity was first introduced in [18]. Definition 6 follows that in [18]. Roughly speaking, a history H that is du-opaque is also du-strictly serializable; additionally, if S is the sequential history which justifies that S is du-strictly serializable, opacity ensures that those transactions in H that are not included in S are also legal. For instance, such transactions are those that have aborted in H (but there may be more).

Definition 6 (du-Opacity [19]). *A history H is du-opaque if there exists a sequential history S equivalent to some history $H' \in Complete(H)$ such that:*

- *S is legal, and*
- *S respects $<_{H'}$.*

An execution α is du-opaque, if H_α is du-opaque. An STM algorithm is du-opaque if each execution α it produces is du-opaque.

In [19], a prefix-closed version of opacity was formally stated. According to it, a history H is du-opaque if the conditions imposed by Definition 6 are satisfied for each prefix H_p of H; this version of du-opacity is stronger than that provided in Definition 6 which is not prefix-closed. Figure 5 illustrates a situation that would be acceptable by the non-prefix-closed version of du-opacity. History H', which is a prefix of history H, does not satisfy du-opacity, as transaction T_2 reads a value written by a transaction which is still not committed. However, as transaction T_1 is committed in history H, H complies with du-opacity. A different formalization of du-opacity as a prefix-closed property was elaborated in [5].

Lemma 5 argues that du-opacity is stronger than du-strict serializability.

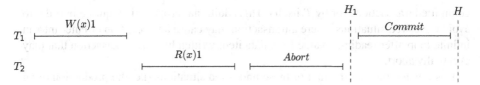

Fig. 5. Example showing that du-opacity is not a prefix-closed property

Lemma 5. *If an execution* α *is du-opaque, then* α *is du-strictly serializable, but not vice versa.*

Proof. Since α is du-opaque, H_α is also du-opaque. Thus, there exists a sequential history S, equivalent to some history $H' \in Complete(H_\alpha)$, such that S is legal and S respects $<_{H'}$.

Let S' be the subsequence of S consisting of all events in S issued or received by transactions in $comm(H')$. Then, the following hold:

- Since S is equivalent to H', it follows that S' is equivalent to $comm(H')$.
- Since S respects $<_{H'}$, it follows that S' respects $<_{comm(H')}$.
- Since S is legal, it follows that each transaction in S is legal. Since S is equivalent to H' and S' is comprised of the events of all transactions in $comm(H')$, it follows that S' is legal.

Thus, H' and S' satisfy the properties of Definition 2 and, therefore, H_α is du-strictly serializable. So, α is du-strictly serializable.

Figure 6 shows an example of a history that is not du-opaque but is du-strictly serializable. This history is not du-opaque because it violates the first condition of Definition 6; specifically, transaction T_2 cannot be legal.

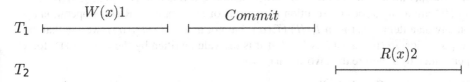

Fig. 6. A du-strictly serializable history which is not du-opaque

Lemmas 2 and 5 imply the following corollary.

Corollary 1. *If an execution* α *is du-opaque, then* α *is e-strictly serializable.*

Consider an execution α which is du-strictly serializable, and let S be the sequential history that justifies that α is du-strictly serializable. Strict serializability doesn't impose any restrictions on those transactions in α that are not included in S, whereas (roughly speaking) du-opacity requires that all reads of each such transaction T (independently of whether the transaction is aborted or live in α) read values written by previously committed transactions (or by T itself). This additional property is required in order to avoid undesired situations where a transaction may cause an exception or enter into an infinite loop after reading a value for a data item written by a live transaction that may eventually abort.

It is remarkable that the first of these undesired situations (i.e. the production of an exception or an error code) can be avoided even by STM systems that ensure only strict serializability if we make the following simple assumptions in our model. An exception (or an error code) that has been resulted by the execution of a t-operation op is considered as a response for op. A transaction that has experienced an exception or has received an error code as a response to one of its t-operations, is considered to be complete (but not aborted). Then, a (e- or du-) strictly serializable STM implementation will never produce such exceptions (or error codes). Notice that the second undesirable situation, namely having some transaction enter an infinite loop, will not appear in STM systems that ensure standard progress properties, like lock-freedom, starvation-freedom, etc. A thread p experiences *starvation* in an execution α, if p takes infinitely many steps in α and it receives only a finite number of commit responses for the transactions that it initiates; an STM algorithm is *starvation-free*, if, in every execution that it produces, no thread ever experiences starvation. *Obstruction-freedom* ensures that for each thread p, if p runs solo starting from any configuration C in α, it eventually completes the execution of its transaction successfully within a finite number of steps.

We continue to present eager opacity (e-opacity). Consider any history H and a transaction T in H. An instance op of READ for some data item x executed by T is *global* if T has not invoked WRITE on x in H before invoking op. Let $H|T|read$ be the longest subsequence of $H|T$ consisting of those invocations of READ (and their responses) for which there is a response and this response is not A_T, followed by COMMIT$_T$, C_T. Let $H|T|read_g$ be the subsequence of $H|T|read$ consisting only of the invocations of the *global* instances of READ and their responses, followed by COMMIT$_T$, C_T. We denote by $T_r(H)$ a transaction that invokes the same t-operations (and in the same order) as those invoked in $H|T|read$. Similarly, denote by $T_{gr}(H)$ a transaction that invokes the same t-operations (and in the same order) as those invoked in $H|T|read_g$. $T_r(H)$ and $T_{gr}(H)$ are defined for an execution α in terms of H_α. For each READ t-operation op on any data item x that is in $T_r(H)$ $(T_r(\alpha))$ but not in $T_{gr}(H)$ $(T_{gr}(\alpha))$, we say that the response for op (if it exists) is *legal*, if it is the value written by the last WRITE for x performed by T before the invocation of op.

Definition 7 (e-Opacity). *We say that an execution α is e-opaque if there exists a set B of live transactions in α and some sequential execution σ which justify that α is e-strictly serializable, and all of the following hold:*

1. *We can extend the history H_σ of σ to get a sequential history H'_σ such that:*
    - *if A is the set of complete transactions in α that are not aborted, for each transaction T in α that is not in $A \cup B$ (i.e. for each transaction T in α that is not in σ), H'_σ contains $H_\alpha|T|read_g$,*
    - *if $<$ is the partial order which is induced by the real time order $<_{H_\alpha}$ in such a way that for each transaction T in α that is not in σ, we replace each instance of T in the set of pairs of $<_{H_\alpha}$ with transaction $T_{gr}(\alpha)$, then H'_σ respects $<$, and*

- H'_σ is legal.

2. For each transaction T in α that is not in σ, and for each invocation of a READ operation op which is in $H_\alpha|T|read$ but not in $H_\alpha|T|read_g$, the response for op is legal.

An STM algorithm is e-opaque *if each execution α it produces is e-opaque.*

Lemma 6 proves that du-opacity is stronger than e-opacity.

Lemma 6. *If an execution α is du-opaque, then α is e-opaque, but not vice versa.*

Sketch of proof. Since α is du-opaque, H_α is also du-opaque. Thus, there exists a sequential history S, equivalent to some history $H' \in Complete(H_\alpha)$, such that S is legal and S respects $<_{H'}$.

Let S' be the subsequence of S consisting of all events in S issued or received by transactions in $comm(H')$. Then, by following similar arguments as in the proof of Lemma 5 we argue that H' and S' satisfy the properties of Definition 2 and, therefore, H_α is du-strictly serializable. So, α is du-strictly serializable.

Let B be those commit-pending transactions in H_α that are committed in H'. Let σ be the sequential execution, starting from the initial configuration, in which each transaction in S' is serially executed, in the order it appears in S'. We follow similar arguments as in the proof of Lemma 1 to argue that σ justifies that α is execution-based du-ss. Thus, Lemma 2 implies that α is e-strictly serializable; moreover, we argue that $H_\sigma = S'$.

Denote by A the set of complete transactions in H_α that are not aborted. Let H'_σ be the subsequence of S such that H'_σ contains all events in S', and for each transaction $T \notin A \cup B$, H'_σ additionally contains each event in $H|T|read_g$. Since S and S' are legal, it follows that H'_σ is also legal. Also, since S respects $<_{H'}$, it follows that S' respects $<$ (as defined in item 1 of Definition 7). Thus, H'_σ (which is equal to S') respects $<$.

Finally, legality of S implies that for each transaction T in α that is not in σ, and for each t-operation op in $T|read$ that is not in $T|read_g$, the response for op is legal. We conclude that α is e-opaque.

Figure 6 shows an example of a history that is not du-opaque but is du-strictly serializable (and therefore also e-strictly serializable, by Lemma 2). This history is not du-opaque because it violates the first condition of Definition 6; specifically, transaction T_2 cannot be legal. $\qquad\qquad\qquad\qquad\qquad\qquad\qquad\qquad\qquad\qquad\qquad\square$

We remark that most STM algorithms presented in the literature are opaque.

3.4 Causality-Related Consistency Conditions

Consider any operation-wise sequential history S_{op} that is equivalent to H. Since S_{op} is equivalent to H, there are the same transactions in S_{op} as in H. We define a binary relation with respect to S_{op}, called *reads-from* and denoted by $<^r_{S_{op}}$, between *transactions* in H such that, for any two transactions T_1, T_2 in H, $T_1 <^r_{S_{op}} T_2$ only if:

- T_2 executes a READ t-operation op that reads some data item x and returns a value v for it,

- T_1 is the transaction in S_{op} which executes the last WRITE t-operation that writes v for x and precedes op.

Notice that each operation-wise sequential history S_{op} that is equivalent to H, induces a *reads-from* relation for H. We denote by $\mathscr{R}_H$ the set of all reads-from relations that can be induced for H.

For each $<^r$ in $\mathscr{R}_H$, we define the *causal* relation for $<^r$ on transactions in H to be the transitive closure of $\bigcup_i \left(<_{H|p_i}\right) \cup <^r$. We define $\mathscr{C}_H$ to be the set of all causal relations in H.

Causal Consistency. Causal consistency was informally introduced as a shared memory consistency condition in [23], and it was formally defined in [2]. Roughly speaking, an execution α is causally consistent if for each thread p_i, there exists a sequential execution σ_i of the complete transactions that are not aborted (as well as of some of the live transactions) in α such that in σ_i each of these transactions invokes the same t-operations and gets the same responses as in α. Thus, causal consistency allows the sequential executions to be different for different threads. However, it imposes the additional constraint that all sequential executions respect the same causal relation.

As in the previous sections, we provide two formal definitions of causal consistency for STM computing.

Definition 8 (e-Causal Consistency). *Consider an execution α and let A be the set of all complete transactions in α that are not aborted. We say that α is e-causally-consistent if there exists a subset B of live transactions in α and a causal relation $<^c$ in $\mathscr{C}_{H'_\alpha}$, where H'_α is the subsequence of H_α consisting of the events (in H_α) issued and received for the transactions in $A \cup B$, such that, for each thread p_i, it is possible to do the following:*
For each transaction $T \in A \cup B$, to associate with T a point $*^i_T$ in α. Let σ_i be the sequential execution we get by serially executing (the code of) each transaction $T \in A \cup B$ at the place that its point has been selected (for p_i) in α starting from the initial configuration. The set B, and the points of transactions in $A \cup B$ should be selected (for p_i) so that:

- *H_{σ_i} respects $<^c$,*
- *for each transaction $T \in A$, the same t-operations, as in α, are invoked by T in σ_i and the response of each such t-operation in σ_i is the same as that in α, and*
- *for each transaction $T \in B$, a prefix of the t-operations invoked by T in σ_i is the same as the sequence of t-operations invoked by T in α, and the response of each such t-operation in σ_i is the same as that in α (if it exists in α).*

An STM algorithm is e-causally-consistent if each execution α it produces is e-causally-consistent.

We continue with the presentation of the du-version of causal consistency.

Definition 9 (du-Causal Consistency). *A history H is du-causally consistent if there exists a history $H' \in Complete(H)$ and a causal relation $<^c$ in $\mathscr{C}_{comm(H')}$ such that, for each thread p_i, there exists a sequential history S_i such that:*

- S_i is equivalent to comm(H'),
- S_i respects the causality order $<^c$, and
- every transaction executed by p_i in S_i is legal.

An execution α is du-causally consistent, if H_α is du-causally consistent. An STM algorithm is du-causally consistent if each execution α it produces is du-causally consistent.

By following similar arguments as in the proof of Lemma 2, it can be proved that du-causal consistency is stronger than e-causal consistency.

Lemma 7. *If an execution α is du-causally consistent then α is e-causally consistent, but not vice versa.*

Lemma 8 argues that serializability is stronger than causal consistency.

Lemma 8. *If an execution α is serializable then α is causally consistent, but not vice versa.*

Sketch of proof. We prove the claim for the e-versions of the consistency conditions. The proof of the claim for the du-variants of them can be performed using similar reasoning.

Let A be the set of complete transactions in α that are not aborted. Moreover, let B and σ be the set of live transactions in α and the sequential execution, respectively, which justify that α is serializable. By Definition 4, the following hold for σ:

- for each transaction $T \in A$, the same t-operations, as in α, are invoked by T in σ and the response of each such t-operation in σ is the same as that in α, and
- for each transaction $T \in B$, a prefix of the t-operations invoked by T in σ is the same as the sequence of t-operations invoked by T in α, and the response of each such t-operation in σ is the same as that in α (if it exists in α).

Let H'_σ be the subsequence of H_σ in which, for each transaction $T \in B$, we exclude those events issued or produced for T in σ that are not in α. Then, H'_σ is equivalent to H'_α, where H'_α is the subsequence of H_α containing just the events of transactions in $A \cup B$. Since H'_σ is sequential, it is also operation-wise sequential, so $<^r_{H'_\sigma}$ is well-defined. Let $<^c$ be the causal relation for $<^r_{H'_\sigma}$. Then, by letting $\sigma_i = \sigma$, for each thread p_i, all conditions of Definition 8 hold.

Figure 7 shows an example of a history which is du-causally consistent (and therefore also e-causally consistent, by Lemma 7) but not e-serializable. In this history both transactions T_1 and T_2 should be serialized before transactions T_3 and T_4, because both T_1 and T_2 read 0 from data item y which is written by T_3 and T_4. Regardless of how the serialization points for T_1 and T_2 are ordered, both T_3 and T_4 should read the same value for data item x. Thus, this history is not e-serializable (and therefore it is not e-serializable, by Lemma 3). However, it is du-causally consistent because threads running T_3 and T_4 may see writes executed by threads running T_1 and T_2 in a different order.

□

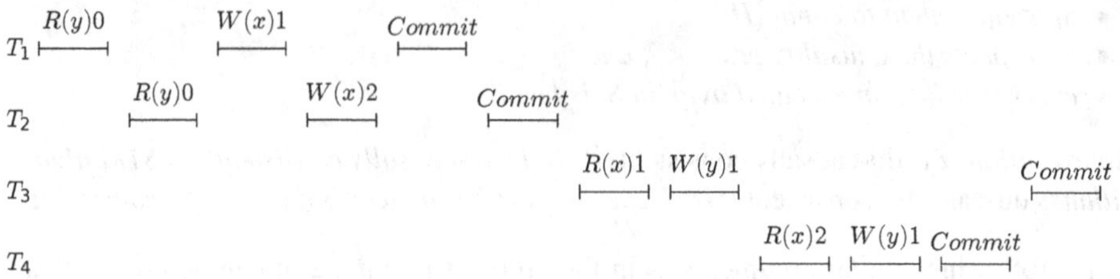

$$
\begin{array}{l}
R(y)0 W(x)1 Commit \\
T_1 \vdash\!\!\dashv \vdash\!\!\dashv \vdash\!\!\dashv
\end{array}
$$

Fig. 7. A du-causally consistent history which is not e-serializable

Causal Serializability. Causal serializability was introduced in [31] as a consistency condition which is stronger than causal consistency but weaker than serializability. Informally, in addition to the constraints imposed by causal consistency, the following constraint must also be satisfied: all transactions that update the same data item must be perceived in the same order by all threads.

Definition 10 (e-Causal Serializability). *Consider an execution α and let A be the set of all complete transactions in α that are not aborted. We say that α is e-causally serializable if there exists a subset B of live transactions in α and a causal relation $<^c$ in $\mathscr{C}_{H'_\alpha}$ where H'_α is the subsequence of H_α consisting of the events (in H_α) issued and received for the transactions in $A \cup B$, such that, for each thread p_i, it is possible to do the following:*
For each transaction $T \in A \cup B$, to associate with T a point $*^i_T$ in α. Let σ_i be the sequential execution we get by serially executing (the code of) each transaction $T \in A \cup B$ at the place that its point has been selected (for p_i) in α starting from the initial configuration. The set B, and the points of transactions in $A \cup B$ should be selected (for p_i) so that:

- *H_{σ_i} respects $<^c$,*
- *for each transaction $T \in A$, the same t-operations, as in α, are invoked by T in σ_i and the response of each such t-operation in σ_i is the same as that in α,*
- *for each transaction $T \in B$, a prefix of the t-operations invoked by T in σ_i are the same as the sequence of t-operations invoked by T in α, the response of each such t-operation in σ_i is the same as that in α (if it exists in α).*
- *for each pair of transactions $T_1, T_2 \in A \cup B$ that write to the same data item, if $T_1 <_{H_{\sigma_i}} T_2$, then for each $j \in \{1, \ldots, n\}$, it holds that $T_1 <_{H_{\sigma_j}} T_2$.*

An STM algorithm is e-causally serializable if each execution α it produces is e-causally serializable.

We continue with the presentation of the du-version of causal serializability.

Definition 11 (du-Causal Serializability). *A history H is du-causally serializable if there exists a history $H' \in Complete(H)$ and a causal relation $<^c$ in $\mathscr{C}_{comm(H')}$ such that, for each thread p_i, there exists a sequential history S_i for which the following hold:*

- S_i is equivalent to comm(H'),
- S_i respects the causality order $<^c$,
- every transaction executed by p_i in S_i is legal, and
- for each pair of transactions T_1 and T_2 in comm(H') that write to the same data item, if $T_1 <_{S_i} T_2$, then for each $j \in \{1,\ldots,n\}$, it holds that $T_1 <_{S_j} T_2$.

An execution α is du-causally serializable, if H_α is du-causally serializable. An STM algorithm is du-causally serializable if each execution α it produces is du-causally serializable.

By following similar arguments as in the proof of Lemma 2, it can be proved that du-causal serializability is stronger than e-causal serializability.

Lemma 9. If an execution α is du-causally serializable then α is e-causally serializable, but not vice versa.

Obviously, every (e- or du-) causally serializable history satisfies the properties of (e- or du-, respectively) causal consistency, but the opposite is not true. For instance, the du-causally consistent history shown in Figure 7 is not e-causally serializable, since threads executing transactions T_3 and T_4 do not see writes from T_1 and T_2 to data item x in the same order.

Lemma 10. If an execution α is causally serializable then α is causally consistent, but not vice versa.

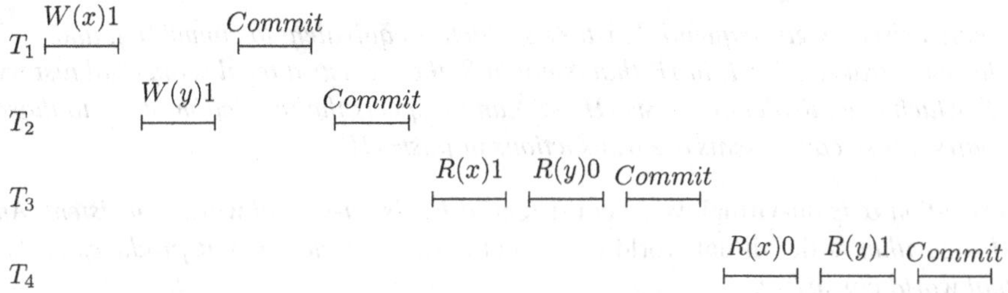

Fig. 8. A du-causally serializable history which is not e-serializable

Using similar arguments as those in the proof of Lemma 8, it can be easily proved that causal serializability is weaker than serializability. However, the opposite does not hold. Figure 8 shows an example of a history H which is du-causally serializable (and therefore also e-causally serializable, by Lemma 9) but not e-serializable (and therefore not du-serializable, by Lemma 3). In H, if transaction T_1 is serialized before T_2 (the opposite case is symmetrical), then it is not possible to serialize transaction T_4. However, by definition of causal serializability, sequential histories constructed for threads p_3 and p_4 may include transactions T_1 and T_2 in different orders.

Lemma 11. *If an execution α is serializable then α is causally serializable, but not vice versa.*

In STM research, causal consistency, as well as causal serializability, are interesting in the context of proving impossibility results [9,10] and lower bounds. We remark that when proving such results, considering a weak consistency condition makes the result stronger. It is therefore an interesting open problem to see whether some of the STM impossibility results (e.g. [6,11,16]) that have been proved assuming some strong consistency condition, like opacity, strict serializability or serializability, can be extended to hold for weaker consistency conditions like those formulated in this or later sections. For instance in this avenue, the impossibility result proved in [17] assuming serializability is extended in [9,10] to hold for a much weaker consistency condition.

Virtual World Consistency. Virtual World Consistency (VWC) was defined in [24] as a family of consistency conditions. Informally, VWC ensures serializability or strict serializability for the committed (and some of the commit-pending) transactions but a weaker condition than that imposed by opacity for the rest of the transactions.

For each transaction T in history H and each causal relation $<_H^c$ in $\mathscr{C}_H$, we define the *causal past* of T denoted by $past_T(H, <_H^c)$ as the subsequence of all events of H issued or produced either for transaction T itself or for any transaction T_i in H such that $T_i <_H^c T$.

Definition 12 (du-Virtual World Consistency). *A history H is* du-virtual world consistent *if there exists a history $H' \in Complete(H)$ and a causal relation $<^c$ in $\mathscr{C}_{H'}$ such that:*

- *there exists a legal sequential history S which is equivalent to $comm(H')$, and*
- *for each transaction T_i in H' that is not in S, there exists a legal sequential history S_i which is equivalent to $past_{T_i}(H', <^c)$ and respects the restriction of $<^c$ to those pairs whose components are transactions in $past_{T_i}(H', <^c)$.*

An execution α is du-virtual world consistent, *if H_α is du-virtual world consistent. An STM algorithm is* du-virtual world consistent *if each execution α it produces is du-virtual world consistent.*

Definition 13 (du-Strong Virtual World Consistency). *A history H is* du-strongly virtual world consistent *if there exists a history $H' \in Complete(H)$ and a causal relation $<^c$ in $\mathscr{C}_{H'}$ such that:*

- *there exists a legal sequential history S which is equivalent to $comm(H')$ and respects $<_{comm(H')}$, and*
- *for each transaction T_i in H' that is not in S, there exists a legal sequential history S_i which is equivalent to $past_{T_i}(H', <^c)$ and respects the restriction of $<^c$ to those pairs whose components are transactions in $past_{T_i}(H', <^c)$.*

An execution α is du-strongly virtual world consistent, *if H_α is du-strongly virtual world consistent. An STM algorithm is* du-strongly virtual world consistent *if each execution α it produces is du-strongly virtual world consistent.*

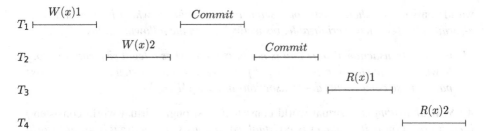

Fig. 9. A du-virtual world consistent history which is not du-opaque

By comparing Definitions 12 and 13 with Definitions 5 and 2, respectively, it is straightforward to see that du-virtual world consistency is stronger than du-serializability and du-strong virtual world consistency is stronger than du-strict serializability.

Lemma 12. *If an execution α is du-virtual world consistent (du-strongly virtual world consistent) then α is du-serializable (du-strictly serializable), but not vice versa.*

Du-strong virtual world consistency (and therefore also du-virtual world consistency) is weaker than du-opacity.

Lemma 13. *If an execution α is du-opaque then α is du-strongly virtual world consistent, but not vice versa.*

Sketch of proof. Since α is du-opaque, H_α is also du-opaque. Thus, there exists a sequential history S, equivalent to some history $H' \in Complete(H_\alpha)$, such that S is legal and S respects $<_{H'}$. Let S' be the subsequence of S consisting of all events in S issued or received by transactions in $comm(H')$. Then, S' is a legal sequential history, equivalent to $comm(H')$, which respects $<_{comm(H')}$.

Since S is sequential, it is also operation-wise sequential, so $<_S^r$ is well-defined. Let $<^c$ be the causal relation for $<_S^r$. Consider any transaction T_i in H' that is not in S'. Then, $past_{T_i}(H', <^c)$ is the subsequence of all events of H' issued or produced either for transaction T_i itself or for any transaction T_j in H' such that $T_j <^c T_i$.

Let S_i be the subsequence of S consisting of all events issued or produced for transactions in $past_{T_i}(H', <^c)$. Since S is equivalent to H', it follows that S_i is equivalent to $past_T(H', <^c)$. Since S_i is a subsequence of S and $<^c$ is the causal relation for $<_S^r$, it follows that S_i respects the restriction of $<^c$ to those pairs whose components are transactions in $past_{T_i}(H', <^c)$. Since S is legal and S_i is a subsequence of S equivalent to $past_T(H', <^c)$, it follows that S_i is legal. Thus, all conditions of Definition 13 hold.

The history shown in Figure 9 is du-strongly virtual world consistent but not du-opaque: regardless of the order of the serialization points of transactions T_1 and T_2, it is not possible to derive a sequential history where both transaction T_3 and T_4 are legal. □

We continue to present the eager versions of virtual world consistency and strong virtual world consistency.

Definition 14 (e-Virtual World Consistency and e-Strong Virtual World Consistency). *We say that an execution α is e-virtual world consistent (e-strongly virtual*

world consistent) *if there exists some sequential execution* σ *which justifies that* α *is e-serializable (e-strictly serializable, respectively), and the following holds:*

1. *for each transaction* T_i *in* α *that is not in* σ *there exists a legal sequential history* S_i *which is equivalent to* $past_{T_i}(H', <^c)$ *and respects the restriction of* $<^c$ *to those pairs whose components are transactions in* $past_{T_i}(H', <^c)$.

An STM algorithm is e-virtual world consistent *(e-strongly virtual world consistent) if each execution* α *it produces is e-virtual world consistent (e-strongly virtual world consistent).*

Using similar arguments as in the proof of Lemma 6, we can prove that du-virtual world consistency is stronger than e-virtual world consistency.

Lemma 14. *If an execution* α *is du-virtual world consistent (du-strongly virtual world consistent) then* α *is e-virtual world consistent (e-strongly virtual world consistent), but not vice versa.*

The following lemma is an immediate consequence of Definition 14.

Lemma 15. *If an execution* α *is e-virtual world consistent (e-strongly virtual world consistent) then* α *is e-serializable (e-strictly serializable), but not vice versa.*

Using similar reasoning as that in the proof of Lemma 13, we can prove that e-opacity is stronger than e-strong virtual world consistency.

Lemma 16. *If an execution* α *is e-opaque then* α *is e-strongly virtual world consistent, but not vice versa.*

Strong consistency conditions such as opacity ensure the safe execution of non-committed transactions by imposing on them the same correctness demands as those that committed transactions are required to obey. This has been criticized in [24] to result in STM algorithms that produce histories in which live transactions are forced to abort in order to preserve the consistency of other transactions that are deemed to also abort. Virtual world consistency relaxes the correctness property used for non-committed transactions in order to avoid such scenarios in several cases, and by consequence, allow for more live transactions to commit than an STM algorithm that implements a stronger consistency condition would.

3.5 Snapshot Isolation

Snapshot isolation was originally introduced as a consistency condition in the database world [7,28]. Snapshot isolation is an appealing property for STM computing [3,13,32] since it provides the potential to increase throughput for workloads with long transactions [32]. The first formal definitions for STM snapshot isolation was given in [9,10].

Consider a history H and let T be a transaction that either commits or is commit-pending in H. Recall that we have already defined the sequences $H|T|read$, $H|T|read_g$, as well as transactions $T_r(H)$ and $T_{gr}(H)$ in Section 3.3. Let $H|T|other$ be the sub-sequence of $H|T$ that consists of all invocations performed by T (and their matching responses) in H other than those comprising $H|T|read_g$, followed by COMMIT_T, C_T. Let $T_o(H)$ be a transaction that invokes the same t-operations (and in the same order) as those invoked in $H|T|other$; for an execution α $T_o(\alpha)$ is defined in terms of H_α in the same way.

Definition 15 (du-Snapshot isolation [10]). *An execution α satisfies du-snapshot isolation, if there exists a set D consisting of all committed and some of the commit-pending transactions in α for which the following holds:*
For each transaction $T \in D$, it is possible to insert (in α) a point $*_{T,gr}$, called the global read point *of T, and a point $*_{T,w}$, called the* write point *for T, so that if δ_α is the sequence defined by these serialization points, the following hold:*

1. *$*_{T,gr}$ precedes $*_{T,w}$ in δ_α,*
2. *both $*_{T,gr}$ and $*_{T,w}$ are inserted within the execution interval of T,*
3. *if H_{δ_α} is the history we get by replacing each $*_{T,gr}$ with $H_\alpha|T|read_g$ and each $*_{T,w}$ with $H_\alpha|T|other$ in δ_α, then H_{δ_α} is legal.*

An STM algorithm satisfies du-snapshot isolation *if each execution α it produces satisfies du-snapshot isolation.*

We now present eager snapshot isolation. Consider a legal execution α and let $C(\alpha)$ be the set of all legal executions such that each execution $\alpha' \in C(\alpha)$ is an extension of α such that the same transactions are executed in α and α' and no transaction is live in α'.

Definition 16 (e-Snapshot Isolation). *Consider an execution α. We say that α satisfies e-snapshot isolation, if there exists an execution $\alpha' \in C(\alpha)$ for which the following holds: if A is the set of transactions that commit in α' then for each transaction $T \in A$, it is possible to insert a point $*_{T,gr}$, called* global read point *of T, and a point $*_{T,w}$, called* write point *of T, in α, so that:*

1. *$*_{T,gr}$ precedes $*_{T,w}$,*
2. *both $*_{T,gr}$ and $*_{T,w}$ are inserted somewhere between T's first invocation of a t-operation and T's last response of a t-operation in α', and*
3. *if σ is the sequential execution that we get when for each transaction $T \in A$, we serially execute transactions $T_{gr}(\alpha)$ and $T_o(\alpha)$ at the points that $*_{T,gr}$ and $*_{T,w}$, respectively, have been inserted, then for each transaction $T \in A$, the response of each t-operation invoked by $T_{gr}(\alpha)$ and $T_o(\alpha)$ in σ is the same as that of the corresponding t-operation in $H_\alpha|T|read_g$ and $H_\alpha|T|other$, respectively.*

An STM algorithm satisfies e-snapshot isolation *if each execution α it produces satisfies e-snapshot isolation.*

Lemma 17 argues that du-snapshot isolation is stronger than e-snapshot isolation.

Lemma 17. *If an execution α satisfies du-snapshot isolation then α satisfies e-snapshot isolation, but not vice versa.*

Lemma 18 argues that strict serializability is stronger than snapshot isolation.

Table 1. A quick reference guide showing the relationships between consistency conditions. We remark that a consistency condition determines a set of histories, namely those histories that satisfy the constraints imposed by the condition. Each row and each column of the table represents a consistency condition. Each cell of the table shows the relationship between the consistency condition of the row and the consistency condition of the column that the cell belongs to. For example, the cell that is found in the crossing between the row of e-s (e-serializability) and the column of du-s (du-serializability) contains $\supseteq$. This means that e-s is a superset of du-s, i.e., that e-s is weaker than du-s. The inverse relation is denoted by $\subseteq$, as can be seen in the cell that is found in the crossing between the row of e-ss and the column of e-s: e-ss is stronger than e-s, and thus, it is a subset of e-s. Equality of two conditions is denoted by $=$. Incomparability between them is denoted by $\neq$.

	e-ss	du-ss	e-s	du-s	e-op	du-op	e-cc	du-cc	e-cs	du-cs	e-vwc	du-vwc	e-svwc	du-svwc	e-si	du-si
e-ss	$=$	$\supseteq$	$\subseteq$	$\subseteq$	$\subseteq$	$\subseteq$	$\subseteq$	$\subseteq$	$\subseteq$	$\subseteq$	$\subseteq$	$\subseteq$	$\subseteq$	$\subseteq$	$\subseteq$	$\subseteq$
du-ss		$=$	$\supseteq$	$\supseteq$	$\supseteq$	$\supseteq$	$\supseteq$	$\supseteq$	$\supseteq$	$\supseteq$	$\supseteq$	$\supseteq$	$\supseteq$	$\supseteq$	$\supseteq$	
e-s			$=$	$\supseteq$	$\supseteq$	$\supseteq$	$\subseteq$	$\subseteq$	$\subseteq$	$\subseteq$	$\subseteq$	$\subseteq$	$\subseteq$	$\subseteq$		
du-s				$=$	$\supseteq$	$\supseteq$	$\subseteq$	$\supseteq$	$\subseteq$	$\supseteq$	$\subseteq$	$\supseteq$	$\subseteq$	$\supseteq$		
e-op					$=$	$\supseteq$	$\subseteq$	$\subseteq$	$\subseteq$	$\subseteq$	$\subseteq$	$\subseteq$	$\subseteq$	$\subseteq$		
du-op						$=$	$\subseteq$	$\subseteq$	$\subseteq$	$\subseteq$	$\subseteq$	$\subseteq$	$\subseteq$	$\subseteq$		
e-cc							$=$	$\supseteq$	$\supseteq$	$\supseteq$	$\supseteq$	$\supseteq$	$\supseteq$	$\supseteq$		
du-cc								$=$	$\supseteq$	$\supseteq$	$\supseteq$	$\supseteq$	$\supseteq$	$\supseteq$		
e-cs									$=$	$\supseteq$	$\subseteq$	$\subseteq$	$\supseteq$	$\supseteq$		
du-cs										$=$	$\subseteq$	$\subseteq$	$\supseteq$	$\supseteq$		
e-vwc											$=$	$\supseteq$	$\subseteq$	$\supseteq$		
du-vwc												$=$	$\subseteq$	$\supseteq$		
e-svwc													$=$	$\supseteq$		
du-svwc														$=$		
e-si															$=$	$\supseteq$
du-si																$=$

e-ss:	e-strict serializability
du-ss:	du-strict serializability
e-s:	e-serializability
du-s:	du-serializability
e-op:	e-opacity
du-op:	du-opacity
e-cc:	e-causal consistency
du-cc:	du-causal consistency
e-cs:	e-causal serializability
du-cs:	du-causal serializability
e-vwc:	e-virtual world consistency
du-vwc:	du-virtual world consistency
e-svwc:	e-strong virtual world consistency
du-svwc:	du-strong virtual world consistency
e-si:	e-snapshot isolation
du-si:	du-snapshot isolation

Lemma 18. *If an execution α satisfies e-strict serializability (du-strict serializability) then α satisfies e-snapshot isolation (du-snapshot isolation), but not vice versa.*

Since strict virtual world consistency and opacity are stronger than strict serializability, Lemma 18 implies that they are stronger than snapshot isolation.

Snapshot isolation is incomparable to virtual world consistency, serializability, causal consistency and causal serializability. For instance, there is an execution which is serializable that does not satisfy snapshot isolation. An example of a history that satisfies snapshot isolation but not serializability is given in Figure 10.

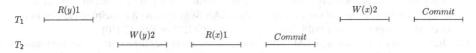

Fig. 10. A history complying with snapshot isolation which is not serializable

Acknowledgments. This work has been supported by the European Commission under the 7th Framework Program through the TransForm (FP7-MC-ITN-238639) project and by the ARISTEIA Action of the Operational Programme Education and Lifelong Learning which is co-funded by the European Social Fund (ESF) and National Resources through the GreenVM project.

We would like to thank Victor Bushkov for his valuable comments in a preliminary version of this chapter and Eleftherios Kosmas for several useful discussions that motivated this work. Many thanks also to Hagit Attiya Petr Kuznetsov, and Sandeep Hans for their comments on a previous version of this article.

References

1. Afek, Y., Avni, H., Dice, D., Shavit, N.: Efficient lock free privatization. In: Lu, C., Masuzawa, T., Mosbah, M. (eds.) OPODIS 2010. LNCS, vol. 6490, pp. 333–347. Springer, Heidelberg (2010)
2. Ahamad, M., Neiger, G., Burns, J.E., Kohli, P., Hutto, P.W.: Causal memory: definitions, implementation, and programming. Distributed Computing 9(1), 37–49 (1995)
3. Ardekani, M.S., Sutra, P., Shapiro, M.: The impossibility of ensuring snapshot isolation in genuine replicated stms. In: TransForm/Euro-TM WTTM 3rd Workshop on the Theory of Transactional Memory, WTTM 2011 (2011)
4. Attiya, H., Hans, S.: Transactions are Back-but How Different They Are? In: 7th ACM SIGPLAN Workshop on Transactional Computing, New Orleans, LA, USA (February 2012)
5. Attiya, H., Hans, S., Kuznetsov, P., Ravi, S.: Safety of deferred update in transactional memory. In: Proceedings of the 33rd International Conference on Distributed Computing Systems, ICDCS 2013, pp. 601–610. IEEE (2013)
6. Attiya, H., Hillel, E., Milani, A.: Inherent limitations on disjoint-access parallel implementations of transactional memory. In: Proceedings of the 21st ACM Symposium on Parallel Algorithms and Architectures, SPAA 2009, pp. 69–78. ACM, New York (2009)
7. Berenson, H., Bernstein, P., Gray, J., Melton, J., O'Neil, E., O'Neil, P.: A critique of ansi sql isolation levels. SIGMOD Rec. 24(2), 1–10 (1995)

8. Bernstein, P.A., Hadzilacos, V., Goodman, N.: Concurrency control and recovery in database systems. Addison-Wesley Longman Publishing Co., Inc., Boston (1987)

9. Bushkov, V., Dziuma, D., Fatourou, P., Guerraoui, R.: Snapshot isolation does not scale either. Tech. Rep. TR-437, Foundation of Research and Technology – Hellas (FORTH) (October 2013)

10. Bushkov, V., Dziuma, D., Fatourou, P., Guerraoui, R.: The pcl theorem - transactions cannot be parallel, consistent and live. In: Proceedings of the 4th ACM Symposium on Parallelism in Algorithms and Architectures, SPAA 2014, pp. 178–187. ACM, New York (2014)

11. Bushkov, V., Guerraoui, R., Kapałka, M.: On the liveness of transactional memory. In: Proceedings of the 31st ACM Symposium on Principles of Distributed Computing, PODC 2012, pp. 9–18. ACM, New York (2012)

12. Dalessandro, L., Spear, M.F., Scott, M.L.: Norec: streamlining stm by abolishing ownership records. In: Proceedings of the 15th ACM SIGPLAN Symposium on Principles and Practice of Parallel Programming, PPoPP 2010, pp. 67–78. ACM, New York (2010)

13. Dias, R.J., Seco, J., Lourenço, J.M.: Snapshot isolation anomalies detection in software transactional memory. In: Proceedings of INForum Simpósio de Informática (InForum 2010). Universidade do Minho, Braga (2010)

14. Dice, D., Shavit, N.: What really makes transactions faster? In: 1st ACM SIGPLAN Workshop on Languages Compilers, and Hardware Support for Transactional Computing, TRANSACT 2006 (2006)

15. Doherty, S., Groves, L., Luchangco, V., Moir, M.: Towards formally specifying and verifying transactional memory. Formal Aspects of Computing 25(5), 1–31 (2012)

16. Ellen, F., Fatourou, P., Kosmas, E., Milani, A., Travers, C.: Universal constructions that ensure disjoint-access parallelism and wait-freedom. In: Proceedings of the 31st ACM Symposium on Principles of Distributed Computing, PODC 2012, pp. 115–124. ACM, New York (2012)

17. Guerraoui, R., Kapalka, M.: On obstruction-free transactions. In: Proceedings of the Twentieth Annual Symposium on Parallelism in Algorithms and Architectures, SPAA 2008, pp. 304–313. ACM, New York (2008)

18. Guerraoui, R., Kapalka, M.: On the correctness of transactional memory. In: Proceedings of the 13th ACM SIGPLAN Symposium on Principles and Practice of Parallel Programming, PPoPP 2008, pp. 175–184. ACM, New York (2008)

19. Guerraoui, R., Kapalka, M.: Principles of Transactional Memory (Synthesis Lectures on Distributed Computing Theory). Morgan and Claypool Publishers (2010)

20. Harris, T., Larus, J., Rajwar, R.: Transactional Memory, 2nd edn. Morgan and Claypool Publishers (2010)

21. Herlihy, M., Moss, J.E.B.: Transactional memory: architectural support for lock-free data structures. SIGARCH Comput. Archit. News 21(2), 289–300 (1993)

22. Herlihy, M.P., Wing, J.M.: Linearizability: a correctness condition for concurrent objects. ACM Transactions on Programming Languages and Systems 12(3), 463–492 (1990)

23. Hutto, P., Ahamad, M.: Slow memory: Weakening consistency to enhance concurrency in distributed shared memories. In: Proceedings of the 10th International Conference on Distributed Computing Systems, ICDCS 1990, pp. 302–309. IEEE (1990)

24. Imbs, D., Raynal, M.: Virtual world consistency: A condition for STM systems (with a versatile protocol with invisible read operations). Theoretical Computer Science 444(0), 113–127 (2009), Structural Information and Communication Complexity (SIROCCO) 2009

25. Maessen, J.: Arvind: Store atomicity for transactional memory. Electr. Notes Theor. Comput. Sci. 174(9), 117–137 (2007)

26. Marathe, V.J., Spear, M.F., Scott, M.L.: Scalable techniques for transparent privatization in software transactional memory. In: Proceedings of the 37th International Conference on Parallel Processing (ICPP), pp. 67–74. IEEE Computer Society (2008)

27. Martin, M.M.K., Blundell, C., Lewis, E.: Subtleties of transactional memory atomicity semantics. Computer Architecture Letters 5(2) (2006)
28. Normann, R., Østby, L.T.: A theoretical study of 'snapshot isolation'. In: Proceedings of the 13th International Conference on Database Theory, ICDT 2010, pp. 44–49. ACM, New York (2010)
29. Papadimitriou, C.H.: The serializability of concurrent database updates. Journal of the ACM 26(4), 631–653 (1979)
30. Ramadan, H.E., Roy, I., Herlihy, M., Witchel, E.: Committing conflicting transactions in an stm. In: Proceedings of the 14th ACM SIGPLAN Symposium on Principles and Practice of Parallel Programming, PPoPP 2009, pp. 163–172. ACM, New York (2009)
31. Raynal, M., Thia-Kime, G., Ahamad, M.: From serializable to causal transactions for collaborative applications. In: Proceedings of the 23rd EUROMICRO Conference, EUROMICRO 1997, pp. 314–321. IEEE (1997)
32. Riegel, T., Fetzer, C., Felber, P.: Snapshot isolation for software transactional memory. In: 1st ACM SIGPLAN Workshop on Languages Compilers, and Hardware Support for Transactional Computing, TRANSACT 2006 (2006)
33. Riegel, T., Fetzer, C., Felber, P.: Time-based transactional memory with scalable time bases. In: Proceedings of the 19th ACM Symposium on Parallel Algorithms and Architectures, SPAA 2007, pp. 221–228. ACM, New York (2007)
34. Scott, M.L., Spear, M.F., Dalessandro, L., Marathe, V.J.: Transactions and privatization in delaunay triangulation. In: Proceedings of the 26th ACM Symposium on Principles of Distributed Computing (PODC), pp. 336–337. ACM, New York (2007)
35. Shavit, N., Touitou, D.: Software transactional memory. In: Proceedings of the 14th ACM Symposium on Principles of Distributed Computing, PODC 1995, pp. 204–213. ACM, New York (1995)
36. Siek, K., Wojciechowski, P.T.: Brief announcement: Towards a fully-articulated pessimistic distributed transactional memory. In: Proceedings of SPAA 2013: The 25th ACM Symposium on Parallelism in Algorithms and Architectures, Montreal, Canada, pp. 111–114. ACM (July 2013)
37. Siek, K., Wojciechowski, P.T.: Zen and the art of concurrency control: An exploration of tm safety property space with early release in mind. In: Euro-TM WTTM 6th Workshop on the Theory of Transactional Memory, WTTM 2014 (2014)
38. Spear, M.F., Marathe, V.J., Dalessandro, L., Scott, M.L.: Privatization techniques for software transactional memory. In: Proceedings of the 26th ACM Symposium on Principles of Distributed Computing (PODC), pp. 338–339. ACM, New York (2007)
39. Spear, M.F., Michael, M.M., von Praun, C.: Ringstm: scalable transactions with a single atomic instruction. In: Proceedings of the 20th ACM Symposium on Parallel Algorithms and Architectures, SPAA 2008, pp. 275–284. ACM, New York (2008)
40. Weikum, G., Vossen, G.: Transactional Information Systems: Theory, Algorithms, and the Practice of Concurrency Control and Recovery. Morgan Kaufmann Publishers (2002)

Liveness in Transactional Memory

Victor Bushkov and Rachid Guerraoui

EPFL, IC, LPD, Lausanne, Switzerland
{victor.bushkov,rachid.guerraoui}@epfl.ch

Abstract. In this chapter we give a formal overview of liveness properties of transactional memory (TM) systems. Unlike safety properties, which require some 'bad' events not to occur, liveness properties require some 'good' events to eventually occur. Usually, liveness properties of shared memory systems require some operations to eventually return a response (terminate). However, in the context of TM systems operation termination is not enough to ensure meaningful progress. It is necessary to require some transactions to eventually commit. In this chapter we give precise definitions of liveness properties and what it means for a TM systems to satisfy a liveness property. Using the defined formal framework we give some impossibility results. We show that it is impossible to guarantee both local progress, the strongest TM liveness property that requires every correct transaction to eventually commit, and common TM safety properties such as strict serializability or opacity in a fault prone system.

1 Introduction

Transactional memory (TM) [13, 16, 26] is a concurrency control paradigm that aims at simplifying concurrent programming. It provides non-expert programmers with an abstraction, called *transaction*, such that transactions concurrently execute atomic pieces of sequential code of some application. Each transaction is executed by some process (thread) and contains transactional operations. A transactional operation is either an access (read or write) to a transactional variable (data item) or a request to commit the transaction. If the transaction is committed, then the effects of its operations become visible to subsequent transactions, and if it is aborted, then the effects are rolled back. Transactions are viewed as a simple way to write concurrent programs and hence leverage multicore architectures. Not surprisingly, a large body of work has been dedicated to implementing the paradigm and reducing its overheads.

Most of the work on the theory of transactional memory focused solely on *safety* (consistency), i.e., on what TMs *should not do*. Indeed, correctness conditions for TMs have been proposed in [11, 18, 5, 6, 8] and programming language level semantics of specific classes of TM implementations have been determined, e.g., in [1, 19, 22, 23]. Most those efforts, however, focused solely on *safety*, i.e., on what TMs *should not do*. Clearly, a TM that ensures only a safety property can trivially be implemented by aborting all operations. To be meaningful, a TM has to ensure that some transactions should eventually commit which is captured by a *liveness* property [2].

Generally, in shared-memory systems, a liveness property states when a certain process that invokes an operation on a shared object is guaranteed to return from this

R. Guerraoui and P. Romano (Eds.): Transactional Memory, LNCS 8913, pp. 32–49, 2015.

operation, i.e. makes progress [17]. One of the widely studied such property is *wait-freedom* [14]. It ensures, intuitively, that *every* process invoking an operation on a shared object eventually returns from this operation, even if other processes crash. It is the ultimate liveness property in concurrent computing as it ensures that every process makes progress and forms the consensus number hierarchy of shared objects [14]. However, requiring TM systems to ensure only wait-freedom would, however, not be enough to ensure any meaningful progress: processes of which all transactions are *aborted* might be satisfying wait-freedom (since every transactional operation returns a response) but would not be making any real progress. To ensure meaningful progress, a TM liveness property should require transaction *commitment*, beyond operation *termination*. In other words, it should require certain processes to eventually commit some of their transactions. One would expect from a TM that every process that keeps executing transactions eventually commits some of them—a property that we call *local progress* and that is similar in spirit to wait-freedom. Not satisfying this property means that some processes might never commit any of their transactions starting from some point in time.

A TM implementation that protects every transaction using a single fair global lock could ensure local progress: such a TM would execute all transactions sequentially, thus avoiding conflicts between transactions. Yet, such a TM would force processes to wait for each other, preventing them from progressing independently. A process that acquires a global lock and gets suspended for a long time, or that enters an infinite loop and keeps running forever without releasing the lock, would prevent all other processes from making any progress. This would go against the very essence of wait-freedom. Hence, to be really meaningful a TM liveness property should enforce some "independent" progress.

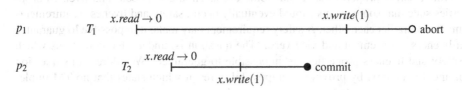

Fig. 1. An illustration of the difficulty of ensuring local progress. The scenario can be repeated infinitely many times preventing transaction T_1 from ever committing.

The classical way of modeling shared-memory systems in which processes can make progress independently, i.e., without waiting for each other, is to consider *asynchronous* systems in which processes can be arbitrarily slow and can fail by *crashing*. A TM implementation that is resilient to crashes enables the progress of a process even if other processes are suspended for a long time or crashed.

However, resiliency against crashes is not enough. Consider a transaction that holds a global lock which does not crash and never invokes a commit request. Such a transaction would prevent all other transactions from making progress. Therefore, one should also ensure progress in the face of *parasitic* processes—those that keep executing transactional operations without ever attempting to commit. These model long-running processes whose duration cannot be anticipated by the system, e.g., because of an infinite loop.

To illustrate the underlying challenges, consider the following example, shown in Figure 1. Two processes, p_1 and p_2, execute transactions T_1 and T_2, respectively. Process p_1 reads value 0 from a shared variable x and then gets suspended for a long time. Then, process p_2 also reads value 0 from x, writes value 1 to x, and attempts to commit. Because of asynchrony, the processes can be arbitrarily delayed. Hence, the TM does not know whether p_1 has crashed or is just very slow, and so, in order to ensure the progress of process p_2, the TM might eventually allow process p_2 to commit T_2. But then, if process p_1 writes value 1 to x and attempts to commit T_1, the TM cannot allow process p_1 to commit, as this would violate safety. A similar situation can occur in the case of parasitic processes, say if p_1 keeps repeatedly reading from variable x. If the maximum length of a transaction is not known, the TM cannot say whether p_1 is parasitic or not, and thus may eventually allow process p_2 to commit T_2, forcing process p_1 to abort T_1 later.

We consider a set-based definition of liveness, i.e. we consider a *TM-liveness* property L as a set of fair histories, so that a TM implementation ensures the property if every fair history of the implementation belongs to L. A history is basically a sequence of invocations and responses of operations executed within transactions, and a fair history is a history augmented with *crash* events. The focus on fair histories is necessary because a TM-liveness property should not require progress from processes which do not take any steps in an execution, i.e. crash in that execution. So, to distinguish crashed processes from processes that take infinitely many steps without returning a response of a transactional operation, we augment histories with crash events. Like fairness properties are defined in [27], we define a TM-liveness property as a weakening of local progress, which has the strongest progress requirement among TM-liveness properties.

Since safety properties state that some events should not occur and liveness properties state that some events should eventually occur, safety and liveness requirements might contradict each other. A safety requirement may make it impossible to guarantee a liveness requirement and vice versa. The question is, under what conditions which safety and liveness properties are impossible to guarantee? We address this question in the TM context by proving an impossibility result which states that no TM implementation can ensure both *local progress* and *opacity* in any fault-prone system, i.e. in a system in which any number of processes can crash or be parasitic. Opacity is the safety property ensured by most TM implementations. It states that every transaction (even aborted or live) observes a consistent state of the system. Local progress is a TM-liveness property, highlighted above, which states that every correct process, i.e. a process which is not parasitic and does not crash, eventually commits its transactions. In fact, we prove a more general result stating that no TM implementation can ensure any safety property that is at least as strong as strict serializability together with the progress of at least two correct processes and any correct process that runs alone.

2 Preliminaries

2.1 System Model

We consider a system of n *asynchronous processes* $p_1, \ldots, p_n$ that communicate with each other by executing operations on *shared objects* (which represent the shared memory, e.g., provided in hardware). A *shared object* is a higher-level abstraction provided to processes, and implemented typically in software using a set of *base objects*. Base objects are shared objects which are accessed via *atomic* operations called *primitives*.

For instance, if base objects are memory locations with basic operations such as read, write, and compare-and-swap, then shared objects could be shared data structures such as linked lists or hash tables. When a process p_i invokes an operation op on a shared object O, then p_i follows the implementation of O, possibly accessing some number of base objects and executing local computations, until p_i is returned the result of op. We assume that processes are sequential; that is, whenever a process p_i invokes an operation op on any shared object, p_i does not invoke another operation on any shared object until p_i returns from op. Invocations and responses on shared objects operations are called (invocation and response) *events*.

2.2 Histories and Executions

Let I be an implementation of a shared object O. A *configuration* C of I determines the current state of each process and of each base object used in I. The *initial configuration* C_0 of I is a configuration when all processes and all base objects are at their initial states. A *step* s (executed by some process p_i) of I can be one of the following: (i) an invocation event of some operation on O, (ii) a response event of some operation from O, (iii) a single primitive operation and one or more computations local to p_i. An *execution* $\alpha = C_0 \cdot s_1 \cdot C_1 \cdot s_2 \cdot C_2 \ldots$ of I is a (finite or infinite) sequence of alternating configurations and steps of I such that: (i) C_0 is the initial configuration, and for any C_i, s_i, and C_{i+1} in α the execution of step s_i by I at configuration C_i results in the new configuration C_{i+1}. We define a *projection* $\alpha|p_k$ of an execution α on a process p_k as the longest subsequence of α consisting only of steps of p_k.

The order in which processes take steps is determined by a *scheduler*. Processes and TM implementations have no control over a scheduler. The scheduler decides which process is allowed to execute a step at a given point in time. These decisions form a *schedule* which is a finite or an infinite sequence of process identifiers.

The longest subsequence of an execution α of I consisting only of invocation and response events is called a *history* of I, and is denoted by H_α. We define a *projection* $H|p_k$ of a history H on a process p_k as the longest subsequence of H consisting of invocation and response events associated with p_k.

2.3 Transactional Memory

Transactional memory allows processes to execute pieces of sequential code within transactions. The code contains accesses to *transactional variables* (t-variables for short) which represent shared data. For presentation simplicity, we focus on t-variables that support *read* and *write* operations. Let K be the set of *process identifiers*, $P = \{p_k | k \in K\}$ be the set of processes, and let X be the set of *t-variables*. Each t-variable can take values from a set V. To write a value v to a t-variable x process p_k invokes $x.write^k(v)$ and receives as a response either ok, if the write was successful, or an abort event A^k if the transaction has to be aborted. To read a value from a t-variable x process p_k invokes $x.read^k$ and receives as a response either the value of t-variable v or an abort event A^k if the transaction has to be aborted. To commit a transaction process p_k invokes a commit request $tryC^k$ and receives as a response either a commit event C^k or an abort event A^k. Let $Inv_k = \{x.write^k(v)|x \in X \text{ and } v \in V\} \cup \{x.read^k|x \in X\} \cup \{tryC^k\}$ be the set of invocation events of process p_k and $Res_k = \{v^k|v \in V\} \cup \{ok^k, A^k, C^k\}$ be the set of response events of process p_k. Also, let $Inv = \cup_{k \in K} Inv_k$ and $Res = \cup_{k \in K} Res_k$. Usually TM implementations provide additional transactional operations such as the request to start a transaction, the request to create a new t-variable (in the case of dynamic TMs), and a request to abort a transaction. Our theoretical results hold for TM implementations that provide these operations. However, for simplicity, we assume TM implementations that provide only operations to read/write a t-variable and commit a transaction.

Denote by Σ_k a set such that $\Sigma_k = \{x.write^k(v) \cdot ok^k|x.write^k(v) \in Inv_k\} \cup \{x.read^k() \cdot v^k|x.read^k() \in Inv_k \text{ and } v^k \in Res_k\} \cup \{tryC^k \cdot C^k\} \cup \{inv \cdot A^k|inv \in Inv_k\}$, i.e. Σ_k contains concatenations of invocations and their possible responses associated with process p_k. Also, let Σ_k^∞ be the set of all finite and infinite sequences over Σ_k. A history H of a TM implementation is *well-formed* if for every $p_k \in P$ either $H|p_k \in \Sigma_k^\infty$ or $H|p_k \in \Sigma_k^* \cdot Inv_k$ holds, i.e. $H|p_k$ is a sequence of alternating invocation and response events. In the rest of the chapter we assume only well-formed histories.

Given projection $H|p_k$ of history H of some TM implementation, a *transaction* of p_k in H is a subsequence $T = e_1 \cdot \ldots \cdot e_m$ of $H|p_k$ such that:

- either e_1 is the first event in $H|p_k$, or the event e' which precedes e_1 in $H|p_k$ is either A^k or C^k, and
- e_m is either A^k or C^k or the last event in $H|p_k$, and
- no event in T, except e_m, is A^k or C^k.

Transaction T is *committed* (*aborted*) if the last event in T is a commit (abort) event. Given transactions T_1 and T_2 in history H, we say that T_1 *precedes* T_2 in H, denoted by $T_1 <_H T_2$, if T_1 is committing or aborting and the last event of T_1 precedes the first event of T_2 in H. Transactions T_1 and T_2 are *concurrent* if T_1 does not precede T_2 and T_2 does not precede T_1. History H is *sequential* if no two transactions in H are concurrent to each other.

Processes communicate with each other only through a TM implementation by invoking concurrently requests (read, write, and commit requests) and receiving corresponding responses from the implementation. Processes send commit requests to the TM implementation that decides which transactions should be committed or aborted. To reduce contention between transactions, a TM implementation may use a logically separate module called a contention manager. A contention manager can force the TM implementation to abort or delay some transactions. In this work we consider a contention manager as an integral part of a TM implementation. That is, all the results of the paper apply to the entire TM, including the contention manager.

2.4 Process Failures

Let α be an infinite execution. Process p_k *crashes* in α if $\alpha|p_k$ is finite. That is, a process crashes in an infinite execution if it stops taking steps in the execution.

Intuitively, a parasitic process is a process that keeps executing transactional operations but, from some point in time, never attempts to commit (by invoking operation *tryC*) when given a chance to do so. Note that if starting from some moment in time every transaction executed by the process is prematurely aborted, i.e. aborted before the process invokes a commit request, in general, we cannot tell whether the process intended to eventually invoke a commit request or not. Therefore, we consider such processes as not parasitic.

Let α be an infinite execution. Process p_k is *parasitic* in α, if there is a suffix α' of α such that: (i) p_k executes infinitely many transactional operations in α', (ii) α' does not contain A^k events, and (iii) α' does not contain $tryC^k$ requests.

Process p_k is *correct* in an infinite execution α if p_k is not parasitic in α and does not crash in α.

We define a *crash-prone system* (respectively, *parasitic-prone system*) Sys to be a system of processes in which any process can crash (respectively, be parasitic). A *fault-prone system* Sys is a system which is crash-prone or parasitic-prone. Note that a fault-prone system can have both crashed and parasitic processes.

2.5   Safety Properties of TM

Intuitively a safety property of TM implementations should capture the fact that all events within a transaction appear to other transactions as if they occur instantaneously. If a transaction is committed, then all the changes made by write operations within the transaction are made visible to other transactions; otherwise all the changes are rolled back. We consider two safety properties of TM implementations: strict serializability and opacity. Intuitively, strict serializability requires every committed transaction to observe a consistent state of the system [24], while opacity requires every transaction (even aborted or unfinished) to observe a consistent state of the system [12].

We say that history H is *equivalent* to history H' if for every process $p_k \in P$ we have $H|p_k = H'|p_k$. A transaction T in history H is *commit-pending* if T ends with a commit request *tryC*. A transaction T in history H is *live* if T is not commit-pending, aborted, or committed. We obtain a completion of a finite history H by aborting every live transaction and by committing or aborting every commit-pending transaction. Formally a *completion comp(H)* of a history H is a history derived from H by appending the following events:

- for every live transaction T (executed by p^k) we append $tryC^k \cdot A^k$
- for every commit pending transaction T (executed by p^k) we append either C^k or A^k.

If $comp(H) = H$, then H is a *complete* history. We say that a history H' *preserves the real time order* of a history H if for any two transactions T_1 and T_2 in H if $T_1 <_H T_2$, then $T_1 <_{H'} T_2$. Let H_s be a complete sequential history and T_j be a transaction in H. Denote by *visible*(T_j) the longest subsequence of H_s such that for every transaction T_i in the subsequence, either $j = i$ or $T_i <_{H_s} T_j$. Transaction T_j is *legal* in H_s if for every t-variable $x \in X$ history *visible*(T_j) respects the sequential specification of x, i.e. for every transaction T_i in *visible*(T_j) and every response event v^k in T_i, v is the value of the previous write to x invocation event within a committing transaction in *visible*(T_j) or v is the initial value of x if there are no write to x invocation events within any committing transaction in *visible*(T_j) before v^k.

A finite history H is *opaque*[1] if there exists a sequential history H_s equivalent to $comp(H)$, such that H_s preserves the real-time order of $comp(H)$, and every transaction in H_s is legal. A finite history H is *strictly serializable* if there exists a sequential history H_s equivalent to H', where H' is obtained from H by removing every aborted and live transaction and some of the commit-pending transactions and appending to H a commit event for every commit-pending transaction which is not removed, such that H_s preserves the real-time order of H, and every transaction in H_s is legal. A TM implementation I ensures opacity (respectively, strict serializability) if for every execution α of I, H_α is opaque (respectively, strictly serializable).

For example, the history in Figure 1 is opaque, while the history in Figure 2 is not opaque but strictly serializable.

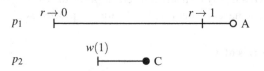

Fig. 2. A history which is not opaque but strictly serializable. All operations access the same t-variable. For simplicity, $r \rightarrow v$ denotes both the invocation of a read operation and its response v, $w(v)$ denotes both the invocation of a write operation (with value v) and its response ok, C denotes both the invocation of a commit request and a commit event, A denotes both the invocation of a commit request and an abort event.

3   Liveness of a TM

3.1   TM-Liveness Properties

Basically, a TM-liveness property states whether some process p_k should make progress in some execution α. Clearly, progress cannot be required for crashed or parasitic processes: these processes have executions with a finite number of *tryC* operation invocations. Thus, we should require progress only for correct processes (which basically captures the fairness requirement). Like a fairness property is defined in [27], we define a TM-liveness property as a weakening of the strongest TM-liveness property. The strongest TM-liveness property that we can require of a TM system is to ensure that every correct process makes progress.

Next we introduce the notion of a fair history in order to distinguish a process that crashes from a process that takes infinitely many steps without returning a response when defining a liveness property. We derive a fair history F_α by augmenting a history H_α, of some execution α, with *crash* events. Formally, we derive a *fair history* F_α in the following way: for every process p_k that crashes in α we insert a crash event $crash^k$ between the last event e of p_k and the event that follows after e in H_α. A process p_k is

---

[1] Since the way we define opacity is not prefix-closed it is not exactly a safety property. However, for the sake of simplicity, we do not consider a prefix-closed definition of opacity since in terms of TM implementations a prefix-closed definition is equivalent to a non-prefix-closed one (i.e. every TM implementation which ensures non-prefix-closed also ensure a prefix-closed one).

correct in a fair history F_α, if p_k is correct in α. Herein, if α is clear from the context, we omit α from the notation of a (fair) history H_α and use just H instead. A process p_k *makes progress* in a fair history F, if F contains infinitely many commit events C^k.

A fair history F ensures *local progress* if every correct process makes progress in F, or F does not have any correct processes. Let L_{local} denote the set of all possible fair histories that satisfy local progress. Then, a *TM-liveness* property L is a set of fair histories such that $L_{local} \subseteq L$. Given two TM-liveness properties L_1 and L_2, we say that L_1 is weaker (stronger) than L_2 if $L_2 \subseteq L_1$ ($L_1 \subseteq L_2$). A fair history F ensures a TM-liveness property L iff $H \in L$. A TM implementation I *ensures a TM-liveness property* L if for every execution α of I its corresponding fair history F_α ensures L.

3.2 Examples of TM-Liveness Properties

Local Progress. Roughly speaking, a TM implementation I ensures local progress if I guarantees that *every* correct process in a fair history makes progress, i.e. has infinitely many of its transactions committed. Note that local progress requirements also imply the requirement of wait-freedom of individual transactional operations. Therefore, every TM-implementation that ensures local progress also ensures wait-freedom [14], which requires each individual transactional operation to receive a response. However, a TM-implementation might ensure wait-freedom without ensuring local progress, e.g. when all transactional operations receive a response each transaction is aborted.

For example, Figure 3 shows an infinite history which ensures local progress in a system with two processes and one t-variable. Both processes make progress in the history.

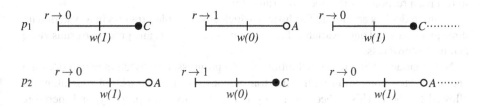

Fig. 3. An infinite fair history with two processes and one t-variable that ensures local progress. Each process executes an infinite number of transactions that either read value 0 and write value 1 or read value 1 and write value 0.

Global Progress. A TM implementation I ensures *global progress* if I guarantees that *some* correct process in a fair history makes progress, i.e. has infinitely many of its transactions committed. Formally, we define global progress, as a TM-liveness property L_{global} such that a fair history F belongs to L_{global} iff at least one correct process in F makes progress in F, or F does not have correct processes. Note that every TM-implementation that ensures global progress also ensures lock-freedom [14], which requires some individual transactional operation to receive a response.

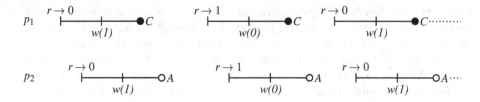

Fig. 4. An infinite fair history with two processes and one t-variable that ensures global progress. Processes execute an infinite number of transactions that either read value 0 and write value 1 or read value 1 and write value 0.

Figure 4 shows an infinite fair history which ensures global progress in a system of two processes and one t-variable. Both of the processes are correct in the history. However, only process p_1 makes progress in the history.

Solo Progress. A TM implementation I ensures *solo progress* if I guarantees that every correct process which runs alone in a fair history makes progress, i.e. has infinitely many of its transactions committed. A correct process runs alone if starting from some point in time it is the only process that takes steps in an execution. Formally, a process p_k *runs alone* in an infinite fair history F if p_k is correct in F and all other processes crash in F (i.e. stop taking steps in the corresponding execution). We define solo progress, as a TM-liveness property L_{solo} such that a fair history F belongs to L_{solo} iff a process that runs alone in F makes progress in H, or F does not have a process that runs alone in F. Note that every TM-implementation that ensures solo progress also ensures obstruction-freedom [15], which requires each individual transactional operation to receive a response if the operation runs alone.

Figure 5 depicts an infinite fair history which ensures solo progress in a system with three processes and one t-variable. Processes p_1 and p_2 crash, and process p_3 runs alone and makes progress.

Note that according to the definition of solo progress, a transaction which does not encounter step contention with other transactions, i.e. the transaction runs alone, is allowed to abort. This is because solo progress is a liveness property, and therefore it should allow any possible finite fair history (by the definition of a liveness property [2, 25]). If we change the definition of solo progress so that the new definition requires every transaction which runs alone to commit, then the resulting new definition would not be a liveness property.

Obstruction-free TM implementations [12, 15] ensure solo progress in systems that are not parasitic-prone. Lock-based TM implementations, such as TinySTM [9] and SwissTM [7], ensure solo progress in systems that are not crash-prone. However, lock-based TMs that use lazy acquire, such as TL2 [4], ensure solo progress in systems that are not crash-prone.

Using the same formal framework we can define other kinds of TM-liveness properties. For example, in [3] we define a stronger version of solo progress which requires progress from a process if all other processes either crash or become parasitic starting

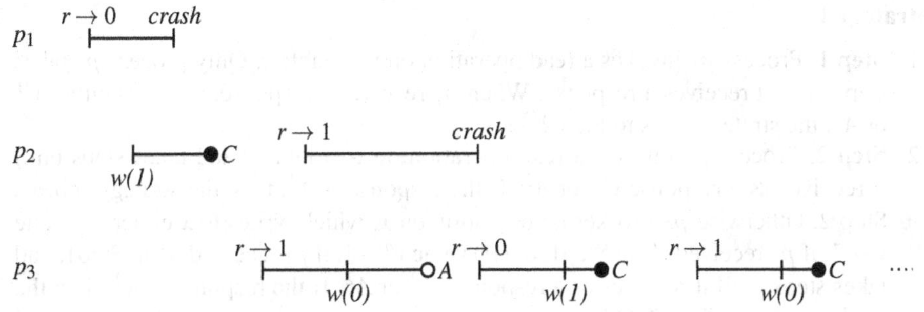

Fig. 5. An infinite fair history with three processes and one t-variable that ensures solo progress. Process p_1 starts a transaction by invoking a read operations, but then it crashes. Process p_2 executes two transactions, but it crashes during the execution of the second transaction. Process p_3 executes an infinite number of transactions that either read value 0 and write value 1 or read value 1 and write value 0.

from some point in time. Basically, such TM-liveness property states that if no other processes attempt to commit their transactions then the only correct process should make progress.

4   Impossibility of Local Progress

Like in any distributed problem, each execution of a TM implementation can be thought of as a game between the environment and the implementation. The *environment* consisting of processes and a scheduler decides on inputs (operation invocations) given to the implementation and schedule of steps and the implementation decides on outputs (responses) returned to the environment. To prove that there is no TM implementation that ensures both opacity and local progress in a fault prone system we use the environment as an adversary that acts against the implementation. The environment wins the game against a TM implementation, if the resulting infinite fair history violates local progress. To prove the impossibility result, we show a wining strategy for the environment.

Theorem 1. *For every fault-prone system, there does not exist a TM implementation that ensures both local progress and opacity in that system.*

Proof. Assume otherwise, i.e. that there exists a fault-prone system Sys for which there exists a TM implementation I that ensures local progress and opacity in Sys. To find a contradiction, we exhibit a winning strategy (Strategies 1 and 2 below) for the environment resulting in an infinite fair history of I which does not ensure local progress.

By its definition, a fault-prone system Sys is a system in which any number of processes can crash or be parasitic. We thus consider two different cases:

Sys is Crash-Prone
Consider two processes p_1 and p_2 and the environment that interacts with I using Strategy 1.

Strategy 1

1. **Step 1.** Process p_1 invokes a read operation on t-variable x. Only process p_1 takes steps until it receives a response. When p_1 receives a response, which is either v'^1 or A^1, the strategy goes to Step 2.
2. **Step 2.** Process p_2 invokes a read operation on t-variable x and takes steps until it receives as a response v''^2 or A^2. If the response is A^2, then the strategy repeats Step 2. Otherwise p_2 invokes an operation on x, which writes to x either (I) value $v' + 1$, if p_1 received v'^1 in Step 1, or (II) value $v'' + 1$, if p_1 received A^1 in Step 1, and takes steps until it receives as a response ok^2 or A^2. If the response is A^2, then the strategy repeats Step 2. Otherwise p_2 invokes $tryC^2$ operation and takes steps until it receives a response C^2 or A^2. If the response is A^2, the strategy repeats Step 2. Otherwise the strategy goes to Step 3. Only process p_2 takes steps until it receives C^2 as a response.
3. **Step 3.** If p_1 received A^1 in Step 1, then the strategy goes to Step 1. Otherwise process p_1 resumes taking steps by invoking a write operation on t-variable x which writes value $v'' + 1$ to x, and then executes until it receives a response. If the response is A^1, then the strategy goes to Step 1. Otherwise p_1 invokes $tryC^1$ operation and executes the operation until it receives a response. If the response is A^1, the strategy goes to Step 1. Otherwise the strategy stops.

First, we prove that processes p_1 and p_2 cannot be parasitic in any execution corresponding to Strategy 1. This is because Strategy 1 does not have loops in which some process invokes infinitely many operations within the same transaction without ever invoking a commit request or receiving an abort event. Note that according to the strategy, process p_1 can crash when transactions of process p_2 are repeatedly aborted in Step 2. Therefore, the strategy does not describe the behavior of processes in a crash-free system, i.e. system in which no process is allowed to crash.

Next, we show that there exists an infinite fair history F of I corresponding to some execution of I according to Strategy 1. To do so, we prove that Strategy 1 never terminates. We first prove that the individual transactional operations of I are obstruction-free, i.e. we prove that each operation in Strategy 1 eventually returns a response. If in Strategy 1 some process p_k, where $k \in \{1, 2\}$, executing a transactional operation, does not return a response, then p_k takes infinitely many steps, and consequently p_k is correct. However, p_k does not make progress: a contradiction to the fact that I ensures local progress. Since individual operations of the implementation are obstruction-free, then the strategy terminates iff at Step 3 process p_1 is returned C^1 by I.

Assume some finite history H_f of I corresponding to an execution according to Strategy 1 such that the last event in H_f is C^1 (Figure 6). Since I ensures opacity, there exists a sequential finite history H_s which is equivalent to $comp(H_f)$, preserves the real-time order of $comp(H_f)$, and every transaction in H_s is legal. Since history H_f has no transactions which are either live or commit-pending, then $comp(H_f) = H_f$. Hence H_s is equivalent to H_f and preserves the real-time order of H_f. Since H_s is a sequential history and preserves the real-time order of H_f, then H_s could only have one of the following forms, where H'_s is a prefix of H_s:

1. $H_s = H'_s \cdot x.read^1() \cdot v'^1 \cdot x.write^1(v'' + 1) \cdot ok^1 \cdot tryC^1 \cdot C^1 \cdot x.read^2() \cdot v''^2 \cdot x.write^2(v' + 1) \cdot ok^2 \cdot tryC^2 \cdot C^2$

2. $H_s = H'_s \cdot x.read^2() \cdot v''^2 \cdot x.write^2(v'+1) \cdot ok^2 \cdot tryC^2 \cdot C^2 \cdot x.read^1() \cdot v'^1 \cdot x.write^1(v''+1) \cdot ok^1 \cdot tryC^1 \cdot C^1.$

In the first case, the last transaction executed by process p_2 is not legal in H_s, because p_2 reads value v'' from t-variable x the value of which is $v''+1$. In the second case, the last transaction executed by process p_1 is not legal in H_s, because p_1 reads value v' from t-variable x the value of which is $v'+1$. Thus, H_f is not opaque. Since every history H_f of I that ends with a commit event C^1 is not opaque and I ensures opacity, then H_f is not a history of I corresponding to Strategy 1. In other words, every history of I corresponding to some execution according to Strategy 1 is infinite.

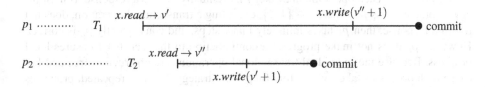

Fig. 6. A suffix of history H_f corresponding to an execution according to Strategy 1 (and Strategy 2) with the last two transactions of p_1 and p_2

Consider some infinite execution α of I corresponding to Strategy 1. Since process p_1 never receives commit event C^1 from I, then p_1 does not make progress in the corresponding infinite fair history F_α. Since *Sys* is crash-prone, then process p_1 either crashes in α or does not. Therefore, we focus on the following two cases:

- **Process p_1 crashes in α.** According to the strategy, process p_1 crashes in F_α iff starting from some point in time the strategy executes infinitely many iterations of Step 2 without going to Step 3. Since no process can be parasitic in any execution corresponding to Strategy 1 and p_2 takes infinitely many steps in α, process p_2 is correct in F_α. Since I ensures local progress and p_2 is correct in F_α, then process p_2 eventually receives commit event C^2 in Step 2, and therefore the strategy should eventually go to Step 3: a contradiction.

- **Process p_1 does not crash in α.** Since p_1 cannot be parasitic in α, then p_1 is correct in F_α. Since I ensures local progress, then p_1 makes progress in F_α: a contradiction.

Sys is Parasitic-Prone. Consider two processes p_1 and p_2 and the environment that interacts with I using the following strategy:

Strategy 2

1. **Step 1.** Process p_1 invokes a read operation on t-variable x and takes steps until it receives as a response v'^1 or A^1. Then process p_2 invokes a read operation on x and takes steps until it receives as a response v''^2 or A^2. If the response is A^2, then the strategy repeats Step 1. Otherwise p_2 invokes a write operation which writes to x either (I) value $v'+1$, if p_1 received v'^1, or (II) value $v''+1$, if p_1 received A^1, and then p_2 takes steps until it receives a response. If the response is A^2, then

the strategy repeats Step 1. Otherwise p_2 invokes $tryC^2$ operation and takes steps until it receives a response. If the response is A^2, then the strategy repeats Step 1. Otherwise the strategy goes to Step 2.

2. **Step 2.** If p_1 received A^1 in Step 1, then the strategy goes to Step 1. Otherwise process p_1 invokes a write operation on x which writes value $v'' + 1$ to x, and p_1 takes steps until it receives a response. If the response is A^1, then the strategy goes to Step 1. Otherwise p_1 invokes $tryC^1$ operation and takes steps until it receives a response. If the response is A^1, then the strategy goes to Step 1. Otherwise the strategy stops.

We first prove that the individual transactional operations of I are obstruction-free, i.e. we prove that each operation in Strategy 2 eventually returns a response. If in Strategy 1 some process p_k, where $k \in \{1, 2\}$, executing a transactional operation, does not return a response, then p_k takes infinitely many steps, and consequently p_k is correct. However, p_k does not make progress: a contradiction to the fact that I ensures local progress. Because the individual transactional operations are obstruction-free and because both processes take steps before Step 1 in Strategy 2 can be repeated, processes p_1 and p_2 cannot crash in any execution corresponding to Strategy 2. Note that according to the strategy, process p_1 can become parasitic when transactions of process p_2 are repeatedly aborted in Step 1 and the read operation of p_1 is never aborted. Therefore, the strategy does not describe the behavior of processes in a parasitic-free system, i.e. system in which no process is allowed to be parasitic.

Next, we prove that Strategy 2 never terminates, i.e. that at Step 2 process p_1 is never returned C^1 by I in any history of I corresponding to an execution of the strategy. Assume some finite history H_f of I corresponding to an execution of Strategy 2 such that the last event in H_f is C^1 (Figure 6). Since I ensures opacity, there exists a sequential finite history H_s which is equivalent to $comp(H_f)$, preserves the real-time order of $comp(H_f)$, and every transaction in H_s is legal. Since history H_f has no transaction which are either live or commit-pending, then $comp(H_f) = H_f$. Hence H_s is equivalent to H_f and preserves the real-time order of H_f. Since H_s is a sequential history and preserves the real-time order of H_f, then H_s could only have one of the following forms, where H_s' is a prefix of H_s:

1. $H_s = H_s' \cdot x.read^1() \cdot v'^1 \cdot x.write^1(v'' + 1) \cdot ok^1 \cdot tryC^1 \cdot C^1 \cdot x.read^2() \cdot v''^2 \cdot x.write^2(v' + 1) \cdot ok^2 \cdot tryC^2 \cdot C^2$
2. $H_s = H_s' \cdot x.read^2() \cdot v''^2 \cdot x.write^2(v' + 1) \cdot ok^2 \cdot tryC^2 \cdot C^2 \cdot x.read^1() \cdot v'^1 \cdot x.write^1(v'' + 1) \cdot ok^1 \cdot tryC^1 \cdot C^1$.

In the first case, the last transaction executed by process p_2 is not legal in H_s, because p_2 reads value v'' from t-variable x the value of which is $v'' + 1$. In the second case, the last transaction executed by process p_1 is not legal in H_s, because p_1 reads value v' from t-variable x the value of which is $v' + 1$. Thus, H_f is not opaque. Since every history H_f of I that ends with commit event C^1 is not opaque and I ensures opacity, then H_f is not a history of I corresponding to the execution of the strategy. In other words, every history of I corresponding to the execution of Strategy 2 is infinite.

Consider now some infinite execution α of I corresponding to the execution of the above strategy. Since process p_1 never receives commit event C^1 from I, then p_1 does not make progress in the corresponding infinite fair history F_α. Since *Sys* is parasitic-prone, then process p_1 is either parasitic in α or not. Therefore, we focus on the following two cases:

- **Process p_1 is parasitic in α.** According to the strategy, process p_1 is parasitic in F_α iff starting from some point in time the strategy executes infinitely many iterations of Step 1 without going to Step 2. Strategy 2 repeats Step 1 without going to Step 2 iff process p_2 is repeatedly returned abort event A^2 in Step 1. Since no process can crash in any execution corresponding to Strategy 1 and p_2 receives infinitely many abort events in α, process p_2 is correct in F_α. Since I ensures local progress and p_2 is correct in F_α, then process p_2 shoudl eventually receive commit event C^2 in Step 1, and therefore the strategy should eventually go to Step 2: a contradiction.

- **Process p_1 is not parasitic in α.** Since p_1 does not crash in α, p_1 is correct in F_α. Since I ensures local progress, then p_1 makes progress in F_α: a contradiction.   □

5   Generalizing the Impossibility

In this section we generalize the impossibility result of the previous section. Namely, we determine a larger class of TM-liveness properties that are impossible to implement together with strict serializability, which is weaker than opacity, in fault-prone systems.

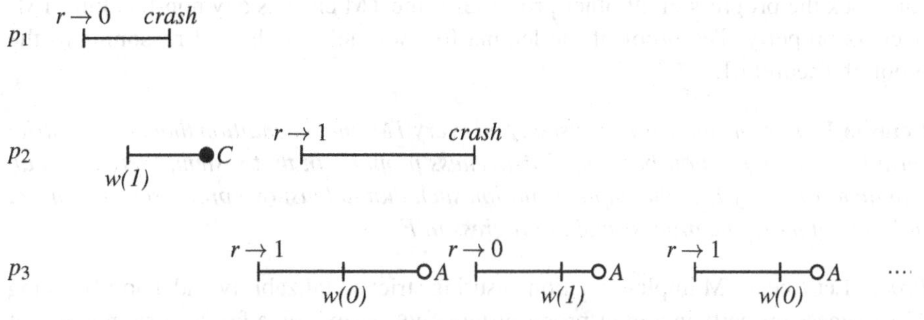

Fig. 7. An infinite fair history with three processes and one t-variable that does not ensure any non-blocking TM-liveness property. Process p_1 starts a transaction by invoking a read operations, but then it crashes. Process p_2 executes two transactions, but it crashes during the execution of the second transaction. Process p_3 executes an infinite number of transactions which read value 0 (read value 1) and write value 1 (write value 0).

5.1   Classes of TM-Liveness Properties

Non-blocking TM-liveness properties. Intuitively, we say that a TM-liveness property is non-blocking if it guarantees progress for every correct process that eventually runs alone. More precisely, a TM-liveness property L is *non-blocking* iff L is stronger than L_{solo}.

For example, Figure 3, Figure 4, and Figure 5 show infinite fair histories which ensure non-blocking TM-liveness properties while Figure 7 shows an infinite fair history which does not ensure any non-blocking TM-liveness property. Local progress, global progress, and solo progress are non-blocking. Note that solo progress is the weakest among non-blocking TM-liveness properties while local progress is the strongest among non-blocking properties.

Biprogressing TM-liveness properties. Intuitively, we say that a TM-liveness property L is a biprogressing property if it requires that at least two correct processes make progress. More precisely, a TM-liveness property L is *biprogressing* if for every $F \in L$ at least two processes are correct in F, only if at least two processes make progress in F.

For example, Figure 3 and Figure 5 show infinite fair histories which ensure a biprogressing property while Figure 4 shows an infinite fair history which does not ensure any biprogressing property. Local progress is a biprogressing property while global progress and solo progress are not biprogressing.

5.2   Generalized Result

In this section we show that TM-liveness properties that are both non-blocking and biprogressing are impossible to implement together with strict serializability in any fault-prone system. We start by stating the following lemma, which says, intuitively, that there exists a fair history in which a process executing infinitely many transactions can block the progress of all other processes if the TM ensures any non-blocking TM-liveness property. The proof of the lemma follows the same line of reasoning as the proof of Theorem 1.

Lemma 1. *For any fault-prone system and every TM implementation that ensures strict serializability and a non-blocking TM-liveness property in that system, there exists an infinite fair history F of the implementation such that at least two processes are correct in F and at most one process makes progress in F.*

Proof. Let I be a TM implementation ensuring strict serializability and a non-blocking TM-liveness property in a fault-prone system **Sys**. To exhibit a fair history in which at least two processes are correct and at most one process makes progress we consider a game between the environment and the implementation. The environment acts against the implementation and wins the game if the resulting history satisfies the requirements of the lemma.

By definition, fault-prone system **Sys** is a system in which any process can crash or be parasitic. We thus consider two different cases:

Sys is Crash-Prone. Consider two processes p_1 and p_2 that interact with I. The environment uses Strategy 1 to win the game. We can show that processes p_1 and p_2 cannot be parasitic in any execution corresponding to Strategy 1 and that Strategy 1 never terminates using the arguments as in Theorem 1 (because those arguments do not involve live or aborted transactions).

Consider some infinite execution α of I corresponding to Strategy 1. Since process p_1 never receives commit event C^1 from I, then p_1 does not make progress in the corresponding infinite fair history F_α. Since *Sys* is crash-prone, then process p_1 either crashes in α or does not.

Assume that process p_1 crashes in fair history F_α. According to the strategy, process p_1 crashes in F_α only if process p_2 invokes infinitely many operations and does not make progress, i.e. only if p_2 is returned an infinite number of abort events at Step 2. Since p_2 is returned an infinite number of abort events and p_2 cannot crash, p_2 is correct in F_α. Because p_2 runs alone in F_α and I ensures a TM-liveness property which is non-blocking, then p_2 makes progress in H: a contradiction. Thus, p_1 does not crash in F_α. Since p_1 is not parasitic in α, p_1 is correct in F_α.

According to the strategy, p_2 does not crash in F_α since Step 2 is repeated infinitely often. Since Step 2 and Step 1 are repeated infinitely often (because p_1 does not crash in F_α), then p_2 receives infinitely many commit events C^2, i.e. p_2 is correct. Thus, in fair history F_α both of the processes are correct and at most one process makes progress (since p_1 is never returned C^1).

Sys is Parasitic-Prone. Consider two processes p_1 and p_2 that interact with I. The environment uses Strategy 2 to win the game. We can show that processes p_1 and p_2 do not crash in any execution corresponding to Strategy 2 and that Strategy 2 never terminates using the same line of reasoning as in Theorem 1.

Consider now some infinite execution α of I corresponding to the execution of the above strategy. Since process p_1 never receives commit event C^1 from I, then p_1 does not make progress in the corresponding infinite fair history F_α. Since *Sys* is parasitic-prone, then process p_1 is either parasitic in α or not.

Assume that p_1 is parasitic in α. According to the strategy, p_1 can be parasitic only if p_2 does not make progress in F_α and is returned A^2 infinitely often (i.e. p_2 is correct in F_α). Since process p_2 runs alone in F_α and I ensures a non-blocking TM-liveness property, then p_2 makes progress in H: a contradiction. Thus, p_1 cannot be parasitic in α. Since p_1 does not crash in α, p_1 is correct in F_α.

Process p_2 cannot be parasitic in α since p_2 either invokes $tryC^2$ or is returned A^2 infinitely often at Step 1. Thus, in history F_α both of the processes are correct and at most one process makes progress (since p_1 is never returned C^1). $\qquad\square$

By definition, a biprogressing TM-liveness property should ensure progress for at least two correct processes in every infinite history. While, by the above lemma, if the property is also non-blocking, then we can find an infinite fair history of any TM implementation in any fault-prone system in which at least two processes are correct and at most one process makes progress: a contradiction. Thus, we have the following theorem.

Theorem 2. *For every fault-prone system and every TM-liveness property L which is non-blocking and biprogressing there is no TM implementation that ensures strict serializability and L in that system.*

6   Conclusion

In this chapter we introduced a set-based framework to formally reason about liveness properties of TM systems. The framework separates liveness properties of transactions from liveness properties of transactional operations. For example, a TM implementation might satisfy global progress, which requires some correct transaction to commit, and wait-freedom, which requires every correct operation within a transaction to return a response. Our definition of a TM-liveness property conforms to standard general definitions of liveness [2, 21, 25] in the sense that (i) it is a *trace* property [21, 25] (i.e. it is defined in terms of invocations and responses which are external events) and (ii) it allows any *finite* execution [2].

We proved that it is impossible to guarantee both local progress, the strongest TM-liveness property, and opacity in any fault-prone system. There are several ways to circumvent our impossibility result. One way is to weaken safety or TM-liveness property requirements, for example, to require only global progress. There are implementations that ensure opacity and global progress, e.g., OSTM [10]. A second way is to assume that all transactions are static and predefined. That is, when a transaction T starts a TM implementation knows exactly which operations, on which t-variables, will be invoked in T, and the operations invoked in T should be the same in any execution. In that case transactions can be viewed as simple operations and one can apply classical universal construction [14] to ensure local progress. A third way is to assume a fault-free system, i.e. assume that no process can crash or be parasitic. However, it was shown in [20] that even in a fault-free system it is impossible to guarantee opacity and local progress when a TM implementation uses a *direct-update* algorithm and the result can be circumvented only for *deferred-update* algorithms. An algorithm is deferred-update if every transaction that writes a value must invoke a commit request before other transactions can read that value; an algorithm which is not deferred-update is called direct-update. A fourth way is to assume a different system model instead of the multi-threaded programming model. For example, [28] shows a TM implementation that ensures local progress in an asynchronous multicore system model which assumes that a transaction can be executed by different processes and that some process crashes are detectable by the runtime system.

References

[1] Abadi, M., Birrell, A., Harris, T., Isard, M.: Semantics of transactional memory and automatic mutual exclusion. ACM Trans. Program. Lang. Syst. 33(1) (2011)
[2] Alpern, B., Schneider, F.B.: Defining liveness. Information Processing Letters 21(4) (1985)
[3] Bushkov, V., Guerraoui, R., Kapałka, M.: On the liveness of transactional memory. In: Proceedings of ACM PODC 2012 (2012)
[4] Dice, D., Shalev, O., Shavit, N.N.: Transactional locking II. In: Dolev, S. (ed.) DISC 2006. LNCS, vol. 4167, pp. 194–208. Springer, Heidelberg (2006)
[5] Doherty, S., Groves, L., Luchangco, V., Moir, M.: Towards formally specifying and verifying transactional memory. Electron. Notes Theor. Comput. Sci. 259 (2009)
[6] Doherty, S., Groves, L., Luchangco, V., Moir, M.: Towards formally specifying and verifying transactional memory. Formal Aspects of Computing 25(5), 769–799 (2013)

[7] Dragojević, A., Guerraoui, R., Kapalka, M.: Stretching transactional memory. SIGPLAN Not 44(6), 155–165 (2009)

[8] Dziuma, D., Fatourou, P., Kanellou, E.: Survey on consistency conditions. Tech. Rep. 439, FORTH-ICS (2013)

[9] Felber, P., Fetzer, C., Riegel, T.: Dynamic performance tuning of word-based software transactional memory. In: ACM PPoPP 2008, pp. 237–246 (2008)

[10] Fraser, K.: Practical lock freedom. PhD thesis, Cambridge University Computer Laboratory (2003)

[11] Guerraoui, R., Kapalka, M.: On the correctness of transactional memory. In: Proceedings of ACM PPoPP 2008 (2008)

[12] Guerraoui, R., Kapalka, M.: Principles of Transactional Memory. Morgan and Claypool (2010)

[13] Harris, T., Larus, J.R., Rajwar, R.: Transactional Memory, 2nd edn. Morgan and Claypool (2010)

[14] Herlihy, M.: Wait-free synchronization. ACM Trans. Program. Lang. Syst. 13(1) (1991)

[15] Herlihy, M., Luchangco, V., Moir, M., Scherer III, W.N.: Software transactional memory for dynamic-sized data structures. In: Proceedings of ACM PODC 2003 (2003)

[16] Herlihy, M., Moss, J.E.B.: Transactional memory: Architectural support for lock-free data structures. SIGARCH Comput. Archit. News 21(2) (1993)

[17] Herlihy, M., Shavit, N.: On the nature of progress. In: Fernàndez Anta, A., Lipari, G., Roy, M. (eds.) OPODIS 2011. LNCS, vol. 7109, pp. 313–328. Springer, Heidelberg (2011)

[18] Imbs, D., de Mendivil, J.R., Raynal, M.: Brief announcement: Virtual world consistency: A new condition for stm systems. In: ACM PODC 2009, pp. 280–281 (2009)

[19] Jagannathan, S., Vitek, J., Welc, A., Hosking, A.: A transactional object calculus. Sci. Comput. Program. 57(2) (2005)

[20] Lesani, M., Palsberg, J.: Proving non-opacity. In: Afek, Y. (ed.) DISC 2013. LNCS, vol. 8205, pp. 106–120. Springer, Heidelberg (2013)

[21] Lynch, N.A.: Distributed Algorithms. Morgan Kaufmann Publishers Inc. (1996)

[22] Menon, V., Balensiefer, S., Shpeisman, T., Adl-Tabatabai, A.R., Hudson, R.L., Saha, B., Welc, A.: Practical weak-atomicity semantics for java stm. In: ACM SPAA 2008, pp. 314–325 (2008)

[23] Moore, K.F., Grossman, D.: High-level small-step operational semantics for transactions. In: ACM POPL 2008, pp. 51–62 (2008)

[24] Papadimitriou, C.H.: The serializability of concurrent database updates. J. ACM 26(4) (1979)

[25] Segala, R., Gawlick, R., Søgaard-Andersen, J., Lynch, N.: Liveness in timed and untimed systems. Inf. Comput. 141(2) (1998)

[26] Shavit, N., Touitou, D.: Software transactional memory. In: Proceedings of ACM PODC 1995 (1995)

[27] Völzer, H., Varacca, D.: Defining fairness in reactive and concurrent systems. J. ACM 59(3) (2012)

[28] Wamhoff, J.T., Fetzer, C.: The universal transactional memory construction. In: TRANSACT 2011. ACM, New York (2011)

Safety and Deferred Update in Transactional Memory

Hagit Attiya[1], Sandeep Hans[1], Petr Kuznetsov[2], and Srivatsan Ravi[3]

[1] Technion
{hagit,sandeep}@cs.technion.ac.il
[2] Télécom ParisTech
petr.kuznetsov@telecom-paristech.fr
[3] TU Berlin
srivatsan@srivatsan.in

Abstract. Transactional memory allows the user to declare sequences of instructions as speculative *transactions* that can either *commit* or *abort*, providing *all-or-nothing* semantics. If a transaction commits, it should appear to execute sequentially, so that the committed transactions constitute a correct sequential execution. If a transaction aborts, none of its instructions should affect other transactions. These semantics allow the programmer to incorporate sequential code within transactions and let the transactional memory care about conflicts between concurrent transactions. In this sense, it is important that the memory is *safe*, i.e., *every* transaction has a *consistent* view even if the transaction aborts later. Otherwise, inconsistencies not predicted by the sequential program may cause a fatal irrecoverable error or an infinite loop. Furthermore, in a general setting, where a transaction may be explicitly aborted by the user or an external contention manager, a transaction should not be allowed to read from a not yet committed transaction, which is often called *deferred-update* semantics. This chapter overviews the scope of consistency criteria proposed so far to capture deferred-update semantics, and shows that—under reasonable conditions—the semantics induces a safety property.

1 Introduction

Resolving conflicts in an efficient and consistent manner is a big challenge in concurrent software design. *Transactional memory* (TM) [10, 19] addresses this challenge by offering an interface in which sequences of shared-memory instructions can be declared as speculative *transactions*. The underlying idea, borrowed from databases, is to treat each transaction as *atomic*: a transaction may either *commit*, in which case it appears as executed sequentially, or *abort*, in which case none of its update instructions affect other transactions. The user can therefore design software having only sequential semantics in mind and let the TM take care of *conflicts* (concurrent reading and writing to the same memory location) resulting from concurrent executions.

In databases, a correct implementation of concurrency control should guarantee that committed transactions constitute a serial execution [9]. Uncommitted transactions can be aborted without invalidating the correctness of committed ones. (In the literature on databases, the latter feature is called *recoverability* [9].)

R. Guerraoui and P. Romano (Eds.): Transactional Memory, LNCS 8913, pp. 50–71, 2015.
© Springer International Publishing Switzerland 2015

In the TM context, intermediate states witnessed by the read operations of an incomplete transaction may affect the application. If the intermediate state is not consistent with any sequential execution, the application may experience a fatal irrecoverable error or enter an infinite loop. Thus, it is important that *each* transaction, including *aborted* ones observes a *consistent* state.

A state should be considered consistent if it could result from a serial application of transactions observed in the current execution. In this sense, every transaction should witness a state that *could have been* observed in *some* execution of the sequential code put by the programmer within the transactions. Additionally, a consistent state should not depend on a transaction that has not started committing yet (referred to as *deferred-update* semantics). This restriction appears desirable, since the ongoing transaction may still abort (explicitly by the user or because of consistency reasons) and, thus, render the read inconsistent. Further, the set of histories specified by the consistency criterion must constitute a *safety property*, as defined by Owicki and Lamport [17], Alpern and Schneider [1] and refined by Lynch [16]: it must be non-empty, *prefix-closed* and *limit-closed*.

In this chapter, we define the notion of deferred-update semantics formally, which we then apply to a spectrum of TM consistency criteria. Additionally, we verify if the resulting TM consistency criterion is a safety property, as defined by Lynch [16].

We first consider the popular criterion of *opacity* [7]. Opacity requires the states observed by all transactions, included uncommitted ones, to be consistent with a global *serialization*, i.e., a serial execution constituted by committed transactions. Moreover, the serialization should respect the *real-time order*: a transaction that completed before (in real time) another transaction started should appear first in the serialization.

By definition, opacity reduces correctness of a history to correctness of all its prefixes, and thus is prefix-closed and limit-closed by definition. Thus, to verify that a history is opaque, one needs to verify that each of its prefixes is consistent with some global serialization. To simplify verification and explicitly introduce deferred-update semantics into a TM correctness criterion, we specify a general criterion of *du-opacity* [3], which requires the global serial execution to respect the deferred-update property. Informally, a du-opaque history must be indistinguishable from a totally-ordered history, with respect to which no transaction reads from a transaction that has not started committing.

Du-opacity is *prefix-closed*, that is, every prefix of a du-opaque history is also du-opaque. We then show that extending opacity (and du-opacity) to infinite histories in a non-trivial way (i.e., requiring that even infinite histories should have proper serializations), does not result in a limit-closed property. However, under certain restrictions, we show that du-opacity is *limit-closed*. In particular, assuming that in an infinite history, every transaction completes each of the operations it invoked, the limit of any sequence of ever extending du-opaque histories is also du-opaque. Therefore, under this assumption, du-opacity is a *safety property* [1, 16, 17], and to prove that a TM implementation that complies with the assumption is du-opaque, it suffices to prove that all its *finite* histories are du-opaque.

One may notice that the intended safety semantics does not require that all transactions observe the same serial execution. Intuitively, we only need that every transaction witnesses *some* consistent state, while the views of different aborted transactions do not have to be consistent with *the same* serial execution. As long as committed transactions constitute a serial execution and every transaction witnesses a consistent state, the execution can be considered "safe": no run-time error that cannot occur in a serial execution can happen. Recently, several definitions adopted this approach: *virtual-world consistency (VWC)* [12] and *Transactional Memory Specifications (TMS)* [5]. We introduce "deferred-update" versions of these proporties and discuss how the resulting properties relate to du-opacity.

The chapter is organized as follows. In Section 2, we introduce our model definitions, recall the notion of safety, and recall the original definition of opacity. In Section 3, we define du-opacity and discuss the property from the safety perspective. In Section 4, we relate du-opacity to the conventional notion of opacity [7]. In Section 5, we compare du-opacity to other TM correctness criteria, such as VWC [12], TMS1 and TMS2 [5], restricted to provide the deferred-update semantics. Section 6 gives a summary of our comparative analysis and concludes the chapter.

2   Preliminaries

A *transactional memory* (in short, *TM*) supports atomic *transactions*. Each transaction is a sequence of accesses, reading from and writing to a set of *transactional* objects (in short, *t-objects*). Each transaction T_k has a unique identifier k.

A transaction T_k accesses t-objects with *t-operations*, each being a matching pair of *invocation* and *response* events: $read_k(X)$ returns a value in some domain V or a special value $A_k \notin V$ (*abort*); $write_k(X,v)$, for a value $v \in V$, returns ok_k or A_k; $tryA_k$ returns A_k; $tryC_k$ returns a special value $C_k \notin V \cup \{A_k\}$ (*commit*) or A_k.

2.1   Implementations and Histories

We consider an asynchronous shared-memory system in which processes communicate via transactions. A TM *implementation* provides processes with algorithms for implementing $read_k$, $write_k$, $tryC_k()$ and $tryA_k()$ of a transaction T_k.

A *history* of a TM implementation is a (possibly infinite) sequence of invocation and response *events* of t-operations.

For every transaction identifier k, $H|k$ denotes the subsequence of H restricted to events of transaction T_k. If $H|k$ is non-empty, we say that T_k *participates* in H, and let $txns(H)$ denote the set of transactions that participate in H. In an infinite history H, we assume that for each $T_k \in txns(H)$, $H|k$ is finite; i.e., transactions do not issue an infinite number of t-operations.

Two histories H and H' are *equivalent* if $txns(H) = txns(H')$ and for every transaction $T_k \in txns(H)$, $H|k = H'|k$.

A history H is *sequential* if every invocation of a t-operation is either the last event in H or is immediately followed by a matching response.

A history is *well-formed* if for all T_k, $H|k$ begins with an invocation of a t-operation, $H|k$ is sequential and has no events after A_k or C_k. For simplicity, we assume that all histories are well-formed, i.e., the client of the transactional memory never invokes a t-operation before receiving a response from the previous one and does not invoke any t-operation op_k after receiving C_k or A_k. Note that the assumption excludes the TM designs providing *nested parallelism* discussed in a dedicated chapter of this book.

The *read set* of a transaction T_k in history H, denoted $Rset(T_k)$, is the set of t-objects that T_k reads in H; the *write set* of T_k in history H, denoted $Wset(T_k)$, is the set of t-objects T_k writes to in H. More specifically, we say that $X \in Rset(T_k)$ (resp., $X \in Wset(T_k)$) in H if H contains an invocation of $read_k(X)$ (resp., $write_k(X,v)$). We avoid parameterizing $Rset(T_k)$ and $Wset(T_k)$ with the history H since it is clear from the usage. If $Wset(T_k) \neq \emptyset$, then T_k is an *updating* transaction.

2.2 Complete Histories and Real-Time Precedence

A transaction $T_k \in txns(H)$ is *complete in* a history H if $H|k$ ends with a response event. A history H is *complete* if all transactions in $txns(H)$ are complete in H.

A transaction $T_k \in txns(H)$ is *t-complete* if $H|k$ ends with A_k or C_k; otherwise, T_k is *t-incomplete*. T_k is *committed* (resp., *aborted*) in H if the last event of T_k is C_k (resp., A_k). The history H is *t-complete* if all transactions in $txns(H)$ are t-complete.

For t-operations op_k, op_j, we say that op_k *precedes* op_j in the *real-time order* of H, denoted $op_k \prec_H^{RT} op_m$, if the response of op_k precedes the invocation of op_j.

We overload the notation and say, for transactions $T_k, T_m \in txns(H)$, that T_k *precedes* T_m in the *real-time order* of H, denoted $T_k \prec_H^{RT} T_m$, if T_k is t-complete in H and the last event of T_k precedes the first event of T_m in H. If neither $T_k \prec_H^{RT} T_m$ nor $T_m \prec_H^{RT} T_k$, then T_k and T_m *overlap* in H. A history H is *t-sequential* if there are no overlapping transactions in H.

For simplicity of presentation, we assume that each history H begins with an "imaginary" t-complete transaction T_0 that writes initial values to all t-objects and commits before any other transaction begins in H.

2.3 Latest Written Value and Legality

Let H be a t-sequential history. For every operation $read_k(X)$ in H, we define the *latest written value* of X as follows: if T_k contains a $write_k(X,v)$ preceding $read_k(X)$, then the latest written value of X is the value of the latest such write to X. Otherwise, the latest written value of X is the value of the argument of the latest $write_m(X,v)$ that precedes $read_k(X)$ and belongs to a committed transaction in H. (This write is well-defined since H starts with T_0 writing to all t-objects.)

We say that $read_k(X)$ is *legal* in a t-sequential history H if it returns the latest written value of X, and H is *legal* if every $read_k(X)$ in H that does not return A_k is legal in H.

We also assume, for simplicity, that the client invokes a $read_k(X)$ at most once within a transaction T_k. This assumption incurs no loss of generality, since a repeated read can be assigned to return a previously returned value without affecting the history's legality.

2.4 Safety

A *property* $\mathscr{P}$ is a set of (transactional) histories.

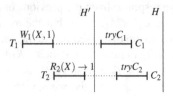

Fig. 1. History H is final-state opaque, while its prefix H' is not final-state opaque

Definition 1 (Lynch [16]). *A property $\mathcal{P}$ is a* safety *property if it satisfies the following two conditions:*

Prefix-closure: *For every history $H \in \mathcal{P}$, every prefix H' of H (i.e., every prefix of the sequence of the events in H) is also in $\mathcal{P}$.*
Limit-closure: *For every infinite sequence of finite histories $H^0, H^1, \ldots$ such that for every i, $H^i \in \mathcal{P}$ and H^i is a prefix of H^{i+1}, the limit of the sequence is also in $\mathcal{P}$.*

Notice that the set of histories produced by a TM implementation M is, by construction, prefix-closed. Therefore, every infinite history of M is the limit of an infinite sequence of ever-extending finite histories of M. Thus, to prove that M satisfies a safety property P, it is enough to show that all finite histories of M are in P. Indeed, limit-closure of P then implies that every infinite history of M is also in P.

2.5 Opacity

Definition 2 (Completions). *Let H be a history. A* completion *of H, denoted $\overline{H}$, is a history derived from H as follows:*

- *First, for every transaction $T_k \in txns(H)$ with an incomplete t-operation op_k in H, if $op_k = read_k \vee write_k$, insert A_k somewhere after the invocation of op_k; otherwise, if $op_k = tryC_k()$, insert C_k or A_k somewhere after the last event of T_k.*
- *After all transactions are complete, for every transaction T_k that is not t-complete, insert $tryC_k \cdot A_k$ after the last event of transaction T_k.*

Definition 3 (Guerraoui and Kapalka [7]). *A finite history H is* final-state opaque *if there is a legal t-complete t-sequential history S, such that*

1. *for any two transactions $T_k, T_m \in txns(H)$, if $T_k \prec_H^{RT} T_m$, then $T_k <_S T_m$, and*
2. *S is equivalent to a completion of H.*

We say that S is a final-state serialization *of H.*

Final-state opacity is not prefix-closed. Figure 1 depicts a t-complete sequential history H that is final-state opaque, with $T_1 \cdot T_2$ being a legal t-complete t-sequential history equivalent to H. Let $H' = write_1(X, 1), read_2(X)$ be a prefix of H in which T_1 and T_2 are t-incomplete. Transaction T_i ($i = 1, 2$) is completed by inserting $tryC_i \cdot A_i$ immediately after the last event of T_i in H. Observe that neither $T_1 \cdot T_2$ nor $T_2 \cdot T_1$ allow us to derive a serialization of H' (we assume that the initial value of X is 0).

A restriction of final-state opacity, which we refer to as *opacity* [7] explicitly filters out histories that are not prefix-closed.

Definition 4 (Guerraoui and Kapalka [7]). *A history H is* opaque *if and only if every finite prefix H' of H (including H itself if it is finite) is final-state opaque.*

It can be easily seen that opacity is prefix- and limit-closed, and, thus, it is a safety property.

3 Deferred-Update Semantics and Its Properties

We now give a formal definition of opacity with deferred-update semantics. Then we show that the property is prefix-closed and, under certain *liveness* restrictions, limit-closed.

3.1 Du-Opacity

Let H be any history and let S be a legal t-complete t-sequential history that is equivalent to some completion of H. Let $<_S$ be the total order on transactions in S.

Definition 5 (Local serialization). *For any $read_k(X)$ that does not return A_k, let $S^{k,X}$ be the prefix of S up to the response of $read_k(X)$ and $H^{k,X}$ be the prefix of H up to the response of $read_k(X)$.*

$S_H^{k,X}$, the local serialization *of $read_k(X)$ with respect to H and S, is the subsequence of $S^{k,X}$ derived by removing from $S^{k,X}$ the events of all transactions $T_m \in txns(H) \setminus \{T_k\}$ such that $H^{k,X}$ does not contain an invocation of $tryC_m()$.*

We are now ready to present our correctness condition, *du-opacity*.

Definition 6. *A history H is* du-opaque *if there is a legal t-complete t-sequential history S such that*

1. *there is a completion of H that is equivalent to S, and*
2. *for every pair of transactions $T_k, T_m \in txns(H)$, if $T_k \prec_H^{RT} T_m$, then $T_k <_S T_m$, i.e., S respects the real-time ordering of transactions in H, and*
3. *each $read_k(X)$ in S that does not return A_k is legal in $S_H^{k,X}$.*

We then say that S is a (du-opaque) serialization *of H.*

Informally, a history H is du-opaque if there is a legal t-sequential history S that is equivalent to H, respects the real-time ordering of transactions in H and every t-read is legal in its local serialization with respect to H and S. The third condition reflects the implementation's deferred-update semantics, i.e., the legality of a t-read in a serialization does not depend on transactions that start committing after the response of the t-read.

For any du-opaque serialization S, $seq(S)$ denotes the *sequence of transactions* in S and $seq(S)[k]$ denotes the kth transaction in this sequence.

3.2   Du-Opacity Is Prefix-Closed

Lemma 1. *Let H be a du-opaque history and let S be a serialization of H. For any $i \in \mathbb{N}$, there is a serialization S^i of H^i (the prefix of H consisting of the first i events), such that $seq(S^i)$ is a subsequence of $seq(S)$.*

Proof. Given H, S and H^i, we construct a t-complete t-sequential history S^i as follows:

- for every transaction T_k that is t-complete in H^i, $S^i|k = S|k$.
- for every transaction T_k that is complete but not t-complete in H^i, $S^i|k$ consists of the sequence of events in $H^i|k$, immediately followed by $tryC_k() \cdot A_k$.
- for every transaction T_k with an incomplete t-operation, $op_k = read_k \vee write_k \vee tryA_k()$ in H^i, $S^i|k$ is the sequence of events in $S|k$ up to the invocation of op_k, immediately followed by A_k.
- for every transaction $T_k \in txns(H^i)$ with an incomplete t-operation, $op_k = tryC_k()$, $S^i|k = S|k$.

By the above construction, S^i is indeed a t-complete history and every transaction that appears in S^i also appears in S. We order transactions in S^i so that $seq(S^i)$ is a subsequence of $seq(S)$.

Note that S^i is derived from events contained in some completion $\overline{H}$ of H that is equivalent to S and some other events to derive a completion of S^i. Since S^i contains events from every complete t-operation in H^i and other events included satisfy Definition 2, there is a completion of H^i that is equivalent to S^i.

We now argue that S^i is a serialization of H^i. First we observe that S^i respects the real-time order of H^i. Indeed, if $T_j \prec_{H^i}^{RT} T_k$, then $T_j \prec_{H}^{RT} T_k$ and $T_j <_S T_k$. Since $seq(S^i)$ is a subsequence of $seq(S)$, we have $T_j <_{S^i} T_k$.

To show that S^i is legal, suppose, by way of contradiction, that there is some $read_k(X)$ that returns $v \neq A_k$ in H^i such that v is not the latest written value of X in S^i. If T_k contains a $write_k(X, v')$ preceding $read_k(X)$ such that $v \neq v'$ and v is not the latest written value for $read_k(X)$ in S^i, it is also not the latest written value for $read_k(X)$ in S, which is a contradiction. Thus, the only case to consider is when $read_k(X)$ should return a value written by another transaction.

Since S is a serialization of H, there is a committed transaction T_m that performs the last $write_m(X, v)$ that precedes $read_k(X)$ in T_k in S. Moreover, since $read_k(X)$ is legal in the local serialization of $read_k(X)$ in H with respect to S, the prefix of H up to the response of $read_k(X)$ must contain an invocation of $tryC_m()$. Thus, $read_k(X) \not\prec_H^{RT} tryC_m()$ and $T_m \in txns(H^i)$. By construction of S^i, $T_m \in txns(S^i)$ and T_m is committed in S^i.

We have assumed, towards a contradiction, that v is not the latest written value for $read_k(X)$ in S^i. Hence, there is a committed transaction T_j that performs $write_j(X, v')$; $v' \neq v$ in S^i such that $T_m <_{S^i} T_j <_{S^i} T_k$. But this is not possible since $seq(S^i)$ is a subsequence of $seq(S)$.

Thus, S^i is a legal t-complete t-sequential history equivalent to some completion of H^i. Now, by the construction of S^i, for every $read_k(X)$ that does not return A_k in S^i, we have $S_{H^i}^{ik,X} = S_H^{k,X}$. Indeed, the transactions that appear before T_k in $S_{H^i}^{ik,X}$ are those with a $tryC$ event before the response of $read_k(X)$ in H and are committed in S. Since $seq(S^i)$ is a subsequence of $seq(S)$, we have $S_{H^i}^{ik,X} = S_H^{k,X}$. Thus, $read_k(X)$ is legal in $S_{H^i}^{ik,X}$. $\square$

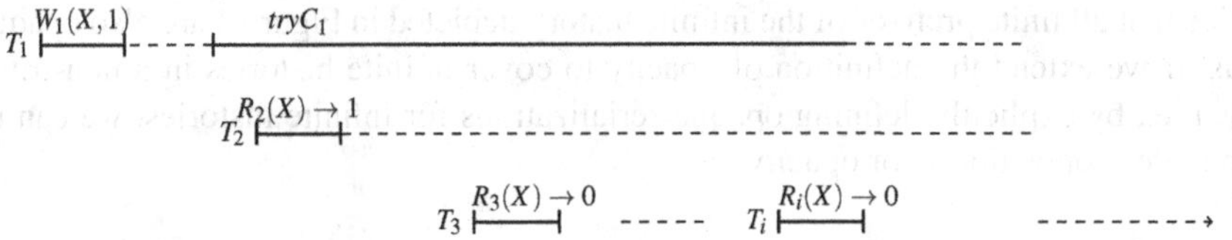

Fig. 2. An infinite history in which $tryC_1$ is incomplete and any two transactions are concurrent. Each finite prefix of the history is du-opaque, but the infinite limit of the ever-extending sequence is not du-opaque.

Lemma 1 implies that every prefix of a du-opaque history has a du-opaque serialization and thus:

Corollary 1. *Du-opacity is a prefix-closed property.*

3.3 The Limit of Du-Opaque Histories

We observe, however, that du-opacity is, in general, not limit-closed. We present an infinite history that is not du-opaque, but each of its prefixes is.

Proposition 1. *Du-opacity is not a limit-closed property.*

Proof. Let H^j denote a finite prefix of H of length j. Consider an infinite history H that is the limit of the histories H^j defined as follows (see Figure 2):

- Transaction T_1 performs a $write_1(X, 1)$ and then invokes $tryC_1()$ that is incomplete in H.
- Transaction T_2 performs a $read_2(X)$ that overlaps with $tryC_1()$ and returns 1.
- There are infinitely many transactions T_i, $i \geq 3$, each of which performing a single $read_i(X)$ that returns 0 such that each T_i overlaps with both T_1 and T_2.

We now prove that, for all $j \in \mathbb{N}$, H^j is a du-opaque history. Clearly, H^0 and H^1 are du-opaque histories. For all $j > 1$, we first derive a completion of H^j as follows:

1. $tryC_1()$ (if it is contained in H^j) is completed by inserting C_1 immediately after its invocation,
2. for all $i \geq 2$, any incomplete $read_i(X)$ that is contained in H^j is completed by inserting A_i and $tryC_i \cdot A_i$ immediately after its invocation, and
3. for all $i \geq 2$ and every complete $read_j(X)$ that is contained in H^j, we include $tryC_i \cdot A_i$ immediately after the response of this $read_j(X)$.

We can now derive a t-complete t-sequential history S^j equivalent to the above derived completion of H^j from the sequence of transactions $T_3, \ldots, T_i, T_1, T_2$ (depending on which of these transactions participate in H^j), where $i \geq 3$. It is easy to observe that S^j so derived is indeed a serialization of H^j.

However, there is no serialization of H. Suppose that such a serialization S exists. Since every transaction that participates in H must participate in S, there exists $n \in \mathbb{N}$ such that $seq(S)[n] = T_1$. Consider the transaction at index $n+1$, say T_i in $seq(S)$. But for any $i \geq 3$, T_i must precede T_1 in any serialization (by legality), which is a contradiction. $\square$

Notice that all finite prefixes of the infinite history depicted in Figure 2 are also opaque. Thus, if we extend the definition of opacity to cover infinite histories in a non-trivial way, i. e., by explicitly defining opaque serializations for infinite histories, we can reformulate Proposition 1 for opacity.

3.4   Du-Opacity is Limit-Closed for Complete Histories

We show now that du-opacity is limit-closed if the only infinite histories we consider are those in which every transaction eventually completes (but not necessarily t-completes).

We first prove an auxiliary lemma on du-opaque serializations. For a transaction $T \in txns(H)$, the *live set of* T *in* H, denoted $Lset_H(T)$ (T included), is defined as follows: every transaction $T' \in txns(H)$ such that neither the last event of T' precedes the first event of T in H nor the last event of T precedes the first event of T' in H is contained in $Lset_H(T)$. We say that transaction $T' \in txns(H)$ *succeeds the live set of* T and we write $T \prec_H^{LS} T'$ if in H, for all $T'' \in Lset_H(T)$, T'' is complete and the last event of T'' precedes the first event of T'.

Lemma 2. *Let H be a finite du-opaque history and assume $T_k \in txns(H)$ is a complete transaction in H, such that every transaction in $Lset_H(T_k)$ is complete in H. Then there is a serialization S of H, such that for all $T_k, T_m \in txns(H)$, if $T_k \prec_H^{LS} T_m$, then $T_k <_S T_m$.*

Proof. Since H is du-opaque, there is a serialization $\tilde{S}$ of H.

Let S be a t-complete t-sequential history such that $txns(\tilde{S}) = txns(S)$, and $\forall\, T_i \in txns(\tilde{S}) : S|i = \tilde{S}|i$. We now perform the following procedure iteratively to derive $seq(S)$ from $seq(\tilde{S})$. Initially $seq(S) = seq(\tilde{S})$. For each $T_k \in txns(H)$, let $T_\ell \in txns(H)$ denote the earliest transaction in $\tilde{S}$ such that $T_k \prec_H^{LS} T_\ell$. If $T_\ell <_{\tilde{S}} T_k$ (implying T_k is not t-complete), then move T_k to immediately precede T_ℓ in $seq(S)$.

By construction, S is equivalent to $\tilde{S}$ and for all $T_k, T_m \in txns(H)$; $T_k \prec_H^{LS} T_m$, $T_k <_S T_m$ We claim that S is a serialization of H. Observe that any two transactions that are complete in H, but not t-complete are not related by real-time order in H. By construction of S, for any transaction $T_k \in txns(H)$, the set of transactions that precede T_k in $\tilde{S}$, but succeed T_k in S are not related to T_k by real-time order. Since $\tilde{S}$ respects the real-time order in H, this holds also for S.

We now show that S is legal. Consider any $read_k(X)$ performed by some transaction T_k that returns $v \in V$ in S and let $T_\ell \in txns(H)$ be the earliest transaction in $\tilde{S}$ such that $T_k \prec_H^{LS} T_\ell$. Suppose, by contradiction, that $read_k(X)$ is not legal in S. Thus, there is a committed transaction T_m that performs $write_m(X, v)$ in $\tilde{S}$ such that $T_m = T_\ell$ or $T_\ell <_{\tilde{S}} T_m <_{\tilde{S}} T_k$. Note that, by our assumption, $read_k(X) \prec_H^{RT} tryC_\ell()$. Since $read_k(X)$ must be legal in its local serialization with respect to H and $\tilde{S}$, $read_k(X) \not\prec_H^{RT} tryC_m()$. Thus, $T_m \in Lset_H(T_k)$. Therefore $T_m \neq T_\ell$. Moreover, T_m is complete, and since it commits in $\tilde{S}$, it is also t-complete in H and the last event of T_m precedes the first event of T_ℓ in H, i.e., $T_m \prec_H^{RT} T_\ell$. Hence, T_ℓ cannot precede T_m in $\tilde{S}$—a contradiction.

Observe also that since T_k is complete in H but not t-complete, H does not contain an invocation of $tryC_k()$. Thus, the legality of any other transaction is unaffected by moving T_k to precede T_ℓ in S. Thus, S is a legal t-complete t-sequential history equivalent to some completion of H. The above arguments also prove that every t-read in S is legal in its local serialization with respect to H and S and, thus, S is a serialization of H.   □

The proof uses König's Path Lemma [13] formulated as follows. Let G on a rooted directed graph and let v_0 be the root of G. We say that v_k, a vertex of G, is *reachable* from v_0, if there is a sequence of vertices $v_0 \ldots, v_k$ such that for each i, there is an edge from v_i to v_{i+1}. G is *connected* if every vertex in G is reachable from v_0. G is *finitely branching* if every vertex in G has a finite out-degree. G is *infinite* if it has infinitely many vertices.

Lemma 3 (König's Path Lemma [13]). *If G is an infinite connected finitely branching rooted directed graph, then G contains an infinite sequence of distinct vertices $v_0, v_1, \ldots$, such that v_0 is the root, and for every $i \geq 0$, there is an edge from v_i to v_{i+1}.*

Theorem 1. *Under the restriction that in any infinite history H, every transaction $T_k \in txns(H)$ is complete, du-opacity is a limit-closed property.*

Proof. We want to show that the limit H of an infinite sequence of finite ever-extending du-opaque histories is du-opaque. By Corollary 1, we can assume the sequence of du-opaque histories to be $H^0, H^1, \ldots H^i, H^{i+1}, \ldots$ such that for all $i \in \mathbb{N}$, H^{i+1} is the one-event extension of H^i.

We construct a rooted directed graph G_H as follows:

1. The root vertex of G_H is (H^0, S^0) where S^0 and H^0 contain the initial transaction T_0.
2. Each non-root vertex of G_H is a tuple (H^i, S^i), where S^i is a du-opaque serialization of H^i that satisfies the condition specified in Lemma 2: for all $T_k, T_m \in txns(H)$; $T_k \prec_{H^i}^{LS} T_m$ implies $T_k <_{S^i} T_m$. Note that there exist several possible serializations for any H^i. For succinctness, in the rest of this proof, when we refer to a specific S^i, it is understood to be associated with the prefix H^i of H.
3. Let $cseq_i(S^j)$, $j \geq i$, denote the subsequence of $seq(S^j)$ restricted to transactions whose last event in H is a response event and it is contained in H^i. For every pair of vertices $v = (H^i, S^i)$ and $v' = (H^{i+1}, S^{i+1})$ in G_H, there is an edge from v to v' if $cseq_i(S^i) = cseq_i(S^{i+1})$.

The out-degree of a vertex $v = (H^i, S^i)$ in G_H is defined by the number of possible serializations of H^{i+1}, bounded by the number of possible permutations of the set $txns(S^{i+1})$, implying that G_H is *finitely branching*.

By Lemma 1, given any serialization S^{i+1} of H^{i+1}, there is a serialization S^i of H^i such that $seq(S^i)$ is a subsequence of $seq(S^{i+1})$. Indeed, the serialization S^i of H^i also respects the restriction specified in Lemma 2. Since $seq(S^{i+1})$ contains every complete transaction that takes its last step in H in H^i, $cseq_i(S^i) = cseq_i(S^{i+1})$. Therefore, for every vertex (H^{i+1}, S^{i+1}), there is a vertex (H^i, S^i) such that $cseq_i(S^i) = cseq_i(S^{i+1})$. Thus, we can iteratively construct a path from (H^0, S^0) to every vertex (H^i, S^i) in G_H, implying that G_H is *connected*.

We now apply König's Path Lemma (Lemma 3) to G_H. Since G_H is an infinite connected finitely branching rooted directed graph, we can derive an infinite sequence of distinct vertices

$$\mathcal{L} = (H^0, S^0), (H^1, S^1), \ldots, (H^i, S^i), \ldots$$

such that $cseq_i(S^i) = cseq_i(S^{i+1})$.

The rest of the proof explains how to use $\mathscr{L}$ to construct a serialization of H. We begin with the following claim concerning $\mathscr{L}$.

Claim. For any $j > i$, $cseq_i(S^i) = cseq_i(S^j)$.

Proof. Recall that $cseq_i(S^i)$ is a prefix of $cseq_i(S^{i+1})$, and $cseq_{i+1}(S^{i+1})$ is a prefix of $cseq_{i+1}(S^{i+2})$. Also, $cseq_i(S^{i+1})$ is a subsequence of $cseq_{i+1}(S^{i+1})$. Hence, $cseq_i(S^i)$ is a subsequence of $cseq_{i+1}(S^{i+2})$. But, $cseq_{i+1}(S^{i+2})$ is a subsequence of $cseq_{i+2}(S^{i+2})$. Thus, $cseq_i(S^i)$ is a subsequence of $cseq_{i+2}(S^{i+2})$. Inductively, for any $j > i$, $cseq_i(S^i)$ is a subsequence of $cseq_j(S^j)$. But $cseq_i(S^j)$ is the subsequence of $cseq_j(S^j)$ restricted to complete transactions in H whose last step is in H^i. Thus, $cseq_i(S^i)$ is indeed equal to $cseq_i(S^j)$. □

Let $f : \mathbb{N} \to txns(H)$ be defined as follows: $f(1) = T_0$. For every integer $k > 1$, let

$$i_k = \min\{\ell \in \mathbb{N} | \forall j > \ell : cseq_\ell(S^\ell)[k] = cseq_j(S^j)[k]\}$$

Then, $f(k) = cseq_{i_k}(S^{i_k})[k]$.

Claim. The function f is *total* and *bijective*.

Proof. (Totality and surjectivity)
Since each transaction $T \in txns(H)$ is complete in some prefix H^i of H, for each $k \in \mathbb{N}$, there exists $i \in \mathbb{N}$ such that $cseq_i(S^i)[k] = T$. By Claim 3.4, for any $j > i$, $cseq_i(S^i) = cseq_i(S^j)$. Since a transaction that is complete in H^i w.r.t H is also complete in H^j w.r.t H, it follows that for every $j > i$, $cseq_j(S^j)[k'] = T$, with $k' \geq k$. By construction of G_H and the assumption that each transaction is complete in H, there exists $i \in \mathbb{N}$ such that each $T \in Lset_{H^i}(T)$ is complete in H and its last step is in H^i, and T precedes in S^i every transaction whose first event succeeds the last event of each $T' \in Lset_{H^i}(T)$ in H^i. Indeed, this implies that for each $k \in \mathbb{N}$, there exists $i \in \mathbb{N}$ such that $cseq_i(S^i)[k] = T$; $\forall j > i : cseq_j(S^j)[k] = T$.

This shows that for every $T \in txns(H)$, there are $i, k \in \mathbb{N}$; $cseq_i(S^i)[k] = T$, such that for every $j > i$, $cseq_j(S^j)[k] = T$. Thus, for every $T \in txns(H)$, there is k such that $f(k) = T$.

(Injectivity)
If $f(k)$ and $f(m)$ are transactions at indices k, m of the same $cseq_i(S^i)$, then clearly $f(k) = f(m)$ implies $k = m$. Suppose $f(k)$ is the transaction at index k in some $cseq_i(S^i)$ and $f(m)$ is the transaction at index m in some $cseq_\ell(S^\ell)$. For every $\ell > i$ and $k < m$, if $cseq_i(S^i)[k] = T$, then $cseq_\ell(S^\ell)[m] \neq T$ since $cseq_i(S^i) = cseq_i(S^\ell)$. If $\ell > i$ and $k > m$, it follows from the definition that $f(k) \neq f(m)$. Similar arguments for the case when $\ell < i$ prove that if $f(k) = f(m)$, then $k = m$. □

By Claim 3.4, $\mathscr{F} = f(1), f(2), \ldots, f(i), \ldots$ is an infinite sequence of transactions. Let S be a t-complete t-sequential history such that $seq(S) = \mathscr{F}$ and for each t-complete transaction T_k in H, $S|k = H|k$; and for transaction that is complete, but not t-complete in H, $S|k$ consists of the sequence of events in $H|k$, immediately followed by $tryA_k() \cdot A_k$. Clearly, there is a completion of H that is equivalent to S.

Let $\mathscr{F}^i$ be the prefix of $\mathscr{F}$ of length i, and $\widehat{S}^i$ be the prefix of S such that $seq(\widehat{S}^i) = \mathscr{F}^i$.

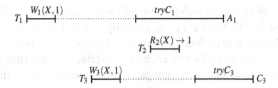

Fig. 3. A history that is opaque, but not du-opaque

Claim. Let $\widehat{H}_i^j$ be a subsequence of H^j reduced to transactions $T_k \in txns(\widehat{S}^i)$ such that the last event of T_k in H is a response event and it is contained in H^j. Then, for every i, there is j such that $\widehat{S}^i$ is a serialization of $\widehat{H}_i^j$.

Proof. Let H^j be the shortest prefix of H (from $\mathscr{L}$) such that for each $T \in txns(\widehat{S}^i)$, if $seq(S^j)[k] = T$, then for every $j' > j$, $seq(S^{j'})[k] = T$. From the construction of $\mathscr{F}$, such j and k exist. Also, we observe that $txns(\widehat{S}^i) \subseteq txns(S^j)$ and $\mathscr{F}^i$ is a subsequence of $seq(S^j)$. Using arguments similar to the proof of Lemma 1, it follows that $\widehat{S}^i$ is indeed a serialization of $\widehat{H}_i^j$. □

Since H is complete, there is exactly one completion of H, where each transaction T_k that is not t-complete in H is completed with $tryC_k \cdot A_k$ after its last event. By Claim 3.4, the limit t-sequential t-complete history is equivalent to this completion, is legal, respects the real-time order of H, and ensures that every read is legal in the corresponding local serialization. Thus, S is a serialization of H. □

Theorem 1 implies the following:

Corollary 2. *Let M be a TM implementation that ensures that in every infinite history H of M, every transaction $T \in txns(H)$ is complete in H. Then, M is du-opaque if and only if every finite history of M is du-opaque.*

4 Du-Opacity vs. Opacity

We now compare our deferred-update requirement with the conventional TM correctness property of opacity [7].

Theorem 2. *Du-opacity $\subsetneqq$ Opacity.*

Proof. We first claim that every finite du-opaque history is opaque. Let H be a finite du-opaque history. By definition, there is a final-state serialization S of H. Since du-opacity is a prefix-closed property, every prefix of H is final-state opaque. Thus, H is opaque.

Again, since every prefix of a du-opaque history is also du-opaque, by Definition 4, every infinite du-opaque history is also opaque.

To show that the inclusion is strict, we present an an opaque history that is not du-opaque. Consider the finite history H depicted in Figure 3: transaction T_2 performs a $read_2(X)$ that returns the value 1. Observe that $read_2(X) \to 1$ is concurrent to $tryC_1$, but precedes $tryC_3$ in real-time order. Although $tryC_1$ returns A_1 in H, the response of $read_2(X)$ can be justified since T_3 concurrently writes 1 to X and commits. Thus, $read_2(X) \to 1$ *reads-from* transaction T_2 in any serialization of H, but since $read_2(X) \prec_H^{RT} tryC_3$, H is not du-opaque even though each of its prefixes is final-state opaque.

We now formally prove that H is opaque. We proceed by examining every prefix of H.

1. Each prefix up to the invocation of $read_2(X)$ is trivially final-state opaque.
2. Consider the prefix, H^i of H where the ith event is the response of $read_2(X)$. Let S^i be a t-complete t-sequential history derived from the sequence T_1, T_2 by inserting C_1 immediately after the invocation of $tryC_1()$. It is easy to see that S^i is a final-state serialization of H^i.
3. Consider the t-complete t-sequential history S derived from the sequence T_1, T_3, T_2 in which each transaction is t-complete in H. Clearly, S is a final-state serialization of H.

Since H and every (proper) prefix of it are final-state opaque, H is opaque.

Clearly, the required final-state serialization S of H is specified by $seq(S) = T_1, T_3, T_2$ in which T_1 is aborted while T_3 is committed in S (the position of T_1 in the serialization does not affect legality). Consider $read_2(X)$ in S; since $H^{2,X}$, the prefix of H up to the response of $read_2(X)$ does not contain an invocation of $tryC_3()$, the local serialization of $read_2(X)$ with respect to H and S, $S_H^{2,X}$ is $T_1 \cdot read_2(X)$. But $read_2(X)$ is not legal in $S_H^{2,X}$, which is a contradiction. Thus, H is not du-opaque. □

4.1 The Unique-Write Case

We now show that du-opacity is equivalent to opacity assuming that no two transactions write identical values to the same t-object ("unique-write" assumption).

Let $Opacity_{uw} \subseteq Opacity$, be a property defined as follows:

1. an infinite opaque history $H \in Opacity_{uw}$ if and only if every transaction $T \in txns(H)$ is complete in H, and
2. an opaque history $H \in Opacity_{uw}$ if and only if for every pair of write operations $write_k(X,v)$ and $write_m(X,v')$, $v \neq v'$.

Theorem 3. $Opacity_{uw} = du\text{-}opacity$.

Proof. We show first that every finite history $H \in Opacity_{uw}$ is also du-opaque. Let H be any finite opaque history such that for every pair of write operations $write_k(X,v)$ and $write_m(X,v)$, performed by transactions $T_k, T_m \in txns(H)$, respectively, $v \neq v'$.

Since H is opaque, there is a final-state serialization S of H. Suppose by contradiction that H is not du-opaque. Thus, there is a $read_k(X)$ that returns a value $v \in V$ in S that is not legal in $S_H^{k,X}$, the local serialization of $read_k(X)$ with respect to H and S. Let $H^{k,X}$ and $S^{k,X}$ denote the prefixes of H and S, respectively, up to the response of $read_k(X)$ in H and S. Recall that $S_H^{k,X}$, the local serialization of $read_k(X)$ with respect to H and S, is the subsequence of $S^{k,X}$ that does not contain events of any transaction $T_i \in txns(H)$ so that the invocation of $tryC_i()$ is not in $H^{k,X}$. Since $read_k(X)$ is legal in S, there is a

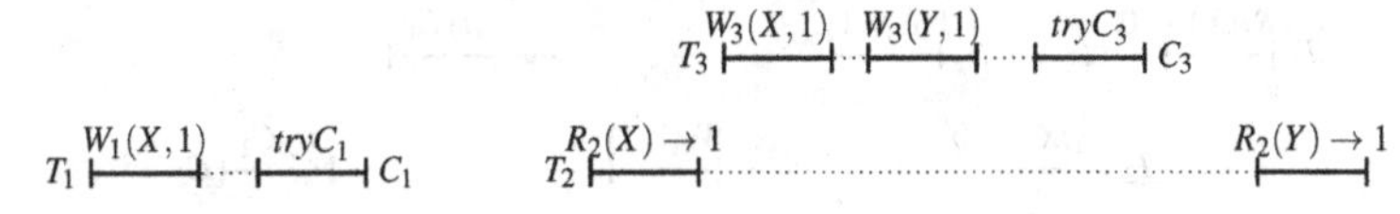

Fig. 4. A sequential du-opaque history, which is not opaque by the definition of [6]

committed transaction $T_m \in txns(H)$ that performs $write_m(X,v)$ that is the latest such write in S that precedes T_k. Thus, if $read_k(X)$ is not legal in $S_H^{k,X}$, the only possibility is that $read_k(X) \prec_H^{RT} tryC_m()$. Under the assumption of unique writes, there does not exist any other transaction $T_j \in txns(H)$ that performs $write_j(X,v)$. Consequently, there does not exist any $\overline{H}^{k,X}$ (some completion of $H^{k,X}$) and a t-complete t-sequential history S', such that S' is equivalent to $\overline{H}^{k,X}$ and S' contains any committed transaction that writes v to X. This is, $H^{k,X}$ is not final-state opaque. However, since H is opaque, every prefix of H must be final-state opaque, which is a contradiction.

By Definition 4, an infinite history H is opaque if every finite prefix of H is final-state opaque. Theorem 1 now implies that Opacity$_{uw} \subseteq$ du-Opacity.

Definition 4 and Corollary 1 imply that du-Opacity $\subseteq$ Opacity$_{uw}$. $\square$

4.2 The Sequential-History Case

The deferred-update semantics was mentioned by Guerraoui et al. [6] and later adopted by Kuznetsov and Ravi [14]. In both papers, opacity is only defined for sequential histories, where every invocation of a t-operation is immediately followed by a matching response. In particular, these definitions require the final-state serialization to respect the *read-commit order*: in these definitions, a history H is opaque if there is a final-state serialization S of H such that if a t-read of a t-object X by a transaction T_k precedes the tryC of a transaction T_m that commits on X in H, then T_k precedes T_m in S. As we observed in Figure 4, this definition is not equivalent to opacity even for sequential histories.

The property considered in [6, 14] is strictly stronger than du-opacity: the sequential history H in Figure 4 is du-opaque (and consequently opaque by Theorem 2): a du-opaque serialization (in fact the only possible one) for this history is T_1, T_3, T_2. However, in the restriction of opacity defined above, T_2 must precede T_3 in any serialization, since the response of $read_2(X)$ precedes the invocation of $tryC_3()$.

5 Du-Opacity vs. Other Deferred-Update Criteria

In this section, we compare du-opacity to other TM correctness conditions, restricted to provide the deferred-update semantics. We first discuss the stronger TMS2 property [5], and then describe deferred-update versions of conditions weaker than opacity, VWC [12] and TMS1 [5].

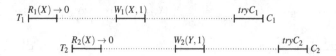

Fig. 5. A history that is du-opaque, but not TMS2 [5]

5.1 TMS2

Transactional Memory Specification (TMS) 1 and 2 were formulated in I/O automata [5]. Following [2], we adapt these definitions to our framework and explicitly introduce the deferred-update requirement. We start with TMS2, a restriction of opacity, and discuss TMS1, a relaxation of du-opacity, in Section 5.3.

Definition 7 (du-TMS2). *A history H is du-TMS2 if there is a legal t-complete t-sequential history S equivalent to some completion, $\overline{H}$ of H such that*

1. *for any two transactions $T_k, T_m \in txns(H)$, such that T_m is a committed updating transaction, if $C_k \prec_H^{RT} tryC_m$ or $A_k \prec_H^{RT} tryC_m$, then $T_k \prec_S T_m$, and*
2. *for any two transactions $T_k, T_m \in txns(H)$, if $T_k \prec_H^{RT} T_m$, then $T_k <_S T_m$, and*
3. *each $read_k(X)$ in S that does not return A_k is legal in $S_H^{k,X}$.*

We refer to S as the du-TMS2 serialization of H.

It has been shown [15] that TMS2 is a strictly stronger property than Opacity, i.e., TMS2 $\subsetneq$ Opacity. We now show that du-TMS2 is strictly stronger than du-opacity. Indeed, from Definition 7, we observe that every history that is du-TMS2 is also du-opaque. The following proposition completes the proof.

Proposition 2. *There is a history that is du-opaque, but not du-TMS2.*

Proof. Figure 5 depicts a history H that is du-opaque, but not du-TMS2. Indeed, there is a du-opaque serialization S of H such that $seq(S) = T_2, T_1$. On the other hand, since T_1 commits before T_2, T_1 must precede T_2 in any du-TMS2 serialization, there does not exist any such serialization that ensures every t-read is legal. Thus, H is not du-TMS2.   □

Theorem 4. *Du-TMS2 is prefix-closed.*

Proof. Let H be any du-TMS2 history. Then, H is also du-opaque. By Corollary 1, for every $i \in \mathbb{N}$, there is a du-opaque serialization S^i for H^i. We now need to prove that, for any two transactions $T_k, T_m \in txns(H^i)$, such that T_m is a committed updating transaction, if $C_k \prec_{H^i}^{RT} tryC_m$ or $A_k \prec_{H^i}^{RT} tryC_m$, there is a du-opaque serialization S^i with the restriction that $T_k \prec_{S^i} T_m$.

Suppose by contradiction that there exist transactions $T_k, T_m \in txns(H^i)$, such that T_m is a committed updating transaction and $C_k \prec_{H^i}^{RT} tryC_m$ or $A_k \prec_{H^i}^{RT} tryC_m$, but T_m must precede T_k in any du-opaque serialization S^i. Since $T_m \not\prec_{H^i}^{RT} T_k$, the only possibility is that T_m performs $write_m(X, v)$ and there is $read_k(X) \rightarrow v$. However, by our assumption,

$write_k(X,v) \prec_{H^i}^{RT} tryC_m$: thus, $read_k(X)$ is not legal in its local serialization with respect to H^i and S^i—contradicting the assumption that S^i is a du-opaque serialization of H^i. Thus, there is a du-TMS2 serialization for H^i, proving that du-TMS2 is a prefix-closed property.   □

Proposition 3. *Du-TMS2 is not limit-closed.*

Proof. The counter-example to establish that du-opacity is not limit-closed (Figure 2) also shows that du-TMS2 is not limit-closed: all histories discussed in the counter-example are in du-TMS2.   □

5.2 Virtual World Consistency (VWC)

Intuitively, VWC [12] and TMS1 [5] achieve intuitively understood safety of each transaction or response, without enforcing a single serialization. Both definitions use the following "deferred-update" version of *strict serializability* [18]:

Definition 8 (Strict serializability). *A finite history H is strictly serializable if there is a legal t-complete t-sequential history S, such that*

1. *there is a completion $\overline{H}$ of H, such that S is equivalent to $cseq(\overline{H})$, where $cseq(\overline{H})$ is the subsequence of $\overline{H}$ reduced to committed transactions in $\overline{H}$,*
2. *for any two transactions $T_k, T_m \in txns(H)$, if $T_k \prec_H^{RT} T_m$, then T_k precedes T_m in S, and*
3. *each $read_k(X)$ in S that does not return A_k is legal in $S_H^{k,X}$.*

We refer to S as the (strictly serializable) serialization of H.

Notice that every du-opaque history is strictly serializable, but not vice-versa. The following result will be instrumental for understanding the properties of du-VWC and du-TMS1.

Theorem 5. *Strict serializability is a safety property.*

Proof. (Sketch) Observe that any serialization of a finite history H does not include events of any transaction that has not invoked $tryC$ in H.

To show prefix-closure, a proof almost identical to that of Lemma 1 implies that, given a strictly serializable history H and a serialization S, there is a serialization S' of H' (H' is some prefix of H) such that $seq(S')$ is a prefix of $seq(S)$.

Consider an infinite sequence of finite histories

$$H^0, \ldots, H^i, H^{i+1}, \ldots,$$

where H^{i+1} is a one-event extension of H^i, we prove that the infinite limit H of this ever-extending sequence is strictly serializable. As in Theorem 1, we construct an infinite rooted directed graph G_H: a vertex is a tuple (H^i, S^i) (note that for each $i \in \mathbb{N}$, there are several such vertices of this form), where S^i is a serialization of H^i and there is an edge from (H^i, S^i) to (H^{i+1}, S^{i+1}) if $seq(S^i)$ is a prefix of $seq(S^{i+1})$. The resulting graph is finitely branching since the out-degree of a vertex is bounded by the number of possible serializations of a history. Observe that for every vertex (H^{i+1}, S^{i+1}), there is a vertex $H^i, S^i)$ such that $seq(S^i)$ is a prefix of $seq(S^{i+1})$. Thus, G_H is connected since we can iteratively construct a path from the root (H^0, S^0) to every vertex (H^i, S^i) in G_H. Applying König's Path Lemma to G_H, we obtain an infinite sequence of distinct vertices, $(H^0, S^0), (H^1, S^1), \ldots, (H^i, S^i), \ldots$. Then, $S = \lim_{i \to \infty} S_i$ gives the desired serialization of H. $\qquad\qquad\square$

Virtual World Consistency (VWC) [12] was proposed as a relaxation of opacity (in our case, du-opacity), where each aborted transaction should be consistent with its *causal past* (but not necessarily with a serialization formed by committed transactions). Intuitively, a transaction T_1 causally precedes T_2 if T_2 reads a value written and committed by T_1. The original definition [12] required that no two write operations are ever invoked with the same argument (the *unique-writes* assumption). Therefore, the causal precedence is unambiguously identified for each transactional read. Below we give a more general definition.

Given a t-sequential legal history S and transactions $T_i, T_j \in txns(S)$, we say that T_i *reads X from* T_j if (1) T_i reads v in X and (2) T_j is the last committed transaction that writes v to X and precedes T_i in S.

Now consider a (not necessarily t-sequential) history H. We say that T_i *could have read X from* T_j *in* H if T_j writes a value v to a t-object X, T_i reads v in X, and $read_i(X)$ $\not\prec_H^{RT} tryC_j()$.

Given $\mathcal{T} \subseteq txns(H)$, let $H^{\mathcal{T}}$ denote the subsequence of H restricted to events of transactions in $\mathcal{T}$.

Definition 9 (du-VWC). *A finite history H is* du-virtual-world consistent *if it is strictly serializable, and for every aborted or t-incomplete transaction $T_i \in txns(H)$, there is $\mathcal{T} \subseteq txns(H)$ including T_i and a t-sequential t-complete legal history S such that:*

1. *S is equivalent to a completion of $H^{\mathcal{T}}$,*
2. *For all $T_j, T_k \in txns(S)$, if T_j reads X from T_k in S, then T_j could have read X from T_k in H,*
3. *S respects the per-process order of H: if T_j and T_k are executed by the same process and $T_j \prec_H^{RT} T_k$, then $T_j \prec_S T_k$.*

We refer to S as a du-VWC serialization *for T_i in H.*

Intuitively, with every t-read on X performed by T_i in H, the du-VWC serialization S associates some transaction T_j from which T_i could have read the value of X. Recursively, with every read performed by T_j, S associates some T_m from which T_j could have read, etc. Altogether, we get a "plausible" causal past of T_i that constitutes a serial history. Notice that to ensure deferred-update semantics, we only allow a transaction T_j to read from a transaction T_k that invoked $tryC_k$ by the time of the read operation of T_j.

We now prove that du-VWC is a strictly weaker property than du-opacity. Since du-TMS2 is strictly weaker than du-opacity (cf. Section 5.1), it follows that Du-TMS2 $\subsetneq$ du-VWC.

Theorem 6. *Du-opacity $\subsetneq$ du-VWC.*

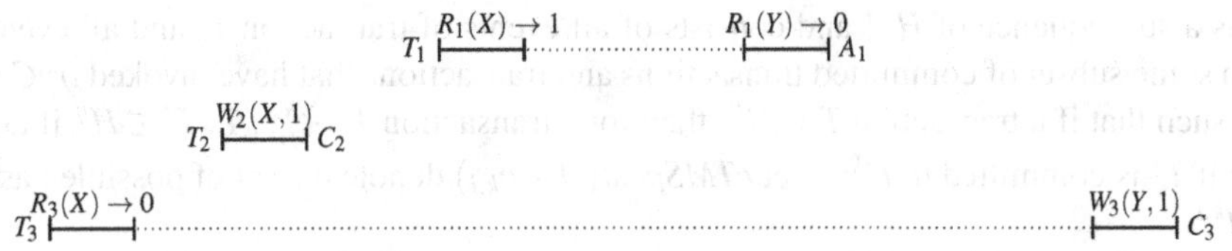

$$T_1 \vdash\!\!\xrightarrow{R_1(X) \to 1}\!\!\dotsb\dotsb\dotsb\dotsb\vdash\!\!\xrightarrow{R_1(Y) \to 0}\!\!\dashv A_1$$

$$T_2 \vdash\!\!\xrightarrow{W_2(X,1)}\!\!\dashv C_2$$

$$T_3 \vdash\!\!\xrightarrow{R_3(X) \to 0}\!\!\dotsb\dotsb\dotsb\dotsb\dotsb\dotsb\dotsb\dotsb\dotsb\dotsb\dotsb\dotsb\dotsb\vdash\!\!\xrightarrow{W_3(Y,1)}\!\!\dashv C_3$$

Fig. 6. A history that is du-VWC, but not du-opaque

Proof. If a history H is du-opaque, then there is a du-opaque serialization S equivalent to $\overline{H}$, where $\overline{H}$ is some completion of H. By construction, S is a total-order on the set of all transactions that participate in S. Trivially, by taking $\mathscr{T} = txns(H)$, we derive that S is a du-VWC serialization for every aborted or t-incomplete transaction $T_i \in txns(H)$. Indeed, S respects the real-time order and, thus, the per-process order of H. Since S respects the deferred-update order in H, every t-read in S "could have happened" in H.

To show that the inclusion is strict, Figure 6 depicts a history H that is du-VWC, but not du-opaque. Clearly, H is strictly serializable. Here T_2, T_1 is the required du-VWC serialization for aborted transaction T_1. However, H has no du-opaque serialization. □

Theorem 7. *Du-VWC is a safety property.*

Proof. By Definition 9, a history H is du-VWC if and only if H is strictly serializable and there is a du-VWC serialization for every transaction $T_i \in txns(H)$ that is aborted or t-incomplete in H.

To prove prefix-closure, recall that strict serializability is a prefix-closed property (Theorem 5). Therefore, any du-VWC serialization S for a transaction T_i in history H is also a du-VWC serialization S for a transaction T_i in any prefix of H that contains events of T_i.

To prove limit-closure, consider an infinite sequence of du-VWC histories H^0, H^1, ..., H^i, H^{i+1}, ..., where each H^{i+1} is the one-event extension of H^i and prove that the infinite limit, H of this sequence is also a du-VWC history. Theorem 5 establishes that there is a strictly serializable serialization for H.

Since, for all $i \in \mathbb{N}$, H^i is du-VWC, for every transaction T_i that is t-incomplete or aborted in H^i, there is a VWC serialization for T_i. Consequently, there is a du-VWC serialization for every aborted or incomplete transaction T_i in H. □

5.3 TMS1

Given a history H, TMS1 requires us to justify the behavior of all committed transactions in H by a legal t-complete t-sequential history that preserves the real-time order in H (strict serializability), and to justify the response of each complete t-operation performed in H by a legal t-complete t-sequential history S. The t-sequential history S used to justify a complete t-operation $op_{i,k}$ (the ith t-operation performed by transaction T_k) includes T_k and a subset of transactions from H whose operations justify $op_{i,k}$. (Our description follows [2].)

Let $H^{k,i}$ denote the prefix of a history H up to (and including) the response of ith t-operation $op_{k,i}$ of transaction T_k. We say that a history H'' is a *possible past* of $H^{k,i}$ if

H'' is a subsequence of $H^{k,i}$ and consists of all events of transaction T_k and all events from some subset of committed transactions and transactions that have invoked $tryC$ in $H^{k,i}$ such that if a transaction $T \in H''$, then for a transaction $T' \prec^{RT}_{H^{k,i}} T$, $T' \in H''$ if and only if T' is committed in $H^{k,i}$. Let $cTMSpast(H, op_{k,i})$ denote the set of possible pasts of $H^{k,i}$.

For any history $H'' \in cTMSpast(H, op_{k,i})$, let $ccomp(H'')$ denote the history generated from H'' by the following procedure: for all $m \neq k$, replace every event A_m by C_m and complete every incomplete $tryC_m$ with including C_m at the end of H''; include $tryC_k \cdot A_k$ at the end of H''.

Definition 10 (du-TMS1). *A history H satisfies* du-TMS1 *if*

1. *H is strictly serializable, and*
2. *for each complete t-read $op_{i,k}$ that returns a non-A_k response in H, there exist a legal t-complete t-sequential history S and a history H' such that:*
   - *$H' = ccomp(H'')$, where $H'' \in cTMSpast(H, op_{k,i})$*
   - *H' is equivalent to S*
   - *for any two transactions T_k and T_m in H', if $T_k \prec^{RT}_{H'} T_m$ then $T_k <_S T_m$*

We refer to S as the du-TMS1 serialization for $op_{i,k}$.

Theorem 8. *Du-TMS1 is a safety property.*

Proof. A history H is du-TMS1 if and only if H is strictly serializable and there is a du-TMS1 serialization for every t-operation $op_{k,i}$ that does not return A_k in H.

To see that du-TMS1 is prefix closed, recall that strict serializability is a prefix-closed property. Let H be any du-TMS1 history and H^i, any prefix of H. We now need to prove that, for every t-operation $op_{k,i} \neq tryC_k$ that returns a non-A_k response in H^i, there is a du-TMS1 serialization for $op_{k,i}$. But this is immediate since the du-TMS1 serialization for $op_{i,k}$ in H is also the required du-TMS1 serialization for $op_{k,i}$ in H^i.

To see that du-TMS1 is limit closed, consider an infinite sequence

$$H^0, H^1, \ldots H^i, H^{i+1}, \ldots$$

of finite du-TMS1 histories, such that H^{i+1} is a one-event extension of H^i. Let let H be the corresponding infinite limit history. We want to show that H is also du-TMS1.

Since strict serializability is a limit-closed property (Theorem 5), H is strictly serializable. By assumption, for all $i \in \mathbb{N}$, H^i is du-TMS1. Thus, for every transaction T_i that participates in H^i, there is a du-TMS1 serialization $S^{i,k}$ for each t-operation $op_{k,i}$. But $S^{i,k}$ is also the required du-TMS1 serialization for $op_{k,1}$ in H. The claim follows. □

It has been shown [15] that Opacity is a strictly stronger property than du-TMS1, that is, Opacity $\subsetneq$ du-TMS1. Since Du-Opacity $\subsetneq$ Opacity (Theorem 2) it follows that Du-Opacity $\subsetneq$ du-TMS1. On the other hand, du-TMS1 is incomparable to du-VWC, as demonstrated by the following examples.

Proposition 4. *There is a history that is du-TMS1, but not du-VWC.*

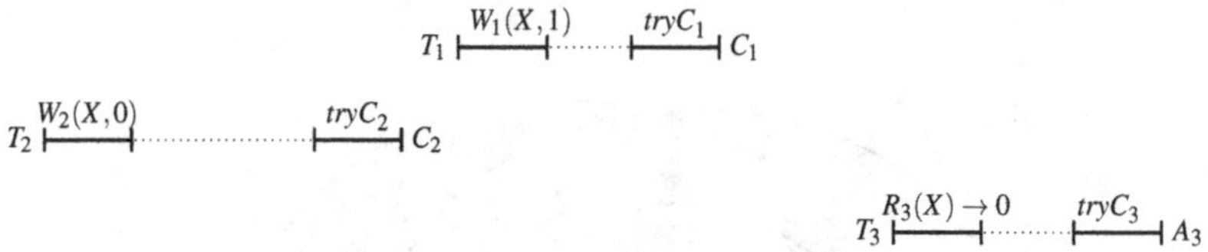

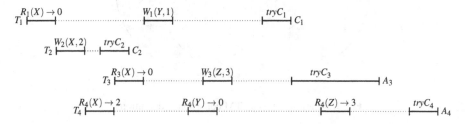

Fig. 7. A history which is du-VWC but not du-TMS1

Fig. 8. A history which is du-TMS1 but not du-VWC

Proof. Figure 8 depicts a history H that is du-TMS1, but not du-VWC. Observe that H is strictly serializable. To prove that H is du-TMS1, we need to prove that there is a TMS1 serialization for each t-read that returns a non-abort response in H. Clearly, the serialization in which only T_3 participates is the required TMS1 serialization for $read_3(X) \to 0$. Now consider the aborted transaction T_4. The TMS1 serialization for $read_4(X) \to 2$ is T_2, T_4, while the TMS1 serialization that justifies the response of $read_4(Y)- > 0$ includes just T_4 itself. The only nontrivial t-read whose response needs to be justified is $read_4(Z) \to 3$. Indeed, $tryC_3$ overlaps with $read_4(Z)$ and thus, the response of $read_4(Z)$ can be justified by choosing transactions in $cTMSpart(H, read_4(Z))$ to be $\{T_3, T_2, T_4\}$ and then deriving a TMS1 serialization $S = T_3, T_2, T_4$ for $read_4(Z) \to 3$ in which $tryC_3$ may be completed by including the commit response.

However, H is not du-VWC. Consider transaction T_3 which returns A_3 in H: T_3 must be aborted in any serialization equivalent to some direct causal past of T_4. But $read_4(Z)$ returns the value 3 that is written by T_3. Thus, $read_4(Z)$ cannot be legal in any du-VWC serialization for T_4. □

Proposition 5. *There is a history that is du-VWC, but not du-TMS1.*

Proof. Figure 7 depicts a history H that is du-VWC, but not du-TMS1. Clearly, H is strictly serializable. Observe that T_3 could have read only from T_1 in H (T_1 writes the value 0 to X that is returned by $read_3(X)$). Therefore, T_1, T_3 is the required du-VWC serialization for aborted transaction T_3.

However, H is not du-TMS1: since both transactions T_1 and T_2 are committed and precede T_3 in real-time order, they must be included in any du-TMS1 serialization for $read_3(X) \to 0$. But there is no such du-TMS1 serialization that would ensure the legality of $read_3(X)$. □

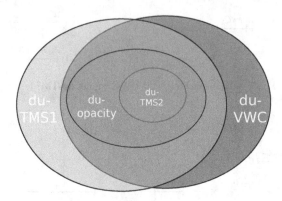

Fig. 9. Relations between TM consistency definitions

6   Concluding Remarks

The properties discussed in this paper explicitly preclude reading from a transaction
that has not yet invoked *tryC*, which makes them prefix-closed and facilitates their verification. We believe that this constructive definition is useful to TM practitioners, since
it streamlines possible implementations of t-read and tryC operations.

We showed that du-opacity is limit-closed under the restriction that every operation
eventually terminates, while du-VWC and du-TMS1 are (unconditionally) limit-closed,
which makes them safety properties [16].

Figure 9 summarizes the containment relations between the properties discussed in
this chapter: opacity, du-opacity, du-VWC, du-TMS1 and du-TMS2.

Linearizability [4, 11], when applied to objects with *finite nondeterminism* (i.e., an
operation applied to a given state may produce only finitely many outcomes) sequential specifications is a safety property [8, 16]. Recently, it has been shown [8] that
linearizability is not limit-closed if the implemented object may expose infinite non-
determinism [8], that is, an operation applied to a given state may produce infinitely
many different outcomes. The limit-closure proof (cf. Theorem 1), using König's
lemma, cannot be applied with infinite non-determinism, because the out-degree of the
graph G_H, constructed for the limit infinite history H, is not finite.

In contrast, the TM abstraction is *deterministic*, since reads and writes behave deterministically in serial executions, yet du-opacity is not limit-closed. It turns out that
the graph G_H for the counter-example history H in Figure 2 is not connected. For example, one of the finite prefixes of H can be serialized as T_3, T_1, T_2, but no prefix has
a serialization T_3, T_1 and, thus, the root is not connected to the corresponding vertex of
G_H. Thus, the precondition of König's lemma does not hold for G_H: the graph is in fact
an infinite set of isolated vertices. This is because du-opacity requires even incomplete
reading transactions, such as T_2, to appear in the serialization, which is not the case for
linearizability, where incomplete operations may be removed from the linearization.

References

1. Alpern, B., Schneider, F.B.: Defining liveness. Information Processing Letters 21(4), 181–185 (1985)
2. Attiya, H., Gotsman, A., Hans, S., Rinetzky, N.: Safety of live transactions in transactional memory: TMS is necessary and sufficient. In: Kuhn, F. (ed.) DISC 2014. LNCS, vol. 8784, pp. 376–390. Springer, Heidelberg (2014)
3. Attiya, H., Hans, S., Kuznetsov, P., Ravi, S.: Safety of deferred update in transactional memory. In: ICDCS, pp. 601–610 (2013)
4. Attiya, H., Welch, J.: Distributed Computing: Fundamentals, Simulations, and Advanced Topics, 2nd edn. Wiley Interscience (2004)
5. Doherty, S., Groves, L., Luchangco, V., Moir, M.: Towards formally specifying and verifying transactional memory. Formal Asp. Comput. 25(5), 769–799 (2013)
6. Guerraoui, R., Henzinger, T.A., Singh, V.: Permissiveness in transactional memories. In: Taubenfeld, G. (ed.) DISC 2008. LNCS, vol. 5218, pp. 305–319. Springer, Heidelberg (2008)
7. Guerraoui, R., Kapalka, M.: Principles of Transactional Memory, Synthesis Lectures on Distributed Computing Theory. Morgan and Claypool (2010)
8. Guerraoui, R., Ruppert, E.: Linearizability is not always a safety property. In: Noubir, G., Raynal, M. (eds.) NETYS 2014. LNCS, vol. 8539, pp. 57–69. Springer, Heidelberg (2014)
9. Hadzilacos, V.: A theory of reliability in database systems. J. ACM 35(1), 121–145 (1988)
10. Herlihy, M., Moss, J.E.B.: Transactional memory: Architectural support for lock-free data structures. SIGARCH Comput. Archit. News 21(2), 289–300 (1993)
11. Herlihy, M., Wing, J.M.: Linearizability: A correctness condition for concurrent objects. ACM Trans. Program. Lang. Syst. 12(3), 463–492 (1990)
12. Imbs, D., Raynal, M.: Virtual world consistency: A condition for STM systems (with a versatile protocol with invisible read operations). Theor. Comput. Sci. 444 (July 2012)
13. König, D.: Theorie der Endlichen und Unendlichen Graphen: Kombinatorische Topologie der Streckenkomplexe. Akad. Verlag (1936)
14. Kuznetsov, P., Ravi, S.: On the cost of concurrency in transactional memory. CoRR, abs/1103.1302 (2011)
15. Lesani, M., Luchangco, V., Moir, M.: Putting opacity in its place. In: WTTM (2012)
16. Lynch, N.A.: Distributed Algorithms. Morgan Kaufmann (1996)
17. Owicki, S.S., Lamport, L.: Proving liveness properties of concurrent programs. ACM Trans. Program. Lang. Syst. 4(3), 455–495 (1982)
18. Papadimitriou, C.H.: The serializability of concurrent database updates. J. ACM 26, 631–653 (1979)
19. Shavit, N., Touitou, D.: Software transactional memory. In: PODC 1995, pp. 204–213 (1995)

Disjoint-Access Parallelism
in Software Transactional Memory

Hagit Attiya[1] and Panagiota Fatourou[2]

[1] Technion, Haifa, Israel
hagit@cs.technion.ac.il
[2] FORTH ICS & University of Crete, Heraklion, Greece
faturu@csd.uoc.gr

Abstract. *Disjoint-access parallelism* captures the requirement that *unrelated* transactions progress *independently*, without interference, even if they occur at the same time. That is, an implementation should not cause two transactions, which are unrelated at the high-level, i.e. they access disjoint sets of data items, to simultaneously access the same low-level shared memory locations. This chapter will formalize this notion and will discuss if and when STM can achieve disjoint-access parallelism, by presenting impossibility results and discussing some of the disjoint-access parallel STM implementations. For example, no *dynamic* STM can be disjoint-access parallel, if it ensures wait-freedom for read-only transactions and a weak liveness property, known as *minimal progress*, for update transactions. In fact, even if transactions are static, STM implementations cannot be disjoint-access parallel, when read-only transactions must be *wait-free* and invisible. These impossibility results hold even when only *snapshot isolation* is required for the STM, and not stronger conditions like *opacity* or *strict serializability*. The second of these impossibility results holds for serializable STM as well.

1 Introduction

As anyone with a laptop or an Internet connection knows, the multi-core revolution is here, since almost any computing appliance contains several processing cores. With the improved hardware comes the need to harness the power of concurrency, since the processing power of individual cores does not increase. Applications must be restructured in order to reap the benefits of multiple processing units, without paying a hefty price for coordination among them.

It has been argued that writing concurrent applications is significantly more challenging than writing sequential ones, and *Transactional Memory* (TM) has been suggested as a way to deal with this difficulty. In the simplest form of TM, the programmer need only wrap code with operations denoting the beginning and end of a transaction. The transactional memory will take care of synchronizing the shared memory accesses so that each transaction seems to execute sequentially and in isolation.

Originally suggested as a hardware platform by Herlihy and Moss [31], TM has resurfaced as a software mechanism a couple of years later. The first software implementation of transactional memory was suggested by Shavit and Touitou [46]; it provided, in essence, support for multi-word synchronization operations on a static set of

R. Guerraoui and P. Romano (Eds.): Transactional Memory, LNCS 8913, pp. 72–97, 2015.

data items, in terms of a unary operation (LL/SC), somewhat optimized over prior implementations, e.g., [8,48]. Shavit and Touitou coined the term *software transactional memory* (STM) to describe their implementation.

Only when the termination condition was relaxed to *obstruction freedom* (see Section 2.2), the first STM handling a dynamic set of data items was presented by Herlihy et al. [30]. Work by Rajwar et al., e.g., [39,44], helped to popularize the TM approach in the programming languages and hardware communities.

Despite its simplicity, or perhaps because of it, transactional memory implementations incur significant cost, as has been discovered in recent theoretical work. This chapter describes several of these impossibility results and lower bounds, and their interaction with various properties of transactional memory. It also discusses some of the disjoint-access parallel STM implementations presented in the literature.

2 Formalizing TM

This section outlines how transactional memory can be formally captured, as well as properties expected of it. A comprehensive in-depth treatment is provided by Guerraoui and Kapałka [27].

The model encompasses at least two levels of abstraction: The high level has *transactions*, each of which is a sequence of *operations* accessing data items. At the low level, the operations are translated into executions in which a sequence of events apply *primitive operations* (or *primitives*) to base objects, containing the data and the metadata needed for the implementation. (See Fig. 1.) A primitive is *non-trivial* if it may change the value of a base object, and *trivial*, otherwise.

A *transaction* is a sequence of operations executed by a single process on a set of *data items*, shared with other transactions. Data items are *accessed* by *read* and *write* operations; a (dynamic) transaction can dynamically create new data items by invoking *create* operations. Some systems also support other operations. The interface additionally includes *try-commit* (*tryC*) and *try-abort* (*tryA*) operations, in which a transaction requests to commit or abort, respectively. If the response of *try-commit* is *commit*, the writes of the transaction are ensured to take effect, and we say that the transaction is *committed* (or has successfully *completed*). Any of these operations, not just *try-abort*, may cause the transaction to abort, in which case, none of its writes take effect and we say that the transaction is *aborted*. If the transaction is aborted not in response to *try-abort*, we say that it is *forcibly* aborted.

A *software implementation of transactional memory* (abbreviated *STM*) provides data representation for transactions and data items using *base objects*, and algorithms, specified as sequences of primitives on the base objects. Specifically, it provides an implementation, for each process, for procedures READ, WRITE, TRYCOMMIT,

Fig. 1. Levels of abstraction in transactional memory

TRYABORT (and CREATE if the STM implementation rely on per-object metadata). These procedures are performed by *asynchronous* processes in order to execute the operations of transactions. The primitives can be simple reads and writes, but also more sophisticated ones, like CAS, typically applied to memory locations, which are the base objects for the implementation.

When processes invoke these procedures, in an interleaved manner, we obtain *executions*, in the standard sense of asynchronous distributed computing (cf. [6]). A *configuration* describes a complete state of the system at some point in time: it is a vector with components comprising the state of each process and the state of each base object. In an *initial configuration*, each process is in an initial state and each base object has an initial value. An execution is a sequence of *events*. An event describes a single *step* by an individual process; a *step* of a process consists of an application of a single primitive to a base object, the response to that primitive, and local computation which may cause the internal state of the process to change. An execution is *legal* starting from a configuration C if the sequence of events caused by each process follows the algorithm for that process (starting from its state in C) and, for each base object, the responses to the primitives performed on the object are in accordance with its specification (and the state of the object at configuration C). An execution α is *indistinguishable* from another execution α' for some processes, if each of these processes causes the same events (i.e. takes the same steps) in α and α'. An execution is *solo* if all its events are caused by the same process.

Consider any execution α produced by an STM implementation I (I may support or not dynamic transactions). The collection of data items read or written by a transaction in α is its *data set* for α; the items written by the transaction are its *write set*, with the other items being its *read set*. A data item is *static* if it exists in the initial configuration. It is dynamic, if it is created dynamically, by invoking CREATE during α.

The *interval of a transaction T* in α is the execution interval that starts at the first event of T and ends at the last event of T in α. If T does not have a last event in α, then the interval of T is the (possibly infinite) suffix of α starting at the first event of T. Two transactions *overlap* if their intervals overlap. We say that a transaction T is *active* in some configuration C, if C is a configuration other than the first and the last in the execution interval of T. A process can have at most one active transaction in a configuration. A configuration is *quiescent* if no transaction is active in the configuration.

2.1 Safety: Consistency Properties of TM

An STM is *serializable* if committed transactions appear to execute sequentially, one after the other [42]. An STM is *strictly serializable* if this serialization order preserves the order of non-overlapping transactions [42]. This notion is called *order-preserving serializability* in [49], and is the analogue of *linearizability* [33] for transactions.[1]

---

[1] *Linearizability*, like *sequential consistency* [38], talks about implementing abstract data structures, and hence they involve one abstraction—from the high-level operations of the data structure to the low level primitives. It also provides the semantics of the operations, and their expected results at the high-level, on the data structure.

Opacity, suggested by Guerraoui and Kapałka [25], further demands that the (global) reads of even partially executed transactions, which may later abort, must be serializable (in an order-preserving manner); a read on a data item is *global* if the transaction executing it has not performed any write on this data item before the read. Opacity also accommodates operations beyond read and write.

While opacity is a stronger condition than strict serializability, *snapshot isolation* [9] is a consistency condition weaker than strict serializability. Roughly stated, snapshot isolation requires that transactions read from some consistent snapshot of the memory which is taken when they begin their execution (Cf. [49, Definition 10.3] and [19].) Riegel et al. [45] proposed to use snapshot isolation for TM.

Virtual World Consistency (VWC), defined by Imbs et al. [34], is a weakening of opacity, tailored for transactional memory. VWC allows aborted (and ongoing) transactions to observe *mutually inconsistent* views of the execution, as long as each of them is consistent with some sequential execution of the committed transactions in their "causal past". A related condition, called *Transactional Memory Specification* (referred to as TMS1), was suggested by Doherty et al. [17]. TMS1 considers each aborted transaction in isolation.

Dziuma *et al.* provide in [19] formal definitions for these and other consistency conditions for transactional memory. Additional discussion of the relations between various TM and database consistency conditions is given by Attiya and Hans [3].

2.2 Progress: Termination Guarantees for TM

One of the innovations of TM is in allowing transactions not to commit, when they are faced with conflicting transactions, namely, transactions that access the same data items. This, however, admits trivial implementations where no progress is ever made. Finding the right balance between nontriviality and efficiency has lead to several progress properties. They are first and foremost distinguished by whether locking is accommodated or not.

When locks are not allowed, the strongest requirement—rarely provided—is of *wait-freedom*, namely, that each transaction has to eventually commit. A weaker property ensures that some transaction eventually commits, or that a transaction commits when it is executed solo for long enough time. The last property is called *obstruction-freedom* [30] (see further discussion in [2]).

A *lock-based* STM (e.g., TL2 [15]) is often required to be *(weakly) progressive* [26], namely, a transaction that does not encounter a conflicting transaction must commit. (There is a *conflict* between two transactions, if both of them access the same data item; if one of these accesses is a write the conflict is *nontrivial*.)

Several lower bounds assume a *minimal progress* property, ensuring that a transaction terminates successfully if it runs alone, from a situation in which no other transaction is pending. This property is implied both by obstruction freedom and by weak progressiveness.

Related definitions [22,26,36] further attempt to capture the distinction between aborts that are necessary in order to maintain the safety properties (e.g., opacity) and *spurious* aborts that are not mandated by the consistency property, and to measure their ratio.

Strong progressiveness [26] ensures that even when there are conflicts, some transaction commits. More specifically, an STM is *strongly progressive* if a transaction without *nontrivial* conflicts, namely, a conflict involving at least one write. is not forcibly aborted, and if a set of transactions have nontrivial conflicts on a single item then not all of them are forcibly aborted. (Recall that a transaction is forcibly aborted, when the abort was not requested by a *try-abort* operation of the transaction, i.e., the abort is in response to *try-commit*, *read* or *write* operations.)

Permissiveness tries to capture the number of unjustified, *spurious* aborts; it requires a transaction to commit unless doing so violates correctness [23]; said otherwise, this means that a transaction can abort or block only if committing may violate correctness. A weaker condition, given by Fan et al. [43], says that an STM is *multi-version (MV)-permissive* if a transaction is forcibly aborted (not because it requests to abort) only if it is an update transaction that has a nontrivial conflict with another update transaction.

Strong progressiveness and MV-permissiveness are incomparable: The former allows a read-only transaction to abort, if it has a conflict with another update transaction, while the latter does not guarantee that at least one transaction is not forcibly aborted in case of a conflict.

Fig. 2 shows the relations between these progress conditions.

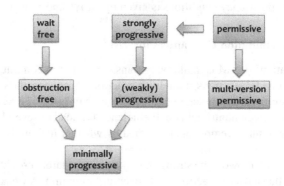

Fig. 2. Relations between progress conditions for transactional memory

Remark 1. Strictly speaking, these properties are not liveness properties in the traditional sense [37], since they can be checked in finite executions.

2.3 Disjoint-Access Parallelism

There has been some theoretical attempts to predict how much parallelism will TM implementations exploit, resulting in definitions that postulate behaviors that are expected to yield superior performance.

The most accepted such notion is *disjoint-access parallelism*, capturing the requirement that unrelated transactions progress *independently*, even if they occur at the same time. That is, an implementation should not cause two transactions, which are unrelated at the high-level, to simultaneously access the same low-level shared memory.

We explain what it means for two transactions to be *unrelated* through a conflict graph that represents the relations between transactions. Consider an execution α and an execution interval I of α. The *conflict graph* of I is an undirected graph, where vertices represent transactions in α whose execution intervals intersect with I, and edges connect those pairs of transactions whose data sets are not disjoint. Two transactions T_1 and T_2 are *disjoint access* in α if there is no path between the vertices representing them in the conflict graph of the minimal execution interval of α containing the execution intervals of both T_1 and T_2; they are *strictly disjoint access* if there is no edge between these vertices.

Fig. 3 illustrates the conflict graph for six transactions: T1 with data set $\{A,B,C\}$, T2 with data set $\{A,D\}$, T3 with data set $\{D,E\}$, T4 with data set $\{F,L\}$, T5 with data set $\{L\}$ and T6 with data set $\{J\}$.

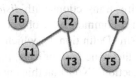

Fig. 3. An example of a conflict graph

In this example, the data sets of T1 and T2 intersect, as do the data sets of T2 and T3, while the data sets of T1 and T3 do not intersect. Hence, T1 and T2 (as well as T2 and T3) are strictly disjoint-access, whereas T1 and T3 are disjoint access but not strictly disjoint access.

Two events *contend* on a base object o if they both access o, and at least one of them applies a nontrivial primitive to o. Transactions *concurrently contend* on a base object o if they have pending events at the same configuration that contend on o.

Definition 1 (Weak Disjoint-Access Parallelism). *An STM implementation is (weakly) disjoint-access parallel if two transactions concurrently contend on the same base object only if they are not disjoint access.*

This definition captures the first condition of the disjoint-access parallelism property of Israeli and Rappoport [35], in accordance with most of the literature (cf. [32]). It is somewhat weaker, as it allows two processes to apply a trivial primitive on the same base object, e.g., read, even when executing disjoint-access transactions. Moreover, this definition only prohibits concurrent contending accesses, allowing disjoint-access transactions to contend on a base object o at different points of the execution. A stronger requirement is:

Definition 2 (Strong Disjoint-access Parallelism). *An STM implementation is disjoint-access parallel if two transactions concurrently access the same base object only if they are not disjoint access.*

The original disjoint-access parallelism definition [35] also restricts the impact of concurrent transactions on the *step complexity* of a transaction. For additional definitions and discussion, see [5].

We remark that, to ensure disjoint-access parallelism, an STM algorithm could cheat, by including in the implementation of each transactional operation fictitious invocations to READ (or WRITE) for all data items. To avoid such fake situations, we make the natural assumption that each STM algorithm executes the code of each transaction as specified by its (enhanced) sequential code and provides implementations for READ, WRITE, CREATE, or TRYCOMMIT which do not contain further invocations of any of these routines.

3 Lower Bounds and Impossibility Results for Providing Disjoint-Access Parallelism

Guerraoui and Kapałka [24] proved that obstruction-free serializable implementations of software transactional memory cannot ensure *strict* disjoint-access parallelism. Strict disjoint-access parallelism requires transactions with *disjoint data sets* (with strict disjoint access) not to contend on a common base object. This notion is stronger than (weak) disjoint-access parallelism (Definition 1), which allows two transactions with disjoint data sets to contend on the same base objects, provided they are connected in the conflict graph via other transactions. Note that this impossibility result does not hold under (weak) disjoint-access parallelism, as Herlihy et al. [30] present an obstruction-free and disjoint-access parallel STM.

The result that obstruction-free implementations of software transactional memory cannot ensure strict disjoint-access parallelism, has been extended in several important ways.

For the stronger case of wait-free *read-only* transactions, the assumption of strict disjoint-access parallelism can be replaced with the assumption that read-only transactions are *invisible* and do not apply non-trivial primitives, e.g., writes. It is expected that many typical applications will generate workloads that include a significant portion of read-only transactions.

Many STMs attempt to optimize read-only transactions, and more generally, the implementation of read operations inside the transaction. By their very nature, read operations, and even more so, read-only transactions, need not leave a mark on the shared memory, and therefore, it is desirable to avoid writing in such transactions, i.e., to make sure that reads are *invisible*, and certainly, that read-only transactions do not write at all.

Remark 2. Dice et al. [14] refer to a transaction as having invisible reads even if it writes, but the information is not sufficiently detailed to supply the exact details about the transaction's data set. (In their words, "the STM does not know which, or even how many, readers are accessing a given memory location.") This behavior is captured by the stronger notion of an *oblivious* STM [4].

Specifically, an STM cannot be disjoint-access parallel and have invisible read-only transactions that always terminate successfully [5], even if update transactions are blocking. A read-only transaction not only has to write, but the number of writes is linear in the size of its read set. These results hold even if the STM supports only static transactions. Both results hold for strict serializability, and hence also for opacity. (See Section 3.1.1.) Section 3.1.3 extends the results to hold for serializability.

In fact, even the original result of Guerraoui and Kapałka [24] holds with consistency weaker than serializability: Bushkov et al. [11] have shown that it is impossible to ensure strict disjoint-access parallelism and obstruction-freedom even if we weaken safety to ensure a property which is weaker than snapshot isolation.

Ellen et al. shows in [18] that dynamic STM implementations (which satisfy a natural property) cannot ensure disjoint-access parallelism, wait-freedom for read-only transactions, and minimal progress for update transactions; this result holds for STM implementations that ensure snapshot isolation (and therefore also for those that ensure any stronger consistency property).

Bushkov *et al.* [12] showed that no TM algorithm (whether or not it is disjoint-access parallel) can ensure local progress. The impossibility results in [5,18] assume weaker progress and safety properties than those of Bushkov *et al.* [12]. Table 1 summarizes these impossibility results.

Table 1. Impossibility of achieving disjoint access parallelism (DAP). The table entry shows the progress condition needed for proving the result.

	Strict DAP	Strong DAP	DAP	Feeble DAP	No DAP
Opacity					wait-freedom [12]
Linearizability				Wait-freedom [18]	
Strict serializability			Invisible, wait-free reads [5]		
Serializability	Obstruction-freedom [24]	Invisible, wait-free reads [5]			
Snapshot isolation	Obstruction-freedom [10]	Invisible, wait-free reads [5]		Wait-free reads [18]	

3.1   Wait-Free, Invisible Reads and Disjoint-Access Parallelism

3.1.1   Strictly Serializable STMs. Formally, a read-only transaction is *invisible* if its algorithm only applies trivial primitives to base objects. Theorem 1 shows that in a disjoint-access parallel STM implementation with invisible read-only transactions, some read-only transaction does not terminate successfully in a finite number of steps.

Specifically, we construct an infinite execution of a read-only transaction. This execution consists of a single read-only transaction with one complete update transaction between any pair of consecutive steps by the read-only transaction; an *update* is a transaction with a singleton write set and an empty read set. We first define a special (finite) execution of this form, called *flippable*, and show that such a read-only transaction cannot terminate successfully. Then we show how a flippable execution can be repeatedly extended to construct successively longer flippable executions.

An execution is called flippable since there are two similar executions in which we flip the position of two update transactions and one of the executions is indistinguishable from the original execution. One type of flipped execution is called a *forward* flip since an update transaction is moved forward in the execution, while other is called a *backward* flip since an update transaction is deferred in the execution. Formally:

$$
\begin{array}{llll}
q: & s_1 & \dots s_{l-1} & s_l & \dots s_k \\
p_0: U_0 & \dots & U_{l-1} & \dots & U_k \\
p_1: & U_1 \dots & & U_l \dots &
\end{array}
$$

Fig. 4. α_k is a flippable execution of length k with two updaters

Definition 3. *A* flippable execution *of length k with t updaters is a finite execution $\alpha_k = U_0 s_1 U_1 \dots s_k U_k$ executed by processes $p_0, \dots, p_{t-1}$ executing update transactions and process q executing a read-only transaction, which reads and returns the value of t data items $\iota_0 \dots \iota_{t-1}$. The execution α_k satisfies all the following conditions:*

1. *for $j = 1, \dots, k$, s_j is a single step by q,*
2. *for $j = 0, \dots, k$, U_j is a solo execution of a complete update transaction, in which process $p_h \in \{p_0, \dots, p_{t-1}\}$, writes $j+1$ to the data item ι_h*
3. *consecutive update transactions are executed by different processes, and*
4. *for any l, $0 < l \leq k$, the execution*

$$
\alpha_k = U_0 s_1 U_1 \dots s_{l-1} U_{l-1} s_l U_l \dots s_k U_k
$$

is indistinguishable to all processes from one of the following executions:

$$
\overleftarrow{\alpha}_l = U_0 s_1 U_1 \dots s_{l-1} U_l U_{l-1} s_l \dots s_k U_k
$$

in which the update transaction U_l is executed before $U_{l-1} s_l$ instead of after $U_{l-1} s_l$ (forward flip) or

$$
\overrightarrow{\alpha}_l = U_0 s_1 U_1 \dots s_{l-1} s_l U_l U_{l-1} \dots s_k U_k
$$

in which the update transaction U_{l-1} is executed after $s_l U_l$ instead of before $s_l U_l$ (backward flip).

Figs. 5(a) and 5(b) present the forward and the backward flips of the execution in Fig. 4.

This definition, and the structure of our proof, is similar to the lower bound of Attiya, Ellen and Fatourou [1] on the step complexity of update operations in implementations of atomic snapshot objects. The main difference is that our definition of a flippable execution has *two* types of flipped executions, and t processes executing update transactions instead of just two.

The next lemma proves that the read-only transaction in a flippable execution does not terminate; it is proved by arguments similar to those applied in [1], extended to handle the possibility of two kinds of flips (forward and backward).

Lemma 1. *If the STM provides strict serializability, then the read-only transaction in a flippable execution does not terminate successfully.*

Proof. Let $\alpha_k = U_0 s_1 U_1 \dots s_k U_k$ be a flippable execution. Assume, towards a contradiction, that q successfully terminates its read-only transaction in α_k, with a result $(v_0, \dots, v_{t-1})$. The proof first fixes the serialization of the update transactions, and then

$$q : \quad s_1 \quad \ldots s_{l-1} \qquad\qquad s_l \ldots s_k$$
$$p_0 : U_0 \qquad \ldots \qquad\quad U_{l-1} \quad \ldots \quad U_k$$
$$p_1 : \qquad U_1 \ldots \qquad \boxed{U_l} \qquad\qquad \ldots$$

(a) Forward flip: U_l is performed before $U_{l-1}s_l$.

$$q : \quad s_1 \quad \ldots s_{l-1} \; s_l \qquad\qquad\quad \ldots s_k$$
$$p_0 : U_0 \qquad \ldots \qquad\qquad \boxed{U_{l-1}} \ldots \quad U_k$$
$$p_1 : \qquad U_1 \ldots \qquad\quad U_l \qquad \ldots$$

(b) Backward flip: U_{l-1} is performed after $s_l U_l$.

Fig. 5. Fig. 5(a) shows the *forward* flip execution of α_k, where the update transaction U_l by process p_1 is executed before the update transaction U_{l-1} by process p_0 and before the step s_l of the read-only transaction; Fig. 5(b) shows the *backward* flip execution of α_k, where the update U_{l-1} by process p_0 is deferred after the update transaction U_l by process p_1 and after the step s_l of the read-only transaction

shows that it is not possible to serialize the read-only transaction among the update transactions, using the forward and backward flip executions, which are indistinguishable to q from α_k.

Since the update transactions in the execution α_k do not overlap, they must be serialized in the order $U_0, \ldots, U_k$. Since all steps of the read-only transaction by q are after U_0 and before U_k, it has a unique serialization point between U_{l-1} and U_l, for some l, $1 \le l \le k$. Let ι_h be the item written by U_{l-1}, and recall that U_{l-1} writes l to ι_h; hence $v_h = l$.

The execution α_k is indistinguishable to process q from β_l, which is either the forward flip

$$\overleftarrow{\alpha}_l = U_0 s_1 U_1 \ldots s_{l-1} U_l U_{l-1} s_l s_{l+1} \ldots U_k$$

in which update U_l is executed before $U_{l-1}s_l$ instead of after $U_{l-1}s_l$; or the backward flip

$$\overrightarrow{\alpha}_l = U_0 s_1 U_1 \ldots s_{l-1} s_l U_l U_{l-1} s_{l+1} \ldots U_k$$

in which update U_{l-1} is executed after $s_l U_l$ instead of before $s_l U_l$. Hence, the read-only transaction executed by q in β_l returns the same vector, $(v_0, \ldots, v_{t-1})$, as in α_k.

Since the update transactions do not overlap in β_l, they are serialized in the order $U_0, \ldots, U_l, U_{l-1}, \ldots, U_k$, that is, the same as for α_k, except that U_{l-1} and U_l are flipped. Since two consecutive update transactions are to different data items, the values of $\{\iota_0, \ldots, \iota_{t-1}\}$ are the same after both update transactions have been executed, no matter which has been executed first. Hence, at all points in the serialization of β_l, except between U_l and U_{l-1}, the value of all items $\{\iota_0, \ldots, \iota_{t-1}\}$ is the same as its value in the corresponding points in the serialization of α_k. Thus, the read-only transaction of q can only be serialized after U_l and before U_{l-1} in β_l. However, since U_{l-1} is the first write of l to ι_h, the value of ι_h is not l before U_{l-1}, and hence, the read-only transaction executed by q cannot be serialized between U_l and U_{l-1}. This contradicts the assumption that the read-only transaction terminates successfully. □

Lemma 3 (below) shows how to inductively construct a flippable execution, when read-only transactions are invisible. The crux of this lemma is quite different from [1], as it relies on weakly disjoint-access parallelism. A critical step in the proof is provided by Lemma 2, showing that in a weakly disjoint-access parallel STM, two consecutive updates by different processes on different items cannot contend on the same base objects. Note that two consecutive update transactions do not contradict weak disjoint-access parallelism since the steps of their executing processes are not interleaved. The proof of the next lemma shows that two such consecutive updates can be perturbed to *concurrently* contend on the same base object.

Lemma 2. *Given a weakly disjoint-access parallel STM implementation and a quiescent configuration C, consider the consecutive execution of two update transactions $U_{j_h} U_{j_{h'}}$, executed by a process p_h on an item ι_h and by process $p_{h'}$ on an item $\iota_{h'}$, $h \neq h'$, respectively, from C. Then p_h and $p_{h'}$ do not contend on the same base object when executing U_{j_h} and $U_{j_{h'}}$.*

Proof. Assume, towards a contradiction, that p_h and $p_{h'}$ contend on a base object when executing $U_{j_h} U_{j_{h'}}$ from a quiescent configuration C. If in U_{j_h}, p_h applies a non-trivial primitive to a base object on which they contend, let ϕ_h be the last event in U_{j_h} in which p_h applies such a primitive, say, to base object o. Let $\phi_{h'}$ be the first event in $U_{j_{h'}}$ that accesses o.

Otherwise, p_h only applies trivial primitives in U_{j_h} to base objects on which it contends with $p_{h'}$ in $U_{j_{h'}}$; let $\phi_{h'}$ be the first event in $U_{j_{h'}}$ in which $p_{h'}$ applies a non-trivial primitive to some base object, say, o, on which they contend. Let ϕ_h be the last event of p_h in U_{j_h} that accesses o.

In both cases, denote by $\alpha_h \phi_h$ the prefix of the execution of U_h from C and by $\alpha_{h'} \phi_{h'}$ the prefix of the execution of $U_{h'}$ after U_h.

We now create an overlapping execution of the update transactions U_{j_h} and $U_{j_{h'}}$, by processes p_h and $p_{h'}$, from C. We argue that p_h and $p_{h'}$ perform the same steps up to the events ϕ_h and $\phi_{h'}$, and p_h and $p_{h'}$ concurrently contend on base object o.

In more detail, consider the execution $\alpha_h \alpha_{h'}$ from C, in which p_h executes U_{j_h} until it is about to perform ϕ_h, and then $p_{h'}$ executes $U_{j_{h'}}$ until it is about to perform $\phi_{h'}$. Clearly, p_h is about to perform ϕ_h also after $\alpha_h \alpha_{h'}$. By construction, the execution interval $\alpha_h \alpha_{h'}$ from C is indistinguishable to $p_{h'}$ from the execution interval $U_{j_h} \alpha_{h'}$ from C. Hence, $p_{h'}$ is about to perform the event $\phi_{h'}$ also after $\alpha_h \alpha_{h'}$, that is, $p_{h'}$ and p_h concurrently contend on o. However, the conflict graph of the execution interval $\alpha_h \alpha_{h'} \phi_{h'} \phi_h$ does not contain a path between the data sets of U_{j_h} and $U_{j_{h'}}$, contradicting the assumption that the implementation is weakly disjoint-access parallel. □

Since two consecutive updates cannot contend on the same base object, we can construct an execution where either the previous update is deferred or the next update is moved forward in the execution without affecting the single step of the read-only transaction in between them. This allows us to inductively construct a flippable execution, in the proof of the next lemma.

Lemma 3. *For every $k \geq 0$, every weakly disjoint-access parallel implementation of an STM with invisible read-only transactions, which is minimally progressive, has a* *flippable execution* $\alpha_k = U_0 s_1 U_1 s_2 \ldots U_k$ *with two updaters* p_0 *and* p_1, *which is indistinguishable to* p_0 *and* p_1 *from the execution* $\alpha'_k = U_0 U_1 \ldots U_k$ *in which only* p_0 *and* p_1 *take steps.*

Proof. The proof is by induction on the length, k, of the flippable execution α_k executed by a process q and two updaters p_0 and p_1 on two items $\{t_0, t_1\}$. In the base case, $k = 0$, the lemma holds with a solo execution of U_0, an update transaction by p_0 that writes 1 to t_0. U_0 successfully terminates since it runs solo from a quiescent configuration.

For the induction step, consider a flippable execution of length $k \geq 1$, $\alpha_k = U_0 s_1 U_1 s_2 \ldots U_k$, which is indistinguishable to p_0 and p_1 from the execution $\alpha'_k = U_0 U_1 \ldots U_k$. We show how to construct a flippable execution of length $k + 1$, which is indistinguishable from an execution in which only p_0 and p_1 take steps.

By Lemma 1, the read-only transaction does not terminate successfully in α_k. Let s_{k+1} be the next step by q. Assume U_k is executed by $p_{h'}$ and let $h = 1 - h'$; note that $h \neq h'$. Let $\alpha_{k+1} = \alpha_k s_{k+1} U_{k+1}$, where process p_h writes $k + 2$ to t_h in the update transaction U_{k+1}. Note that U_{k+1} terminates successfully: The execution $\alpha_k s_{k+1}$ is indistinguishable to p_0 and p_1 from the execution α'_k, because the read-only transaction is invisible. The configuration at the end of α'_k is quiescent, and since the execution of U_{k+1} from the configuration at the end of α'_k must terminate successfully, since the STM is minimally progressive, U_{k+1} must also terminate successfully when executing from the configuration at the end of $\alpha_k s_{k+1}$.

Since the read-only transaction by q is invisible, $\alpha_k s_{k+1} U_{k+1}$ is indistinguishable to p_0 and p_1 from the execution $\alpha'_k U_{k+1}$.

It remains to prove that α_{k+1} is a flippable execution, i.e., that for every l, $0 < l \leq k + 1$, the execution α_{k+1} is indistinguishable to all processes from either $\overleftarrow{\alpha}_l$ or $\overrightarrow{\alpha}_l$. For every l, $0 < l \leq k$, by the inductive assumption, the execution

$$\alpha_k = U_0 s_1 U_1 \ldots s_{l-1} U_{l-1} s_l U_l \ldots s_k U_k$$

is indistinguishable to all processes from the flipped execution β_l which is either

$$\overleftarrow{\alpha}_l = U_0 s_1 U_1 \ldots s_{l-1} U_l U_{l-1} s_l \ldots U_k$$

or

$$\overrightarrow{\alpha}_l = U_0 s_1 U_1 \ldots s_{l-1} s_l U_l U_{l-1} \ldots s_k U_k.$$

In particular, $\alpha_{k+1} = \alpha_k s_{k+1} U_{k+1}$ and $\beta_l s_{k+1} U_{k+1}$ are indistinguishable to all processes.

To prove the condition for $l = k + 1$, let C'_{k-1} be the configuration at the end of α'_{k-1}; C'_{k-1} is quiescent, and Lemma 2 implies that $p_{h'}$ and p_h do not contend on the same base object when executing U_k followed by U_{k+1} from C'_{k-1}, namely, in the suffix of α'_{k+1}. Since α'_{k+1} is indistinguishable to $p_{h'}$ and p_h from α_{k+1}, $p_{h'}$ and p_h do not contend on the same base object while executing U_k and U_{k+1} also in the execution α_{k+1}. Moreover, if q accesses a base object o in s_{k+1}, then either at least one of the two processes p_h or $p_{h'}$ does not access o in U_{k+1} or U_k, respectively, or they both apply a trivial primitive to o. In the former case, if p_h does not access o in U_{k+1} then

$$\overleftarrow{\alpha}_{k+1} = U_0 s_1 U_1 \ldots s_k U_{k+1} U_k s_{k+1}$$

is indistinguishable to all processes from α_{k+1}, while if $p_{h'}$ does not access o in U_k, then

$$\overrightarrow{\alpha}_{k+1} = U_0 s_1 U_1 \ldots s_k s_{k+1} U_{k+1} U_k$$

is indistinguishable to all processes from α_{k+1}. If both p_h and $p_{h'}$ apply a trivial primitive to o, then both flipped executions, $\overleftarrow{\alpha}_{k+1}$ and $\overrightarrow{\alpha}_{k+1}$, are indistinguishable to all processes from α_{k+1}.   □

The impossibility result follows from Lemmas 1 and 3.

Theorem 1. *There is no weakly disjoint-access parallel implementation with invisible read-only transactions of a strictly serializable STM, which is minimally progressive, in which read-only transactions always terminate successfully.*

Theorem 1 holds also for opaque STMs [25], since opacity implies strict serializability.

Theorem 1 can be extended to prove that a read-only transaction with a read set of t items in a disjoint-access parallel STM implementation, which successfully terminates in a finite number of steps, must apply non-trivial primitives to $t - 1$ base objects; this assumes that there are at least $t + 1$ processes. This result was proved by Attiya, Hillel and Milani [5]. It relies on *strong* disjoint-access parallelism, which requires two transactions to be connected (in the conflict graph) even if they both just apply a trivial primitive to the same base object. (Definition 2; this is the definition in [35].) The lower bound holds for strictly serializable STMs, and hence, also for opaque STMs.

3.1.2   STMs with Snapshot Isolation. *Snapshot isolation* [9,40,45,49] decouples the consistency of the reads and the writes. Informally, all read operations in a transaction return the most recent value as of the time the transaction starts. In addition, the write sets of any pair of concurrent transactions must be disjoint. For a formal definition, see [49, Definition 10.3]. Attiya, Hillel and Milani [5] show results for this definition.

A somewhat weaker definition is used in the context of STMs, which requires all read operations to return the values at some point during a transaction, and requires all write operations to appear to occur at some (later) point during the transaction. (See Chapter 5.) Since the transactions used in our proofs are either read-only or write-only (update) this definition boils down to strict serializability and the impossibility result holds for STMs that satisfy this type of snapshot isolation:

Theorem 2. *There is no weakly disjoint-access parallel implementation with invisible read-only transactions of an STM providing snapshot isolation, which is minimally progressive, in which read-only transactions always terminate successfully.*

This theorem can also be extended to a lower bound requiring a read-only transaction to apply a non-trivial primitive to at least $t - 1$ base objects. (See [5].)

3.1.3   Serializable STMs

In this section, we show that Theorem 1 holds for serializable STMs. Recall that an STM is *serializable* if transactions appear to execute sequentially, one after the other;

that transactions of the same process must preserve their order (*per-process* order). This definition should also apply to infinite executions, implying that if a value v is written to a data item o, then repeatedly reading o after the write eventually returns v. (Otherwise, we will have to place an infinite sequence of reads before the write, which cannot be done.)

The proof uses an additional process q'. Given a flippable execution $\alpha_k = U_0 s_1 U_1 \ldots s_k U_k$, we construct an *augmented flippable execution*

$$\widehat{\alpha}_k = U_0 s_1 S_1^* U_1 \ldots s_k S_k^* U_k ,$$

where the additional process q' performs invisible read-only transactions. For every $j \in \{1, \ldots, k\}$, q' performs solo a sequence S_j^* of read-only transactions after the event s_j by process q and before the update U_j. Each read-only transaction in S_j^* accesses the items $\iota_{f_{j-1}}$ and ι_{f_j} updated by U_{j-1} and U_j. The result of the last read-only transaction in the sequence S_j^*, denoted S_j, is the value written by U_{j-1} to $\iota_{f_{j-1}}$ and the last value of ι_{f_j} before U_j updates it.

Fig. 6 shows the augmented flippable execution obtained by augmenting the flippable execution α_k of Fig. 4 with sequences of read-only transactions performed by process q'.

$$
\begin{array}{llllll}
q: & s_1 & \ldots s_{l-1} & s_l & \ldots s_k & \\
p_0: U_0 & & \ldots & U_{l-1} & & \ldots & U_k \\
p_1: & U_1 \ldots & & & U_l \ldots & \\
q': & S_1^* & \ldots & S_{l-1}^* & S_l^* & \ldots & S_k^*
\end{array}
$$

Fig. 6. An augmented flippable execution $\widehat{\alpha}_k$ derived from the flippable execution α_k of Fig. 4

We apply the per-process ordering of transactions to prove that the read-only transactions of q' must eventually read the latest value written in U_{j-1}, and thus, S_j^* is finite.

Lemma 4. *Consider an augmented flippable execution of length $k \geq 0$, $\widehat{\alpha}_k = U_0 s_1 S_1^* U_1 \ldots s_k S_k^* U_k$. In any serialization of $\widehat{\alpha}_k$ that preserves the per-process order, $U_0, U_1, \ldots, U_k$ appear in their order of execution.*

Proof. We show, by induction on ℓ, that $U_0, U_1, \ldots, U_\ell$ appear in their order of execution. In the base case, $k = 0$, the serialization of U_0 is trivial.

For the induction step, consider $U_{\ell+1}$. By the induction assumption, the updates $U_0, U_1, \ldots, U_\ell$ are serialized by their execution order in $\widehat{\alpha}_k$. By construction, $S_{\ell+1}^*$ is a sequence of read-only transactions that access ι_{f_ℓ} and $\iota_{f_{\ell+1}}$, and the last read-only transaction in $S_{\ell+1}^*$, denoted $S_{\ell+1}$, returns the value written by U_ℓ and the last value of $\iota_{f_{\ell+1}}$ before the one written by $U_{\ell+1}$.

The sequence $S_{\ell+1}^*$ is finite since the STM is serializable and so, eventually, some transaction must return the latest values written to ι_{f_ℓ} and $\iota_{f_{\ell+1}}$, and by the induction assumption, U_ℓ is the last to write to ι_{f_ℓ}. Moreover, $S_{\ell+1}$ completes before $U_{\ell+1}$ starts, so it cannot return the value written by $U_{\ell+1}$, since due to serializability, a read operation can not return a value not written.

Since each data item is written by a different process, and due to per-process order, $U_{\ell+1}$ can not be serialized before the last update of $\iota_{f_{\ell+1}}$ preceding $U_{\ell+1}$.

Moreover, $U_{\ell+1}$ can not be serialized after this update and before $S_{\ell+1}$, since $S_{\ell+1}$ does not return the value written by $U_{\ell+1}$. Hence, $U_{\ell+1}$ is serialized after $S_{\ell+1}$. □

We use Lemma 4 to prove an analogue of Lemma 1.

Lemma 5. *Consider an augmented flippable execution of length $k \geq 0$ with t updaters, $\widehat{\alpha}_k = U_0 s_1 S_1^* U_1 \ldots s_k S_k^* U_k$. If the read-only transactions by process q' are invisible, then the read-only transaction by process q does not terminate successfully.*

Proof. Assume, towards a contradiction, that the read-only transaction of process q in $\widehat{\alpha}_k$ terminates successfully and returns a value $(v_0, \ldots, v_{t-1})$, which does not violate serializability. Let the augmented flippable execution $\widehat{\alpha}_k = U_0 s_1 S_1^* U_1 \ldots s_k S_k^* U_k$ correspond to a flippable execution $\alpha_k = U_0 s_1 U_1 \ldots s_k U_k$.

By Lemma 4, the updates in $\widehat{\alpha}_k$ are serialized in the order $U_0, U_1, \ldots, U_k$. The vector $(v_0, \ldots, v_{t-1})$ determines where q's read-only transaction is serialized. In particular, for some l, $0 < l \leq k$, the read-only transaction of q is serialized after U_{l-1} and before U_l, and for each item ι_f in $\{\iota_0 \ldots \iota_{t-1}\}$, either v_f is zero and no update wrote to ι_f before U_l, or the last update to ι_f before U_l wrote v_f to ι_f. Let S be the serialization of execution $\widehat{\alpha}_k$.

Since the read-only transactions executed by process q' are invisible, $\widehat{\alpha}_k$ and α_k are indistinguishable to $p_0, \ldots, p_{t-1}$ and q. Thus, they will execute the same steps in both executions. Note that S is a serialization also for α_k. Since S preserves the real-time order among transactions, α_k is a flippable execution where the read-only transaction terminates and strict serializability is preserved, contradicting Lemma 1. □

As discussed before the lemma, the existence of a flippable execution (guaranteed by Lemma 3) implies there is an augmented flippable execution, and hence, Lemma 5 implies the following impossibility result:

Theorem 3. *There is no weakly disjoint-access parallel implementation with invisible read-only transactions of a serializable STM, which is minimally progressive, in which read-only transactions always terminate successfully.*

When a read-only transaction of $t \geq 2$ data items applies non-trivial primitives to at most $t - 2$ base objects, the read-only transactions of q' in the augmented flippable execution are, in fact, invisible since their read set contains only two data items. This can be used to prove that the read-only transaction must apply non-trivial primitives to at least $t - 1$ base objects, assuming the STM is strongly disjoint-access parallel (Definition 2). (See [5].)

These results also hold for *virtual world consistency*, recently proposed by Imbs et al. [34]. This consistency condition requires serializability or strict serializability of committed transactions, and ensures that aborted transactions always see a consistent state of the memory, although not necessarily consistent with each other. Since our results do not consider the behavior of aborted transactions, they also hold for virtual world consistency.

3.2 Feeble Disjoint-Access Parallelism, Wait-Free Reads and Minimally Progressive Writes

In this section, we present an impossibility result stating that there is no STM implementation which ensures snapshot isolation, wait-freedom for read-only transactions, minimal progress for update transactions, and a weak version of disjoint-access parallelism, called *feeble disjoint-access parallelism*. Feeble disjoint-access parallelism is weaker than all existing disjoint-access parallelism definitions. Thus, the impossibility result still holds if we replace feeble disjoint-access parallelism with any existing definition of disjoint-access parallelism. Definition 4 formally defines feeble disjoint-access parallelism.

The impossibility result was originally presented in [18] for universal constructions [29]. Our presentation below adjusts the presentation in [18] for STM.

Definition 4 (Feeble Disjoint-Access Parallelism [18]). *A STM implementation is feebly disjoint-access parallel if, for every solo execution α_1 of a transaction T_1 and every solo execution α_2 of a transaction T_2, both starting from the same quiescent configuration C, if T_1 and T_2 access disjoint sets of data items in α_1 and α_2, then α_1 and α_2 contend on no base objects.*

To prove the impossibility result, we employ transactions to execute operations on an unsorted singly-linked list of integers. The list supports two operations:

- APPEND(L, k), which appends an element with key k to the end of the list L, and
- SEARCH(L, k), which searches the list L for an element with key k starting from the first element of the list.

Fig. 7 presents C-like pseudo-code for the sequential implementation of this data structure where, for clarity, we use routines READ and WRITE to identify accesses (reads or writes, respectively) to data items. Notice that the data items are the nodes of the singly-linked list and the pointers $L.start$ and $L.end$ which point to the first and the last element of the list, respectively. We assume that READ takes as a parameter a pointer to a data item and returns its value. Similarly, WRITE takes as a parameter a pointer to a data item and the new value for it and applies the change. Notice that in case the data item is a list node, its value is a pair because the node is a struct with two fields. Since the linked list is a dynamic data structure, the data items accessed by an instance of SEARCH in a sequential execution depends on the sequence of nodes that have been previously appended to the list. The *state* of a data structure consists of the collection of data items in the representation and a set of values, one for each of the data items. We remark that the pseudo-code for a transaction executing APPEND (which we will later call a transaction of type APPEND) or a transaction executing SEARCH (which we will later call a transaction of type SEARCH) would look like those presented in Fig. 7 (enhanced with a call to TRYCOMMIT before each *return* statement).

The proof of the impossibility result is by contradiction. So, we consider an arbitrary feebly disjoint-access parallel STM implementation which ensures snapshot isolation, wait-freedom for read-only transactions, and minimal progress for update transactions. We construct an execution α' in which two processes q and p, $p \neq q$, perform two types

```
1     struct NODE {                          12    struct LIST {
2          int key;                          13         NODE* start;
3     }    NODE* next;                        14    }    NODE* end;

4     boolean SEARCH(LIST L, int k) {         15    void APPEND(LIST L, int k) {
5          s = READ(&L.start);                16         new = CREATE(NODE);
6          if (s == NULL) return(false);      17         WRITE(new, ⟨k, NULL⟩);
7          ⟨k′,s⟩ = READ(s);                  18         e = READ(&L.end);
8          while(s ≠ NULL AND k′ ≠ k)         19         if (e ≠ NULL) WRITE(e, ⟨e → key, new⟩);
9               ⟨k′,s⟩ = READ(s);             20         else WRITE(&L.start, new);
10         if (k′ == k) return(true);         21         WRITE(&L.end, new);
11    }    else return(false);                22    }    return;
```

Fig. 7. Sequential implementation of a singly-linked list supporting APPEND and SEARCH

of transactions. Specifically, process p performs an infinite sequence of update transactions of type APPEND to continually append new elements with different values into the list, i.e. the i-th transaction, $i > 0$, initiated by p executes an instance of APPEND(L, i); p may also perform a transaction which executes an instance of APPEND$(L, 0)$. On the other hand, process q performs a single read-only transaction T of type SEARCH which executes an instance of SEARCH$(L, 0)$. We prove that the execution of T takes an infinite number of steps, i.e. T never commits in α'. This violates wait-freedom (of read-only transactions).

Roughly speaking, in α', p performs each instance of its APPEND transactions before q gets to close to the end of the list. In this way, p's knowledge is consistent with the possibility that q's transaction could terminate successfully before it accesses a data item accessed by p's current APPEND transaction. So, disjoint-access parallelism prevents p from communicating to q any information which could help q decide whether it can commit its transaction. Moreover, q cannot determine which nodes were appended by process p after q started its SEARCH transaction.

The proof relies on a natural assumption about STM implementations. To the best of our knowledge, all STM implementations presented thus far satisfy this assumption.

Assumption. 4 (Value-Obliviousness Assumption) *In any STM implementation, the set of base objects accessed by trivial primitives and the set of base objects accessed by non-trivial primitives during any solo execution, starting from a quiescent configuration, of a sequence of consecutive instances of the same (type of) update transaction until each instance successfully completes, do not depend on the second parameter of the WRITE operations they perform.*

Let C_0 be the initial configuration in which L is empty. Let α denote the solo execution by p, starting from C_0, in which p performs an infinite sequence of update transactions $U_1, U_2, \ldots$ of type APPEND; specifically, for each integer $i > 0$, transaction U_i executes APPEND(L, i). Minimal progress (for update transactions) ensures that all these transactions commit after a finite number of steps. For $i \geq 1$, let C_i be the configuration obtained when p successfully completes the execution of U_i starting from configuration C_{i-1}. Let α_i denote the sequence of steps performed in this execution. Let $B(i)$ denote the set of base objects accessed by non-trivial primitives during α_i. Let $A(i)$ denote the set of base objects not in $B(i)$ accessed during α_i, i.e. base objects in $A(i)$ are only accessed by trivial primitives during α_i. In configuration C_i (which is quiescent), the list L consists of i nodes, with values $1, \ldots, i$, in increasing order.

For the proof, an infinite execution α' is built which is indistinguishable from α to process p. In α', q performs a transaction T of type SEARCH. Specifically, T executes a single instance of SEARCH$(L, 0)$, so it is a read-only transaction. The steps taken by process q in α' are chosen from the solo executions by q, starting from C_i, of transactions executing SEARCH$(L, 0)$, for $i \geq 4$.

We start by defining α'. For $i \geq 4$, let $\beta_i = \alpha_i \alpha_{i+1} \cdots$ denote the suffix of α starting from C_{i-1}. The set $\bigcup \{B(k) \mid k \geq i\}$ consists of all base objects to which p applies a non-trivial primitive in β_i and $\bigcup \{A(k) \mid k \geq i\} \cup \bigcup \{B(k) \mid k \geq i\}$ is the set of all base objects accessed by β_i. Let ρ_i be the steps of the solo execution by q, starting from configuration C_i, of a transaction R_i which executes SEARCH$(L, 0)$. Moreover, let π_i be the longest prefix of ρ_i that does not contend with β_i, i.e. in π_i, q does not access any base object in $\bigcup \{B(k) \mid k \geq i\}$ and does not apply non-trivial primitives to any base object in $\bigcup \{A(k) \mid k \geq i\}$.

Lemma 6. *For each* i, i', $4 \leq i \leq i'$, π_i *is a prefix of* $\pi_{i'}$.

Proof. Only base objects in $\bigcup \{B(k) \mid i < k \leq i'\}$ can have different values in configurations C_i and $C_{i'}$. Since π_i does not access any base objects in $\bigcup \{B(k) \mid k \geq i\}$, it follows that π_i is a prefix of $\rho_{i'}$. Since π_i does not contend with β_i and $\beta_{i'}$ is a suffix of β_i, π_i does not contend with $\beta_{i'}$. By definition of $\pi_{i'}$, it follows that π_i is a prefix of $\pi_{i'}$.

For $i \geq 5$, Lemma 6 implies that π_{i-1} is a prefix of π_i. Let ϕ_i be the (possibly empty) suffix of π_i such that $\pi_i = \pi_{i-1} \phi_i$. Let $\alpha' = \alpha_1 \alpha_2 \alpha_3 \alpha_4 \pi_4 \alpha_5 \phi_5 \alpha_6 \phi_6 \cdots$. We argue in Lemma 7 that α' is a legal execution starting from C_0.

Lemma 7. α' *is a legal execution starting from* C_0.

Proof. Since by definition, π_4 does not apply non-trivial primitives to any base objects accessed in $\alpha_4 \alpha_5 \cdots$ and, for $i \geq 5$, $\pi_i = \pi_{i-1} \phi_i$ (and, hence, ϕ_i) does not apply non-trivial primitives to any base object accessed in $\alpha_i \alpha_{i+1} \cdots$, the executions arising from α and α' starting from C_0 are indistinguishable to process p. Furthermore, since π_i and, hence, ϕ_i do not access any base objects to which $\alpha_i \alpha_{i+1} \cdots$ applies non-trivial primitives, it follows that $\alpha_1 \alpha_2 \alpha_3 \alpha_4 \pi_4 \alpha_5 \phi_5 \cdots \alpha_i \phi_i$ and $\alpha_1 \alpha_2 \alpha_3 \alpha_4 \cdots \alpha_i \pi_4 \phi_5 \cdots \phi_i = \alpha_1 \alpha_2 \alpha_3 \alpha_4 \cdots \alpha_i \pi_i$ are indistinguishable to process q for all $i \geq 4$. Thus α' is a legal execution. $\square$

Next, we argue that, for each $i \geq 4$, there exists $i' > i$ such that $\phi_{i'}$ is nonempty; specifically, Lemma 10 proves that $\pi_i \neq \pi_{i+3}$. Fix any arbitrary integer $i \geq 4$. To obtain a contradiction, suppose that $\pi_i = \pi_{i+3}$. We first argue, in Lemma 8, that π_i is a proper prefix of ρ_i. We then use this fact to find an integer $\ell \geq i+3$ and define two executions, namely, $\alpha_{\ell-1}^{\ell-3}$ in which p executes solo a transaction $U_{\ell-1}^{\ell-3}$, and $\rho_{\ell-1}^{\ell-3}$ in which q executes solo a transaction $R_{\ell-1}^{\ell-3}$. We argue, in Lemma 9, that $U_{\ell-1}^{\ell-3}$ and $R_{\ell-1}^{\ell-3}$ access disjoint sets of data items, so feeble disjoint-access parallelism implies that $\rho_{\ell-1}^{\ell-3}$ and $\alpha_{\ell-1}^{\ell-3}$ do not contend on some base object. We then derive a contradiction by arguing, in the proof of Lemma 10, that $\rho_{\ell-1}^{\ell-3}$ and $\alpha_{\ell-1}^{\ell-3}$ do contend on some base object.

Lemma 8. π_i *is a proper prefix of* ρ_i.

Proof. Let C_{i+3}^i be the configuration obtained from configuration C_0 when process p performs the first $i+3$ transactions of execution α, except that the i'th transaction now executes APPEND$(L,0)$ instead of APPEND(L,i). Since the STM implementation is value-oblivious, non-trivial primitives are applied to the same set of base objects during the executions leading to configurations C_{i+3} and C_{i+3}^i. Thus, only base objects in $B(i) \cup B(i+1) \cup B(i+2) \cup B(i+3)$ can have different values in C_{i+3} and C_{i+3}^i. Let ρ_{i+3}^i be the solo execution by q of a transaction R_{i+3}^i which executes SEARCH$(L,0)$ starting from C_{i+3}^i. Since, by definition, π_i is a prefix of ρ_i that does not access any base objects in $B(i) \cup B(i+1) \cup B(i+2) \cup B(i+3)$, it follows that π_i is a prefix of ρ_{i+3}^i. Since we have assumed that $\pi_i = \pi_{i+3}$, it follows that π_{i+3} is a prefix of ρ_{i+3}^i. Snapshot isolation implies that R_{i+3}^i commits in ρ_{i+3}^i with SEARCH$(L,0)$ being successful, whereas R_{i+3} commits in ρ_{i+3} with SEARCH$(L,0)$ being unsuccessful. Thus, T is not completed after π_{i+3}. Since $\pi_i = \pi_{i+3}$, it follows that T is not completed after π_i. Therefore π_i is a proper prefix of ρ_i. □

We next define ℓ. Lemma 8 implies that π_i is a proper prefix of ρ_i. Let b be the base object accessed in the first step following π_i in ρ_i. Since $\pi_i = \pi_{i+3}$, b is also the base object accessed in the first step following π_{i+3} in ρ_{i+3}. By definition of π_{i+3}, there is some $\ell \geq i+3$ such that this step is either an access to $b \in B(\ell)$ or the application of a non-trivial primitive to $b \in A(\ell)$.

We are now ready to define $\rho_{\ell-1}^{\ell-3}$ and $\alpha_{\ell-1}^{\ell-3}$ and argue about their properties, thus concluding the argument. Let $C_{\ell-1}^{\ell-3}$ be the configuration obtained from configuration C_0 when process p performs the first $\ell-1$ transactions of execution α, except that the $(\ell-3)$'rd transaction now executes APPEND$(L,0)$ instead of APPEND$(L,\ell-3)$. Let $\rho_{\ell-1}^{\ell-3}$ be the solo execution by q, starting from $C_{\ell-1}^{\ell-3}$, of a transaction $R_{\ell-1}^{\ell-3}$ which executes SEARCH$(L,0)$. Moreover, let $\alpha_{\ell-1}^{\ell-3}$ be the solo execution by p of a transaction $U_{\ell-1}^{\ell-3}$ which executes APPEND(L,ℓ) starting from $C_{\ell-1}^{\ell-3}$. We argue in Lemma 9 that $\rho_{\ell-1}^{\ell-3}$ and $\alpha_{\ell-1}^{\ell-3}$ do not contend.

Lemma 9. $\rho_{\ell-1}^{\ell-3}$ and $\alpha_{\ell-1}^{\ell-3}$ contend on no base objects.

Proof. Let S denote the state of the data structure in configuration $C_{\ell-1}^{\ell-3}$. In state S, the list has $\ell-1$ nodes and the third last node has value 0. Then, the set of data items accessed by $R_{\ell-1}^{\ell-3}$ in $\rho_{\ell-1}^{\ell-3}$ consists of $L.first$ and the first $\ell-3$ nodes of the list. This is disjoint from the set of data items accessed by $U_{\ell-1}^{\ell-3}$ in $\alpha_{\ell-1}^{\ell-3}$, which consists of $L.end$, the last node of the list, and the newly appended node. Hence, by feeble disjoint-access parallelism, $\rho_{\ell-1}^{\ell-3}$ and $\alpha_{\ell-1}^{\ell-3}$ contend on no base objects. □

Lemma 10. $\pi_i \neq \pi_{i+3}$.

Proof. By Lemma 6, π_i is a prefix of $\pi_{i'}$ for every integer $i' \geq i$. In particular, π_i is a prefix of $\rho_{\ell-1}$. By the value obliviousness assumption, only base objects in $B(\ell-3) \cup B(\ell-2) \cup B(\ell-1)$ can have different values in $C_{\ell-1}$ and $C_{\ell-1}^{\ell-3}$. Since $l \geq i+3$, it follows that $l-3 \geq i$. Thus, π_i does not access any of the objects in $B(\ell-3) \cup B(\ell-2) \cup B(\ell-1)$. It follows that π_i is also a prefix of $\rho_{\ell-1}^{\ell-3}$ and the first step following π_i in this execution is the same as the first step following π_i in ρ_i, i.e. it is either an access to $b \in B(\ell)$ or an application of a non-trivial primitive to $b \in A(\ell)$. By the value obliviousness assumption, $B(\ell)$ is the set of base objects accessed by non-trivial primitives during $\alpha_{\ell-1}^{\ell-3}$ and $A(\ell)$ is the set of base objects not in $B(\ell)$ accessed during that execution. Thus, $\rho_{\ell-1}^{\ell-3}$ and $\alpha_{\ell-1}^{\ell-3}$ contend on b. This contradicts Lemma 9. Hence, $\pi_i \neq \pi_{i+3}$.   □

Lemma 10 implies that ϕ_i is nonempty for infinitely many integers $i > 1$, so in the infinite execution α', process q never commits the read-only transaction T, despite taking an infinite number of steps. This contradicts wait-freedom for read-only transactions. So, the following theorem holds.

Theorem 5. *There is no feebly disjoint-access parallel implementation of a STM, which ensures snapshot isolation, wait-freedom for read-only transactions, and minimal progress for update transactions.*

We presented Theorem 5 and its proof assuming the STM implementation is deterministic. If it is randomized, fixing a sequence of coin tosses for each process and only considering executions using these coin tosses would do [18]. Some generalizations of this impossibility result (including more elaborated versions of the value-obliviousness assumption and some of the definitions presented in Section 2 and here so as to hold for universal constructions), are presented in [18].

4 Disjoint-Access Parallel TM Implementations

In this section, we discuss some of the disjoint-access parallel STM implementations presented in the literature. We remark that the list of STM implementations described below is probably not exhaustive.

4.1 Blocking Disjoint-Access Parallel STM Implementations

In this section, we discuss two blocking STM implementations which are strict disjoint-access parallel.

4.1.1 TL

TL [13] was the first STM implementation in the family of "Transactional Locking" blocking STM implementations [13,15,16,7,20]. (Some of the implementations of this family are described in Chapter 5.)

TL comes in two flavours which are known as *commit mode* and *encounter mode*. The description below focuses on TL's commit mode and presents a version of TL which employs a lock per data item; other versions of TL employ a lock per stripe.

TL stores a monotonically-increasing version number with each data item and implements a lock for it. Each time a transaction T reads a data item, it stores information about it, including its current version, in a (local) read set. TL employs a validation mechanism to ensure the consistency of the data items read. When T validates its read set, the version stored for each data item in the read set is compared to the actual version of the data item stored in shared memory. If, for each data item in T's read-set, these two values are the same and the lock for the data item is free, the validation is successful. If the validation is not successful, T aborts.

Each transaction in TL maintains a (local) write set. Updates of data items take effect at commit time after acquiring the locks for them; each update of a data item x increases the version of x by one.

When READ is invoked by a transaction T for a data item x that has not accessed by T before, READ checks if the lock for x is acquired. If this is the case, then T aborts. Otherwise, T records the data item, its value, and its version in T's read set. If x has been accessed by T before, T finds the value to return for x either in its write set or in its read set. At the end of each READ, T performs a validation to verify consistency of its read set.

When WRITE is invoked by a transaction T for a data item x with value v, if T's write set contains an entry for x, this entry is updated with v, otherwise an entry for x, which records v, is added in T's write set.

During the execution of TRYCOMMIT, T attempts to lock all data items in its write set. Locks may be acquired in some specific order to avoid deadlocks. If lock acquisition fails for any of the data items in T's write set, T aborts after releasing the locks that it has already acquired. If all locks are acquired successfully, T performs a validation of its read set, and if this is successful, it writes the new value for each data item in its write set to shared memory (with its version increased), and commits. Otherwise, it aborts. In either case, T releases the locks it has acquired before it completes.

In TL, there is a transactional record for each transaction T providing access to T's read and write sets. This record is accessed only by T, so the executions of two transactions cannot contend on accessing transactional records. TL implements a data item x by storing its value, its version, and its lock in a record, known as the data item record for x. A transaction accesses the data item record for x, only if it wants to read or to write x. Moreover, reads in TL are invisible. Thus, TL ensures that if the execution of two transactions T and T' contend on the same base object, then there is a data item x which one of the two transactions reads and the other writes. Therefore, there is an edge between T and T' in the conflict graph of the minimal execution interval containing the execution intervals of the two transactions. This implies that TL ensures strict disjoint-access parallelism.

4.1.2 PermiSTM

Attiya and Hillel presented in [3] a strict disjoint-access parallel lock-based STM implementation, called PERMISTM, in which a transaction aborts only if it is an update transaction that conflicts with another update transaction. For each data item, PERMISTM maintains a lock, a version number, and a read counter. Roughly speaking, PERMISTM works in a way similar to TL. However, a read-only transaction announces its existence in each data item it reads by incrementing its read-counter; it decrements this read counter before it commits. Update transactions cannot commit as long as the data items in their write sets have read counter values that are not zero. This design ensures strict disjoint-access parallelism.

4.2   Non-blocking Disjoint-Access Parallel STM Implementations

The first software STM implementation [46] was disjoint-access parallel and lock-free. However, it was restricted to static transactions, i.e. transactions that accessed a pre-determined set of known memory locations, so we will not include its presentation below. The algorithms discussed in this section are presented in Chapter 5 in more detail.

4.2.1   DSTM

DSTM [30] is a disjoint-access parallel obstruction-free STM implementation.

For each active transaction T, DSTM maintains a transactional record that stores the current status of T, which can be ACTIVE, COMMITTED, or ABORTED, and its read set. Moreover, for each data item x, DSTM maintains a *locator*, i.e. a record which has three fields: a pointer *transaction* to the record of the transaction that acquired the ownership of x most recently, and two pointers *oldData* and *newData* to values for x. DSTM also maintains a pointer *start* to the *locator* of x.

When a transaction T invokes READ for x, T finds the *current value* for x by checking the status of the transaction T' that acquired the ownership for x most recently. If the status of T' is ACTIVE, T executes a CAS to forcibly abort T' and reads the status of T' again; this time the status will be either COMMITTED or ABORTED. If the status is ABORTED, then the value for x is found in the *oldData* field of its locator, and if it is COMMITTED, it is found in the *newData* field of it.

When a transaction T invokes WRITE for x with value v, cloning and indirection are employed: a new locator is created for x, its *transaction* field is initialized to point to the transactional record of T, its *oldData* field is initialized to point to the current value for x (which is found following a procedure similar to that described above for READ), and its *newData* field is initialized to point to a newly allocated memory location where v is stored. Then, T attempts to change the *start* pointer for x to point to this new locator. If it does not succeed in doing so, it re-initiates the fields of the locator it has allocated (as described above) and retries.

When T calls TRYCOMMIT, it validates its read set, and if the validation is successful, it executes a CAS to change the value of its status to COMMITTED. If the CAS is successful it commits. If the validation or the CAS are not successful, it aborts.

In DSTM, the executions of two transactions T and T' may contend if they both access pointer *start*, the *locator* of the same data item x, or the transactional record to which this locator points to. In the first two cases, both T and T' access x, so there is an edge between T and T' in the conflict graph of the minimal execution interval containing the execution intervals of T and T'. To better explain the third case, assume that a third transactions T'' has acquired the ownerships for two data items x and y. If T invokes WRITE for x and T' invokes WRITE for y, and the executions of these writes occur while T''''s status is ACTIVE, then both T and T' will try to forcibly abort T''. So, the executions of T and T' may contend when they try to change the status of T'' to ABORTED. Notice that in this case, there is no edge connecting T and T' in the conflict graph. However, there is a path from T to T' in it. Thus, DSTM ensures disjoint-access parallelism.

4.2.2   OSTM

OSTM [21] is a lock-free STM which is disjoint-access parallel.

OSTM executes each transaction T in two *phases*. While in its first phase, T is executed speculatively by performing writes locally using a write set. Reads are invisible: a read set is maintained in the transactional record of T and a validation mechanism, similar to that of DSTM, is employed to ensure consistency. Thus, during its first phase, T is invisible to other transactions.

The second phase of T starts when it calls TRYCOMMIT. Then, T becomes visible by announcing its write set, i.e. by making its write set shared. Then, it tries to acquire the ownership for each of the data items in its write set. OSTM associates a *start* pointer with each data item x. In contrast to DSTM though, it does not associate a locator with x. A transaction T acquires the ownership for x by atomically updating the *start* pointer of x to point to the transactional record of T; T releases the ownership for x by updating *start* to point to the value T wrote for x. If T finds that the ownership for x is acquired, it helps the transaction holding the ownership for x to complete, before T continues its execution. We remark that the levels of indirections are reduced by one in OSTM in comparison to DSTM.

OSTM is disjoint-access parallel for the same reasons as in DSTM.

4.2.3 ASTM

ASTM [41] is an *adaptive*, disjoint-access parallel, obstruction-free STM implementation. ASTM resembles a lot DSTM but, when accessing data items in absence of contention, it attempts to reduce the levels of indirection that DSTM introduces. It does so, by associating a status with each data item, which indicates whether the ownership for the data item is acquired or not. In the first case, ASTM simulates the functioning of DSTM (i.e. accesses to data items take place using locators, thus introducing an additional level of indirection). In the opposite case however, *start* is updated to point directly to the data. The adaptive behaviour of ASTM respects disjoint-access parallelism.

We remark that a blocking version of ASTM is also discussed in [41].

4.2.4 NZTM

NZTM [47] stands for Nonblocking Zero-indirection STM. It is a disjoint-access parallel, obstruction-free STM implementation that further reduces, compared to ASTM, the levels of indirection used when accessing data items in the absence of contention. As in ASTM, each data item x is associated with a status, which can be either *deflated* or *inflated*. In contrast to ASTM though, NZTM avoids the use of pointer *start* in absence of contention. So, if the status of x is deflated, its value can be read directly. If, however, the status of x is inflated, x is accessed in a way similar to that of DSTM. The new techniques employed by NZTM ensure disjoint-access parallelism.

4.3 Related Research

Similarly to STM, *universal constructions* [28,29] aim at simplifying parallel programming by providing mechanisms to efficiently execute pieces of sequential code in a concurrent environment. So, we briefly discuss some disjoint-access parallel universal constructions below.

Barnes [8] presented a disjoint-access parallel, lock-free universal construction. Remarkably, OSTM [21] works in a way that resembles the functioning of Barnes' algorithm. In Barnes' algorithm, a process p first simulates locally the execution of the piece of sequential code it wants to execute. It does so using a local dictionary where it stores the data items accessed during the simulation of its piece of code, and their new values. After completing the local simulation, p announces its dictionary (by making it shared), and then attempts to acquire the ownerships of the data items that are stored in it. If this ownership acquisition phase terminates successfully, p applies its modifications to shared memory and releases the ownerships. A process that wants to write a data item x whose ownership is acquired, releases the ownerships it holds, helps the process that owns the ownership of x to finish the piece of code it executes, and re-starts its execution.

Ellen *et al.* presents in [18], a universal construction which produces concurrent implementations that are both wait-free and disjoint-access parallel, when applied to objects that have a bound on the number of data items accessed by each piece of sequential code they perform. Similarly to Barnes' algorithm, in the algorithm of [18], a process executing a piece of code, first simulates its execution locally by using a local dictionary, and then it tries to apply the changes. However, in the algorithm of [18] more advanced helping techniques are required to ensure wait-freedom and disjoint-access parallelism. Moreover, the algorithm of [18], compared to Barnes' algorithm, may detect conflicts at earlier simulation stages, so helping must be introduced earlier.

Acknowledgements. The authors were supported by funding from the European Commission under the 7th Framework Program through the TransForm (FP7-MC-ITN-238639) project and by the ARISTEIA Action of the Operational Programme Education and Lifelong Learning which is co-funded by the European Social Fund (ESF) and Greek National Resources, through the GreenVM project.

References

1. Attiya, H., Ellen, F., Fatourou, P.: The complexity of updating snapshot objects. Journal of Parallel and Distributed Computing 71(12), 1570–1577 (2011)
2. Attiya, H., Guerraoui, R., Hendler, D., Kuznetsov, P.: The complexity of obstruction-free implementations. J. ACM 56(4) (2009)
3. Attiya, H., Hans, S.: Transactions are back—but how different they are? In: TRANSACT 2012 (2012)
4. Attiya, H., Hillel, E.: The cost of privatization in software transactional memory. IEEE Transactions on Computers 62, 2531–2543 (2013)
5. Attiya, H., Hillel, E., Milani, A.: Inherent limitations on disjoint-access parallel implementations of transactional memory. Theory Comput. Syst. 49(4), 698–719 (2011)
6. Attiya, H., Welch, J.L.: Distributed Computing: Fundamentals, Simulations and Advanced Topics, 2nd edn. Wiley (2004)
7. Avni, H., Shavit, N.: Maintaining consistent transactional states without a global clock. In: Shvartsman, A.A., Felber, P. (eds.) SIROCCO 2008. LNCS, vol. 5058, pp. 131–140. Springer, Heidelberg (2008),
   http://dx.doi.org/10.1007/978-3-540-69355-0_12
8. Barnes, G.: A method for implementing lock-free shared-data structures. In: SPAA 1993, pp. 261–270 (1993)
9. Berenson, H., Bernstein, P., Gray, J., Melton, J., O'Neil, E., O'Neil, P.: A critique of ANSI SQL isolation levels. In: Proceedings of the 1995 ACM SIGMOD International Conference on Management of Data (SIGMOD 1995), pp. 1–10 (1995)

10. Bushkov, V., Dziuma, D., Fatourou, P., Guerraoui, R.: Snapshot isolation does not scale either. In: WTTM 2013 (2013)
11. Bushkov, V., Dziuma, D., Fatourou, P., Guerraoui, R.: The pcl theorem: Transactions cannot be parallel, consistent and live. In: Proceedings of the 26th ACM Symposium on Parallelism in Algorithms and Architectures, SPAA 2014, pp. 178–187. ACM, New York (2014), http://doi.acm.org/10.1145/2612669.2612690
12. Bushkov, V., Guerraoui, R., Kapałka, M.: On the liveness of transactional memory. In: ACM Symposium on Principles of Distributed Computing (PODC 2012), pp. 9–18 (2001)
13. Dice, D., Shavit, N.: What really makes transactions faster? In: Proc. of the 1st TRANSACT 2006 Workshop (2006)
14. Dice, D., Matveev, A., Shavit, N.: Implicit privatization using private transactions. In: 5th ACM SIGPLAN Workshop on Transactional Computing (TRANSACT 2010) (2010)
15. Dice, D., Shalev, O., Shavit, N.N.: Transactional locking II. In: Dolev, S. (ed.) DISC 2006. LNCS, vol. 4167, pp. 194–208. Springer, Heidelberg (2006)
16. Dice, D., Shavit, N.: Tlrw: return of the read-write lock. In: Proceedings of the 22nd ACM Symposium on Parallelism in Algorithms and Architectures, SPAA 2010, pp. 284–293. ACM, New York (2010), http://doi.acm.org/10.1145/1810479.1810531
17. Doherty, S., Groves, L., Luchangco, V., Moir, M.: Towards formally specifying and verifying transactional memory. Formal Aspects of Computing 25(5), 769–799 (2013)
18. Ellen, F., Fatourou, P., Kosmas, E., Milani, A., Travers, C.: Universal constructions that ensure disjoint-access parallelism and wait-freedom. In: ACM Symposium on Principles of Distributed Computing (PODC 2012), pp. 115–124 (2012)
19. Fatourou, P., Dziuma, D., Kanellou, E.: Consistency for transactional memory computing. Bulletin of European Association for Theoretical Computer Science (EATCS) 113 (June 2014)
20. Felber, P., Fetzer, C., Riegel, T.: Dynamic performance tuning of word-based software transactional memory. In: Proceedings of the 13th ACM SIGPLAN Symposium on Principles and Practice of Parallel Programming, PPoPP 2008, pp. 237–246. ACM, New York (2008), http://doi.acm.org/10.1145/1345206.1345241
21. Fraser, K.: Practical lock freedom. Ph.D. thesis, Cambridge University Computer Laboratory (2003), also available as Technical Report UCAM-CL-TR-579
22. Gramoli, V., Harmanci, D., Felber, P.: Toward a theory of input acceptance for transactional memories. In: Baker, T.P., Bui, A., Tixeuil, S. (eds.) OPODIS 2008. LNCS, vol. 5401, pp. 527–533. Springer, Heidelberg (2008)
23. Guerraoui, R., Henzinger, T.A., Singh, V.: Permissiveness in transactional memories. In: Taubenfeld, G. (ed.) DISC 2008. LNCS, vol. 5218, pp. 305–319. Springer, Heidelberg (2008)
24. Guerraoui, R., Kapałka, M.: On obstruction-free transactions. In: SPAA 2008, pp. 304–313 (2008)
25. Guerraoui, R., Kapałka, M.: On the correctness of transactional memory. In: Proceedings of the 13th ACM SIGPLAN Symposium on Principles and Practice of Parallel Programming (PPoPP 2008), pp. 175–184 (2008)
26. Guerraoui, R., Kapałka, M.: The semantics of progress in lock-based transactional memory. In: Proceedings of the 36th ACM SIGPLAN-SIGACT Symposium on Principles of Programming Languages (POPL 2009), pp. 404–415 (2009)
27. Guerraoui, R., Kapałka, M.: Principles of Transactional Memory. Synthesis Lectures on Distributed Computing. Morgan & Claypool Publishers (2010)
28. Herlihy, M.: A methodology for implementing highly concurrent data structures. In: Proceedings of the Second ACM SIGPLAN Symposium on Principles & Practice of Parallel Programming, PPOPP 1990, pp. 197–206. ACM, New York (1990), http://doi.acm.org/10.1145/99163.99185
29. Herlihy, M.: Wait-free synchronization. ACM Trans. Program. Lang. Syst. 13(1), 124–149 (1991)

30. Herlihy, M., Luchangco, V., Moir, M., Scherer III, W.N.: Software transactional memory for dynamic-sized data structures. In: Proceedings of the Twenty-Second ACM Symposium on Principles of Distributed Computing (PODC 2003), pp. 92–101 (2003)
31. Herlihy, M., Moss, J.E.B.: Transactional memory: Architectural support for lock-free data structures. In: Proceedings of the 20th Annual International Symposiupm on Computer Architecture (ISCA 1993) (1993)
32. Herlihy, M., Shavit, N.: The Art of Multiprocessor Programming. Morgan Kaufmann (2008)
33. Herlihy, M.P., Wing, J.M.: Linearizability: A correctness condition for concurrent objects. ACM Trans. Program. Lang. Syst. 12(3), 463–492 (1990)
34. Imbs, D., Raynal, M., de Mendivil, J.R.: Brief announcement: virtual world consistency: A new condition for stm systems. In: Proceedings of the 28th Annual ACM Symposium on Principles of Distributed Computing (PODC 2009), pp. 280–281 (2009)
35. Israeli, A., Rappoport, L.: Disjoint-access-parallel implementations of strong shared memory primitives. In: Proceedings of the Twenty-Third Annual ACM Symposium on Principles of Distributed Computing (PODC 2004), pp. 151–160 (2004)
36. Keidar, I., Perelman, D.: On avoiding spare aborts in transactional memory. In: SPAA 2009, pp. 59–68 (2009)
37. Lamport, L.: Proving the correctness of multiprocess programs. IEEE Transactions on Software Engineering SE 3(2), 125–143 (1977)
38. Lamport, L.: How to make a multiprocessor computer that correctly executes multiprocess program. IEEE Transactions on Computers 100(28), 690–691 (1979)
39. Larus, J.R., Rajwar, R.: Transactional Memory. Morgan and Claypool (2007)
40. Lu, S., Bernstein, A., Lewis, P.: Correct execution of transactions at different isolation levels. IEEE Transactions on Knowledge and Data Engineering 16(9), 1070–1081 (2004)
41. Marathe, V.J., Scherer, W.N., Scott, M.L.: Design tradeoffs in modern software transactional memory systems. In: Proceedings of the 7th Workshop on Workshop on Languages, Compilers, and Run-time Support for Scalable Systems, LCR 2004, pp. 1–7. ACM, New York (2004), http://doi.acm.org/10.1145/1066650.1066660
42. Papadimitriou, C.H.: The serializability of concurrent database updates. J. ACM 26(4), 631–653 (1979)
43. Perelman, D., Fan, R., Keidar, I.: On maintaining multiple versions in STM. In: Proceedings of the 29th Annual ACM Symposium on Principles of Distributed Computing (PODC 2010), pp. 16–25 (2010)
44. Rajwar, R., Goodman, J.R.: Transactional lock-free execution of lock-based programs. In: Proceedings of the 10th International Conference on Architectural Support for Programming Languages and Operating Systems (ASPLOS 2002), pp. 5–17 (2002)
45. Riegel, T., Fetzer, Ç., Felber, P.: Snapshot isolation for software transactional memory. In: First ACM SIGPLAN Workshop on Languages, Compilers, and Hardware Support for Transactional Computing (TRANSACT 2006) (2006)
46. Shavit, N., Touitou, D.: Software transactional memory. In: PODC 1995, pp. 204–213 (1995)
47. Tabba, F., Moir, M., Goodman, J.R., Hay, A.W., Wang, C.: Nztm: nonblocking zero-indirection transactional memory. In: Proceedings of the Twenty-first Annual Symposium on Parallelism in Algorithms and Architectures, SPAA 2009, pp. 204–213. ACM, New York (2009), http://doi.acm.org/10.1145/1583991.1584048
48. Turek, J., Shasha, D., Prakash, S.: Locking without blocking: making lock based concurrent data structure algorithms nonblocking. In: Proceedings of the Eleventh ACM SIGACT-SIGMOD-SIGART Symposium on Principles of Database Systems (PODS 1992), pp. 212–222 (1992)
49. Weikum, G., Vossen, G.: Transactional Information Systems: Theory, Algorithms, and the Practice of Concurrency Control and Recovery. Morgan Kaufmann, San Francisco (2001)

Algorithms

Algorithmic Techniques in STM Design

Panagiota Fatourou[1], Mykhailo Iaremko[2], Eleni Kanellou[3], and Eleftherios Kosmas[1]

[1] FORTH ICS & University of Crete, Heraklion (Crete), Greece
{faturu,ekosmas}@csd.uoc.gr
[2] FORTH ICS, Heraklion (Crete), Greece
mykhailo.iaremko@gmail.com
[3] FORTH ICS, Heraklion (Crete), Greece & University of Rennes 1, Rennes, France
kanellou@ics.forth.gr

Abstract. The Transactional Memory paradigm has gained a lot of momentum in recent years. This is evidenced by the plethora of software transactional memory (STM) algorithms that can be found in the literature. Although their goal is common - to offer the transaction abstraction to the programmer - the implementations that they provide for this abstraction show a great variation among them. This variation appears as different algorithms aim at exhibiting different additional properties, such as offering specific liveness guarantees or good performance or both. In this chapter, we identify the basic characteristics of STM algorithms and the mechanisms that they are made up from. In conjunction with the design decisions, and in order to outline how they are used, we present in detail some representative STM algorithms. We also briefly discuss a lot of other STM algorithms found in the literature.

1 Introduction

Software transactional Memory (STM) [34,57] attempts to simplify parallel programming by taking much of the pain out of writing concurrent programs. Specifically, the naive programmer is relieved from the burden of using locks or developing efficient non-blocking algorithms. In order to achieve this, STM employs transactions. A *transaction* executes a block of code that accesses pieces of data, called *data items*. Data items may be accessed through several concurrent transactions. When a transaction is executed, it may either *commit* or *abort*. If it commits, all its updates take effect, whereas if it aborts, its updates are discarded.

The design of an STM algorithm is performed by a concurrency expert with the major goal to hide the implementation details of the STM from the naive programmer who has just to enhance its sequential code appropriately so that it can serve as a transaction. This enhancement is relatively simple to achieve since a transaction's code usually resembles a lot its sequential analog. For specific workloads, the STM algorithm exhibits better performance than running the transaction in a sequential setting.

An *STM algorithm* guarantees that accesses of transactions on data items are executed consistently. The design of an STM algorithm is not an easy task since all problems encountered when concurrency is employed must be taken into consideration by the STM designer, in order to come up with an algorithm that is correct, live and efficient. To ensure liveness, deadlocks, livelocks or other progress limitations must probably be prevented, and to ensure efficiency, appropriate implementation decisions must

R. Guerraoui and P. Romano (Eds.): Transactional Memory, LNCS 8913, pp. 101–126, 2015.

be taken depending on the characteristics of the high-level parallel applications that may run on top.

In this chapter, we aim at providing an introduction to STM algorithms. Specifically, we describe the main problems encountered when designing an STM algorithm and summarize possible solutions. We also discuss main characteristics and synchronization mechanisms met in some of the well-known STM algorithms. In conjunction with the design decisions, and in order to outline how they are used, we present in detail some representative STM algorithms. We also briefly discuss other STM algorithms found in the literature. So, this chapter provides the necessary machinery for a non-expert who wants to become familiar with the basics of STM algorithms.

The STM algorithms in this chapter are presented from a theoretical point of view, in order to trace a high-level overview of synchronization issues that occur in STM computing and of how they are solved algorithmically. Therefore, the present chapter does not attempt to delve into implementation-related characteristics and problems, or to provide any critical evaluation of the algorithms that are discussed in terms of their performance. We also do not touch several interesting issues of STM design such as the privatization problem [3,41,43,45,56,59,62], the details of irrevocable transactions [47,65], language level semantics [1,2,30], nesting in STM [5,46], distributed STM algorithms [54], and others. We solely focus on software transactional memory so we do not cover hardware or hybrid transactional memory (TM) implementations. A comprehensive discussion of some of these issues, including more detailed presentations of some of the algorithms presented in this chapter, is provided in [31].

The rest of this chapter is organized as follows. Section 2 gives a brief description of the system model, while Section 3 presents the STM model. STM design decisions and mechanisms are explored in Section 4. Section 5 provides an interface for transactional operations which is implemented by the STM algorithms presented in this chapter. Finally, Sections 6, 7, and 8 present some case studies and discuss some STM algorithms from three representative categories, namely those of non-blocking, blocking, and pessimistic STMs.

2   The System

We consider an *asynchronous shared memory* system of threads communicating by accessing base objects. A *base object* has a *state* and supports a set of *primitives* through which a thread may access (read or update) the state of the object. The simplest base object is a *read-write* (R/W) object O that stores a value from some set and supports two atomic primitives: *read*(O), which returns the value of O leaving its content unchanged, and *write*(O,v), which writes the value v into O and returns an acknowledgement.

Stronger objects, like Fetch&Inc and CAS, are usually also provided by the hardware.

A Fetch&Inc object O stores a value from some set and supports, in addition to *read*(O), the atomic primitive Fetch&Inc(O) that increments the value of O by one and returns the previous value of O.

A CAS object O stores a value from some set and supports the atomic primitives read and CAS; read(O) returns the value of O and CAS(O,u,v) checks whether the value of O is u and, if so, it sets the value of O to v and returns `true`, otherwise, the value of O does not change and `false` is returned. Similarly to CAS, a LL/SC *object* O stores a value from some set and supports the atomic primitives LL and SC. $LL(O)$ returns the current value of O. With $SC(O, v)$, a thread p_i sets the value of O to v only if no thread has changed the value of O since the execution of p_i's latest LL on O. In this case, `true` is returned and we say that the SC is *successful*; otherwise, the value of O does not change, `false` is returned, and we say that the SC is *unsuccessful*. A primitive is *non-trivial* if it may change the value of the base object, for example CAS is a non-trivial primitive; otherwise, the primitive is called *trivial*, for instance a *read* is a trivial primitive.

A *configuration* provides a global view of the system at some point in time; it consists of the state of each thread and the state of each base object. In an *initial configuration*, threads and base objects are in initial states. A *step* consists of a primitive applied to a base object by a thread plus probably some local computation by that thread. An *execution* is a (finite or infinite) sequence of alternating configurations and steps starting from an initial configuration. An execution is *legal* starting from a configuration C if the sequence of steps performed by each thread follows the algorithm for that thread (starting from its state in C) and, for each base object, the responses to the primitives performed on the object are in accordance with its specification (and the state of the object at configuration C). An *execution interval* of an execution α is a subsequence of consecutive steps and configurations of α, starting (and ending) with a configuration. An execution (or an execution interval) is *solo* if every step is performed by the same thread.

We assume that threads may experience *crash failures*, i.e., they may stop running at any point during their execution. If a thread p does not fail in some execution α, we say that p is *alive* in α, otherwise the thread is *faulty* in α.

3 Transactional Memory Model

3.1 Transactions

A *transaction* executes a block of code that accesses pieces of data, called *data items* or *t-variables*. A transaction may either *commit* or *abort*. A transaction that is committed or aborted is called *completed*. A transaction that is not completed is *live*. During an execution, each thread may execute a sequence of *transactions*. A transaction may *read* or *write* several data items.

An STM algorithm provides a *shared representation* for each data item; this representation may consist of several base objects. An STM algorithm also provides, for each process, implementations for the routines: (i) READDI for a data item x which returns a value for x or a special value *abort* (which indicates that the transaction which called READDI has to abort), (ii) WRITEDI for a data item x which takes as a parameter a value v for x, updates x with the value v, and returns either *ack* or *abort*, (iii) BEGINTX, which is called when a transaction starts and returns *ack*, (iv) COMMITTX which is called when a transaction tries to commit and returns either a special value *commit* (which indicates that the transaction which called COMMITTX has committed) or *abort*, and (v) ABORTTX which aborts the transaction and returns *ack*. Additionally, an STM algorithm might provide an implementation for a routine, called CREATEDI for creating a data item, when transactions are not static (i.e. when they create data items dynamically). We call these routines *transactional operations*. Each time a process p executing a transaction T calls an instance op of a transactional operation in some execution, we say that p (or T) *invokes* op and we call the return value of op its *response*. We remark that invocations and responses of transactional operations are also considered as steps.

Consider an execution α of an STM algorithm. We say that a transaction T *is* in α, if there is an invocation of BEGINTX in α for T. If T invokes a transactional operation op in α and there is no response for op in α, we say that op (as well as T) is *active* in α. The sequence of transactional operations invoked by each transaction T in α is of the following form: BEGINTX(CREATEDI, READDI, WRITEDI)* (COMMITTX|ABORTTX). We remark that each thread may perform several transactions in α, but these transactions are executed sequentially, i.e. a thread cannot have two transactional operations active at the same point in time. Also, no transaction invokes any operation once it receives *commit* or *abort* as a response.

A transaction T is *forcibly aborted* in α if T invokes a transactional operation other than ABORTTX in α which returns *abort*. This may happen, for instance, if the transaction has performed some action which may violate consistency or if it discovers that the set of values for the data items it has read thus far is inconsistent.

We say that T *creates* a data item initialized with some value v in α, if it invokes CREATEDI for v in α. We say that T *reads* or *writes* a data item x in α, if α contains an invocation of READDI or WRITEDI, respectively, by T on x; then, we say that T *accesses* x in α.

The set of data items read by T in α is called the *read-set* of T, while the set of data items written by T in α is called its *write-set*. Together the read-set and the write-set of T constitute the *data-set* of T (in α). If T performs only read (write) accesses is called a *read-only* (or a *write-only*) transaction. Assume that T reads data item x in α. If T has not written x before this read, we call this read a *global read*. A transaction is *static*, if it never calls CREATEDI in any legal execution it is executed. A transaction that is not *static* is *dynamic*.

The *execution interval* of a transaction T in α is a subsequence of α which starts with the invocation of BEGINTX for T; this invocation is also called the *invocation* of T in α. If T is active in α, its execution interval is the suffix of α starting with the invocation of BEGINTX for T. If T is completed in α, its execution interval ends with the *abort* or *commit* response to the last operation it invoked; this response is called the *response* of T in α. We say that a transaction T *precedes* a transaction T' in α, if T is completed in α and the response of T precedes the invocation of T'. We say that transactions T and T' are *concurrent* (or that their execution intervals *overlap*) if neither T precedes T' nor vice versa.

3.2　STM Correctness

Two well-known *consistency conditions* for database transactions are *serializability* and its stricter variation, *strict serializability*, which were first introduced in [49]. The definition provided below is based on [21].

Definition 1 (Strict Serializability). We say that an execution α is *strictly serializable* if it is possible to do all of the following:

- If A is the set of all complete transactions in α that are not aborted, for each transaction $T \in A$, to associate with T a point $*_T$ somewhere between T's first invocation of a transactional operation and T's last response for a transactional operation in α.
- To choose a subset B of the live transactions in α and, for each transaction $T \in B$, associate with T a point $*_T$ somewhere after T's first invocation of a transactional operation in α.

For each $T \in A \cup B$, the point associated with T is called the *serialization point* of T. Let σ be the sequential execution we get by serially executing each transaction $T \in A \cup B$ at the place that its serialization point has been selected in α. The set B and the serialization points of transactions in $A \cup B$ should be selected so that:

- for each transaction $T \in A$, the same transactional operations, as in α, are invoked by T in σ and the response of each such operation in σ is the same as that in α, and
- for each transaction $T \in B$, a prefix of the operations[1] invoked by T in σ is the same as the sequence of operations invoked by T in α and the response of each such operation in σ is the same as that in α.

An STM algorithm is strictly serializable if all the executions it produces are strictly serializable. Serializability differs from strict serializability in that it does not ensure that the real-time order of transactions is respected by the sequential history defined by the serialization points. Thus, every execution that is strictly serializable is also serializable but not vice versa.

Consider a strictly serializable execution α and let A and B be the sets of transactions which justify that α is serializable. Opacity [29] is a well-known consistency condition for STM which imposes the additional property that even transactions outside $A \cup B$ must read consistent values. Roughly speaking, for some execution α of an STM algorithm, opacity requires that *each* transaction T that accesses a data item sees only changes performed on the data item by transactions that have committed before T starts its execution (or by the transaction itself). This additional property is required in order to avoid undesired situations where a transaction may cause an exception or enter into an infinite loop after reading a value for a data item written by a live transaction that may eventually abort.

The production of an exception or an error code can be avoided by STM algorithms that ensure strict serializability if we consider (1) an exception (or an error code) that has been resulted by the execution of a transactional operation op as the response for op and (2) a transaction that has experienced an exception or has received an error code as a response to one of its operations, as completed (and not aborted). Then, a strictly serializable STM algorithm would never produce exceptions or error codes. Additionally, no transaction will ever enter an infinite loop in executions produced by STM algorithms that ensure standard liveness properties, like obstruction-freedom, livelock-freedom, or

---

[1] Notice that since σ is a sequential execution, each transaction $T \in B$ commits in σ.

any other standard liveness property (see Section 3.3 for formal definitions of some of these properties).

Other consistency conditions for STM have been presented in [8,12,17,36,50] (this list is not exhaustive).

3.3 STM Liveness

An STM algorithm is called *blocking* if it produces executions in which threads may *block* waiting for some other thread to perform a step. Notice that if some thread p crashes all threads may block. Let α be an infinite execution of a blocking STM algorithm. We say that a thread p experiences *starvation* (or *starves*) in α, if p takes infinitely many steps in α and it receives only a finite number of commit responses for the transactions that it initiates. We say that there is a *livelock* in α, if all threads that take an infinite number of steps in α, experience starvation. We say that a set of threads experiences *deadlock* in α, if there is a configuration C in α in which each of these threads has an active transaction in α, yet all of those threads are blocked in α.

Non-blocking algorithms produce executions in which threads never have to wait for other threads. Consider now an execution α of a non-blocking STM algorithm. *Obstruction-freedom* ensures that for each thread p, if p runs solo starting from any configuration C in α, it eventually completes the execution of its transaction successfully (or of a newly initiated transaction if p does not have an active transaction at C) within a finite number of steps. Thus, obstruction-freedom guarantees progress only if a thread executes solo for sufficiently long. *Lock-freedom* is a stronger property which ensures that *some* non-faulty thread successfully completes the execution of a transaction within a finite number of steps (independently of whether it runs solo or not). Finally, *wait-freedom ensures* that *each* non-faulty thread completes the execution of each of its transactions within a finite number of steps.

3.4 Conflicts

We say that two transactions T_1 and T_2 *conflict* in an execution α (or experience a *conflict* in α) if they both access the same data item x, one of these accesses writes the data item, and their execution intervals are overlapping in α. We describe some execution scenarios in which conflicts may result to violations of consistency.

If both T_1 and T_2 write x, we say that T_1 and T_2 experience a W–W conflict. Denote by W_1 an instance of WRITEDI executed for x by T_1 and let v_1 be the value that W_1 writes for x. Similarly, let W_2 be an instance of WRITEDI executed for x by T_2 and let v_2 be the value that W_2 writes for x. Suppose that T_1 additionally executes an instance W_1' of WRITEDI to update some data item y with a value v_1'. Assume that T_2 also performs an instance W_2' of WRITEDI to update y with a value v_2'. Assume that both T_1 and T_2 commit in α and let T be a third transaction that is initiated after the completion of T_1 and T_2 and reads x and y. To ensure consistency, an STM algorithm should take actions to guarantee that if T commits, it reads values v_1 and v_1' or v_2 and v_2' for x and y, respectively, i.e. that the values it reads for x and y are written by the same transaction.

Consider next the following scenario. Suppose that T_1 executes an instance W of WRITEDI writing a distinct value v for x, T_2 executes an instance R of READDI on x, and R returns the value v written by W. Then, we say that T_1 and T_2 experience a W-R conflict. If this happens, we say that T_1 performs a *dirty read* [7]. Most STM algorithms ensure that this does not occur since T_1 eventually aborts. Specifically, dirty reads never occur in executions produced by opaque algorithms.

Finally, consider the following scenario. Suppose that T_1 executes an instance W_1 of WRITEDI writing a distinct value v for x, and assume that another transaction T_3 executes an instance W_3 of WRITEDI writing a distinct value v' for x. Let T_2 perform two instances R_1 and R_2 of READDI on x, and assume that R_1 returns the value v written by W_1 whereas R_2 returns the value v' written by W_3. Notice that T_2 experiences W-R conflicts with both T_1 and T_3. In addition however, T_2 experiences a R-W conflict with T_3 since T_2's first read returns a value other than v'. A R-W conflict appears also if a transaction T_1 performs a WRITEDI on x and T_2 performs a READDI on x so that the response of READDI occurs before the invocation of WRITEDI.

We say that an STM algorithm uses a *conflict prevention mechanism*, if it prevents a conflict from occurring. We say that it uses a *conflict detection mechanism*, if it detects a conflict once it occurs and takes appropriate actions to resolve it.

4 STM Design Decisions and Mechanisms

4.1 Ownerships

Most existing TM algorithms employ some *ownership acquisition* mechanism to ensure that data items are atomically accessed by each transaction. Specifically, before effectuating a write to a data item x, a transaction T acquires the *write ownership* of x. If T holds the ownership of x, no other transaction can update x. In some TM algorithms, T must additionally acquire the *read-ownership* of each data item it reads. Notice that in this case, a transaction T must acquire the read-ownerships just of the data items it globally reads since any read that T performs on a data item after writing it, must return the value written by T itself in order to ensure consistency. A transaction that holds the ownership of a data item x at a configuration C is referred to as the *owner* of x at C.

The implementation of ownerships varies in different TM implementations. Blocking TM algorithms usually implement ownerships using (non-preemptive) locks. So, as long as a thread p holds the ownership of a data item x, it blocks all other threads from updating (or even reading) x. Thus, in blocking algorithms ownership is usually *non-preemptive*.

On the contrary, in non-blocking TM algorithms no thread is ever blocked waiting for other threads. Non-blocking algorithms usually implement a *helping mechanism* which allows threads to help each other finishing their transactions, or a mechanism of forcibly aborting other transactions in order to get the ownerships that they hold. In this way, all ownerships held by a thread can be released even if the thread fails, so in non-blocking algorithms ownerships are *preemptive*.

A simple blocking TM algorithm presented in [13] uses a coarse-grain lock to implement the ownerships of all data items. However, several TM algorithms [14,15,24,33] provide a distinct ownership for each data item. This approach is called *per data item* ownership assignment. Another approach is the *per set of data items* ownership assignment (or *per stripe*), where a mapping is determined between a concrete number of ownerships and a number of disjoint sets of data items that cover the data items universe. This mapping can be accomplished using hashing.

In existing blocking TM algorithms, the representation of some data item x stores just a boolean which describes whether the data item is occupied or free. This way a transaction can acquire (release) x's ownership by changing its state to occupied (free). So, the representation of a data item is *thread-unaware*, i.e. it does not contain the information of its owner at each configuration. In non-blocking algorithms, a thread must discover which transaction T holds the ownership of some data item it wants to access and either help T to complete or forcibly abort it. This information is usually maintained in the representation of the data item; we then say that the representation is *thread-aware*. We say that a TM implementation employs *invisible reads*, if in all executions that it produces, no instance of READDI writes to any base object. A TM implementation that does not employ invisible reads, employs *visible* reads.

A transaction usually acquires the ownership of some data item x either when accessing x for the first time, or at commit time (during the execution of COMMITTX). In the former case, we say that the TM algorithm uses *eager acquisition* (or *encounter-time acquisition*) of ownerships, while in the latter case it uses *lazy acquisition* of ownerships.

A transaction usually implements two sets, namely its *read-set* and its *write-set*. In TM algorithms that use eager acquisition, each transaction T updates the value of some data item x that writes, directly, during the execution of the corresponding WRITEDI routine it invokes for x. Then, T maintains the old values of the data items it has updated in its write-set, so that it can restore the memory to a previous consistent state if it aborts. Such updates are called *direct updates*. On the other hand, in the lazy ownership acquisition, a transaction effectuates the update of some data item at commit time. Updates performed in this way are called *deferred updates*. When deferred updates are used, transactions maintain the new values for each data item they update in their write-set, so that to be able to effectuate these updates at commit time.

The ownerships are usually released when the corresponding transaction completes (independently of whether it commits or aborts).

4.2 Mechanisms for Preventing, Detecting and Resolving Conflicts

A TM algorithm that employs invisible reads (or visible reads with lazy acquisition for read ownerships), must take some care for ensuring consistency. Such TM algorithms usually implement a *validation mechanism* that ensures that each transaction has read consistent values for the data items in its read-set.

The validation mechanism can be implemented in several different ways. Most TM algorithms introduce the notion of a *version* for each data item but implement versions in different ways. Some of them store a version together with the metadata of a data item [14,15,33].

A transaction that updates some data item must update also its version, so that another transaction can determine if the data item's value has changed. Each transaction T must maintain, for each data item x it reads, x's version in its read-set. This way T can check at each point in time if the value read by T for x is still consistent by checking whether its version has changed since it was accessed for the first time by T.

The validation mechanism performs the previous check for all the data items read by T and returns `true` if none of them has changed; otherwise, it returns `false`.

To ensure strict serializability, each transaction may execute the validation mechanism only once at commit time. However, in order to avoid reading inconsistent values which may result in performing illegal actions, the validation mechanism must be executed more often. We refer to a transaction that has read inconsistent values as a *doomed* transaction: such a transaction is fated to eventually abort although it is still running. A doomed transaction may cause an exception which may result in the abnormal termination of the entire execution.

Existing TM algorithms execute the validation mechanism in different time periods. Some of them [15,22,33,38] execute this mechanism each time a transaction reads a data item. This is called *incremental validation* because each time the mechanism is executed it has to validate one more data item. Incremental validation has been implemented in [15] by using a global timestamp. Riegel et al. show in [52] how the global timestamp can be replaced by an external physical clock that can be accessed efficiently or by multiple synchronized physical clocks. The timestamp mechanism has been used since then in many algorithms [24,58,64].

Other TM algorithms, such as TL [14] execute the validation mechanism after a specified number of read operations have been performed, although this does not ensure full prevention from all possible inconsistencies. Other algorithms [25] transfer to the user the responsibility of calling the validation mechanism whenever she believes it is necessary. This form of validation is called *manual*. A validation mechanism that is not manual is *automatic*.

RINGSTM [61] uses a ring as a shared ordered set, and employs a bit-vector technique, like Bloom filters [11] to allow each transaction to announce, in a space-efficient way, its write-set in the shared set. A transaction then validates its read-set by checking whether there are any conflicts among its read-set and other announced write-sets. Other algorithms that use the Bloom filters technique for implementing their validation mechanism are presented in [26]. We remark that this chapter does not aim at describing different implementations of validation mechanisms (or versions) in detail.

The actions that TM algorithms take when they detect a conflict vary. In a blocking TM algorithm, a transaction T_1 that has discovered a conflict with a transaction T_2 may either wait for T_2 to complete or it may abort. In a non-blocking TM algorithm, T_1 may either cause T_2 to abort or it may help T_2 to complete. Which of the two actions will occur usually depends on the liveness property that the TM algorithm ensures. In some TM algorithms, when T_1 can cause T_2 to abort, T_1 may consult a software entity, called *contention manager*. The contention manager then decides whether T_1 should indeed forcefully abort T_2 or whether T_1 should wait for a particular period of time before proceeding to any action. In such systems, it is the contention manager that is responsible to guarantee progress. Contention managers have been studied in [6,27,28,55,58].

The prevention (or detection) of a conflict can be *eager* or *lazy*. When eager prevention (or detection) is employed the conflict is prevented (or detected) at the point it arises in the execution. In contrast, when lazy prevention (or detection) is employed the conflict is prevented (or detected) at a later point in the execution, e.g. at commit time. For example, STM algorithms that eagerly (or lazily) acquire write ownerships for data items can prevent (or detect) W-W and W-R conflicts. Also, an STM algorithm that acquires write-ownerships to data items, uses visible reads, and employs eager acquisition of read ownerships, can prevent R-W conflicts from occurring. Another strategy for preventing R-W conflicts employs the technique of letting the read-only transactions, accessing a data item, commit before the update transactions that are writing to it [4,9,20,44].

To resolve a conflict between two transactions T_1 and T_2, one of them, let's say T_1 may wait, abort or help T_2 to complete. Each of these cases introduces a performance penalty which is paid by T_1 even if T_2 aborts later on, in which case we call this penalty *needless*. We remark that there exists a trade-off when choosing between eager and lazy prevention (detection) of conflicts: the eager approach enables fast detection of doomed transactions but it may lead to false positives when deciding which transactions are doomed. On the other hand, the lazy approach decreases the possibility of needless payments and allows more transactions to commit.

4.3 Levels of Indirection and In-Place Updates

TM algorithms follow two main approaches to represent data items and maintain their values. The first stores, for each data item, the extra state required by the algorithm, together with the data item's value in a single record in memory. We call this approach *in-place*. The second approach requires a thread executing a read or a write on some data item x to perform a number of intermediate memory accesses in order to find the memory address in which x's value is stored. Then, we say that the TM algorithm employs *indirection*. The number of intermediate memory accesses that are performed in this case is called *indirection level*. To reduce performance overheads, the indirection level should be as small as possible. In some algorithms [33], performing the intermediate memory accesses is done by following a path of intermediate pointers. Moreover, some algorithms [33,38] have to retrieve the state of the last transaction that has acquired the ownership of x in order to determine the current value of x. In other algorithms [25,63], the indirection level is different if the ownership of x is acquired at the time that a transaction tries to read the value of x from if it is not. Finally, other algorithms adjust the indirection level at execution time based either on the contention incurred on the data items [63] or on statistics [38]. This last class of algorithms are called *adaptive*.

5   Interface for Transactional Operations

For uniformity of presentation, we assume that all TM algorithms presented in this chapter implement the following interface for transactional operations:

- $T = \text{BEGINTX}()$: when invoked by a thread p, it identifies the beginning of a new transaction T by p; it is used to allocate state variables that may be required to execute the transaction. It returns a handle T that identifies the transaction through which its state variables are accessed. Notice that we abuse notation by using T to refer to both the transaction itself and its handle.

- $x = \text{CREATEDI}(T,v)$: it is used for the allocation of a new data item x by transaction T. This routine initiates the shared representation for the data item and returns a handle x for it which is passed as a parameter to READDI or WRITEDI when they are invoked for x. Notice that we abuse notation by using x to refer to the data item itself and its handle. The argument v of CREATEDI specifies the initial value for x.
- $(b,v) = \text{READDI}(T,x)$: it is called whenever transaction T wants to read the value of a data item x; it returns the value v for x as well as a boolean value b, which is `true` when the read operation completes successfully. On the other hand, if READDI discovers that T is doomed to abort (e.g. because the values for some of the data items that it has read are not consistent any longer) then READDI completes unsuccessfully by returning `false` for b.
- $b = \text{WRITEDI}(T,x,v)$: it is called whenever transaction T wants to update the value of a data item x with the value v; it returns a boolean value b, which is either `true` to identify that the write was successful or `false` to identify that the write was unsuccessful in which case T is doomed to abort.
- $b = \text{COMMITTX}(T)$: it requests the termination of T as committed. It returns a boolean value b, which is `true` if the commit attempt was successful and `false` otherwise.
- $\text{ABORTTX}(t)$: causes the termination of T as aborted.

A TM transaction resembles more an atomic code block than a database transaction. For this reason, whenever a thread initiates a transaction, it would like it to commit. So, the functionality of ABORTTX is not necessary. We also remark that CREATEDI is provided only by STM algorithms that rely on per-object metadata. Both ABORTTX and CREATEDI are included in the list above for the sake of completeness.

6 Non-blocking Algorithms

In this section, we discuss non-blocking STM algorithms. We start by presenting DSTM, the first non-blocking STM algorithm presented in the literature for dynamic transactions. We then provide shorter discussions of other non-blocking STM algorithms.

6.1 Case Study: DSTM

DSTM [33] was the first algorithm to support dynamic transactions. DSTM is an obstruction-free algorithm.

6.1.1 Data Structures

DSTM associates a record, called *transactional record*, with each transaction T; we call T the owner of this transactional record. The transactional record of T consists of two fields: *status* which is a CAS object storing the status of T and *readList* which implements the read-set of T. The status of T can be either ACTIVE, COMMITTED or ABORTED. We abuse notation and use T to refer to both the transaction itself and its transactional record.

DSTM uses ownership assignment per data item. Specifically, DSTM associates a CAS object, called *start*, with each data item x. This object stores a pointer to a structure called *locator*. The *locator* of x contains a pointer *tran* which points to the transactional record of the transaction that either holds the ownership of x or was the last transaction that acquired the ownership of x. Assume that *tran* points to some transaction T. If the status of T is ACTIVE, then T holds the ownership of x; otherwise, no transaction holds the ownership of x. The *locator* of x additionally stores two pointers, called *oldData* and *newData*, respectively. They both point to values for x. The *oldData* field points to a value that has been written for x by a transaction other than T, whereas *newData* points to a value written for x by T itself. The representation of a data item x is illustrated in Figure 1.

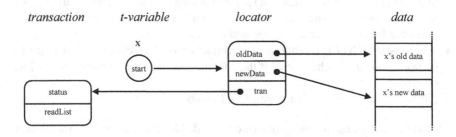

Fig. 1. The representation of a data item x in DSTM

DSTM uses invisible reads: it maintains a read-set for each transaction T and implements a validation mechanism to ensure the consistency of the values of the data items that are contained in its read-set. Specifically, T maintains in its read-set a version for each data item x that it reads. This version is the memory address of the value read by T for x.

6.1.2 Implementation

In DSTM, a transaction T starts its execution with its status ACTIVE and its read-set empty. Each time T calls CREATEDI to create a new data item x, T allocates a new *locator* whose *tran* field points to T (to indicate that T is the owner of x), its *oldData* field is equal to NULL, and its *newData* field points to the initial value for x. T also allocates a new pointer *start* for x and set *start* to point to the new *locator*. We remark that pointer *start* for x will not always point to the same *locator* record.

Since the *locator* of each data item x stores pointers, namely *oldData* and *newData*, to two values for x, whenever a transaction T wants to read the value for x, it has to take appropriate actions to determine which of these two values it should consider as the current value for x. To determine this, it reads the *status* field of the transactional record pointed to by *tran* in x's *locator*. Let T' be the owner of this transactional record.

If the status of T' is COMMITTED (ABORTED), then the current value for x is the value pointed to by the *newData* field (*oldData* field, respectively) of x's *locator*. Notice that in either case, T' is not the owner of x; specifically, x does not have an owner at the current point in time. However, if the status of T' is ACTIVE, then T' is the current owner of x and the current value for x cannot consistently be determined until T' completes. So, T tries to forcibly abort T': it executes a CAS on T''s status to change the status of T' to ABORTED. If it succeeds, then it reads the value for x pointed to by *oldData*; otherwise, some other CAS has been successfully executed on T''s status and therefore the status of T' has been already updated to COMMITTED or ABORTED. So, T reads again T''s status and, depending on whether its value is COMMITTED or ABORTED, it reads the value for x pointed to by *newData* or *oldData*, respectively.

This feature of allowing a transaction to forcibly abort another transaction, makes DSTM an obstruction-free algorithm. The procedure described above to determine the current value for a data item, implies that DSTM uses indirection with two indirection levels.

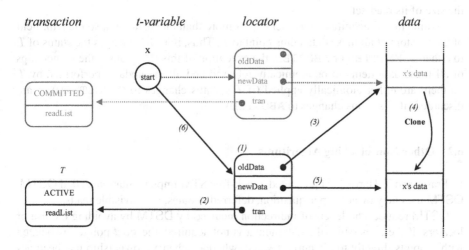

Fig. 2. The procedure of ownership acquisition and cloning, followed by DSTM

DSTM uses eager acquisition of ownerships and direct updates. So, in order for some transaction T to update the value for a data item x, it first has to acquire its ownership. The procedure executed by DSTM for the acquisition of x's ownership by T is illustrated in Figure 2. The gray color part of the figure illustrates the representation of x before the acquisition of its ownership by T, whereas the black color part illustrates its representation right after. Notice that we have assumed that the last transaction to acquire the ownership for x before T, has committed by the time that T tries to acquire x's ownership.

To acquire the ownership for x, T creates a new *locator* for x (step 1) and initializes it so that *tran* points to T (step 2), *oldData* points to the current value for x (step 3), and *newData* points to a copy of the current value for x (step 5). Thus, T uses cloning to copy the current value for x (step 4) in a new memory location pointed to by the *newData* field of the black locator. Any updates of T on x will be performed on this copy. Notice that the current value for x is the value pointed to by the *newData* pointer in the gray *locator* (since the transaction that created that *locator* has committed). Finally, the *start* pointer of x is atomically updated (using CAS) so that it points to the new *locator* (step 6). After the successful execution of this CAS, and as long as T's status is ACTIVE, T holds the ownership for x.

To ensure opacity, each transaction T validates its read-set each time it globally reads a data item and a last time before it commits. The validation mechanism checks whether the value for each data item x maintained in T's read-set is still consistent, i.e., it finds the current value for x (with the procedure described above) and checks whether it is the same with the one maintained for x in T's read-set. If at least one of the values maintained in its read-set is not consistent, T aborts by executing a CAS to change its status to ABORTED. So, DSTM employs an automatic and incremental validation mechanism. Since the validation is performed on all elements of the read-set each time a new data item is accessed, it incurs an overhead of $O(r^2)$ to a transaction, where r is the size of its read-set.

Assume that T acquires the ownership of more than one data item, so the *tran* field of the locators of all these data items point to T. Thus, if a CAS changes the status of T to either COMMITTED or ABORTED, the execution of this CAS causes the ownerships of all these data items to be atomically released and all the updates performed by T on them are either atomically applied (if T's status changes to COMMITTED) or are discarded (if T's status changes to ABORTED).

6.2 Other Non-blocking Algorithms

K. Fraser and T. Harris [25] presented a lock-free STM implementation, called OSTM. OSTM uses lazy ownership acquisition, deferred updates, and invisible reads.

OSTM reduces the levels of indirection incurred by DSTM by avoiding the use of locators: if the ownership of a data item x is not acquired, the *start* pointer associated with x points directly to x's current value, whereas when x's ownership has been acquired, *start* points to the transactional record of the transaction that has acquired the ownership of x.

In order to achieve lock-freedom, OSTM executes each transaction T in two *phases*. During the first phase, T simulates its execution using local versions of the data items that it accesses. It does so in an invisible way by maintaining a read-set and a write-set. Thus, during its first phase, T is invisible to other transactions. Its second phase starts when T calls COMMITTX. Then, T becomes visible by making its write-set shared and tries to acquire the ownerships of the data items in its write-set, it validates its read-set, updates the data items in its write-set and releases the ownerships it acquired. Deadlocks can be avoided by acquiring ownerships based on some order, which is determined by sorting the memory addresses of the data items.

Since T becomes visible at commit time, its data-set does not change until it completes. OSTM employs a recursive helping mechanism to ensure that at each point in time at least one of the transactions will complete successfully within a finite number of steps. Specifically, if T discovers that the ownership of a data item x it has accessed is already taken by some transaction T', it releases the ownerships it has acquired, helps the process executing T' to complete the execution of T', and aborts. This helping mechanism is recursive. Specifically, if T' conflicts with a third transaction T'', then while helping T', T may also help T''.

This helping mechanism can result in livelocks as follows. Consider a transactions T that reads a data item x and writes a data item y. Let T' be another transaction that reads y and writes x. At commit-time, and specifically during the validation of their read-sets, both T and T' will discover that there is a conflict between them, so they may (recursively) help each other for ever. To avoid such livelocks, OSTM defines a total order on transactions, which determines transactions' priorities. If T discovers a conflict with T' and T has priority over T', T causes T' to abort, otherwise, T helps T' to complete and aborts.

A second lock-free STM implementation, called NBSTM, was presented in [37]. NBSTM employs the same data item representation as DSTM. However, it replaces DSTM's mechanism for forcibly aborting conflicting transactions with a recursive helping mechanism similar to that of OSTM [25]. As in OSTM, each transaction T is executed in two *phases*. In contrast to OSTM however, during its second phase, each transaction in NBSTM acquires a read-ownership for each data item in its read-set, in addition to acquiring the ownership for each data item in its write-set. By employing read-ownerships, livelocks can easily be avoided through the helping mechanism and the final validation is done implicitly when acquiring the read ownership of each data item. However, more CAS instructions are executed to acquire the extra ownerships. NBSTM ensures that all acquired ownerships by a transaction T can be released, and all its updates can be applied (if T commits) or discarded (if T aborts), by performing a single write primitive. This is more efficient than in DSTM which requires a CAS primitive for the same purpose. OSTM requires two CAS primitives to change the status of a transaction from ACTIVE to COMMITTED and $O(w)$ write primitives, where w is the size of the write-set, to update the data items and release their ownerships.

As in DSTM, each access of some data item in NBSTM faces two levels of indirection. OSTM faces just one level of indirection when the data item's ownership is not acquired. Assume now that the ownership of a data item is acquired. In this case, OSTM may face indirections up to a number proportional to the size of the write-set of this transaction, whereas NBSTM pays only two indirections. We also remark that in the case where the ownership of a data item is not acquired, NBSTM can exhibit just one level of indirection, as OSTM does, by employing a similar technique as that of OSTM.

ASTM [39] and NZTM [63] are obstruction-free STM algorithms that attempt to reduce the levels of indirection faced by DSTM. They both originate from DSTM, so they greatly follow the techniques of DSTM.

ASTM [39] is adaptive, i.e. it adjusts the way it works based on the characteristics of the workload it executes. In ASTM, the *start* pointer of a data item x whose ownership has not been acquired is updated so that it points directly to the value of x. This is performed lazily as follows. Whenever a transaction reads a data item that is currently non-acquired and its *start* pointer points to a locator, this pointer is updated so that it directly points to the data item's current data. If now the ownership of x is acquired, ASTM follows the same indirection technique as DSTM, i.e. *start* is updated to point to a locator for x, so two levels of indirection are then introduced.

This technique has the following implication. In read-dominated workloads, data items tend to stay in the non-acquired state. Then, performance is improved since the levels of indirection are reduced. However, in update-dominated workloads, data items tend to stay in the acquired state, so then the technique does not have any significant impact in performance. ASTM implements both eager and lazy ownership acquisition and adaptively alternates between these two modes based on a simple threshold-based heuristic regarding the average number of WRITEDI executed by each transaction.

In NZTM [63], transactions access data items (whose ownership is not acquired) without facing indirection. NZTM uses visible reads (i.e., a transaction acquires the ownership of each data item it reads) and eager ownership acquisition. In NZTM, each data item has a status. A data item x can have its status either equal to *deflated* and then its value can be read directly, or equal to *inflated* and then the representation of x is the same as that in DSTM. Initially, the status of each data item is deflated. When a transaction wants to acquire the ownership of a data item with deflated status, it can simply mark it as acquired. In case some transaction T wants to acquire the ownership of a data item x that is marked as acquired by a transaction T', T informs T' to abort and checks whether T''s status indeed changed to ABORTED. If this is so, T can proceed to acquire the ownership of the variable itself. If however T' is slow in updating its status, instead of blocking, T *inflates* the data item, i.e. x's state changes to inflated. While x is in inflated state, NZTM handles it in a way similar to that employed by DSTM. When later T' aborts, the state of x may change again to deflated.

Similarly to ASTM and NZTM, RSTM [40] is an STM algorithm that aims at reducing the levels of indirection for the common case. In RSTM, a data item x is accessed through an *object header*, which is a structure that contains a pointer to the data item new metadata record. Apart from the value of the data item, the metadata record contains a pointer to the transaction record of the transaction that has write ownership of x, as well as a pointer to the immediately previous metadata record of x. The object header further contains a limited list of *visible readers*. A transaction T that wishes to access x as a visible reader, attempts to install a pointer to its descriptor into this list. A further transaction T' which acquires the ownership of x for writing, aborts transactions that it finds in x's visible readers list. Thus, in cases like this, T may be spared the quadratic overhead of read-set validation.

MM-STM [42] is another non-blocking STM algorithm. MM-STM is lock-free and uses a record, called *orec*, to store the metadata of a data item and information about the transaction that has ownership of it. In case a transaction T wishes to acquire ownership of a data item x that is already owned by some other transaction T', MM-STM lets T "steal" the orec from T' instead of aborting T'. T is then in charge of performing T' update on x, apart from its own, provided that T' has not aborted in the meanwhile.

7   Blocking Algorithms

In this section, we discuss blocking STM implementations. We start by presenting two case studies, NOrec [13] and TLII [15] in Sections 7.1 and 7.2, respectively. A short discussion of additional blocking STM implementations is provided in Section 7.3.

7.1 Case Study 1: NOrec

NOrec [13] is a simple blocking STM implementation presented by L. Dalessandro *et al.* It employs value-based validation, as does JudoSTM [48]. NOrec is livelock-free but it does not necessarily avoid starvation.

7.1.1 Data Structures and Design Decisions

NOrec employs a shared CAS object which implements a coarse-grain lock L. L is used to ensure that at most one transaction has the write ownership of the entire space of data items at any given point in time. L is implemented as an integer which is initially zero and its consecutive values are strictly increasing. If the value of L is odd, then L is locked by some transaction, otherwise it is unlocked. During the commit phase each write transaction tries to acquire the lock, by incrementing it, thus changing its parity. Only one transaction will succeed in acquiring the lock, ensuring that update transactions cannot modify data items concurrently. The transaction that manages to acquire the lock, stores its updates into the shared memory and increments L, changing its parity once again which results in releasing the lock. NOrec implements no indirection and performs deferred updates.

One of the main characteristics of NOrec is that it does not store any metadata for the data items; for each data item x, it stores only the value *val* for x. NOrec maintains a transactional record for each transaction T. In addition to the pointers to T's read-set and write-set, this record contains a local copy of L which is used to validate the consistency of T's read-set. Specifically, after every read operation, T checks if L has a different value than its local copy and if this is so, it waits until the lock is released and then performs value-based validation of the data items in its read-set; the value of each data item x in T's read-set is compared to the current value of x stored in shared memory. If these two values are the same for all data items in T's read-set, then the validation succeeds, in which case T updates its local copy of L to the current value of L to avoid unnecessary validations in the future.

7.1.2 Implementation

When a transaction T starts, it first initializes its transactional record so that its read and write-sets are empty and the current value of L, if even, is stored in its local copy. If the value of L is odd, T spins on L until it reads an even value in it. It does so, since if T starts its execution while the lock is acquired, it may read inconsistent values for data items.

The local copy of L is used to implement incremental validation, each time T globally reads a data item. Validation compares T's local copy of L against the current value of L. If the values are the same, the validation terminates successfully. Otherwise, T checks whether the value of L is odd. If this is so, T performs spinning until it reads an even value in L. In either case, T parses its read-set and for each data item in it, it compares the locally stored value with the data item's current value. If discrepancies are found, T aborts. T repeats this validation, if the value of L changes in the meantime. If none of these cases occurs, the validation is successful. After each successful validation, T updates the local copy of L with the value it last read in L.

When T performs a read of a data item x, it first checks whether an entry for x already exists in T's write-set, in which case it returns the value stored there. After each read operation, T compares the current value of L with the value of the copy it maintains for it and, if they are different, it performs a validation. If the validation is unsuccessful, T aborts. Otherwise, T creates a new entry for x and adds it in its read-set (if it is not already there).

When T writes a value to a data item x, it stores a pointer to it and the new value in its write-set, if x is not already there; otherwise, it updates the already existing entry for x with the new value.

During COMMITTX, a read-only transaction commits without any further action. This is safe since the last incremental validation that is performed by the transaction ensured that its read-set is consistent. An update transaction T first tries to acquire the global lock. It does so by using CAS to increment L. A failed CAS indicates that a different transaction T' has entered its commit phase. In this case, some data item in T's read-set may be invalidated by some of the updates of T', which is why T re-validates its read-set before it tries to acquire the lock again. An unsuccessful validation leads T to abort. If validation succeeds and T manages to acquire the lock, T performs its updates and releases the lock.

7.2   Case Study 2: TLII

Transactional Locking II (TLII), proposed by Dice *et al.* [15], is a blocking TM algorithm which employs a two-phase locking scheme. Each transaction T in TLII is executed in two phases: (1) T is first executed speculatively, i.e., its execution is simulated locally using its read-set and write-set, and (2) T then attempts to acquire the ownerships of all data items in its write-set and if it does so successfully, it applies its changes, releases the ownerships it has acquired, and commits. Some of the ideas employed by TLII are also found in the algorithm presented in [35] (which was inspired by Ennals's STM algorithm [23]).

7.2.1   Data Structures and Design Decisions

TLII implements ownership assignment per stripe by employing fine-grained locking. Reads are invisible and data items have in-place, thread-unaware representations. TLII associates a version with each data item in order to perform validation. Moreover, it relies on a global Fetch&Inc variable, GVC, which is used as a global versioning clock.

TLII employs lazy ownership acquisition and deferred updates. To update the versions of the data items in its write-set, an update transaction performs a Fetch&Inc on GVC at commit time, and assigns the value that this Fetch&Inc returns as the new version of each data item it updates. The transactional record of each transaction T stores the following data:

- A *read version number* which stores the value that T read from GVC at the beginning of its execution. Each time T reads a data item x, x's current version is compared against the read version number of T and T may only proceed if x's version is less than its read version number. Furthermore, when T validates its read-set,

T reads the current version for each data item in its read-set and compares it with T's read version number. T aborts if the current version of any of these data items is greater than T's read version number.

- A *write version number* which is the value of GVC that T obtained as the return value of the Fetch&Inc it performs on it at commit time. This number is used as the new version of the data items that T updates.
- Two pointers, one to T's read-set and one to T's write-set.

7.2.2 Implementation

A transaction T starts by reading GVC to obtain its read version number and initializing its read- and write-sets to empty.

To carry out a global read of a data item x, T verifies that x is neither owned by another transaction, i.e. x is not locked, nor has a version number greater than the read version number of T. If the version number of x is greater than the read version number of T, then between the time that T initiated its read version number and the time that it read x, some update transaction incremented GVC and updated x. Thus, if T proceeds, it runs the risk of reading inconsistent data. The same danger holds when T finds out that x is owned by some other transaction. T therefore aborts in both those cases. The described validation procedure is referred to as *post-validation*. It is remarkable that T does not validate the consistency of its entire read-set each time it performs a global read. So, validation in TLII is fast. Notice also that read-only transactions in TLII do not need to perform a final validation of their entire read-set before committing, since the post-validation procedure that takes place at each read ensures that their read-set remains consistent.

If T is not aborted during the validation procedure, it creates an entry for x in its read-set. If the read is not global, x is contained in T's write-set (or read-set), in which case T must read the value for x that is recorded there.

As in all algorithms that employ deferred updates, when writing to a data item x, a transaction T either creates a new entry for x in its write-set (if there is no such an entry in it) and stores the intended value there , or updates the entry for x in its write-set (if there is such an entry there).

If T is an update transaction, it first tries to obtain the ownership of each data item in its write-set. Ownership acquisition of a data item x is performed by acquiring the lock for x. If x is already locked, T releases all ownerships it has already acquired and aborts. If ownership acquisition is successful, then T performs the final validation of its read-set. If validation is successful, T obtains its write version number by incrementing GVC and proceeds to applying its intended updates to shared memory. For each data item whose value T updates in shared memory, it also sets its version to T's write version number. Once all of T's intended updates have been performed, T releases the data item ownerships and commits. To avoid deadlock, ownership acquisition may be performed in some order. TLII chooses not to do so for performance reasons. TLII is not starvation-free.

7.3 Other Blocking Algorithms

TLII is an indicative example of a family of algorithms that use fine-grained locking in order to implement write ownership. TLII itself is a development of TL, a previous blocking algorithm presented by Dice and Shavit in [14]. The important difference between TL and TLII is that TL does not employ a global lock. Instead, data items have a version number which is incremented each time the data item is updated. This characteristic hinders efficient incremental validation, which is why it was replaced with the global version clock in TLII. A further difference is that TL offers the option of operating in two different modes, the *commit* mode and the *encounter* mode. In commit mode, TL employs deferred updates and must therefore implement a redo log. Conversely, when it operates in encounter mode, TL executes direct updates and it must implement an undo log.

TLC, presented by Avni and Shavit in [10], is another member of the family of transactional locking algorithms. TLC is a variation of TL/TLII that attempts to provide better scaling prospects by avoiding contention on a single resource, such as the shared counter GVC in TLII. Instead, the TLC scheme uses a local version counter for each thread. Validation is then implemented through a mechanism which employs vector clocks.

One more algorithm which employs transactional locking is TLRW [16]. In TLRW, each data item x is equipped with a read counter which is incremented by each transaction before it accesses x for reading. After the read, the transaction decrements the read counter of the data item. Thus, TLRW employs read ownerships resulting in visible read-only transactions. TLRW implements thread-aware write ownerships. An update transaction that has obtained write ownership of x requires the read counter to be 0 in order to update x. Read set consistency is ensured because a transaction is not able to obtain read ownership of x, if some other transaction has a write ownership for it. For the implementation of ownership, TLRW introduces *byte locks*, which are read/write locks conceived to perform and scale well even in workloads with high amount of read-only transactions.

Further algorithms in the family of TL and TLII are presented in [32,51,58,64] (this list is probably not exhaustive).

Another well-known candidate of STM blocking algorithms is TINYSTM, presented by Felber *et. al* in [24]. Like TL, it also supports two different modes, called *write-through* and *write-back*. The write-through mode implements the same update policy as the encounter mode in TL, i.e. direct updates, while the write-back mode implements the same update policy as the commit mode in TL, i.e. deferred updates. Contrary to TL, however, TINYSTM employs eager ownership acquisition in either mode. TINYSTM uses a global version clock in the fashion of TLII. However, each time a read operation executes a successful post-validation of the data item it is reading, it updates the corresponding transaction's read version number with the current value of the global version clock. This way TINYSTM enhances a transaction's possibility of committing.

8   Pessimistic STM Implementations

STM algorithms presented thus far have employed an *optimistic* approach to conflict resolution. This means that transactions execute as if they were expecting to encounter no conflicts and deal with conflicts only after they arise. *Pessimistic* STM algorithms, on the other hand, take appropriate actions, so that transactions do not encounter any conflicts when accessing data items. This leads to algorithms where transactions never abort.

8.1   Pessimistic Software Lock Elision

Pessimistic Software Lock Elision (PLE) is a technique that was introduced by Afek, Matveev and Shavit in [4]. PLE implements read-only transactions that are wait-free but it does so by serializing the execution of update transactions.

PLE uses a coarse-grain lock WL which an update transaction T must acquire in order to obtain ownership of the entire space of data items. Ownership acquisition is eager as T attempts to lock WL when it starts its execution. Thus, as long as T holds the lock, no other update transaction can make progress. Therefore, the execution of update transactions is totally serialized.

PLE assigns versions per stripe with an additional shared variable, called GV, to serve as a version counter. PLE employs direct updates. However, T maintains a write-set in its transactional record where it stores the previous value and version of each data item it updates. The data items representation is in-place and thread-aware; once T acquires the lock, it writes the identifier of the thread that initiated T into a shared variable, called WID. This enables read-only transactions that conflict with T to have access to T's write-set (where they can find previous values for the data items updated by T). After T has acquired WL and written the identifier of its initiator thread into WID, it copies locally the current value of GV. It next (locally) increments this value to obtain its write version number. Then, T performs its updates in a direct way and sets the version of each data item it writes to be equal with its write version number.

PLE employs a global announce array A where read-only transactions announce themselves. Thus, read-only transactions are visible. A read-only transaction T' reads the value of GV when it starts its execution and stores this value - which will act as its read version number - in the element of A that corresponds to the thread that initiated T'. When T' accesses a data item x, it compares x's version against its own read version number. If they are the same, T' reads the value of x directly. If they are not, then some update transaction T has updated x while T' was executing. In this case, to preserve the consistency of its read-set, T' must read the value that x had before the update by T. T' can find this value in T's write-set. To access T's write-set, T' reads the identifier of the thread that initiated T' in WID. In order for this to be safe, at commit time, T first writes its write version number into GV and then scans the announce array until all read-only transactions that have a read version number less than T's write version number, have terminated. At commit time, a read-only transaction simply sets its announce array element to the maximal possible value (so as not to cause any update transaction to wait for it) and terminates.

8.2   Other Pessimistic STM Algorithms

PLE [4] is a successor of a pessimistic STM algorithm presented in [44]. Characteristics similar to theirs were previously exhibited by techniques such as [65], which enhances an STM algorithm with the possibility of rendering one transaction at a time irrevocable using a fine-grained technique. More coarse-grained techniques are explored in [47,53]. A broader spectrum of implementations was discussed in [60]. Once a transaction becomes irrevocable, it is guaranteed not to abort. It eagerly acquires write ownerships and executes visible reads. It can perform its update on a data item once it ensures that it is not concurrently accessed by other transactions, aborting them if necessary. However, a transaction does not start as irrevocable and has to compete during the course of its execution in order to attempt to gain irrevocability. A failed attempt can lead it to abort.

An opaque STM system, called SEMANTICTM, that executes transactions without ever causing any aborts is presented in [18,19]. SEMANTICTM uses a set of *t-var lists*, one for each transactional variable. The instructions of each transaction are placed in the appropriate t-var lists based on which data item each of them accesses. A set of worker threads execute these instructions. SEMANTICTM ensures that no conflict ever occurs and exhibits fine-grained parallelism at the level of transactional instructions (instead of at the level of transactions themselves). SEMANTICTM works well for simple transactions that access a known set of data items, and their codes contain READDI and WRITEDI instructions on them, conditionals, loops, and function calls. For such transactions, SEMANTICTM ensures wait-freedom. The authors of [18,19] also present ideas for extending SEMANTICTM to work for more complicated transactions.

Acknowledgments. The authors were supported by funding from project "IRAKLITOS II - University of Crete" of the Operational Programme for Education and Lifelong Learning 2007 - 2013 (E.P.E.D.V.M.) of the NSRF (2007 - 2013), which is co-funded by the European Union (European Social Fund) and National Resources. They were also supported by the European Commission under the 7th Framework Program through the TransForm (FP7-MC-ITN-238639) project and by the ARISTEIA Action of the Operational Programme Education and Lifelong Learning which is co-funded by the European Social Fund (ESF) and National Resources through the GreenVM project.

References

1. Abadi, M., Birrell, A., Harris, T., Isard, M.: Semantics of transactional memory and automatic mutual exclusion. ACM Trans. Program. Lang. Syst. 33(1), 2:1–2:50 (2011)
2. Adl-Tabatabai, A.R., Lewis, B.T., Menon, V., Murphy, B.R., Saha, B., Shpeisman, T.: Compiler and runtime support for efficient software transactional memory. SIGPLAN Not 41(6), 26–37 (2006)
3. Afek, Y., Avni, H., Dice, D., Shavit, N.: Efficient lock free privatization. In: Lu, C., Masuzawa, T., Mosbah, M. (eds.) OPODIS 2010. LNCS, vol. 6490, pp. 333–347. Springer, Heidelberg (2010)
4. Afek, Y., Matveev, A., Shavit, N.: Pessimistic software lock-elision. In: Aguilera, M.K. (ed.) DISC 2012. LNCS, vol. 7611, pp. 297–311. Springer, Heidelberg (2012)

5. Agrawal, K., Fineman, J.T., Sukha, J.: Nested parallelism in transactional memory. In: Proceedings of the 13th ACM SIGPLAN Symposium on Principles and Practice of Parallel Programming (PPoPP), pp. 163–174. ACM, New York (2008)

6. Attiya, H., Epstein, L., Shachnai, H., Tamir, T.: Transactional contention management as a non-clairvoyant scheduling problem. In: Proceedings of the 25th ACM Symposium on Principles of Distributed Computing (PODC), pp. 308–315. ACM, New York (2006)

7. Attiya, H., Hans, S.: Transactions are back—but how different they are? In: 7th ACM SIGPLAN Workshop on Transactional Computing (Transact), New Orleans, LA, USA (February 2012)

8. Attiya, H., Hans, S., Kuznetsov, P., Ravi, S.: Safety of deferred update in transactional memory. CoRR abs/1301.6297 (2013), http://arxiv.org/abs/1301.6297

9. Attiya, H., Hillel, E.: A single-version STM that is multi-versioned permissive. Theory Comput. Syst. 51(4), 425–446 (2012)

10. Avni, H., Shavit, N.N.: Maintaining consistent transactional states without a global clock. In: Shvartsman, A.A., Felber, P. (eds.) SIROCCO 2008. LNCS, vol. 5058, pp. 131–140. Springer, Heidelberg (2008)

11. Bloom, B.H.: Space/time trade-offs in hash coding with allowable errors. Commun. ACM 13(7), 422–426 (1970)

12. Bushkov, V., Dziuma, D., Fatourou, P., Guerraoui, R.: The pcl theorem: Transactions cannot be parallel, consistent and live. In: Proceedings of the 26th ACM Symposium on Parallelism in Algorithms and Architectures (SPAA), pp. 178–187. ACM, New York (2014)

13. Dalessandro, L., Spear, M.F., Scott, M.L.: Norec: streamlining stm by abolishing ownership records. In: Proceedings of the 15th ACM SIGPLAN Symposium on Principles and Practice of Parallel Programming (PPoPP), pp. 67–78. ACM, New York (2010)

14. Dice, D., Shavit, N.: What really makes transactions faster? In: 1st ACM SIGPLAN Workshop on Transactional Computing (Transact), Ottawa, Canada (June 2006)

15. Dice, D., Shalev, O., Shavit, N.: Transactional locking II. In: Dolev, S. (ed.) DISC 2006. LNCS, vol. 4167, pp. 194–208. Springer, Heidelberg (2006)

16. Dice, D., Shavit, N.: Tlrw: return of the read-write lock. In: Proceedings of the 22nd ACM symposium on Parallelism in Algorithms and Architectures (SPAA), pp. 284–293. ACM, New York (2010)

17. Doherty, S., Groves, L., Luchangco, V., Moir, M.: Towards formally specifying and verifying transactional memory. Formal Aspects of Computing 25(5), 769–799 (2013)

18. Dolev, S., Fatourou, P., Kosmas, E.: Abort free SemanticTM by dependency aware scheduling of transactional instructions. In: 8th ACM SIGPLAN Workshop on Transactional Computing (Transact), Houston, TX, USA (March 2013)

19. Avni, H., Dolev, S., Fatourou, P., Kosmas, E.: Abort free semanticTM by dependency aware scheduling of transactional instructions. In: Noubir, G., Raynal, M. (eds.) NETYS 2013. LNCS, vol. 8593, pp. 25–40. Springer, Heidelberg (2014)

20. Dragojevic, A., Guerraoui, R., Kapalka, M.: Stretching transactional memory. In: Proceedings of the 2009 ACM SIGPLAN Conference on Programming Language Design and Implementation (PLDI), pp. 155–165. ACM, New York (2009)

21. Dziuma, D., Fatourou, P., Kanellou, E.: Consistency for transactional memory computing. Bulletin of European Association for Theoretical Computer Science (EATCS) 113, 112–135 (2014)

22. Ennals, R.: Cache sensitive software transactional memory. Tech. rep., Intel Research, Cambridge, United Kingdom (2005)

23. Ennals, R.: Software transactional memory should not be obstruction-free. Tech. Rep. IRC-TR–06–052, Intel Corporation (January 2006)

24. Felber, P., Fetzer, C., Riegel, T.: Dynamic performance tuning of word-based software transactional memory. In: Proceedings of the 13th ACM SIGPLAN Symposium on Principles and Practice of Parallel Programming (PPoPP), pp. 237–246. ACM, New York (2008)
25. Fraser, K.: Practical lock freedom. Ph.D. thesis, Cambridge University Computer Laboratory (2003), also available as Technical Report UCAM-CL-TR-579
26. Gottschlich, J.E., Vachharajani, M., Siek, J.G.: An efficient software transactional memory using commit-time invalidation. In: Proceedings of the 8th Annual IEEE/ACM International Symposium on Code Generation and Optimization (CGO), pp. 101–110. IEEE Computer Society, ACM, New York (2010)
27. Guerraoui, R., Herlihy, M., Kapalka, M., Pochon, B.: Robust contention management in software transactional memory. In: Workshop on Synchronization and Concurrency in Object-Oriented Lanugages (SCOOL) (2005)
28. Guerraoui, R., Herlihy, M., Pochon, B.: Toward a theory of transactional contention managers. In: Proceedings of the 24th ACM Symposium on Principles of Distributed Computing (PODC), pp. 258–264. ACM, New York (2005)
29. Guerraoui, R., Kapalka, M.: On the correctness of transactional memory. In: Proceedings of the 13th ACM SIGPLAN Symposium on Principles and Practice of Parallel Programming (PPoPP), pp. 175–184. ACM, New York (2008)
30. Harris, T., Fraser, K.: Language support for lightweight transactions. SIGPLAN Not 38(11), 388–402 (2003)
31. Harris, T., Larus, J., Rajwar, R.: Transactional Memory, 2nd edn. Morgan and Claypool Publishers (2010)
32. Harris, T., Plesko, M., Shinnar, A., Tarditi, D.: Optimizing memory transactions. In: Proceedings of the 2006 ACM SIGPLAN Conference on Programming Language Design and Implementation (PLDI), pp. 14–25. ACM, New York (2006)
33. Herlihy, M., Luchangco, V., Moir, M., Scherer III, W.N.: Software transactional memory for dynamic-sized data structures. In: Proceedings of the 22nd ACM Symposium on Principles of Distributed Computing (PODC), pp. 92–101. ACM, New York (2003)
34. Herlihy, M., Moss, J.E.B.: Transactional memory: architectural support for lock-free data structures. SIGARCH Comput. Archit. News 21, 289–300 (1993)
35. Hudson, R.L., Saha, B., Adl-Tabatabai, A.R., Hertzberg, B.C.: Mcrt-malloc: A scalable transactional memory allocator. In: Proceedings of the 5th International Symposium on Memory Management (ISMM), pp. 74–83. ACM, New York (2006)
36. Imbs, D., Raynal, M.: Virtual world consistency: A condition for stm systems (with a versatile protocol with invisible read operations). Theor. Comput. Sci. 444, 113–127 (2012)
37. Kosmas, E.: Software Transactional Memory. Master's thesis, University of Ioannina (October 2008) (in Greek)
38. Marathe, V.J., Scherer III, W.N., Scott, M.L.: Design tradeoffs in modern software transactional memory systems. In: Proceedings of the 7th Workshop on Workshop on Languages, Compilers, and Run-time Support for Scalable Systems (LCR), pp. 1–7. ACM, New York (2004)
39. Marathe, V.J., Scherer III, W.N., Scott, M.L.: Adaptive software transactional memory. In: Fraigniaud, P. (ed.) DISC 2005. LNCS, vol. 3724, pp. 354–368. Springer, Heidelberg (2005)
40. Marathe, V.J., Spear, M.F., Heriot, C., Acharya, A., Eisenstat, D., Scherer III, W.N., Scott, M.L.: Lowering the overhead of nonblocking software transactional memory. Tech. Rep. 893, Department of Computer Science, University of Rochester (May 2006)
41. Marathe, V.J., Spear, M.F., Scott, M.L.: Scalable techniques for transparent privatization in software transactional memory. In: Proceedings of the 37th International Conference on Parallel Processing (ICPP), pp. 67–74. IEEE Computer Society (2008)

42. Marathe, V.J., Moir, M.: Toward high performance nonblocking software transactional memory. In: Proceedings of the 13th ACM SIGPLAN Symposium on Principles and Practice of Parallel Programming (PPoPP), pp. 227–236. ACM, New York (2008)
43. Martin, M.M.K., Blundell, C., Lewis, E.: Subtleties of transactional memory atomicity semantics. Computer Architecture Letters 5(2) (2006)
44. Matveev, A., Shavit, N.: Towards a fully pessimistic stm model. In: 7th ACM SIGPLAN Workshop on Transactional Computing (Transact), New Orleans, LA, USA (February 2012)
45. Minh, C.C., Trautmann, M., Chung, J., McDonald, A., Bronson, N., Casper, J., Kozyrakis, C., Olukotun, K.: An effective hybrid transactional memory system with strong isolation guarantees. In: Proceedings of the 34th Annual International Symposium on Computer Architecture (ISCA), pp. 69–80. ACM, New York (2007)
46. Moss, J.E.B., Hosking, A.L.: Nested transactional memory: Model and architecture sketches. Sci. Comput. Program. 63(2), 186–201 (2006),
    http://dx.doi.org/10.1016/j.scico.2006.05.010
47. Ni, Y., Welc, A., Adl-Tabatabai, A., Bach, M., Berkowits, S., Cownie, J., Geva, R., Kozhukow, S., Narayanaswamy, R., Olivier, J., Preis, S., Saha, B., Tal, A., Tian, X.: Design and implementation of transactional constructs for C/C++. In: Proceedings of the 23rd Annual ACM SIGPLAN Conference on Object-Oriented Programming, Systems, Languages, and Applications (OOPSLA), pp. 195–212. ACM, New York (2008)
48. Olszewski, M., Cutler, J., Steffan, J.G.: Judostm: A dynamic binary-rewriting approach to software transactional memory. In: Proceedings of the 16th International Conference on Parallel Architecture and Compilation Techniques (PACT), pp. 365–375. IEEE Computer Society, Washington, DC (2007)
49. Papadimitriou, C.H.: The serializability of concurrent database updates. J. ACM 26, 631–653 (1979)
50. Riegel, T.: Snapshot isolation for software transactional memory. In: 1st ACM SIGPLAN Workshop on Transactional Computing (Transact), Ottawa, Canada (March 2006)
51. Riegel, T., Felber, P., Fetzer, C.: A lazy snapshot algorithm with eager validation. In: Dolev, S. (ed.) DISC 2006. LNCS, vol. 4167, pp. 284–298. Springer, Heidelberg (2006)
52. Riegel, T., Fetzer, C., Felber, P.: Time-based transactional memory with scalable time bases. In: Proceedings of the 19th ACM Symposium on Parallel Algorithms and Architectures (SPAA), pp. 221–228. ACM, New York (2007)
53. Riegel, T., Fetzer, C., Felber, P.: Automatic data partitioning in software transactional memories. In: Proceedings of the 20th ACM Symposium on Parallelism in Algorithms and Architectures (SPAA), pp. 152–159. ACM, New York (2008)
54. Romano, P., Carvalho, N., Rodrigues, L.: Towards distributed software transactional memory systems. In: Proceedings of the 2nd Workshop on Large-Scale Distributed Systems and Middleware (LADIS), pp. 4:1–4:4. ACM, New York (2008)
55. Scherer III, W.N., Scott, M.L.: Advanced contention management for dynamic software transactional memory. In: Proceedings of the 24th ACM Symposium on Principles of Distributed Computing (PODC), pp. 240–248. ACM, New York (2005)
56. Scott, M.L., Spear, M.F., Dalessandro, L., Marathe, V.J.: Transactions and privatization in delaunay triangulation. In: Proceedings of the 26th ACM Symposium on Principles of Distributed Computing (PODC), pp. 336–337. ACM, New York (2007)
57. Shavit, N., Touitou, D.: Software transactional memory. In: Proceedings of the 14th ACM Symposium on Principles of Distributed Computing (PODC), pp. 204–213. ACM, New York (1995)
58. Spear, M.F., Dalessandro, L., Marathe, V.J., Scott, M.L.: A comprehensive strategy for contention management in software transactional memory. In: Proceedings of the 14th ACM SIGPLAN Symposium on Principles and Practice of Parallel Programming (PPoPP), pp. 141–150. ACM, New York (2009)

59. Spear, M.F., Marathe, V.J., Dalessandro, L., Scott, M.L.: Privatization techniques for software transactional memory. In: Proceedings of the 26th ACM Symposium on Principles of Distributed Computing (PODC), pp. 338–339. ACM, New York (2007)

60. Spear, M.F., Michael, M., Scott, M.L.: Inevitability mechanisms for software transactional memory. In: 3rd ACM SIGPLAN Workshop on Transactional Computing (Transact), Salt Lake City, Utah, USA (February 2008)

61. Spear, M.F., Michael, M.M., von Praun, C.: Ringstm: scalable transactions with a single atomic instruction. In: Proceedings of the 20th ACM Symposium on Parallelism in Algorithms and Architectures (SPAA), pp. 275–284. ACM, New York (2008)

62. Spear, M.F., Dalessandro, L., Marathe, V.J., Scott, M.L.: Ordering-based semantics for software transactional memory. In: Baker, T.P., Bui, A., Tixeuil, S. (eds.) OPODIS 2008. LNCS, vol. 5401, pp. 275–294. Springer, Heidelberg (2008)

63. Tabba, F., Moir, M., Goodman, J.R., Hay, A.W., Wang, C.: Nztm: Nonblocking zero-indirection transactional memory. In: Proceedings of the 21st ACM Symposium on Parallelism in Algorithms and Architectures (SPAA), pp. 204–213. ACM, New York (2009)

64. Wang, C., Chen, W.Y., Wu, Y., Saha, B., Adl-Tabatabai, A.R.: Code generation and optimization for transactional memory constructs in an unmanaged language. In: Proceedings of the 5th Annual IEEE/ACM International Symposium on Code Generation and Optimization (CGO), pp. 34–48. IEEE Computer Society, ACM, New York, USA (2007)

65. Welc, A., Saha, B., Adl-Tabatabai, A.R.: Irrevocable transactions and their applications. In: Proceedings of the 20th ACM Symposium on Parallelism in Algorithms and Architectures (SPAA), pp. 285–296. ACM, New York (2008)

Conflict Detection in Hardware Transactional Memory

Ricardo Quislant, Eladio Gutierrez, Emilio L. Zapata, and Oscar Plata

Dept. Computer Architecture, University of Malaga, E-29071, Malaga, Spain
{quislant,eladio,zapata,oplata}@uma.es

Abstract. This chapter is dedicated to the conflict detection mechanism in the context of hardware transactional memory (HTM) systems. An effective mechanism is needed to detect conflicts amongst transactions, thus ensuring atomicity while allowing concurrency. Together with version management and conflict resolution, the conflict detection mechanism is one of the main design choices in HTM systems.

In this chapter, the two most common ways of detecting conflicts are described: eager and lazy. Then, we discuss the main HTM approaches to conflict detection, from the very first system proposed by Herlihy and Moss in 1993, to the commercial systems delivered by Intel or IBM, amongst others. Finally, a survey on conflict detection virtualization, i.e. support for unbounded transactions, is presented, emphasizing the signature topic.

1 Introduction

One of the most important design choices in hardware transactional memory (HTM) systems is how to address the conflict detection problem. Transactions must be perceived by the user as though they were a single, indivisible instruction. That is, the HTM system must ensure the *atomicity* property of transactions. A single global lock is able to provide atomicity, but eliminates concurrency. In order for a HTM system to exploit potential parallelism, an effective mechanism must be designed that keeps track of every memory access issued by transactions to detect conflicts amongst them and preserve atomicity.

Conflict detection mechanisms can be classified into two main categories depending on when data conflicts are detected: *eager* and *lazy*.

Eager Conflict Detection

When conflicts are detected eagerly, the HTM system has to intercept each memory access so that the conflict is detected just before it occurs. This way of detecting conflicts is *conservative* since it keeps transactions from working with stale data, thus reducing the amount of useless computation.

Eager conflict detection can be combined with either form of version management, also categorized as *eager* and *lazy*, where eager version management updates transactional data directly to memory, and lazy version management isolates transactional writes into a private buffer. We can therefore find eager-eager HTM approaches [4,19] and eager-lazy ones [2,15,26].

R. Guerraoui and P. Romano (Eds.): Transactional Memory, LNCS 8913, pp. 127–149, 2015.

Most HTM systems rely on the cache coherence mechanism to detect conflicts early [2,15,19,27]. Note that having transactional state together with each cache block allows the conflict detection mechanism to check for conflicts in an effective way. Although the cache coherence protocol is a critical element of a multicore processor, which is difficult to specify and verify [31], this is a common way to address eager conflict detection implementation.

As far as conflict resolution is concerned, eager conflict detection enables another alternative than aborting transactions, which is *stalling* them [19]. As conflicts are detected just before happening, the HTM system might as well delay the resolution of the conflicting memory access until it is not a conflict anymore. The involved transaction is then stalled and its work preserved unless the transaction has to be aborted eventually, either to ensure forward progress or to avoid performance pathologies [5].

Lazy Conflict Detection

With lazy conflict detection the HTM system allows transactions to access shared data concurrently regardless of conflicts, whose detection is deferred to commit time. This kind of conflict detection is *optimistic*, as it encourages parallelism. However, the lazy approach could readily serialize execution when conflicts are often encountered, because the only conflict resolution possibility is to abort one of the conflicting transactions. In general, stalling is impossible with lazy conflict detection. The increased level of speculation translates into an increased amount of discarded computation in case of conflict. On the other hand, anti-dependencies (WAR) and output dependencies (WAW) can be filtered out as the instructions of the committing transaction are considered sequentially earlier than the instructions of the other transactions that have not yet committed.

Unlike eager conflict detection, lazy conflict detection can be coupled only with lazy version management. Otherwise, the isolation property of transactions would not be enforced as conflicts are not detected until commit time. We can find several lazy-lazy HTM systems in the literature [7,14].

The lazy conflict detection mechanism can simplify the implementation of the HTM system by minimizing added complexity to the cache coherence protocol and primary caches. Private buffers are often used to keep new versions of the data accessed by a transaction. But the system must deal with an increased interconnection network traffic as the transactional state of a transaction has to be broadcast in order for the rest of processors to detect conflicts.

A third form of conflict detection can be considered for those systems that allow validations inside transactions. *Conflict validation* consists of checking that the data accessed by a transaction have not been updated by other transactions, and it can be thought of as a way to attain a trade-off between eager and lazy conflict detection, since it can be performed at any point in the transaction. Although validation is more frequent in software transactional memory (STM) systems, we can also find it in HTM systems [15], where the conflict is detected eagerly but users can be notified whenever they ask for validation.

HTM system proposals can also be classified by the amount of transactional accesses they are able to track. This can be determined by either the conflict detection or the version management mechanism. Depending on whether or not HTM systems can cope with transactions of any duration and size, they can be classified into *unbounded* and *bounded* HTM systems. Bounded systems, also known as best-effort HTM systems, are able to deal with transactions that do not overflow their hardware resources or do not survive operating system events. Some of them burden programmers with the task of handling overflow events, which defeats a key TM motivation: reducing the difficulty of parallel programming. Conversely, unbounded systems deploy mechanisms to tackle transactions of any size and duration, thus facilitating the task of transactional programming.

In this chapter, we focus on hardware conflict detection from the point of view of bounded and unbounded HTM systems. Section 2 discusses the main HTM proposals with bounded conflict detection mechanisms. The recent approaches of main hardware manufacturers are also surveyed. Section 3 is devoted to the unbounded HTM system proposals and their conflict detection mechanisms, with special interest in signatures as the means to effective conflict detection virtualization. Finally, Section 4 draws the conclusions.

2 Bounded Conflict Detection

This section discusses several HTM systems that implements bounded conflict detection mechanisms. These *best-effort* systems execute transactions properly as long as certain events do not occur during the execution.

The main events that can abort transactions in a bounded HTM system, apart from conflicts, are those coming from the operating system (OS) and the ones caused by hardware overflow. In regard to OS events, virtual memory paging can cause the relocation of pages that contain transactional data, which means that the physical address of the data has changed and the conflict detection mechanism loses track of the locations accessed by a transaction. Also, context switches caused by descheduling or thread migration are difficult to manage if the transactional information is not visible to the OS. As far as hardware overflow is concerned, bounded HTM systems are not able to execute transactions whose data set (DS) is larger than the hardware structures used to hold it. Usually, the response to these events is to abort the transaction in the hope that they do not happen again. This can work in case of OS events. However, overflow events are likely to recur, thus risking livelock whenever a fall-back solution is not provided.

The remainder of this section deals with bounded conflict detection in bounded HTM systems that use the cache coherence protocol to enforce atomicity (Section 2.1). We also discuss those systems that use alternative methods to implement the conflict detection mechanism (Section 2.2). We then review the main approaches taken by hardware manufacturers (Section 2.3).

2.1 Leveraging the Cache Coherence Protocol

There are several bounded HTM system proposals in the literature that modify the cache coherence protocol to implement the conflict detection mechanism [2,15,19,27].

They usually implement eager conflict detection. Next, the most relevant characteristics of them are described.

Herlihy and Moss [15] were the first to propose a HTM implementation leveraging the cache coherence protocol to detect conflicts amongst transactions and ensure atomicity. Figure 1 depicts the hardware needed to implement their proposal. They use a *transactional cache* besides the private primary cache to keep track of the data accessed by transactions, both old and new values. New transactional states are added to those of the coherence protocol to indicate whether the entry is old or new. Data updates are performed over the new version. Old versions are discarded (invalidated) on commits, and new versions are invalidated on aborts. The transactional cache is fully associative and has additional logic to perform commits and aborts in a single cache cycle, as they assume a few entries are needed per transaction. The primary cache and the transactional cache are exclusive, so a location can only be in one of them at a time, and the coherence protocol probes both caches in parallel.

Herlihy and Moss modify an invalidation-based snoopy coherence protocol [13] to add three more messages related to transactional accesses. One of the new messages requests a location needed by a transactional load, the second one is for requesting a location needed by a transactional exclusive load or a transactional store, and the third message signals a conflict for requested transactional locations (busy message). When a transaction loads a location, its transactional cache is searched just in case the location was previously written by the same transaction. In case of a miss, a transactional load message is broadcast to check all the transactional caches. This is done in one cycle, as transactional caches are fully associative. If there is at least one hit in the transactional caches, a busy message is sent to the requesting core. Then, the requesting core sets a flag to false (aborted), indicating that the transaction conflicted and must abort. Subsequent transactional loads and stores of the conflicting transaction do not cause network traffic and may return arbitrary values. Therefore, conflict detection can be said to be eager, although the conflict does not resolve until the program executes a commit/abort/validate instruction that checks the abort flag.

The use of a fully-associative cache is an important implementation constraint due to its higher hardware requirements and the slower access time compared with other implementations. Also, a bus-based coherence protocol limits scalability.

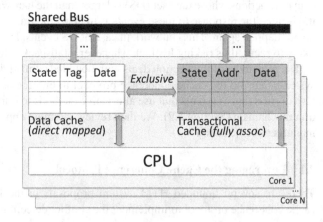

Fig. 1. Herlihy and Moss HTM implementation. Transactional data are stored in an exclusive transactional cache apart from the private primary cache. The snooping coherence protocol probes both caches in parallel on request. The cache coherence protocol is modified to detect conflicts eagerly.

Another approach to bounded conflict detection is that of Moore et al. [19]. They propose LogTM, a HTM system implementation devised to provide better scalability and to support larger transactions than the Herlihy and Moss proposal. LogTM virtualizes version management by using the concept of *before-image log* taken from the data base field, where old values are saved in a per-thread log in cacheable virtual memory. New values are kept in place and isolation is ensured by the coherence protocol. The log allows unbounded version management, unlike the fully-associative cache of Herlihy and Moss, but it has the disadvantage of slow aborts, as the log has to be *undone* to restore old versions. Nevertheless, LogTM is bounded because of the conflict detection mechanism.

Figure 2 shows the hardware needed to implement conflict detection in LogTM. Private caches are augmented with transactional read (R) and write (W) bits per cache block. These bits are set whenever a location is read or written by a transaction to keep track of its *read set* (RS) and *write set* (WS). The cache must support flash clear of these bits to reset them when a transaction commits. The system implements a directory that holds a bit vector of sharers per memory block so that the coherence protocol knows which cores share the block (multiple readers) or which one owns it (one writer). When a transaction running in core X requests a block that has been written by another transaction running in core A, the coherence protocol (by means of the directory) forwards the request to core A, which checks the block against its private caches. If the check is a hit and the W bit is set, then core A accessed the block transactionally. Therefore, core A sends a NACK message (like Herlihy's busy message) to core X, which has to manage the conflict.

LogTM deals with transaction overflow in a peculiar manner. A novel "sticky" state is defined for those blocks in the directory that were evicted from the second level cache (L2) during the execution of a transaction. Hence, subsequent requests for those blocks are still forwarded to that core. The core should check its caches on a forwarded request for an evicted block. However, the block is not in the caches anymore, so the core should respond with an ACK, which would result in an atomicity violation. The Overflow bit is used to avoid this situation. The bit is set whenever a transactional block is evicted, and

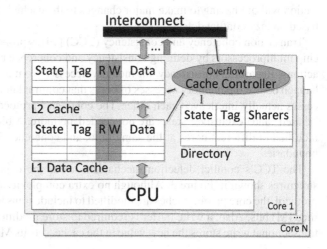

Fig. 2. LogTM implementation. Transactional state is supported by R/W bits per cache block. The directory is not updated when a cache block is evicted. Instead, the block state is changed to "sticky", and requests are still forwarded to the core ensuring atomicity. The cache controller's Overflow flag is set when transactional data are evicted.

the controller checks the bit when a block is not in the caches. If the Overflow bit is set, the core conservatively NACKs the requester. Sticky states are cleaned lazily once the transaction has committed. A forwarded request due to a stale sticky state is responded with a message to clean the sticky state as long as the Overflow bit of the core is cleared. Otherwise, false conflicts can arise because of overlapping of stale sticky states from an earlier transactions with an overflowed current one.

Although LogTM can cope with larger transactions it is still a bounded HTM system. OS events cannot be survived because conflict detection information is not persistent since it cannot be saved in a context change. Furthermore, LogTM does not resolve replacements of sticky blocks in the directory.

Having transactional bits or tags to label cache blocks that have been accessed by transactions, along with the modification of the cache coherence protocol to maintain atomicity are the main techniques when it comes to implementing the conflict detection mechanism in these bounded systems. Some approaches before LogTM have used these same techniques although with certain subtleties. Speculative lock elision (SLE) [27] associates an Access bit with each cache block that interacts with the coherence protocol. The difference is that SLE accepts code with locks as input, elides the lock and speculatively executes the critical section enclosed by the lock as though it is a transaction. In case of repeated speculation failure because of conflicts, the lock is acquired and progress guaranteed. Large transactional memory (LTM) [2] has a T bit per cache block to label transactional data. The cache coherence protocol uses NACK messages to hint conflicts. LTM is different from LogTM in the way it deals with cache overflows. Each cache set is extended with an overflow bit that is set when the block is evicted. Then, the block moves into an uncached hash table in memory that has to be traversed by the core on each request from other cores.

2.2 Alternatives to Cache Coherence Protocol Modification

Adding complexity to an already complex mechanism like the cache coherence protocol or to a fine-tuned structure like a cache memory could bring implementation issues. Some alternative implementations have been proposed to manage conflict detection without having to make major changes to the cache hierarchy. They are usually based on lazy conflict detection [7,14].

Transaction coherency and consistency (TCC) [14] is proposed to ease the design of chip multiprocessors by defining consistency and coherence at the granularity of transactions. Regarding consistency, all memory accesses from a core that commits earlier happen before the memory accesses of cores that commit later, regardless of if such accesses actually interleaved each other. The coherence protocol is also simplified since "shared" and "exclusive" states are not needed anymore. A block can be unmodified or modified in different cores at the same time, and coherency is enforced at transaction boundaries.

The TCC's conflict detection mechanism needs the deployment of the hardware structures shown in Figure 3. Although no extra complexity is added to the coherence protocol, the core private caches are modified to include transactional read (R) and modified (M) bits. Also, a write buffer is required to store modified data addresses. Thus, a transactional write stores the new value in the cache, sets its M bit and stores the address in the write buffer. Transactional loads simply set the R bit. Once the transaction comes to commit, the core broadcasts the write buffer for the other cores to check it against their R bits (notice that WAR and WAW dependencies are filtered out). If a core finds a conflict, it invalidates its modified data by transferring (through NOT gates) the W bits to the valid bits (V) of the cache, thus keeping caches coherent. An alternative implementation broadcasts addresses and data to update other caches instead of invalidating their copies of the data. TCC also suggests an optimization by means of the Rename bit field that avoids false conflicts because of false sharing of cache blocks. It extends the M bit to each word or byte in the cache block.

Hammond et al.'s TCC conflict detection mechanism is bounded by the size of the cache and the write buffer. If these structures overflow, they propose to request commit permission, which ensures that all earlier transactions have committed and no other has begun, so there is no need to track transactional information anymore. However, this can be severely detrimental to the system performance. Also, the commit phase may suppose a bottleneck to scalability as addresses have to be broadcast one by one, or in packets. The network bandwidth requirements could increase dramatically, specially if data are transferred as well.

Qian et al. present OmniOrder [21], a lazy-lazy HTM system that keeps the cache coherence protocol untouched and conflict-serializes transactions to avoid unnecessary aborts. The history of transactional stores to a memory block is maintained in a per-processor fully associative buffer called speculative version buffer (SVB). The SVB's information for a memory block is moved piggybacked on coherence messages on each block's transition to the M state in a directory-based MESI coherence protocol [30]. From these transitions, each core figures out the processors that are executing predecessor and successor transactions to the one it is executing, and stores that information into bitmask registers. Thus, if processor P1 updates block B, the coherence protocol brings B to P1's cache an set the B's state to M. The new value of B is also stored in the P1's SVB. When another processor, P2, updates B, the unmodified coherence protocol moves B to P2's cache and invalidates the block in the P1's cache. P1 piggybacks the SVB's entry for B in the coherence message and P2 is now responsible for it. Also,

Fig. 3. TCC implementation. A write buffer is added to store the addresses of transactional modified data. Such a buffer is broadcast on commit for other cores to check it against their transactional read bits (R). In case of conflict, their modified data (M) is invalidated (V). Alternatively, the write buffer can be broadcast together with the modified values in order to update instead of invalidating.

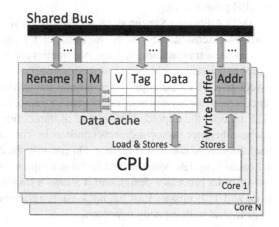

P1 is marked as predecessor of P2 so that P2 must commit after P1 filtering out the WAW output dependence. In case of a cycle where a group of processors are both in the predecessor and the successor list of each other, one transaction must be aborted to break the cycle. On L1 cache evictions, OmniOrder aborts the transaction and restarts it in a conventional transactional mode that does not expose its transactional state to other transactions.

2.3 Hardware Manufacturers' Approaches

Hardware manufacturers include HTM support in their multiprocessors that is bounded and based on the cache hierarchy. Below we describe the main HTM extensions focusing on the implementation of the conflict detection mechanism.

Sun Microsystems' Rock multicore processor was the first production processor to include HTM support [8], although it was never distributed commercially as a result of Sun acquisition by Oracle. Each Rock core has hardware support to run two threads simultaneously. Rock implements a form of speculative threading that uses the second thread to execute the code whose data is not yet available because of long-latency instructions. Rock leverages the speculative threading hardware to support HTM. In addition, two new instructions have been added to the instruction set: checkpoint fail-pc to denote the beginning of a transaction, which accepts a pointer to compensating action code used in case of abort, and commit to denote the end of the transaction. Also, cache lines include a bit to mark lines as transactional. Stores within the transaction are placed in the store queue and sent to the L2 cache, which tracks conflicts with loads and stores from other threads. If the L2 cache detects a conflict, it reports the conflict to the core, which aborts the transaction. When the commit instruction begins, the L2 cache locks all lines being written by the transaction. Locked lines cannot be read or written by any other threads, thus ensuring atomicity. Rock's TM supports efficient execution of moderately sized transactions that fit within the hardware resources. However, a wide variety of events may abort a transaction: invalidation or replacement of cache lines marked as transactional, interrupts and processor exceptions, TLB misses, context switches, divide instructions, etc. These constraints make it difficult to predict and reason about why transactions abort, thus complicating parallel programming.

AMD Advanced Synchronization Facility (ASF) [11] is proposed as an eager-lazy AMD64 extension. ASF adds two bits per L1 cache line to mark read and written data inside a transaction. Besides, two queues are used to hold transactional loads and stores to guarantee a higher minimum transaction length. This is because a 4-way set-associative L1 cache implies a minimum transaction size of 4 different cache blocks, since a mapping miss in a set might cause a transaction to abort. With this design choice ASF reduces the unpredictable nature of transactions, unlike Rock's HTM. The AMD cache coherence protocol detects conflicts by checking the cache transactional bits on each forwarded coherence request. On commit, the cache bits are flash-cleared and the L1 cache is update with the data in the store queue. ASF is designed to coexist with an out-of-order processor design and it allows a transaction to survive branch mispredictions and TLB misses. Last but not least, programmers need to write software fallback code to deal with capacity overflows.

Intel has released its Transactional Synchronization Extensions (TSX) [28] on the multicore processor code-named *Haswell*. TSX provides two interfaces to denote transactional code. The first one is known as Hardware Lock Elision (HLE — similar to SLE described in Section 2.1), and involves two prefixes for instructions: XACQUIRE and XRELEASE. HLE is compatible with the conventional lock-based programming model. So, software written using the HLE prefixes can run on both legacy hardware without TSX and new hardware with TSX, since the prefixes correspond to the REPNE/REPE IA-32 prefixes which are ignored on the instructions where XACQUIRE and XRELEASE are valid. Thus, the programmer uses the XACQUIRE prefix in front of the instruction that is used to acquire the lock which is protecting the critical section. The processor treats the indication as a hint to elide the write associated with the lock acquire operation, and a transaction is started instead. If the transaction aborts, the processor will roll back the execution and then resume it non-transactionally. In case of a processor not supporting TSX, the lock is acquired normally, and the execution is serialized. The second interface provided by TSX is known as Restricted Transactional Memory (RTM) and allows more flexibility in transaction declaration than HLE. RTM adds three new instruction to the ISA: XBEGIN, XEND and XABORT. Intel does not provide implementation details of TSX, but gives some hints which suggest that TSX is a *best effort* approach to HTM, like Sun's Rock and AMD's ASF. That is, they do not guarantee successful execution of transactions of any size and duration, and they abort transactions that exceed on-chip resources for HTM, or encounter certain events like page faults, cache misses or interrupts. Thus, Intel enumerates a list of runtime events that may cause transactional execution to abort, namely, synchronous and asynchronous exceptions, memory operations other than write-back cacheable type operations, executing self-modifying code, excessive sizes for transactional regions, non-transactional requests to a cache line accessed within a transaction (*strong atomicity* [17] is ensured), and so on.

IBM BlueGene/Q hardware support for TM [33] leverages the L2 cache to implement the main transactional mechanisms. The shared L2 cache is 16-way set-associative and it is *multi-versioned*, to allow multiple versions (old and new speculative data) of the same physical memory block. Each L2 cache set guarantees up to 10 ways to be used for transactional writes, so it can handle a maximum transaction size of up to 20MB, out of the 32MB shared L2 cache. However, a transaction might be aborted with just 11 speculative blocks due to mapping misses. The L2 directory maintains read, write, and speculative bits per block of the cache, and it also holds a transaction ID to identify the transaction that read or wrote the block. There are 128 transaction IDs and a scrubbing process is executed every 132 cycles to recover IDs of aborted or committed transactions. The conflict detection mechanism uses the read/write bits of the directory to detect RAW, WAR and WAW conflicts among transactions through the cache coherence protocol. Also, a conflict is detected when non-transactional code writes a memory location that was previously accessed by a transaction (BlueGene/Q ensures strong atomicity). Transactional threads involved in a conflict are hardware interrupted and the conflict handler resolves the conflict. A special conflict register is set to indicate the cause of the conflict.

BlueGene/Q extends a pre-existing core design and therefore private L1 caches are not modified. To ensure forward progress without bothering the programmer, Blue-Gene/Q uses *irrevocability* [34], a special transactional mode that, once engaged, ensures transaction commit with the impossibility of being aborted. With the irrevocable mode, transactions can handle I/O irreversible operations, hardware overflows and other events. A runtime algorithm can make a transaction irrevocable after being aborted a fixed number of times. Also, if the aborting ratio for that transaction surpasses a threshold, subsequent executions will be performed in irrevocable mode after only one abort.

A different implementation approach to HTM has been used in IBM's System z mainframe computers with the microprocessor generation zEC12 [16]. Each IBM zEC12 chip has 6 cores with 2 levels of private caches that share a 3rd-level cache. Six of these Central Processing (CP) chips are connected to an off-chip 4th-level cache, thus forming a multi-chip module (MCM) with 36 cores. Up to 4 MCM's can form a coherent SMP system with up to 144 cores. Coherency is managed with a MESI protocol variant.

Unlike BlueGene/Q, System z chips implement HTM by leveraging the L1 private cache instead of the shared one. Figure 4 depicts the core organization with the transactional state highlighted. The L1 cache directory is augmented with two transactional state bits per cache line (tx-read and tx-dirty bits) with flash-clear support to reset all bits in one cycle on transaction commit. Also, tx-dirty bits are connected to the valid bits so that every transactional store can be flash-invalidated on aborts. L1 and L2 caches are store-through caches, so every store causes an L3 access. To hide L1 and L2 store miss latencies, the core has a store queue and a store cache respectively. Both buffers are augmented with a tx-dirty bit and are probed in parallel with the caches by the coherence protocol. In case of conflict, that is, an exclusive or demote (from exclusive to shared) coherence request is received, then the core rejects the request back to the sender which will repeat the coherence request. This mechanism, called *stiff-arming* [16] or stall [19], gives more time to the requested core in the hope of finishing its transaction. The number of rejects is determined by a counter that triggers a transaction abort when a threshold is exceeded. Thereby, deadlock is prevented.

Fig. 4. IBM System z HTM implementation. The L1 cache and the store buffers (both the store queue and the store cache are used to hide the store miss latency) maintain the transactional state that comprises a tx-read bit (tx-r) and a tx-dirty bit (tx-d). The valid bit is tied to the tx-dirty bit to flush-invalidate cache entries in case of abort. The L1 cache and the buffers are probed in parallel on a coherency request.

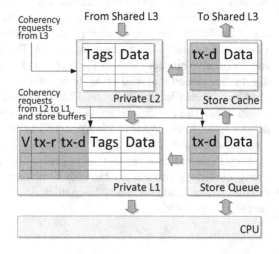

IBM zEC12 processor's L1 cache is a 96KB cache organized in 64 sets with 6 ways and 256 byte lines. Its latency is 4 cycles. On the other hand, the private L2 cache is a 1MB 8-way associative cache with a 7 cycle L1 miss penalty. On abort, the tx-dirty lines in L1 are invalidated (new values), and the old values are very close in L2 at 7 cycle L1 miss penalty. In order for transactions not to be limited by L1 size and associativity, a special bit per L1 set is asserted whenever a transactional line is evicted from L1. Thus, transactional footprint capability is extended to L2 size and associativity without modifying L2, and to the store cache size, at the cost of false positives. The special eviction bits in the L1 cache do not store address information, so every coherence request for an address that maps to a set whose eviction bit is set will abort the transaction regardless of whether the address was transactional or not. Therefore, a false positive might occur. However, the system can track much larger transactions, specially on the read set. The write set is limited to the size of the store cache (64 x 128 bytes).

Finally, IBM has added a HTM facility to the POWER8 processor [1,6] from which few implementation-specific details have been revealed. Each POWER8 core has two data private caches, L1 and L2, and one bank of a larger shared L3 cache. Unlike Blue-Gene/Q and System z, the POWER8 processor keeps track of transactional state in the private L2 cache [1]. When the transaction commits, the new values stored in L2 are committed to the memory sub-system. POWER8 introduces the concept of *suspended transactional mode* [6] to allow for transactions to survive interruptions (context switches, hypervisor, debuggers,....). In this mode, memory accesses are performed non-transactionally and cannot be undone if the transaction eventually aborts. The initiation of a new transaction is prevented, and the hardware tracks conflicts with the transactional data of the suspended transaction. Stores to memory locations that were transactionally accessed by the same thread will abort the suspended transaction.

3   Unbounded Conflict Detection

Programming a bounded HTM system might become a difficult task if the hardware is overflowed persistently, and it can happen more frequently than expected. Table 1 shows the number of overflowed transactions and the average number of evicted blocks for the STAMP benchmark suite [18]. Those figures have been obtained from an *implicitly transactional* system, where only the boundaries of transactions have to be defined and all memory accesses within them are tracked[1], and 32KB L1D caches. As a result, none of the benchmarks would have been able to complete in a bounded HTM system that uses the primary cache to provide transactional support.

Increasing the size of caches does not always guarantee that the HTM system can handle larger transactions, since an eviction can happen because of mapping misses regardless of whether the cache is full or empty. Bounded HTM systems usually provide a fallback mechanism to tackle overflowing situations, which might involve the programmer. However, next we describe several unbounded HTM proposals that are able to handle transactions of arbitrary size and duration, even in the presence of OS events, without further programming effort.

---

[1] Conversely, *explicitly transactional* systems urge the programmer to explicitly identify transactional memory accesses.

Table 1. Number of transactions that overflow the L1D cache and the number of cache blocks replaced on average, both read and written within a transaction

Benchmark	Overflowed Transactions	Average Number of Block Evictions	
		Read	Written
Bayes	102	68.2	100.8
Genome	447	78.7	1.8
Intruder	4511	2.1	0.1
Kmeans	387	1.0	0
Labyrinth	48	62.9	76.8
Vacation	2710	7	0.1
Yada	816	117.2	73.2

3.1 Persistent Meta-Data Systems

The unbounded HTM systems described in this section hold transactional meta-data (the information needed to perform conflict detection and version management) in virtual memory that persists hardware overflows and OS events.

Unbounded transactional memory (UTM) [2] holds, in virtual memory, a structure called XSTATE that represents the state of all transactions running in the system. Besides, each memory block is augmented with a transactional read/write bit and a pointer to the old value of the block that resides in an entry of the XSTATE structure. Such an entry of the XSTATE structure, in turn, has a pointer to the memory block. So, the XSTATE structure holds a linked list of memory blocks whose transactional read/write bits are set. Conflict detection is carried out eagerly, so every memory access operation must check the pointer and bits of the memory block to detect any conflict. The access to the XSTATE and memory block meta-data is done by means of several hardware registers that hold pointers to their base and bounds. For non-overflowed transactions, UTM implements a conventional cache-based HTM to accelerate execution, called LTM (see Section 2.1).

Virtual transactional memory (VTM) [26] assigns each transaction a status word (XSW), which is used to commit or abort the transaction by modifying it atomically with a CAS instruction. VTM also defines a transaction address data table (XADT), which is the shared log for holding overflowed transactional data. Both structures reside in the application's virtual address space. However, they are invisible to the user. The VTM system, implemented in either hardware or microcode, manages these structures by means of new registers added to each thread context that point to them and are initialized by the application. When a transaction issues a memory operation that is a cache miss, it must be checked against overflowed addresses by traversing the XADT. Traversing the XADT might be too slow, so VTM provides two mechanisms for not interfering with transactions that do not overflow. First, an XADT overflow counter records the number of overflowed entries. If it is set to zero, no traffic is needed as it is locally cached at each processor. Second, an XADT filter (XF), implemented as a software counting Bloom filter [12] that allows deletions, provides fast detection of conflicts. A miss in the filter guarantees that the address does not conflict, and a hit triggers an XADT walk.

TokenTM [4] is an unbounded, eager conflict detection HTM system that augments each memory block with transactional meta-data. As depicted in Figure 5, the meta-data consist of a Token and a thread identifier, TID. The system must comply with the following invariant for each memory block: a block can be non-transactional, part of the RS of one or more transactions, or part of the WS of only one transaction. Therefore, a block that is non-transactional will have 0 tokens, and the TID is not necessary. A block read by one transaction will have 1 token and the TID of the thread executing such a transaction. A block read by n transactions will have n tokens, and the TID is not necessary. And a block written by one transaction will have all the tokens, T, and the TID of the thread that issued the transactional write. So, if a transaction reads a block with (Token=T,TID=X) and the TID does not match its own TID (the TID is stored in a CPU register, see Figure 5) a conflict is detected with the thread X. Also, if a transaction writes a block with (1,Y), a conflict is detected with the thread Y. However, if a transaction writes a block with (n,-), the conflict is quickly detected, but the resolution can be costly, as the TIDs of the n sharers cannot be stored in the TID field. In this case, if all shared copies of the block were in the cache hierarchy, the coherence protocol would provide the TIDs of the conflicting transactions. Otherwise, the system has to traverse the thread logs, that hold old data versions and precise meta-data, in order to find that information. The coherence protocol is not modified except for piggybacking the transactional meta-data (Token, TID) in each coherence message. Then, to maintain meta-data coherency, as multiple copies of a block can coexist in the cache hierarchy, TokenTM defines simple rules to fission and fusion transactional meta-data.

As transactional meta-data is attached to each memory block, transactions can overflow the caches without losing transactional state. Also, conflict detection suffers no false conflicts unlike other unbounded proposals (see Section 3.2). TokenTM handles paging and context switches easily by initializing, saving, restoring meta-data, and flash-clearing/ORing meta-data in L1 cache. Finally, by means of a Fast Release (this CPU bit is set when none of the locations in the WS have been evicted, so Fast Release is safe), small transactions that fit in the cache can commit at full hardware speed, just by flash-clearing their tokens. Larger transactions must walk the log to reset all their tokens on commit.

Fig. 5. TokenTM implementation. Each memory block is augmented with a field holding a token number, and another field for the thread ID, TID, of the transaction. Caches are also modified to hold such meta-data, but the coherence protocol is not modified. Meta-data is piggybacked on coherence messages.

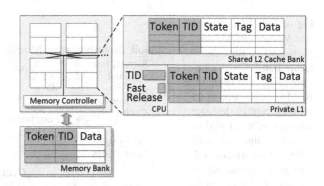

3.2 Signature-Based Systems

Ceze et al. [7] propose Bulk as a mechanism to detach conflict detection from caches, and they manage to implement an unbounded conflict detection mechanism based on *signatures* that is able to track an indeterminate number of addresses and survive certain OS events like context switches.

Bulk is a lazy-lazy HTM system that presumes an invalidation-based coherence protocol that works unmodified when dealing with non-transactional data, and puts off invalidations until commit time when dealing with transactional data. Bulk is similar to TCC (Section 2.2), but the latter only supports transactional data, thus simplifying the cache coherence protocol specification. Unlike TCC, Bulk does not hold transactional state in primary caches. Instead, a Bulk Disambiguation Module (BDM) is defined per core which supports unbounded conflict detection.

Figure 6 shows the architecture of the BDM. The main part of the module consists of a set of signatures. *Signatures* are defined as Bloom filters (see Section 3.2.1), time and space-efficient hash structures that are implemented as a bit array and a set of hash functions. Such functions are a surjection between a larger set of addresses, the memory space, and a smaller set of indexes, the bit array, so the signature represents a superset of the real RS and WS of transactions. Hence, aliases or false positives can arise that do not compromise correctness but can hurt system performance as transactions get larger.

Bulk broadcasts fixed-sized signatures on commit for the other cores to invalidate stale data, just as TCC does, but with the difference that addresses are compacted in the signature instead of having a write set with individual addresses. The Bulk Functional Units implement operations, like signature intersection, to quickly perform the disambiguation of addresses. Thus, when a core receives the WS signature from other core that attempts to commit, the former intersects the received signature with its RS signature. If the result is not empty the conflict has to be resolved, so the receiver invalidates its modified data. To invalidate the speculatively written data, the BDM could walk the cache sets, retrieve the tags of valid entries and perform a membership query to its WS signature. This could be very inefficient if the number of valid lines is small. Instead, the BDM has a bit array (Current W Cache Sets) of length the number of sets in the cache, that holds the valid written sets of the cache and is calculated from the

Fig. 6. Bulk Disambiguation Module (BDM) implementation. Bulk detaches transactional state from caches and defines the BDM to implement an unbounded conflict detection mechanism. It is based on signatures, time and space-efficient hash structures that are able to store an indefinite number of addresses at the cost of false positives.

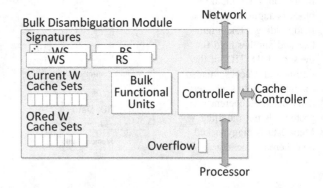

WS signature with a decoding operation of the Bulk Functional Units. Invalidations are done sequentially, regardless of that optimization.

The BDM has a set of signatures to support context switches and to keep on detecting conflicts with a transaction that has been preempted. In case that the private caches evict a transactional block, the overflow bit is set. Checking for conflicts with evicted cache blocks does not necessarily imply traversing an overflow memory space as the information is in the signature. However, if the module runs out of signatures, the signature of one thread is moved to the overflow memory space and conflict detection is carried out like in VTM (see Section 3.1) until one transaction commits and clears one signature. There is another bit array, the ORed W Cache Sets, that stores the union of each written cache sets of every signature managed by the BDM, both current and preempted. These bit arrays also help to maintain the *set restriction* property introduced by Bulk, by which each cache set must only contain transactional or non-transactional blocks.

Although Bulk can be considered as unbounded from the conflict detection mechanism point of view, it does not clarify what happens on a page relocation or a thread migration.

LogTM-SE [35] is the unbounded extension of LogTM. Unlike Bulk, LogTM-SE is an eager-eager HTM system with an architecture that fully supports unbounded transactions that can survive thread migration, paging, context switches and transactions of indeterminate size. LogTM-SE stands for LogTM Signature Edition, so it is based on Bulk signatures, although the eager nature of the conflict detection mechanism simplifies the implementation.

The Bulk's BDM implements Bulk Functional Units that provide intersect, decode, and other operations to deal with address disambiguation. The BDM holds the cache sets of transactionally modified blocks and implements a finite state machine to invalidate those blocks on abort, as lazy conflict detection implies bulk disambiguation at commit time. However, LogTM-SE does not need such a complex hardware surrounding the signature since addresses are disambiguated individually and eagerly by the coherence protocol. When a core, A, reads a block within a transaction, the cache coherence protocol forwards the request to the owner of the block, B. Core B checks its WS signature and responds with an ACK or a NACK message depending on whether it was a miss or a hit in the signature. If the block is not in the cache hierarchy, it is fetched from main memory and a signature check is broadcast for the directory to rebuild the block state in cache. If a core hits its signature, its bit in the bit vector of sharers is set, and a conflict is signaled if the owner was not core A.

In order to support context switches and migrations, LogTM-SE proposes to add an additional hardware *summary* signature per thread context that holds the union of the signatures from all descheduled threads. In addition, the signatures are saved to the transaction's log header to be reinstalled in the normal signature when the thread is rescheduled. The summary signature is maintained by the OS in software, which is in charge of interrupting all threads of the same process to set their hardware summary signature to the global software summary signature. The hardware summary signature is checked before loads and stores reach the primary cache, so coherence requests do not have to check the summary signature because that early checking filters out conflicts

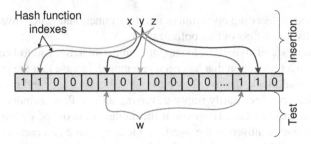

Fig. 7. Design of a Bloom filter. A false positive scenario.

with descheduled transactions. When a conflict is detected in the summary signature, the OS traps to a conflict handler since normal hardware conflict resolution is not valid as one of the conflicting transactions is not running in the system.

With virtual memory paging the problem lies in the fact that signatures operates on physical memory addresses, so if a page is relocated to a different address space, false negatives can arise risking incorrect conflict detection. LogTM-SE proposes to interrupt all threads to update their signatures whenever a page relocation occurs. This signature update consists in decoding the signature to get the addresses inserted in it and check if those addresses belonged to the old page. If so, the addresses are reinserted with the new page address.

LogTM-SE support for virtualization is costly and can be very detrimental to performance if large transactions become the norm. Otherwise, if these OS events are not frequent, the described mechanisms prove to be an effective solution.

3.2.1 Signature Implementation Enhancements

Signatures have been proved an effective mechanism to implement unbounded conflict detection. They are implemented as Bloom filters [3], proposed by Burton H. Bloom in 1970 as a time and space-efficient hash coding method with allowable errors. Figure 7 shows the design of a Bloom filter. It comprises a bit array of 2^m bits and k different hash functions that map elements into k randomly distributed bits of the array. Such an array is initially set to 0, and inserting an element into the filter consists in setting to 1 the k bits indexed by the hash functions. Test for membership consists in checking that those k bits are asserted. As the array is fixed-sized there exists the possibility of errors of testing, called *false positives*. For instance, in Figure 7, elements x, y and z are inserted in the filter and the bits indexed by the hash functions ($k = 2$ in this case) are set to 1. When we test for element w, it happens to be mapped into bits that have already been set to 1, so the test is a false positive. However, false negatives are not possible.

The probability of false positives rises as signature fills, and it might cause substantial performance degradation because of false conflicts or false contention. Figure 8 shows the probability of false positives for a signature implemented as a Bloom filter [3] with a 1Kbit array and different number of hash functions. The false positive rate is given by the equation:

$$p_{FP}(M,n,k) = \left(1 - \left(1 - \frac{1}{M}\right)^{nk}\right)^k \approx \left(1 - e^{-\frac{nk}{M}}\right)^k, \tag{1}$$

where M is the signature size, n the number of insertions and k the number of hash functions. And p_{FP} can be simplified by using the Taylor series expansion of the exponential function, $e^x = \sum_{n=0}^{\infty} \frac{1}{n!}x^n$ [29]. We can see that better false positive probability is expected for low populated filters and a high number of hash functions ($k \in \{4,8\}$). However, the more hash functions the Bloom filter has, the earlier the filter populates and the higher the false positive probability is expected for high populated filters.

We can find manifold signature implementation proposals in the literature that try to enhance signature performance by reducing both the false positive rate and the hardware budget as well.

Bloom filter signatures can be implemented as a k-ported SRAM in its regular version. However, Sanchez et al. [29] proposed *parallel signatures* as an alternative hardware-efficient implementation to regular Bloom filter signatures. Multiported SRAMs require much hardware as they grow quadratically with the number of ports. Figure 9 shows the implementation of both regular and parallel filters. Whereas the regular filter is implemented as a k-ported SRAM, the parallel one consists of k subfilters implemented as single-ported SRAMs, yielding the same or better false positive rate.

Cuckoo-Bloom signatures are also proposed in [29]. They are intended to perform like high-k Bloom filters for small transactions, while yielding the false positive rate of Bloom filters with few hash functions when transactions are large, i.e. Cuckoo-Bloom signatures try to get the lowest false positive rate in each situation. Cuckoo-Bloom filters act like a hash table at the beginning of the transaction. Addresses are stored as if in a set-associative cache, where tags and data are the result of hashing the address with two independent hash functions, and sets are indexed by other hash function. When a set is full, the filter executes a sequence of evictions and re-insertions to store the incoming address. If such a sequence takes too long, the set is converted into a regular Bloom filter with low k, after storing the addresses into a separate storage space. Then such addresses are hashed into the newly converted Bloom filter. Lookups are fast, but insertions are more complicate, and the filter needs certain control logic, additional storage, a bit array to signal whether a set has been converted into a Bloom filter or not, and other structures (comparators,...) that complicate the design and might rise the hardware budget.

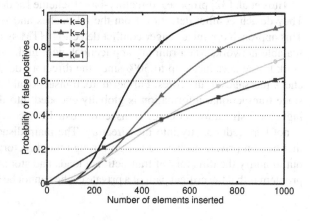

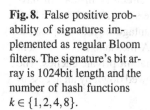

Fig. 8. False positive probability of signatures implemented as regular Bloom filters. The signature's bit array is 1024bit length and the number of hash functions $k \in \{1,2,4,8\}$.

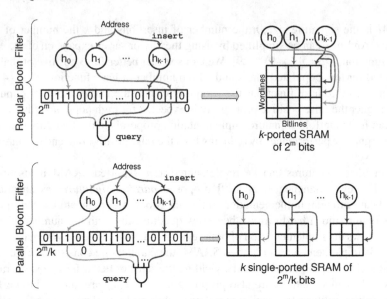

Fig. 9. Regular Bloom filter vs. parallel Bloom filter design and implementation. The bit array is implemented as a bidimensional SRAM where the most significant bits of the hash index select the wordline and the less significant bits select the bitline within the word.

An alternative hardware-efficient implementation of hash functions, Page-Block-XOR hashing (PBX), is proposed in [36]. They use the concept of entropy to find the highest randomness bits of the address, to allow reducing the hardware complexity of hash functions, that are usually implemented as a tree of XOR gates per hash index bit. PBX compacts those trees to a single XOR gate per hash bit, although it requires a profiling of the application to find the most random address bits. Notary [36] also proposes a technique to reduce the number of asserted bits in the signature. Their approach is based on segregating addresses into private and shared sets. Then, only the shared addresses are recorded. This solution requires support at the compiler, runtime/library and operating system levels. In addition, the programmer must define which objects are private or shared, which might be a difficult and error-prone task.

Titos et al. [32] propose a directory-based scheme for detection of conflicts in HTM. They detach conflict detection from the L1 caches and shift it to the directory level. This approach optimizes eager conflict detection HTM systems with an unordered and scalable network, when running applications with high number of conflicts. The network traffic is reduced up to 30% since the directory does not have to send signature check messages to the cores. Furthermore, transactional bookkeeping is more efficient since transactional information is globally encoded into the directory instead of having a local signature per core. Transactions usually access the same shared data which is not kept redundantly into the directory. The main disadvantage of this proposal is that hits on private caches do not go through the directory. A message has to be sent out to notify the directory of transactional loads and stores that hit private caches. The problem is that the critical path of a private cache cannot be slowed down by an access to the directory, so the communication between cache and directory is set asynchronously, thus introducing races in conflict detection.

Orosa et al. [20] propose *FlexSig* as a flexible hardware signature implementation to change dynamically the amount of signatures per core according to system requirements. FlexSig groups all signatures in the system into a pool of signatures and assigns them to the cores on demand. It relies in the fact that all cores are not always running transactional code at the same time. Thus, if there are only two transactions running in the system, they will use half of the signature pool each. If other cores start a transaction, they demand signature allocation to the pool and it is repartitioned to meet the necessities of all the cores running transactions in the system, without incurring false positives.

Choi and Draper [9] propose adaptive grain signatures, that keep the history of transaction aborts and dynamically changes the input bit range to the hash functions on the abort history. The aim of this design is to reduce the number of false positives that harm the execution performance.

Quislant et al. [22,25] propose locality-sensitive signatures, LS-Sig, that exploit the spatial locality property of memory references to reduce the probability of false conflicts. LS-Sig defines new maps for hash functions to reduce the number of bits inserted in the filter (occupancy) for those addresses with spatial locality. That is, nearby memory locations share some bits of the Bloom filter. As a result, false conflicts are significantly reduced in transactions that exhibit spatial locality in their read or write sets, but the false conflict rate remains unalterable for transactions that do not exhibit locality at all. This is favorable particularly for large transactions that usually present a significant amount of spatial locality. In addition, as the proposal is based on new locality-aware hash maps, its implementation does not require extra hardware.

The probability of false positives for LS-Sig can be expressed as follows:

$$p_{FP}^{local}(M,n,k) = \left(1 - \left(1 - \frac{1}{M}\right)^{n\sum_{t=1}^{k} t f_t}\right)^k, \tag{2}$$

where the exponent nk of Equation 1, which stands for the number of bits of the array that are set after n insertions, is replaced by $n\sum_{t=1}^{k} t f_t$. Now, inserting an address in the filter does not necessarily set k bits as fewer bits can be set depending on locality. f_t is the probability that an insertion only sets t bits in the filter because a nearby address was already inserted.

Figure 10 shows the analytical evaluation of false positive probability for the generic Bloom filter given by Equation 1 with several k values, and the proposed LS-Sig scheme (Equation 2) for $k = 4$. To parameterize the evaluation, $f = \sum_{t=1}^{k-1} f_t$ was introduced as the probability of an address being near to some inserted address. Consequently, $1 - f = f_k$ is the probability of being far from those already in the filter. With a generic Bloom filter low values of k are advantageous for large transactions and high values of k for small ones. However, it can be inferred from Figure 10 that the LS-Sig scheme can achieve the benefits of both situations if the address sequence exhibits medium/high spatial locality.

Unified [10], Multiset and Asymmetric [23,24] signatures are proposed to deal with asymmetry in transactional data sets. Read and write signatures are usually

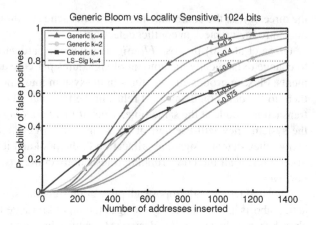

Fig. 10. Probability of false positives of generic and LS-Sig varying the parameter $f = \sum_{t=1}^{3} f_t$ (the higher the f, the more the locality).

Fig. 11. Unified (UNI), Multiset Shared (MS s) and Asymmetric (ASYM) signature configurations studied in [10,23]. UNI blind is the same as MS s=4 (the number of hash functions is set to 4 and s=4 means that all hashes are shared between the RS and the WS). ASYM a=7 devotes 7 subfilters to the RS and 1 to the WS. SEP is the conventional separate parallel signature proposed in [29].

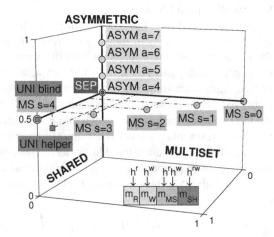

implemented as two separate, same-sized Bloom filters. In contrast, transactions frequently exhibit read and write sets of uneven cardinality. In addition, both sets are not disjoint, as data can be read and also written. This mismatch between data sets and hardware storage introduces inefficiencies in the use of signatures that have some impact on performance, as, for example, read signatures may populate earlier than write ones, increasing the expected false positive rate.

Figure 11 shows all the signature configurations explored in [10,23]. There are three orthogonal axes: asymmetric, shared or unified, and multiset. Asymmetric signatures are implemented using parallel Bloom filters, where the number of subfilters devoted to the RS and the WS can be configured via a reconfiguration register that can be set by a new instruction of the ISA or by the HTM system. A profiled RS to WS ratio can be computed for each application to configure the asymmetric signature. Multiset signatures merge RS and WS bit arrays into a common array while keeping their hash functions separate one another. However, sharing/unifying the hash functions of the RS and the WS is also proposed and it proves to be a good and general solution to the problem of asymmetry in data sets. Shared/Unified signatures have the problem of introducing read-read dependencies, since they share all hash functions so they cannot distinguish between read and written locations. In [10], it is proposed to augment the signature with an extra register to filter out read-read dependencies, called the helper register, where only writes are stored. The same helper register effect is achieved with multiset shared signatures by segregating one hash function per set while sharing the rest (the number of hash functions is assumed greater than one). Last but not least, a study of the different combinations of multiset shared signatures with LS-Sig is carried out in [23].

4 Conclusions

The conflict detection mechanism is a key element in the design and implementation of a HTM system, as it is the means to attain atomicity while providing optimistic parallelism. In this chapter, we have surveyed the main approaches to hardware conflict detection implementation and we have classified them into two big groups: bounded and unbounded.

Whereas unbounded HTM conflict detection mechanisms release the programmers from worrying about HTM limitations and restrictions, they may require a significant multicore architecture modification that could compromise overall system performance. Signature-based proposals try to keep the hardware simple but suffers from false-positives on conflict detection that can be detrimental for the performance.

On the other hand, bounded HTM conflict detection is more feasible from the point of view of the hardware design and implementation. Several approaches have been explored that either leverage the cache hierarchy or use alternative implementation solutions. Hardware manufactures have adopted this bounded approach and some of them are releasing commercial processors with bounded HTM support. However, these HTM extensions could fail to comply with one of the main features that transactional memory systems claim to deliver, i.e. simplifying concurrent programming. Thus, effective unbounded HTM systems, and unbounded conflict detection in particular, could help to ease multicore processor programming so that transactional memory becomes the paradigm to use.

Acknowledgement. This work has been supported by the Government of Spain with project CICYT TIN2010-16144.

References

1. Adir, A., Goodman, D., Hershcovich, D., Hershkovitz, O., Hickerson, B., Holtz, K., Kadry, W., Koyfman, A., Ludden, J., Meissner, C., Nahir, A., Pratt, R.R., Schiffli, M., St. Onge, B., Thompto, B., Tsanko, E., Ziv, A.: Verification of Transactional Memory in Power8. In: 51st Ann. Design Automation Conference (DAC 2014), pp. 1–6 (2014)
2. Ananian, C., Asanovic, K., Kuszmaul, B., Leiserson, C., Lie, S.: Unbounded transactional memory. In: 11th Int'l. Symp. on High-Performance Computer Architecture (HPCA 2005), pp. 316–327 (2005)

3. Bloom, B.: Space/time trade-offs in hash coding with allowable errors. Communications of the ACM 13(7), 422–426 (1970)
4. Bobba, J., Goyal, N., Hill, M., Swift, M., Wood, D.: TokenTM: Efficient execution of large transactions with hardware transactional memory. In: 35th Ann. Int'l. Symp. on Computer Architecture (ISCA 2008), pp. 127–138 (2008)
5. Bobba, J., Moore, K.E., Volos, H., Yen, L., Hill, M.D., Swift, M.M., Wood, D.A.: Performance pathologies in hardware transactional memory. In: 34th Ann. Int'l. Symp. on Computer Architecture (ISCA 2007), pp. 81–91 (2007)
6. Cain, H.W., Michael, M.M., Frey, B., May, C., Williams, D., Le, H.: Robust architectural support for transactional memory in the power architecture. In: 40th Ann. Int'l. Symp. on Computer Architecture (ISCA 2013), pp. 225–236 (2013)
7. Ceze, L., Tuck, J., Torrellas, J., Cascaval, C.: Bulk disambiguation of speculative threads in multiprocessors. In: 33th Ann. Int'l. Symp. on Computer Architecture (ISCA 2006), pp. 227–238 (2006)
8. Chaudhry, S., Cypher, R., Ekman, M., Karlsson, M., Landin, A., Yip, S., Zeffer, H., Tremblay, M.: Rock: A high-performance sparc cmt processor. IEEE Micro 29(2), 6–16 (2009)
9. Choi, W., Draper, J.: Locality-aware adaptive grain signatures for transactional memories. In: IEEE Int'l. Symp. on Parallel and Distributed Processing (IPDPS 2010), pp. 1–10 (2010)
10. Choi, W., Draper, J.: Unified signatures for improving performance in transactional memory. In: IEEE Int'l. Parallel Distributed Processing Symp. (IPDPS 2011), pp. 817–827 (May 2011)
11. Chung, J., Yen, L., Diestelhorst, S., Pohlack, M., Hohmuth, M., Christie, D., Grossman, D.: Asf: Amd64 extension for lock-free data structures and transactional memory. In: 43rd Ann. Int'l. Symp. on Microarchitecture (MICRO 43), pp. 39–50 (2010)
12. Fan, L., Cao, P., Almeida, J., Broder, A.: Summary cache: A scalable wide-area web cache sharing protocol. IEEE/ACM Trans. on Networking 8(3), 281–293 (2000)
13. Goodman, J.R.: Using cache memory to reduce processor-memory traffic. In: 10th Ann. Int'l. Symp. on Computer Architecture (ISCA 1983), pp. 124–131 (1983)
14. Hammond, L., Wong, V., Chen, M., Carlstrom, B., Davis, J., Hertzberg, B., Prabhu, M., Wijaya, H., Kozyrakis, C., Olukotun, K.: Transactional memory coherence and consistency. In: 31th Ann. Int'l. Symp. on Computer Architecture (ISCA 2004), pp. 102–113 (2004)
15. Herlihy, M., Moss, J.: Transactional memory: Architectural support for lock-free data structures. In: 20th Ann. Int'l. Symp. on Computer Architecture (ISCA 1993), pp. 289–300 (1993)
16. Jacobi, C., Slegel, T., Greiner, D.: Transactional memory architecture and implementation for ibm system z. In: 45th Ann. Int'l Symp. on Microarchitecture (MICRO 45), pp. 25–36 (2012)
17. Martin, M., Blundell, C., Lewis, E.: Subtleties of transactional memory atomicity semantics. IEEE Computer Architecture Letters 5(2), 17–20 (2006)
18. Minh, C., Chung, J., Kozyrakis, C., Olukotun, K.: STAMP: Stanford Transactional Applications for Multi-Processing. In: IEEE Int'l Symp. on Workload Characterization (IISWC 2008), pp. 35–46 (2008)
19. Moore, K., Bobba, J., Moravan, M., Hill, M., Wood, D.: LogTM: Log-based transactional memory. In: 12th Int'l. Symp. on High-Performance Computer Architecture (HPCA 2006), pp. 254–265 (2006)
20. Orosa, L., Antelo, E., Bruguera, J.: FlexSig: Implementing flexible hardware signatures. ACM Trans. on Architecture and Code Optimization 8(4), 30:1–30:20 (2012)
21. Qian, X., Sahelices, B., Torrellas, J.: Omniorder: Directory-based conflict serialization of transactions. In: 41th Ann. Int'l. Symp. on Computer Architecture (ISCA 2014) (2014)
22. Quislant, R., Gutierrez, E., Plata, O., Zapata, E.L.: Improving signatures by locality exploitation for transactional memory. In: Int'l Conf. on Parallel Architectures and Compilation Techniques (PACT 2009), pp. 303–312 (2009)

23. Quislant, R., Gutierrez, E., Plata, O., Zapata, E.L.: Hardware signature designs to deal with asymmetry in transactional data sets. IEEE Trans. on Parallel and Distributed Systems 24(3), 506–519 (2013)

24. Quislant, R., Gutierrez, E., Plata, O., Zapata, E.L.: Multiset signatures for transactional memory. In: Int'l. Conf. on Supercomputing (ICS 2011), pp. 43–52 (2011)

25. Quislant, R., Gutierrez, E., Plata, O., Zapata, E.L.: LS-Sig: Locality-sensitive signatures for transactional memory. IEEE Trans. on Computers 62(2), 322–335 (2013)

26. Rajwar, R., Herlihy, M., Lai, K.: Virtualizing transactional memory. In: 32th Ann. Int'l. Symp. on Computer Architecture (ISCA 2005), pp. 494–505 (2005)

27. Rajwar, R., Goodman, J.R.: Speculative lock elision: Enabling highly concurrent multi-threaded execution. In: 34th Ann. Int'l. Symp. on Microarchitecture (MICRO 34), pp. 294–305 (2001)

28. Reinders, J.: Transactional synchronization in Haswell. Intel's software blogs (2012), http://software.intel.com/en-us/blogs/2012/02/07/transactional-synchronization-in-haswell/

29. Sanchez, D., Yen, L., Hill, M., Sankaralingam, K.: Implementing signatures for transactional memory. In: 40th Ann. Int'l Symp. on Microarchitecture (MICRO 2007), pp. 123–133 (2007)

30. Sorin, D.J., Hill, M.D., Wood, D.A.: A Primer on Memory Consistency and Cache Coherence, 1st edn. Morgan & Claypool Publishers (2011)

31. Sorin, D.J., Plakal, M., Condon, A.E., Hill, M.D., Martin, M.M.K., Wood, D.A.: Specifying and verifying a broadcast and a multicast snooping cache coherence protocol. IEEE Trans. Parallel and Distributed Systems 13(6), 556–578 (2002)

32. Titos, R., Acacio, M.E., García, J.M.: Directory-based conflict detection in hardware transactional memory. In: Sadayappan, P., Parashar, M., Badrinath, R., Prasanna, V.K. (eds.) HiPC 2008. LNCS, vol. 5374, pp. 541–554. Springer, Heidelberg (2008)

33. Wang, A., Gaudet, M., Wu, P., Amaral, J.N., Ohmacht, M., Barton, C., Silvera, R., Michael, M.: Evaluation of Blue Gene/Q hardware support for transactional memories. In: 21st Int'l Conf. on Parallel Architectures and Compilation Techniques (PACT 2012), pp. 127–136 (2012)

34. Welc, A., Bratin, S., Adl-Tabatabai, A.R.: Irrevocable transactions and their applications. In: 20th Symp. on Parallelism in Algorithms and Architectures (SPAA 2008), pp. 285–296 (June 2008)

35. Yen, L., Bobba, J., Marty, M., Moore, K., Volos, H., Hill, M., Swift, M., Wood, D.: LogTM-SE: Decoupling hardware transactional memory from caches. In: 13th Int'l. Symp. on High-Performance Computer Architecture (HPCA 2007), pp. 261–272 (2007)

36. Yen, L., Draper, S., Hill, M.: Notary: Hardware techniques to enhance signatures. In: 41st Ann. Int'l Symp. on Microarchitecture (MICRO 2008), pp. 234–245 (2008)

Multi-versioning in Transactional Memory

Idit Keidar[1] and Dmitri Perelman[2]

[1] Technion, Israel Institute of Technology
idish@ee.technion.ac.il
[2] Facebook Inc.
dmitrip@fb.com

Abstract. Reducing the number of aborts is one of the biggest challenges of most transactional systems: existing TMs may abort many transactions that could, in fact, commit without violating correctness. Historically, the commonly used method for reducing the abort rate was maintaining multiple object versions. Multiversion concurrency control is a classical approach for providing concurrent access to the database in database management systems. Its idea is to let a reading transaction obtain a consistent snapshot corresponding to an arbitrary point in time (e.g., defined at the beginning of a transaction) – concurrent updates are isolated through maintaining old versions rather than via scheduling decisions.

Multi-versioning was adopted by transactional memory algorithms as well. In this chapter we overview the multi-versioning approach by studying the inherent properties of STMs that use multiple versions to guarantee successful commits of all read-only transactions. We first consider the challenges of garbage collecting of old object versions, and show that no STM can be optimal in the number of previous versions kept, while following the naïve approach of keeping a constant number of last versions per object might lead to an exponential memory growth. We then show the potential performance challenges of multi-versioned STMs, including disjoint-access parallelism and visibility of read-only transactions.

We demonstrate the advantages of implementing multi-versioned STMs in managed memory environments by presenting Selective Multi-Versioning (SMV) algorithm. SMV relies on automatic garbage collection, and thus efficiently deals with old versions while still allowing invisible read-only transactions.

1 Why Multiple Versions

1.1 Because Read-Only Transactions Matter

Frequent aborts, especially in the presence of long-running transactions, may have a devastating effect on performance and predictability of the execution [3,11,18].

Of particular interest in this context is reducing the abort rate of read-only transactions (transactions with empty write-sets). Read-only transactions play a significant role in various types of applications, including linearizable data structures with a strong prevalence of read-only operations [19], or client-server applications where an STM infrastructure replaces a traditional DBMS approach (e.g., FenixEDU web application [8]). Particularly long read-only transactions are employed for taking consistent snapshots of dynamically updated systems, which are then used for checkpointing, process replication, monitoring program execution, gathering system statistics, etc.

R. Guerraoui and P. Romano (Eds.): Transactional Memory, LNCS 8913, pp. 150–165, 2015.

Unfortunately, long read-only transactions might be repeatedly aborted for arbitrarily long periods of time. As we show in [26], the time for completing such a transaction varies significantly under contention, to the point that some read-only transactions simply cannot be executed without "stopping the world". This kind of instability becomes a practical disadvantage for STM adoption in the real-world systems.

Historically, one of the commonly used methods for reducing the number of aborts was maintaining multiple object versions. Multiversion concurrency control is a classical approach for providing concurrent access to the database in database management systems [6,25]. Its idea is to let a reading transaction obtain a *consistent snapshot* [5] corresponding to an arbitrary point in time (typically defined at the beginning of a transaction) – concurrent updates are isolated through maintaining old versions rather than through a process of locks or mutexes.

Multi-versioning technique was adopted by transactional memory algorithms as well [3,24,14,7,26]. By keeping multiple versions it is possible to ensure that every read-only transaction successfully commits. Consider, for example, the scenario depicted in Figure 1. [1] In this run transaction T_2 reads an object o_1, then another transaction T_3 updates objects o_1 and o_2, and commits. Assume that T_2 now tries to read o_2. Reading the value o_2^2 written by T_3 would violate correctness, since T_2 does not read the value o_1^1 written by T_3. In a single-versioned STM, illustrated in Figure 1(a), T_2 must abort. However, a multi-versioned STM may keep both versions o_2^1 and o_2^2 of o_2, and may return o_2^1 to T_2, as illustrated in Figure 1(b). This allows T_2 to successfully commit, in spite of its conflict with T_3.

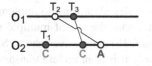
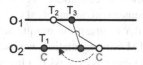

(a) Single-versioned TM, T_2
aborts.

(b) Multi-versioned TM, T_2
commits.

Fig. 1. Keeping multiple versions avoids aborts, which are inevitable in STMs with only one object version

1.2 Formalizing the Advantages of Multi-versioned Solutions

As mentioned earlier, keeping multiple versions has a potential to significantly improve STM's performance and predictability: we now need rigorous metrics to grasp

---

[1] We depict transactional histories in the style of [29]. An object o_i's state in time is represented as a horizontal line, with time proceeding left to right. Transactions are drawn as polylines, with circles representing accesses to objects. Filled circles indicate writes, and empty circles indicate reads. A commit is indicated by the letter **C**, and an abort by the letter **A**. A read operation returning an old value of an object is indicated by a dotted arc line. The initial value of object o_i is denoted by o_i^0, and the value written to o_i by the j'th write is denoted by o_i^j.

this intuition. At a high level, we can talk about two aspects of transactional performance: 1) *responsiveness*, for measuring the progress of individual transactional operations, and 2) *permissiveness*, for measuring the wasted operations belonging to aborted transactions.

Responsiveness

We say that a TM is *responsive* if it guarantees that each operation invocation eventually gets a response, even if all other threads do not invoke new transactional operations. This limits the responsive TM's behavior upon operation invocation, so that it may either return an operation response, or abort a transaction, but cannot wait for other transactions to invoke new transactional operations. Note that we do allow for a responsive TM to wait for concurrent transactional operations to complete, for example TL2 [9] is responsive in spite of the use of locks. One may say that a responsive TM provides lock-freedom at the level of transactional operations.

Multi-versioned Permissiveness

We can capture the amount of spuriously aborted transactions using the notion of *permissiveness*, first introduced by Guerraoui et al. [17]. Intuitively, permissiveness defines properties of transactional histories for which no aborts are allowed. Various levels of permissiveness have been defined. *Single-version π-permissiveness* [17] focuses on a model with single-version objects and thus allows many spurious aborts. Another permissiveness condition, *online π-permissiveness* [20], prevents all spurious aborts, which comes with an inherent cost of extremely complex algorithms to implement.

In order to grasp the unique advantages coming with the use of multiple versions in an STM implementation, we use *multi-versioned (MV)* permissiveness: an STM satisfies MV-permissiveness if a transaction aborts only if it is an update transaction that conflicts with another update transaction. In other words, with MV-permissiveness read-only transactions never abort and do not cause aborts of update transactions. We say that an STM satisfying MV-permissiveness is MV-permissive.

Multi-versioning Alternatives: Losing Responsiveness

Besides multi-versioning, there exist multiple approaches for avoiding aborts of read-only transactions, demonstrating the richness of the solution space defined by responsiveness and permissiveness. As a trivial example, we can think of an STM implemented with a single global lock acquired in the beginning of each transaction and released upon commit: while being highly permissive (zero aborted transactions), the global-lock STM is non-responsive (all transactions are mutually exclusive).

There exist various real STMs that avoid aborts of read-only transactions without being multi-versioned:

- Dependence-aware transactional memory [28] reduces the number of aborts by allowing transactions to read uncommitted values and then waiting for the successful commit of the writer.

- TLRW [10] reduces the aborts of read-only transactions by using read-write locks to block in case of concurrency.
- PermiSTM [1] provides MV-permissiveness by having every update transaction being blocked until the termination of all the conflicting readers.

Note that in all the cases mentioned above we lose different degrees of responsiveness (transactions cannot always progress independently) for the sake of reduced overhead and abort rate.

2 Memory Management Challenges of Multi-versioned STMs

One of the key aspects to maintaining multiple versions is a mechanism for garbage collecting (GC) old object versions. In this section we show that while keeping a constant number of versions per object might be suboptimal, a space optimal solution is impossible as well.

2.1 STMs with a Constant Number of Versions for Every Object

The simplest multi-versioning STM approach is to keep a constant preconfigured number of old versions for every object. However, this technique has two main issues.

First, we lose a premise that every read-only transaction successfully commits in a non-blocking manner (responsive MV-permissiveness). Indeed, for every constant number k of object versions, there exists a scenario in which some hot object is updated $k+1$ times after a read of a read-only transaction T_r, such that the old version corresponding to the consistent snapshot of T_r is deleted and the reader has to abort.

Secondly, keeping a constant number of object versions causes an inherent memory consumption problem. A naïve assessment of the memory consumption of a k-versioned STM would probably estimate that it takes up to k times as much more memory as a single-versioned STM.

However, in [26] we demonstrate that, in fact, the memory consumption of a k-versioned STM in runs with n transactional objects might grow like k^n. Intuitively, this happens because previous object versions continue to keep references to already deleted objects, which causes deleted objects to be pinned in memory.

Consider, for example, a 2-versioned STM in the scenario depicted in Figure 2. The STM keeps a linked list of three nodes. When removing node 30 and inserting a new node 40 instead, node 30 is still kept as the previous version of 20.*next*. Next, when node 20 is replaced with node 25, node 30 is still pinned in memory, as it is referenced by node 20. After several additional node replacements, we see that there is a complete binary tree in memory, although only a linked list is used in the application.

More generally, with a k-versioned STM, a linked list of length n could lead to $\Omega(k^n)$ node versions being pinned in memory (though being still linear to the number of write operations). This demonstrates an inherent limitation of keeping a constant number of versions per object. Our observation is confirmed by the empirical results shown in [26], where the algorithms keeping k versions cannot terminate in the runs with a limited heap size.

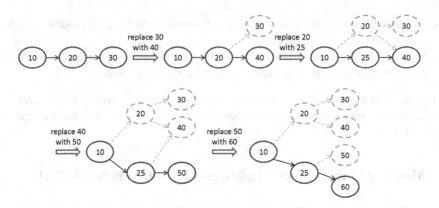

Fig. 2. Example demonstrating exponential memory growth for an STM keeping 2 versions of each object. A linked list implementation creates a whole binary tree to be pinned in memory because previous node versions continue keeping references to already deleted nodes.

2.2 Impossibility of Space Optimal STM

While keeping a constant number of versions does not work, we need a smarter way to manage old object versions. Unfortunately, responsive MV-permissive cannot be space optimal as we show below.

Definition 1. *A responsive MV-permissive STM $\mathcal{X}$ is online space optimal, if for any other responsive MV-permissive STM $\mathcal{X}'$ and any transactional history H, the number of versions kept by $\mathcal{X}$ at any point of time during H is less than or equal to the number of versions kept by $\mathcal{X}'$.*

Theorem 1. *No responsive MV-permissive STM can be online space optimal.*

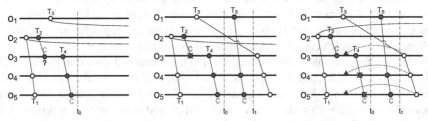

(a) An STM does not know whether to remove o_3^1.

(b) Removing o_3^1 leads to keeping the versions of o_4 and o_5 after they are overwritten.

(c) Keeping o_3^1 allows removing the versions of o_4 and o_5 after they are overwritten.

Fig. 3. No STM can be online space optimal — it is not known at time t_0 whether to remove the version of o_3 written by T_2

Proof (full proof in [27]). The main idea is to construct a transactional history in which any STM that keeps the minimum number of object versions at a time t_0 will keep more than the minimum number of object versions at time $t_1 > t_0$. Consider the transactional history H depicted in Figure 3(a). At time t_0, $\mathcal{X}$ should either remove object version o_3^1 or keep it. In [27] we show that for either one of these decisions, there exists a responsive MV-permissive STM that keeps fewer versions than $\mathcal{X}$ during H or an extension of H. Thus, no STM can keep the minimum number of versions at all times, and so is not online space optimal.

2.3 Garbage Collecting Useless Prefixes

Though we have just seen that no responsive MV-permissive STM is online space optimal, we would still like an STM to manage old versions better than a constant number of object versions approach. Intuitively, we want to garbage collect as many old versions as we can by truncating the whole prefix of a versions list. To this end, we define the following.

Definition 2. *An MV-permissive STM satisfies useless-prefix (UP) GC if at any point in a transactional history H, an object version o_i^j is kept only if there exists an extension of H with an active transaction T_i, such that (1) T_i can read o_i^j, and (2) T_i cannot read any version written after o_i^j.*

In other words an STM satisfying UP GC, removes the longest possible prefix of versions for each object at any point in time and keeps the shortest suffix of versions that might be needed by read-only transactions.

Note that STMs satisfying UP GC are going to keep all the versions of an object that have been added since the snapshot time of the oldest read-only transaction. Therefore, the number of old versions of an object is defined by the ratio of its update rate to the duration time of read-only transactions in the system: rarely updated objects will usually keep the last version only, while hot objects might still keep a lot of previous versions if a long read-only transaction is stuck.

3   Performance Challenges of Multi-versioned STMs

3.1   Disjoint-Access Parallelism

In shared memory systems, cache contention due to concurrent memory accesses, and especially concurrent writes, is a significant performance bottleneck. Thus, it is desirable to try to separate the memory locations accessed by different transactions as much as possible. One natural requirement seems to be that transactions that access different transactional objects access only different base objects. This property is formally captured by the notion of *weak disjoint-access parallelism* [2], which is defined below.

Let T_1, T_2 be transactions, and let α be an execution. Let $\mathcal{T}$ be the set of all transactions whose execution interval overlaps with the execution interval of $\{T_1, T_2\}$ in α. Let X be the set of transactional objects accessed by $\mathcal{T}$. Let $G(T_1, T_2, \alpha)$ be an undirected graph with vertex set X, and an edge between vertices $x_1, x_2 \in X$ whenever there is a transaction $T \in \mathscr{T}$ accessing both x_1 and x_2. We say T_1, T_2 are *disjoint-access* in α if there is no path between T_1 and T_2 in $G(T_1, T_2, \alpha)$. Given two sets of base steps, we say they *contend* if there is a base object that is accessed by both sets of steps, and at least one of the accesses changes the state of the object.

Definition 3. *An STM is* weakly disjoint-access parallel (weakly DAP) *if, given any execution α, and transactions T_1, T_2 that are disjoint-access in α, the base steps for T_1 and T_2 in α do not contend.*

Theorem 2. *A responsive STM satisfying MV-permissiveness cannot be weakly disjoint-access parallel.*

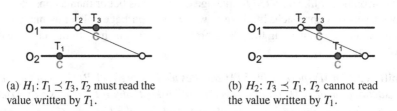

(a) H_1: $T_1 \preceq T_3$, T_2 must read the value written by T_1.

(b) H_2: $T_3 \preceq T_1$, T_2 cannot read the value written by T_1.

Fig. 4. In a weakly DAP STM T_1 does not distinguish between H_1 and H_2 and cannot be MV-permissive

Proof (full proof in [27]). Suppose for contradiction that there exists a responsive STM satisfying MV-permissiveness that is weakly DAP. Consider the transactional histories in Figure 4. In both H_1 and H_2, transactions T_2 and T_3 conflict on object o_1: T_3 writes to o_1 and commits, overriding the value read by an active transaction T_2. Note that since an STM is responsive and satisfies MV-permissiveness, T_3 neither aborts nor waits for T_2's termination upon a write to o_1. In [27] we prove the following claims: (1) The second step of T_2 returns o_2^1 in H_1. (2) The second step of T_2 returns o_2^1 in H_2. (3) The first step of T_2 returns o_1^0 in H_2. (4) H_2 is not strictly serializable if the first step of T_2 returns o_1^0, and the second step returns o_2^1. Conclusion (4) contradicts the strict serializability of the STM, which proves that there is no responsive STM that is both MV-permissive and weakly DAP.

It is interesting to note that the previous result stems from the real-time order requirement of opacity used as our correctness criterion: independent transactions still need a common base object to designate their real-time order. If we are ready to tolerate real-time order violation of disjoint transactions, we can imagine an implementation of DAP multi-versioned STM.

3.2 Read Visibility

Another desirable property for an STM is not to update shared memory during read-only transactions. Such STMs are said to use *invisible reads*. It is easy to show that an

STM satisfying MV-permissiveness and UP GC cannot use invisible reads. Indeed, UP GC requires knowing about existing read-only transactions, in order to determine which object versions to GC; such knowledge cannot be obtained unless read-only transactions write.

However, it is possible to show a much stronger statement: UP GC is impossible even if we allow read-only transactions to write, and only require that the external configurations before and after the transaction are the same. In other words, UP GC requires read-only transactions to leave some trace of their existence, even *after* they have committed. In particular, even keeping active readers lists for the objects [15], or using non-zero indicators for conflict detection [12] does not suffice.

Theorem 3. *Suppose a responsive STM satisfies MV permissiveness and UP GC. Consider a read-only transaction whose execution interval does not contain base steps of any other transaction. Then the configuration external to the transaction, immediately before and after the transaction, cannot be the same.*

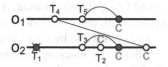 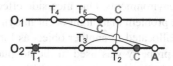

(a) H_1: o_2^1 is GCed, T_4 can read o_2^2 and commits.

(b) H_2: o_2^1 is GCed, T_4 cannot read o_2^2 and aborts.

Fig. 5. H_1 and H_2 are indistinguishable if a read-only transaction T_2 does not leave any trace after its execution

Proof (full proof in [27]). Suppose for contradiction that there exists a responsive STM satisfying MV-permissiveness and UP GC, in which the external configurations before and after a read-only transaction are the same, when the transaction's interval does not overlap the steps of any other transaction. Consider the transactional histories in Figure 5. In [27] we prove the the following claims: (1) o_2^1 is GCed in H_1. (2) o_2^1 is GCed in H_2. (3) T_4 aborts in H_2. Conclusion (3) is a contradiction, because T_4 is a read-only transaction, and cannot abort because of MV-permissiveness.

4   Multi-versioned STM in Managed Memory Environments

4.1   Concurrent Algorithms Are Simpler with Garbage Collection

As demonstrated in Sections 2 and 3, maintaining multiple versions in an STM is a challenging task. Space optimality is impossible and even with a non-optimal uselessprefix garbage collection, read-only transactions must leave a trace of their existence, which might devastate STM performance.

Combining invisible readers with effective garbage collection is problematic — if read-only transactions are invisible, then other transactions have no way of telling whether potential readers of an old version still exist! Some STM implementations take the approach of special cleanup threads, like JVSTM [7]: in this case the visibility of the readers' operations can be limited to cleanup threads only. However, in garbage collected environments it is possible to exploit the designated GC threads, which are running in the system anyway. GC threads have access to all the threads' private memories, so that even operations that are invisible to other transactions are visible to the garbage collector.

We now give a brief reminder of the garbage collection mechanism. An object can be reclaimed by the garbage collector once it becomes unreachable from the call stack or global variables. Reachability is a transitive closure over *strong* memory references: if a reachable object o_1 has a strong reference to o_2, then o_2 is reachable as well (strong references are the default ones). In contrast, *weak references* [16] do not protect the referenced object from being GCed; an object referenced by weak references only is considered unreachable and may be removed.

Generally speaking, an automatic deletion of unreachable objects in garbage collected environments plays a significant role in various concurrent systems way beyond the STM world, dramatically simplifying the algorithmic part in comparison with native environments. One nice side effect of an automated GC is the elimination of the ABA problem that might occur in dynamic data structures [22]: object memory cannot be reallocated to another object as long as this memory is reachable by a live thread. This property was used in the adaptation of Michael-Scott non-blocking concurrent queue [23] to Java concurrency library, as well as in CAFÉ, scalable producer consumer Java library [4].

4.2 Selective Multi-Versioning (SMV) STM

We now want to exemplify the principles discussed earlier in this section, in which garbage collection of old versions is delegated to the already existing GC mechanisms of the managed environment. For that purpose we present *Selective Multi-Versioning (SMV)* [26], an STM which keeps old object versions that are still useful to potential readers, while allowing read-only transactions to remain invisible by ensuring that old object versions become *garbage collectible* once there are no transactions that can safely read them.

SMV is especially efficient for read-dominated workloads with long read-only transactions, in situations where other transactions would either repeatedly abort readers or block update transactions for extended periods of time.

4.2.1 Overview of Data Structures

SMV's main goal is to reduce aborts in workloads with read-only transactions, without introducing high space or computational overheads. SMV is based on the following design choices: 1) Read-only transactions do not affect the memory that can be accessed by other transactions. This property is important for performance in multi-core systems, as it avoids cache thrashing issues [13,30]. 2) Read-only transactions always commit. A read-only transaction T_i observes a consistent snapshot corresponding to T_i's start time — when T_i reads object o_j, it finds the latest version of o_j that has been written before T_i's start. 3) Old object versions are removed once there are no live read-only transactions that can consistently read them. To achieve this with invisible reads, SMV relies on the omniscient GC mechanism available in managed memory systems.

As in other object-based STMs, transactional objects in SMV are accessed via *object handles*. An object handle includes a history of object values, where each value keeps a *versioned lock* [9] – a data structure with a version number and a lock bit. In order to facilitate automatic garbage collection, object handles in SMV keep strong references only to the latest (current) versions of each object, and use weak references to point to other versions.

Each transaction is associated with a *transactional descriptor*, which holds the relevant transactional data, including a read-set, a write-set, status, etc. In addition, transactional descriptors play an important role in keeping strong references to old object versions, as we explain below.

Version numbers are generated using a global version clock, where transactional descriptors act as "time points" organized in a one-directional linked list. Upon commit, an update transaction appends its transactional descriptor to the end of the list (a special global variable *curPoint* points to the latest descriptor in this list). For example, if the current global version is 100, a committing update transaction sets the time point value in its transactional descriptor to 101 and adds a pointer to this descriptor from the descriptor holding 100.

Version management is based on the idea that old object versions are pointed to by the descriptors of transactions that over-wrote these versions (see Figure 6). A committing transaction T_w includes in its transactional descriptor a strong reference to the previous version of every object in its write set before diverting the respective object handle to the new version.

When a read-only transaction T_i begins, it keeps (in its local variable *startTP*) a pointer to the latest transactional descriptor in the list of committed transactions. This pointer is cleared upon commit, making old transactional descriptors at the head of the list GCable.

This way, active read-only transaction T_r keeps a reference chain to version o_i^j if this version was over-written after T_r's start, thus preventing o_i^j's garbage collection. Once there are no active read-only transactions that started before o_i^j was over-written, this version stops being referenced and thus becomes GCable .

Figure 6 illustrates the commit of an update transaction T_w that writes to object o_1 (the use of *readyPoint* variable will be explained in Section 4.2.3). In this example, T_w and a read-only transaction T_r both start at time 9, and hence T_r references the transactional descriptor of time point 9. The previous update of o_1 was associated with version 5. When T_w commits, it inserts its transactional descriptor at the end of the time points list with value 10. T_w's descriptor references the previous value of o_1. This way, the algorithm creates a reference chain from T_r to the previous version of o_1 via T_w's descriptor, which ensures that the needed version will not be GCed as long as T_r is active.

4.2.2 Basic Algorithm

We now describe the SMV algorithm. For the sake of simplicity, we present the algorithm in this section using a global lock for treating concurrency on commit — in Section 4.2.3 we show how to remove this lock.

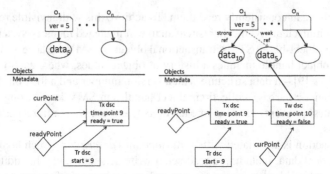

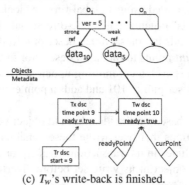

(a) T_r's descriptor points to the latest committed transaction.

(b) T_w commits and begins write-back.

(c) T_w's write-back is finished.

Fig. 6. Transactional descriptor of T_w references the over-written version of o_1 ($data_5$). This way, read-only transaction T_r keeps a reference chain to the versions that have been overwritten after T_r's start.

SMV handles read-only and update transactions differently. We assume that transaction's type can be provided to the algorithm beforehand by a compiler or via special program annotations. If not, each transaction can be started as read-only and then restarted as update upon the first occurrence of a write operation.

Handling Update Transactions

The protocol for update transaction T_i is depicted in Algorithm 1. The general idea is similar to the one used in TL2 [9]. An update transaction T_i aborts if some object o_j read by T_i is over-written after T_i begins and before T_i commits. Upon starting, T_i saves the value of the latest time point in a local variable *startTime*, which holds the latest time at which an object in T_i's read-set is allowed to be over-written.

A read operation of object o_j reads the latest value of o_j, and then post-validates its version (function *validateRead*. The validation procedure checks that the version is not locked and it is not greater than T_i.startTime, otherwise the transaction is aborted.

A write operation (lines 12–14) creates a copy of the object's latest version and adds it to T_i's local write set.

Algorithm 1. SMV algorithm for update transaction T_i.

```
 1: Upon Startup:
 2:    T_i.startTime ← curPoint.commitTime

 3: Read o_j:
 4:    if (o_j ∈ T_i.writeSet)
 5:       then return T_i.writeSet[o_j]
 6:    data ← o_j.latest
 7:    if ¬validateRead(o_j) then abort
 8:    readSet.put(o_j)
 9:    return data

10: Write to o_j:
11:    if (o_j ∈ T_i.writeSet)
12:       then update T_i.writeSet.get(o_j); return
13:    localCopy ← o_j.latest.clone()
14:    update localCopy; writeSet[o_j] ← localCopy

15: Function validateReadSet
16:    foreach o_j ∈ T_i.readSet do:
17:       if ¬validateRead(o_j) then return false
18:    return true

19: Commit:
20:    foreach o_j ∈ T_i.writeSet do: o_j.lock()
21:    if ¬validateReadSet() then abort
         ▷ txn dsc should reference the over-written data
22:    foreach o_j ∈ T_i.writeSet do:
23:       T_i.prevVersions.put(⟨o_j, o_j.latest⟩)
24:    timeLock.lock()
25:    T_i.commitTime ← curPoint.commitTime + 1
         ▷ update and unlock the objects
26:    foreach ⟨o_j, data⟩ ∈ T_i.writeSet do:
27:       o_j.version ← T_i.commitTime
28:       o_j.weak_references.append(o_j.latest)
29:       o_j.latest ← data; o_j.unlock()
30:    curPoint.next ← T_i; curPoint ← T_i
31:    timeLock.unlock()

32: Function validateRead(Object o_j)
33:    return (¬o_j.isLocked ∧ o_j.version ≤ T_i.startTime)
```

Commit (lines 20–31) consists of the following steps:

1. Lock the objects in the write set (line 20). Deadlocks can be detected using standard mechanisms (e.g., timeouts or Dreadlocks [21]), or may be avoided if acquired in the same order by every transaction.
2. Validate the read set (function *validateReadSet*).

3. Insert strong references to the over-written versions to T_i's descriptor (line 23). This way the algorithm guarantees that the over-written versions stay in the memory as long as T_i's descriptor is referenced by some read-only transaction.
4. Lock the time points list (line 24). Recall that this is a simplification; in Section 4.2.3 we show how to avoid such locking.
5. Set the commit time of T_i to one plus the value of the commit time of the descriptor referenced by *curPoint*.
6. Update and unlock the objects in the write set (lines 26–29). Set their new version numbers to the value of T_i.commitTime. Keep weak references to old versions.
7. Insert T_i's descriptor to the end of the time points list and unlock the list (line 30).

Handling Read-Only Transactions

Algorithm 2. SMV algorithm for read-only transaction T_i.

1: **Upon Startup:**
2:    T_i.startTP ← curPoint

3: **Read** o_j:
4:    latestData ← o_j.latest
5:    **if** (o_j.version ≤ T_i.startTP.commitTime) **then return** latestData
6:    **return** the latest version *ver* in o_j.weak_references, s.t.
7:       *ver*.version ≤ T_i.startTP.commitTime

8: **Commit:**
9:    T_i.startTP ← ⊥

The pseudo-code for read-only transactions appears in Algorithm 2. Such transactions always commit without waiting for other transactions to invoke any operations. The general idea is to construct a consistent snapshot based on the start time of T_i. At startup, T_i.*startTP* points to the latest installed transactional descriptor (line 2); we refer to the time value of startTP as T_i's *start time*.

For each object o_j, T_i reads the latest version of o_j written before T_i's start time. When T_i reads an object o_j whose latest version is greater than its start time, it continues to read older versions until it finds one with a version number older than its start time. Some old enough version is guaranteed to be found, because the updating transaction T_w that over-wrote o_j has added T_w's descriptor referencing the over-written version somewhere after T_i's starting point, preventing GC.

The commit procedure for read-only transactions merely removes the pointer to the starting time point, in order to make it GCable, and always commits.

4.2.3   Allowing Concurrent Access to the Time Points List

We show now how to avoid locking the time points list (lines 24, 31 in Algorithm 1), so that update transactions with disjoint write-sets may commit concurrently.

We first explain the reason for using the lock. In order to update the objects in the write-set, the updating transaction has to know the new version number to use. However, if a transaction exposes its descriptor before it finishes updating the write-set, then some read-only transaction might observe an inconsistent state. Consider, for example, transaction T_w that updates objects o_1 and o_2. The value of *curPoint* at the beginning of T_w's commit is 9. Assume T_w first inserts its descriptor with value 10 to the list, then updates object o_1 and pauses. At this point, $o_1.version = 10$, $o_2.version < 10$ and *curPoint* $\rightarrow$ *commitTime* $= 10$. If a new read-only transaction starts with time 10, it can successfully read the new value of o_1 and the old value of o_2, because they are both less than or equal to 10. Intuitively, the problem is that the new time point becomes available to the readers as a potential starting time before all the objects of the committing transaction are updated.

To preserve consistency without locking the time points list, we add an additional boolean field *ready* to the descriptor's structure, which becomes *true* only after the committing transaction finishes updating all objects in its write-set. In addition to the global *curPoint* variable referencing the latest time point, we keep a global *readyPoint* variable, which references the latest time point in the *ready prefix* of the list (see Figure 6).

When a new read-only transaction starts, its *startTP* variable references *readyPoint*. In the example above, a new transaction T_r begins with a start time equal to 9, because the new time point with value 10 is still not ready. Generally, the use of *readyPoint* guarantees that if a transaction reads an object version written by T_w, then T_w and all its preceding transactions had finished writing their write-sets.

Note, however, that when using ready points we should not violate the real time order — if a read-only transaction T_r starts after T_w terminates, then T_r must have a start time value not less than T_w's commit time. This property might be violated if update transactions become ready in an order that differs from their time points order, thus leaving an unready transaction between ready ones in the list.

In [26] we have implemented two approaches to enforce real-time order: 1) An update transaction does not terminate until the ready point reaches its descriptor. A similar approach was previously used by RingSTM [31] and JVSTM [14]. 2) A new read-only transaction notes the time point of the latest terminated transaction and then waits until the *readyPoint* reaches this point before starting. Note that unlike the first alternative, read-only transactions in the second approach are not wait-free.

According to [26], both techniques demonstrate similar results. The waiting period remains negligible as long as the number of transactional threads does not exceed the number of available cores; when the number of threads is two times the number of cores, waiting causes a $10 - 15\%$ throughput degradation (depending on the workload) — this is the cost we pay for maintaining real-time order.

5   Conclusions

An effective way to reduce the number of aborts in transactional memory is keeping multiple versions of transactional objects. We studied the inherent properties of STMs that use multiple versions to guarantee successful commits of all read-only transactions (we call such STMs MV-permissive). We presented the challenge of efficient garbage collection of old object versions by demonstrating that the memory consumption of algorithms keeping a constant number of versions for each object can grow exponentially. We then showed that no responsive MV-permissive STM can be optimal in the number of previous versions kept and that no responsive MV-permissive STM can be disjoint-access parallel. We defined an achievable garbage collection property, useless-prefix GC, and showed that in a responsive MV-permissive STM satisfying UP GC, even read-only transactions must make lasting changes to the system state.

Theoretical study of multi-versioning in STM is far from being complete. There are clear tradeoffs between the quality of garbage collection, permissiveness and the computational complexity of transactional operations: we believe that understanding these tradeoffs may be valuable to improving the performance and utility of transactional memory.

We referred to practical implications of multi-versioning by discussing SMV, a multi-versioned STM that achieves high performance in the presence of read-only transactions. Despite keeping multiple versions, SMV can work well in memory constrained environments. It keeps old object versions as long as they might be useful while still allowing read-only transactions to remain invisible by relying on automatic garbage collection to dispose of obsolete versions.

SMV exemplifies the idea of delegating disposal responsibilities to the independent GC module that is being developed and upgraded by a very large community. We think that this approach can be the key to achieving good performance not only in STMs, but also in a range of concurrent data structures.

References

1. Attiya, H., Hillel, E.: Single-version STMs can be multi-version permissive (Extended abstract). In: Aguilera, M.K., Yu, H., Vaidya, N.H., Srinivasan, V., Choudhury, R.R. (eds.) ICDCN 2011. LNCS, vol. 6522, pp. 83–94. Springer, Heidelberg (2011), http://dl.acm.org/citation.cfm?id=1946143.1946151
2. Attiya, H., Hillel, E., Milani, A.: Inherent limitations on disjoint-access parallel implementations of transactional memory. In: Proceedings of the Twenty-first Annual Symposium on Parallelism in Algorithms and Architectures, SPAA 2009, pp. 69–78. ACM, New York (2009), http://doi.acm.org/10.1145/1583991.1584015
3. Aydonat, U., Abdelrahman, T.: Serializability of transactions in software transactional memory. In: Second ACM SIGPLAN Workshop on Transactional Computing (2008)
4. Basin, D., Fan, R., Keidar, I., Kiselov, O., Perelman, D.: CAFÉ: Scalable task pools with adjustable fairness and contention. In: Peleg, D. (ed.) DISC 2011. LNCS, vol. 6950, pp. 475–488. Springer, Heidelberg (2011)
5. Berenson, H., Bernstein, P., Gray, J., Melton, J., O'Neil, E., O'Neil, P.: A critique of ANSI SQL isolation levels. In: Proceedings of the 1995 ACM SIGMOD International Conference on Management of Data, pp. 1–10 (1995)
6. Bernstein, P.A., Hadzilacos, V., Goodman, N.: Concurrency Control and Recovery in Database Systems. Addison-Wesley (1987)
7. Cachopo, J., Rito-Silva, A.: Versioned boxes as the basis for memory transactions. Science of Computer Programming 63(2), 172–185 (2006)
8. Carvalho, N., Cachopo, J., Rodrigues, L., Rito-Silva, A.: Versioned transactional shared memory for the FenixEDU web application. In: Proceedings of the 2nd Workshop on Dependable Distributed Data Management, pp. 15–18 (2008)
9. Dice, D., Shalev, O., Shavit, N.: Transactional locking II. In: Dolev, S. (ed.) DISC 2006. LNCS, vol. 4167, pp. 194–208. Springer, Heidelberg (2006)

10. Dice, D., Shavit, N.: TLRW: Return of the read-write lock. In: TRANSACT 2009: 4th Work-shop on Transactional Computing (February 2009)
11. Dragojević, A., Harris, T.: Stm in the small: Trading generality for performance in software transactional memory. In: Proceedings of the 7th ACM European Conference on Computer Systems, EuroSys 2012, pp. 1–14. ACM, New York (2012),
    http://doi.acm.org/10.1145/2168836.2168838
12. Ellen, F., Lev, Y., Luchangco, V., Moir, M.: Snzi: Scalable nonzero indicators. In: PODC 2007: Proceedings of the Twenty-Sixth Annual ACM Symposium on Principles of Dis-tributed Computing, pp. 13–22. ACM, New York (2007)
13. Ennals, R.: Cache sensitive software transactional memory. Tech. rep.
14. Fernandes, S.M., Cachopo, J.A.: Lock-free and Scalable Multi-Version Software Transac-tional Memory. In: PPoPP 2011, pp. 179–188 (2011)
15. Fraser, K.: Practical lock freedom. Ph.D. thesis, Cambridge University Computer Laboratory (2003)
16. Gosling, J., Joy, B., Steele, G., Bracha, G.: The Java Language Specification, 3rd edn. Addison-Wesley Longman (2005)
17. Guerraoui, R., Henzinger, T.A., Singh, V.: Permissiveness in Transactional Memories. In: Taubenfeld, G. (ed.) DISC 2008. LNCS, vol. 5218, pp. 305–319. Springer, Heidelberg (2008)
18. Heber, T., Hendler, D., Suissa, A.: On the impact of serializing contention management on stm performance. J. Parallel Distrib. Comput. 72(6), 739–750 (2012),
    http://dx.doi.org/10.1016/j.jpdc.2012.02.009
19. Herlihy, M., Shavit, N.: The Art of Multiprocessor Programming. Morgan Kaufmann (2008)
20. Keidar, I., Perelman, D.: On avoiding spare aborts in transactional memory. In: SPAA 2009, pp. 59–68 (2009)
21. Koskinen, E., Herlihy, M.: Dreadlocks: Efficient deadlock detection. In: Proceedings of the Twentieth Annual Symposium on Parallelism in Algorithms and Architectures, pp. 297–303 (2008)
22. Michael, M.M.: Hazard pointers: Safe memory reclamation for lock-free objects. IEEE Trans. Parallel Distrib. Syst. 15, 491–504 (2004)
23. Michael, M.M., Scott, M.L.: Simple, fast, and practical non-blocking and blocking concur-rent queue algorithms. In: Proceedings of the Fifteenth Annual ACM Symposium on Princi-ples of Distributed Computing, PODC 1996, pp. 267–275 (1996)
24. Napper, J., Alvisi, L.: Lock-free serializable transactions. Tech. rep., The University of Texas at Austin (2005)
25. Papadimitriou, C.H., Kanellakis, P.C.: On concurrency control by multiple versions. ACM Trans. Database Syst., 89–99 (1984)
26. Perelman, D., Byshevsky, A., Litmanovich, O., Keidar, I.: SMV: Selective multi-versioning STM. In: Peleg, D. (ed.) DISC 2011. LNCS, vol. 6950, pp. 125–140. Springer, Heidelberg (2011)
27. Perelman, D., Fan, R., Keidar, I.: On maintaining multiple versions in STM. In: Proceedings of the 22nd ACM Symposium on Parallelism in Algorithms and Architectures, PODC 2001, pp. 16–25 (2010)
28. Ramadan, H.E., Roy, I., Herlihy, M., Witchel, E.: Committing conflicting transactions in an STM. SIGPLAN Not 44(4), 163–172 (2009)
29. Riegel, T., Fetzer, C., Sturzrehm, H., Felber, P.: From causal to z-linearizable transactional memory. In: Proceedings of the 26th Annual ACM Symposium on Principles of Distributed Computing, pp. 340–341 (2007)
30. Riegel, T., Felber, P., Fetzer, C.: A lazy snapshot algorithm with eager validation. In: Proceed-ings of the 20th International Symposium on Distributed Computing, pp. 284–298 (2006)
31. Spear, M.F., Michael, M.M., von Praun, C.: RingSTM: Scalable transactions with a single atomic instruction. In: SPAA 2008, pp. 275–284 (2008)

Framework Support for the Efficient Implementation of Multi-version Algorithms

Ricardo J. Dias, Tiago M. Vale, and João M. Lourenço

CITI — Universidade Nova de Lisboa, Quinta da Torre, 2829-516 Caparica, Portugal
{ricardo.dias,joao.lourenco}@fct.unl.pt,
t.vale@campus.fct.unl.pt

Abstract. Software Transactional Memory algorithms associate metadata with the memory locations accessed during a transaction's lifetime. This metadata may be stored in an external table and accessed by way of a function that maps the address of each memory location with the table entry that keeps its metadata (this is the out-place or external scheme); or alternatively may be stored adjacent to the associated memory cell by wrapping them together (the in-place scheme). In transactional memory multi-version algorithms, several versions of the same memory location may exist. The efficient implementation of these algorithms requires a one-to-one correspondence between each memory location and its list of past versions, which is stored as metadata. In this chapter we address the matter of the efficient implementation of multi-version algorithms in Java by proposing and evaluating a novel in-place metadata scheme for the Deuce framework. This new scheme is based in Java Bytecode transformation techniques and its use requires no changes to the application code. Experimentation indicates that multi-versioning STM algorithms implemented using our new in-place scheme are in average $6\times$ faster than when implemented with the out-place scheme.

1 Introduction

Software Transactional Memory (STM) algorithms differ in the properties and in the guarantees they provide. Among other differences, one can refer distinct strategies used to read (visible or invisible) and update memory (direct or deferred), the consistency (opacity or snapshot isolation) and progress guarantees (solo, global and local progress), the policies applied to conflict resolution (contention management), and the sensitivity to interactions with non-transactional code (weak or strong atomicity). Some STM frameworks, e.g., DSTM2 [10] and Deuce [11], address the need of experimenting with new algorithms and their comparative evaluation by providing a single transactional interface over which the STM algorithms are built. However, the internal architecture each STM framework tends to favor the performance of some classes of STM algorithms and disfavor others. For instance, the Deuce framework stores the metadata in an external table and favors algorithms like TL2 [6] and LSA [14], which are resilient to the false sharing of transactional metadata (such as ownership records), and disfavor multi-version algorithms, which require unique metadata per memory location.

STM algorithms manage information per transaction (frequently referred to as the *transaction descriptor*), and per memory location (or object reference) accessed within

R. Guerraoui and P. Romano (Eds.): Transactional Memory, LNCS 8913, pp. 166–191, 2015.

that transaction. The transaction descriptor is typically stored in a thread-local memory space and keeps the information required to validate and commit the transaction, e.g., the read- and write-sets. The per memory location information, henceforth be referred as *metadata*, depends on the nature of the STM algorithm and may contain locks, timestamps, version lists. Metadata is stored either adjacent to each memory location (*in-place* scheme), or in an external table (*out-place* or *external* scheme). STM libraries for imperative languages, such as C, frequently use the out-place scheme, while those addressing object-oriented languages bias towards the in-place scheme.

The out-place scheme is implemented by using a table-like data structure that efficiently maps memory references to its metadata. Storing the metadata in such a pre-allocated table avoids the overhead of dynamic memory allocation, but incurs in the overhead for evaluating the location-to-metadata mapping function. The bounded size of the external table also induces a false sharing situation, where multiple memory locations share the same table entry and hence the same metadata, in a *many-to-one* relation between memory locations and metadata units. The in-place scheme is usually implemented using the *decorator* design pattern [8], by extending the functionality of an original class by wrapping it in a *decorator* class that contains the required metadata. This scheme implements a *one-to-one* relation between memory locations and metadata units, thus no false sharing occurs. It allows the direct access to the object metadata without significant overhead, but is very intrusive to the application code, which must be heavily rewritten to use the decorator classes instead of the original ones. The *decorator* pattern based technique bears two other problems: additional overhead for non-transactional code, and multiple difficulties while working with primitive and array types. Riegel et al. [15] briefly describe the trade-offs of using in-place *versus* out-place strategies.

Deuce is among the most efficient STM frameworks for the Java programming language and provides a well defined interface that is used to implement several STM algorithms. On the application developer's side, a memory transaction is defined by adding the annotation @Atomic to a Java method, and the framework automatically instruments the application's bytecode to intercept the read and write memory accesses by injecting call-backs to the STM algorithm. These call-backs receive the referenced memory address as argument, hence limiting the range of viable STM algorithms to be implemented by forcing an out-place scheme. Implementing in Deuce an algorithm that requires a one-to-one relation between metadata and memory locations, such as a multi-version algorithm, requires the use of an external table to handles collisions, which significantly degrades the throughput of the algorithm.

In the remaining of this Chapter we present a novel approach to support the in-place metadata scheme that does not use the decorator pattern, and thoroughly evaluate its implementation in Deuce. This extension allows the efficient implementation of multi-version algorithms, which require a one-to-one relation between metadata and memory locations. The developed extension has the following properties:

Efficiency. The extension fully supports primitive types, even in transactional code. Transactional code does not require the extra memory dereference imposed by the decorator pattern. Non-transactional code is in general oblivious to the presence of metadata in objects, hence no significant performance overhead is introduced.

And we propose a solution for supporting transactional n-dimensional arrays with a negligible overhead for non-transactional code.

Flexibility. The extension supports both the original out-place and the new in-place strategies simultaneously, hence it is fully backwards compatible and imposes no restrictions on the nature of the STM algorithms to be used, nor on their implementation strategies.

Transparency. The extension automatically identifies, creates and initializes all the necessary additional metadata fields in objects. No source code changes are required, although we apply some light transformations to the non-transactional bytecode.

Compatibility. Our extension is fully backwards compatible and the already existing implementations of STM algorithms are executed with no changes, and with zero or negligible performance overhead.

Compliance. The extension and bytecode transformations are fully-compliant with the Java specification, hence supported by standard Java compilers and JVMs.

The Deuce framework assumes a weak atomicity model, i.e., transactions are atomic only with respect to other transactions, and hence their execution may be interleaved with non-transactional code. Multi-version algorithms update objects (memory locations) by writing the new value to the object (memory cell) metadata (which contain the lists or past values), and therefore transactional accesses cannot see non-transactional updates, and vice-versa. We tackle this problem by proposing an algorithmic adaptation for multi-version algorithms that enables the support of a weak atomicity model for multi-version algorithms with meaningless impact in the overall performance.

This chapter follows with a description of the Deuce framework and its out-place scheme in Section 2. Section 3 describes properties of the in-place scheme, its implementation, and its limitations as an extension to Deuce. We present an evaluation of the extension's implementation using several metrics in Section 4. Section 5 describes the implementation of several state-of-the-art STM multi-version algorithms using our proposed extension. In Section 6 we show how to adapt the multi-version algorithms to support a weak-atomicity model. Finally, we present a comparison between different single- and multi-version algorithms using standard benchmarks in Section 7.

2   The Deuce Framework

Deuce supplies a single @Atomic Java annotation, and relies heavily on bytecode instrumentation to provide a transparent transactional interface to application developers, which are unaware of how the STM algorithms are implemented and which strategies they use to store the transactional metadata. Algorithms such as TL2 [6] or LSA [14] use an out-place scheme by resorting to a very fast hashing function and storing a single lock in each table entry. Due to performance issues, the mapping table does not avoid hash collisions and thus two memory locations may be mapped to the same table entry, resulting in the false sharing of a lock by two different memory locations. In these algorithms, false sharing may have some impact in the performance but does not affect the correctness. To implement multi-version algorithms with the out-place scheme, one has to manage collision lists in the table, which significantly degrades performance.

```
public interface Context {
    void init(int atomicBlockId, String metainf);
    boolean commit();
    void rollback();
    void beforeReadAccess(Object obj, long field);
    int onReadAccess(Object obj, int value, long field);
    // ... onReadAccess for the remaining types
    void onWriteAccess(Object obj, int value, long field);
    // ... onWriteAccess for the remaining types
}
```

Fig. 1. Context interface for implementing an STM algorithm

To support the out-place scheme, Deuce identifies an object's field by the object reference and the field's logical offset. This logical offset is computed at compile time, and for every field f in every class C an extra static field f^o is added to that class, whose value represents the logical offset of f in class C. No extra fields are added for array cells, as the logical offset of each cell corresponds to its index. Within a memory transaction, when there is a read or write memory access to a field f of an object O, or to the array element $A[i]$, the runtime passes the pair (O, f^o) or (A, i) respectively as the argument to the call-back function. The STM algorithm shall not differentiate between field and array accesses. If an algorithm wants to, e.g., associate a lock with a field, it has to store the lock in an external table indexed by the hash value of the pair (O, f^o) or (A, i). STM algorithm implementations must comply with a well defined Java interface, as depicted in Figure 1. The methods specified in the interface are the call-back functions that are injected by the instrumentation process in the application code. For each read and write of a field of an object, the methods onReadAccess and onWriteAccess, are invoked respectively. The method beforeReadAccess is called before the actual read of an object's field.

3   Supporting the In-Place Scheme in Deuce

In our approach to extend Deuce to support the in-place scheme, we replace the previous pair of arguments to call-back functions (O, f^o) with a new metadata object f^m, whose class is specified by the STM algorithm's programmer. We guarantee that there is a unique metadata object f^m for each field f of each object O, and hence the use of f^m to identify an object's field is equivalent to the pair (O, f^o). The same applies to arrays, where we ensure that there is a unique metadata object a^m for each position of any array A.

3.1   Implementation

Although the implementation of the support for in-place metadata objects differs considerably for class fields and array elements, a common interface is used to interact with the STM algorithm implementation. This common interface is supported by a well defined hierarchy of metadata classes, illustrated in Figure 2, where the rounded rectangle classes are defined by the STM algorithm developer.

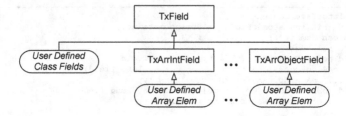

Fig. 2. Metadata classes hierarchy

```
public class TxField {
    public Object ref;
    public final long offset;
    public TxField(Object ref, long offset) {
        this.ref = ref;
        this.offset = offset;
    }
}
```

Fig. 3. TxField class

```
public interface ContextMetadata {
    void init(int atomicBlockId, String metainf);
    boolean commit();
    void rollback();
    void beforeReadAccess(TxField field);
    int onReadAccess(int value, TxField field);
    // ... onReadAccess for the remaining types
    void onWriteAccess(int value, TxField field);
    // ... onWriteAccess for the remaining types
}
```

Fig. 4. Context interface for implementing an STM algorithm supporting in-place metadata

All metadata classes associated with class fields extend directly from the top class TxField (see Figure 3). The constructor of TxField class receives the object reference and the logical offset of the field. All subclasses must call this constructor. For array elements, we created specialized metadata classes for each primitive type in Java, the TxArr*Field classes, where * ranges over the Java primitive types[1]. All the TxArr*Field classes extend from TxField, providing the STM algorithm with a simple and uniform interface for call-back functions.

We defined a new interface for the call-back methods (see Figure 4). In this new interface, the read and write call-back functions (onReadAccess and onWriteAcess respectively) receive only the metadata TxField object, not the object reference and logical offset of the Context interface. This new interface coexists with the original one in Deuce, allowing new STM algorithms to access the in-place metadata while ensuring backward compatibility.

The TxField class can be extended by the STM algorithm programmer to include additional information required by the algorithm for, e.g., locks, timestamps, or

---

[1] int, long, float, double, short, char, byte, boolean, and Object.

```
@InPlaceMetadata(
    fieldObjectClass="TL2ObjField",
    fieldIntClass="TL2IntField",
    ...
    arrayObjectClass="TL2ArrObjectField",
    arrayIntClass="TL2ArrIntField",
    ...
)
public class TL2Context implements ContextMetadata {
    ...
}
```

Fig. 5. Declaration of the STM algorithm specific metadata

```
class C {
    int a;
    Object b;
}
```
$\Longrightarrow$
```
class C {
    int a;
    Object b;
    final TxField a_metadata;
    final TxField b_metadata;
}
```

Fig. 6. Example transformation of a class with the in-place scheme

version lists. The newly defined metadata classes need to be registered in our framework to enable its use by the instrumentation process, using a Java annotation in the class that implements the STM algorithm, as exemplified in Figure 5. The programmer may register a different metadata class for each kind of data type, either for class field types or array types. As shown in the example of Figure 5, the programmer registers the metadata implementation class `TL2IntField` for the fields of **int** type, by assigning the name of the class to the `fieldIntClass` annotation property.

The STM algorithm must implement the `ContextMetadata` interface (Figure 4) that includes a call-back function for the read and write operations on each Java type. These functions always receive an instance of the super class `TxField`, but no confusion arises from there, as each algorithm knows precisely which metadata subclass was actually used to instantiate the metadata object.

Lets now see where and how the metadata objects are stored, and how they are used on the invocation of the call-back functions. We will explain separately the management of metadata objects for class fields and for array elements.

3.1.1 Adding Metadata to Class Fields

During the execution of a transaction, there must be a metadata object f^m for each accessed field f of object O. Ideally, this metadata object f^m is accessible by a single dereference operation from object O, which can be achieved by adding a new metadata field (of the corresponding type) for each field declared in a class C. The general rule for this process can be described as: given a class C that has a set of declared fields $F = \{f_1, \ldots, f_n\}$, for each field $f_i \in F$ we add a new metadata object field f_{i+n}^m to C, such that the class ends with the set of fields $F^m = \{f_1, \ldots, f_n, f_{1+n}^m, \ldots, f_{n+n}^m\}$, where each field f_i is associated with the metadata field f_{i+n}^m for any $i \leq n$. In Figure 6 we show a concrete example of the transformation of a class with two fields.

Instance and static fields are expected to have instance and static metadata fields, respectively. Thus, instance metadata fields are initialized in the class constructor, while static metadata fields are initialized in the static initializer (`static { ... }`). This ensures that whenever a new instance of a class is created, the corresponding metadata objects are also new and unique, while static metadata objects are the same in all instances. Since a class can declare multiple constructors that can call each other, using the *telescoping constructor* pattern [1], blindly instantiating the metadata fields in all constructors would be redundant and impose unnecessary stress on the garbage collector. Therefore, the creation and initialization of metadata objects only takes place in the constructors that do not rely in another constructor to initialize its target.

Opposed to the transformation approach based in the *decorator* pattern, where primitive types must be replaced with their object equivalents (e.g., in Java an `int` field is replaced by an `Integer` object), our transformation approach keeps the primitive type fields untouched, simplifying the interaction with non-transactional code, limiting the code instrumentation and avoiding auto-boxing and its overhead.

3.1.2   Adding Metadata to Array Elements

The structure of an array is very strict. Each array cell contains a single value of a well defined type and no other information can be added to those cells. The common approach to overcome this limitation, and add some more information to each cell, is to change the original array to an array of objects that wrap the original value and also contain the additional information. This straight forward transformation has many implications in the application code, as statements accessing the original array, or array elements, will now have to be rewritten to use the new array type, or wrapping class, respectively. This problem is even more complex if the new arrays with wrapped elements are to be manipulated by non-instrumented libraries, such as the JDK libraries, which are unaware of the new array types.

We address this matter by changing the type of the array to be manipulated by the instrumented application code, but with minimal impact on the performance of non-instrumented code. We keep all the values in the original array, and have a sibling second array, only manipulated by the instrumented code, that contains the additional information and references to the original array. The type in the declaration of the base array is changed to the type of the corresponding sibling array (`TxArr*Field`), as shown in Figure 7. This Figure also illustrates the general structure of the sibling `TxArr*Field` arrays (in this case, a `TxArrIntField` array). Each cell of the sibling array has the metadata information required by the STM algorithm, its own position/index in the array, and a reference to the original array where the data is stored (i.e., where the reads and updates take place). This scheme allows the sibling array to keep a metadata object for each element of the original array, while maintaining the original array always updated and compatible with non-instrumented legacy code. With this approach, the original array can still be retrieved with a minimal overhead by dereferencing twice the sibling `TxArr*Field` array. Since the original array serves as the backing store, no memory allocation or copies need to be performed, even when array elements are changed by non-instrumented code.

Non-transactional methods that have arrays as parameters are also instrumented to replace the array type by the corresponding sibling `TxArr*Field`. For non-instrumented methods, the method signature does not provide information enough to know if there is the need to revert to primitive arrays. Take, for example, the

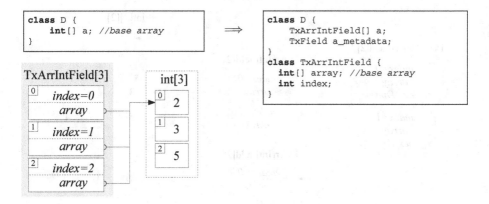

```
class D {
    int[] a; //base array
}
```

$\Longrightarrow$

```
class D {
    TxArrIntField[] a;
    TxField a_metadata;
}
class TxArrIntField {
    int[] array; //base array
    int index;
}
```

TxArrIntField[3]

0	index=0
	array
1	index=1
	array
2	index=2
	array

int[3]

0	2
1	3
2	5

Fig. 7. Memory structure of a `TxArrIntField` array

```
void foo(int[] a) {
    // ...
    t = a[i];
}
```

$\Longrightarrow$

```
void foo(TxArrIntField[] a) {
    // ...
    t = a[0].array[i];
}
```

Fig. 8. Example transformation of array access in the in-place scheme

`System.arraycopy(Object, int, Object, int, int)` method from the Java platform. The signature refers `Object` but it actually receives arrays as arguments. We identify these situations by inspecting the type of the arguments on a *virtual stack*[2] and if an array is found, despite the method's signature, we revert to primitive arrays. The value of an array element is then obtained by dereferencing the pointer to the original array kept in the sibling, as illustrated in Figure 8. When passing an array as argument to an non-instrumented method (e.g., from the JDK library), we can just pass the original array instance. Although the instrumentation of non-transactional code adds an extra dereference operation when accessing an array, we still do avoid the auto-boxing of primitive types, which would impose a much higher overhead.

3.1.3 Adding Metadata to Multi-dimensional Arrays

The special case of multi-dimensional arrays is tackled using the `TxArrObjectField` class, which has a different implementation from the other specialized metadata array classes. This class has an additional field, `nextDim`, which may be null in the case of a unidimensional reference type array, or may hold the reference of the next array dimension by pointing to another array of type `TxArr*Field`. Once again, the original multi-dimensional array is always up to date and can be safely used by non-instrumented code. Figure 9 depicts the memory structure of a bi-dimensional array of integers. Each element of the first dimension of the sibling array has a reference to the original integer matrix. The elements of the second dimension of the sibling array have a reference to the second dimension of the matrix array.

---

[2] During the instrumentation process we keep the type information of the operand stack.

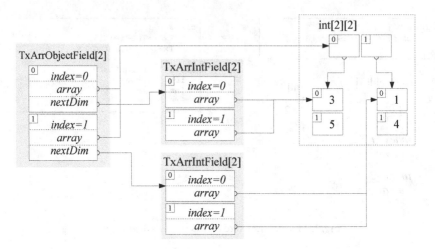

Fig. 9. Memory structure of a multi-dimensional `TxArrIntField` array

The limitations of our support for in-place metadata for single- and multi-dimensional arrays in Deuce are discussed with further detail in [5].

4   Evaluation of the In-Place Scheme

The implementation of the proposed Deuce extension, described in the previous sections, introduces more complexity to the transactional processing when comparing with the original Deuce implementation. This complexity, in the form of additional memory operations and allocations, may slowdown the performance in some cases. In our first step to assess the extension implementation performance, we evaluate the overhead of the new implementation by comparing it with the original Deuce implementation.

In a second step we evaluate the performance speedup of using our extension to implement a multi-version STM algorithm, against an implementation of the same algorithm using the original Deuce interface. We chose a well known multi-version STM algorithm, JVSTM, described in [3], and implemented two versions of the algorithm, one using the original Deuce interface and an out-place scheme (referred to as `jvstm-outplace`), and another using our new interface and extension supporting an in-place scheme (referred to as `jvstm-inplace`).

Both the overhead and speedup evaluations are preformed using several micro- and macro-benchmarks. Micro-benchmarks are composed by the Linked List, Red-Black Tree, and Skip-List data structures. Macro-benchmarks are composed by the STAMP [4] benchmark suite and the STMBench7 [9] benchmark. All these benchmarks were executed in our extension of Deuce with in-place metadata with no changes whatsoever, as all the necessary bytecode transformations were performed automatically by our instrumentation process. The benchmarks were executed on a computer with four AMD Opteron 6272 16-Core processors @ 2.1 GHz with 8×2 MB of L2 cache, 16 MB of L3 cache, and 64 GB of RAM, running Debian Linux 3.2.41 x86_64, and Java 1.7.0_21.

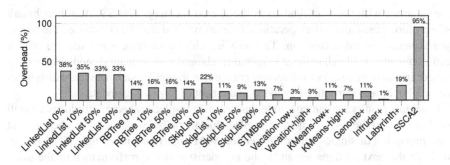

Fig. 10. Performance overhead measure of the usage of metadata objects relative to out-place TL2

In the following sections we describe in detail, and present the results, of the overhead evaluation as well as the speedup evaluation.

4.1 Overhead Evaluation

To evaluate the overhead introduced by the management of the metadata object fields and sibling arrays as required by our extension, we measured and compared the performance of two very similar implementations of the TL2 algorithm, which only differ in which API (context interface) is used to implement the algorithm: one uses the original API as provided by the Deuce distribution, and another (named tl2-overhead) uses the new interface of our modified Deuce (as described in Figure 4 in page 170). The change of API requires the additional management of metadata objects (allocation, and array manipulation), and two additional dereferences on the metadata object to obtain the field's object reference and the field offset, for each read and write operation.

Figure 10 depicts the average overhead introduced by the tl2-overhead implementation with respect to the original Deuce TL2 implementation. The Figure reports on several benchmarks, with each benchmark aggregating results from executions ranging form 1 to 64 threads. The overhead of the additional management of metadata objects and sibling arrays is in average about 20%. The benchmarks that use metadata arrays (SkipList, Kmeans, Genome, Labyrinth, SSCA2) have in general a higher overhead than those that only use metadata objects for class fields (RBTree, STMBench7, Vacation, Intruder). The micro-benchmarks (Linked List, Red-Black Tree and Skip-List) were all tested in four scenarios: with a read-only workload (0% of updates), and read-write workloads with 10%, 50%, and 90% of updates. These micro-benchmarks are composed of small transactions which only perform read and write accesses to shared memory, and thus, the overhead is more visible. The higher overhead in the LinkedList micro-benchmark is due to the long running transactions that perform a very large number of read operations, and our extension requires an external table lookup and an additional object dereference to retrieve the metadata object for each memory read operation.

The STAMP benchmarks, show relatively low overhead, except for the SSCA2+ benchmark. These benchmarks have medium sized transactions which perform some computations with the data read from the shared memory. The SSCA2+ benchmark only preforms read and write operations over arrays, and may be considered the worst-case scenario for our extension. The STMBench7 benchmark was executed with a read-dominant workload, without long-traversals, and with structural modifications activated. In this benchmarks transactions are computationally much heavier, which hides the small overhead introduced by the management of in-place metadata.

From this results we can conclude that out new in-place scheme introduces a small overhead due to the management of in-place metadata, but it also enables the efficient implementation of single- and multi-version STM algorithms in a single STM framework. In the next sections we show the comparison of the performance of the same multi-version algorithm implemented using the original Deuce framework and our extension.

4.2   Implementing a Multi-versioning Algorithm: JVSTM

The JVSTM algorithm defines the notion of version box (*vbox*), which maintains a pointer to the head of an unbounded list of versions, where each version is composed by a timestamp and the data value. Each version box represents a distinct memory location. The timestamp in each version corresponds to the timestamp of the transaction that created that version, and the head of the version list always points to the most recent version. During the execution of a transaction, the read and write operations are done in versioned boxes, which hold the data values. For each write operation a new version is created and tagged with the transaction timestamp. For read operations, the version box returns the version with the highest timestamp less than or equal to the transaction's timestamp. A particularity of this algorithm is that read-only transactions never abort. To commit a transaction, a global lock must be acquired to ensure mutual exclusion with all other concurrent transactions. Once the global lock is acquired, the transaction validates the read-set, and in case of success, creates the new version for each memory location that was written, and finally releases the global lock. To prevent version lists from growing indefinitely, versions that are no more necessary are cleaned up by a *vbox* garbage collector.

To implement the JVSTM algorithm, we need to associate a *vbox* with each field of each object. For the sake of the correctness of the algorithm, this association must guarantee a relation of *one-to-one* between the *vbox* and the object's field. We will detail the implementation of this association for both, the out-place and the in-place strategies.

4.2.1   Out-Place Scheme
To implement JVSTM algorithm in the original Deuce framework, which only supports the out-place scheme, the *vboxes* must be stored in an external table[3]. The *vboxes* are indexed by a unique identifier for the object's field, composed by the object reference and the field's logical offset. Whenever a transaction performs a read or write operation on an object's field, the respective *vbox* must be retrieved from the table. In the case where the *vbox* does not exists, we must create one and add it into the table. These two steps, verifying if a *vbox* is present in the table and creating and inserting a new one

---

[3] We opted to use a concurrent hash table from the `java.util.concurrent` package.

```
public class VBox extends TxField {
    protected VBoxBody body;
    public VBox(Object ref, long offset) {
        super(ref, offset);
        body = new VBoxBody(read(), 0, null);
    }
    // ... methods to access and commit versions
}
```

Fig. 11. VBox in-place implementation

if not, must be performed atomically, otherwise we would incur in the case where two different *vboxes* may be created for the same object's field. Once the *vbox* is retrieved from the table, either it is a read operation and we look for the appropriate version using the transaction's timestamp and return the version's value, or it is a write operation and we add an entry to the transaction's write-set.

We use weak references in the table indices to reference the *vbox* objects and not hamper the garbage collector from collecting old objects. Whenever an object is collected our algorithm is notified in order to remove the respective entry from the table.

Despite using a concurrent hash map, this implementation suffers from a high overhead penalty when accessing the table, since it is a point of synchronization for all the transactions running concurrently. This implementation (jvstm-outplace) will be used as a base reference when comparing with the implementation of the same JVSTM algorithm using the in-place scheme (jvstm-inplace).

4.2.2 In-Place Scheme
The in-place version of JVSTM algorithm makes use of the metadata classes to hold the same information as the *vbox* in the out-place variant. This will allow direct access to the version list whenever a transaction is reading or writing.

We extend the *vbox* class from the TxField class as shown in Figure 11. The actual implementation creates a VBox class for each Java type in order to prevent the boxing and unboxing of primitive types. When the constructor is executed, a new version with timestamp zero is created, containing the current value of the field identified by object ref and logical offset offset. The value is retrieved using the private method read(). The code to create these VBox objects during the execution of the application is inserted automatically by our bytecode instrumentation process. The lifetime of an instance of the class VBox is the same as the lifetime of the object ref. When the garbage collector decides to collect the object ref, all metadata objects of class VBox associated with each field of the object ref, are also collected.

Our comparison evaluation shows that the direct access to the version list allowed by the in-place scheme will greatly benefit the performance of the algorithm. We present the comparison results in the next section by presenting the speedup of the in-place version with respect to the out-place version.

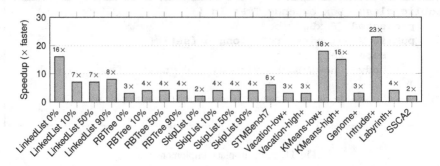

Fig. 12. In-place over Out-place scheme speedup: the case of JVSTM

4.3 Speedup Evaluation

From the evaluation of the in-place management overhead, we concluded that this scheme is a viable option for implementing algorithms biased to in-place transactional metadata. Hence, we implemented and evaluated two versions of the JVSTM algorithm as proposed in [3], one in the original Deuce using the native out-place scheme (jvstm-outplace), and another in the extended Deuce using our in-place scheme (jvstm-inplace), as described in the previous Section.

Figure 12 depicts the average speedup of our two implementations of the JVSTM algorithm: one In-Place (jvstm-inplace) and another Out-Place (jvstm-outplace). We used the same set of benchmarks and configuration that was used for the overhead evaluation in Section 4.1. In The in-place version of the JVSTM algorithm is in average 7 times faster than its dual out-place version. The speedup observed for the micro-benchmarks, where transactions are small and contention is low, shows that the multi-versioning algorithms greatly benefit from our in-place support. In the case of the STAMP benchmarks, where transactions are submitted to workloads of intensive contention, the in-place version is much faster than the out-place approach as it avoids completely the use of a shared external table, which becomes a serious bottleneck in the presence of high contention. In the special case of KMeans and Intruder benchmarks, the overhead of managing a shared external table drastically increases the probability of transaction aborts as depicted in Figure 13, which in turn makes the transactional throughput to decrease. The STMBench7 macro-benchmark has many long-running transactions and the overall throughput for both algorithms is relatively low. Even so, the in-place algorithm is in average 6× faster.

5 State-of-the-Art Multi-version Algorithm's Implementations

Our main purpose for extending Deuce with support for in-place metadata was to allow the efficient implementation of a class of STM algorithms that require a *one-to-one* relation between memory locations and their metadata. Multi-version based algorithms fit into that class, as they associate a list of versions (holding past values) with each memory location. With the support for in-place metadata we can implement and compare the state-of-the-art multi-version algorithms, both between themselves and with single-version algorithms.

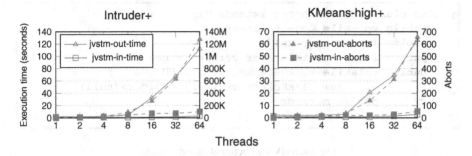

Fig. 13. Performance and transaction aborts of JVSTM-Inplace/Outplace for the Intruder and KMeans benchmarks

To support this fact, we implemented two state-of-the-art multi-version algorithms: SMV [12] and JVSTM-LockFree [7]. These algorithms are significantly different, although both are MV-*permissive* [13]. They differ on the progress guarantees, e.g., JVSTM-LockFree implements a commit algorithm that is lock-free, while SMV uses write-set locking, and also differ on the technique used to garbage collect unnecessary versions, where JVSTM-LockFree uses a custom parallel garbage collector, while SMV resorts to the JVM garbage collector by using weak-references. In the following sections we describe the implementation details of each of the above algorithms.

5.1 SMV – Selective Multi-Versioning STM

The SMV algorithm described in [12] is an MV-*permissive* multi-version algorithm, which uses the JVM garbage collector to automatically collect unreachable versions. The implementation of this algorithm in our extension of Deuce was based on the original source code released by the authors[4]. The original algorithm is object-based, opposite to Deuce, and our extension, which only supports word-based STMs, and hence we adapted the SMV algorithm to work as a word-base STM.

The transactional metadata required by SMV can be depicted in Figure 14. This is a direct adaptation of the `SMVAdapterLight` class provided by the original source code. Also, we used the same source code that implements the behavior of read- and update-transactions with minimal changes. We did this by implementing our extension's interface `ContextMetadata` as an adapter of the original source code, each transactional operation (read, write, commit, abort) is forward to the original implementation.

The change from an object-based to a word-based approach only required minimal changes on the read and write procedures. In the case of a read operation, instead of returning an object, is returned a field's value. And in the case of a write operation, instead of cloning the object to be written and storing in the transaction's write-set, the tentative value of a field is stored in the write-set. The overall adaptation of the original source code to our framework was very easy and fast, which proves the flexibility of our support for implementing different STM algorithms.

---

[4] http://tx.technion.ac.il/ dima39/sourcecode/
SMVLib-29-06-11.zip

```
public class SMVObjAdapter extends TxField {
    public volatile Object latest;
    public int creatorTxnId;
    public final AtomicInteger version = new AtomicInteger(1);
    public volatile WeakReference<VersionHolder> prev =
                new WeakReference<VersionHolder>(null);
    // ... public methods
}
```

Fig. 14. SMV transactional metadata class

```
public class VBoxAdapter extends TxField {
    protected VBox<Object> vbox;
    // ... public methods
}
```

Fig. 15. JVSTM-LockFree transactional metadata class

5.2 JVSTM Lock Free

The JVSTM-LockFree [7] is an adaptation of the original JVSTM algorithm [3], which enhances the commit procedure using a lock-free algorithm, instead of using a global lock, and also improves the garbage collector algorithm by the use of a parallel collecting approach. Once again, we based our implementation in the original source code[5].

We created a metadata object containing a reference to a vbox, as implemented originally by the JVSTM-LockFree algorithm. We show the object metadata implementation in Figure 15. The context class was implemented as an adapter to the original implementation of the read-only and update transactions. Actually, we used the JVSTM-LockFree implementation as an external library (JAR file), and the Deuce context class only forwards the transactional calls to the external library. This approach was possible because there was no need to make any changes to the JVSTM-LockFree algorithm, for it to work in our framework extension.

6   Supporting Efficient Non-transactional code

Multi-version algorithms read and write the data values from and into the list of versions. This implies that all accesses to fields in shared objects must be done inside a memory transaction, and thus multi-version algorithms require a *strong atomicity* model [2]. Deuce does not provide a strong atomicity model as memory accesses done outside of transactions are not instrumented, and hence it is possible to have non-transactional accesses to fields of objects that were also accessed inside memory transactions. This hinders the usage of multi-version algorithms in Deuce. This problem can be circumvented by rewriting the existing benchmarks to wrap all accesses to shared

---

[5] https://github.com/inesc-id-esw/jvstm

objects inside an atomic method, but such code changes are always a cumbersome and error prone process. We addressed this problem by proposing an adaptation to the multi-version algorithms that makes them compatible with the *weak atomicity* model.

When using a weak atomicity model with a multi-version scheme, updates made by non-transactional code to object fields are not seen by transactional code and, on the other way around, updates made by transactional code are not seen by non-transactional code. The key idea for our solution is to store the value of the latest version in the object's field instead of in the node at the head of the version list. When a transaction needs to read a field of an object, it requests the version corresponding to the transaction timestamp. If it receives the head version, then it reads the value directly from the object's field, otherwise it reads the value from the version node.

The main issue with this approach is how to guarantee the atomicity of the commit of a new version, because now we have two steps: adding a new version node to the head of the list and updating the field's value. These two steps must be atomic with respect to the other concurrent transactions. Our solution is to create a temporary new version with an infinite timestamp, making it unreachable for other concurrent transactions, until we update the value and then change the timestamp to its proper value. The algorithmic adaptation that we propose is not intended to support a workload of intertwined non-transactional and transactional accesses, but rather a phased workload where non-transactional code does not execute concurrently with transactional code. Many of the transactional benchmarks we used exhibit such a phased workload, because the data structures are initialized in the program startup using non-transactional code. After this initialization, the transactional code can now operate over the data previously installed by non-transactional code. After the transactional processing, non-transactional code may also post-process the data, such as in a case of a validation procedure.

6.1 Read Access Adaptation

In a multi-version scheme, read-only transactions always search for a correct version to return its value. Each version container holds the timestamp (or version number) and the respective value. When the transaction finds the correct version, it returns the value contained in the version.

To support non-transactional accesses mixed with a multi-version scheme, the latest value of an object's field is stored in-place, and therefore the head version might not have the correct value because of a previous non-transactional update. The read procedure of a multi-version transaction must be adapted to reflect the new location of the latest value. When a transaction queries for a version, and receives the head version, corresponding to the latest value, it has to return the value directly from the object's field. The pseudo-code of this adaptation is presented below, where the additional operations are denoted in underline.

1. $\underline{val := \mathsf{read}()}$
2. $ver := \mathsf{find\_version}()$
3. return $\begin{cases} \underline{val} & \text{if } \underline{\mathsf{is\_head\_version}(ver)} \\ ver.val & \text{otherwise} \end{cases}$

The read() function returns the value from the object's field, the find_version function retrieves the corresponding version according to the transaction timestamp, and the is_head_version function asserts if version *ver* is the head version. This small change introduces the additional shared memory access performed in step 1. The correctness of this adaptation can only be assessed with the explanation of the commit adaptation, which guarantees that whenever the is_head_version function returns true the value *val* is correct.

6.2 Commit Adaptation

The commit operation is typical composed by a validation phase and write-back phase. In the write-back phase, for each new value present in the write-set, a new version is created and is stored as the head version. The write-back phase must be atomic, and this can be achieved using a global lock (JVSTM), a write-set entry locking (SMV), or even a lock-free algorithm (JVSTM-LockFree).

Our adaptation only makes changes to the write-back phase. In each iteration of the write-back phase, a new version is installed as the head version of the version list associated with the object's field being written. The version contains the commit timestamp, which defines the commit ordering, and the new value. Additionally, to support the weak-atomicity model, we also need to write the new value directly to the object's field. The problem that arises with this additional operation is that concurrent transactions need to see the update on the version list, and the update of the object's value as a single operation. The key idea to solve this problem is to create a version with a temporary infinite timestamp, which will prevent concurrent transactions from accessing the head version, and consequently the object's field value.

Below we present the pseudo-code of the adaptation to the commit of a new version, where t_c is the timestamp of the transaction that is performing the commit, t_∞ is the highest timestamp, *val* is the value to be written, and ver_h is the pointer to the head version. For the sake of simplicity, we assume that these steps execute in mutual exclusion with respect to other concurrent commits (in Section 6.2.3 we explain how to apply these steps to a lock-free context as in the JVSTM-LockFree algorithm).

1. $ver_h.value := \underline{\text{read}()}$
2. $ver_n := \text{create\_version}(new\_val, t_\infty, ver_h)$
3. $ver_h := ver_n$
4. $\text{write}(\underline{new\_val})$
5. $\underline{ver_h.timestamp := t_c}$

Once again, the additional changes are denoted in underline. The first step is to update the value of the head version with the current value of the object's field. This update is safe because until this point transactions that retrieve the head version read the value directly from the object's field, as described in the previous section. Then we create a new version with an infinite timestamp and the new value to be written in the object's field, and the pointer to the current head version. In the third step, we make the new version ver_n the current head version and it becomes visible to all concurrent transactions. This version will never be accessed by any concurrent transaction because of the infinite timestamp. Then we can safely update the object's field value in the fourth step

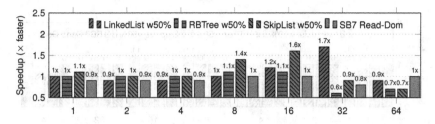

Fig. 16. Performance comparison between original JVSTM and adapted JVSTM

because no concurrent transaction gets the head version (the head version still has an infinite timestamp up to this point). In the last step we change the timestamp of the current head version to its proper value making accessible to concurrent transactions.

The adaptation of the commit operation introduces three new shared memory accesses, where two of them are write accesses. Thus, this adaptation is expected to slightly lower the throughput of the multi-version algorithm. We applied this adaptation to the multi-version algorithms that we described previously, and compared the performance of both versions of each. In the next section we report the experience of adapting each algorithm.

6.2.1 JVSTM

The JVSTM algorithms preform the commit operation in mutual exclusion with other concurrent committing transactions. The adaptation of these algorithms to support a weak-atomicity model is straightforward. The changes that we presented in the previous section to modify the read and commit operation can be applied directly to both implementations. Moreover, the Deuce framework already provides the memory value when a read access is issued (see Figure 4 in page 170), which simplifies the first step of the read procedure described in Section 6.1.

Figure 16 depicts the performance comparison between the original and adapted versions of JVSTM. The comparison is done by showing the relative performance of the adapted version over the original version. The adapted version of JVSTM shows a performance very similar to the original versions. Sometimes, the adapted version can even outperform the original version. This is due to the specificity of the Deuce framework that already provides the memory value for each read access callback. In the case of the adapted version, most of the times that value is used, opposed to the original version where the value is always obtained by dereferencing a version container.

6.2.2 SMV

The SMV algorithm defines a different memory layout for the version list. In SMV, the value of the latest version is stored outside of the version list, which reassembles our adaptation proposal of storing the latest value directly on the memory location. To apply the support for a weak-atomicity model, we simply moved the value of the latest version from an auxiliary variable (used in SMV original implementation) directly to the associated memory location.

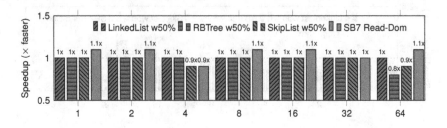

Fig. 17. Performance comparison between original SMV and adapted SMV

This modification has consequences in the commit operation, which must also be adapted to atomically update the latest version information and the memory location value. The first step in the SMV commit operation is to move the latest value and timestamp to a newly created version container and add it to the head of the version list. We change this step by using the latest value stored in memory. In the last step of the SMV commit operation the variable containing the latest value is updated with the new tentative value. We changed this step by writing the tentative value directly to memory. The changes made to the SMV algorithm are minimal and thus we expect that the performance differences between the two versions to be also minimal. The results depicted in Figure 17 confirm our expectations, showing minimal differences between the original version and adapted version.

6.2.3 JVSTM-LockFree

The JVSTM-LockFree implements a lock free commit operation. The assumption to apply the adaptation for the commit procedure, presented in Section 6.2, is that the commit should be done in mutual exclusion. This assumption is true for the previous algorithms but not for the JVSTM-LockFree. In this algorithm, the commit of a single version can be done by more than one thread at the same time by resorting to atomic primitives such as compare-and-swap.

The adaptation of the read procedure is straightforward as in the JVSTM algorithm. The adaptation of the commit procedure is rather complex and requires additional atomic operations to ensure the correctness of the algorithm. Figure 18 depicts a simplified version of the original commit. The method commit preforms a compare-and-swap to install the new version. Other threads may be executing the same method for the same *vbox*, but only one of them will install the new version. Further details on how the JVSTM-LockFree commit algorithm works can be found in [7].

Figure 19 depicts the adapted version of the JVSTM-LockFree commit algorithm to support a weak-atomicity model. The new algorithm has roughly three times more operations than the original one. We explain this adapted version by describing how each step of the adaptation described in Section 6.2 is related to the code listed in the Figure 19.

The first step $ver_h.value :=$ read() is preformed by lines 5 and 7-9. The update of the head version's value (line 8) is done inside a conditional statement because other concurrent thread may had already preformed the same update. The creation of a new version in the second step $ver_n :=$ create_version(new_val, t_∞, ver_h) is preformed in

```
1   public void commit(Object newValue, int txNumber) {
2       Version currHead = this.head;
3       Version existingVersion = currHead.getVersion(txNumber);
4       if (existingBody.version < txNumber) {
5           Version newVer = new Version(newValue, txNumber, currHead);
6           compare_and_swap(this.head, currHead, newVer);
7       }
8   }
```

Fig. 18. JVSTM-LockFree original commit operation

```
1   public void commit(Object newValue, int txNumber) {
2       Version currHead = this.head;
3       Version existingVersion = currHead.getVersion(txNumber);
4
5       Object latest = read(memory_location);
6       if (existingVersion == currHead
7               && existingVersion.version < txNumber) {
8           if (this.head == existingVersion) {
9               currHead.value = latest;
10          }
11          Version newVer = new Version(newValue, Integer.MAX_VALUE,
12                  currHead);
13          if (compare_and_swap(this.head, currHead, newVer)) {
14              existingVersion = newVer;
15          } else {
16              existingVersion = this.head;
17              Version tmpVer = existingVersion.getVersion(txNumber);
18              if (tmpVer.version == txNumber) {
19                  existingVersion = tmpVer;
20              }
21          }
22          if (existingVersion.version == Integer.MAX_VALUE) {
23              compare_and_swap(memory_location, latest, newValue);
24          }
25          existingVersion.version = txNumber;
26      }
27      else {
28          if (existingVersion.version < txNumber) {
29              existingVersion = currHead;
30              if (existingVersion.version == Integer.MAX_VALUE)
31                  compare_and_swap(memory_location, latest, newValue);
32              existingVersion.version = txNumber;
33          }
34      }
35  }
```

Fig. 19. JVSTM-LockFree adapted commit operation

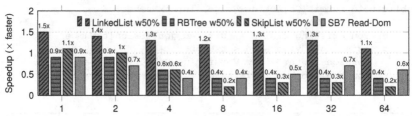

Fig. 20. Performance comparison between original JVSTM-LockFree and adapted JVSTM-LockFree

line 10. The publication of the new version in the third step $ver_h := ver_n$ is preformed in lines 11-19. In this step we preform a compare-and-swap, as in the original algorithm, to publicize the new version, but if other concurrent thread already publicize the new version, then we need to get a pointer to the new version. This is done in lines 14 to 18. Using this pointer we can preform the final fourth and fifth steps write(*new_val*) and $ver_h.timestamp := t_c$, which are done in lines 20-23. The writing of the new value directly to memory (line 21) is done using a compare-and-swap atomic operation to prevent lost updates. The update of the version number (line 23) is safe because we always have a pointer to the correct version container. These last two steps are also preformed in lines 28-31, in the case when a thread attempting to commit finds out, in line 6, that other concurrent thread already publicized the new version, and therefore it helps finishing the commit. Another source of overhead is caused by a limitation of the compare-and-swap operation, which can only be preformed for reference and integer types. Thus, for other primitive type such as **float**, or **byte**, the compare-and-swap operations preformed in lines 21 and 29, must be substituted by some mutual exclusion block. Fortunately the use of compare-and-swap non-supported types in the benchmarks is rare.

Figure 20 presents the results of comparing the adapted version over the original version of JVSTM-LockFree. In the case of the LinkedList micro-benchmark, the transactions generate small write-sets (the add and remove operations only write to a single object), and typically the commit rate is low due to the long duration of the lookup of a node, which is linear with the size of the list. As so, the adapted version outperforms the original version, due to the read accesses that use value directly from memory and are immediately provided by the Deuce framework. In the case of the SkipList and RBTree micro-benchmarks, the adapted commit overhead is more notorious when the contention increases with the number of threads. These benchmarks generate a high rate of commit operations, although still with small write-sets per transaction. In the STMBench7 benchmark, known to generate very large read- and write-sets, the adapted version can only achieve half the performance of the original version. The results confirm our performance expectations, and also confirm that the overhead introduced by adapting a multi-version algorithm to support a weak-atomicity model is almost nil for algorithms that preform the commit of versions in mutual exclusion, and has a considerable cost otherwise.

7   Performance Comparison of STM Algorithms

In this chapter we presented an extension of the Deuce framework to support the efficient implementation of STM algorithms that require a one-to-one relation between memory locations and transactional metadata, being multi-version algorithms an instance of this class of algorithms. We evaluated the extension considering the implications in both performance and memory consumption. The results were very satisfactory and thus we implemented two state-of-the-art multi-version algorithms (SMV and JVSTM-LockFree).

Given this support for very different classes of STM algorithms, we may now aim at a fair comparison of their performance, i.e., compare the algorithms implemented in the same framework and with the same benchmarks. In this section we show the direct comparison between several out-place and in-place STM algorithms. The list of STM algorithms chosen for comparison are TL2, JVSTM, JVSTM-LockFree, and SMV. In the case of TL2 we use two versions: the out-place version (TL2-Outplace) which is distributed with Deuce, and an in-place version (TL2-Inplace) which we implemented in our extension. The in-place version moves the locks from the external lock table to the transactional metadata, and completely avoids the false-sharing on locks. In the case of multi-version algorithms our measurements were conducted under two settings. The first setup consisted on executing the (unmodified) benchmarks combined with the weak-atomicity-adapted multi-version algorithms. In the second setup, we executed a modified version of the micro-benchmarks and STMBench7 combined with the original multi-version algorithms that do not support weak-atomicity. In the comparison results, we will only use the best of the results of the original and the adapted versions of each multi-version algorithm. As in the extension evaluation, the benchmarks were executed on a computer with four AMD Opteron 6272 16-Core processors @ 2.1 GHz with 8×2 MB of L2 cache, 16 MB of L3 cache, and 64 GB of RAM, running Debian Linux 3.2.41 x86_64, and Java 1.7.0_21.

Figure 21 shows the results of the execution of the micro-benchmarks Linked List, Red-Black Tree, and Skip List. The Linked List benchmark is characterized by transactions with large read-sets and by a high abort rate. In this benchmark the algorithms do not scale well with the increase in the number of threads. The single-version algorithms TL2-Outplace and TL2-Inplace exhibit better performance. These algorithms have very efficient implementations and the read accesses are very lightweight. Additionally, in the case of read-only transactions, each read access is checked for consistency but the transaction can safely commit without further verification. To support multiple versions per memory location, the multi-version algorithms add a high number of extra computations when reading a value from a memory location, with the benefit of avoiding spurious transaction aborts and hence avoid the re-execution of transactions. Although, in the micro-benchmarks this possible benefit is not observed. In the Red-Black Tree and Skip List benchmarks, transactions are very small and fast, and have a low conflict probability, except in the Red-Black Tree when tree rotations are preformed. These benchmarks hide even more the advantages of multi-version algorithms when compared with single-version algorithms. The poor performance of SMV when compared to the

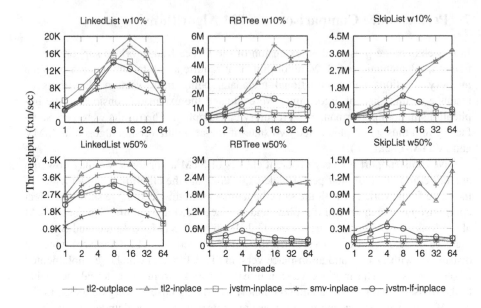

Fig. 21. Micro-benchmarks comparison

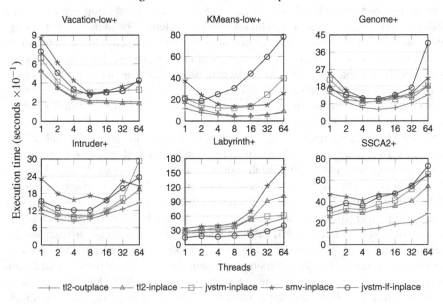

Fig. 22. STAMP benchmarks comparison

other multi-version algorithms is due to the strain imposed on the Java garbage collector: the micro-benchmarks generate millions of transactions per second, generating a lot of activity of the Java garbage collector.

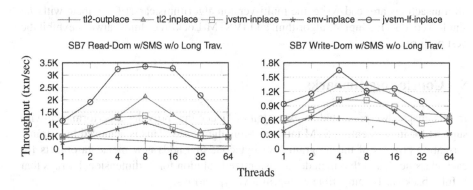

Fig. 23. STMBench7 comparison

The comparison results for the STAMP benchmarking suite are depicted in Figure 22. In these results the y-axis represents execution time and therefore lower values are better. The benchmarks in this suite exhibit very different workloads, some of them even generate such high contention that hinders the scaling for all of the tested algorithms. The benchmarks KMeans, Genome, and Intruder, exposes the corner cases of the *adapted* JVSTM-LockFree algorithm, hence its performance is strongly penalized. We believe that the original JVSTM-LockFree algorithm would perform much better than the adapted version in these particular benchmarks. The TL2 based algorithms overall exhibit a very good performance. In the Labyrinth benchmark the multi-version algorithm JVSTM-LockFree presents a very good result. This algorithm has a low abort rate when compared with the other algorithms, which allows it to not waist so much work in transaction restarts. In the SSCA2 benchmark all the in-place algorithms suffer from the high overhead of transactional metadata management shown in Figure 10 of Section 4.1.

In Figure 23 we show the results for the STMBench7 benchmarks. This benchmark generate CPU-intensive transactions with large read-sets and write-sets. This benchmarks allows to exploit the benefits of multi-version algorithms which can avoid spurious aborts and thus achieve better performance than single-version algorithms. The JVSTM-Lockfree algorithm achieves a good performance, higher than the remaining algorithms, confirming the advantages of using an MV-*permissive* algorithm in this kind of workload. In this benchmark, there is a significant performance difference between the out-place and in-place versions of TL2 algorithm. The out-place version does not even scale with the number of threads. The reason of this behavior may be due to cache locality issues. The in-place version is much more cache-friendly than the out-place version. The in-place version has a high probability of having the metadata in the same cache line as the memory location. This does not happen in the out-place version, and in the special case of STMBench7, where transactions perform a large number of reads and writes, the out-place version must read many entries from the external lock table, which may not fit in the cache and requiring much more page transfers from main memory to the cache. In the write-dominated workload of STMBench7, all algorithms have similar performance with the exception of TL2-Outplace. Although almost all transactions are read-write, the multi-version algorithms can still compete with the single-version TL2-Inplace algorithm, and JVSTM-LockFree almost always exhibit the best performance.

8   Concluding Remarks

In this chapter we presented an extension of Deuce that provides a performance-wise support for implementing STM multi-version algorithms. This is achieved by a transformation process of the program Java bytecode that adds new metadata objects for each class field, and that includes a customized solution for N-dimensional arrays that is fully backwards compatible with primitive type arrays.

We evaluated the proposed system by measuring the overhead introduced by the new in-place scheme with respect to the original Deuce implementation. Although we can observe a light slowdown caused by the in-place metadata management, the slowdown is quickly absorbed by the performance gains achieved when using the in-place scheme to store the STM algorithms metadata.

The new efficient implementation support for STM multi-version algorithms allowed to implement two state-of-the-art multi-version algorithms SMV and JVSTM-LockFree. Moreover, we present the first performance comparison between the two.

Finally, we proposed an algorithmic adaptation for multi-version algorithms to support the weak-atomicity model as provided in the Deuce framework. We reported the experience of adapting several state-of-the-art multi-version algorithms and evaluate their performance. In general, multi-version algorithms can be adapted to support the weak-atomicity model without a performance penalty, except the case of the algorithms that implement a lock-free commit operation.

Acknowledgments. This research was partially supported by the EU COST Action IC1001 (Euro-TM) and the Portuguese *Fundação para a Ciência e Tecnologia* in the research project PTDC/EIA-EIA/113613/2009 (Synergy-VM), and the research grants SFRH/BD/41765/2007 and SFRH/BD/84497/2012.

References

1. Bloch, J.: Effective Java, 2nd edn. Addison-Wesley (2008)
2. Blundell, C., Lewis, E.C., Martin, M.M.K.: Deconstructing transactions: The subtleties of atomicity. In: Fourth Annual Workshop on Duplicating, Deconstructing, and Debunking, (WDDD) (2005)
3. Cachopo, J., Rito-Silva, A.: Versioned boxes as the basis for memory transactions. Sci. Comput. Program. 63(2), 172–185 (2006)
4. Cao Minh, C., Chung, J., Kozyrakis, C., Olukotun, K.: STAMP: Stanford transactional applications for multi-processing. In: 4th IEEE International Symposium on Workload Characterization (IISWC). IEEE (2008)
5. Dias, R.J., Vale, T.M., Lourenço, J.M.: Efficient support for in-place metadata in java software transactional memory. Concurrency and Computation: Practice and Experience 25(17), 2394–2411 (2013)

6. Dice, D., Shalev, O., Shavit, N.N.: Transactional locking II. In: Dolev, S. (ed.) DISC 2006. LNCS, vol. 4167, pp. 194–208. Springer, Heidelberg (2006)
7. Fernandes, S.M., Cachopo, J.A.: Lock-free and scalable multi-version software transactional memory. In: 16th ACM SIGPLAN Symposium on Principles and Practice of Parallel Programming (PPoPP), pp. 179–188. ACM (2011)
8. Gamma, E., Helm, R., Johnson, R., Vlissides, J.: Design Patterns: Elements of Reusable Object-Oriented Software. Addison-Wesley Professional (1994)
9. Guerraoui, R., Kapalka, M., Vitek, J.: STMBench7: A benchmark for software transactional memory. In: 2nd EuroSys Conference (EuroSys), pp. 315–324. ACM (2007)
10. Herlihy, M., Luchangco, V., Moir, M.: A flexible framework for implementing software transactional memory. In: 21th Annual ACM SIGPLAN Conference on Object-Oriented Programming, Systems, Languages, and Applications (OOPSLA), pp. 253–262. ACM (2006)
11. Korland, G., Shavit, N., Felber, P.: Deuce: Noninvasive software transactional memory. Transactions on HiPEAC 5(2) (2010)
12. Perelman, D., Byshevsky, A., Litmanovich, O., Keidar, I.: SMV: Selective multi-versioning STM. In: Peleg, D. (ed.) DISC 2011. LNCS, vol. 6950, pp. 125–140. Springer, Heidelberg (2011)
13. Perelman, D., Fan, R., Keidar, I.: On maintaining multiple versions in STM. In: 29th Annual ACM Symposium on Principles of Distributed Computing (PODC), pp. 16–25. ACM (2010)
14. Riegel, T., Fetzer, C., Felber, P.: Snapshot isolation for software transactional memory. In: 1st ACM SIGPLAN Workshop on Transactional Computing (TRANSACT) (2006)
15. Riegel, T., Brum, D.B.D.: Making object-based STM practical in unmanaged environments. In: 3rd ACM SIGPLAN Workshop on Transactional Computing (TRANSACT) (2008)

Nested Parallelism in Transactional Memory

Ricardo Filipe and João Barreto

Instituto Superior Técnico, Universidade de Lisboa /INESC-ID
{rfilipe,jpbarreto}@gsd.inesc-id.pt

Abstract. We are witnessing an increase in the parallel power of computers for the foreseeable future, which requires parallel programming tools and models that can take advantage of the higher number of hardware threads. For some applications, reaching up to such high parallelism requires going beyond the typical monolithic parallel model: it calls for exposing fine-grained parallel tasks that might exist in a program, possibly nested within memory transactions.

While most current mainstream transactional memory (TM) systems do not yet support nested parallel transactions, recent research has proposed approaches that leverage TM with support for fine-grained parallel transactional nesting. These novel solutions promise to unleash the parallel power of TM to unprecedented levels. This chapter addresses parallel nesting models in transactional memory from two distinct perspectives.

We start from the programmer's perspective, studying the spectrum of parallel-nested models that are available to programmers, and giving a practical tutorial on the utility of each model, as well as the languages, tools and frameworks that help programmers build nested-parallel programs. We then turn to the perspective of a TM runtime designer, focusing on state-of-the art algorithms that support nested parallelism.

1 Introduction

Harnessing the parallel power of today's computers calls for concurrent programs that expose and exploit as much parallelism as the ever increasing hardware thread count. More than easily coding concurrent programs that yield *some* parallelism, we want concurrent programs that expose *as much parallelism as the ever increasing hardware thread count.*

This goal becomes dramatically more challenging as affordable multicore machines include more and more cores each year. While 4-core processors supporting up to eight simultaneous hardware threads are already regarded as commodity hardware, 8-core, 16-core and even chips with tens or hundreds of cores promise to be an affordable reality soon [1].

Achieving such parallelism levels will not always be possible with the traditional monolithic organization of coarse-grained parallel threads. For many real applications, the programmer may not be able to find enough coarse-grained top-level parallelism to fork. Hence, the alternative is to recursively expose the fine-grained parallel tasks that might exist within coarser-grain parallel tasks in the program. This leads to *nested-parallel* programs.

R. Guerraoui and P. Romano (Eds.): Transactional Memory, LNCS 8913, pp. 192–209, 2015.

As a motivational example, let us assume that a programmer building an application finds different tasks that, according to the application semantics, can safely run in parallel threads. Furthermore, inside such tasks, the programmer finds that some sub-tasks of a same task can also be parallelized in a fork-join fashion. Proceeding recursively with this approach, the final application will comprise a dynamic tree of nested fork-join tasks, each of which can run in concurrent threads to exploit the available hardware resources. This tree can even be deeper if we consider that some tasks may invoke functions from other modules (e.g., a library call) that may themselves be implemented by nested-parallel programs.

If the tasks work on shared data, then the above application will most likely have concurrent accesses to that data. Concurrency in traditional parallel programming is well known to be a hard problem to tackle, as we need to correctly synchronize access to shared data. Shifting to nested-parallel programming can further complicate synchronization to dantesque levels.

Nested-parallel programs comprise dynamic trees of tasks, running at concurrent threads, where correct synchronization depends on ancestor-descendant relations. On the one hand, data contention between concurrent threads needs to be synchronized. But, on the other hand, tasks that are ancestor/descendant of each other need to be treated differently: for instance, a nested task trying to access some memory location locked by some ancestor may be allowed to proceed with the access. Further, deadlock situations are more likely and harder to prevent, as they may happen between tasks at any nesting depths.

Relying on the programmer to explicitly solve such intricate synchronization challenges (e.g., using lock-based programming) is usually unrealistic for the average programmer. Except for embarrassingly parallel programs, the programmer is strongly discouraged to explore into the possibilities of nested-parallel programming.

Memory transactions, in contrast, are an elegant and effective solution to hide the hard synchronization parallel programming, especially if nested, away from the programmer. This makes transactional memory (TM) a promising paradigm to leverage fine-grained nested parallelism in tomorrow's multi/many-core machines.

Hereafter, let us designate the original non-nested TM programming model as *flat-parallel* (in contrast to the nested-parallel counterpart). The key insight is that the flat-parallel TM programming model is easily extensible to support nested transactions [2], an extension that has been introduced well earlier in the context of database transactions [3]. Essentially, a nested transaction is one whose execution is contained inside another transaction's execution. A program may hence recursively create nested transaction trees while executing.

When building a parallel-nested program, the programmer simply needs to apply the same rule that she was required to follow in traditional flat-parallel programming: to identify each code region that needs to run atomically and wrap it inside a transaction. Since transactions are composable [4], if all the atomic regions in a task have been properly defined, then executing such a task nested within a nested-parallel program will be correct. This holds true even if some of the tasks in a nested-parallel program belong to different modules, whose implementation the programmer does not know about (e.g. a call to a parallelized library function).

Programming in a nested-parallel fashion using TM, when compared to flat-parallel programming, introduces new challenges that programmers must be aware of in order to build correct and efficient programs. Firstly, the nested-parallel model is more complex than the flat one. Secondly, starting nested tasks may be cumbersome, error-prone and lead to inefficient, slow and not scalable programs if is not handled correctly. Finally, not of all today's mainstream TM runtimes support a fully nested-parallel model. Instead, many TM runtimes support limited nesting models, which need to be taken into account by the programmer.

This chapter approaches parallel nesting models in TM from two distinct perspectives. We start from the programmer's perspective. Section 2 studies the spectrum of parallel-nested models that are available to programmers, and gives a practical tutorial on the utility of each model. Section 3 then surveys languages, tools and frameworks that help programmers build nested-parallel programs in TM. Section 4 then focuses on the inner works of TM runtimes that support parallel nesting, describing state-of-the art algorithms. Finally, Section 5 summarizes.

2   Nested Parallelism Models in Transactional Memory

In theory, the TM model is extensible to support parallel-nested programs [5]. This extension implies redefining the correctness guarantees that were originally defined in the context of flat-parallel programming in TM.

The key insight is that correctness must now consider the ancestor-descendant relationships between parallel transactions, as we shall detail next.

However, supporting parallel nesting also implies changes to the TM runtime that may introduce substantial overheads or limit scalability. For this reason, many current mainstream TM runtimes opt for limited nesting models. For the sake of efficiency of flat-parallel programs, these typically restrict the nested parallelism that programmers can actually extract from their programs.

Hence, the reality is that, instead of a single nested-parallel model, TM runtimes actually offer a spectrum of models. It is, of course, important that the programmer understands each model in order to produce programs that, while ensuring correctness, are able to fully exploit the model supported by the underlying runtime.

This section presents and discusses each different model in the spectrum of nested models for TM. We start by focusing on the pure parallel-nested model, before delving in restricted variants of such a model in the subsequent subsections.

2.1   Parallel Nesting

Simply put, the nested-parallel model for TM means that the TM runtime supports nested transactions and allows the child transactions of a common parent to run in parallel. This model is a straightforward extension of the closed nesting model proposed by Moss and Hosking [2].

Conceptually, the execution of a nested-parallel program yields a dynamic tree of active transactions, inter-connected by child-parent relations. At any moment, some of the transactions will be running, while others will be waiting (for instance, for some processor to become available, or waiting for their children to commit).

Algorithm 1. Example of parallel nested transactions

```
1  function sb7-longTraversal(root)
2     atomic {
3        parallel {
4           sb7-traverseComplexAssembly(root.leaf1);
5           sb7-traverseComplexAssembly(root.leaf2);
6           sb7-traverseComplexAssembly(root.leaf3);
7        }
8     }
```

We illustrate with an excerpt taken from a modified long transaction of the popular STMBench7 benchmark [6], presented in Algorithm 1. Method sb7-longTraversal includes an atomic region (i.e. encloses a transaction), which calls the sb7-traverseComplexAssembly method for each leaf of the root data item. The sb7-traverseComplexAssembly method also executes a transaction inside of it. In this example the programmer is calling methods within the same program, but they could be calls to an external library.

In the above example, the programmer calls the sb7-traverseComplexAssembly methods in parallel threads, thereby building a nested-parallel program. These methods will perform accesses that may conflict with transactions running concurrently at other threads. Furthermore, the parallel-nested threads may also contend for shared memory locations. If that is the case, the programmer should have identified the code regions at the called methods that need to run atomically and created transactions to ensure the necessary synchronization.

The transactions defined by the atomic regions within sb7-traverseComplexAssembly will compose with the parent transaction initiated at method sb7-longTraversal. In other words, the sb7-traverseComplexAssembly methods will start nested transactions. We call each such nested transaction a *child* of the parent transaction from sb7-longTraversal. By extension, we say that two transactions are *siblings* if they have a common parent transaction. Furthermore, we define that transaction t is an *ancestor* of transaction s if t is included in the path from s's node to the root node in the tree of nested transactions.

For model simplicity, most definitions of the nested-parallel transactional model (e.g. [5]) assume that the parent transaction halts until all the threads that it spawned (and the inherent nested transactions) complete. Only after all children tasks finish does the parent's execution continue. We adopt such assumption too. Hence, when a given nested task is running, all its ancestors' threads are waiting. Accordingly, when a nested transaction is active, all its ancestor transactions are waiting.

A nested transaction is seen as executing after all the accesses that its ancestors have performed so far. In particular, when some transaction t reads from a memory location that has been written by any of its ancestors, t should observe the most recently written value by its ancestors.

Each nested transaction runs in isolation relatively to any other concurrent transaction. More precisely, the concurrent transactions of a given transaction include its own siblings and all its ancestors' siblings and their descendants (including the root transactions that are concurrent to the transaction's root ancestor).Note that a transaction never runs concurrently with its descendants, as it waits for the descendants to complete.

Conceptually, a nested transaction has its own read set and write set. This enables rolling back the nested transaction without having to roll back its entire root transaction.

On commit, a nested transaction's read and write sets are inherited by the transaction's parent. In other words, the reads and writes of the committed nested transaction are, from that moment on, considered to have been performed on behalf of the parent transaction.

Committing a nested transaction does not make its writes visible to the rest of the world. [1] Instead, committing a nested transaction means that the committed writes become visible to its active siblings and to its ancestors (which are blocked until all children commit). Following this rule recursively, the writes of a nested transaction become gradually visible to other transactions, starting at the set of siblings of the transaction and then going upwards the nesting tree.

The nested-parallel transactional model is very powerful to ease programmers' lives when exploiting nested parallelism in their programs. The key insight is that the nested-parallel model retains the composability of the traditional flat model. Hence, when shifting from the flat-parallel model to the nested-parallel one, the programmer is required to apply the very same principle as before: to identify regions within the program that are atomic and wrap them in transactions. Having done that, correct synchronization is ensured by the TM runtime even for a program that has been structured in a nested-parallel fashion. This holds true even if some of the tasks in a nested-parallel program belong to different modules, whose implementation the programmer does not know about (e.g. a call to a parallelized library function).

However, porting a flat parallel program with monolithic coarse-grained threads to a nested-parallel alternative that exposes more fine-grained parallelism is not transparent and requires caution from the programmer. Let us consider a thread that executes a seguence of tasks. Before parallelizing such tasks, the programmer needs to carefully confirm that:

- The candidate tasks to parallelize safely commute. Parallelizing them can yield executions where the serialized order of the transactions within the parallelized tasks is different than the serial order in the original flat thread's program. Whether such a reordering of such tasks is safe or not depends on the semantics of the operations being performed at each candidate task.
  When two or more tasks are not commutable, spawning them inside nested-parallel threads is not a safe choice.
- The tasks to parallelize should be long enough to compensate the overheads associated with nesting. Namely, the cost of forking/joining the new threads to run each task in parallel, the costs of beginning and committing nested transactions, the additional overheads of deeper nesting in the transactional tree, among others.

---

[1] This means that we consider only a closed nesting model. An alternative is the open nesting model introduced briefly in Section 2.3. We leave that alternative out of the scope of this chapter, since no research work on parallel nesting support includes open nesting. In theory, however, open nesting is applicable to both parallel and linear nesting models.

Nested tasks should only be parallelized when the associated speed-ups clearly compensate the above costs.

- There are available hardware contexts to run each task in parallel. Of course, exposing additional fine-grained parallelism is advantageous as long as there are idle hardware contexts to run the spawned nested tasks. Blindly spawning nested tasks may lead to pathological executions where spawned tasks are actually condemned to spend substantial periods waiting for an available core. Furthermore, it increases thread preemption cost.

Ensuring the above conditions is not trivial and is, perhaps, the key obstacle to building efficient nested-parallel programs. There are, however, tools, frameworks and language support that assist the programmer with some of the above issues. We describe some examples of such items in the following sections.

Although appealing in theory, only a few of today's state-of-the-art TMs support this nested-parallel model. As we shall discuss in Section 4, the nested-parallel model brings about a number of technical challenges that can substantially complicate the implementation of a TM runtime. Hence, many TMs offer support for nesting but introduce restrictions that do not exist in the pure nested-parallel model we described previously.

We address such restricted models next.

2.2 Shallow Parallel Nesting

Volos et al. [7] define one poorer variant of the nested-parallel model, which they call *shallow nesting*. In shallow nesting, a transaction can have several threads executing, in parallel, parts of the transaction's code. However, no nested transactions are allowed.

The memory accesses performed by the threads running on behalf of a common (parallelized) transaction are added to the transaction's read and write set. However, the TM does not guarantee that such threads run in isolation.

Hence, the programmer's role is harder, since shallow nesting places the burden of ensuring correct synchronization among the parallel threads running on behalf of a same transaction. Shallow nesting is, though, a nice fit for parallelizing long transactions that perform multiple independent operations (e.g. a loop on disjoint data).

2.3 Nesting with Restricted Parallelism

Other variants of the nested-parallel model restrict the allowed parallelism among nested tasks (and transactions).

Hierarchical Lock Atomicity. One such model consists in disallowing sibling transactions (i.e., nested transactions descending from a common parent) to run in parallel. Volos et al. [7] define this as the *Hierarchical Lock Atomicity* (HLA) model. In concept, it is as if each parent transaction has a single lock, which the children transactions need to obtain before proceeding. More precisely, let us consider that some transaction spawned a set of threads. When any of such threads wishes to begin a (nested) transaction, it needs to wait until there is no other sibling or any sibling's descendant transaction running.

Note that, like shallow nesting, HLA also allows a transaction to effectively run in parallel - as long as such parallel threads do not begin simultaneous nested transactions. Hence, in long transactions that can be parallelized into tasks that contain few and short transactions, HLA is able to yield parallel executions that resemble those of the pure nested-parallel model.

Linear Nesting. For implementation simplicity, many mainstream TMs support nested transactions but simply disallow a transaction to spawn any threads. In other words, if some parent transaction creates child transactions, then the children will run in the same thread that runs the parent transaction, one after another. This is called the *linear nesting* model.

Linear nesting imposes a decisive limitation on the potential parallelism that is made available to programmers, who can only create threads in code locations that lie out-side atomic blocks. Hence, it severely restricts composability of parallel programs [16], as a program cannot call a parallel library function from inside a transaction without serializing the function [1]. Or, alternatively, the programmer cannot decompose long transactions into parts that do not conflict among each other (at least not too much).

We can actually identify three main variants of the linear nesting model, as follows:

- Flat Nesting.
  The parent transaction sees all modifications to program state made by inner trans-actions, since child and parent transactions are coupled onto a single transaction. This is the simpler approach, since aborting the child transaction will also abort the parent, but committing the child transaction has no effect until the parent trans-action also commits. Flattened transactions are easy to implement, since there is only one transaction in execution coupled with a nesting depth counter. However, this is a poor programming abstraction, since if an explicit abort is issued in a li-brary routine that contains transactions, all surrounding transactions must terminate execution.
- Closed Nesting.
  A closed transaction behaves similarly to a flattening one, except the inner transac-tion can abort without terminating its parent transaction. When a closed transaction commits or aborts, control passes to its parent. If the inner transaction commits, its changes become visible to the parent. However, they only become visible to other threads when the parent transaction commits. Hence, closed nesting ensures the same correctness properties as flat nesting.
- Open Nesting.
  When an open transaction commits, its changes become visible to all other trans-actions in the system, even if the parent transaction is still executing. Further-more, if the parent transaction aborts, the results of the nested open transactions remain committed. Thus, open nesting allows greater concurrency between transac-tions. For example, it allows concurrent transactions to increment a shared counter without provoking a conflict for the whole parent transaction. While using open transactions allows for greater concurrency in the application, they can subvert the

isolation of a parent transaction, thus requiring extra care. For instance, consider the case where a child transaction reads data tentatively written by the parent; then the child transaction commits but the parent transaction later aborts. Now there is some inconsistent global state which depends on a write operation that actually never occurred. Another problematic case is the one where the parent transaction reads some location that the child transaction writes to. The child can commit a new value to that location, and then the parent may abort and read the value that was updated by its child transaction upon re-execution.

2.4   Nested-Parallelism with Thread-Level Speculation

As discussed earlier in this section, the nested-parallelism model requires careful reasoning about the semantics of the parent task being parallelized. Namely, the programmer must assert if the work performed by the parallel children tasks is actually commutative.

This assertion may not be trivial for all applications. For the average programmer, this may pose a significant effort and introduce a non-negligible risk of errors due to parallelizing tasks that, after all, were not semantically commutable. At the end, most programmers will most likely feel discouraged from exposing fine-grained parallelism lying within their applications.

Furthermore, some tasks are simply not commutable, as the application's semantics require them to run accordingly to the sequential program's order. That is, any task reordering that leads to different results is simply prohibited by the semantics. However, this does not mean that running the tasks in parallel will always lead to such undesirable executions. Consider, for instance, a sequence of tasks that work on some shared data structure (e.g., a large array or matrix) such that some tasks may occasionally read or write to the same elements in the shared structure. Any task reading from an element that other tasks in the sequence write to should obtain the value updated by the most recent task that, in program order, precedes the reader. Hence, parallelizing these tasks as sibling nested transactions may violate this condition, as the nested-parallel model may serialize siblings in a different order than that of the original program.

A recent research direction has proposed a variant of the nested-parallel model that address the two above issues [8]. This new model combines TM and thread-level speculation (TLS) [9].

As in the nested-parallel model, the programmer can sub-divide a transaction into parallel tasks. The key difference in the hybrid TM+TLS model is that runtime is responsible for ensuring that any data dependencies stemming from the original sequential program order are respected in the speculatively parallelized execution.

This hybrid model eliminates the two issues discussed above. On the one hand, the programmer in doubt about task commutativity can conservatively parallelize a transaction using this hybrid model. Since the underlying runtime guarantees that the parallelized execution will be equivalent to a sequential execution of the same transaction, the parallelized program is correct no matter if the tasks were actually commutable or not. On the other hand, situations where the sequence of tasks in a transaction is not commutable may now be safely parallelized, since the TM ensures that such tasks will be serialized according to program order.

Algorithm 2. Example of nested-parallel programs with TFJ

```
 9  function sb7-longTraversal-TFJ(root)
10      transaction(proc, params) {
11          onacid;
12              proc(params);
13          commit;
14      }
15      onacid;
16          spawn transaction(sb7-traverseComplexAssembly, root.leaf1);
17          spawn transaction(sb7-traverseComplexAssembly, root.leaf2);
18          spawn transaction(sb7-traverseComplexAssembly, root.leaf3);
19      commit;
20      }
```

It is thus pertinent to compare the the hybrid TM+TLS model with the nested-parallel model. The TM+TLS model is perhaps more appealing to the average programmer, as it strongly simplifies programming fine-grained parallel programs where the tasks do not commute or the programmer simply is not sure that they commute.

However, the main question is which model is able to actually deliver higher parallelism. In fact, each model can, in theory, achieve more parallelism than the other, depending on the program being parallelized. As discussed above, the TM+TLS model can expose parallelism in situations where the pure nested-parallel model cannot.

However, in situations where the nested-parallel tasks are commutable, the TM+TLS model is limited. Whereas the pure nested-parallel model is free to serialize the sibling tasks in any order, the TM+TLS model will always enforce the sequential program order. Unfortunately, the sequential program order may not be the serialization order that allows for highest parallelism, when considered among the remaining possible serialization orderings.

3 Support

In order to aid the programmer in building nested parallel programs it should be easy for him to: i) create nested tasks in a fork-join pattern; ii) protect the accesses to regions of shared data using transactions. Recently several frameworks in different programming languages have added support for such mechanisms, which we will now address.

The flat-nesting TM API makes use of functions to start and end transactional code, e.g. tx-begin() and tx-commit(), or simply use an annotation or construct that surrounds the transactional code, e.g. @*Atomic* or *atomic* { }. When using nested transactions there is, usually, a need for an extended TM API that supports each of the models described in Section 2.

The first framework support for parallel nested transactions was proposed by Vitek et al. in Transactional Featherweight Java (TFJ) [10]. TFJ used a *spawn* keyword to create a new thread for executing a transaction, an *onacid* keyword that represents the start of a transaction and a *commit* keyword for ending a transaction (example Algorithm 2).

Algorithm 3. Example of nested-parallel programs with Cilk

```
21  function sb7-longTraversal-Cilk(root)
22      atomic {
23          parallel {
24              atomic {
25                  traverseComplexAssembly(root.leaf1);
26              }
27              atomic {
28                  traverseComplexAssembly(root.leaf2);
29              }
30              atomic {
31                  traverseComplexAssembly(root.leaf3);
32              }
33          }
34      }
```

They proceed to define the semantics in which such keywords can be used to program parallel nested applications. Then, they describe theoretical proofs that validate these keywords as building blocks for any model of nested transactions.

The work on TFJ was followed by Agrawal et al. [5] implementing similar constructs in Cilk, a dynamic multi-threaded language. Cilk already supported executing parallel sections of code, using a *parallel* { } construct, to tell the runtime that there exists a possibility for parallelism, and transactions, using the *atomic* { } construct. The combination of these two constructs allowed for the specification of parallel nested transactions, with an unbounded nesting depth (example Algorithm 3).

The support for parallel nested transactions on TFJ and Cilk executed all sibling transactions independently, as most parallel nested transactions' models require. However, Ramadan et al. [11] argued that this execution model was not expressive enough, and that siblings should affect each other's outcomes. They introduced coordinated sibling transactions in Xfork, a programming construct that allowed TM programmers to express intra-transaction concurrency. Inside an *atomic* { } construct, a TM programmer could define parallel transactions with the construct *xfork (form, numForks, xforkProcedure, data)*, where:

- form : the form of sibling coordination (AND, OR, XOR)
- numForks: the number of concurrent sibling transactions to spawn
- xforkProcedure: a list of procedures to execute inside sibling transactions
- data: a list of arguments for each of the procedures

Xfork supports three forms of coordinated sibling transactions:

- AND: All sibling transactions must succeed, or none succeed
- OR: Sibling transactions succeed or fail independently
- XOR: Only one sibling transaction must succeed

Algorithm 4. Example of nested-parallel programs with xFork

```
35  function sb7-longTraversal-xFork(root)
36      atomic {
37          xfork (AND, 3, { traverseComplexAssembly, traverseComplexAssembly,
            traverseComplexAssembly }, {root.leaf1, root.leaf2, root.leaf3});
38      }
```

Algorithm 5. Example of nested-parallel programs with JVSTM

```
39  @Atomic
40  function sb7-longTraversal-JVSTM(root)
41      @Parallel
42      for each leaf in root do
43          traverseComplexAssembly(leaf);
```

The AND form is used for regular nested parallel transactions (Example Function 4). The OR form emulates independent nested transactions, where all successfully completed siblings will commit. The XOR form allows for speculative parallel nested transactions, where if some sibling is successful the parent is also successful. Non-speculatively, the XOR form can execute several transactions in parallel when the programmer knows that only one sibling will commit successfully (e.g. when doing a parallel search for an item on a data structure).

Finally, the work by Diegues et al. [12] uses the annotations *@Atomic* and *@Parallel*, identical to the constructs of Agrawal et al. and DeuceSTM [13], in the Java programming language. These annotations are enough to fully program parallel nested transactions, with an unbounded nesting depth, in JVSTM [12] (example Algorithm 5).

4   Algorithms

Extending a TM runtime with parallel nested transactions support is not trivial. Conflict detection, in particular, becomes much more complex. Not only does the TM need to detect conflicts between concurrent running transactions accessing the same data object, but now the TM must also allow accesses from child transactions to objects written to and commited by its siblings. Handling such accesses in an efficient manner requires a re-organization of the TM data structures.

Therefore, for a TM runtime to fully support nested parallel transactions it has to tackle several challenges that did not exist in the traditional flat nesting scenario:

1. To support partial rollback of child transactions, without affecting the parent
2. To handle concurrent data structures correctly, such as the parent-child read and write sets
3. To coordinate the commit or abort of parent and child transactions
4. To detect conflicts by verifying ancestor-descendant relationships, which may be complicated for deep nested trees

This section addresses several state of the art algorithms for the nested parallel transactions models we presented in Section 2. Since this chapter focuses on parallel nesting models, we omit algorithms that support only linear nesting. A survey of linear nesting algorithms can be found in the technical report of Diegues [14].

Each of the following algorithms solves some or all of the previous challenges in different ways, with different complexity degrees. As discussed in Section 2, some solutions opt for limited models in exchange for better performance or scalability.

4.1 CWSTM

This approach builds on Cilk, a dynamic multi-threaded language that allows the programmer to use special constructs to create new threads with assigned tasks. The CW-STM [5] dynamically unfolds the program execution into a computation tree that is used for conflict detection. This structure serves as the basis for a work-stealing algorithm that allows the exploration of a transaction's inner parallelism.

The work-stealing technique is a means of distributing a set of tasks to threads: Each thread maintains a double-ended queue of tasks; when the thread runs out of work, it reaches the top of another thread's dequeue and steals a task to execute on that thread's behalf. Given the uniform random access for stealing, there should never exist any contention in accessing a dequeue, as long as there is work left to be done.

CWSTM uses the aforementioned computation tree for eager conflict detection, with a computational intensity that is independent of the nesting depth. Each transactional object has an associated access stack in which entries correspond to accesses performed by active transactions. The content of these stacks is a form of multiple-readers-single-writer locking scheme: The last entry always corresponds to the youngest descendant writer transaction, or a set of reader transactions all descendant of a common writer ancestor. Therefore, below the first stack entry there may only exist accesses of descendants of the last access owner. This way, as soon as a transaction accesses an object, that transaction may eagerly detect a conflict.

However, maintaining these per-object stacks is very inefficient. Hence, their effort only resulted in providing a STM specification and a theoretical upper bound for the execution time of a parallel nested transaction. No complete implementation of such design was achieved for this paper, albeit the proposed design solves all of the challenges we described.

4.2 PNSTM

The Parallel Nesting STM (PNSTM) [15] followed the approach of Agrawal et al. and succeeded in implementing an algorithm for parallel nested transactions support. PNSTM provides a simple work-stealing approach with a single global queue, into which the application's blocks may be enqueued for concurrent transactional execution.

Moreover, each transactional object is associated with a stack that contains all the accesses (both reads and writes) performed by active transactions. To achieve constant time ancestor queries for eager conflict detection, the per-object stack is represented by a memory word that has each bit assigned to a transaction (called a *bitnum*). When two transactions access the same object, a conflict is easily detected by performing a bitwise operation on the object's stack.

By using a memory word for this representation they achieved performance improvements but limit the maximum number of transactions on the system at all times. As a workaround, PNSTM uses a mechanism that allows for new transactions to reuse *bit-nums* of completed transactions.

The system is limited to a determined maximum number of concurrent transactions. However, PNSTM claims that no more parallelism would be achieved over that limit if it is larger than the maximum number of worker threads.

When a transaction commits, it leaves behind traces in all the objects it accessed, namely the stack frames stating its ownership. To avoid having to go through all the objects in the write-set by locking and merging the frame with the previous entry, PNSTM does that lazily, similarly to Agrawal's algorithm. This may lead to false conflicts when some transaction accesses an object and finds an entry in the stack that corresponds to an already committed but not yet reclaimed transaction. The authors show that it is possible to avoid it by resorting to a global structure maintaining data about all committed transactions.

This was the first implementation of parallel nesting with constant time ancestor queries, for an arbitrary nesting depth. It solves all of the challenges we presented in a more efficient way, at the cost of a bound in the active threads count.

4.3   NePalTM

The Nested Parallelism for Transactional Memory (NePalTM) [16] provides in-place updates with strict two-phase locking for writes. Memory addresses are mapped to transactional records with a granularity of several addresses.

The transactional records may be read in two modes: in pessimistic mode they have to acquire a lock in read-mode, or by using version timestamps which are accessed by optimistic readers. Therefore, it actually provides both visible and invisible readers.

NePalTM supports the Shallow Nesting model, described in Section 2, by having each member of an atomic region store its own transactional logs (read, write and undo logs). This way, no synchronization is required to access the logs of an atomic region, and they are all used only at commit time of that atomic region.

NePalTM also supports the Hierarchical Lock Atomicity model, defined in Section 2. In this case, NePalTM has a major limitation of requiring such sibling transactions to run in mutual exclusion. Hence, it does not support parallel nesting entirely. Thus, NePalTM solves the first challenge, of supporting partial rollback, since there is no concurrency between parent and child transactions. It also solves the second challenge, since in shallow nesting members of an atomic region are concurrently logging transactional data.

4.4   NeSTM

The Nested STM (NeSTM) [17] is based on McRT-STM [18]. McRT-STM is a traditional blocking STM, with eager conflict detection, with undo logs for writes at the word granularity. In the extension of McRT-STM to support parallel nesting, the focus point was that it should not interfere with the performance of workloads in which nesting is not used. They were also driven by the intent of keeping the memory footprint as close to constant as possible, regardless of the nesting depth in use.

The original McRT-STM assumed that no other transaction could access a locked variable. With nested-parallel transactions this is no longer the case: due to the parallel nested transactions, other transactions can correctly access the locked object as long as they are descendants of the owner. When a transaction accesses an object, it locks such an object. That object's lock includes a new field with information about its current owner. This way, when another transaction wishes to access the same object, it may confirm if it is a descendant of the lock's owner.

Similarly, the version number of an object must also be visible at all times, in order to serialize conflicting transactions. Consequently, the lock variable now has some reserved bits to identify the transaction owning it, and the rest of the bits are used for the version number. This scheme allows visible readers even when the object is locked. This leads to two practical consequences: first, there is a maximum number of concurrent transactions at a given time, since the transaction identifier is just a few bits long; second, the transaction identifier overflows several orders of magnitude faster than normal.

At transaction start, the global clock is used to timestamp the transaction. Reads will cause an abort if an object was written since the transaction started. This might cause unnecessary aborts: picture two transactions T_i and T_k; T_i did not perform any access, T_k commits values, T_i reads one of the values and will abort. When writing a value, the transaction will attempt to acquire the lock corresponding to the variable and then it will validate the object: The transaction attempting to write, as well as its ancestors, must not have a timestamp smaller than the object's timestamp, in case they read it previously.

To reduce the work needed for this validation, only transactions that were not ancestors of the previous owner of the object must go through the check. Yet, this mechanism yields considerable costs in terms of computation at deeper levels.

Given that the nested commit procedure requires validating the reads across the transaction and its ancestors, followed by the merge of the sets into the parent, this set of actions must be atomic in the algorithm. This is meant to prevent concurrent siblings from committing simultaneously and breaking serializability. This was solved by introducing a lock at each transaction and making nested transactions acquire their parent's lock in mutual exclusion with their siblings.

In addition, NeSTM is subject to livelocks at the level of nested transactions. Picture two transactions, T_1 who writes to x and T_2 who writes to y, they will both have acquired ownership of the respective objects. Now if the T_1 spawns $T_{1:1}$ while T_2 spawns $T_{2:1}$ and both these nested transactions cross-access y and x, respectively, they will abort since those variables are neither owned by them or their ancestors. However, they will have mutually blocked each other unless one of their ancestors aborts as well and releases the corresponding variable. The authors placed a mechanism to avoid this in which they heuristically count consecutive aborts and abort the parent as well.

NeSTM solves all of the challenges we identified, in a more efficient manner than PNSTM, but still with several limitations. Baek et al. [19] and Liu et al. [20] studied how hardware acceleration could improve the performance of nested transactional systems, using NeSTM as a baseline.

4.5   HParSTM

The Hierarchy-based Parallel STM (HParSTM) [21] allows a parent to execute concurrently with its children nested transactions. The advantage of this is that it allows more nodes in the transactional tree to be active in computations concurrently, which enhances the distribution of tasks.

The same protocol used for top-level transactions is extended for nesting by replicating most control data structures. The baseline STM design promotes a mixed invalidation strategy with visible readers and lazy lock acquisition and write-back on commit time.

To achieve this, a global structure is used to register transactions that are doomed to abort. This is accomplished by having a transaction's commit procedure invalidate active readers of objects that it is writing-back in the aforementioned structure. Any transaction has to check that it does not belong to the doomed transactions list prior to commit.

Furthermore, this information is also scattered across the shared objects which have a forbidden set associated to them, better defined by an example: if T_1 read x and T_2 wrote x and y followed by commit, it not only adds T_1 to the global doomed set, but also to the forbidden set of x and y. If T_1 attempts to read y it will fail to do so, in order to prevent an inconsistent view state.

This procedure is used by nested transactions, except that they must ensure that these invalidation sets contain neither the nested transaction's identifier or any of its ancestors'. The control data structures of nested parallel transactions are merged into the parent transaction by concurrent siblings (and the parent's execution itself) with mutual exclusion.

HparSTM goes even further in the design space of parallel nested transactions algorithms. Although it solves all our challenges, HparSTM still has some limitations when supporting higher levels of nested transactions.

4.6   JVSTM

The first STM to solve all challenges we described in an efficient manner was the work by Diegues et al. in JVSTM [12]. They extended the original JVSTM [22] with parallel nesting support, assuming that each top-level transaction may unfold a nesting tree in which a transaction performs transactional accesses only when all its children are no longer active.

Their approach is to extend VBoxes (JVSTM's placeholders for transactional locations' values) such that transactions may now write directly to the VBoxes, rather than having to maintain a private write set mapping each location written to its new value. In order to distinguish between globally committed values and the tentative values of ongoing transactions, a VBox now contains both values. A permanent value has been consolidated via a commit of some top-level transaction, whereas a tentative value belongs to an active top-level transaction (or any of its children nested transactions), and is thus part of its write-set.

Additionally, each tentative write points to an ownership record (*orec*) that encapsulates the transaction that owns it, the version of the write, and the status of the owner. Each writing transaction creates one such *orec* and propagates it to the transaction's parent when it commits. Through these *orecs* a nested transaction can perform the ancestor query, which depends only on the number of tentative writes on the location.

The algorithm proposed in this work has three major features that make it efficient: a fast path in the read operation that is performed in constant time (independently of the nesting depth); a fast mode for writing, backed up by a slow mode for fallbacks; and a commit operation that is independent of the write-set size.

The fast read path is achieved by checking if the read operation being performed is not a read-after-write. In that case the read operation can be done directly from the last permanent write, and avoid the ancestor query. The fast path for writing occurs when the transaction that is writing to a location already owns that location, thus it can simply overwrite the tentative value. The commit operation of nested transactions simply changes the ownership of *orecs* that the child transaction owns to its parent. The set of location *orecs* is usually smaller than the whole write-set.

4.7 TLSTM

TLSTM is the first algorithm to tackle the challenges of nested-parallelism using thread level speculation. TLSTM extends an existing STM, SwissTM [23]. The key insight is that a SwissTM transaction is used as the speculative execution unit that supports two concepts: STM transactions (defined by the user) and TLS speculative tasks (automatically created at compile time). An STM transaction is seen as a sequence of one or more TLS speculative tasks, which can run out-of-order in a speculative fashion, until they commit sequentially.

Most of the maintenance load of STM and TLS that typically dominates the associated execution overheads is, in fact, common to both approaches. Namely, conflict detection, speculative reads and writes, read-log and write-log maintenance, commit and rollback are issues that both STM and TLS must handle. Hence, by combining both STM and TLS in TLSTM, the overhead associated with the above aspects remains comparable to the overhead of stand-alone STM, rather than doubling.

Cross-transaction conflict detection follows the original approach of SwissTM: using eager, lock-based conflict detection for write/write conflicts, and lazy counter-based validation for read/write conflicts. Within each top-level transaction, cross-task conflict detection relies on the very data structures maintained for cross-transaction conflict detection, with the addition of a task read-set for speculative cross-task reads. TLSTM allows only one task to write on each location at a time, also using eager, lock-based write-write conflict detection. TLSTM validates the task and transaction read-sets at write and commit time, looking for cross-task Write after Read conflicts. Furthermore, TLSTM only allow speculative reads from completed tasks within a transaction.

5 Summary

For many real applications, harnessing the hardware parallelism of modern multi- and many-core machines calls for exposing fine-grained parallel tasks, possibly nested within memory transactions. Memory transactions, being a composable abstraction, are a promising way to enable the average programmer to exploit nested-parallel programming.

This chapter has given an insight into the concepts, techniques and challenges behind nested-parallel programming. We started with a view from the programmer's point of view, describing the nested-parallel model in transactional memory and its variants. Complementarily, we surveyed available support to build and run nested-parallel programs. We then turn to the perspective of a TM runtime designer, studying the state-of-the art algorithms that support currently nested parallelism.

References

1. Howard, J., Dighe, S., Hoskote, Y., Vangal, S., Finan, D., Ruhl, G., Jenkins, D., Wilson, H., Borkar, N., Schrom, G., Pailet, F., Jain, S., Jacob, T., Yada, S., Marella, S., Salihundam, P., Erraguntla, V., Konow, M., Riepen, M., Droege, G., Lindemann, J., Gries, M., Apel, T., Henriss, K., Lund-Larsen, T., Steibl, S., Borkar, S., De, V., Van Der Wijngaart, R., Mattson, T.: A 48-core ia-32 message-passing processor with dvfs in 45nm cmos. In: 2010 IEEE International on Solid-State Circuits Conference Digest of Technical Papers (ISSCC), pp. 108–109 (February 2010)
2. Moss, J.E.B., Hosking, A.L.: Nested transactional memory: Model and architecture sketches. Sci. Comput. Program. 63, 186–201 (2006)
3. Gray, J., Reuter, A.: Transaction Processing: Concepts and Techniques, 1st edn. Morgan Kaufmann Publishers Inc., San Francisco (1992)
4. Harris, T., Marlow, S., Peyton-Jones, S., Herlihy, M.: Composable memory transactions. In: Proceedings of the Tenth ACM SIGPLAN Symposium on Principles and Practice of Parallel Programming, PPoPP 2005, pp. 48–60. ACM, New York (2005)
5. Agrawal, K., Fineman, J.T., Sukha, J.: Nested parallelism in transactional memory. In: Proceedings of the 13th ACM SIGPLAN Symposium on Principles and Practice of Parallel Programming, PPoPP 2008, pp. 163–174. ACM, New York (2008)
6. Guerraoui, R., Kapalka, M., Vitek, J.: Stmbench7: A benchmark for software transactional memory. In: Proceedings of the 2nd ACM SIGOPS/EuroSys European Conference on Computer Systems, EuroSys 2007, pp. 315–324. ACM, New York (2007)
7. Volos, H., Welc, A., Adl-Tabatabai, A.-R., Shpeisman, T., Tian, X., Narayanaswamy, R.: NePaLTM: Design and Implementation of Nested Parallelism for Transactional Memory Systems. In: Drossopoulou, S. (ed.) ECOOP 2009. LNCS, vol. 5653, pp. 123–147. Springer, Heidelberg (2009)
8. Barreto, J., Dragojevic, A., Ferreira, P., Filipe, R., Guerraoui, R.: Unifying thread-level speculation and transactional memory. In: Narasimhan, P., Triantafillou, P. (eds.) Middleware 2012. LNCS, vol. 7662, pp. 187–207. Springer, Heidelberg (2012)
9. Sohi, G.S., Breach, S.E., Vijaykumar, T.N.: Multiscalar processors. In: 25 Years of the International Symposia on Computer Architecture (Selected Papers), ISCA 1998, pp. 521–532. ACM, New York (1998)
10. Vitek, J., Jagannathan, S., Welc, A., Hosking, A.L.: A semantic framework for designer transactions. In: Schmidt, D. (ed.) ESOP 2004. LNCS, vol. 2986, pp. 249–263. Springer, Heidelberg (2004)

11. Ramadan, H., Witchel, E.: The xfork in the road to coordinated sibling transactions. In: 4th ACM SIGPLAN Workshop on Transactional Computing (TRANSACT 2009) (2009)
12. Diegues, N., Cachopo, J.: Practical parallel nesting for software transactional memory. In: Afek, Y. (ed.) DISC 2013. LNCS, vol. 8205, pp. 149–163. Springer, Heidelberg (2013)
13. Korland, G., Shavit, N., Felber, P.: Noninvasive concurrency with java stm. In: Third Workshop on Programmability Issues for Multi-Core Computers (MULTIPROG) (2010)
14. Diegues, N., Cachopo, J.: Review of nesting in transactional memory. Tech. rep., Technical Report RT/1/2012, Instituto Superior Técnico/INESC-ID (2012)
15. Barreto, J.A., Dragojević, A., Ferreira, P., Guerraoui, R., Kapalka, M.: Leveraging parallel nesting in transactional memory. SIGPLAN Not 45, 91–100 (2010)
16. Volos, H., Welc, A., Adl-Tabatabai, A.-R., Shpeisman, T., Tian, X., Narayanaswamy, R.: NePaLTM: Design and Implementation of Nested Parallelism for Transactional Memory Systems. In: Drossopoulou, S. (ed.) ECOOP 2009. LNCS, vol. 5653, pp. 123–147. Springer, Heidelberg (2009)
17. Baek, W., Kozyrakis, C.: NesTM: Implementing and Evaluating Nested Parallelism in Software Transactional Memory. In: Proceedings of the 9th International Conference on Parallel Architectures and Compilation Techniques (PACT) (2009)
18. Saha, B., Adl-Tabatabai, A.-R., Hudson, R.L., Minh, C.C., Hertzberg, B.: Mcrt-stm: A high performance software transactional memory system for a multi-core runtime. In: Proceedings of the Eleventh ACM SIGPLAN Symposium on Principles and Practice of Parallel Programming, PPoPP 2006, pp. 187–197. ACM, New York (2006)
19. Baek, W., Bronson, N., Kozyrakis, C., Olukotun, K.: Making nested parallel transactions practical using lightweight hardware support. In: Proceedings of the 24th ACM International Conference on Supercomputing, pp. 61–71. ACM (2010)
20. Liu, Y., Diestelhorst, S., Spear, M.: Delegation and nesting in best-effort hardware transactional memory. In: Proceedings of the Twenty-fourth Annual ACM Symposium on Parallelism in Algorithms and Architectures, pp. 38–47. ACM (2012)
21. Kumar, R., Vidyasankar, K.: Hparstm: A hierarchy-based stm protocol for supporting nested parallelism. In: The 6th ACM SIGPLAN Workshop on Transactional Computing (TRANSACT 2011) (2011)
22. Cachopo, J.A., Rito-Silva, A.: Versioned boxes as the basis for memory transactions. Sci. Comput. Program. 63, 172–185 (2006)
23. Dragojević, A., Guerraoui, R., Kapalka, M.: Stretching transactional memory. In: Proceedings of the 2009 ACM SIGPLAN Conference on Programming Language Design and Implementation, PLDI 2009, pp. 155–165. ACM (2009)

Contention Management
and Scheduling

Scheduling-Based Contention Management Techniques for Transactional Memory

Danny Hendler[1] and Adi Suissa-Peleg[2]

[1] Department of Computer Science, Ben-Gurion University of the Negev
hendlerd@cs.bgu.ac.il
[2] School of Engineering and Applied Sciences, Harvard University, Cambridge
adisuis@seas.harvard.edu

Abstract. *Contention management* refers to the mechanisms used by transactional memory (TM) implementations "to ensure forward progress – to avoid livelock and starvation, and to promote throughput and fairness" [1]. Without effective contention management mechanisms, TM implementations are susceptible to performance degradation caused by numerous transaction collisions.

Early work on contention management focused on the narrower problem of *conflict resolution*. When two transactions collide, one transaction (the *winner transaction*) is allowed to proceed, while the other (the *loser transaction*) must wait and/or be aborted. Conflict resolution policies decide which transaction should win and which should lose and for how long the losing transaction should be delayed. However, it was shown that conflict resolution alone is insufficient for guaranteeing reasonable performance for high-contention TM workloads.

The key idea underlying *transaction schedulers*, introduced a few years ago, is that the execution of conflicting transactions must be serialized in the face of high contention and, more generally, that the level of parallelism between transactional threads should be controlled by the contention manager and dynamically adjusted. Transaction scheduling allows not only to resolve conflicts after they occur, but also to proactively reduce their probability, thus improving performance. This chapter provides a survey of the key approaches and techniques used by transaction schedulers.

1 Introduction

A TM implementation can allow two concurrent transactions to successfully commit if the write-set of neither of them intersects with the data-set of the other transaction. Otherwise, the two transactions are said to be in *conflict* and at most one can successfully commit, while the other must wait before it is allowed to proceed, or must abort, and retry after possibly waiting for some period of time.

Herlihy et al. [2] introduced contention management as a mechanism for ensuring progress in DSTM, the first obstruction-free [3] Software TM (STM) implementation. Early work by Scherer and Scott [1, 4] defined the contention

R. Guerraoui and P. Romano (Eds.): Transactional Memory, LNCS 8913, pp. 213–227, 2015.
© Springer International Publishing Switzerland 2015

management problem as follows: "When two or more transactions attempt to access transactional data concurrently, at least one transaction must be aborted. The decision of which transaction to abort, and under what conditions, is the contention management problem." This definition is too narrow, however, as there are contention managers (CMs) that attempt not only to resolve collisions once they occur but also to avoid them in the first place.

Spear et al. [5] define contention management as: "The mechanisms used to ensure forward progress – to avoid livelock and starvation and to promote throughput and fairness". According to this broader definition, which we adopt in this chapter, contention management does not only address the resolution of conflicts once they occur, but also takes proactive measures in order to avoid them altogether.

We distinguish between contention managers that have full control of the scheduling of threads executing transactions, called *transaction schedulers*, and *conventional contention managers*, where transactional threads are directly controlled by a system scheduler which is unaware of transactions. Our work focuses on scheduling-based CMs.

The key premise of transaction scheduling is that the thread scheduler must be TM-aware — thread scheduling decisions must take into consideration whether a thread is transactional or not and, if it is, what the state of the transaction is. The advantage of transaction schedulers over conventional conflict resolution is that they have more options for coping with transactional conflicts and are very effective for managing high-contention transactional workloads.

In this chapter, we provide an overview of transaction schedulers. We start with a short description of conventional contention managers. We then discuss the key ideas underlying transaction scheduling and describe a few key scheduler implementations. This is followed by a brief survey of theoretical results. We conclude the chapter with a discussion.

2   Conventional Contention Managers

STM implementations typically delegate the task of conflict resolution to a separate *contention manager* (CM) module [2]. The CM tries to resolve transaction conflicts once they are detected. When a transaction detects a conflict with another transaction, it consults the CM in order to determine how to proceed. The CM can then decide which of the two conflicting transactions should continue, and when and how the other transaction should be resumed.

Herilhy et al. [2] introduced Dynamic STM (DSTM), the first STM that supports a separate contention manager module. DSTM consults the CM module when a conflict occurs in order to decide whether a transaction should be forced to abort. To this end, DSTM emits transactional events to the CM. For instance, DSTM may emit an event whenever a transaction starts, a transactional object is accessed, or a transaction commits.

In particular, DSTM notifies the CM when a transactional conflict is detected. In this case, the CM can decide, based on the events communicated to it, which of the conflicting transactions can continue (the *winner transaction*) and whether the other transaction (the *loser transaction*) should be aborted or delayed. The CM can also determine how long a loser transaction must wait before it can restart or resume its execution.

Other STM implementations, such as [6–8], also provide their own contention manager interface, which typically extends the interface provided with DSTM. Figure 1 depicts the workflow of a TM System that uses a CM module when a conflict is detected.

Conventional contention management implementations [2, 4, 9–11] have only a few alternatives for dealing with transaction conflicts. They can only decide which of the conflicting transactions can continue (the winner transaction) and whether the other transaction (the loser transaction) will be aborted or delayed. A conventional CM can also determine how long a loser transaction must wait before it can restart or resume execution.

The scalability of STM implementations directly depends on the characteristics of the workload at hand. It has been shown that STMs scale well on multiple cores when the transactional workloads behave "well", i.e., when there is a relatively small number of transaction conflicts [12, 13]. Unfortunately, this is not always the case.

Two transactional workload types often exhibit poor performance with conventional CM. First, workloads characterized by transactions that conflict frequently will trigger many aborts, sometimes even creating a livelock situation in which the same pair of transactions may collide again and again (a.k.a. *repeated aborts*). This is often the case with long running transactions. Second, when the number of threads exceeds the number of cores, threads are frequently preempted while executing transactions. This increases the transaction's duration by one or more scheduling time slices, which is often several orders of magnitude longer than the actual computation time of the transaction, thus drastically increasing the risk of conflicts. For these workload types, transaction throughput (i.e., commit rate) will be relatively low. An important challenge faced by STM implementations is to handle such scenarios gracefully.

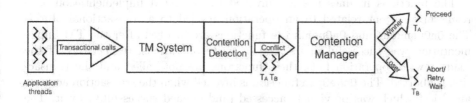

Fig. 1. A TM System workflow. Application threads interact with the TM System using transactional calls. The TM System detects conflicts and delegates their resolution to a separate contention manager module. The contention manager arbitrates the conflict by deciding which transaction should win and proceed in its execution, and which transaction should lose.

```
    // Transaction related events
1   void OnBeginTransaction();
2   void OnTryCommitTransaction();
3   void OnTransactionCommitted();
4   void OnTransactionAborted();

    // Object related events
5   void OnOpenRead();
6   void OnOpenWrite();
7   void OnReOpen();
8   void OnContention();

    // Contention management functions
9   boolean ShouldAbort(ContentionManager* enemy, void * objectID);
```

Fig. 2. A contention manager interface (RSTM)

The rest of this section is organized as follows. We describe the interface between the TM system and contention managers in Section 2.1. In Section 2.2, we describe two sample contention managers.

2.1   Contention Manager Interface

Marathe et al. [8] presented a contention manager interface as part of their RSTM implementation. The key functions of this interface are shown in Fig. 2.[1] Each transaction is associated with a unique contention manager instance. A contention manager can also store transaction-specific data that can be modified or queried by the implementation of these functions. With the exception of ShouldAbort, the implementation of all these functions is optional. If no function is provided, then no action is performed upon the occurrence of the respective events.

The functions in lines 1–4 are invoked by the STM implementation after a transaction-related event occurs. Specifically, the OnBeginTransaction, OnTryCommitTransaction, OnTransactionCommitted, and OnTransactionAborted (lines 1–4) are invoked when a transaction starts, attempts to commit, commits successfully, or aborts, respectively.

The functions in lines 5–8 are invoked by the STM implementation as a result of an event related to an operation applied to a transactional object. The OnOpenRead and OnOpenWrite functions are invoked after the TM implementation was successful in its read or write operations, respectively. If the read or write operation fails, these functions are not called and the transaction is aborted. The OnReOpen function is invoked when the transaction accesses an object which was previously accessed (and opened successfully) by it. The OnContention function is invoked when the STM implementation detects that the current transaction attempts to access an object that is currently in another transaction's data-set.

---

[1] This is the interface used by RSTM-v3, which can be downloaded from:
http://www.cs.rochester.edu/research/synchronization/rstm/index.shtml.

Finally, the ShouldAbort function (line 9) must be implemented by a contention manager. It is invoked by the STM implementation after it detects a transactional conflict. More specifically, if, during the execution of a transactional operation (such as read, write, or commit) by some transaction T_A, the STM implementation detects a conflict with transaction T_B, then T_A's ShouldAbort function is invoked and receives as arguments a pointer to T_B and a pointer to the object accessed by T_A that is in T_B's data-set. The function returns true if the STM implementation should try to abort transaction T_B, or false, otherwise. In the latter case, T_A calls the OnContention function, and retries accessing the object again, possibly after waiting for some period of time.[2]

If the ShouldAbort function returns true, the STM implementation attempts to change the status of T_B to ABORTED using a compare-and-swap (CAS) operation. If the CAS operation fails (implying that T_B already committed or aborted), or the function returns false, then the OnContention function is called and the transaction continues its execution.

2.2 Sample Contention Managers

The Karma contention manager [1] keeps track of how many objects were accessed by a transaction during its execution, and favors transactions that have accessed more objects. This is done by adding a counter to each transactional context, that is set to one when the transaction starts and is incremented in the OnOpenRead and OnOpenWrite functions. Upon a conflict, the counters of the two transactions are compared in the ShouldAbort function. If the value of the counter of the current transaction is larger than that of the other transaction, a value of *true* is returned and the other transaction is aborted. If a transaction attempts to access an object that was accessed by another transaction and should not be aborted, the transaction is delayed for one second.

Another example is the Polite contention manager. Polite employs exponential backoff to reduce the number of aborts. To this end, the contention manager counts the number of times an access to an object encountered contention without a successful object access. Let t be this number, then the transaction is set to wait for $2^{(t+c)}$ nanoseconds, where c is an architectural tuning constant. The OnOpenRead, OnOpenWrite, and OnReOpen functions reset the counter. The OnContention function first waits for some random period of time and then increments the number of times a contended object was accessed. Finally, the ShouldAbort function aborts the other transaction if the counter of the current transaction is bigger than some predefined algorithm parameter constant (i.e., the number of times the current transaction waited was too large). Many additional conventional contention managers are described in the literature [1, 4, 5, 10, 11, 14].

---

[2] Later versions of RSTM allowed this function to return one of three values, indicating that the TM implementation should either 1) abort the current transaction, 2) abort the other transaction, or 3) wait for some time before retrying to access the object and avoid aborting any of these two transactions.

Guerraoui, Herlihy and Pochon showed that which contention manager works best depends on various characteristics of the workload and the execution context, such as transaction lengths, data access patterns and concurrency levels [15]. They concluded that there is no universal contention management algorithm. Maldonado et al. [16] evaluated both user-level and kernel-level contention management mechanisms and reached similar conclusions.[3] This motivated *polymorphic contention management*, a mechanism that allows applications to dynamically associate different contention managers with different transaction types [15] .

3   Scheduling-Based Contention Managers

The contention management algorithms described in Section 2 have no control of transaction threads, which remain under the supervision of the system's transaction-unaware scheduler. Consequently, these "conventional" (i.e., nonscheduling) contention managers can only decide which of two conflicting transactions should win, and whether the loser transaction will be aborted or delayed. They may also determine the length of the waiting period of the loser transaction.

Conventional CMs have been found to often provide poor performance with many workloads commonly used to evaluate STMs [1, 4]. They suffer from: (i) too many aborts, e.g., when a long running transaction conflicts with shorter transactions; (ii) lack of precision, since a thread whose transaction was aborted may wait for too long after the commit of the conflicting transaction to restart its own transaction; and (iii) unpredictable benefits, as delaying the restart of a long transaction does not necessarily guarantee its success, unless all other conflicting transactions have completed or are delayed even longer. These problems are particularly acute when there are more threads than cores, as can be desirable for the execution of server-type applications where threads can block in nontransactional code. In this case, a transaction that repeatedly aborts prevents other useful work from being performed on the same core.

In recent years, researchers considered various contention management policies performing some variant of *serializing contention management*, in which the thread running a loser transaction is moved to a waiting-queue until the winner transaction completes.

The rationale behind serializing CM is the following: once a pair of transactions conflict, they are likely to conflict again if allowed to execute concurrently. It follows that the execution of a loser transaction concurrently with a transaction with which it conflicted before is likely to waste CPU cycles.

Using serializing CM enables increasing the effectiveness of contention management by allowing the TM implementation to directly control thread scheduling. Scheduling-based contention managers are able to serialize the execution of conflicting transactions. This is done by having the loser thread (the one executing the loser transaction) wait in a waiting-queue managed by the CM until the winner transaction completes its execution.

---

[3] Refer to Section 3.3 for more details on kernel-level contention management.

Scheduling-based contention management has the potential of providing better performance than conventional CMs, since it allows resuming the execution of the loser transaction immediately after the winner transaction commits. To exemplify this point, consider a collision between transactions T_1 and T_2. Assume that a conventional CM decides that T_1 is the winner and so T_2 must wait.

- If T_2 is allowed to resume execution too soon (the waiting period is too short), it is likely to collide with T_1 again. In this case, either T_1 has to resume waiting (typically for a longer period of time), or, alternatively, the CM may now decide that T_1 wins and so T_2 must wait. In the latter case, T_1 and T_2 may end up repeatedly failing each other in a livelock manner without making any progress.
- On the other hand, if the waiting period of T_1 is too long, then T_1 may be unnecessarily delayed beyond the point when T_2 terminates.

Contrary to conventional contention managers that rely on waiting for a predetermined period of time, with scheduling-based contention management the system is capable of resuming the execution of T_2 immediately after T_1 terminates, resulting in better performance.

The rest of this section is organized as follows. We describe serializing contention management algorithms in Section 3.1. In Section 3.2, we describe proactive scheduling-based mechanisms for collision avoidance. Section 3.3 surveys kernel scheduling-based contention management support.

3.1 Serializing Contention Management

Three works that appeared more-or-less at the same time were the first to present transaction schedulers. These are the Adaptive Transactions scheduler (ATS) algorithm by Yoo and Lee [17], CAR-STM by Dolev et al. [18], and Steal-on-abort by Ansari et al. [19]. Although there are many differences between these transaction schedulers, the key idea underlying them is that the execution of conflicting transactions is serialized by the TM system and that the level of parallelism between transactional threads is controlled by the contention manager and dynamically adjusted. We now provide a brief description of these schedulers.

Yoo and Lee [17] introduced *ATS* – a simple user-level transaction scheduler, and incorporated it into RSTM [8] – a TM implementation from the University of Rochester – and into LogTM [20], a simulation of a hardware-based TM system. ATS uses a *local* (per thread) mechanism to monitor the level of contention (called *contention intensity*) which is used to adaptively determine whether transactions should be serialized or not. When a thread's level of contention exceeds a parameter threshold value, its transactions are serialized to *a single global* scheduling queue. As they show, this adaptive approach can improve performance when workloads lack parallelism. To the best of our knowledge, ATS was the first adaptive scheduling-based CM algorithm.

Dolev, Hendler and Suissa [18] introduced CAR-STM, a user-level scheduler for collision avoidance and resolution in STM implementations. CAR-STM maintains *per-core transaction queues*. Whenever a thread starts a transaction (we say that the thread becomes *transactional*), CAR-STM assumes control of the transactional thread instead of the system scheduler. Upon detecting a collision between two concurrently executing transactions, CAR-STM aborts one transaction and moves it to the transactions queue of the core on which the other transaction is running; this effectively serializes their execution and ensures they will not collide again.

Ansari et al. [19] proposed *steal-on-abort*, a transaction scheduler that avoids wasted work by allowing transactions to "steal" conflicting transactions so that they execute serially. Steal-on-abort was implemented in DSTM2 [21]. It creates a number of *worker threads*, each of which is associated with a single double-ended work queue (a.k.a. *dequeue*) storing transactional jobs. Similarly to CAR-STM, each queue entry holds the information required to execute an associated transaction. A worker thread consumes transactions from the head of its dequeue. It also inserts newly generated transactions to the head of the dequeue. Whenever a dequeue becomes empty, the corresponding worker thread randomly selects another dequeue and attempts to steal a transaction from its tail. A transaction that identifies a collision attempts to abort the other transaction and to insert it to a private (per-thread) queue of "abort-stolen" transactions. This guarantees that the execution of the conflicting transactions will be serialized.

Later work on serializing contention management targeted reducing their overhead and avoiding excessive parallelism reduction (see, e.g., [22–30]).

Attiya and Milani [23] investigated scheduling transactions under read-dominated workloads. They presented *BIMODAL*, a transactions scheduler that targets workloads consisting of read-only and early-write transactions. Its architecture is similar to that of CAR-STM, as each core is associated with a work queue and serialization is employed upon conflicts between writing transactions. BIMODAL also maintains a single global FIFO queue for read-only transactions. It promotes progress by alternating between periods in which it favors the execution of writing transactions and periods in which it favors the execution of read-only transactions. They show that BIMODAL has an optimal competitive ratio compared to any non-clairvoyant scheduler for these workloads.

Heber et al. [27] implemented and evaluated several adaptive algorithms that control the activation of a serializing CM according to measured contention level. Both *local-adaptive* (in which each thread adapts its behavior independently of other threads) and *global-adaptive* (in which transitions between serializing and conventional operation modes are applied to the system as a whole) policies were considered. The algorithms are based on a low-overhead serializing CM implementation they introduced. Their empirical evaluation showed that adaptive contention managers are susceptible to a phenomenon of *mode oscillations*, in which the adaptive algorithm oscillates between serializing and conventional modes of operation. They showed that these mode oscillations hurt performance, thus highlighting the importance of *stabilized* adaptive algorithms that mitigate mode oscillations and improve performance.

Nicácio et al. [28] presented *LUTS*, a lightweight user-level transaction scheduler. LUTS implements a cooperative scheduler for transactional threads. Their scheduler guarantees that a transactional thread is never preempted by another transactional thread in the midst of execution a transaction, thus reducing the window of vulnerability to collisions. They observe that there is a tradeoff between the effectiveness and overhead of conflict-avoidance scheduling heuristics. As the adverse impact of conflict-avoidance overhead on short transactions is more pronounced, they propose different heuristics for short and long transactions.

3.2 Proactive Collision Avoidance

Rather than handle conflicts post factum (i.e., after the transactions doomed to conflict have already started their execution), some schedulers attempt to avoid possible conflicts before they occur in a proactive manner. The TM system attempts to avoid concurrent execution of pairs of transactions that are more likely to collide. Implementations vary according to the mechanisms by which information on the likelihood of collisions is obtained and the manner in which concurrent execution is restricted.

CAR-STM implements a proactive collision avoidance mechanism that pre-assigns transactions that are more likely to collide to the same core. The rationale behind this approach is that transactions that execute on the same core cannot fail each other. Information about conflict probability is provided by the programmer. This is facilitated by extending the interface between applications and the STM so that an application-specific *conflict probability method* can be communicated to the STM. This method receives two transactional contexts and computes an estimate of the probability that the two transactions will conflict.

Another work, by Dragojevic et al. [31], introduced a scheduler called *Shrink* that implements a different approach to collision avoidance. Whereas in CAR-STM it is up to the programmer to provide information regarding the collision probability of transactions, Shrink performs collision avoidance by predicting the future memory accesses of a transaction based on transactional accesses that were made by the same thread in the past.

Dragojevic et al. conducted experiments showing that for many workloads, the read-set of the next transaction can be predicted fairly accurately based on past transactions performed by the thread, regardless of whether these transactions were committed or aborted, and they call this heuristic *temporal locality*. As for the write-set, it is typically much smaller, and according to their experiments, can be predicted based on the immediately preceding aborted transactions. The resulting predicted sets are used by Shrink to decide whether or not to serialize a new transaction.

Another heuristic employed by Shrink serializes a transaction with probability proportional to the number of transactions that are already in the serialization queue. They call this heuristic *serialization affinity*. This is a global measure of contention, unlike contention intensity which is a local (per-thread) measure.

Upon high contention, Shrink checks, before a transaction starts, whether variables in its predicted sets are in the write set of other threads. Only in this case, the transaction will be serialized to the global serialization queue.

Similarly to Shrink, the *RELSTM* transaction scheduler [32], proposed by Sainz and Attiya, tracks conflict patterns between transactions. In addition to avoiding the concurrent execution of transactions that were found to directly conflict with each other, it also avoids executing a transaction when many of its *second-hop* conflicting transactions (transactions that conflict through an intermediate transaction) are running. They show that this approach is useful in highly-contended workloads, when many cores are used.

Several proposals provide proactive collision avoidance by directly adjusting the allowed number of concurrently executing transactional threads (henceforth referred to as the *concurrency level*) adaptively.

Di Sanzo et al. [30] employ a machine-learning based approach that self-regulates the concurrency level by predicting the scalability of the STM application as a function of features derived from the actual workload profile.

Ansari et al. [33] introduce several concurrency control algorithms, with the goal of obtaining a predefined Transaction Commit Rate (TCR) threshold. Their best performing algorithm is named the *P-only Concurrency Control* (PoCC) algorithm. PoCC periodically samples the number of transactions that were committed during a sampling time-window of predefined length. It then compares the TCR of that period with the threshold TCR. The concurrency level is increased if the observed TCR value is greater than the TCR threshold, and is decreased otherwise.

Didona et al. [26] show that adaptively adjusting the concurrency level can improve the performance of both shared-memory and distributed STMs. For shared-memory STMs, a hill-climbing exploration based algorithm is used for optimizing the concurrency level. Their algorithm for distributed STMs is more complex, as it has to adjust both the number of nodes and the number of transactional threads per node. It combines an analytic performance model for optimizing the number of nodes and an exploration-based approach for optimizing the number of node threads. They show that their algorithms adjust quickly to workload changes and reduce the number of aborted transactions.

Rughetti et al. [34] introduce a technique that combines an analytical model for concurrency level prediction and a machine-learning algorithm. Their hybrid approach improves performance by reducing the training time of the machine-learning algorithm and by increasing the accuracy of the analytical model. They evaluate their implementation using the STAMP benchmark suite [35] and compare it to a pure analytical model algorithm and a pure machine-learning algorithm. They show that their implementation obtains higher throughput and reduces energy consumption.

3.3   Kernel-Assisted Scheduling-Based Contention Management

Maldonado et al. [16] presented techniques for improving the performance of software transactional memory by implementing TM contention management support in the kernels of the Linux and OpenSolaris operating systems. They implemented and evaluated "soft" forms of serialization in which the loser thread is not prevented from executing, but only has its priority reduced. They also proposed a new contention management strategy that is based on extending the time slice of a thread running a transaction, to reduce its window of vulnerability. This strategy is orthogonal to serialization and can be combined with either regular or soft serialization algorithms. In addition to system calls, they evaluated the use of a shared memory segment to provide lightweight communication between the user-level STM library and the kernel-level scheduler.

Their competitive analysis established that communication via a segment of shared memory allows defining a serialization strategy that is efficient for short transactions with high contention, that soft serialization is beneficial for transactions that may be nondeterministic, and that time slice extension can improve scalability for some contention management strategies. Collectively, their results show that kernel scheduling-based support is effective in many situations where an application-level contention manager cannot provide satisfactory performance.

Maldonado et al. [36] investigated the transactional support required by reactive applications and propose mechanisms that enable real-time transactions associated with deadlines. Among other contributions, they have extended the Linux scheduler so that it disables the preemption and migration of threads that are in the midst of executing transactions that have deadlines.

4 Theoretical Results

A few works investigate the asymptotic complexity of online scheduling-based contention management algorithms. The worst-case and average-case bounds they derived provide better understanding of the potential scalability of such algorithms.

An online scheduling algorithm is often measured by its *makespan*, the total duration of time it takes to perform a set of transactions. The makespan of an online algorithm is compared to the makespan of an optimal, clairvoyant scheduler that schedules transactions with a-priori knowledge of transactions' release times and durations, and their transactional object access patterns. The worst-case ratio between the makespan of an online algorithm and the makespan of the optimal scheduler is the *competitive ratio* of the algorithm and we seek to minimize it.

In [9], Attiya et al. show that $\Omega(s)$ is a lower bound on the competitive ratio of any deterministic online transaction scheduling algorithm, where s denotes the number of shared objects accessed by a transaction.

In later work [23] Attiya and Milani show that this bound holds for *bimodal* workloads, consisting of *read-only* and *early-write* transactions. They present the Bimodal scheduler (described in Section 3.1), that has a tight $O(s)$ competitive ratio. Bimodal alternates between read-only and non read-only epochs, in which it boosts the relative priority of read-only and non read-only transactions, respectively.

As previously mentioned, in [31], Dragojevic et al. present a scheduler called *Shrink*. They show that both CAR-STM and ATS are $O(n)$-competitive, where n is the number of transactions. In addition, they present *Restart*, an online clairvoyant scheduler that is 2-competitive, which assumes complete knowledge (in terms of execution times, release times, and conflict relations) of all transactions that have already started execution.

Sharma and Busch [37] analyze the behavior of contention management algorithms under a window-based scheduling model, that allows the execution of *windows of transactions*. In every window, each thread performs exactly N transactions. The window-based model restricts the number of conflicts that can occur in the course of the transactional workload's execution.

They present a few randomized greedy algorithms that are $O(s + log(n \cdot N))$-competitive and $O(s \cdot log(n \cdot N) + log^2(n \cdot N))$-competitive, respectively, w.r.t an offline (clairvoyant) and an online (non-clairvoyant) algorithms, respectively.

In another work [38], Sharma and Busch presented the *balanced workload model*, which is able to express bimodal workloads. Under this workload, the number of write operations that are performed by any non read-only transaction is guaranteed to be at most a constant fraction of its total read and write operations. They present a deterministic clairvoyant scheduler that is $O(\sqrt{s})$-competitive, and a randomized non-clairvoyant scheduler that is $O(\sqrt{s} \cdot log(n))$-competitive.

5   Discussion

Conventional contention managers (CMs) have been found to often provide poor performance for highly-contended workloads, due to repeated collisions that may cause throughput to drop below that of using single-lock synchronization. Scheduling-based CMs have the potential of providing better performance than conventional CMs on such workloads, since they allow resuming the execution of a loser transaction immediately after the respective winner transaction commits.

The key idea underlying transaction schedulers, introduced a few years ago, is that the execution of conflicting transactions must be serialized in the face of high contention and, more generally, that the level of parallelism between transactional threads should be controlled by the contention manager and dynamically adjusted.

Most of the transaction schedulers that have been proposed implement some variant of serializing contention management, in which the thread running a loser transaction is moved to a waiting-queue until the winner transaction completes.

Rather than handle conflicts post factum, some schedulers attempt to avoid possible conflicts before they occur in a proactive manner. Implementations of such proactive collision avoidance mechanisms vary according to how the information on the likelihood of collisions is obtained and the manner in which concurrent execution is restricted.

Researchers implemented and investigated scheduling-based contention management mechanisms both in operating system kernels and in user mode. In general, which scheduling strategy is best depends on the workload and the execution context. Dynamically determining the most appropriate scheduling strategy for a given workloads is therefore desired, but this seems to be a non-trivial challenge.

References

1. Scherer III, W.N., Scott, M.L.: Contention management in dynamic software transactional memory. In: Proceedings of the PODC Workshop on Concurrency and Synchronization in Java Programs (2004)
2. Herlihy, M., Luchangco, V., Moir, M., Scherer III, W.N.: Software transactional memory for dynamic-sized data structures. In: Proceedings of the Twenty-second Annual Symposium on Principles of Distributed Computing, PODC 2003, pp. 92–101. ACM, New York (2003)
3. Herlihy, M., Luchangco, V., Moir, M.: Obstruction-free synchronization: Double-ended queues as an example. In: Proceedings of the 23rd IEEE International Conference on Distributed Computing Systems (ICDCS 2003), pp. 522–529 (2003)
4. Scherer III, W.N., Scott, M.L.: Advanced contention management for dynamic software transactional memory. In: Proceedings of the Twenty-fourth Annual ACM Symposium on Principles of Distributed Computing, PODC 2005, pp. 240–248. ACM, New York (2005)
5. Spear, M.F., Dalessandro, L., Marathe, V.J., Scott, M.L.: A comprehensive strategy for contention management in software transactional memory. In: Proceedings of the 14th ACM SIGPLAN Symposium on Principles and Practice of Parallel Programming, PPoPP 2009, pp. 141–150. ACM, New York (2009)
6. Dragojević, A., Guerraoui, R., Kapalka, M.: Stretching transactional memory. In: Proceedings of the 2009 ACM SIGPLAN Conference on Programming Language Design and Implementation, PLDI 2009, pp. 155–165. ACM, New York (2009)
7. Felber, P., Riegel, T., Fetzer, C.: Dynamic performance tuning of word-based software transactional memory. In: 13th ACM SIGPLAN Symposium on Principles and Practice of Parallel Programming (PPOPP), pp. 237–246 (2008)
8. Marathe, V.J., Spear, M.F., Heriot, C., Acharya, A., Eisenstat, D., Scherer III, W.N., Scott, M.L.: Lowering the overhead of nonblocking software transactional memory. In: Workshop on Languages, Compilers, and Hardware Support for Transactional Computing (TRANSACT 2006) (2006)
9. Attiya, H., Epstein, L., Shachnai, H., Tamir, T.: Transactional contention management as a non-clairvoyant scheduling problem. In: Proceedings of the Twenty-fifth Annual ACM Symposium on Principles of Distributed Computing, PODC 2006, pp. 308–315. ACM, New York (2006)
10. Guerraoui, R., Herlihy, M., Pochon, B.: Toward a theory of transactional contention managers. In: Proceedings of the Twenty-fourth Annual ACM Symposium on Principles of Distributed Computing, PODC 2005, pp. 258–264. ACM, New York (2005)
11. Guerraoui, R., Herlihy, M., Pochon, B.: Towards a theory of transactional contention managers. In: Proceedings of the Twenty-fifth Annual ACM Symposium on Principles of Distributed Computing, PODC 2006, pp. 316–317. ACM, New York (2006)

12. Adl-Tabatabai, A.R., Kozyrakis, C., Saha, B.: Unlocking concurrency. Queue 4, 24–33 (2007)

13. Harris, T., Larus, J., Rajwar, R.: Transactional Memory, 2nd edn. Morgan and Claypool Publishers (2010)

14. Bai, T., Shen, X., Zhang, C., Scherer III, W.N., Ding, C., Scott, M.L.: A key-based adaptive transactional memory executor. In: IPDPS, pp. 1–8 (2007)

15. Guerraoui, R., Herlihy, M.P., Pochon, B.: Polymorphic contention management. In: Fraigniaud, P. (ed.) DISC 2005. LNCS, vol. 3724, pp. 303–323. Springer, Heidelberg (2005)

16. Maldonado, W., Marlier, P., Felber, P., Suissa, A., Hendler, D., Fedorova, A., Lawall, J.L., Muller, G.: Scheduling support for transactional memory contention management. In: PPoPP 2010: Proceedings of the 15th ACM SIGPLAN Symposium on Principles and Practice of Parallel Programming, pp. 79–90. ACM, New York (2010)

17. Yoo, R.M., Lee, H.H.S.: Adaptive transaction scheduling for transactional memory systems. In: SPAA, pp. 169–178 (2008)

18. Dolev, S., Hendler, D., Suissa, A.: CAR-STM: scheduling-based collision avoidance and resolution for software transactional memory. In: Twenty-Seventh Annual ACM Symposium on Principles of Distributed Computing (PODC), pp. 125–134 (2008)

19. Ansari, M., Luján, M., Kotselidis, C., Jarvis, K., Kirkham, C., Watson, I.: Steal-on-abort: Improving transactional memory performance through dynamic transaction reordering. In: Seznec, A., Emer, J., O'Boyle, M., Martonosi, M., Ungerer, T. (eds.) HiPEAC 2009. LNCS, vol. 5409, pp. 4–18. Springer, Heidelberg (2009)

20. Moore, K.E., Bobba, J., Moravan, M.J., Hill, M.D., Wood, D.A.: Logtm: Log-based transactional memory. In: Proceedings of the 12th International Conference on High Performance Computer Architecture, pp. 254–265 (2006)

21. Herlihy, M., Luchangco, V., Moir, M.: A flexible framework for implementing software transactional memory. In: Proceedings of the 21st Annual ACM SIGPLAN Conference on Object-oriented Programming Systems, Languages, and Applications, OOPSLA 2006, pp. 253–262. ACM, New York (2006)

22. Atoofian, E.: Improving performance of software transactional memory through contention locality. The Journal of Supercomputing 64, 527–547 (2013)

23. Attiya, H., Milani, A.: Transactional scheduling for read-dominated workloads. Journal of Parallel and Distributed Computing 72, 1386–1396 (2012)

24. Blake, G., Dreslinski, R.G., Mudge, T.N.: Proactive transaction scheduling for contention management. In: MICRO, pp. 156–167 (2009)

25. Blake, G., Dreslinski, R.G., Mudge, T.N.: Bloom filter guided transaction scheduling. In: HPCA, pp. 75–86 (2011)

26. Didona, D., Felber, P., Harmanci, D., Romano, P., Schenker, J.: Identifying the optimal level of parallelism in transactional memory applications. In: NETYS, pp. 233–247 (2013)

27. Heber, T., Hendler, D., Suissa, A.: On the impact of serializing contention management on stm performance. Journal of Parallel and Distributed Computing 72, 739–750 (2012)

28. Nicácio, D., Baldassin, A., Araujo, G.: Transaction scheduling using dynamic conflict avoidance. International Journal of Parallel Programming 41, 89–110 (2013)

29. Pereira, M.M., Baldassin, A., Araujo, G., Buzato, L.E.: Transaction scheduling using conflict avoidance and contention intensity. In: HiPC, pp. 236–245 (2013)

30. di Sanzo, P., Re, F.D., Rughetti, D., Ciciani, B., Quaglia, F.: Regulating concurrency in software transactional memory: An effective model-based approach. In: SASO, pp. 31–40 (2013)

31. Dragojević, A., Guerraoui, R., Singh, A.V., Singh, V.: Preventing versus curing: Avoiding conflicts in transactional memories. In: Proceeding of the 28th ACM Symposium on Principles of Distributed Computing, pp. 7–16. ACM (2009)

32. Sainz, D., Attiya, H.: Relstm: A proactive transactional memory scheduler. In: TRANSACT 2013. ACM, New York (2013)

33. Ansari, M., Kotselidis, C., Jarvis, K., Luján, M., Kirkham, C.C., Watson, I.: Advanced concurrency control for transactional memory using transaction commit rate, pp. 719–728 (2008)

34. Rughetti, D., di Sanzo, P., Ciciani, B., Quaglia, F.: Analytical/ml mixed approach for concurrency regulation in software transactional memory. In: 2014 14th IEEE/ACM International Symposium on Cluster, Cloud and Grid Computing, Chicago, IL, USA, May 26-29, pp. 81–91 (2014)

35. Cao Minh, C., Chung, J., Kozyrakis, C., Olukotun, K.: STAMP: Stanford transactional applications for multi-processing. In: IISWC 2008: Proceedings of the IEEE International Symposium on Workload Characterization (2008)

36. Maldonado, W., Marlier, P., Felber, P., Lawall, J.L., Muller, G., Riviere, E.: Deadline-aware scheduling for software transactional memory. In: DSN, pp. 257–268 (2011)

37. Sharma, G., Busch, C.: Window-based greedy contention management for transactional memory: Theory and practice. Distributed Computing 25, 225–248 (2012)

38. Sharma, G., Busch, C.: A competitive analysis for balanced transactional memory workloads. Algorithmica 63, 296–322 (2012)

Proactive Contention Avoidance

Hillel Avni[1], Shlomi Dolev[1], and Eleftherios Kosmas[2]

[1] Department of Computer Science, Ben-Gurion University of the Negev
{shlomi.dolev,hillel.avni}@gmail.com
[2] FORTH ICS & University of Crete
ekosmas@csd.uoc.gr

Abstract. In current TM systems, both STM and HTM, if two transactions access the same address, and, one of them writes it, at least one of the two is aborted. However, many times, the aborted transaction was in a valid state, and work was lost for no good reason. In the first part of the chapter we discuss lowering such contention. We focus on methods that never lock-out a transaction, thus, we exclude approaches that serialize writing transaction to allow irrevocable transactions, for example. We are interested only in mechanisms that avoid conflicts and not in contention managers which resolves them. This part is about using the TM that exists, both in hardware and the compiler. The second part of the chapter is about SemanticTM, an algorithm that manages to eliminate the need for aborts, while maintaining parallelism. SemanticTM allows the application to maintain a consistent state without locks and aborts, but is currently restricted to specific scenarios.

1 Introduction

In this chapter we discuss two lines of work that tackle the unwanted phenomenon of cancelled transactions. One is practical, and aims to lower the amount of potential contention in state of the art TM systems. This is necessary because a lot of effort, thousands of man years, was already invested in TM. It is present in its abort prone form, in GCC compiler, and in the hardware of the major vendors, and, least for the near future, this infrastructure will be used.

The second part of the chapter shows a TM algorithm that never aborts. It marks a new direction that is not optimistic (does not take risk of failure), but not pessimistic (does not add serialization to any workload). We show the first such algorithm, SemanticTM, and discuss its correctness and scope of usage.

1.1 Proactive Aborts Reduction

The simplest way to avoid contention is to grab a lock and run with mutual exclusion. However, this solution also abolishes parallelism. Previous work on reducing aborts without global serialization, yielded several solutions. However, some of these solutions are specific to certain data structures, while other assume features in the TM system that are not feasible in realistic HTM hardware or TM compiler support. The only approach which do work with the TM industrial tools, and attempts to be general is COP, which we discuss in Section 2.

R. Guerraoui and P. Romano (Eds.): Transactional Memory, LNCS 8913, pp. 228–241, 2015.

1.1.1   TM's Inherent Limitations

The introduction of TM into compilers and hardware might seem to imply that transactions are easy to use, and that a programmer only needs to mark the atomic sections with transaction delimiters. It is implied that creating efficient concurrent data structures is especially easy. Simply take a good sequential implementation of the data structure, and put each operation in a transaction. Moreover, it is implied that the many techniques in concurrent data structures, developed throughout the past thirty years of research, can each be dismissed and replaced by TM. These implications might be true in theory, but, in practice, TM has fundamental limitations, especially in hardware and in the compiler.

A TM transaction maintains read and write sets, either through software (in software transactional memory, STM) or in hardware (in hardware transactional memory, HTM). At commit time, the TM infrastructure must verify that the read set is a snapshot, and must atomically update the write set, relevant to that snapshot [19,?,?]. This order of operation implies certain limitations, both in performance and in adaptation. As the TM must log every access, it must either fit in the hardware cache for HTM or be explicitly logged by software. This logging forces STM to call a function per access, i.e., instrumentation. If a transaction overflows the cache in HTM, it fails, while, in STM, an instrumentation makes a memory access consume many more resources than the original load or store had demanded.

Once the TM transaction has logged the accessed address, it continuously monitors all future accesses in the system in order to verify that the address is not externally modified. If a monitored address is written by another concurrent thread, the monitoring transaction fails, due to the conflict. If the written address is no longer being used by the failed transaction, this failure is unjustified.

1.1.2   Previous Approaches to Overcoming TM Limitations

TM's practical problems have motivated various research efforts, including TM algorithms and tailored TM-friendly data structures.

The boosting [15] family of STM algorithms only uses TM as an operation composition method. It assumes that every method has an inverse, and it creates transactions that are built by these methods. This approach relies upon the efficiency of existing data structures to bypass the overhead of TM. It resolves conflicts by semantic locking, in which each method protects the area in the data that it is going to access. In this way, TM is only dealing with semantic conflicts, while the actual interleaving of the accesses is being managed by underlying methods. This approach yields high performance, but it is limited to reversible methods, and it does not benefit from hardware and compiler support.

Another STM algorithm that only supports composition is transactional predication [8]. Like [15], it relies upon existing concurrent libraries, but, instead of logging reverse operations, it logs specific locations at which data should be updated by the transaction. If the transaction fails, their value remains unchanged or is replaced by an empty slot, in the case of insertion. Although this approach reduces aborts that arise from arbitrary read sets, it yields highly complicated algorithms, and, as no method has yet been offered for releasing the empty slots, it uses an uncontrollable amount of memory.

A set of algorithms was developed to reduce the overhead of STM. These algorithms relax some of the correctness requirements of the original TM, and, in exchange, save some of the overhead and the false conflicts. Elastic [12], and view transactions [3] do not log some of the accessed addresses, thus avoiding a part of the transactional work. These algorithms improve performance, but they preserve much of the overhead and grant an application access to transactional logs, which places a burden on the developer, and is not possible with GCC compiler architecture. These algorithms therefore are unlikely to be part of a practical STM solution. In [10], they use small HTM transactions to create concurrent algorithms for queues that are simpler than their non transactional counterparts. While this method demonstrates the power of HTM, it is not targeting the aborts issue. TM-friendly data structures are using other techniques to reduce conflicts. For example, [9] is decoupling the balancing of the binary tree from the updates, which manages to avoid some of the conflicts in highly contentious workloads, introduces restrictions like relax balancing or single updater, and are tailored exclusively for specific data structure.

To benefit from the compiler support for STM and from HTM, COP [1] and, later, [22] and [21] are leaving the read-only prefix of the atomic operation out of the transaction. This lazy approach stretches the usability of TM, while utilizing the hardware and compiler support.

1.1.3   COP in a Nutshell

COP takes advantage of both TM and contemporary research developments of data structures. In a sense, it uses TM to generalize the lazy locking approach. Consequently, it permits a relatively simple conversion of sequential operations to efficient, scalable and composable concurrent operations. COP enables the developer to design such operations for complex data structures that do not yet have any known concurrent version.

The developer uses knowledge of the data structure algorithm to extract a read- only prefix (ROP) of the operation, and to verify that this prefix does not crash or hit an infinite loop, when no synchronization is involved. This prefix returns an output that either is the output of the operation or the input to the completion of the operation. Completion, here, means any updates necessary to finish the operation. In an insert function of an RB-Tree, for example, the updates may include connecting a new node to the tree and balancing it.

After extracting the ROP, the developer uses a TM transaction to perform two actions atomically, to verify that the ROP output is valid, and to complete the updates. At this point, the transaction may continue to execute any other code.

1.2   No Aborts and No Serialization

Since the nature of TM is optimistic, conflicts occur between transactions. To avoid possible inconsistencies, most TM systems abort one of the conflicting transactions; the work performed by this transaction is discarded and it is later re-executed as a new transaction. This has a negative effect on performance. On the other hand, if either no conflicts ever occur or transactions never abort, then no work is ever discarded.

In order to guarantee progress, all transactions should eventually commit. However, most TM systems do not even ensure that transactions abort only when they violate the considered consistency condition (this property is known as *permissiveness* [13]).

In terms of achieving good performance, the system should additionally guarantee that parallelism is achieved. So, transactions should not be executed sequentially and global contention points should be avoided.

The design of TM algorithms that never abort transactions is highly desirable since they additionally support transactions that perform irrevocable operations such as I/O operations.

1.2.1 Prior TM Algorithms for Abort Elimination

TM algorithms that never abort transactions has been presented in [2,2]. They use ideas from [20] where a TM system is presented which supports the execution of irrevocable transactions. In the algorithms of [2,2], read-only transactions are *wait-free*, i.e. each of them is completed successfully within a finite number of steps; a *read-only* transaction never writes a t-variable in contrast to an *update* transaction that performs write operations on such variables. However, these algorithms restrict parallelism by executing all update transactions sequentially using a global lock.

Moreover, TM systems that never abort read-only transactions are presented in [18,4]. The STM algorithm of [18] supports wait-free read-only transactions by maintaining the previously written values to each t-variable; i.e., multiple versions for each t-variable are maintained. Then, a read-only transaction is always able to read a consistent value for each t-variable x, by choosing either the current value of x or one of the previously written values to x. In order to reduce its space requirements, [18] maintains only a subset of the previous versions of each t-variable. More specifically, each of the previously written values to some t-variable is discarded only after determining that no read-only transaction will access (or choose) it, thereafter.

Avoiding the high space complexity of [18], PrmiSTM, the STM algorithm presented in [4], supports obstruction-free read-only transactions by maintaining a single version for each t-variable, that is its current value. For each t-variable x, PermiSTM maintains a dedicated read-counter for x. Then, while accessing x, a read-only transaction T_r starts by announcing that it is going to read the value of x by atomically incrementing the read-counter of x. Upon committing, T_r atomically decrements the read-counter of x (and the read-counter of any other t-variable in its write-set). So, an update transaction that wants to write x is able to figure out the presence of read-only transactions which are concurrently reading x and postpone applying its update on x until no read-only transaction is present.

Update transactions in [18,4] may abort and they require locks to execute some of the transactional instructions.

In [11], CAR-STM has been presented which succeeds to reduce aborts (but not to eliminate them) by implementing two general transactional scheduling techniques, which can also be incorporated by any other STM algorithm. In CAR-STM, each processes has an associated *transactions queue* from which it dequeues transactions in order and execute them one by one. With its first proposed scheduling technique, CAR-STM tries to reduce conflicts by probabilistically avoiding some of them. More specifically, whenever a new transaction is initialized, a *dispatcher* process undertakes the role to enqueue it to the appropriate transactions queue. To do so, the dispatcher uses information provided during transaction's initialization to predict its *conflict-probabilities*, i.e., the probabilities that the new transaction will conflict with any of the transactions already executing in the system. Then, the dispatcher chooses to enqueue it in the same transactions queue with the transaction that is most likely to conflict. Notice that the corresponding process will execute these transactions sequentially one after the other; so, they can not conflict.

Whenever a conflict is detected between two transactions T_1 and T_2, CAR-STM aborts the newer one; let it be T_1. Then, according to the second scheduling technique of CAR-STM, when T_1 is re-initialized, the dispatcher chooses to enqueue it in the same transactions queue with T_2, in order to reduce the probability that they will conflict again. However, during its execution, T_2 may conflict with an older transaction T_3, contained in some other transactions queue. So, T_2 is moved to T_3's transaction's queue, and T_1 and T_2 may conflict again. In order to ensure that T_1 and T_2 will never conflict again, when T_1 is moved to T_2's transactions queue, CAR-STM groups them together. Later, when T_2 is enqueued in T_3's transactions queue, T_1 is also moved to the same queue. Notice that at the end of the example we consider, T_1, T_2, and T_3 are all grouped together.

1.2.2 SemanticTM in a Nutshell

In this paragraph, we present SemanticTM [5] an opaque [14] STM algorithm. In contrast to [2,2,18,4], SemanticTM does not use locks and guarantees that no transaction aborts while exploiting parallelism between both writers and readers. More specifically, SemanticTM ensures that both read-only and update transactions are wait-free (i.e., they complete within a finite number of steps and never abort). In addition, SemanticTM achieve fine-grain parallelism at the transactional instruction level, executing concurrently both to instructions of different transactions, and to instructions of the same transaction that do not depend on each other.

SemanticTM employs a list for each t-variable, called *t-var list*. The instructions of each transaction are placed in the appropriate lists in FIFO order. Since each instruction is executed on a single t-variable, it is placed in the list of the t-variable that it accesses. Transactions are inserted into t-var lists, one after the other; more specifically, all the instructions of each transaction are placed in the t-var lists before the instructions of any subsequent transaction. We remark that several dependencies may exist among the instructions of a single transaction. Specifically, if the execution of an instruction requires the result of the execution of another instruction, then there is a *dependency* between them. A single instruction may have several dependencies. The dependencies that may originate from or leading to some instruction are stored together with this instruction in the corresponding t-var list.

An instruction is *ready* to be executed when all the instructions preceding it in its t-var list have been executed and its dependencies are resolved. Each of the workers repeatedly chooses a t-var list and executes the ready instructions of this list, in order, starting from the first one. Processing transactions in this way ensures that conflicts never occur; so, transactions never abort. Since several workers threads may choose the same t-var list, the algorithm is highly fault-tolerant; all transactions whose instructions have been placed in the t-var lists will be executed, as long as at least one process does not fail. On the other hand, several workers may (concurrently) execute the same instructions; so, SemanticTM employs synchronization techniques to ensure the correct execution of each instruction.

SemanticTM focuses on simple *static* transactions (i.e. the set of t-variables accessed is known a priori, before the transaction's execution) that contain Read and Write instructions, conditionals (i.e. if, else if, and else), loops (i.e. for, while, etc.), and function calls. Using compiler support, these dependencies become known before the beginning of the execution of the transactions; SemanticTM can make use of any work on dataflow analysis to extract them.

2 Consistency Oblivious Programming

The principle behind COP is simple: Just execute the read-only prefix (ROP) of a data structure operation as part of a transaction, but without the overhead of the transaction. This implies that the ROP will perform un instrumented accesses to shared memory in STM, and that its accesses will not leave a transaction footprint in HTM, and will not subsequently be monitored in the transaction. Conversely, the ROP must see any value that had been written in the transaction before the COP operation started. After the ROP has run and generated output, a transaction starts or continues, verifies the output, and uses it to perform any updates.

This chapter provides a general template for a COP operation algorithm and correctness proof, and elaborates on the composition of COP operations in STM compiler support and HTM.

2.1 The COP Template

The COP algorithms work with any HTM and STM implementation, but the actual TM realizations have their own limitations and characteristics that demand specific tailoring. The template in this section is for a TM block where non transactional read accesses inside a transaction are supported, and assumes every transaction eventually succeeds.

2.1.1 Operation Structure

Let K (kappa) be a function, which is a sequential operation on a data structure. K can be written as a sequential function, as KComplete(KROP()), where KROP() is the read-only prefix of K and it generates KROPOutput.

The template for a COP version of K is given in Figure 1.

To adapt K to COP, we extract a read-only prefix of it into KROP() (line 4). KROP() calculates KROPOutput, in an unsafe mode, i.e., without any synchronization, even though it resides in a transaction. Thus KROPOutput might be inconsistent and wrong, due to conflicts with a concurrent transactions.

After calculating KROPOutput, we resume the transaction in line 5, and call KVerify(KROPOutput) in line 8. If KVerify sees KROPOutput is inconsistent, it will abort and retry the transaction. If KOutput is consistent, the transaction continues to execute KComplete(KROPOutput). KComplete(KROPOutput) will use KROPOutput and performs any updates, assuming that KROPOutput is correct.

If the transaction aborts, due to explicit **abort_transaction** or because of a conflict, it will automatically retry, and, if there are too many retries, the TM mechanism must execute it solo in order to verify progress, as if it were a transaction that does not include any COP operations.

General COP Template for Function K
1 **start_transaction**;
2 ANY CODE;
3 **suspend_transaction**;
4 KROPOutput ← KROP();
5 **resume_transaction**;
6 **if** ¬($\kappa Verify(\kappa ROPOutput)$) **then**
7 | **abort_transaction**;
8 KComplete(KROPOutput);
9 ANY CODE;
10 **end_transaction**;

Fig. 1. Generic COP template

2.1.2 Correctness Proof Method

A correct COP version of K requires that the underlying TM and the the KROP() will not produce arbitrary executions:

Property 1. **Transactional Regular Registers:** transactional locations are regular, in the sense of regular-registers [16], i.e., if a thread reads a location L in non-transactional context concurrently with a transaction T, which writes V to L, it will read from L, either V, or the value that was in L when T started, but not an arbitrary value.

All variables, parameters and return value of KROP() are transactional regular registers.

Transactional regular registers are safety related, in the sense that the ROP can not read arbitrary values, thus, it is possible to reason about its output. In addition, if the COP version of K demonstrates the following properties, it is correct and will not deadlock.

Property 2. **Obliviousness:** KROP() must complete without faults, regardless of concurrent executions, and finishes in a finite number of steps if executes alone.

Obliviousness is progress related, as if KROP() will crash or get stuck in an infinite loop, no work will be done. The following two properties imply the correctness of the COP operation.

Property 3. **Verifiability:** KROPOutput has attributes, that can be tested locally, and that imply KROPOutput is consistent, and KVerify is checking these attributes.

Property 4. **Separation:** KComplete is using KROPOutput but is not aware of any other data collected by KROP().

Verifiability imply that the consistency of KROPOutput can be checked locally, by looking at its attributes. This may require adding to the sequential K code, without changing its functionality. As the KVerify and KComplete are in the same transaction, we know that KROPOutput stays consistent until commit, and as KComplete executes in a transaction, and according to **Separation**, KComplete accesses only consistent data, thus, we have a serializable, COP version of K.

The system model here is a global lock model where a code segment that executes in a transaction that is semantically protected by a global lock will have all its necessary barriers inserted by the TM.

Now, if we want to implement a COP version of a function ϕ, we only need to show ϕROP, ϕVerify and ϕComplete. If, for example, we want to demonstrate a COP implementation of an RB-Tree Insert function, we will present ROP, InsertVerify and InsertComplete. After creating the COP version, we have to show that it has the three properties described above.

2.2 Composable COP Requires Non Transactional Loads

A COP operation, is based on a data-structure operation op. We split op to a read only prefix op^{ROP} and to the writing suffix op^C. To run op inside a transaction just execute op^C after op^{ROP}. However, the COP version of op, which is embedded in a transaction T, T_{op}, performs the following steps:

- **In non-transactional mode:** Execute $T_{op^{ROP}}$ and record its output. This part is done without any synchronization, and may pass through inconsistent states and return inconsistent output.
- **In transactional mode:** Verify that ROP output is consistent, and if it is not, abort, otherwise execute T_{op^C}.

We remind the reader that the verification not only ensures T that the op^{ROP} output was consistent, but also adds the addresses that prove it to the read set for monitoring of this consistency.

The only way to compose COP operations without non transactional loads (NTL), is the one proposed by [21], i.e., execute all ROP parts of the composed operations before starting the transaction, then, inside the transaction, verify their output and complete updates. This method allows composition only if an operation is not writing data that may later be accessed by another operation in the same transaction.

To demonstrate this restriction, we split each COP operation op_k, which executes in transaction T, T_{op_k}, to $T_{op_k^{ROP}}$ and $T_{op_k^C}$ (verify and complete). Now, assume op_1 precedes op_2, and op_1 is writing data that op_2 is reading. According to [21], the transaction T, which executes op_1 and then op_2, will execute the following sequence. **tm_start** means the TM, either STM or HTM, goes into transactional mode, and **tm_end** is TM commit:

$$T_{op_1^{ROP}} \rightarrow T_{op_2^{ROP}} \rightarrow \textbf{tm\_start} \rightarrow T_{op_1^C} \rightarrow T_{op_2^C} \rightarrow \textbf{tm\_end}$$

As $T_{op_2^{ROP}}$ must execute before $T_{op_1^C}$, op_1 will not see op_2 updates, and T will not be correct.

If instead of op_1, T will execute any other transactional code, we will have to call **tm_start** before op_2, so op_2^{ROP} will be in transactional mode. For example, if T dequeues V and then inserts V to a RB-Tree with a COP operation, then this operation will not benefit from the usage of COP.

Using NTL allows the composition of any COP operation, with any other operations, by using NTL in the ROP. Now T will execute the ROP with NTL, so we call the ROP of op op^{ROP-N}. If T tries to execute the COP operation op_2 after the COP operation op_1, it will go through the following sequence:

$$\textbf{tm\_start} \rightarrow T_{op_1}{}^{ROP-N} \rightarrow T_{op_1}{}^C \rightarrow T_{op_2}{}^{ROP-N} \rightarrow T_{op_2}{}^C \rightarrow \textbf{tm\_end}$$

As $T_{op_1}{}^C$ executes before $T_{op_2}{}^{ROP-N}$, and as both $T_{op_1}{}^C$ and $T_{op_2}{}^{ROP-N}$ execute in the context of T, $T_{op_2}{}^{ROP-N}$, which executes after $T_{op_1}{}^C$ performed its updates in the context of T, can see these updates in the local cache and T is correct.

2.3   COP Data Structure

We have COP versions to linked-list, red-black tree, and a skip-list.In addition, [6] presents a Leaplist, which is a probabilistic flavor of a T-Tree, tailored for range queries in main-memory databases. As shown, COP is yielding great performance on many tree data structures, and in STM, also on data structures such as union-find, which would be extremely contentious without the incorporation of COP.

However, COP is not the silver bullet when global operations are involved. For example, if the data structure has a prune operation, e.g., there is an option to split the structure at any arbitrary node, COP becomes awkward. It remains an open question how to adjust COP to supporting these global operations in an efficient way.

2.4   Evaluation of COP in Applications

To examine the potential contribution of COP to applications, we added the COP RB-Tree from [1] to the STAMP testing suite. We implement the NTL over GCC STM, by using TM-Pure [7] attribute for the ROP function. Our goal is to demonstrate the benefit of NTL and COP in some applications.

We execute the standard configuration of Vacation (*vacation-high* from [17]). Each transaction in this application is accessing several 1M RB trees, several times each, and these transactions are a significant portion of the workloads.

	GCC-COP	GCC-STM
Transactional Loads	0.4 G	2.4 G
Aborts Rate	0.5%	3.0%

Fig. 2. STAMP Vacation Statistics ($G = 10^9$)

In Figure 2 we count transactional loads and aborts for the Vacation benchmark. We count the transactional loads when the whole application is executing on a single thread, to get the most accurate number. The aborts count is taken when all eight hardware threads execute. We see that plain STM is performing more than five times the transactional loads of COP with NTL, and there are six times more aborts in plain STM.

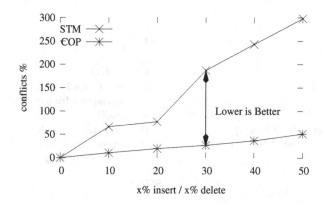

Fig. 3. Aborts vs. update rates on a small red-black that executes on eight threads

In Figure 3 we compare the conflicts rate on a COP red-black tree vs. plain STM one. The tree keys range is 1K and it is half full, thus it is small and has a lot of mutations, which cause relatively high contention. Each update, i.e., insert or delete is a transaction that consists of the update and four lookups, to demonstrate COP operations composition. As each transaction is retried up to 20 times, the number of conflict aborts can be higher that the number of successful transactions. We can see that contention on the plain STM is rising much faster and on 100% updates, i.e., 50% inserts and 50% deletes, STM has 6 times more aborts than COP.

3 SemanticTM

In SemanticTM, instead of executing the transactional instructions of some transaction, each process executes the transactional instructions applied on some t-variable. To do this, SemanticTM maintains a t-var list for each t-variable, the instructions of each transaction are placed in the appropriate t-var lists (based on which t-variable each of them accesses), and each process chooses a t-var list and executes its ready instructions. Each *entry* of a t-var list, additionally to the instruction to be applied, records also any dependencies that may originate from or lead to this instruction. Recall that compiler support is employed to know the dependencies of each instruction.

It is important that transactions are inserted into t-var lists one after the other; i.e., the instructions of some transactions are inserted into t-var lists before the instructions of any subsequent transaction. For example, consider transactions T_1 and T_2 of Figure 4; also, the instructions of these transactions together with their dependencies are presented. Without loss of generality, assume that the instructions of T_1 are placed in the t-var lists first. Then, the write instruction on z of T_1 (line 3) will be placed in the t-var list for z before the read instruction on z by T_2 (line 10). Similarly, the read instruction on x by T_1 (line 4) will be placed in the t-var list for x before the read and write instructions on x by T_2 (lines 8 and 9). Finally, the write instruction on y by T_1 (line 5) will be placed in the t-var list for y before the write instructions on y by T_2 (line 11). Since processes respect the order in which instructions have been inserted in the t-var

1    $z := 1$
2    $y := 2^x$
     T_1

3    $write(z, 1)$
4    $read(x)$
5    $write(y, 2^x)$ with
     dependency from $read(x)$
           Instructions of T_1

6    $x := x + 1$
7    $y := z + 1$
     T_2

8    $read(x)$
9    $write(x, x + 1)$ with
     dependency from $read(x)$
10   $read(z)$
11   $write(y, z + 1)$ with
     dependency from $read(z)$
           Instructions of T_2

Fig. 4. Transactions

lists when they execute them, the instructions of T_1 on each t-variable will be executed before the instructions of T_2 on this t-variable, and thus no conflict between them will ever occur.

The conditionals and loops are called *control flow statements* , and the instruction cond is used to refer to such a statement. Each cond instruction is associated with a *block* of instructions, that is the set of instructions in the body of a control flow statement. A dependency that either leads to or originates from a cond instruction is called *control* dependency. For each cond instruction, SemanticTM maintains a control dependency from cond to each instruction of the block associated with it. An an example, consider the if ... then ... else statements. The two conds (for the if and the else statement) and their blocks' transactional instructions will be placed in the appropriate t-var lists. Then, at runtime, one of the two cond instructions will be evaluated as false and its block's instructions will be invalidated, so that they are never executed. Notice that a cond instruction can be inserted in any t-var list, since its execution affects no t-variable.

Consider now a cond instruction that describes a loop statement. Although a loop may be executed several times, the number of its iterations may only become known at runtime. So, SemanticTM places the instructions of the loop's body in the appropriate t-var lists exactly once and associates an *iteration number* with the cond, describing the current loop iteration. In SemanticTM the next iteration of a loop starts only after all the instructions of this loop have been executed for the current loop iteration. In order to be able to understand this, it associates an iteration number also with each instruction in loop's block, describing the iteration for which this instruction has been executed.

For example consider a t-var list that contains 2 instructions of the same loop (the cond of this loop could be one of them). Then, assume that a process has executed the first of them for the first iteration, but not the second one, since it is not ready (its dependencies are still unresolved for the first iteration). So, when another process choose the same t-var list, it uses the iteration numbers of these instructions to understand that the second instruction has not yet be executed for the current loop iteration. So, the cond instruction of the loop initiates a new loop iteration by incrementing its iteration number by one. Then, whenever an instruction of this loop has been executed for the current loop iteration, it increments by one its iteration number (so that it equals the iteration number of the loop's cond).

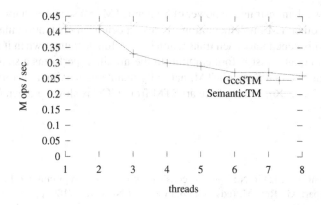

Fig. 5. Operations for a workload with a counter

Recall that the entry of each instruction in some t-var list, contains also its dependencies. Since, SemanticTM uses a single entry for each instruction of the loop, whenever a new iteration of the loop is initiated, the dependencies of this loop should be re-initialized as unresolved for the new iteration. To do this, an iteration number is also associated with each of the dependencies of these instructions. A dependency is resolved for the current loop iteration (that is described by the iteration number of this loop's cond instruction) when its iteration number is equal to the current loop iteration; otherwise, (it can only be smaller) it is unresolved for the current loop iteration. So, whenever a process resolves the dependencies of an instruction that participates in some loop, it also update its iteration number (specifically, it increments it by one) so that it equals to the current loop iteration.

Since several processes may choose the same t-var list, the same instruction may (concurrently) be executed by several processes, SemanticTM employs synchronization techniques to ensure the correct execution of each instruction. More specifically, the status of each instruction is maintained (in its entry), which is initially ACTIVE, indicating that e has not yet been performed, and becomes DONE, when a process completes its execution. Moreover, in order to atomically update each t-variable, its value is maintained in a CAS object together with a *version number*; an unsigned integer that is incremented by one, each time a new value is written to this t-variable.

Moreover, the iteration numbers of instructions that participate in some loop are maintained in CAS objects; also, each dependency of these instructions, is maintained together with its iteration number in a CAS object. Before updating a t-variable x, each process has to read its old value. When several processes are executing a write instruction on x that participates in some loop, they should use the same old value for x, so that x is updated consistently, and they should calculate the same new value for x, for the current loop iteration. To ensure this, the old value of x is maintained in a CAS object together with an iteration number, describing the iteration on which this old value has been read. It is worth mentioning that each process consistently calculates the new value of x on each iteration, since it uses the values of the resolved dependencies of this write instruction for this iteration.

In Figure 5 we demonstrate the power of SemanticTM in a scenario that will reach a live-lock in all other TM implementations, unless specialized contention management is involved. In this benchmark each transaction is sampling a counter when it starts, and increments that counter just before commit. In the middle it performs a small amount of work. We can see that SemanticTM, naturally maintains maximal performance for this serial workload, while state of the art STM from GCC is slowing down linearly as parallelism grows.

References

1. Afek, Y., Avni, H., Shavit, N.: Towards consistency oblivious programming. In: Fernàndez Anta, A., Lipari, G., Roy, M. (eds.) OPODIS 2011. LNCS, vol. 7109, pp. 65–79. Springer, Heidelberg (2011)
2. Afek, Y., Matveev, A., Shavit, N.: Pessimistic software lock-elision. In: Aguilera, M.K. (ed.) DISC 2012. LNCS, vol. 7611, pp. 297–311. Springer, Heidelberg (2012)
3. Afek, Y., Morrison, A., Tzafrir, M.: Brief announcement: view transactions: Transactional model with relaxed consistency checks. In: PODC, pp. 65–66 (2010)
4. Attiya, H., Hillel, E.: A single-version stm that is multi-versioned permissive. Theory Comput. Syst. 51(4), 425–446 (2012)
5. Avni, H., Dolev, S., Fatourou, P., Kosmas, E.: Abort free semantictm by dependency aware scheduling of transactional instructions. In: NETYS, vol. 51(4), pp. 425–446 (2014)
6. Avni, H., Shavit, N., Suissa, A.: Leaplist: lessons learned in designing tm-supported range queries. In: ACM Symposium on Principles of Distributed Computing, PODC 2013, Montreal, QC, Canada, July 22-24, pp. 299–308 (2013)
7. Avni, H., Suissa, A.: Brief announcement: Cop composition using transaction suspension in the compiler. In: DISC 2014 (2014)
8. Bronson, N.G., Casper, J., Chafi, H., Olukotun, K.: Transactional predication: high-performance concurrent sets and maps for stm. In: PODC, pp. 6–15 (2010)
9. Crain, T., Gramoli, V., Raynal, M.: A speculation-friendly binary search tree. In: PPOPP, pp. 161–170 (2012)
10. Dice, D., Lev, Y., Marathe, V.J., Moir, M., Nussbaum, D., Olszewski, M.: Simplifying concurrent algorithms by exploiting hardware transactional memory. In: SPAA, pp. 325–334 (2010)
11. Dolev, S., Hendler, D., Suissa, A.: Car-stm: Scheduling-based collision avoidance and resolution for software transactional memory. In: Proceedings of the Twenty-seventh ACM Symposium on Principles of Distributed Computing, PODC 2008 pp. 125–134 (2008)
12. Felber, P., Gramoli, V., Guerraoui, R.: Elastic transactions. In: DISC, pp. 93–107 (2009)
13. Guerraoui, R., Henzinger, T.A., Singh, V.: Permissiveness in transactional memories. In: Taubenfeld, G. (ed.) DISC 2008. LNCS, vol. 5218, pp. 305–319. Springer, Heidelberg (2008)
14. Guerraoui, R., Kapalka, M.: On the correctness of transactional memory. In: Proceedings of the 13th ACM SIGPLAN Symposium on Principles and Practice of Parallel Programming, PPoPP 2008, pp. 175–184. ACM, New York (2008),
    http://doi.acm.org/10.1145/1345206.1345233
15. Herlihy, M., Koskinen, E.: Transactional boosting: A methodology for highly-concurrent transactional objects. In: Proceedings of the 13th ACM SIGPLAN Symposium on Principles and Practice of Parallel Programming, PPoPP 2008, pp. 207–216 (2008)
16. Herlihy, M., Shavit, N.: The art of multiprocessor programming. Morgan Kaufmann (2008)
17. Minh, C.C., Chung, J., Kozyrakis, C., Olukotun, K.: Stamp: Stanford transactional applications for multi-processing. In: IISWC, pp. 35–46 (2008)

18. Perelman, D., Fan, R., Keidar, I.: On maintaining multiple versions in stm. In: Proceedings of the 29th ACM SIGACT-SIGOPS Symposium on Principles of Distributed Computing, PODC 2010, pp. 16–25 (2010)
19. Shavit, N., Touitou, D.: Software transactional memory. Distributed Computing 10(2), 99–116 (1997)
20. Welc, A., Saha, B., Adl-Tabatabai, A.R.: Irrevocable transactions and their applications. In: Proceedings of the Twentieth Annual Symposium on Parallelism in Algorithms and Architectures, SPAA 2008, pp. 285–296. ACM, New York (2008), http://doi.acm.org/10.1145/1378533.1378584
21. Xiang, L., Scott, M.L.: Composable partitioned transactions. In: WTTM (2013)
22. Xiang, L., Scott, M.L.: Compiler aided manual speculation for high performance concurrent data structures. In: Proceedings of the 18th ACM SIGPLAN Symposium on Principles and Practice of Parallel Programmig, PPoPP 2013, pp. 47–56 (2013)

Transactional Memory and Reliability

Safe Exception Handling with Transactional Memory*

Pascal Felber[1], Christof Fetzer[2], Vincent Gramoli[3,**],
Derin Harmanci[1], and Martin Nowack[2]

[1] University of Neuchatel, Switzerland
pascal.felber@unine.ch, derin.harmanci@gmail.com
[2] Technische Universität Dresden, Germany
{christof.fetzer,martin_nowack}@tu-dresden.de
[3] NICTA and University of Sydney, Australia
vincent.gramoli@sydney.edu.au

Abstract. Exception handling is notoriously difficult for programmers whereas transactional memory has been instrumental in simplifying concurrent programming. In this chapter, we describe how the transactional syntactic sugar simplifies the exception handling problems both when writing sequential and concurrent applications. We survey exception handling solutions to prevent applications from reaching an inconsistent state in a sequential environment on the one hand, and extend these solutions to also prevent concurrent execution of multiple threads from reaching an inconsistent state, on the other hand. The resulting technique greatly simplifies exception handling and is shown surprisingly efficient.

1 Introduction

Developing robust software is a challenging, yet essential, task. A robust program has to be able to detect and recover from a variety of faults such as the temporary disconnection of communication links, resource exhaustion, and memory corruption. With the advent of multi-cores, other forms of errors appear in multi-threaded software. For example, raising an exception in one thread does not prevent others from operating on an inconsistent shared state. Instead, faults should ideally be handled in coordination by all the threads that are affected by their cause. Ideally, robust software, be it sequential or concurrent, has to tolerate runtime errors without a substantial increase in the code complexity. Indeed, this would augment the probability of design and coding faults and thus decrease the robustness of the application.

Exception handling has been proposed as a powerful mechanism for dealing with failures at runtime. It simplifies the development of robust programs by allowing the programmer to implement recovery actions and tolerate non-fatal errors. Furthermore it relieves the programmer of the burden of specifying one action in response to each individual error. Instead, it allows the programmer to handle errors with only one test

* Parts of Sections 3 and 4 already appeared in the proceedings of ECOOP'11 [1]. This chapter covers exception handling in the more general context of sequential/concurrent programming.
** NICTA is funded by the Australian Government through the Department of Communications and the Australian Research Council through the ICT Centre of Excellence Program.

R. Guerraoui and P. Romano (Eds.): Transactional Memory, LNCS 8913, pp. 245–267, 2015.
© Springer International Publishing Switzerland 2015

per block (compared to error return codes requiring at least one check for each function call). Another major advantage of this technique is that it cleanly separates the application business logic from error handling code.

Yet, exception handling is difficult to get right. In fact, the code dealing with errors tends to be complex and lengthy [2,3]. However, neither complexity nor high volume of code is desirable for error handling since this *(i)* increases the potential of bugs in the error handling code, as well as *(ii)* introducing substantial development effort only to handle (erroneous) cases that rarely occur. In particular, even though more than 4% of the total source code is dedicated to exception handling, it is clearly neglected: in most of the cases exception handling consists of either terminating the program or ignoring the exception [4]. It is therefore important to reduce the complexity of writing exception handling code while, at the same time, making sure it is correct.

In this chapter, we explore the use of transactional memory language constructs to achieve this goal. Transactional memory has gained momentum as a technique to simplify concurrent programming. It encapsulates regions of code within transactions guaranteeing that either all their changes take effect, when transactions commit, or none of their changes take effect, when transactions abort. By exploiting this semantics, one can offer failure atomicity making sure that the problematic states resulting from or causing the exception can be rolled back. Although in the context of concurrent programming, the decision to abort a transaction is based on conflicting shared accesses, we used exception to decide when to roll back the effect of transactions.

The complexity of exception handling code results from several factors:

Inconsistent State: When an exception is raised, there are high chances that the application is in an inconsistent state. Recovery is often based on retrying failed methods. But before retrying, the program might first have to correct the runtime error condition to increase the probability of success. However, for a retry to succeed, a failed method also has to leave changed objects in a consistent state. Consistency can be ensured if any modification performed by the method prior to the occurrence of the exception is reverted, before the exception is propagated to the calling method. This can be tricky because restoring a previous state may require compensating actions to be provided (just for the sake of handling errors). Even if the compensating actions are provided for methods, if several of them need to be combined to achieve an atomic action (i.e., an action where either all functions appear executed or none of them are executed), it remains difficult to determine the function triggering the raised exception and to apply the compensating actions correctly and in the correct order. Another consistency issue that appears by raising exceptions is that exceptions can result in implicit disposal of data on the stack as the stack is unwinded until the exception is called. In such cases there is no guarantee that all resources are cleaned up correctly.

Complex CONTROL-Flow: Exceptions modify the flow control of the application in a way similar to a `goto` statement – that is known to be dangerous – but the destination of the jump is not known a priori. This makes exception handling code more complex, and the situation gets worse if the exception handling code can itself raise exceptions.

Incorrectness: Exception handling code is rarely exercised and not well tested [5,2]. This fact together with the complexity of exception handling makes exception handling code to be more likely to contain software bugs than other parts of the application code.

Lack of Composability: Although different functions may raise different exceptions, it is generally hard to handle exceptions raised potentially by multiple functions. In the case where a code region calls multiple functions, determining the precise cause of the exception or the point in the execution where it was raised is not trivial. The exception handling code for composed functions requires many checks making it harder to parse.

Race Condition: In settings where applications can access shared resources concurrently, more intricate inconsistency issues related to exception handling appear. One such issue occurs when an exception handling code performs compensating actions to restore shared state. If not properly designed there can be race conditions between the compensating actions and other business logic code leading the application into inconsistent state.

Shared Inconsistent States: Another issue that is generally overlooked is that an exception raised by one thread can terminate safely its own execution but cannot prevent other threads from accessing an inconsistent shared state because other threads may not be aware of the raised exception. Such an exception should ideally be detected by all the threads that operate on the same shared state because they can be affected by its cause.

Consider the following code in Figure 1. The figure presents a naive implementation of a classifier program where multiple threads concurrently evaluate nodes from the unclassifiedNodes list, process them, and move them to the target class using the assignToClass method. Note that we assume that both the unclassifiedNodes list and the target classes class[N] are shared by all threads.

```
1   Class NodeClassifier {
2     int N;                    // number of classes
3     List unclassifiedNodes;   // shared
4     Set class[N];             // shared
5     ...
6     public void assignToClass(int srcPos, int targetClass) {
7       synchronized(this) {
8         Node selectedNode = unclassifiedNodes.remove(srcPos);
9         selectedNode.transform();
10        class[targetClass].add(selectedNode);
11      }
12    }
13  }
```

Fig. 1. A concurrent code that may end up in an inconsistent state if an exception is raised while the selected node's representation is being transformed as required by the target class object in selectedNode.transform()

When an exception is raised on line 9, the system reaches an inconsistent shared state if the exception is not handled: the selectedNode gets lost as it is neither in the unclassifiedNodes nor in its target class. For correct execution of the program, the exception should be handled and this should be performed before any of the other threads, unaware of the raised exception, access either the unclassifiedNodes list or the target class, which are inconsistent. Hence, the handling of the exception should take the existence of concurrent threads into account.

This example, albeit naive, clearly shows that exception handling becomes a first class design consideration in development of correct concurrent programs. This fact highlights the need for solutions that will simplify concurrent programming under exceptional situations.

All the above factors indicate that programmers using exception handling should think of many issues other than how to recover from the exceptional situation. The major objectives of a programmer regarding exception handling are: *a*) to keep the application in a consistent state, and *b*) to cope with the reasons of the exceptional state. For programmers to apply an error handling solution more readily, we need to offer them a simple-to-use mechanism. The purpose of this chapter is to present advanced exception handling solutions that offer safe execution of programs in both a sequential and a concurrent environments.

Contribution

We show how programs - both, sequential and concurrent - can *effortlessly* be brought to a known consistent state after an exception is raised. Obtaining consistent state without effort removes part of the complexity of treating an exception and, hence, exception handling can be used much more effectively to recover from errors.

We show how TM can be utilized to remove inconsistencies upon an exception by reverting the effects of a code portion up to a point known to be consistent. And we extend this concept to multi-threaded applications. As explained in the previous section, for concurrent programs handling exceptions should be part of the main application design and development in order to not jeopardize the application correctness. However, there are no widespread mechanisms that allow the notification and coordination of threads upon the raise of an exception in order to safely resume the application. In this chapter, we explain how such a mechanism can be provided on top of atomic blocks and show how this can relieve the burden from the programmer.

For the sake of simplicity, we will focus on Java to demonstrate our language extensions. Nevertheless, the proposed extension can be adapted to other languages as well.

Roadmap

We start by describing sequential exception handling and how one can leverage atomic blocks to simplify it (Section 2). Then we extend our proposition for coordinated exception handling (Section 3), the abox construct and compare it to *failbox* [6] that prevents the system from running in an inconsistent state. The failbox language construct allows us to demarcate a block of code in which if a thread raises an exception, then any other thread gets prevented from executing the same failbox. The abox goes a step further in ensuring failure atomicity, i.e., executing its content fully or reverting its modifications back as if nothing has executed. To this end it uses a software transactional memory algorithm; and we will finish with an evaluation of both concepts (Section 4) and conclusion (Section 5).

2   From Exception Handling to Atomic Exception Handling

We start with introducing the *atomic exception handling* mechanism, which automatically maintains an application in a consistent state, even in case of unexpected errors.

In order to provide this exception handling behavior we propose to enclose the code that needs to be consistent within so-called *atomic box* blocks. These blocks provide the "all-or-nothing" semantics for exceptions, also known as *failure atomicity*, i.e., either their content executes fully (and no uncaught exception is raised within the block) or an uncaught exception is raised and none of the code within the block appears to be executed. We propose to use transactional memory (TM) for this purpose. The only modification needed on top of TM is that in case an exception is raised but not caught inside an atomic block, the rollback of the atomic box gets triggered.

Before we delve into semantic details, we introduce an example code (Figure 2), which we later use to explain different aspects of atomic boxes. The example represents a multi-threaded application with a shared task queue taskQueue from which threads get tasks to process. All threads execute the same code. Once a thread obtains a task, it first performs pre-computation work (getting necessary inputs and configuring the task accordingly) in the prepare method. The execution of the task is performed in the execute method of the thread, by calling sequentially the process and generateOutput methods of the task. We assume that generateOutput can add new tasks in the taskQueue.

In what follows, we will mainly focus on the execute method of the thread. The code of the method is given without any exception handling. The traditional approach would be to use a try-catch statement enclosing the content of the execute method. However, when an exception is caught, one cannot easily determine at what point the execution of the method was interrupted and hence, in general, it is difficult to revert to the state at the beginning of the method. In such a case the task object could stay in an inconsistent state, possibly even affecting the state shared with other threads, and it would not be possible to simply put the task back into the taskQueue for later re-processing. The loss of a task might require other threads to reconfigure, or to stop execution altogether for safety or performance reasons: shared state may be inconsistent, incomplete processing would be worthless. We will see in the next sections using this example how abox and atomic boxes prevent the loss of the task and how they allow us to correct the cause of the exception and coordinate threads for the program to recover.

For the following part, we focus on syntax and semantics for sequential executed programs.

```
1    public void run() {
2      Task task = null;
3      while(true) {
4        synchronized(taskQueue) {
5          task = taskQueue.remove();
6        }
7        if (task == null) break;
8        prepare(task);
9        execute(task);
10     }
11   }
12
13   public void prepare(Task task) {
14     task.getInput();
15     task.configure();
16   }
17
18   // No exception handling
19   public void execute(Task task) {
20     task.process();
21     task.generateOutput();
22   }
```

Fig. 2. A simple example where multiple threads process tasks from a common task queue and that would benefit from atomic and concurrent exception handling

2.1   Syntax and Semantics

Basically, an atomic box block is composed of two consecutive blocks: the first block is called `abox` and the second `recover`. The precise syntax is as follows:

> **abox**
> { S }
> [**recover**(ABoxException <exceptionName>)
> { S' }]

`abox` and `recover` are keywords, *S* and *S'* are sequences of statements (that may include atomic box blocks and additional keywords `or` `retry` and `leave` that are later introduced). For the sake of simplicity, in this paper we do not consider Java statements that perform irrevocable actions (e.g., I/O operation or system calls) in an `abox` because most underlying TM implementations do not support transactional execution for such actions. There exist however practical solutions to this limitation (e.g., in [7,8,9]).

In its simplest form (i.e., when its optional parameters are omitted) the syntax for an `abox` is

> **abox** { S }

We distinguish two different operation modes for an `abox-recover` statement: *normal mode* and *failure mode*. The normal mode is associated with `abox` and the failure mode is associated with the `recover` block. An `abox` executes in normal mode, i.e., an `abox` executes as long as no exceptions are raised or until an exception raised inside `abox` propagates outside of the block. Note that if the code inside `abox` raises an exception, and this exception is caught in the block itself, the `abox` still executes in normal mode.

When an exception is propagated out of `abox` boundaries (i.e., when an unhandled exception is raised in the `abox`), the `abox` is said to fail and its `abox-recover` statement switches to failure mode.

Although the functionality of the code inserted in an `abox` is not modified, an `abox` has different semantics compared to traditional blocks: `abox` executes as a transaction. That way, the modifications performed by the code inside the `abox` are only guaranteed to be effective if the `abox` successfully terminates (hence, if it successfully commits without switching to failure mode). Otherwise none of the modifications performed in the context of the `abox` are visible by code outside the `abox`. Therefore, the code in an `abox` executes atomically and in isolation.

Recover Blocks. The non-transactional `recover`-block allows the programmer to describe the actions that should be taken if an atomic box block could not be executed (Fig. 4). Changes inside this block (if not nested inside an atomic box block) cannot be rolled back and therefore, just one non-transactional recover block per atomic box can be provided.

The use of a `throw` statement inside the `abox` raises an exception in the block as in plain Java. If the exception is handled inside the `abox` the behavior of the `throw` statement is unchanged. However, if the exception is not handled in the `abox`, the `abox` (and the corresponding active atomic box block) switches to failure mode. In that case, instead of the original exception, an ABoxException is thrown.

The **ABoxException**. The structure of the ABoxException is as follows:

```
public class ABoxException {
  Class causeClass;
  String message;
  // Fields used in concurrent setting
  Thread source;
  String aboxName;
  int   handlingContext;
  // Methods omitted...
}
```

where the `causeClass` field stores the class of the exception raised by the `abox` that failed (initiator `abox`), the `message` field is the message of the original exception (the rest of the fields of the exception are used for concurrent exception handling and will be explained later). Note that the ABoxException stores the class of the original exception object that initiated the atomic box failure rather than its reference. This is a deliberate choice since the original exception object can include references to other objects that are allocated inside the initiator `abox` and that will be invalidated by the rollback performed upon the failure of the atomic box.

However, failure atomicity per se does not provide a complete error recovery solution. For example, if the reason for the uncaught exception still persists, the re-execution of the atomic box will fail again. Therefore, we need further language constructs and mechanisms to provide error recovery. Which are:

- Alternative execution path: allows the programmer to define alternatives in case of an exception
- Transactional control flow keywords to guide to alternative execution paths or recover blocks
- support for different exception-throw behaviors, namely *commit-and-throw* and *abort-and-throw semantics*.

Alternative Execution Paths. With the ability to automatically rollback changes, it becomes easy to provide cleanly separated alternatives. The typical use case of alternative execution paths is to provide different strategies for solving a problem ordered by less desired properties.

To allow alternative execution paths or is introduced as one new keyword to the language, which concatenates two abox-recover statements (Figure 3). During execution, the runtime environment tries to execute the first atomic box. In case it fails, it rolls back the changes and continues with the next or block until the final alternative is reached. If that fails as well the whole atomic box can be retried.

```
1    public void execute(Task task) {
2        abox {
3            abox {
4                task.processFast();
5            } or {
6                task.processMemoryEfficient();
7            }
8            task.generateOutput();
9        }
10   }
```

Fig. 3. Example of the alternative execution path construct with or. The task is processed with a fast but memory intensive algorithm. The slow but memory efficient method is used in case the first fails. Furthermore, this code shows how atomic boxes can be nested.

Atomic box Control Flow Keywords. Three new keywords are introduced for this purpose: retry, next, and leave. They can be used both - inside aboxes and inside recovery blocks. If used inside an atomic box block, they will abort the box immediately, rollback the chances, executes the associated recovery block (if available), and transfer the control according to the selected keyword.

The leave keyword is used to abort the surrounding abox (i.e., to cancel all the effects of the abox). A typical use case is upon a serious error where the software should stop execution immediately. But it can also be used in a recovery block of a nested atomic box block in case recovery on that level is not possible, the parent atomic box will be aborted and associated recovery options applied. If `leave` is used inside a non-nested `recovery`-block, the control flow is transferred beyond the last alternative.

The other keywords give more control to the programmer in determining the control flow inside an atomic box block. Using `retry` aborts the `abox`, executes the associated recovery block (if available), and re-executes the box from its beginning. This is useful in handling exceptions which typically happen in temporarily critical situations, e.g. due to resource constraints. The `next` is similar to `retry` but transfers control flow to the following `abox` alternative if available otherwise control flow will be transferred beyond the end of the alternatives.

In general, keywords used in the `recovery` block have precedence over the `abox`.

Exceptional Control Flow Constructs. The usual mechanism to control the flow of an application that raised an exception is to use a `try-catch` block. With the use of atomic box blocks, this mechanism can still be used (even inside an `abox` or `recover` block). However, `abox-recover` introduces a second mechanism for exceptional control flow. Due to the "all-or-nothing" semantics of an `abox` block, the way the exception should propagate out of an `abox` block is a debatable issue. There are two well-known behaviors though: *commit-and-throw* and *abort-and-throw*. The behaviors differ in the visibility of the effects of the atomic box block when the exception is propagated out of it. With commit-and-throw behavior the effects of the atomic box up to the point where the exception is raised are made permanent. In other words, commit-and-throw allows partial execution of `abox` blocks. The abort-and-throw behavior, however, rolls back all the effects of `abox` blocks and only then throws the exception.

Since commit-and-throw behavior allows the partial effects of an `abox` block to be visible to other threads at the time an exception is raised, the all-or-nothing guarantee of the `abox` block will be violated upon an exception. Abort-and-throw behavior avoids such a problem by throwing the exception only after aborting the `abox` block. However, with this behavior exception object cannot carry information about the actions performed inside the `abox` block, which is sometimes useful for recovery.

In order to have the "all-or-nothing" guarantee together with the ability to propagate information out of `abox`es, we propose the following behavior: an exception that is raised and uncaught within an `abox` causes the generation of an `ABoxException` which carries only the class of the exception originally raised. Due to the raised exception, the `abox` block is aborted and the generated `ABoxException` is propagated out of the block. Syntactically, this exception propagation behavior is provided with the usual exception `throw` statement. However, an `abox` block without a `recover` block aborts and retries the `abox` block automatically (without any exception propagation). In order to provide the usual exception propagation behavior the programmer needs to provide a `recover` block to propagate the exception further.

3   Concurrent Atomic Exception Handling

Our language extension for multi-threaded use cases deals mainly with code blocks that can run in parallel but are dependent on each other in the sense that if a statement in one of the blocks raises an exception not handled within the block, none of the other code blocks should continue executing. We call such blocks *dependent blocks*. An *atomic box* is a group of dependent code blocks that can act together to recover from an exception that is raised in at least one of the code blocks. In order to express the fact that abox-recover blocks belong to the same atomic box, they get the same name assigned (as a parameter).

The already known syntax of the abox-recover statement is extended in the following way:

> **abox** [(*"name"*, <handlingContext>)]
> { S }
> [**recover**(ABoxException <exceptionName>)
> { S' }]

As one can notice the only addition to the syntax to support atomic box are the name and <handlingContext>, which are parameters of the associated abox keyword. The dependency relation between aboxes statements is established by naming abox-recover blocks with a common name (or with names of descendants).

Contrarily to the simplest form of abox, the named form implies that upon failure of an abox the exception handling should be coordinated across the atomic box (i.e. across all aboxes which run in parallel and belong to the same atomic box).

3.1 Semantics

The atomic box provides following semantics:

- *Failure atomicity:* An abox of an abox-recover statement can be rolled back, i.e., either the contents of the abox performs all of its modifications successfully (thus none of the aboxes that belong to the same atomic box fail at any point), or the abox acts as if it has not performed any modifications.
- *Dependency-safety:* An atomic box ensures dependency safety; i.e., if a statement fails and raises an exception, all statements that depend on the failing statement do not execute. The dependency-safety is ensured by two properties of abox-recover block: *i)* An abox executes in a transaction, thus its execution is isolated from all dependent code in the system until it commits. In other words, none of the dependent code blocks see the effects of each other as long as code blocks do not commit. *ii)* If an exception is not handled in an abox it rolls back its changes and recovery actions are taken only after all the aboxes of an atomic box are rolled back. Thus, in no situation it is possible for a dependent code block to see partial modifications of another dependent block that is in inconsistent state.
- *Coordinated exception handling:* A try-catch statement offers a recovery from exception only for the thread on which the exception occurs. The abox-recover statement allows the programmer to inform concurrently executing threads of an exception raised in one of the threads. Moreover, through the recover block of the abox-recover statement it is possible to recover from that exception in a coordinated manner. Note that the coordination is possible among recover blocks because they do not execute in a transaction.

The failure model of the `abox-recover` statement for concurrent utilization is such that when the block `abox` fails, its associated atomic box also fails (because the atomic box acts as a single entity upon an exception). Thus, all the `abox-recover` statements associated to the atomic box switch to failure mode upon the failure of an `abox`. The failure of an `abox` also triggers the failure of the descendent atomic boxes.

In the failure mode all the threads that execute in the atomic box coordinate together. They wait for each other to ensure that all the associated `abox-recover` statements switch to failure mode and all the `aboxes` are rolled back. Then they perform recovery actions as specified by the `abox` where the exception is raised. After the recovery actions are terminated all the threads decide locally how to redirect their local control flow using the keywords introduced Section 2.1.

In the rest of this section, we will discuss the semantics of the `abox-recover` statement under concurrently raised exceptions.

The simplest form of an `abox` is considered as an indication that the block is the only block in an atomic box, and thus it does not have any dependencies on other parts of the code. For such `abox` the exception handling is done locally without any coordination with any other `abox`. Hence, this form is suitable for exception handling in single-threaded applications as well as handling of exceptions for code blocks of multi-threaded applications that do not have any implications on other running threads.

As an example of such scenario, assume that an `OutOfMemoryError` is raised during the execution of the `execute` method of Figure 2. If for the running multi-threaded application, it is known that most of the tasks have small memory footprint but occasionally some tasks can have large memory footprint (but never exceeding the heap size allocated by the JVM), it is possible to clean up some resources or wait for a while before restarting execution. This would solve the problem if memory is freed when a task with a possibly large footprint finishes executing. Using the simple form of `abox`, the code for this solution would be as in Figure 4. Note that this solution is

```
1   public void execute(Task task) {
2     abox {
3       task.process();
4       task.generateOutput();
5     } recover(ABoxException e) {
6       if(e.getCauseClass() == OutOfMemoryError.getClass()) {
7         // Back off (sleep) upon OutOfMemoryError
8         backOff();
9       } // Implicit restart
10    }
11  }
```

Fig. 4. Local recovery for an `OutOfMemoryError` using the simple form of `abox`

not possible with either a `try-catch` block or a failbox since the state of the `task` object cannot be rolled back to its initial state.

We can slightly change the conditions to the example for which `abox` provided a solution in Figure 4 and generate a different scenario. Let us assume that in the example there are not many solutions for solving the OutOfMemoryError and the programmer simply wants to stop all the threads when such an exception is raised. The code that will provide this solution would be as in Figure 5.

```
1    public void execute(Task task) {
2      abox("killAll", all) {
3        task.process();
4        task.generateOutput();
5      } recover(ABoxException e) {
6        if(e.getCauseClass() == OutOfMemoryError.getClass()) {
7          // Upon OutOfMemoryError, propagate to terminate thread
8          throw e;
9        }
10     }
11   }
```

Fig. 5. Coordinated termination of a multi-threaded application upon an OutOfMemoryError. The named form of abox can be used to provide such recovery.

Note that all the threads are running the same code. The code in Figure 5 uses the named form of abox. The <handlingContext> parameter is given as all, which means that when the OutOfMemoryError is raised on one thread, all the threads running in the atomic box will execute their recover blocks. In the recover block an exception is raised so that the currently executing thread dies (since the threads are assumed to be running the code in Figure 2, the exception will not be caught and each thread will be terminated). This solution is again not possible with a try-catch statement. Since the objective in this example is to stop the application, the failbox approach would also work: one could enclose the content of the execute method in an enter block, which would specify that the code enters a failbox common to all threads.

We can also think about a variant of the above example that cannot be resolved using the failbox approach. Let us assume that, as the task object can configure itself before execution, it is also possible to reconfigure it to perform the same job using less memory but slower (e.g., by disabling an object pool). In such a case, the named form of the abox allows us to resolve the problem with the code in Figure 6 (again only by changing the content of the execute method). This solution is possible with the named form of abox since the abox-recover statement including the abox provides failure atomicity and coordinated exception handling. The failure atomicity property of the abox-recover statement allows the modifications of the execution inside the abox to be rolled back, thus the task object can be reverted to a consistent state where it can be reconfigured. The coordinated exception handling provided by the abox-recover statement allows the same behavior to be performed on all threads in a synchronized way and remedy the problem in a single step.

```
1    public void execute(Task task) {
2      abox("reconfigure", all) {
3        task.process();
4        task.generateOutput();
5      } recover(ABoxException e) {
6        if(e.getCauseClass() == OutOfMemoryError.getClass()) {
7          // Upon OutOfMemoryError, reconfigure and restart
8          task.reconfigure();
9        }
10     }
11   }
```

Fig. 6. Coordinated recovery to reconfigure tasks (for decreasing their memory footprint) upon OutOfMemoryError

3.2 Failure Mode Constructs

Since an atomic box corresponds to dependent code blocks, when an abox fails, its associated atomic box also fails. We call the atomic box that fails upon the failure of an abox an *active* atomic box. An active atomic box is defined as the set of aboxes of the same atomic box that have started executing and that have not yet started committing. This set is defined as long as at least one thread executes in the atomic box.

We argue that in terms of failure it is enough to consider an active atomic box rather than all the statically defined atomic boxes to ensure dependency-safety and failure atomicity. Since aboxes that have started committing are guaranteed not to execute on any inconsistent state that can be generated by the aboxes of the active atomic box (aboxes execute in isolation), their exclusion does not harm dependency-safety. Moreover, the consistency of data is ensured as long as the commit of aboxes that have started committing are allowed to finish before the aboxes of the active atomic box start performing recovery actions. So the rollback of an active atomic box does not require aboxes that have already started committing to rollback. Hence, it is safe to provide failure atomicity only for an active atomic box.

To have better understanding of the concept of active atomic box consider the solution proposed in Figure 5. For this solution if we think that the tasks executed by all of the threads have more or less the same load, the threads will generally be executing the execute method at about the same time periods. However, if we think of a scenario where tasks have variable load, this may not be true. So when the OutOfMemoryError is raised, some threads may be executing in the content of the abox, while some others may be still committing the abox in the execute method and some others maybe fetching a new task from the taskQueue (these threads have not yet entered in an abox). In such a case, the proposed solution may not stop all the threads since not all may be executing in the active atomic box when the OutOfMemoryError is raised. However, for these non-terminated threads the execution continues safely; threads that were committing while the exception is raised in active atomic box do not have any more dependence on the aboxes of the atomic box, and threads that have not yet entered execution in the atomic box may not raise an OutOfMemoryError if there is enough memory once the threads of the active atomic box get killed. Even if an OutOfMemoryError is again raised, this will be resolved by the active atomic box defined at the time of the second exception. Hence, we see that by applying the failure atomicity and dependency-safety only on the active atomic box it is also possible to provide safe executions.

The failure of an active atomic box results in the following coordinated behavior in the aboxes that constitute the active atomic box:

1. The aboxes that constitute an active atomic box switch to failure mode. This triggers the coordinated failure behavior of the atomic box.
2. All the aboxes that switch to failure mode automatically rollback. At the same time all aboxes that have started committing terminate their commit.
3. All the threads executing in an active atomic box are notified of a special exception ABoxException (the structure of this exception is explained later).
4. All the threads executing in an active atomic box wait for each other to make sure that they all rolled back and received the ABoxException notification. The threads in the active atomic box also wait for threads running an abox that have already started committing to finish their commit operation (which may not succeed and trigger an abort).
5. All the aboxes that constitute an active atomic box perform the recovery actions in the associated recover blocks according to the ABoxException they receive. Entry in the atomic box is forbidden for any thread during recovery.
6. All the threads executing in an active atomic box wait for each other to terminate their recovery actions. Once all recovery actions are terminated each of the threads executing in the active atomic box decide locally how to redirect their control after failure.

The *recover* block - revisited. The additional fields of an AboxException are: the source field is the reference to the Thread object executing the initiator abox, aboxName is the name of the failing atomic box and handlingContext is an integer value that defines which of the corresponding recover blocks associated to the atomic box will be executed. The value of the handlingContext corresponds to the <handlingContext> parameter of the initiator abox (the details for the values of handlingContext are explained below together with the recover block).

A recover block encloses recovery actions to be executed when the abox it is associated to fails. Since the recover block is related to failure of an atomic box, it is only part of failure mode execution. Note also that the recover block does not execute in a transactional context; it always executes after its corresponding abox rolls back. The decision of whether the recover block will be executed depends on the handlingContext parameter of ABoxException sent by the initiator abox. Two values exist for the parameter handlingContext: local and all. With the local option, only the recover block of the initiator abox will be executed, other threads will not execute any recovery action. If the all option is chosen all the threads executing in the atomic box execute their respective recover blocks.

Whichever of the handlingContext options is chosen, once the recover block executions are terminated each of the threads executing in the atomic box take their own

```
1    public void execute(Task task) {
2      abox("killSome", local) {
3        task.process();
4        task.generateOutput();
5      } recover(ABoxException e) {
6        if(e.getCauseClass() == OutOfMemoryError.getClass()) {
7          // Upon OutOfMemoryError, propagate to terminate local thread
8          throw e;
9        }
10     }
11   }
```

Fig. 7. Coordinated recovery to decrease the memory used by the multi-threaded application by only killing some of the threads upon OutOfMemoryError

control flow decision. If the handlingContext parameter has the value local, the initiator abox redirects the control flow according the control flow keyword used in its recover block (for the control flow keywords see Section 2.1). All the other threads in the atomic box re-execute the abox for which they perform recovery actions. If the handlingContext parameter has the value all, each of the threads redirects the control flow according the control flow keyword used in its respective recover block.

If the recover block of abox-recover statement has been omitted, the thread executing this abox-recover statement performs no recovery and re-executes the abox of the abox-recover statement.

Having analyzed most of the properties of the normal and failure modes, it would be appropriate to analyze the mechanisms described above in an example. At this point we can use another variant of the running example of Figure 2 with an OutOfMemoryError being raised during the execution of the execute method. Suppose, in this case, that the programmer knows that he is using too many threads and if the heap allocated by the JVM is not enough, it would be enough for him to kill only some of the worker threads. This would effectively handle the exception while keeping the parallelism of thread execution at a reasonable level. Since the programmer would not know the size of the memory allocated in advance he can choose to implement the solution in Figure 7 using the atomic boxes.

The solution shown in Figure 7 is the same as the code in Figure 5 except that the name of the <handlingContext> parameter is set to local instead of all. With this change each time an OutOfMemoryError is raised only the thread raising the exception executes the throw statement and kills itself. This solution works better than a simple try-catch because with the try-catch solution multiple threads could have raised the same exception at the same time and, being unaware of the exceptions raised in other threads, all of these threads would kill themselves leaving a smaller amount of threads running in the system, rather than gradually decreasing the amount of concurrency. Gradual decrease is possible thanks to the coordinated nature of the exception handling: coordination imposes the threads to abort their aboxes (instead of killing themselves) and restart execution after the thread of the initiator abox is killed. Thanks to the failure atomicity provided by atomic boxes, this can safely be repeated as many times as required until the required number of threads are killed.

3.3 Nesting of Atomic Boxes

The failure of an `abox` can also trigger the failure of an atomic box other than the one it belongs to. For example, if the failing `abox` contains another `abox`, also the contained `abox` fails. This, furthermore, leads to their associated atomic boxes to fail as well. In contrast, when a child atomic box fails, its parent atomic box does not fail, thus the child atomic box switches to failure mode, while the parent atomic box does not.

The fact that atomic boxes have ascendants or descendants is reflected by a hierarchical naming of `abox`es. The `name` parameter of an `abox` can be a list of strings of the form `x.y.z` following the naming convention of Java package names [1].

3.4 Resolution of Concurrently Raised Exceptions

Up to this point we have considered only the case where a single `abox` initiates an atomic box failure. If an exception needs to be treated by an `abox`, this is most probably because the exception concerns all the threads executing in the atomic box. So it is not surprising to expect that multiple `abox`es raise the same exception and fail the atomic box. It is also perfectly possible that different `abox`es of the same atomic box, concurrently raise the different exceptions and cause the atomic box to fail.

The atomic box takes a very simple approach to resolve concurrently raised exceptions thanks to its failure atomicity property: an atomic box allows only one exception (the first one to be caught) to be treated in failure mode and ignores all the concurrently raised exceptions during failure mode.

The atomic box does not consider all the concurrently raised exceptions together. By handling one exception and removing its cause before re-execution, one may avoid other concurrent exceptions to occur again. During re-execution, if the cause of the concurrently raised exceptions are not removed they will again manifest and fail the atomic box. They will thus be treated during re-execution.

As can be noticed, among other advantages, the atomic box approach brings an elegant solution to the concurrent exception handling problem thanks to its failure atomicity property. Actually, the solution presented in Figure 7 is a good example illustrating the resolution of concurrently raised exceptions. In this example, other than the coordinated nature of the exception handling, it is the simple concurrent exception handling approach taken by atomic boxes that allows us to kill only as many threads as required.

3.5 Evolution of Code

The simple structure and composability of atomic boxes and `abox`es allows a programmer to evolve her/his application code in an easy way. Starting from the very first beginning, a simple `abox` allows to mark critical code to be executed atomic avoiding any inconsistent state—the programmer just has to concentrate on fixing reasons for failures if needed. If e.g. new special purpose libraries become available, they can be easily integrated with the `or` statement. Furthermore, if the programmer decides to parallelize the application, the transition is easy. By adding a name to an `abox`, it allows

---

[1] For simplicity, we just use one string instead of a list in our examples. Referencing boxes can also be done relatively with a leading dot, e.g. `.y.z`.

to group multiple boxes into one atomic box allowing them to orchestrate their effort. Which again helps to ease the development as the coordination of recovery for different threads does not have to be implemented. This can speed up the development process tremendously.

3.6 Implementation

We have implemented a concurrent exception handling compiler framework, called CXH, which supports the language constructs proposed in Section 2 and 3. The CXH compiler framework produces bytecode that is executable by any Java virtual machine in a three-step process. First it runs our pre-compiler, TMJAVA that converts the extended language into annotated Java code. The annotations are used to detect in the bytecode, which parts of the code have the abox semantics. Second our CXH embeds the LSA transactional memory library [10] that provides wrappers to shared memory accesses. Our aboxes benefit from the speculative execution of TMs to ensure that no exceptions are raised before applying any change in the shared memory. Third, CXH uses an existing bytecode instrumentation framework, Deuce [11], which redirects calls within annotated methods to transactional wrappers.

We implemented TMJAVA, a Java pre-compiler that converts abox-recover constructs in annotated Java code. This allows us to compile the resulting code using any Java compiler. TMJAVA converts each abox into a dedicated method that is annotated with an @Atomic keyword. More precisely, TMJAVA analyzes the code to find the aboxes (abox keyword) inside class methods. Then, for each such abox it creates a new method whose body is the content of the corresponding abox and replaces the original abox with a call to this new method. The conversion of an abox a into a method m requires passing some variables to the produced method m to address the following issues:

1. Variables that belong to the context of the method enclosing the abox a should also be accessible inside the scope of the produced method m.
2. Variables that belong to the context of the method enclosing the abox a and that are modified inside a should have their modifications effective outside the produced method m (as it would be for abox a).

To ensure that variables are still visible inside the produced methods, the variables whose scope are out of abox context are passed as input parameters to the corresponding method. For the state of variables to be reflected outside the scope of the abox, these variables are passed as parameters using arrays (if the variables are of primitive types). When the method returns, we copy back these array elements into the corresponding variables.

Our abox leverages memory transactions that execute speculatively on shared data. The main difference between aboxes and the transactions lies in the fact that each abox decides whether to abort or commit its changes also depending on (concurrent) exceptions raised. Before committing, an abox makes sure that no exception was raised inside the block or by a dependent abox.

Each memory transaction executes speculatively by buffering its modifications. If the transaction reaches its end without having aborted, it attempts to commit by applying its modifications to shared memory. More precisely, when a transaction starts it records the value of a global time base, implemented as a shared counter. Upon writing a shared location, the transaction acquires an associated ownership record, buffers the write into a log, and continues executing subsequent accesses. At the end, when the transaction tries to commit, it reports all the logged writes in memory by writing the value, incrementing the global counter, and associating its new version to all written locations as part of the ownership records. Upon reading a shared location, it first checks if the location is locked (and aborts if locked), then compares the version of the location to the counter value it has seen. If the location has a higher version than this value, this means that a concurrent transaction has modified the location, indicating a conflict.

After compilation we obtain a bytecode where annotated methods directly access the memory. To ensure that these annotated methods, which correspond to the original `abox`es, execute speculatively we have to redirect their memory accesses to the transactional memory. To that end, we use the Deuce framework [11] to instrument the annotated method calls at load time. Deuce instruments class methods annotated with `@Atomic` such that accesses to shared data inside those methods are performed transactionally. This bytecode instrumentation redirects all `abox` memory accesses to LSA so that each `abox` executes as a transaction.

4 Evaluation

We compare our `abox` solution against failbox [6] on an Intel Core2 CPU running at 2.13GHz. It has 8-way associative L1 caches of 32KB and an 8-way associative L2 cache of 2MB. For `abox` we implemented the compiler framework as explained in Section 3.6 whereas for failboxes we reused the original code from [6].

4.1 Producer-Consumer Example

Our first experiments consist of a simple producer-consumer application, where one thread pushes an item to a shared stack while another pops the topmost item from the same stack. For the sake of evaluation, the stack `push()` method raises an exception if adding the new item to the stack would exceed its capacity. We evaluated two versions of the same program: one using failbox, the other using our `abox`. The execution time of these two versions has been evaluated in normal cases (where we fill the stack prior to execution such that no exceptions are raised) and for handling exceptions (where we try to push an item to an already full stack). Results are averaged over 100 executions.

Table 1 reports the minimum, maximum and average execution time in microseconds, respectively without and with exceptions. On the one hand, we observe that our solution executes about $2\times$ faster (on average) than failboxes in normal executions. This is due to a cache effect observed with failbox approach. Each time a failbox is entered a shared variable is checked to verify whether it has failed. Since this experiment requires very frequent entries to a failbox by multiple threads the failbox entries are serialized. Our implementation does not suffer from this problem since the check for the failure of an `abox` does not need to be verified often (an `abox` is executed in isolation from other code).

Table 1. Execution times of `abox` and failbox in microseconds on a multi-threaded producer-consumer application when no exception is raised (left) and if an exception is raised (right)

	no exception raised			exception raised		
	min	max	average	min	max	average
`abox`	7.27	11.67	8.92	1.40	2.62	2.22
failbox	15.70	34.97	18.58	32.167	47.23	34.55
speedup of `abox`	1.34	4.81	2.08	12.28	33.74	**15.7**

On the other hand, our solution performs more than 15× faster (on average) than fail-boxes to handle exceptions. We conjecture that it is due to the fact that failbox approach uses the `interrupt` mechanism to communicate the exception on one thread to the other threads. The `abox` approach communicates over the shared memory, resulting in a faster notification. It is worth mentioning that our `abox`es permit both `push()` and `pop()` methods to recover from exception, allowing the program to resume, while fail-box simply stops the program upon the first exception raised. Considering this desirable behavior and the observed overhead, `abox` clearly represents a promising approach.

4.2 Sorting Examples

Our second experiments rely on two single-threaded sorting applications (quick-sort and bubble-sort) coded in 3 ways: *(i)* using plain Java (with no extensions), *(ii)* inside failboxes, and *(iii)* inside `abox` blocks. The plain Java version is used to measure the

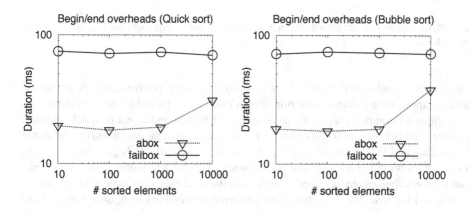

Fig. 8. Comparison of the overhead produced when starting and terminating an `abox` and a fail-box (note the logarithmic scales on both axes)

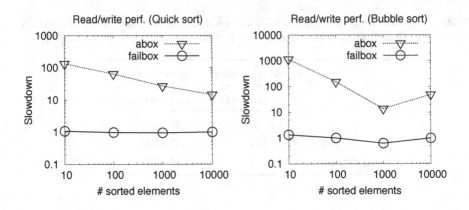

Fig. 9. Comparison of the overhead due to accessing the shared memory in abox and failbox (note the logarithmic scales on both axes)

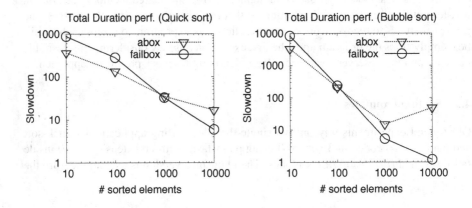

Fig. 10. Comparison of the total duration time of abox and failbox (note the logarithmic scales on both axes)

inherent overhead of failbox and abox versions. The sort is performed inside a function and the application can choose to run either a *quick-sort* or a *bubble-sort* function.

Figures 8 through 10 depict the performance of failbox and abox on quick-sort (left column) and bubble-sort (right column). Figure 8 compares the execution overhead due to entering and leaving an abox block or a failbox (we call this *begin/end overhead*). Figure 9 shows the execution time performance of abox and failbox executions without the *begin/end overhead*. Figure 10 depicts the total execution time performance of abox and failbox. The execution time performance depicted in figures 9 and 10 are given as the slowdown with respect to the performance of the plain Java version, which does not have any begin/end overhead. Each point in the graphs corresponds to the average of 10 runs.

The results show that although the failbox approach performs as good as plain Java inside the failbox, its begin/end overhead is quite high. We attribute this high overhead of the failbox approach to the memory allocation performed to generate a new failbox (be it a child or a new failbox) before entering the failbox. Figure 10 also illustrates that abox blocks perform better than the failbox approach for input arrays of up to about 1000 elements. This demonstrates that our abox implementation, although using transactions to sort array elements, performs well even compared to simpler approaches that do not roll back state changes.

5 Conclusion

In this chapter, we have shown how a simple language extension can be provided to handle exceptions correctly. The language extension addresses consistency issues that can arise in both sequential and concurrent programs using a new abox language construct based on software transactional memory.

In sequential programs, abox offers a "all-or-nothing" semantics. Hence the inconsistent state that results from or causes the exception is automatically rolled back and alternative actions can be safely taken in a subsequent recovery block. In concurrent programs, the abox parameters also allow for one thread to propagate the exception to other threads to prevent others from accessing inconsistent data but also to coordinate the recovery among multiple threads.

We also discussed another tentative solution to propagate exceptions to other threads. Even though this solution does not provide coordination among threads, it is significantly slower than our technique, precisely because abox exploits the recent research results in software transactional memory.

6 Bibliographic Notes

Transactional memory was initially used in the exception handling context about a decade ago. Harris [12] proposed to commit by default all changes when an exception is thrown. The notion of atomic exception handling described in Section 2 was proposed to extend the approach of Harris, for example by rolling back the exception [13].

Figure 1 is inspired by a similar example from Stelting [14]. Failboxes were proposed by Jacobs and Piessens as a mechanism to prevent the system from running in such an inconsistent state. The key idea is that, if one thread raises an exception in a failbox, any other thread is prevented from executing in the same failbox [6]. Instead of letting the system run in an inconsistent state, a failbox simply halts all concurrent threads accessing the same failbox. However, failboxes neither revert the system to a consistent state nor help the programmer recover from the error.

Atomic boxes were presented two years later [1]. They rely on LSA [10], an efficient time-based software transactional memory algorithm that maps each shared memory location with a timestamp. The LSA algorithm allows the transaction to commit despite such a conflict thanks to incremental validation: if all previously read values are still consistent, i.e., their versions have not changed since they have been read, the transaction has a valid consistent snapshot and can resume without aborting.

The Java pre-compiler TMJAVA is available for download at http://tmware.org/tmjava. Even though LSA is key to the lightweight and efficient implementation of abox we have experimented, other software transactional memory libraries could be used. In particular, TMJAVA relies on Deuce [11] to automatically instrument shared memory accesses within aboxes at the bytecode level. Hence, one could easily define different abox semantics depending on their parameters by using polymorphic transactional memory [15].

Shinnar et al. [16] proposed a try_all block for C#, which is basically a try block capable of undoing the actions performed inside the block. Cabral and Marques [17] similarly proposed to augment the try block with transactional semantics (using transactional memory as the underlying mechanism) to allow the retry of a try block when necessary.

Other work proposed richer atomic block constructs that build upon TM and that help with exception handling [18,12,13,11,19]. However, all the existing implementations for the above work focus on sequential executions, hence being unable to cope with coordinated exception handling. When a thread raises an exception, it can either rollback or propagate the exception. If the exception is not caught correctly, the thread may stop and leave the memory in a corrupted state that other threads may access.

References

1. Harmanci, D., Gramoli, V., Felber, P.: Atomic boxes: Coordinated exception handling with transactional memory. In: Mezini, M. (ed.) ECOOP 2011. LNCS, vol. 6813, pp. 634–657. Springer, Heidelberg (2011)
2. Cristian, F.: Exception handling and tolerance of software faults. In: Lyu, M.R. (ed.) Software Fault Tolerance, pp. 81–107. John Wiley & Sons, Inc., New York (1995)
3. Utas, G.: Robust Communications Software: Extreme Availability, Reliability and Scalability for Carrier-Grade Systems. Wiley, Chichester (2005)
4. Cabral, B., Marques, P.: Exception handling: A field study in java and.NET. In: Ernst, E. (ed.) ECOOP 2007. LNCS, vol. 4609, pp. 151–175. Springer, Heidelberg (2007)
5. Broadwell, P., Sastry, N., Traupman, J.: Fig: A prototype tool for online verification of recovery. In: Workshop on Self-Healing, Adaptive and Self-Managed Systems (2002)
6. Jacobs, B., Piessens, F.: Failboxes: Provably safe exception handling. In: Drossopoulou, S. (ed.) ECOOP 2009. LNCS, vol. 5653, pp. 470–494. Springer, Heidelberg (2009)
7. Volos, H., Tack, A.J., Goyal, N., Swift, M.M., Welc, A.: xCalls: safe I/O in memory transactions. In: EuroSys, pp. 247–260 (2009)
8. Porter, D.E., Hofmann, O.S., Rossbach, C.J., Benn, A., Witchel, E.: Operating system transactions. In: SOSP, pp. 161–176 (2009)
9. Smiljkovic, V., Nowack, M., Miletic, N., Harris, T., Unsal, O., Cristal, A., Valero, M.: Tm-dietlibc: A tm-aware real-world system library. In: 2013 IEEE 27th International Symposium on Parallel Distributed Processing (IPDPS), pp. 1266–1274 (May 2013)
10. Riegel, T., Felber, P., Fetzer, C.: A lazy snapshot algorithm with eager validation. In: Dolev, S. (ed.) DISC 2006. LNCS, vol. 4167, pp. 284–298. Springer, Heidelberg (2006)
11. Korland, G., Shavit, N., Felber, P.: Deuce: Noninvasive software transactional memory in Java. Transactions on HiPEAC 5(2) (2010)
12. Harris, T., Marlow, S., Peyton-Jones, S., Herlihy, M.: Composable memory transactions. In: Proceedings of the Tenth ACM SIGPLAN Symposium on Principles and Practice of Parallel Programming, PPoPP 2005, pp. 48–60. ACM, New York (2005)

13. Fetzer, C., Felber, P.: Improving program correctness with atomic exception handling. J. of Universal Computer Science 13(8), 1047–1072 (2007)
14. Stelting, S.: Robust Java: Exception Handling, Testing and Debugging. Prentice Hall, New Jersey (2005)
15. Gramoli, V., Guerraoui, R.: Democratizing transactional programming. Commun. ACM 57(1), 86–93 (2014)
16. Shinnar, A., Tarditi, D., Plesko, M., Steensgaard, B.: Integrating support for undo with exception handling. Technical Report MSR-TR-2004-140, Microsoft Research (2004)
17. Cabral, B., Marques, P.: Implementing retry - featuring AOP. In: Fourth Latin-American Symposium on Dependable Computing, pp. 73–80 (2009)
18. Harris, T.: Exceptions and side-effects in atomic blocks. Sci. Comput. Program. 58(3), 325–343 (2005)
19. Gramoli, V., Guerraoui, R.: Reusable concurrent data types. In: Jones, R. (ed.) ECOOP 2014. LNCS, vol. 8586, pp. 182–206. Springer, Heidelberg (2014)

Transactional Memory for Reliability

Gulay Yalcin and Osman Unsal

Barcelona Supercomputing Center, Spain
{gyalcin,ounsal}@bsc.es

Abstract. It is foreseen that technology trends will increase the transient and permanent fault rates in future processors. Thus providing reliability for both the applications running on personal computers and running on mission-critical systems is becoming an absolute necessity. A reliable system requires the inclusion of two key capabilities: 1) error detection and 2) error recovery mechanisms. Transactional Memory (TM) provides an ideal base for both error detection and error recovery. First, TM provides mechanisms to abort transactions in case of a conflict, thus they discard or undo all the tentative memory updates and restart the execution from the beginning of the transaction. Thus, a transaction's start can be viewed as a locally checkpointed stable state which can be used for error recovery. Second, transactional semantics allows the error detection to be deferred until a transaction commits (or the value becomes externally visible), so that the cost of error detection can be reduced compared to traditional error detection schemes (in which error detection is conducted et every instruction [26]) while its efficiency can be increased.

In this chapter, we first explain the hardware faults and aspects of reliability schemes such as error detection and error recovery. Then, we explain the major requirements of reliability schemes and the similarities between these requirements and transactional memory basics. Finally, we present current research landscape for reliability schemes using transactional memory.

1   Fault Categorization

In a computer system, a hardware defect is termed as a *fault*. Errors are the manifestation of faults. This means that an error is caused by faults but not all faults lead to errors. Also, fault within a particular scope (i.e. circuit, architecture, operating system) may not appear as an error outside the scope if the fault is either masked or tolerated within the scope. Failure is defined as a system malfunction that causes the system to not meet its correctness, performance, or other guarantees.

Faults experienced by semiconductor devices fall into three main categories: transient, intermittent and permanent. Moreover, when these faults affect more than a bit at a time, multi-bit faults occur. A *transient fault* (also known as Soft Error: a transient fault cause an error) is a bit flip due to some radiation event or power supply noise. Obviously, these radiation events are unpredictable and it is not easy to mitigate them through circuit design. The faulty data bit stays corrupted until it is overwritten, thus, these faults are temporal (transient) [5]. As transistor dimensions and operating voltages shrink, sensitivity to radiation increases dramatically. Thus, it is foreseen that future systems will be more prone to transient faults. Despite the fact that transient

R. Guerraoui and P. Romano (Eds.): Transactional Memory, LNCS 8913, pp. 268–282, 2015.

faults are nondestructive functional errors and that they can be fixed by re-setting or re-writing of the device, they may cause dramatic impact on computer systems unless they are mitigated [6]. For instance, in 2005,Hewlett-Packard acknowledged that a large installed base of a 2048-CPU server system in Los Alamos National Laboratory which is located at about 7000 feet above sea level, crashed frequently because of cosmic ray strikes to its parity-protected cache tag array [18]. It is reported that HP's ASC Q super-computer was crashing 15 times a week due to the inability of software and hardware to collaborate in fault recovery [18].

Irreversible physical changes in the semiconductor devices are called *permanent faults*. Permanent faults tend to occur early in the processor lifetime due to manufac-turing defects (called "infant mortality"), or late in the lifetime due to thermal and pro-cess related stress. Thus they are typically characterized by the classic bathtub curve as shown in Figure 1. Initially, the error rate is typically high because of either bugs in the system or latent hardware defects. Beyond the infant mortality phase, a system typ-ically works properly until the end of its useful lifetime is reached. Then, the wearout accelerates causing significantly higher error rates. Reliability mechanisms usually dis-connect the faulty structures hit by permanent faults, and replace them with fault-free spare structures. Systems having these mechanisms tolerate permanent faults. In fact, the lifetime reliability of a system is defined by its ability to tolerate these faults. A per-manent fault can be detected by performing built-in self test (BIST) [3]. For instance, to check that if there is a permanently faulty bit in a memory structure producing always '0' or always '1' (i.e. stuck-at-zero or stuck-at-1), first '0's are written to the memory structure and read back to see if they are read correctly. Then the process is repeated with writing all '1's to the memory structure.

Typically faults in the wear-out epoch are manifested first as intermittent faults, then progress to permanent faults. Intermittent faults occur when process variation or in-progress wear-out, combined with voltage and temperature fluctuations cause a burst of frequent faults that last from several cycles to several seconds. An intermittent fault occurs repeatedly at the same location; It tends to occur in bursts for a period of time when the fault is activated. The replacement of the offending circuit mitigates the inter-mittent fault [11,4]. It has been suggested that intermittent faults have the potential to impact program execution to a greater extent when compared with transient faults [22].

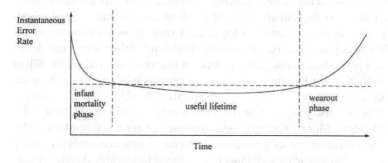

Fig. 1. The bathtub curve showing the relationship between the hard-errors (i.e. infant mortality and wearout errors) and lifetime [21]

In this sense, intermittent faults can be considered as similar to permanent faults. However, similarly to transient faults, it is hard to diagnose an intermittent fault by hardware/software tests because intermittent faults do not persist and the conditions that caused the fault are hard to regenerate.

Besides this classification (i.e. transient, permanent, intermittent), faults are also classified according to their outcomes [29]. If a fault disappears or masked without being noticed by the user, it is termed as *benign*. Obviously, if the fault is not benign, it leads to an error unless it is detected and corrected. If an error is not caught by the system, it leads to a Silent Data Corruption (SDC). In another case, an error can be caught by the system but it can not be corrected. In this case, the error is termed as Detected Unrecoverable Error (DUE). Mission-critical systems such as airplanes must have extremely low SDC and DUE because human life may be at stake.

In order to characterize the behaviour of a system in the presence of a fault, two attributes are defined: *Reliability* and *Availability*. The reliability of a system is the probability that the system does not experience a user-visible error. Availability, on the other hand, is the probability that a system is functioning correctly at a particular time. *Fault-Tolerance* is the ability of a computer system to survive in the presence of faults. In the literature, Fault Tolerance and Reliability tend to be used interchangeably.

2 Aspects of Reliability

A reliable system should have two main aspects in order to avoid errors: Error Detection and Error Recovery. *Error Detection* is the process of discovering that an error has occurred. *Error Recovery* is the process of restoring the system's integrity after the occurrence of an error.

In this section, we cover microarchitectural error detection and recovery schemes.

2.1 Error Detection

Typical error detection schemes in the literature are: (1) Redundant Execution, (2) Encoded Processing and (3) Monitoring Error Symptoms.

Redundant Execution is the most common error detection solution satisfying strict reliability requirements of mission-critical systems [15,20,26,30]. The instruction stream is executed redundantly and the value is generated multiple times with a single or multiple resources. Later, a voting circuit checks if result of the executions are identical. If results diverge, a recovery mechanism is triggered. Executing instruction streams redundantly in chip multi processors (CMP) provides higher reliability since it can detect both transient and permanent faults. Thus, redundant execution can reduce the Silent Data Corruption (SDC) rate to almost zero for components it is covering. However, when the executions are compared in the fine-granularity, redundant execution can also increase the rate of the false positive case (i.e. error recovery is triggered although the detected fault is benign). More essentially, the comparison of execution results in order to detect divergent execution causes synchronization/comparison overheads especially if the inter-processor communication channel has a limited bandwidth. Another disadvantage of redundancy is that it is difficult to provide reliability to non-deterministic programs since replicas may observe different results from different random seeds.

Encoded Processing adds redundancy by applying arithmetic codes (which are similar to parity bits used in memory redundancy) to the values processed by the application. All operations must preserve the encoding which result in more computations and high energy consumption. Encoded Processing adds redundancy (i.e. arithmetic codes) to values in the application so that values are transformed into a larger domain where only a small subset of values are valid. This process is termed as Encode. In the error-free execution of the application, all values always stay in the valid state. In case of an error such as a bit-flip in the operand or the operation of an instruction, it is highly likely that results would diverge to the invalid state. The Decode process of the encoded processing determines this divergence and detects the error which might have affected the data during the storage, transport, or operation. The main advantage of encoded processing over replication is that it allows executions of non-deterministic applications.

Monitoring error symptoms (e.g. fatal traps, miss-predictions) for error detection is proposed to provide a low-cost error detection by avoiding redundancy. However, their error coverage is limited and they do not mitigate Silent Data Corruptions (SDCs). For instance, a fault may cause an erroneous amount of money to be transferred to a bank account. Thus, these schemes are not convenient to be used in mission-critical systems.

2.2 Error Recovery

Checkpoint/Recovery is the most well-known error recovery technique which stores an error-free state of the system (checkpointing) and reverts the system state upon error detection (recovery). Checkpointing strategies are classified into three groups [2]: (1) Global (2) Coordinated-local and (3) Uncoordinated-Local checkpointing.

Global checkpointing schemes create system-wide checkpoints periodically. The scalability of these schemes is limited due to two main difficulties. First, typically they perform relatively complex barrier synchronization at checkpointing at which some processors may stay idle if load is not properly balanced among them. Second, when recovery is required, they rollback all processors to an earlier validated state which causes unnecessary rollbacks of error-free processors.

Coordinated-local Checkpointing synchronize only the set of processors which communicated during the checkpoint interval before creating a checkpoint. Similarly, when the recovery is required, only the cores which communicated with the erroneous core rollback. Thus, coordinated-local checkpointing typically outperform global checkpointing.

Uncoordinated-local checkpointing performs checkpointing locally at each processor without any synchronization. It only stores the interactions between processors in order to rollback to a consistent checkpoint. This approach is interesting for executions where processors communicate rarely.

In addition to the performance degradation in the error-free execution, recovery schemes require supplementary hardware. Moreover, this hardware is non-functional for performance, it is only utilized for reliability (e.g buffers to save checkpoints). These structures increase system verification and test complexity.

3   Reliability with Transactional Memory

Transactional Memory (TM) is one of the most promising approach for concurrent programming. Also, several key characteristics of TM are notably suitable for developing a reliable system [14].

TM provides mechanisms to abort transactions in case of a conflict. Transactions record their tentative reads and writes in a read-set and write-set respectively. In order to abort a transactions, TM systems discard or undo all the tentative memory updates and restart the execution from the beginning of the transaction. Thus, a transaction's start can be viewed as a checkpointed state.

A reliable system should ensure that faulty tasks do not negatively affect other tasks in the system. Hence, it should provide a failure isolation which is not easy to achieve since tasks need to communicate. TM executes transactions atomically and in isolation which also supports the isolation of failures.

Error detection presents a performance overhead in reliable systems every time it is triggered. Moreover, if it is frequently triggered, the possibility that a benign fault cause an error recovery is increased. Transactional semantics allows the error detection to be deferred until a transaction commits (or the value becomes externally visible), so that the cost of error detection can be reduced while its efficiency can be increased.

One of the main challenges in TM is how to cope with external actions such as system calls or I/O operations. Note that external operations are an issue for reliable systems as well and they are mostly deferred after validating that all operations are error-free. Besides external actions, TM systems have inefficiency at executing large transactions. However, when transactions are not used for concurrency control (i.e. reliability purposed transactions), transaction demarcation can be changed and these two disadvantages of TM can be eliminated for reliable systems. Thus, the size of reliability-purposed transactions can be limited and those transactions can be committed before system calls and I/O operations. From now on, we use the term transaction for the reliability purposed transactions unless it is determined otherwise.

In this section, we present the previous reliability schemes combining an error detection scheme with TM recovery.

3.1   Symptom-Based Error Detection and Recovery with TM

Symptom-based error detection mechanisms using transactions to recover from application crashes have been proposed in SymptomTM [34] and disclosed in a patent filed by IBM [10] (See Figure 3 for the basic design of SymptomTM). In this approach, applications are executed in back-to-back, reliability purposed transactions which are monitored to detect if there are any symptoms of hardware errors, which typically result in fatal traps (e.g., undefined opcode). Unless any fatal trap exception is raised in the transaction, the write-set is committed to shared memory at the end of the transaction. Otherwise, the system aborts and restarts the execution from the beginning of the transaction. If there is no symptom at the end of the second restarted execution, that means that the error was transient and that it was corrected. If the second execution raises the fatal trap exception signal again, this could be due to a permanent fault. In this

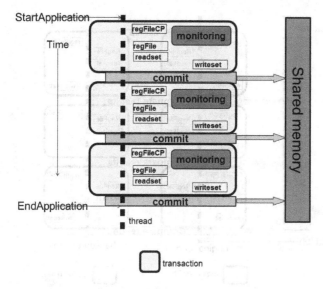

Fig. 2. Basic design of SymptomTM [34]

case, SymptomTM allocates another core, copies the checkpointed state of the trans-action to the second core and re-executes the transaction. If the second core does not raise an exception, that means the first core had a permanent fault and finally it should be disconnected from the system. Otherwise, either the error is caused by software or SymptomTM can not recover from it.

Since there is no replication, the scheme has virtually no area/energy overheads in the error-free execution. It has, however, limited error coverage since it cannot detect silent data corruptions (SDC) and, further, exceptions can be raised after the commit of the transaction. Both SymptomTM and [10] are build on top of a HTM that features lazy conflict detection and lazy data versioning.

Some symptoms can be observed very efficiently (e.g., catching exceptions) and symptom-based error detection can be easily combined with other error detection mech-anisms. Some other symptoms such as mispredictions in the high confidence branches can also be used as symptoms of faults. However, they may cause false positive impact (i.e. a misprediction which are not due to a fault) unlike fatal traps, thus, they are not convenient to be used for permanent fault detection. Similarly, those symptoms (e.g., infinite loops due to a corruption of the stop condition) may require an instrumentation of the code or support by the operating system (e.g, adding timeouts).

3.2 Redundancy Based Error Detection and Recovery with TM

FaulTM [31,32] and Log-Based Redundant Architecture (LBRA) [25] propose utiliz-ing redundant transactions for error detection and leveraging the abort mechanism of transactional memory for error recovery in order to provide high reliability for mission-critical systems.

The FaulTM approach is built on top of a HTM that features lazy conflict detection and lazy data versioning (See Figure 3 for the basic design of FaulTM).

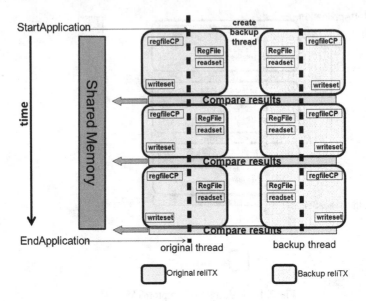

Fig. 3. Basic design of FaulTM [31]

At the beginning of the execution, FaulTM creates a backup thread which executes the identical instruction stream to the original thread. Then the original and backup threads are executed as two separate transactions. Each transaction independently sends load request to shared memory or read-sets. In FaulTM, there are no conflicts between the original and the backup transaction, because the backup transaction is only for validation of error-free execution and it does not modify shared memory. Note that, an original transaction may conflict with other transactions (reliability or concurrence purposed) except its pair transaction. When a transaction aborts to resolve a conflict, its pair transaction also aborts and restarts. Original and backup transactions wait for each other (spin) to reach the commit stage. Then, the transaction pair compare their write-sets and register files through the comparators in the backup transaction. If they match, the original transaction commits its changes to memory, and the backup transaction is cleared as if it aborts and it does not re-execute. Mismatch means an error due to a hardware fault in one of the transaction that starts the recovery in which both the original and backup transactions abort and they restart execution. If they match in the second execution, that means that there was a transient fault either in one of the cores or in the comparators in the first execution. Two successive mismatch signals between the same original and backup transactions signify that either one of the cores or the comparators has a permanent fault. In this case, FaulTM executes the transaction in a third core to detect the source of the permanent fault by comparing the results with this third core's comparators.

FaulTM has three main advantages provided by lazy data versioning of TM. First, FaulTM reduces the comparison overhead compared to the previous redundancy-based fault-detection schemes due to two reasons. First, it compares the write-sets (instead of each store values) which have a fewer amount of entries than the total number of store instructions due to multiple stores to the same address. Second, register file comparison is done only at the commit stage of reliTXs (instead of after each instruction). Furthermore, comparison only at the commit point reduces the probability of detecting benign faults; because if a fault is masked within the reliTX, its effect is eliminated before the end of the reliTX. Second, FaulTM eliminates the requirement of separate input replication mechanisms (a mechanism that satisfies that pair transactions load the same data) since memory is not modified until commit and a thread perceives memory as its pair thread. Third, FaulTM avoids the propagation of a fault to the rest of the system, thus, it provides a very fast error recovery.

However, in FaulTM the execution is stalled at the commit stages of the transactions since transaction pairs are tightly coupled. Also, after the verification of the correct execution of transactions, buffered values must be visible to the rest of the system. This commit process presents a pressure over the memory hierarchy and the performance of the system. In order to provide an alternative design overcoming these limitations, Log-Based Redundant Architecture (LBRA), a reliability scheme build on a eager data versioning HTM system is proposed.

In LBRA, the thread pairs are termed master-slave threads akin to original-backup threads of FaulTM. The master thread executes the transaction but, additionally, it keeps the results of its progress (i.e. Verification Signature which summarizes the computation performed during the execution of the transaction) in a pair-shared log. By means of this log, the slave verifies that the results produced by master are correct. Using the eager-eager HTM, LBRA decouples the pair transactions so that master transaction can commit without being stalled for the execution of the slave transaction to be finished. However, it requires additional implementation of 3 mechanisms: i) *input replication*: Since master and slave transactions are not decoupled, the execution of redundant memory instructions would probably lead to input incoherence. Input replication is required to solve this issue. LBRA extends the log area provided by the TM to contain the history related to memory operations for the purpose of keeping track of the data values that the master thread accesses. The load instruction of the slave transaction is served through this log (in program order), thus, slave thread obtain the same value as its master-pair. ii)*Providing a stable recovery state*: As memory values are allowed to be shared and shared memory is eagerly updated in LBRA, potential faults could be propagated across the system. Thus, when a fault is detected in a transaction and this transaction aborts, all other transactions using the data produced by this faulty transaction (i.e. consumer of the faulty transaction) should also abort. To this purpose, in LBRA, master thread track the producer/consumer dependencies with other threads in the system by means of the conflict detection support provided by TM. Thus, when a faulty transaction aborts, it also sends an abort request to all its consumers. iii) *output comparison*: If a thread is the consumer of another thread, the validation of the consumer thread is accomplished after the validation of its producers.

Replication can also be utilized in distributed systems for reliability. Distributed Software Transactional Memory (DSTM) systems are usually object-based. Having these transactions execute on distinct address spaces makes it appealing to duplicate objects for reliability. There is a wide body of previous work that aim to develop duplicate DSTMs [9,7,8,12,24,17]; these papers are inspired by the fault tolerance properties of

```
MAIN
    out = WrapperFunction ( val)
    Print (out)


function WraperFunctionA (val)
    BEGIN_TX
        val_enc = ENCODE (val)
        outenc = FunctionA (val_enc)
        out = DECODE (out_enc)
    END_TX


function FunctionA(val_enc)
    ...
    READ_TX(addr_enc)
    WRITE_TX(addr_enc, val_enc)
    ...
    return out_enc
```

```
function DECODE (val_enc)
    if NotValid(val_enc)
        ABORT


function READ_TX (addr_enc)
    addr = DECODE (addr_enc)
    .....
    val = get (addr)
    return ENCODE (val)


function WRITE_TX (addr_enc, val_enc)
    addr = DECODE (addr_enc)
    val = DECODE (val_enc)
    ....
    put(addr, val)
```

Fig. 4. Algorithm for eager error detection for Transactional Encoding simplified from [28]

database replication schemes. In addition, [13] investigates how checkpointing and flat nesting could be employed to increase the scalability of these replication mechanisms.

3.3   Encoded Processing for Error Detection and Recovery with TM

Wamhoff at el [28] proposed Transactional Encoding which combines arithmetic codes for error detection and STM for error recovery. They provide the design for both lazy and eager conflict detections. They use AN arithmetic codes together with symptom-based error detection. Besides the advantage of encoding processing that allows executing non-deterministic applications, the software-based Transactional Encoding also provide achieving reliability using unreliable commodity hardware. However, software-only solutions can not guarantee the detection or the recovery of permanent errors since replicas or recovered executions can be issued to the same hardware structures.

In the transactional encoding, first, the application written in C is transformed to the encoded version by using an encoding compiler (see Figure 4). During this transformation, the main module initializing the application is not encoded. Also, encoded versions of public functions and wrappers of those functions are added to the encoded application. Wrappers encode the parameters for the function, call the encoded version of the function and then decode the returned value (if there is any). In the second step of the transactional encoding, transactional memory semantics are added to the encoded version. In this sense, Transaction Begin/End instructions are added to the wrapper. Also, all accesses to the state are redirected to the TM by invoking read and write operations from the encoded functions. Also, before reading/writing to/from memory, the memory address is decoded so that the correct memory location can be accessed.

The error detection can be accomplished in either lazy or eager manner similar to the conflict detection of TM. If the error detection is accomplished eagerly, all transactional writes conduct decode operation of encoded processing for the written data. Otherwise, if the error detection is deferred until transaction commit, the entire write-set is decoded only in the commit stage. If transactional encoding detects a divergence of any value from the valid state, it aborts the transaction and starts it from the beginning. Otherwise, the transaction commits and all the memory operations can visible by the system.

4 Discussion: Pros and Cons of TM Design Parameters for Reliability

Although TM (and especially STM) is known to have a high overhead for certain work-loads, a significant portion of this overhead is due to data synchronization when detecting whether different threads accessed common data. For error recovery purposes, however, only the checkpoint/rollback behavior is necessary and the synchronization requirement is therefore largely reduced. Hence, it is possible to design cost-effective TM for error recovery by providing minimal synchronization.

TM systems can be implemented in the software, in the hardware or in a hybrid fashion. On the other side, TM proposals implement two key mechanisms, data versioning and conflict detection. Each of these mechanisms can be implemented either in lazy or eager policies. In this section, we discuss the effects of these design parameters when transactions are leveraged for the reliability purpose. At the end of the section, we also present possible programming modelling extensions.

4.1 TM in Software or in Hardware

Reliability is becoming one of the essential design constraint in computer systems due to the increasing fault rate in each technology nodes. Reliability can be accomplished in the software or in the hardware level. Software-based reliability schemes have been proposed in order to avoid new hardware design. However, besides that they present higher performance degradation than hardware-based schemes, also they are not capable of detecting permanent faults. Moreover, they require the recompilation of the source code.

On the other side, there have been many hardware-based academic reliability proposals. However, most of them have not been implemented in real hardware. This is because, these proposals require supplementary hardware and design of this extra hardware such as checkpoint buffer for restart is dedicated only for reliability. Thus, these structures increase system implementation and test complexity. To the best of our knowledge, lockstepping is one of the few redundancy-based error detection proposals with a real implementation [26,30]. We believe that building reliable systems on HTM systems is an appealing approach and appealing topic to study due to two reasons. First, the hardware structures required for reliability are also implemented in HTM systems for optimistic concurrency. Second, HTM is already implemented in mainstream processors and available from large system integrators [1,35].

Although there are HTM systems available, conducting reliability experiments on those real-systems presents several challenges. Thus, the initial real-system experiments are conducted in STM systems which presents high overhead similar to software-based reliability schemes. In this section, we explain the challenges of running reliability experiments in HTM systems.

First of all, the code that requires recovery should be executed within transactions regardless of whether the original code includes transactions or not (i.e. transactification). In TM systems, the begin/end point of parallelism purposed transactions are defined by the programmer and passed to the hardware via allocated instructions in the ISA. In reliable systems, it is expected that HTM does the transactification transparently in hardware so that transaction granularity can be arranged automatically not to exceed the HTM limitations while not introducing many delays caused between transactions. Moreover, in this way, not only the application but also operating system can run in reliable transactions.

Secondly, when the replication is used for error detection, replicated transactions require exchanging data for comparing the result of the transactions. However, in an unmodified HTM, this exchange causes a conflict since one transaction reads the data written by another transaction. One solution could be to run the replicated code in another process (instead of another thread) thus in another address space and then compare results, but this could lead to considerable overhead.

4.2   Conflict Detection and Data Versioning Policies

TM proposals implement two key mechanisms: data versioning and conflict detection. Each of these mechanisms can be implemented either in lazy or eager policies. Out of four possible combinations of these policies, the lazy-lazy [16], lazy-eager [27], and eager-eager [19] schemes are the most popular implementations. In the rest of this section, we provide a succinct discussion of the impact of TM policies on reliability by considering five desirable features for a reliable system:

Table 1. Reliability attributes of different TM implementations (Bold is Better)

	Data Versioning - Conflict Detection		
	lazy-lazy	lazy-eager	eager-eager
Checkpointing Overhead	High	High	**Low**
Recovery Overhead	**Low**	**Low**	High
Error Containment	**High**	**High**	Low
Error Detection Latency	High	**Low**	**Low**
Error Detection Overhead	**Low**	High	High

(1) Low checkpointing overhead,
(2) low recovery overhead,
(3) high error containment, to limit the propagation of errors in the system,
(4) low error detection latency, to detect errors as soon as possible, and
(5) low error detection overhead.

In Table 1, we summarize effects of the data versioning and conflict detection policies on reliability. As we show in the table (bolds typeface denotes the desired properties), none of the possible three TM policy combinations has all these features.

The cost of providing checkpoint/rollback behavior depends mainly on the data versioning strategy. *Lazy data versioning* works in two stages, a pre-commit phase and a commit phase. In the pre-commit phase the modifications are made on private copies and at the commit phase these modifications are written to the memory. Since the modifications within transactions are repeated—at least once for the private copy and once for the shared memory—a significant overhead is introduced for checkpointing even for error-free executions. However, it provides a very fast error recovery. *Eager data versioning* performs in-place memory updates during transaction execution and introduces overhead only upon abort, i.e., upon error recovery. The abort overhead is caused by the replacement of modified versions of data with their versions prior to the transaction. Thus, eager data versioning presents less overhead for checkpointing compared to lazy data versioning, however, its recovery overhead is much higher than lazy data versioning. Eager data versioning is preferable in terms of performance and energy efficiency when the error rate is low and the system presents few rollback. On the contrary, when the error rate is high (e.g in low Vdd or when the hardware is located in a high attitude), using lazy data versioning is preferable since the system would require many rollbacks and a rollback for lazy data versioning is cheaper in comparison to eager data versioning.

In TM implementations with eager data versioning, main memory keeps the latest speculative version of the data. If we use eager data versioning for reliability, some data in the shared memory which is not validated for being error-free, can be read by other cores. Assuming any of these data or any address is erroneous, this error might then easily propagate to concurrently executing tasks. Therefore, error propagation in eager data versioning is high while lazy data versioning presents high error containment. Thus, eager data versioning requires additional synchronization mechanisms for error recovery in order to rollback the communicating tasks when an error is detected in a transaction. Due to the error propagation, all transactions executing in the systems may require recovery. On the contrary, in lazy data versioning, only error-free data is written to the shared memory, therefore any error occurring in a certain transaction does not propagate to the other transactions through memory. Thus, only the erroneous transaction rolls back while the rest of the system keeps running without wasting any error-free work done. A possible benefit of using eager data versioning can be detecting errors in the shared memory besides the errors in the pipeline structures. However, it requires a detailed design which may present a higher overhead.

For Error Detection, from time to time the normal process should stop and the error detection operations (e.g. in redundancy-based error detection, comparing the results of instructions) should be carried out. Thus, the higher the number of error detection is triggered, the higher the potential performance degradation due to error detection is presented. In TM systems, error detection is accomplished during the conflict detection time of TM. For instance in a redundancy-based reliable system utilizing TM with lazy conflict detection (e.g. FaulTM), the comparison operation is carried out at the commit stage of the transaction. On the contrary, for eager conflict detection, the error detection should be carried out at every time the shared memory is updated (i.e. every write operation). Therefore, we could conclude that potential performance degradation of lazy conflict detection is lower.

On the other hand, in lazy conflict detection any error occurring earlier in the transaction will only be detected at the commit stage, so error detection latency will be higher. In eager conflict detection, however, the error could be detected earlier when a transactional store containing the error is compared.

4.3   Possible Programming Model and Software Extensions

Reliability requirements of systems depend on the application. A suitable programming modelling featuring programmer reliability annotations can reduce resilience costs for reliable systems [33]. To this end, FaulTM adds the keyword "vulnerable"to denote sections of code that should be protected by FaulTM against hardware errors instead of duplicating the entire application. Using these keywords, programmers only need to define the vulnerable sections in their applications. They can insert vulnerability boundaries as if they define atomic sections in TM applications. The vulnerable sections can be either fine-grained, lasting for a few instructions or coarse-grained such as the entire application. While the fine-grained approach causes less performance degradation, coarse-grained approach provides more reliability. For instance, for an airplane control application, the programmer could identify that the code that is responsible for controlling the flaps should be protected coarsely, whereas the code regarding the on-flight entertainment system is not protected at all. Alternatively in the fine grained version of flap controlling code, the programmer decides to protect only the calculation of desired flap angle but he leaves the graphic user interface unprotected.

Riegel et al [23] also proposes programming modelling extensions for recovering from hardware errors and software exceptions by using atomic blocks. In this study, when an atomic block fails, the Recovery Manager controls if the atomic block should be retried and, if so, how often it should be retried. This mechanism can be utilized to recover from transient and intermittent faults since those faults may disappear in the second retry.

5   Conclusion and Future Direction

Reliability is becoming one of the essential design constraint in computer systems due to increasing fault rate in each technology nodes. However, it presents high performance and design costs, thus, providing reliability is expensive.

On the other side, mechanisms such as checkpointing and abort are already implemented in transactional memory to support optimistic concurrency. We believe these schemes can be leveraged for reliability. In this study, we present the similarities between TM and reliability requirements as well as design challenges of adapting TM for reliability purpose. We also present several previous proposals in this area with their benefits and drawbacks from the reliability point of view.

Acknowledgement. This work was supported in part by the Montblanc: European scalable and power efficient HPC platform based on low-power embedded technology project of call FP7-ICT-2011-7 under the contract number 288777.

References

1. Adir, A., Goodman, D., Hershcovich, D., Hershkovitz, O., Hickerson, B., Holtz, K., Kadry, W., Koyfman, A., Ludden, J., Meissner, C., Nahir, A., Pratt, R.R., Schiffli, M., Onge, B., Thompto, B., Tsanko, E., Ziv, A.: Verification of transactional memory in power8. In: Proceedings of the The 51st Annual Design Automation Conference on Design Automation Conference, pp. 58:1–58:6 (2014)
2. Agarwal, R., Garg, P., Torrellas, J.: Rebound: scalable checkpointing for coherent shared memory. In: Proceedings of the 38th Annual International Symposium on Computer Architecture, ISCA 2011, pp. 153–164 (2011)
3. Franklin, M., et al.: Built-in Self-Testing of Random-Access Memories. IEEE Computer 23(10) (October1990)
4. Wells., P.M., et al.: Adapting to Intermittent Faults in Multicore Systems. In: Proceedings of the 13th ASPLOS, pp. 255–264 (2008)
5. Baumann, R.: Soft errors in advanced computer systems. IEEE Design and Test 22, 258–266 (2005)
6. Bidokhti, N.: SEU Concept to Reality (Allocation, Prediction, Mitigation). In: RAMS (2010)
7. Bieniusa, A., Fuhrmann, T.: Consistency in hindsight: A fully decentralized stm algorithm, pp. 1–12 (2010)
8. Bocchino, R.L., Adve, V.S., Chamberlain, B.L.: Software transactional memory for large scale clusters. In: Proceedings of the 13th ACM SIGPLAN Symposium on Principles and Practice of Parallel Programming, pp. 247–258 (2008)
9. Carvalho, N., Romano, P., Rodrigues, L.: A generic framework for replicated software transactional memories. In: Proceedings of the Tenth IEEE International Symposium on Networking Computing and Applications, pp. 271–274 (2011)
10. Chen, D.: Local Rollback for Fault-Tolerance in Parallel Computing systems, United States Patent Application, 12/696780 (2011)
11. Constantinescu, C.: Trends and challenges in vlsi circuit reliability. IEEE Micro 23, 14–19 (2003)
12. Couceiro, M., Romano, P., Carvalho, N., Rodrigues, L.: D2stm: Dependable distributed software transactional memory. In: Proceedings of the 2009 15th IEEE Pacific Rim International Symposium on Dependable Computing, pp. 307–313 (2009)
13. Dhoke, A., Ravindran, B., Zhang, B.: On closed nesting and checkpointing in fault-tolerant distributed transactional memory. In: IEEE International Symposium on Parallel and Distributed Processing, pp. 41–52 (2013)
14. Fetzer, C., Felber, P.: Transactional memory for dependable embedded systems. In: 7th Workshop on Hot Topics in System Dependability (HotDep), pp. 223–227. IEEE (2011)
15. Gong, R., Dai, K., Wang, Z.: Transient Fault Recovery on Chip Multiprocessor based on Dual Core Redundancy and Context Saving. In: International Conference for Young Computer Scientists, pp. 148–153 (2008)
16. Hammond, L., Wong, V., Chen, M., Carlstrom, B.D., Davis, J.D., Hertzberg, B., Prabhu, M.K., Wijaya, H., Kozyrakis, C., Olukotun, K.: Transactional memory coherence and consistency. SIGARCH Computer Architecture News 32(2), 102 (2004)
17. Kotselidis, C., Ansari, M., Jarvis, K., Lujn, M., Kirkham, C., Watson, I.: Distm: A software transactional memory framework for clusters. In: Proceedings of the International Conference on Parallel Processing (ICPP), pp. 51–58 (2008)
18. Michalak, S.E., Harris, K.W., Hengartner, N.W., Takala, B.E., Wender, S.A.: Predicting the Number of Fatal Soft Errors in Los Alamos National Labratory's ASC Q Computer. IEEE Transactions on Device and Materials Reliability 5, 329–335 (2005)

19. Moore, K., Bobba, J., Moravan, M., Hill, M., Wood, D.: LogTM: log-based transactional memory, vol. 12, pp. 254–265. Austin, Texas (2006)
20. Mukherjee, S.S., Kontz, M., Reinhardt, S.K.: Detailed Design and Evaluation of Redundant Multithreading Alternatives. In: Proceedings of the International Symposium on Computer Architecture, pp. 99–110 (2002)
21. Mukherjee, S.: Architecture Design for Soft Errors (2008)
22. Rashid, L., Pattabiraman, K., Gopalakrishnan, S.: Towards understanding the effects of intermittent hardware faults on programs. Dependable Systems and Networks Workshops, 101–106 (2010)
23. Riegel, T., Felber, P., Fetzer, C.: Composable error recovery with transactional memory. Bulletin of the European Association for Theoretical Computer Science (BEATCS) 99 (2009)
24. Romano, P., Rodrigues, L., Carvalho, N., Cachopo, J.: Cloud-tm: Harnessing the cloud with distributed transactional memories. SIGOPS Oper. Syst. Rev. 44(2), 1–6 (2010)
25. Sanchez, D., Cebrian, J.M., Garcia, J.M., Aragon, J.L.: Soft-error mitigation by means of decoupled transactional memory threads. Distributed Computing, 1–16 (2014)
26. Slegel, T.J.A.: IBM's S/390 G5 Microprocessor Design. IEEE Micro 19, 12–23 (1999)
27. Tomić, S., Perfumo, C., Kulkarni, C., Armejach, A., Cristal, A., Unsal, O., Harris, T., Valero, M.: Eazyhtm: eager-lazy hardware transactional memory. In: Micro-42: Proceedings of the 42nd Annual IEEE/ACM International Symposium on Microarchitecture, New York, NY, USA, pp. 145–155 (2009)
28. Wamhoff, J.-T., Schwalbe, M., Faqeh, R., Fetzer, C., Felber, P.: Transactional encoding for tolerating transient hardware errors. In: Higashino, T., Katayama, Y., Masuzawa, T., Potop-Butucaru, M., Yamashita, M. (eds.) SSS 2013. LNCS, vol. 8255, pp. 1–16. Springer, Heidelberg (2013)
29. Weaver, C., Emer, J., Mukherjee, S.S., Reinhardt, S.K.: Techniques to Reduce the Soft Error Rate of a High-Performance Microprocessor. In: Proceedings of the 31st Annual International Symposium on Computer Architecture, pp. 264–275 (2004)
30. Wood, A., Jardine, R., Bartlett, W.: Data integrity in HP NonStop servers. In: Workshop on SELSE (2006)
31. Yalcin, G., Unsal, O., Cristal, A.: FaulTM: Fault-Tolerance Using Hardware Transactional Memory. In: Design, Automation and Test in Europe DATE (2012)
32. Yalcin, G., Unsal, O., Cristal, A.: Fault Tolerance for Multi-Threaded Applications by Leveraging Hardware Transactional Memory. In: International Conference on Computing Frontiers (2013)
33. Yalcin, G., Unsal, O., Cristal, A., Hur, I., Valero, M.: FaulTM: Fault-Tolerance Using Hardware Transactional Memory. In: Workshop on Parallel Execution of Sequential Programs on Multi-Core Architecture PESPMA (2010)
34. Yalcin, G., Unsal, O.S., Cristal, A., Hur, I., Valero, M.: SymptomTM: Symptom-Based Error Detection and Recovery Using Hardware Transactional Memory. In: International Conference on Parallel Architectures and Compilation Techniques (PACT), pp. 199–200. IEEE (2011)
35. Yoo, R.M., Hughes, C.J., Lai, K., Rajwar, R.: Performance evaluation of intel transactional synchronization extensions for high-performance computing. In: Proceedings of the International Conference on High Performance Computing, Networking, Storage and Analysis, pp. 19:1-19:11 (2013)

Verification Tools for Transactional Programs

Adrian Cristal[1], Burcu Kulahcioglu Ozkan[2], Ernie Cohen, Gokcen Kestor[3],
Ismail Kuru[2], Osman Unsal[1], Serdar Tasiran[2],
Suha Orhun Mutluergil[2], and Tayfun Elmas[4]

[1] Barcelona Supercomputing Center, Barcelona, Spain
[2] Koc University, Istanbul, Turkey
[3] Pacific Northwest National Laboratory, Richland, WA
[4] Google, Mountain View, CA

Abstract. While transactional memory has been investigated intensively, its use as a programming primitive by application and system builders is only recently becoming widespread, especially with the availability of hardware support in mainstream commercial CPUs. One key benefit of using transactional memory while writing applications is the simplicity of not having to reason at a low level about synchronization. For this to be possible, verification tools that are aware of atomic blocks and their semantics are needed. While such tools are clearly needed for the adoption of transactional memory in real systems, research in this area is quite preliminary. In this chapter, we provide highlights of our previous work on verification tools for transactional programs.

1 Introduction

The verification of both sequential and concurrent programs using static and dynamic methods has been a field of intense study. Much research has also concentrated on specifying and verifying transactional memory (TM) algorithms and implementations. However, for transactional programs, whether the transactions employed are TM, database or distributed-system transactions, verification tool support is quite preliminary. This is not only the case for verifying data structure and program invariants, but also for simpler generic safety properties such as race freedom or the absence of null pointer dereferences. In this chapter, as representative of research in this space, we give an overview of three approaches we have worked on for verifying programs that mix transactional and non-transactional accesses.

In Section 2, we motivate the problem of verifying assertions, data structure and program invariants for transactional programs. Since the few concurrent program verification tools that can handle practical programming languages are not aware of even strong atomicity semantics for transactions, the work described in this section is the first of its kind that provides a workable tool to TM users. The static verification of properties for transactional programs becomes both more involved and more necessary when the TM platform being used provides more relaxed consistency guarantees such as snapshot isolation for performance reasons.

R. Guerraoui and P. Romano (Eds.): Transactional Memory, LNCS 8913, pp. 283–306, 2015.

The technique presented in Section 2 builds on the VCC tool for verifying concurrent C programs and provides tool support for transactional programs running on relaxed platforms.

Section 3 focuses on dynamic techniques for detecting concurrency errors for programs that mix transactional and non-transactional accesses. A variety of programming disciplines and platform support for this setting have been investigated. In this section, we provide highlights of two dynamic race-detection techniques and tools that have been applied successfully. While the Goldilocks race and transaction-aware runtime described in Section 3.1 provides DataRaceException as a programming language construct for transactional program, the T-Rex tool in Section 3.2 is intended to be a debugging tool used to avoid undesirable interference between transactional and non-transactional accesses.

This chapter is not intended to exhaustively cover the literature on verifying properties of transactional programs. Rather, by presenting at some length three approaches we have worked on, we intend to highlight both the correctness and the tool-building concerns in this area. As transactional programs find wider use, especially because of commonly-available hardware TM support on general-purpose CPUs, we believe the need for such tools will intensify.

2   Static Verification for Transactional Programs

Transactions provide a convenient, composable mechanism for writing concurrent and distributed programs. A transactional execution platform can provide a strong or more relaxed programming semantics. The former simplifies program construction and verification, while the latter provides better performance and availability. This section is about a technique for verifying transactional programs that operate under relaxed semantics.

Static tools for code verification targeted at sequential programs [8,19,17], and the VCC verification tool [12] for verifying concurrent C programs have been quite successful. These tools are (when applicable) thread, function and object-modular, and scale well to large programs. For programmers interested in formally, exhaustively verifying formal specifications ranging from simple partial specifications such as the absence of null-pointer dereferences and out-of-bounds array accesses, to program invariants, assertions, procedure pre- and post-conditions these tools are indispensable. We present an overview of a prototype tool [29] for carrying out static, modular verification of assertions and invariants.

For transactional platforms, existing static verification tools cannot be used as is, since they are not aware of transactions or possible relaxed consistency semantics that may be offered by a transactional platform. The goal of the technique presented in this section is to provide a verification environment exactly like that of VCC but for programs running on transactional platforms. The verification approach provides scalability and modularity, as VCC does, but requires programmer annotations for procedure pre- and post-conditions and loops in the same way all existing modular static code verification tools do.

For performance reasons, many practical transactional platforms provide a weaker consistency guarantee than atomic, serializable transactions and non-transactional accesses. One very widely used such consistency model is snapshot isolation (SI), where the entire transaction is not guaranteed to be atomic, but all of the read accesses in the transaction are atomic and all the updates performed by the transaction are atomic. Many popular databases provide SI as the default consistency mode. Relaxed semantics and relaxed conflict detection schemes other than SI, such as programmer-defined conflict detection [39], and early release of read set entries [36] have been investigated in the database, software and hardware transactional memory communities. For distributed transactional programs, relaxed consistency semantics such as session SI [14] and parallel SI [37] have been investigated (See per-record time line consistency [11] and prefix consistency [38] for examples). In the rest of this section, for brevity, we focus on the SI relaxed consistency model.

When a transactional execution platform provides strong consistency and serializable transactions, the code of a transaction can be treated as sequential code. This significantly simplifies writing and verifying applications. For the increasingly common transactional execution platforms with relaxed semantics, one way to retrieve the simplicity of sequential reasoning is to enforce serializability via additional analyses or instrumentation, e.g. by preventing or avoiding write-skew anomalies. This approach can be useful some of the time, but, for many examples, may result in a loss of performance or availability and defeat the purpose of relaxed semantics. On platforms with relaxed semantics, much of the time, it is the application author's intent to implement a transactional program that is correct, e.g. satisfies assertions and invariants, without enforcing strong consistency or serializability. Typically, the way relaxed consistency exhibits itself in transactional code is in the form of "stale reads"' – data read by the transaction may not be the most recent version later during the transaction, or even at the time of the read access, in the case of geo-replicated databases. The verification technique presented in this section can handle such transactional programs.

We take a transactional program and the relaxed consistency semantics SI. Using the transactional program and the relaxed consistency model, we produce an augmented C program with VCC annotations. The program our approach outputs has the same structure as the input program, but includes an encoding of the relaxed transactional semantics and allows exactly the executions and interleavings specified by the relaxed semantics through the use of auxiliary variables in VCC. This program transformation can be viewed as augmenting the program with a high-level implementation of the transactional platform. The transformation is designed with special attention towards preserving the thread, function and object modularity of the verification of the sequential version of the program in VCC.

2.1   Motivating Examples

To motivate our approach, in this section, we use (Figure 1) the Labyrinth benchmark from the STAMP benchmark suite, one of the four benchmark programs we applied our method to. The Labyrinth program satisfies the desired invariants and procedure post-conditions despite its executions not being serializable. Enforcing serializability (as is typically accomplished by enforcing conflict serializability [31]) would be an unnecessary restriction that hurts performance.

Labyrinth is an example of a common parallel programming pattern. Transactions each read a large portion of the shared data, perform local computation and update only a small portion of the shared data.

```
// Program invariant:
// forall int i; 0<=i && i< pathlist->num_paths
//     ==> isValidPath(grid, pathsList->paths[i])

FindRoute(p1, p2) {
 transaction {
 1:    localGridSnapshot = makeCopy(grid);
 2:                    // Take snapshot of entire grid

 3:    // Local, possibly long computation
 4:    onePath = shortestPath(p1, p2, localGridSnapshot);

 5:    // Desired post-conditions of shortestPath:
 6:    assert(isValidPath(onePath, localGridSnapshot))
 7:    assert(isConnectingPath(onePath, p1, p2);
 8:
 9:    // Register points on onePath as "taken" on grid
 10:   // Add onePath to pathsList
 11:   gridAddPathIfOK(grid, pathsList, onePath);
 12:
 13:   // FindRoute must ensure program invariants,
 14    // and the post-condition
 15:   //    onePath in pathsList &&
 16:   //          IsConnectingPath(onePath, p1, p2)
 } }
```

Fig. 1. Outline for FindRoute code and specification

As shown in 1, each concurrent transaction runs an instance of the function FindRoute to route a wire in a three-dimensional grid (grid) from point p1 to point p2. Wires are represented as paths: lists of points with integer x, y, and z coordinates, where consecutive entries in the list must be adjacent in the grid. The grid is represented as a three-dimensional array, where each entry [i][j][k] is the unique ID of the path (wire). A data structure pathList keeps pointers to all paths in an array.

Each execution of `FindRoute(p1,p2)` first takes a snapshot of the grid (line 1) by traversing it and then performs local computation using this local snapshot to compute a path (`onePath`, line 4) from `p1` to `p2`. Observe that, during this local computation, other executions of `FindRoute` may complete and modify the grid. In other words, `localGridSnapshot` may be stale snapshot of `grid`. SI guarantees in this example that (i) the read of the entire grid in line 4 is atomic, (ii) that the updates to `pathsList` and `grid` in line 11 are atomic, but does *not* guarantee that the entire transaction is atomic.

Specification. Desired properties for this program are that (i) the `grid` is filled correctly by the information, and that (ii) no two paths overlap. The latter of these is implicitly ensured because each grid point contains a single wire ID number. The former is formally expressed below

```
isValidPath(int ***grid, path_t* p) =
  (forall int i; 0<= i < path->path_len ==>
    p->ID == grid[p->x[i]][p->y[i]][p->z[i]])
  forall int i; 0<= i < path->path_len-1 ==>
    isAdjacent(p->x[i],  p->y[i],  p->z[i],
               p->x[i+1], p->y[i+1], p->z[i+1])
```

`FindRoute` must preserve this invariant for all paths on `pathList` in addition to the post-conditions that `onePath` is a valid path that connects `p1` to `p2` and is in `pathList`.

Static Verification of Sequential `FindRoute`: When `FindRoute` is viewed as if it is running sequentially, with no interference from other transactions, it is straightforward to verify using VCC. The following are the key steps taken:

- We verify that the code for `shortestPath` (not shown) satisfies the post-conditions in lines 6 and 7.
- Using this fact, we verify that `gridAddPathIfOK`, if and when it terminates, satisfies the program invariant (no two paths overlap and `pathsList` and `grid` are consistent), and the desired post-conditions in 14.

To carry out the verification tasks above, static code verification tools, including VCC, require the programmer to write loop invariants as annotations. The rest of the verification of function post-conditions is carried out automatically.

Verifying `FindRoute` Under Relaxed Consistency: The verification of `FindRoute` under SI rests on the key observation that the conditions listed above for correctness of `FindRoute` under SI remain correct even when thread interference as described by SI occurs. The technique described in this section allows us to verify that this is the case mechanically using VCC.

In a given instance of `FindRoute`, if `gridAddPathIfOK` detects that `onePath` overlaps an existing wire, it explicitly aborts the transaction. Instances of `FindRoute` that complete do so because they have computed a path `onePath` that not only does not overlap any of the wires in the initial snapshot `localGridSnapshot`, but also does not overlap any of the paths added to the grid since.

The intuition behind `FindRoute` being correct while running under SI is as follows:

1. SI ensures that the traversal and copying of the grid in line 1 is carried out atomically.
2. SI ensures that the updates to `pathList` and `grid` performed by `gridAddPathIfOK` are carried out atomically.
3. To verify that an atomic, terminating execution of `gridAddPathIfOK` establishes the desired program invariant and post-condition, it is sufficient to know that the post-conditions established by `shortestPath` in lines 6 and 7 still hold at the time `gridAddPathIfOK` starts running. New paths that may have been added to `grid` since `grid` was copied into `localGridSnapshot` do not cause invariant violations, since the atomically-executed `gridAddPathIfOK` explicitly aborts the transaction if it detects that `shortestPaths` overlaps one of the paths in `grid`.

In our technique, we transform and augment the code for `FindRoute` to obtain another C program with VCC annotations. Verifying the resulting program in VCC amounts to checking that (3) continues to hold under thread interleavings constrained by (1) and (2).

Our technique accomplishes this as follows.

- The encoded program has exactly the set of thread interleavings allowed by SI. The auxiliary variables (e.g., version numbers for each grid element and wire, fictitious locks, etc.) and constraints ("assume" statements) on these variables built into the encoded program only allow executions where all read accesses in a transaction are carried out atomically and all write accesses are carried out atomically. There are no other restrictions on how the threads are interleaved.
- When VCC verifies the object and global invariants and procedure post-conditions (e.g., the `FindRoute` program invariant or post-condition of `shortestPath`) in the encoded concurrent program, it checks whether they are preserved under thread interference possible in the encoded program. Since the encoded program (an ordinary concurrent C program) allows exactly the interleavings specified by SI, this amounts to verifying that properties of the original program running under SI hold.

The encoded program preserves the structure of the original program, and does not inline code from other possibly interfering transactions.

2.2   Preliminiaries: Transactional Programs

The user provides the code for a transaction as a C function. The beginning and end of a transaction are indicated by calls to the `beginTrans()` and `endTrans()` functions. We make the committing of a transaction syntactically visible by a call to `commitTrans(t, inv)` in order to allow the programmer to specify an invariant that holds when the transaction is committed. Data shared by transactions is represented by aliasing among arguments of functions calls representing different transactions. Unless indicated otherwise, function arguments of the same type are treated as possibly aliasing to the same address. Shared data is represented by aliasing among arguments of functions calls representing different transactions. Transaction are not allowed to be nested.

We define states and the transition relation of a program under SI as follows: A *global state* is a tuple $GS = (GlVar, GlMem, TtoLcSts)$ such that

- $GlVar$ is the set of global variables, i.e., shared objects (structs) that multiple transactions hold references to in GS,
- $GlMem : GlVar \rightarrow Val$ maps global variables to their values in the memory, and
- $TtoLcSts : Tid \rightarrow L$ keeps local states of each transaction.

The local state of a transaction t contains $LcVar$, the set of objects local to t, $RSet \subseteq GlVar$ ($WSet \subseteq GlVar$) the set of global variables that have been read (written) by t since the beginning of the transaction.

An *action* is a unique execution of a statement by a transaction t in a state s. An *execution prefix* of a program P_{SI} is a tuple $E_N = (s, \alpha)$ where α is a finite sequence of actions $\alpha_0, \alpha_1, \ldots, \alpha_{N-1}$ and $s = s_0, s_1, \ldots, s_N$ is a finite sequence of states such that $(s_i, \alpha_i) \rightarrow s_{i+1}$ for all $i < N$. An execution has the form:

$$s_0 \xrightarrow{\alpha_0} s_1 \xrightarrow{\alpha_1} s_2 \xrightarrow{\alpha_2} \ldots \xrightarrow{\alpha_{N-1}} s_N$$

The transaction consistency semantics and conflict detection scheme, such as serial execution of transactions, conflict serializability, and SI specify which interleavings of actions from different transactions are allowed in an execution.

2.3   SI and Other Relaxed Conflict Detection

We write $Idx_E(\alpha_i)$ to refer to the index i of action α_i in the execution, and $Tr_E(\alpha_i)$ to refer to the transaction performing α_i. To make precise the sets of executions of a program allowed by different relaxed conflict-detection schemes, we define the *protected span* of a shared variable x within a transaction t for a given consistency model M. Intuitively, this span is a set of indices of actions with the property that, according to the consistency model, at none of these indices can an update to x in shared memory take place due to the commit action of a transactions other than t.

The following definition of snapshot isolation makes two simplifying assumptions. First, we assume that if a transaction both reads and writes to a variable, then the read comes before the write. Second, we assume that the effects of transactions that have not committed or do not commit are not visible to other transactions. We also take as implicit the usual requirement that of two concurrent transactions with write-write conflicts, at least one must abort.

Definition 1. *An execution E is said to obey snapshot isolation iff for all committed transactions t, (i) all read accesses performed by t are atomic, (ii) all write accesses performed by t are atomic, and (iii) if t both reads and writes to a variable x, the value of x in shared memory is not changed between the first access to x by t and the commit action of t.*

To specify snapshot isolation in terms of spans within an execution, we first define the snapshot read span of a variable x read by a transaction t. Let α_i be the first read action (of any variable) in a transaction t, and let α_j be the last read of a variable x by t. Then, the *snapshot read span* of x in t is the interval $[i, j]$. If x is never read in t, its snapshot read span is the empty interval. The protected span of a variable x in snapshot isolation is defined as follows:

- If x is only read by the transaction, the protected span of x is the snapshot read span of x.
- If x is both read and written to, then the protected span is the interval $[i, j]$ where i is the index of the first access of the transaction to x, and j is the index of the commit action of t.
- If x is only written to, the protected span is defined to be the write span of x, which is the interval $[i, j]$, where i is the index of the first write access to x by t, and j is the index of the commit action of t.
- Otherwise the protected span is empty.

Snapshot isolation requires that the protected span of each variable x does not contain any commit actions by other threads that write to x. Due to space restrictions, we omit a proof of the fact that this formulation of SI in terms of protected spans, which describes how certain implementations of SI operate, implies Definition 1.

Other related relaxed transactional semantics, such as !WAR can be defined using the concepts of read and write spans, version numbers, fictitious locks and assume statements in a similar way.

Relaxing Write-After-Read Conflict Detection. This semantics specifies the executions provided by a transactional memory with relaxed detection of conflicts using the !WAR annotation as described in [39]. In this semantics, the programmer annotates certain read actions to be *relaxed reads*. The protected span of a variable x in t is defined as the interval $[i, Idx(commit(t))]$, where α_i is the first regular (not relaxed) read action or write action accessing x as part of t. A relaxed read of x in t is simply required to return the result of the last write to x. Differently from serializable semantics, in read-relaxed semantics, after a relaxed read of x by t but before t commits other transactions are allowed to commit and update the value of x. However, conflicting writes are never allowed between a write access and the corresponding commit action.

2.4 Concurrency, VCC and Modular Verification

In this section, we informally introduce the VCC mechanisms and conventions we make use of in our approach. VCC allows programmers to think C structs as objects and other base C types (int, char, double etc.,) as primitive types. VCC allows programmer to create ghost objects or declare ghost structs which can not modify the concrete program state but can be used for verification tasks. ghost structs can be C structs defined in the program or special types provided by VCC.

Each object has a unique owner at any given time. The concept of ownership is one mechanism using which access to objects shared between threads is coordinated, and invariants spanning multiple objects are stated and maintained. Objects can be annotated with any number of two-state transition invariants: first-order formulas in terms of any variables.

VCC allows the introduction of ghost variables of all types, including all C types, and more complex ones such as sets or maps. Ghost variables are (auxiliary) history variables, and they do not affect the execution of the program and values of program variables.

VCC performs modular verification in the following manner. Each function is annotated with pre- and post-conditions. Each loop is annotated with a loop invariant. Every struct may be annotated with two-state transition invariants. Code may also be annotated with assertions in VCC's first-order specification logic, in terms of the program and ghost variables in scope. VCC then verifies the code for one function at a time, using pre-post condition pairs to model function calls, loop invariants to model executions of loops, and "sequential" or "atomic" access, as described below, to model interference from concurrent threads. In "sequential" access, the thread accessing a variable obtains exclusive access to a variable aVar by obtaining ownership of aVar. Another way to coordinate access to shared variables in VCC is to mark them volatile and to require that any state transition of the program must adhere to the transition invariants of these objects.

2.5 Source-to-source Transformation for Simulating SI

In this section, we present our source-to-source transformation. We have chosen to implement our verification approach in this manner in order to expose to the users the constructs used in the encoding. Currently, this transformation is carried out manually following the procedure described in this section. In future work, we plan to provide tool support for this transformation.

The input to our transformation is C program P_{SI}. P_{SI} contains the program text and the correctness specifications. In VCC, these specifications are provided as

- an invariant for user-defined data types (structs),
- desired function pre- and post-conditions, given as boolean expressions in terms of variables in scope at function entry and exit,
- assertions, given as boolean expressions over transaction-local or shared variables

A global invariant that is to hold at the time a transaction commits can also be specified.

The output of the transformation is a program $\widetilde{P_{SI}} = Encode(P_{SI})$ that will be verified using VCC. It runs under ordinary C semantics and contains the kinds of VCC annotations described in Section 2.4. Verifying $\widetilde{P_{SI}}$ under ordinary VCC semantics is equivalent to verifying P_{SI} under transactional SI semantics.

The encoding is obtained via a high-level modelling of the operational semantics of SI. Since only the effects of succeding transactions are visible to other
transactions, the high-level model does not include mechanisms such as rolling
transactions back or aborted transactions. The transformation is described for
SI. While a simpler transformation would have sufficed for SI, the construction
we present here is necessary to generalize to other relaxed consistency models,
such as early release of read entries, programmer-defined conflict detection, e.g.
ignoring write-after-read conflicts.

$\widetilde{P_{SI}}$, the encoded version of a program P_{SI} is constructed as follows.

$\widetilde{P_{SI}}$ makes use of VCC statements of the form assume(ϕ). A thread in a
program can take a state transition by executing assume(ϕ) only at a state s
that satisfies ϕ, in which case, program control moves on to the next statement.
Interleavings disallowed by the consistency model M are expressed as a formula
ψ in terms of objects' version numbers, and statements of the form assume $\neg\psi$
are used in the encoding.

Transforming Data Types: Each primitive C type used in the original program is replaced by a "wrapper" struct type. This is necessary so we can coordinate access to these variables using mechanisms provided by VCC.

For simplicity, we present the transformation for programs that only use int
s as primitive types. In the transformation, each shared variable of type int is
replaced with a variable of type PInt as shown below:

```
PInt{
    int inMem;          int inMemVNo;
    int inTM[Trans];    int inTMVNo[Trans];
    Lock lock;
    _(invariant \unchanged(inMemVNo) ==> \unchanged(inMem))
    _(invariant \forall int t;
            \unchanged(inTMVNo[t]) ==> \unchanged(inTM[t]))
};
```

In the definition above PInt stands for struct Int*. The "wrapper" type PInt
holds the following information:

- a field inMem value that corresponds to the value of the variable in shared
  memory,
- a version number inMemVNo that gets incremented atomically each time the
  inMem field is written to,
- a (ghost) field inTM[Trans] which is a map from Tid to integers. inTM[t]
  holds the value of the transaction-local copy of the integer
- a (ghost) field inTMVNo[Trans] which is a map from Tid to integers. inTMVNo[t]
  is incremented atomically with each update of inTM[t]
- a (ghost) field lock that is used to convey to VCC when a transaction has
  exclusive access to the int variable

This wrapper type has an important invariant that indicates that a field's value
remains unchanged if its version number remains unchanged. This invariant,

along with `assume` statements involving version numbers allows us to represent constraints such as the value of a variable remaining unchanged between two accesses within a transaction.

For each global variable of type `int` in P_{SI}, the encoded program $\widetilde{P_{SI}}$ has a global variable of type `PInt`. For each global `int` variable (a) in P_{SI}, we denote the corresponding `PInt` variable in $\widetilde{P_{SI}}$ by $\tilde{a}$. When transforming the program syntactically, we use lowercase variables a to refer to variables of type `int` in the original program, and uppercase versions (A) to refer to the corresponding wrapper variable of type `PInt` in the encoded program.

To implement transactional semantics, we create an instance of the `Trans` struct per transaction.

```
Trans{
    bool holding[PInt];
    bool readSetInt[PInt];
    bool writeSetInt[PInt];
};
```

Fields of `Trans` are ghost maps. `readSetInt` and `writeSetInt` are maps that store `Int` objects read and written to by this transaction.

If there are struct declarations in the original program, `Trans` contains three maps for each field of these structs used following the same approach for `Int` s. The structs and their fields are flattened into maps.

Transforming a Transaction. The transformation is described assuming that the code has been decomposed so that each statement accesses a global variable at most once, as is typical in transactional applications. The code transformation makes use of a number of C functions whose pre- and post-conditions are presented later in this section. We only provide highlights of the transformation rules:

- Statements of the form `beginTrans`(t) remain unchanged in the transformed version. (see pre and post-conditions of this function below)
- Statements that only assign a value *val* to a local variable or a local variable to a local variable remain unchanged in the transformation.
- Statements that create a new shared variable A of type `Int` are transformed to `newPInt(A)`. This is similar for creating new shared variable of other types.
- Each statement `l = v` by transaction t that reads a global variable v into local variable l is transformed to an atomically-executed statement that performs the equivalent of the following VCC code atomically.

```
assume( \forall PInt P;
            trans->readSet[P] ==>
                trans->inTMVNo[P] == P->inMemVNo);
l = transReadInt(trans, V);
```

The specifics of `transReadInt` are described later in this section.
- Each statement `V = l` that writes the value of a local variable `l` to a shared variable `V` is transformed to atomically-executed statements that perform the equivalent of the following VCC code.

```
assume(V->\owner == t || V->\owner == NULL);
acquireLock(V,t);
assume(V->inTMVNo[t] == V->inMemVNo);
//V has not been written to since it was read by t.
transWrite(V, 1, t);
```

This code enforces (as per SI semantics) if V is in the transaction's read set and write set, then V have not changed since a snapshot was taken.

- Each statement commitTrans(t, inv), is transformed to the following atomically-executed sequence of statements:

```
assume( \forall PInt P;
          t->writeSetInt[P] ==>
              P->inTMVNo == P->inMemVNo + 1);
commitTrans(t);
assert(inv);
```

- For each statement endTrans(t), in the encoded version, we replace the statement with endAndCleanTrans(t).
- Each statement assert(p), where p is a boolean expression in terms of local variables, is left as is in the encoded version. Each boolean expression e involved in a loop invariant, and function pre- and post-condition is transformed to a boolean expression E, where each appearance of a global variable v is replaced with a reference to the transaction-local copy v->inTM[t].

The functions used in the encoded program are listed below together with their pre-conditions and post-conditions:

- beginTrans(t) creates a Trans structure for thread t. This function has no pre-condition and has the post-condition that the read and write sets of t and the set of variables t has exclusive ownership of are empty, i.e.,

```
\forall PInt P; !t->readSetInt[P] &&
              !t->writeSetInt[P] && !t->holding[P]
```

- acquireLock(V, t) is used to obtain exclusive access to V by transaction t. This is accomplished by using the fictitious (ghost) lock V->lock. Since we are verifying only succeeding executions of transactions (and assuming that aborted transactions have no visible effect), we call acquireLock in the encoded program only at a state where it will successfully complete. Thus, this function has the pre-condition that the global variable V has no owner or is owned by t, and the post-condition that the owner of V is the transaction t. The post-condition of acquireLock(V,t) also requires that t->holding[V] be true.
- transRelaxedRead(V,t) reads V in a transaction t. This function does not require V to be owned by t and has the post-condition that

```
t->readSetInt[V] == true &&
V->inTM[t] == V->inMEM &&
V->inTMVMo[t] == V->inMEMVNo
```

- `newPInt(V)` is used to create a new PInt variable. This function has the post-condition that `V->owner` is `t`. All version numbers associated with `V` are initialized to 0.
- `transWrite(V, l,t)` writes the value of the local variable `l` to the `inMem` field of `V` and atomically increments `v->inTMVNo[t]`. If `V` has been read previously by `t`, then this function requires that `V`'s version number has not changed since. These are expressed by the pre-condition

```
V->\owner == t && V->inMemVNo == V->inTMVNo[t]
```

and the post-condition

```
t->writeSetInt[V] == true &&
t->inTM[t] == l &&
t->inTMVNo[t] == old(t->inTMVNo[t]) + 1
```

- `commitTrans(t)` commits a transaction by writing the updates performed by the transaction into the memory. Note that a valid execution can have only local statements (that only effect local state) after `commitTrans(t)` statement until it ends the transaction. This function is better explained by the following pseudocode

```
_(atomic t {
      \foreach PInt P;
          if (ptrans->writeSetInt[P]) {
              P->inMEM = P->inTM[t];
              P->verNoInMEM = P->verNoInTM[t];
          }
})
```

Since VCC currently does not support loops inside `atomic` statements, the state update corresponding to the loop above is expressed as the function post-condition for `commitTrans` and the atomicity of the commit is accomplished using fictitious locks for objects for which `holding` is true.
- `endAndCleanTrans(t)` ends a transaction `t` by releasing the locks that the transaction holds, cleaning its read and write sets. It has the post-condition that `t` releases ownership of all objects it owns, and the `readSetInt`, `writesSetInt`, and `holding` are all reset to maps corresponding to empty sets.

The following theorem states the soundness of our verification approach.

Theorem 1 (Soundness). *Let P_{SI} be a transactional program and $\widetilde{P_{SI}}$ be the augmented program obtained from P_{SI} as described above. Then $\widetilde{P_{SI}}$ satisfies its specifications (assertions, invariants, function pre- and post-conditions) if and only if P_{SI} satisfies its specifications.*

It follows from this theorem that users can start with the program P, provide the desired specifications, and additional proof annotations. Then, to verify properties of P_{SI}, users can follow the source-to-source transformation approach described in this section and obtain $\widetilde{P_{SI}}$. Verifying the transformed specifications with the transformed annotations on $\widetilde{P_{SI}}$ is equivalent to verifying the specifications of P_{SI}, by the soundness theorem.

The source-to-source code transformation preserves the thread, function, and object structure of the original program. The newly-introduced objects representing transactions are local to each thread or transaction. All additional invariants introduced are per-object. There is no inlining of code from other, possibly interfering transactions, and the size of the transformed code is linear in the size of the original code.

2.6   Verifying Transformed Program with VCC

In this part, we explain how verification of the transformed program is performed on the grid example. For the grid, user provides the program invariant both as the pre-condition and post-condition of findRoute and specifications between lines 13-16 as post-condition for the original program.

Generally, program pre- and post-conditions are not enough for verification and the user may need extra ghost variables or annotations. Especially for the loops or other code blocks enclosed with curly parentheses, user should provide conditions about user defined shared or local objects that are satisfied throughout the code block and helps verification of the post-conditions. Since findRoute does not contain such code blocks. Hence, no extra annotation is needed.

Moreover, the user may need to provide extra annotations although the function does not contain any such code blocks. These annotations reflect the correctness intuition of the program. To our experience with SI, user should provide a condition that holds right after end of the read phase (after snapshot has been taken) such that this condition is preserved although other transactions interfere and modify data. In the grid example, assertions on lines 6,7 reflect the correctness intuition. onePath is a valid and connecting path for localGrid and grid when the snapshot was taken. It continues to hold during execution although other transactions interfere and modify grid. This information is enough for VCC to verify post-conditions of findRoute: Since onePath is a valid and connecting path on the localGrid and points on the onePath stays the same in grid, onePath becomes a valid and connecting path after call to addGridPathIfOK.

Note that the assertions added for verification on lines 6,7 do not include variables, fields or calls to functions introduced by the transformation. Therefore, user does not need any knowledge about transformation and these extra program parts. This is the case we encountered during the verification of examples. Correctness intuition based on local and shared user variables are enough for verification.

If the initial correctness intuition is not enough for verification for function post-conditions, user may come up with tighter and stricter annotations for verification of assertions or program post-conditions until the function is verified.

2.7   Experimental Demonstration

We applied our technique to the Genome, Labyrinth and Self-Organizing Map benchmarks as implemented in [39] and a StringBuffer pool example that we wrote ourselves. These examples have pre-annotated transactional code blocks which can be run under relaxed transactional semantics. We made precise and formally verified the correctness arguments for these implementations and for the StringBuffer example. Our work makes formal the correctness arguments in the work of Titos et al. [39] about the correctness of the transactions in the benchmarks and provides evidence that the intuitive reasoning about why programs can function correctly under TM relaxations can be expressed and verified systematically.

For each benchmark, we wrote partial specifications and statically verified that they hold for transactional code running with the regarding relaxed consistency semantics, starting from a VCC verification of the specifications on a sequential interpretation of the benchmark.

```
struct node_t { int key; node_t* next; ghost Set reach;}
 1   bool list_insert(list_t *listPtr,
 2                    node_t *node) {
 3     node_t *prev, *curr = listPtr->head;
 4
 5     do {
 6       prev = curr;
 7       curr = curr->next;
 8     } while (curr != NULL
 9             && key > curr->key);
10     _(invariant loopInv(prev, curr, head, node))
11     // loopInv(prev, curr, head, node) ==
12     //        prevKey < key && prevKey < curKey
13     //        && prev reachable from head
14     //        && curr reachable from head
15
16     // assert(prev->next == curr);
17     node->next = curr;
18     prev->next = node;
19     return true; // key was not present
20   }
```

Fig. 2. The insertion operation of a sorted linked list

- **Genome:** Figure 2 shows the pseudocode for a linked list implementation used in the Genome benchmark [10]. The code in the figure has been simplified for ease of presentation. In the part of this benchmark where relaxed consistency is used, concurrent transactions insert into a shared linked list. Transactions run under programmer-defined conflict detection, where write-after-read conflicts are ignored (!WAR), i.e., do not cause transactions to abort.

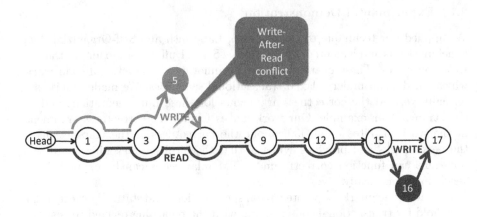

Fig. 3. Sorted linked list and a write-after-read conflict

Figure 3 illustrates how concurrent insertions experience write-after-read (!WAR) conflicts, and how, intuitively, it would be correct implementation to let an insertion commit even though it experiences a WAR conflict. Following [39], the body of list_insert is marked with the !WAR annotation to indicate that write-after-read conflicts should be ignored.

We verify that the linked list maintains two invariants under interference : (i) its nodes are in ascending order and (ii) linked list is not circular. We further verify that the addNode(newNode) Function satisfies the post-condition that the node it adds (newNode) is reachable from the head of the linked list. The read (traversal) phase of the addNode function finds a node prev in the list after which newNode is to be inserted. The assertion that prev is reachable from the head of the list and that the appropriate place for newNode to be inserted is right after prev is preserved despite interference caused by ignoring write-after-read conflicts.

- **SOM:** In this benchmark, concurrent transactions run the learning phase of the machine learning algorithm SOM. SOM contains a shared grid of which nodes are n-dimensional vectors. The learning function solve takes an n-dimensional vector v and the grid as input, calculates the Euclidean distance of v to each grid nodes, picks the closest one v' and moves nodes in a neighbourhood of v' closer to v.

- **StringBuffer** In this example, a pool of StringBuffer objects are implemented as a collection. Transactions to allocate or free a string buffer perform relaxed read on the shared collection. When a transaction finds a suitable object and wants to allocate it, it can commit ignoring other possible write operations (that allocate or free a string buffer object) on the collection. The example is written using programmer-defined conflict detection, in particular, using !WAR semantics. We verified that a data structure invariant and post-conditions of the Allocate and Free functions are satisfied.

- **Labyrinth:** This example and its verification process was described earlier in the section.

We have demonstrated the applicability of our verification approach on these examples that were written without assuming serializability and satisfied their specifications despite this. In each of these examples, our encoding facilitates thread- and procedure-modular correctness proofs that hold for an arbitrary number of threads. Programmer annotations on encoded program makes no reference to auxiliary encoding variables. Our experience with the SI and !WAR relaxed consistency models, which are very similar to other relaxed consistency models described earlier leads us to believe that our static verification technique is a useful tool for a programmer building applications in these settings.

2.8 Related Work

Relaxed Conflict Detection. Relaxed conflict detection has been devised to improve concurrent performance by reducing the number of aborted transactions. Titos et al. [39] introduce and investigate conflict-defined blocks and language construct to realize custom conflict definition. Our work builds on this work, and provides a formal reasoning and verification method for such programs. As we have shown with SI and !WAR, we believe that our method can easily be adapted to support other relaxed conflict detection schemes.

Enforcing (conflict) Serializability, Detecting Write-Skew Anomalies. There is a large body of research on verifying or ensuring conflict or view serializability of transactions even while the transactional platform is carrying out relaxed conflict detection [15,7,5,9,3,18]. In this work, we enable programmers to verify properties of transactional code on SI even when executions may not be serializable. This allows the user to prove the correctness of and use transactional code that allows more concurrency.

Linearizability. One way to allow low-level conflicts while preserving application-level guarantees is to use linearizability as the correctness criterion [26]. To prove linearizability of a transactional program P running under SI, one could use the encoded program we construct, $\widehat{P}$ as the starting point in a linearizability or other abstraction/refinement proof. In this work, we have chosen not to do so for two reasons. First, abstract specifications with respect to which an entire program is linearizable may not exist or may be hard to write. Second, programmers would like to verify partial specifications such as assertions into their program in terms of the concrete program variables in scope. Verifying linearizability does not help the programmer with this task.

Encodings, Source-to-Source Transformations. As a mechanism for transforming a problem into one for which there exist efficient verification tools, source-to-source code transformations are widely-used in the programming languages and software verification communities. The work along these lines that is closest to ours in spirit involves verifying properties of programs running under weak memory models by transforming them into programs that run under sequential consistency semantics [6,4]. Our work also makes use of a source-to-source translation in order to transform the problem of verifying a transactional program running under SI to a generic C program that can be verified using VCC. Our transformation results in only a linear increase in code size. While we perform an encoding for representing different semantics from these studies, our encoding itself has some features that distinguish it from encodings devised for different verification purposes. During the transformation, the thread, object and procedure structure of the original program is preserved. No inlining of extra code modeling interference from other transactions is involved. We also have the practically important advantage that while verifying his code under SI, the user does not have to provide extra annotations in terms of the extra auxiliary variables in the encoded program.

3   Dynamic Verification for Transactional Programs

While there has been some preliminary work on temporal specifications for programs that use optimistic concurrency, including transactional programs [35,34], the vast majority of research on dynamic verification techniques for transactional programs has focused on detecting races. As with ordinary concurrent programs, race conditions are undesirable for two reasons. First, they result in non-deterministic outcomes for read accesses even for a given fixed execution and thread interleaving. Second, race conditions are symptomatic of higher-level programming errors, such as a certain concurrency discipline not being followed or the intended atomicity not being accomplished by the program.

As with most concurrent programming settings, there is much discussion on the definition of race conditions for transactional programs. In this section, we first provide an overview of various definitions of race conditions that are the most interesting from the point of view of an application programmer. We then highlight two race detection tools for transactional programs from the literature: the Goldilocks tool for precisely detecting races in transactional Java programs, and the T-Rex tool for dynamic detection of potentially-harmful pairs of transactional and non-transactional conflicting accesses to a shared variable.

One category of race detection approaches are based on a precise definition of a happens-before relationship between actions in a transactional program. In such approaches, synchronization primitives in the transactional program are modeled in the same way as the programming language being used so that the definition of the happens-before relation is backwards compatible. There are several different ways of defining the happens-before relationship between software transactions in the literature [23,20,22,25,24]. Different definitions of happens before make different choices on whether two transactions are considered to synchronize with each other, usually based on what variables are accessed within the transactions.

Some definitions of the happens-before relationship in the literature are obtained by using an analogy to lock-protected programs. For instance, in the *Single Global Lock Atomicity* (SGLA) semantics [30], the happens-before relationship is defined as if all transactionally-executed code blocks are protected by the same, single global lock. This definition naturally integrates the happens-before relationship of the underlying programming language and the happens-before relationsips induced by the TM platform. On transactional platforms that implement this semantics, Dalesandro et al. [13] call a program *transactional data race free* (TDRF) if any two accesses to the same variable one of which is a write are ordered by the happens before relationship as defined in SGLA.

A race detection algorithm can either be explicitly based on a choice of a particular definition of a happens-before relationship in a transactional execution, or can formulate undesirable intereference between accesses without making explicit the underlying happens-before model. The former approach has the advantage of precision, even when the race detection algorithm makes the choice to allow false positives or negatives, since what exactly constitutes a false warning is known. The latter approach may be more applicable for use in conjunction with a wider variety of TM implementations. Goldilocks [16] is an example of the former category of approaches while T-Rex [28] is an example of the latter category.

In the transaction semantics used in Goldilocks, pairs of shared variable accesses where both accesses take place within the same transaction are considered to be race-free. A linearization of the projection of the happens-before ordering onto the commit actions corresponds to the atomic order of transactions as defined in [20]. Naturally, pairs of accesses executed transactionally are considered race free, reflecting the fact that these accesses are managed by the TM implementation and the programmer and the dynamic race checker should not be concerned with them.

3.1 Transaction-Aware, Precise Race Detection

The Goldilocks runtime is precise about when it throws DataRaceException in the presence of software transactions that manage a portion of the shared data. This issue brings about two challenges. First, for portions of the execution not contained in transactions, transactions become yet another synchronization primitive to be taken into account. Second, it is desirable to trust the correctness of a TM implementation and to avoid the cost of checking at runtime that it performs proper synchronization for its implementation variables and for accesses performed transactionally.

Goldilocks builds upon the Java Memory Model, which does not specify which happens-before edges (must) arise due to transactions and atomic code blocks. As observed in [21], there is not yet a consensus about the interaction between the semantics of transactions and the Java Memory Model. Such a specification serves as an interface between the implementers and users of TM. The TM implementer must guarantee, among other things, at least the existence of the required synchronization edges using Java language or lower-level primitives. The actual implementation (e.g. [27]) may actually provide more synchronization than required.

Goldilocks is based on the following interpretation of strongly-atomic transactions. All transactions, along with other synchronization operations are part of the global *synchronization order* of the Java memory model. Given two transactions Tx1 and Tx2, Goldilocks requires that Tx1 happens-before Tx2 if and only if there exists a shared variable x that Tx1 writes and Tx2 reads. This does not include variables involved in the TM implementation but not visible to the programmer. The actual transaction manager may be performing stronger synchronization and may be using some of the same locks and/or volatile variables as the application program, but, proper synchronization of the application program should not rely on this. The Goldilocks approach is able to accomodate other, similar definitions of when a transaction happens-before another. For instance, it can handle the case where Tx1 happens before Tx2 if and only if there is a variable x that Tx1 reads or writes and Tx2 reads or writes.

To detect races at runtime, Goldilocks requires a transaction manager to provide or make possible for the runtime to collect the following information for each transaction:

- the shared variables read by the transaction
- the shared variables written by the transaction
- the place of commit point of the transaction in the global synchronization order

Goldilocks race-aware runtime makes use of the implementation of transactional (atomic) blocks via source-to-source translation of Hindman et. al. [27]. In this implementation, all shared variable reads and writes that are part of a transaction come after the first lock acquire associated with the transaction, and they come before the first lock release, which also constitutes the commit point of the transaction. Goldilocks extends the lockset update rules for the base precise race detection algorithm for Java in order to handle transactions. The nature of the lockset rules and the implementation made it possible to integrate this feature without significant restructuring. In [16], we demonstrate this way of handling transactions in our runtime on a hand-coded transactional data structure.

3.2   Detecting Potential Races in Transactional Programs

Dynamic race detection algorithms that precisely check a happens-before relationship handle many styles of synchronization. This often results in high computational overhead for both transactional and non-transactional programs. A happens-before-based algorithm needs to keep track of and synchronize access to a large amount of analysis metadata in order to precisely capture the execution and synchronization history. One other possible undesirable feature of such algorithms is that actual execution order of memory accesses and source program order may not co-incide because hardware and compiler instruction re-ordering may break this correspondence. Compiler optimizations such as the elimination of certain unnecessary accesses or, say, empty transactions may have significant consequences regarding the happens-before relationship. While the source program appears to have certain happens-before relationships, the actual execution might not. Since a programmer would ideally like to base correctness reasoning about the program on the program source, a discrepancy between source code and execution happens-before relationships can be dangerous.

While a runtime such as Goldilocks must precisely keep track of the happens-before relationships observed in an execution, for a debugging tool, this precision, even ignoring the computational cost, may not be desirable. A programmer might want to know about potential race conditions in executions that are similar to the one observed, even if the observed execution itself does not experience a race condition. Race detectors such as ones based on Eraser [32] for non-transactional programs, or the T-Rex [28] race detection tool for transactional programs instead track adherence to a certain concurrency discipline.

For transactional programs, race detection approaches based on a happens-before relationship necessarily make strong assumptions about TM implementations. For instance, since privatization and publication, based on program source code and a happens-before relationship, are expected to be safe patterns. However, in practice, especially for software TM implementations, for performance reasons, privatization and publication may not be safely supported [28]. For software TM implementations that do not support safe privatization and publication, speculative reads, buffered writes or the abort mechanism in the TM implementation may result in data races introduced by the TM implementation itself [28]. Kestor et al. [28] provide examples of programs in which updates can be lost or zombie transactions may have harmful effects on other transactions – effects that are not visible when only the source code of the transactional program and a precise happens-before relationship based on read and write-sets of succesful transactions are considered. As a result, race detection based on the happens-before relationship may not be the most appropriate practical approach for debugging transactional programs. Such programs may experience data corruption or even program crashes even if they appear to be free of races judging by a happens-before relationship and the program source code. Researchers have investigated concurrent programming disciplines to avoid undesirable interactions between non-transactional and transactional accesses [1,2]. These disciplines may be enforced by a compiler, a runtime, or by requiring the programmer's collaboration by notifying the compiler or runtime of transitions of variables between transactional and non-transactional access modes.

Instead, in T-Rex [28], Kestor et al. employ a correctness criterion that is less dependent on particular TM implementations, and, in particular, does not rely for correctness on a safe implementation of privatization and publication idioms. T-Rex defines a transactional data race so that in a correctly synchronized program, for a pair of accesses to the same shared variable at least one of which is a write, the following hold.

- Either both accesses take place within transactions, or
- the two accesses are separated by a global (i.e., involving all threads) synchronization operation such as a barrier or thread fork or join, and
- it is not the case that one of the accesses takes place in a fragment of the execution during which there is only one live thread

This definition of transactional data race is defined based on the set of accesses observed during an execution, and, in many ways, is independent of the particular interleaving of actions. Similar to data race detectors based on lock-set algorithms, this definition does not need to witness a concurrent access to a shared memory location in particular program execution to report a potential race [33]. Consider a program that fails to protect a particular data access by enclosing it within a transaction. Race detection tools that track the precise happens-before relationship would signal an error only in some executions of this program, whereas our algorithm would signal a transactional data race in all executions of this program.

Using this pragmatic definition of correct synchronization, T-Rex is able to both be computationally efficient and detect noteworthy violations of the correctness criterion above in STAMP benchmarks.

4 Conclusion

The tools and techniques described in this chapter represent important but preliminary steps towards building software engineering and verification tools for programs that make use of transactional memory. Mature software engineering tools for transactional programs will need to be developed and integrated into the program authoring, compilation, testing and debugging toolchain as TM finds wider use. As language primitives implemented using TM become widespread, it is expected that semantics of TM-supported programming primitives will find their way into language and memory-model specifications.

References

1. Abadi, M., Birrell, A., Harris, T., Isard, M.: Semantics of transactional memory and automatic mutual exclusion. SIGPLAN Not. 43(1), 63–74 (2008)
2. Abadi, M., Harris, T., Moore, K.F.: A model of dynamic separation for transactional memory. In: van Breugel, F., Chechik, M. (eds.) CONCUR 2008. LNCS, vol. 5201, pp. 6–20. Springer, Heidelberg (2008)
3. Adya, A.: Weak consistency: a generalized theory and optimistic implementations for distributed transactions. PhD thesis, AAI0800775 (1999)
4. Alglave, J., Kroening, D., Nimal, V., Tautschnig, M.: Software Verification for Weak Memory via Program Transformation. In: Felleisen, M., Gardner, P. (eds.) Programming Languages and Systems. LNCS, vol. 7792, pp. 512–532. Springer, Heidelberg (2013)
5. Alomari, M., Fekete, A., Röhm, U.: A robust technique to ensure serializable executions with snapshot isolation dbms. In: Proceedings of the 2009 IEEE International Conference on Data Engineering, ICDE 2009, pp. 341–352. IEEE Computer Society, Washington, DC (2009)
6. Atig, M.F., Bouajjani, A., Parlato, G.: Getting rid of store-buffers in TSO analysis. In: Gopalakrishnan, G., Qadeer, S. (eds.) CAV 2011. LNCS, vol. 6806, pp. 99–115. Springer, Heidelberg (2011)
7. Attiya, H., Ramalingam, G., Rinetzky, N.: Sequential verification of serializability. SIGPLAN Not 45, 31–42 (2010)

8. Barnett, M., Leino, K.R.M., Schulte, W.: The Spec# Programming System: An Overview. In: Barthe, G., Burdy, L., Huisman, M., Lanet, J.-L., Muntean, T. (eds.) CASSIS 2004. LNCS, vol. 3362, pp. 49–69. Springer, Heidelberg (2005)

9. Cahill, M.J., Röhm, U., Fekete, A.D.: Serializable isolation for snapshot databases. In: Proceedings of the 2008 ACM SIGMOD International Conference on Management of Data, SIGMOD 2008, pp. 729–738. ACM, New York (2008)

10. Minh, C.C., Chung, J.W., Kozyrakis, C., Olukotun, K.: STAMP: Stanford transactional applications for multi-processing. In: Proc. of the IEEE International Symposium on Workload Characterization, IISWC 2008 (September 2008)

11. Cooper, B.F., Ramakrishnan, R., Srivastava, U., Silberstein, A., Bohannon, P., Jacobsen, H.-A., Puz, N., Weaver, D., Yerneni, R.: Pnuts: Yahoo!'s hosted data serving platform. Proceedings of the VLDB Endowment 1(2), 1277–1288 (2008)

12. Dahlweid, M., Moskal, M., Santen, T., Tobies, S., Schulte, W.: Vcc: Contract-based modular verification of concurrent c. In: ICSE-Companion 2009, pp. 429–430 (May 2009)

13. Dalessandro, L., Scott, M.L., Spear, M.F.: Transactions as the Foundation of a Memory Consistency Model. In: Lynch, N.A., Shvartsman, A.A. (eds.) DISC 2010. LNCS, vol. 6343, pp. 20–34. Springer, Heidelberg (2010)

14. Daudjee, K., Salem, K.: Lazy database replication with snapshot isolation. In: Proceedings of the 32nd International Conference on Very Large Data Bases, pp. 715–726. VLDB Endowment (2006)

15. Dias, R.J., Distefano, D., Seco, J.C., Lourenço, J.M.: Verification of Snapshot Isolation in Transactional Memory Java Programs. In: Noble, J. (ed.) ECOOP 2012. LNCS, vol. 7313, pp. 640–664. Springer, Heidelberg (2012)

16. Elmas, T., Qadeer, S., Tasiran, S.: Goldilocks: a race and transaction-aware java runtime. In: PLDI 2007: Proc. of the 2007 ACM SIGPLAN Conference on Programming Language Design and Implementation, pp. 245–255. ACM, New York (2007)

17. Fähndrich, M.: Static Verification for Code Contracts. In: Cousot, R., Martel, M. (eds.) SAS 2010. LNCS, vol. 6337, pp. 2–5. Springer, Heidelberg (2010)

18. Fekete, A., Liarokapis, D., O'Neil, E., O'Neil, P., Shasha, D.: Making snapshot isolation serializable. ACM Transactions on Database Systems (TODS) 30(2), 492–528 (2005)

19. Flanagan, C., Leino, K.R.M., Lillibridge, M., Nelson, G., Saxe, J.B., Stata, R.: Extended static checking for Java. In: PLDI 2002, pp. 234–245. ACM Press, New York (2002)

20. Grossman, D., Manson, J., Pugh, W.: What do high-level memory models mean for transactions? In: MSPC 2006: Proc. of the 2006 Workshop on Memory System Performance and Correctness, pp. 62–69. ACM Press, New York (2006)

21. Grossman, D., Manson, J., Pugh, W.: What do high-level memory models mean for transactions? In: Proceedings of the 2006 Workshop on Memory System Performance and Correctness, MSPC 2006, pp. 62–69. ACM, New York (2006)

22. Harris, T., Fraser, K.: Language support for lightweight transactions. In: OOPSLA 2003: Proc. of the 18th Annual ACM SIGPLAN Conference on Object-Oriented Programing, Systems, Languages, and Applications, pp. 388–402. ACM Press, New York (2003)

23. Harris, T., Marlow, S., Peyton-Jones, S., Herlihy, M.: Composable memory transactions. In: PPoPP 2005: Proc. of the Tenth ACM SIGPLAN Symposium on Principles and Practice of Parallel Programming, pp. 48–60. ACM Press, New York (2005)

24. Herlihy, M.: SXM1.1: Software transactional memory package for c#. Tech. rep., Brown University & Microsoft Research (May 2005)
25. Herlihy, M., Moss, J.E.B.: Transactional memory: Architectural support for lock-free data structures. In: Proc. of the Twentieth Annual International Symposium on Computer Architecture (1993)
26. Herlihy, M.P., Wing, J.M.: Linearizability: a correctness condition for concurrent objects. ACM Trans. Program. Lang. Syst. 12(3), 463–492 (1990)
27. Hindman, B., Grossman, D.: Atomicity via source-to-source translation. In: Proceedings of the 2006 Workshop on Memory System Performance and Correctness, MSPC 2006, pp. 82–91. ACM, New York (2006)
28. Kestor, G., Unsal, O.S., Cristal, A., Tasiran, S.: T-rex: A dynamic race detection tool for c/c++ transactional memory applications. In: Proceedings of the Ninth European Conference on Computer Systems, EuroSys 2014, pp. 20:1–20:12. ACM, New York (2014)
29. Kuru, I., Ozkan, B.K., Mutluergil, S.O., Tasiran, S., Elmas, T., Cohen, E.: Verifying programs under snapshot isolation and similar relaxed consistency models. In: Workshop on Transactional Computing, TRANSACT (2014)
30. Menon, V., Balensiefer, S., Shpeisman, T., Adl-Tabatabai, A.-R., Hudson, R.L., Saha, B., Welc, A.: Practical weak-atomicity semantics for java stm. In: Proceedings of the Twentieth Annual Symposium on Parallelism in Algorithms and Architectures, SPAA 2008, pp. 314–325. ACM, New York (2008)
31. Papadimitriou, C.: The theory of database concurrency control. Computer Science Press (1986)
32. Savage, S., Burrows, M., Nelson, G., Sobalvarro, P., Anderson, T.: Eraser: a dynamic data race detector for multithreaded programs. ACM Trans. Comput. Syst. 15(4), 391–411 (1997)
33. Savage, S., Burrows, M., Nelson, G., Sobalvarro, P., Anderson, T.: Eraser: A dynamic data race detector for multithreaded programs. ACM Trans. Comput. Syst. 15(4), 391–411 (1997)
34. Sezgin, A., Tasiran, S., Muslu, K., Qadeer, S.: Run-time verification of optimistic concurrency. In: Barringer, H., Falcone, Y., Finkbeiner, B., Havelund, K., Lee, I., Pace, G., Roşu, G., Sokolsky, O., Tillmann, N. (eds.) RV 2010. LNCS, vol. 6418, pp. 384–398. Springer, Heidelberg (2010)
35. Sezgin, A., Tasiran, S., Qadeer, S.: Tressa: Claiming the future. In: Leavens, G.T., O'Hearn, P., Rajamani, S.K. (eds.) VSTTE 2010. LNCS, vol. 6217, pp. 25–39. Springer, Heidelberg (2010)
36. Skare, T., Kozyrakis, C.: Early release: Friend or foe?. In: Workshop on Transactional Memory Workloads (June 2006)
37. Sovran, Y., Power, R., Aguilera, M.K., Li, J.: Transactional storage for geo-replicated systems. In: Proceedings of the Twenty-Third ACM Symposium on Operating Systems Principles, pp. 385–400. ACM (2011)
38. Terry, D.B., Theimer, M.M., Petersen, K., Demers, A.J., Spreitzer, M.J., Hauser, C.H.: Managing update conflicts in bayou, a weakly connected replicated storage system. ACM SIGOPS Operating Systems Review 29(5), 172–182 (1995)
39. Titos, R., Acacio, M.E., García, J.M., Harris, T., Cristal, A., Unsal, O., Valero, M.: Hardware transactional memory with software-defined conflicts. In: High-Performance and Embedded Architectures and Compilation (HiPEAC 2012) (January 2012)

Distributed Transactional Memory

Introduction to Transactional Replication

Tadeusz Kobus, Maciej Kokociński, and Paweł T. Wojciechowski

Institute of Computing Science, Poznan University of Technology
Poznań, Poland
{Tadeusz.Kobus,Maciej.Kokocinski,
Pawel.T.Wojciechowski}@cs.put.edu.pl

Abstract. Transactional replication is a new enabling technology for service replication. Service replication means that a service runs on a group of processes (service replicas) that work together to execute requests issued by external clients. The characteristic feature of transactional replication is that client requests can be processed on a single replica concurrently as atomic transactions that can read or modify local state. Our goal is to provide an introduction to the transactional replication algorithms. We begin by discussing state machine replication and then present several algorithms that provide full transactional semantics such as deferred update replication and many variants of thereof. Finally, we compare their properties and performance as well as show their strong and weak points.

1 Introduction

Replication is a popular method to increase service reliability and accessibility. It means deployment of a service on several interconnected server machines, each of which may fail independently, and coordination of the service replicas, so that each replica maintains a consistent state view despite failures of communication links or crashes of other replicas. The state is kept by every replica in its local store (the main memory and, optionally, nonvolatile memory).

In this chapter, we survey distributed algorithms that can be used for full replication of services with strong consistency guarantees, without resorting to any central coordinator. An example application is a geo-replicated storage system that ensures strong consistency among all service replicas. Distribution and replication can improve locality and availability of a service by, respectively, moving data closer to the users and processing many requests in parallel. The common feature of the presented algorithms is that they all rely on the fault-tolerant total order (atomic) broadcast primitive (defined in Section 3) that is used to make the state updates consistent among all the replicas despite any crashes. We begin with a simple algorithm of this sort that implements the classical replication scheme relying on atomic broadcast, called *state machine replication (SMR)* [34]. In this approach, a stream of client requests is agreed among all service replicas (that must be deterministic state machines) and processed sequentially by each replica.

Next, we describe example replication algorithms that fall into a different category which we call *transactional replication (TR)* [37]. They can be used to implement a replicated storage system which is then used by replicated services (processes) to process multiple client requests as concurrent transactions. Transactions can read or modify local state and they are executed atomically—completely and successfully or not

R. Guerraoui and P. Romano (Eds.): Transactional Memory, LNCS 8913, pp. 309–340, 2015.

at all, much like in transactional memory systems, but the local state is replicated and kept consistent on many servers. We only focus on one TR scheme relying on atomic broadcast, which is called *deferred update replication (DUR)* [7], and present several algorithms that optimize DUR in various ways. In this approach, a client request can be processed optimistically by any one replica using an atomic transaction, in parallel with other requests (transactions) processed on the same or other replicas. Any state updates are deferred and consistently applied on all replicas on transaction commit.

In the TR systems that provide transactional memory and support full transactional semantics, many transactions can be executed on a single node in parallel. They can perform arbitrary operations (with possible restrictions, such as the use of irrevocable operations) and may also commit or abort (and possibly restart) on demand. On the other hand, pure SMR does not offer full transactional semantics—on each node there is only one transaction executed at a time (spawned for processing a client request) that is only allowed to commit and its code must be deterministic. However, we largely ignore the semantic differences and give, in Section 3, a common specification of the SMR and TR schemes in terms of properties describing the inter-replica and client-replica interactions.

In the chapter, we discuss the following replication algorithms:

1. SMR – state machine replication based on total order broadcast; the algorithm resembles the original idea proposed in [17,33] but was modified to optimize the read-only transactions, as in [29];
2. DUR – deferred update replication that follows the idea presented in [7];
3. MvDUR – deferred update replication with multiversioning; it extends the previous algorithm with an optimization technique that dates back to first database systems [4];
4. HTR – a hybrid state-machine-based and deferred-update replication scheme proposed in [14], which seamlessly combines SMR and DUR with multiversioning into one replication scheme;
5. Postgres-R – an algorithm proposed in [12] that aims at improving DUR by reducing the amount of data transmitted via a network;
6. EDUR – executive deferred update replication proposed in [15], which uses a leader of the broadcast protocol to streamline transaction certification.

Interestingly, replication schemes designed for database systems often are not suitable for replication of services (processes) or software transactional memory (see e.g., [30,25]). This is because typical workloads in TR systems are much different than those in SQL database systems, in which transactions are relatively long, require time-consuming optimizations of queries, and perform costly I/O operations. On the contrary, transactions performed by a replicated service are usually very short (take a fraction of a millisecond to execute) and access few shared objects. The crucial observation here is that, usually, the transaction execution times are much shorter than the latency caused by the network communication. Hence, the main design aspect of TR systems is minimizing the inter-replica synchronization footprint, both in terms of the communication steps as well as the amount of data that need to be communicated between replicas.

We aim our chapter at developers of replication frameworks and all those who would like to learn about transactional replication. We therefore explain the algorithms and their properties in detail. Each algorithm is presented by giving its pseudocode. We then compare the algorithms taking into account their semantics, the overhead due to concurrency control and transaction certification, the number of communication steps, the number and volume of network transmissions, and the expected performace under different workload types.

The structure of the chapter is as follows. We begin by defining the system model and transactional replication properties in Section 2 and discuss problems that face the designers of such systems in Section 3. Then, we present the SMR algorithm in Section 4. Next, we describe DUR in Section 5 and various ways this scheme can be optimized (the MvDUR, HTR, Postgres-R, and EDUR algorithms) in Sections 6–9. Then, we compare the presented algorithms in Section 10, and finally conclude and give references to related work in Section 11.

2   System Model and Properties

In this section, we describe the system model and properties. A *replicated process* $P = \{P_1, ..., P_n\}$ consists of n service processes (replicas) P_i $(i = 1..n)$ running on independent machines (nodes) connected via a network. Each process P_i has access to its own volatile memory and stable storage; the combined content of the two constitutes *local state*. $S = \{S_1, ..., S_n\}$ is a *replicated state*, where S_i is a local state of process P_i $(i = 1..n)$. A transaction executed by process P_i can only access objects that belong to local state S_i.

We assume a crash-recovery failure model in which processes may crash independently and later on recover and rejoin computation. Processes can recover its local state either from stable storage or other replicas (as in e.g. JPaxos [16]). However, the recovery algorithms are beyond the scope of this chapter. A process is said to be *up* if it correctly executes its program. Upon crash, a process fails by ceasing communication with any other processes and becomes a *down* process. It can rejoin distributed computation upon a recovery event which requires executing a recovery procedure. A process is said to be *unstable* if it crashes and recovers infinitely many times. A process is *correct* if it is eventually permanently up (there is a time after which it never crashes). Otherwise, it is *faulty*, i.e. unstable or eventually permanently down (there is a time when it crashes and later never recovers).

Our replication algorithms are aimed at distributed asynchronous systems which can be characterized as follows. There is no central coordinator and the processes communicate solely by exchanging messages using bidirectional *fair-loss links* [2]. For simplicity, however, all presented algorithms use *perfect links* (no messages are lost) since they can be easily implemented on top of fair-loss links (see e.g., [5]). Messages may be lost and no upper bound on message transmission is known. The failure pattern of messages is independent from the one of processes. No assumption is also made on the relative computation speeds of the processes. However, we assume availability of a failure detector Ω [6], which is the weakest failure detector capable of solving consensus in a distributed asynchronous system in which processes or communication links may fail.

In addition to service processes we consider an unspecified number of external client processes. We assume that the clients are independent and they do not communicate

Properties of a replicated process P:

R1: *Validity:* If a process P_j modifies object o with v during state update, then $w(o^k)v$ was executed by some process P_i ($i = j$ or $i \neq j$) as part of some transaction that commits.

R2: *Termination:* On commit of a transaction T, every correct process P_i eventually applies $T's$ updates (modified objects) to its local state S_i.

R3: *Integrity:* No process updates its state twice as the result of executing a transaction T.

R4: *Agreement:* No two correct processes update their state differently as the result of executing a transaction T.

R5: *Atomicity:* Operations of a transaction T and any T's updates to S are performed atomically.

R6: *Causal order:* No process P_i updates state S_i as the result of request r_2 unless P_i has already updated S_i as the result of any update request r_1, such that $r_1 \overset{c}{\rightarrow} r_2$.

R7: *Total order:* Let r_1 and r_2 be any two requests. Let P_i and P_j be any two processes that update state as the result of r_2. If P_i updates state on r_1 before r_2 then P_j updates state on r_1 before r_2.

Properties of client-P interaction:

C1: *Validity:* If a client sends a request r to a correct process P_i then replicated process P executes T and eventually returns the response to r to the client.

C2: *No creation:* If a request r is handled by some process P_i, then r was previously sent by some client.

C3: *No duplication:* No response is delivered more than once.

C4: *Causal order:* Let r_1 and r_2 be any two requests such that $r_1 \overset{c}{\rightarrow} r_2$. If res_1 and res_2 are responses to these requests (r_1 and r_2, respectively) delivered to the client, then res_1 is delivered before res_2.

Fig. 1. Properties of transactional replication

with each other directly. The only possible client interaction is through the replicated service. They can submit requests to any of the service processes and await responses. A client may submit only one request at a time. If a client does not receive any response after submitting a request, it can choose a different replica and issue the request again. Such a situation can occur if a replica is down or a timeout was reached due to high communication latency. Each request is processed by an atomic transaction. In case of optimistic replication schemes, such as DUR, transactions are executed in parallel and some of them may conflict. The conflicting transactions are reexecuted until they finally commit (or explicitly abort). However, the clients are not aware of transaction reexecutions.

We assume a simple communication interface: to communicate with a replicated service, a client sends a request message $\langle$Request $| \ (id, LC, code, args)\rangle$, denoted r, which is then handled by a replicated process P by executing an atomic transaction T identified by $r.code$, where T can use arguments $args$; id is the message identifier and LC will be explained in Section 3. Then, replicated process P will return to the client a response to request r using a message $\langle$Response $| \ (r.id, LC, res)\rangle$, where result res

depends on the local state read by transaction T. We use a notation $r.a$ to denote a record field a of message r.

In general, transactions can execute any legal program containing operations $r(o^k)v$, $w(o^k)v$, **abort**, and **retry**, which respectively, read or write a value v to object o in version k, and abort or retry T. Writes of transaction T to object versions on replica P_i can be seen by other transactions on P_i only after P_i *updates* state S_i with the modified objects. All transactions (including retried) eventually *commit* or *abort*. On commit, T updates a replicated state S (with modified objects) and returns result res. On abort, T returns $\emptyset$.

In Figure 1, we define the properties of a transactional replication system, taking into account the handling of requests by a replicated process P (rules **R1-R7**) and the interaction between the clients and P (rules **C1-C4**). All algorithms described in this chapter guarantee these properties. In the specification, we use the symbol $\overset{c}{\rightarrow}$ to denote a causal order relation defined as follows: if $r_1 \overset{c}{\rightarrow} r_2$, then request r_2 depends on result res returned by r_1.

3   Replicated Algorithm Design Problems

Replication of a service means maintaining the service's code and state on a number of machines, so when some of them fail, others can continue to provide the service and process clients' requests. The *service's state* consists of all data which the service and the replication protocol operate on and their current status of execution. Developing replication frameworks is challenging due to some known fundamental problems in distributed systems. Below we discuss the problems which are related to inter-replica and client-replicas synchronization, and fault-tolerance.

Inter-replica synchronization.   In order to guarantee consistency of state updates, replicas must synchronize, which is inherently difficult in a distributed system. Formally, many such problems can be reduced to the problem of *consensus*, i.e. reaching agreement among a group of distributed processes on a single value proposed by one of them. It has been proven that this problem is impossible to solve in a fully asynchronous distributed system [10]. However, some additional assumptions can be made about the system (e.g., the existence of partial synchrony and failure detectors) which make this problem solvable. Solving the consensus problem efficiently is essential for performance of TR schemes described in this chapter. The best known algorithm of this sort is Paxos [18], which solves the consensus problem assuming that the majority of processes is not faulty (meaning not down). If a "faulty process" is as defined in Section 2, then also some additional mechanism is required to support process recovery (see e.g., [16]). In fact, Paxos can solve an infinite sequence of consensus instances. Thus, distributed processes can use this protocol to propose (in multiple consensus instances) and agree upon a common set and order of messages. This semantics is captured by *Total Order Broadcast (TOB)* [5,9]. This primitive enables reliable broadcast of messages with a guarantee that all messages are delivered by all non-faulty processes in the same order. All algorithms discussed in this chapter rely on TOB or protocols derived from it. This, in turn, allowed us to directly compare them.

Client-replicas synchronization.   The interaction between the external clients and the replicated service is not trivial. Imagine a client who issues a request r_1 to one of the replicas, say P_i. P_i handles r_1 and sends a response back to the client. The response to request r_1 can only be sent after the request is *stable* in the system, which means that P_i has updated its local state and it is sure that all other non-faulty replicas will also *eventually* update state. Therefore, some of the replicas may lag behind others. It is possible, then, that upon receiving a response to r_1, the client issues a new request r_2 to a replica P_j that lags behind P_i. If P_j subsequently executes r_2 and r_2 is causally dependent on r_1 (which is typical), then inconsistencies may be introduced to the system.

Fortunately, this problem can be easily solved using logical clocks LC_i that are maintained by replicas P_i ($i = 1..n$). Every replica P_i will increment LC_i each time it has updated local state S_i. A replica P_i which is handling a client request r_1 will return to the client the current value of LC_i in response to r_1 just after r_1 is stable. The client can attach the obtained clock value to a subsequent request r_2 (in a field $r_2.clock$). Since the clock values are monotonically increased, a replica handling r_2 can check whether its state is up-to-date and so it can execute the request, or it has to postpone its processing until it synchronizes with the rest of the replicas. All algorithms presented in this chapter feature this mechanism.

Consider yet another troublesome scenario. A client sends a request r to a replica P_i and awaits the response. P_i crashes before sending reply to the client, or it takes exceptionally long time for the replica to reply to the client. The client may become impatient and issue request r again, but this time to another replica. In effect, the request may be executed twice. To prevent this undesirable behavior, a history could be maintained (and garbage collected after some time) of all requests sent by each client, which will allow detection of duplicates. However, for brevity, we omit this code in the presentation of the algorithms.

Fault-tolerance. The transactional replication systems must be robust against failures. Ideally, a replicated service should be operational when all machines except one crash. However, this requirement is usually too strong since systems fulfilling it cannot be implemented efficiently. It is because the replicas would have to extensively use stable storage in order to be able to recover in the event of failures. On the other hand, if majority of processes is up and running at any time, recovery of failed processes can be very efficient and does not require replicas to access stable storage during the normal (non-faulty) operation. All of the replication schemes discussed in this chapter fall into the latter category.

4   State Machine Replication

State Machine Replication (SMR) [17,33] is one of the simplest replication schemes. It does not support full transactional semantics, but we included SMR in our discussion as it serves as a base for some optimized TR schemes. In this replication scheme, a service replica (process) begins execution on every server from the same initial state and advances by processing all client requests sequentially. Note that each process has to be deterministic. Otherwise, consistency among replicas could not be preserved as the replicas might diverge. Then, the crucial element of SMR is the protocol which is used for dissemination of requests to be executed by all processes in the same order. The required semantics is provided by the Total Order Broadcast (TOB) protocol defined in Section 3.

Algorithm 1. State Machine Replication for process p_i

1: integer $LC \leftarrow 0$

Thread q on request r from client c (executed on one replica)
2:   response $res \leftarrow \perp$
3:   **upon** INIT
4:       **if** $r.code$ is read-only **then**
5:           **wait until** $LC \geq r.clock$
6:           **lock** { $res \leftarrow$ execute $r.code$ with $r.args$ }
7:       **else**
8:           TO-BROADCAST r
9:           wait for res
10:     return $(r.id, LC, res)$ to client c

The main thread of SMR (executed on all replicas)
11: response $res \leftarrow \perp$
12: **upon** TO-DELIVER (request r)
13:     **lock** { $res \leftarrow$ execute $r.code$ with $r.args$
14:         $LC \leftarrow LC + 1$ }
15:     **if** request with $r.id$ handled locally by thread q **then**
16:         pass res to thread q

Algorithm. In Algorithm 1, we show an optimized version of SMR which differentiates between updating and read-only requests [29], thus allowing for some level of parallelism in the execution of requests. For simplicity, we assume that each incoming request is handled in a separate thread. Depending on whether the request is read-only or not, the replica either executes it locally, or broadcasts it to all processes. As for broadcast, a replica uses the *TO-Broadcast* primitive of TOB (line 8). The request is delivered by each replica (through the *TO-Deliver* event) and independently executed by the replica's main thread (line 13). Finally, the replica that received the request, sends the response back to the client (line 10).

On the other hand, if the request is read-only, the replica has to first make sure that it is aware of the changes performed by all requests issued by the same client earlier (this procedure pertains to the problem described in Section 3). For this purpose, each replica stores a logical clock variable LC and attaches its current value to every response message that is sent to the client. This value is then enclosed in the subsequent request message issued by the client (in the field *clock*) and is used to check whether the replica that handles the request is up-to-date, so that its execution will not result in any inconsistencies (line 5).

In the presented algorithm, replicas do not perform the above check for updating requests since the execution order of the updating requests is determined in SMR by TOB and so it is the same at every replica. In effect, if r_1 and r_2 are any two requests, such that r_2 causally depends on r_1, then r_2 can be executed at each replica only after the replica executed r_1.

In our SMR algorithm, the execution of requests is performed within a critical section, guarded by a lock (lines 6 and 13). It is because read-only requests cannot be processed concurrently with updating requests. Otherwise, they could encounter inconsistencies, since the updating requests do not operate on copies of objects they modify, as it is in other schemes described in this chapter, but instead they perform write operations in place of the old values. It would be possible to run several read-only requests in parallel, but this optimization would require using readers-writers locks to protect critical sections of lines 6 and 13, respectively.

Discussion. The advantages of SMR are obvious. This replication scheme is simple and can handle machine failures well. However, the performance of SMR is limited by the capacity of any replica to process the updating requests sequentially. It can therefore neither benefit from modern multicore architectures nor scale with the increasing number of replicas. Furthermore, the semantics of SMR is not as rich as the one available in the TR scheme, e.g., processing of requests cannot be rolled back or wait for a condition to be met.

5   Deferred Update Replication

In the rest of the chapter, we focus on *multi primary-backup replication* [7] (also called *multi-master replication*), where each request is executed by only one single replica that processes the request and issues updates to other replicas, but all replicas can process requests in parallel. In this approach, we have to be able to resolve any conflicts which take place between concurrent threads that access the same set of objects and at least one of the threads modifies the shared object. Here is where the transaction abstraction comes into play. Then each request is executed as an atomic transaction whose operations logically occur at a single instant in time, so the intermediate states are not visible to other transactions. Furthermore, atomicity prevents updates to the state from occurring only partially.

For efficiency, it is important to limit the amount of synchronization among threads and replicas. Hence, we focus on replication schemes featuring *optimistic concurrency control*. They require much less synchronization than those relying on the *pessimistic* one. It is because transactions are executed without upfront locking of objects that are to be accessed by these transactions but, instead, they operate on their own local copies of the objects. Any object modifications are then applied to the replica state on transaction commit.

Deferred Update Replication (DUR) [7] is the simplest transactional replication scheme of this sort. Typically, DUR supports full replication, and each replica can handle multiple requests in separate threads using optimistic transactions. The transactional semantics ensures that the requests are processed atomically and in isolation. The transaction's execution phase is followed by the committing phase in which the replicas synchronize and certify transactions.

Transaction certification means checking if a committing transaction does not conflict with concurrent transactions. It is the only moment in a transaction's lifetime that requires replica and thread synchronization. Upon successful certification, replicas update their state. Otherwise, the transaction is rolled back and restarted. Many different protocols can be used for transaction certification. In this chapter, we discuss *DUR relying on Total Order Broadcast* (see e.g., [27,26,1] among others). Using TOB avoids blocking and limits the number of costly synchronization steps [1,13,26] (see also [32,11]).

Algorithm. In Algorithm 2, we give pseudocode for DUR that builds on [14]. Each replica maintains two global variables. The first one, *LC*, represents the logical clock

Algorithm 2. Deferred Update Replication for process p_i

```
 1: integer LC ← 0
 2: set Log ← ∅
 3: function GETOBJECT(txDescriptor t, objectId oid)
 4:     if (oid, obj) ∈ t.updates then
 5:         value ← obj
 6:     else
 7:         lock { value ← retrieve object oid }
 8:     return value
 9: function CERTIFY(integer start, set readset)
10:     lock { L ← {t ∈ Log : t.end > start} }
11:     for all t ∈ L do
12:         writeset ← {oid : ∃(oid, obj) ∈ t.updates}
13:         if readset ∩ writeset ≠ ∅ then
14:             return failure
15:     return success
```

Thread q on request r from client c (executed on one replica)

```
16: txDescriptor t ← ⊥                              // type: record (id, start, end, readset, updates)
17: response res ← ⊥
18: upon INIT
19:     wait until LC ≥ r.clock
20:     raise TRANSACTION
21:     return (r.id, LC, res) to client c
22: upon TRANSACTION
23:     t ← (a new unique id, 0, 0, ∅, ∅)
24:     lock { t.start ← LC }
25:     res ← execute r.code with r.args
26:     COMMIT()
27: upon READ(objectId oid)
28:     t.readset ← t.readset ∪ {oid}
29:     if CERTIFY(t.start, {oid}) = failure then
30:         raise RETRY
31:     else
32:         return GETOBJECT(t, oid)
33: upon WRITE(objectId oid, object obj)
34:     t.updates ← {(oid', obj') ∈ t.updates : oid' ≠ oid} ∪ {(oid, obj)}
35: procedure COMMIT
36:     if t.updates = ∅ then
37:         return to INIT
38:     if CERTIFY(t.start, t.readset) = failure then
39:         raise RETRY
40:     TO-BROADCAST t
41:     wait for outcome
42:     if outcome = failure then
43:         raise RETRY
44:     else                                          // outcome = success
45:         return to INIT
46: upon ROLLBACK
47:     stop executing r.code and return to INIT
48: upon RETRY
49:     stop executing r.code
50:     raise TRANSACTION
```

The main thread of DUR (executed on all replicas)

```
51: upon TO-DELIVER (txDescriptor t)
52:     outcome ← CERTIFY(t.start, t.readset)
53:     if outcome = success then
54:         lock { t.end ← LC
55:             Log ← Log ∪ {t}
56:             apply t.updates
57:             LC ← LC + 1 }
58:     if transaction with t.id executed locally by thread q then
59:         pass outcome to thread q
```

which is used in a similar way as in SMR, i.e., LC is incremented every time a replica changes its state (line 57) and enables the replica to track whether its state is recent enough to execute the client's request (line 19). Additionally, LC is used to mark the start and the end of the transaction execution (lines 24 and 54). The transaction's start and end timestamps, stored in the *transaction descriptor* (line 16), allow us to reason about the precedence order between transactions. Let t_1 and t_2 be transaction descriptors of two transactions T_1 and T_2. We say that transaction T_1 *precedes* transaction T_2 (denoted $T_1 \rightarrow T_2$) iff $t_1.end < t_2.start$. If neither $T_1 \rightarrow T_2$ nor $T_2 \rightarrow T_1$, we say that T_1 and T_2 are *concurrent*. The second variable, Log, is a set used to store the transaction descriptors of committed transactions. Maintaining this set is necessary to perform transaction certification.

The DUR algorithm detects any conflicts among transactions by checking whether a given transaction T that is being certified read any stale data. The latter occurs when T read any shared objects that have been modified by a concurrent but already committed transaction. For this purpose, DUR traces the accesses to shared objects independently for each transaction. The identifiers of objects that were read and the modified objects themselves are stored in private, per transaction, memory spaces: *readset* and *updates*. On every read, an object's identifier is added to the *readset* (line 28). Similarly, on every write a pair of the object's identifier and the corresponding object is recorded in the *updates* set (line 34). Then, the CERTIFY function compares the given *readset* against the *updates* of all the committed transactions in Log that are concurrent with the tested transaction. If it finds any non-empty intersection of the sets, the outcome is negative. Otherwise, it is positive (no conflicts detected, the transaction is certified successfully). Note that every time a transaction reads some shared object, a check against conflicts is performed (line 29). This way T is guaranteed to always read from a consistent snapshot. When a conflict is detected, T is forced to retry.

When a transaction's code completes, the COMMIT operation (line 35) is used to end the transaction and initiate the committing phase, which can be explained as follows. If T is a read-only transaction (T did not modify any objects), it can commit straight away, without performing any further conflict checks or replica synchronization, similarly as in SMR (lines 36–37). A read-only transaction does not need to perform certification as the possible conflicts would have been detected earlier, upon read operations (line 29). For update transactions, first, the local certification takes place (line 38), which is not mandatory but allows the replica to detect conflicts earlier, and thus sometimes avoid costly network communication. Next, the transaction's descriptor containing *readset* and *updates* is broadcast to all processes using TO-BROADCAST (line 40). The message is delivered in the main thread, where the final certification takes place (line 52). Upon successful certification of transaction T, replicas apply the updates performed by T and commit it (lines 54–57). Otherwise, T is rolled back and reexecuted by the same replica.

To manage the control flow of a transaction, the programmer can use two additional operations: ROLLBACK and RETRY, whose semantics is similar as in transactional memory systems. The ROLLBACK operation (line 46) stops the execution of a transaction and revokes all the changes it performed so far. The RETRY operation (line 48) forces a transaction to rollback and restart.

For clarity, we made several simplifications. Firstly, note that the operations on LC (lines 24, 54, 57), Log (lines 10 and 55) and the accesses to transactional objects (lines 7 and 56) have to be synchronized. For simplicity, a single global lock is used. For better performance, the implementation can rely on fine-grained locks. Secondly, in our pseudocode, Log can grow indefinitely. In reality, Log can easily be kept small by garbage collecting information about the already committed transactions that ended before the oldest live transaction started in the system.

In the presented algorithm, we use the same certification procedure for both the certification test performed upon every read operation (line 29) and the certification test that happens after a transaction descriptor is delivered to the main thread (line 52). In practice, however, doing so would be very inefficient. It is because for every read operation, we check for the conflicts against all concurrent transactions (line 10), thus performing much of the same work again and again. However, this repeated actions can be easily avoided by associating the accessed shared objects with version numbers—the value of LC at the time the objects were most recently modified.

Discussion. It is easy to see that, at least theoretically, DUR has the potential to perform much better than SMR. The capability of executing requests in parallel is especially valuable for CPU-intensive workloads. Unfortunately, there are also factors that limit the robustness of DUR. Firstly, the system has to monitor transactional accesses to all shared objects, which is costly. This overhead cannot be avoided unless we know *a priori* the conflict pattern of all transactions. Secondly, the volume of data exchanged via a network is high, mainly due to, usually large, *readsets* that have to be broadcast alongside *updates*. Thirdly, transaction certification, which can be a costly operation, is performed independently for every transaction by each process, thus limiting scalability. In the next sections, we present several replication algorithms that address some of the above problems.

6 Deferred Update Replication with Multiversioning

Multiversioning [4] in an important optimization technique which allows for multiple versions of transactional objects that are transparent to the programmer. Only one object version is accessible by a transaction at any time. Object versions are immutable, thus they can be accessed concurrently without any synchronization. Furthermore, since read-only transactions accessing object versions are abort-free, the system does not need to trace accesses to shared objects for transactions *a priori* known to be read-only. The latter feature can greatly improve the overall performance and scalability of the transactional system when workloads are dominated by read-only transactions [30]. All TR algorithms described in this chapter can benefit from this optimization technique.

Algorithm. In Algorithm 3, we present the DUR scheme extended with multiversioning, which we call *Multiversion DUR (MvDUR)*. In MvDUR, the information about already committed transactions is no longer stored in Log, and each object can have many *object versions obj*, each one paired with their corresponding *version numbers ver*. When a transaction commits, the system creates new versions of all objects modified by the transaction (lines 56–57), all having the same version number assigned, which is equal to the current value of logical clock LC.

Algorithm 3. Deferred Update Replication with Multiversioning for process p_i

1: integer $LC \leftarrow 0$
2: **function** GETVERSION(objectId *oid*, integer *notNewerThan*)
3:     **lock** { **return** (obj, ver) such that obj is a version of object *oid* whose version number *ver*
4:                      is the highest available such that $ver \leq notNewerThan$ }
5: **function** GETOBJECT(txDescriptor *t*, objectId *oid*)
6:     **if** $(oid, obj) \in t.updates$ **then**
7:         *value* $\leftarrow obj$
8:     **else**
9:         $(obj, ver) \leftarrow$ GETVERSION$(oid, t.start)$
10:        *value* $\leftarrow obj$
11:     **return** *value*
12: **function** CERTIFY(integer *start*, set *readset*)
13:     **for all** $id \in readset$ **do**
14:         $(obj, ver) \leftarrow$ GETVERSION(id, ∞)
15:         **if** $ver > start$ **then**
16:             **return** *failure*
17:     **return** *success*

Thread q on request r from client c (executed on one replica)
18: txDescriptor $t \leftarrow \perp$ *// type: record (id, start, end, readset, updates)*
19: response $res \leftarrow \perp$
20: **upon** INIT
21:     **wait until** $LC \geq r.clock$
22:     **raise** TRANSACTION
23:     return $(r.id, LC, res)$ to client c
24: **upon** TRANSACTION
25:     $t \leftarrow$ (a new unique $id, 0, 0, \emptyset, \emptyset$)
26:     **lock** { $t.start \leftarrow LC$ }
27:     $res \leftarrow$ execute $r.code$ with $r.args$
28:     COMMIT()
29: **upon** READ(objectId *oid*)
30:     $obj \leftarrow$ GETOBJECT(t, oid)
31:     **if** $r.code$ is not read-only **then**
32:         $t.readset \leftarrow t.readset \cup \{oid\}$
33:     **return** obj
34: **upon** WRITE(objectId *oid*, object *obj*)
35:     $t.updates \leftarrow \{(oid', obj') \in t.updates : oid' \neq oid\} \cup \{(oid, obj)\}$
36: **procedure** COMMIT
37:     **if** $t.updates = \emptyset$ **then**
38:         return to INIT
39:     **if** CERTIFY$(t.start, t.readset) = failure$ **then**
40:         **raise** RETRY
41:     TO-BROADCAST t
42:     wait for *outcome*
43:     **if** *outcome* $= failure$ **then**
44:         **raise** RETRY
45:     **else**   *// outcome = success*
46:         return to INIT
47: **upon** ROLLBACK
48:     stop executing $r.code$ and return to INIT
49: **upon** RETRY
50:     stop executing $r.code$
51:     **raise** TRANSACTION

The main thread of MvDUR (executed on all replicas)
52: **upon** TO-DELIVER (txDescriptor *t*)
53:     *outcome* $\leftarrow$ CERTIFY$(t.start, t.readset)$
54:     **if** *outcome* $= success$ **then**
55:         **lock** { $LC \leftarrow LC + 1$
56:             **for all** $(oid, obj) \in t.updates$
57:                 add obj as a new version of object *oid* with version number LC }
58:     **if** transaction with $t.id$ executed locally by thread q **then**
59:         pass *outcome* to thread q

Compared to DUR, there is also a new function GETVERSION which takes two arguments *oid* and *notNewerThan* and retrieves a version *obj* of an object identified with *oid* that is the most recent among all those object versions that have a version number lower than or equal to *notNewerThan* (lines 2–4). The function can be used to read from a consistent snapshot of the system and return the newest object versions that existed in the system up to a given moment in time. This way all reads which are performed by a transaction are consistent and no conflict checks are necessary. Therefore, read-only transactions are guaranteed to always commit. For this reason, as stated earlier, if a transaction is *a priori* known to be read-only, it does not need to record its accesses in the *readset* (line 31).

The transaction certification phase in MvDUR is different and much more efficient than in DUR. Instead of checking a transaction's *readset* against the *update* sets of (possibly many) committed concurrent transactions, the certification procedure just compares the version numbers of the objects that were read. If the most recent version of a read object has a version number which is higher than the transaction's *start* timestamp, then a conflict exists—i.e., a new version was created after the transaction had already started execution.

The committing phase in MvDUR is similar to DUR's one. Both algorithms differ in the way each replica applies transaction updates. In MvDUR, replicas update their state by adding new object versions (lines 56–57). For this, we have to use locks since these operations must be done atomically. However, in practice MvDUR can be implemented in a way that avoids using locks altogether.

In our pseudocode, no object version is ever removed from the system. However, a simple garbage collection mechanism can be proposed, as follows. Let us consider a replica R, and let t be the transaction descriptor of the oldest live transaction in R ($t.start$ is equal to the the lowest value among all descriptors of live transactions in R). Let d be the set of all object versions in R whose version numbers are lower than or equal $t.start$. Then, for each shared object, all its versions in d but the most recent one can be safely dropped.

7 Hybrid SM-DUR Algorithm

The SMR and DUR (or MvDUR) replication schemes presented in previous sections are based on different premises. In SMR, any sequential program implementing some service can be replicated, and the replication framework simply broadcasts requests using TOB. On the other hand, DUR requires the service's program to be transaction-oriented, but it offers potentially much better scalability due to its capability of processing requests in parallel. The two schemes were compared both theoretically and experimentally in [37]. The main corollary drawn from this comparison is that no scheme can be considered superior.

In SMR, all requests are executed sequentially by all replicas, which does not leave much room for performance improvement. Therefore, it might seem that DUR, which supports parallelism, should always outperform SMR. However, this is not the case for several reasons. Firstly, the size of messages broadcast can be an order of magnitude larger than in SMR since a message contains not only the *updates* that result from the transaction execution but also the *readset*, necessary for transaction certification. Especially the latter set can be of significant size. Also, the cost of bookkeeping *readset* and *updates* is not negligible. On the other hand, a message broadcast in SMR usually only contains a client request with a reference (with some arguments) to a function that executes this request. Therefore, it is sometimes more efficient to broadcast a client request, as in SMR, rather than broadcast the state changes, as in DUR, even at the cost of executing the request n times independently on each replica. Secondly, there is also the aspect of concurrency control and its inherent cost in the optimistic replication schemes. In DUR, transactions may be forced to retry due to conflicts, so a transaction can be executed multiple times before it eventually commits. If the contention level is high, the benefits of parallel execution in DUR may not only be overshadowed but even completely outweighed by the costly transaction reruns. This, in turn, causes the performance of the system to diminish. On the contrary, in SMR no conflicts ever occur.

The SMR and DUR (or MvDUR) replication schemes also differ in the semantics offered to the programmer. Unlike DUR, SMR only supports deterministic services. Otherwise, replicas could diverge when processing the same request and eventually cause the system to run into inconsistencies. On the other hand, the fact that each request (transaction) is executed in SMR exactly once by each process, and is never forcefully retried can be an advantage. For instance, it allows SMR to support operations with side-effects that cannot be easily undone, such as I/O, system calls, etc. On the other hand, the basic DUR scheme cannot deal with irrevocable operations well because each transaction may execute multiple times before it eventually commits. In transactional memory systems, various techniques were developed to deal with this problem, such as buffering or executing irrevocable transactions sequentially w.r.t. other transactions. They can be used to extend DUR accordingly.

These insights led us to merge SMR and DUR into *Hybrid Transactional Replication (HTR)* [14]. In this replication scheme, the programmer can use transactional constructs to encode handlers of client requests as atomic transactions, similarly as in DUR. However, each transaction is executed in one of two execution modes that are selected dynamically: a pessimistic one (*SM mode*) and an optimistic one (*DU mode*). A transaction which is executed in the SM mode is guaranteed an abort-free execution, but its code has to be deterministic. Moreover, HTR makes sure that only one such a transaction is run in the system at a time. On the other hand, a transaction which is executed in the DU mode can run in parallel with any SM transaction and any other DU transactions. Because a DU transaction is executed only by one replica process, it can also contain non-deterministic operations. However, a DU transaction may abort, so the client requests that require irrevocable operations should only be executed as SM transactions.

Algorithm. Before we dive into the details of HTR, let us discuss the key idea of how the two transaction execution modes can coexist. The way SM and DU transactions are executed in HTR closely resembles how the client requests are handled, respectively, by SMR and DUR, but objects are not modified in place as it is in SMR. HTR manages the two modes by serializing the execution of SM transactions with the certification of DU transactions. Therefore, during the execution of a SM transaction, no other transaction can modify the system state. This way a SM transaction operates on consistent state and is guaranteed an abort-free execution. Note that DU transactions execute in isolation on copies of shared objects, so no interference with other transactions is possible. The order in which the main HTR thread certifies DU transactions and executes SM transactions is determined by TOB. Therefore, each replica advances exactly in the same way.

The pseudocode of the HTR algorithm (see Algorithm 4) shares many parts with MvDUR, on which HTR is based. [1] HTR features an abstraction called the *transaction oracle*. After a replica receives a request, the oracle is queried to asses whether to execute the request as a DU or SM transaction (line 25). In practice, the decision made by the oracle relies on hints declared by the programmer as well as on dynamically collected data regarding various aspects of system's performance. Note that, the request execution mode is determined on per transaction execution basis. It means that a request can be first executed multiple times as a DU transaction (due to aborts) and then as a SM transaction (which is guaranteed to always commit).

The execution and committing phases of DU transactions are almost identical as in MvDUR. The only difference lies in feeding the oracle with the statistics regarding transaction execution (lines 54, 57 and 61) which, in turn, allow the oracle to adjust its future decisions. On the other hand, if the oracle determines that a request is to be executed as a SM transaction, it is first broadcast using TOB (line 32). When the request is delivered, it is processed by the same thread that certifies DU transactions and applies their updates (lines 76–79). A SM transaction does not execute directly on the shared objects as in SMR. Instead, it uses shared object copies as a DU transaction does. By doing so, a SM transaction can be easily rolled back on demand at any time. Moreover, SM transactions produce versions of objects that can be used by other transactions (including the read-only ones) exactly the same way as the versions produced by regular DU transactions. For this purpose, HTR features the appropriate upon statements (TRANSACTION, READ, WRITE, ROLLBACK, and RETRY) in the main thread section. Since a SM transaction is guaranteed to commit, it does not need to maintain *readset* (line 86). A SM transaction commits by simply applying the updates it produced (lines 90–92) and returning the result to the thread that originally received the request (lines 78–79).

Discussion. HTR brings together the best features of both SMR and DUR. It offers rich transactional semantics, also when the client requests are executed in the SM mode. Additionally, it supports irrevocable operations, which is not typical in replication schemes featuring optimistic concurrency control. In terms of performance, HTR is at least as good as either SMR or DUR. Moreover, HTR can dynamically adapt to a changing workload because the oracle can monitor the system's performance and adjust its decisions accordingly. However, for HTR to perform well, the oracle has to be tailored to the application in question. In [14], we outline the most important aspects of a good oracle design and describe example oracles for several benchmark applications.

---

[1] HTR does not require multiversioning in order to work. However, the only existing implementation of HTR is based on MvDUR [14].

Algorithm 4. Hybrid Transactional Replication for process p_i (part 1)

```
 1: integer LC ← 0
 2: function GETVERSION(objectId oid, integer notNewerThan)
 3:     lock { return (obj, ver) such that obj is a version of object oid whose version number ver
 4:                        is the highest available such that ver ≤ notNewerThan }
 5: function GETOBJECT(txDescriptor t, objectId oid)
 6:     if (oid, obj) ∈ t.updates then
 7:         value ← obj
 8:     else
 9:         (obj, ver) ← GETVERSION(oid, t.start)
10:         value ← obj
11:     return value
12: function CERTIFY(integer start, set readset)
13:     for all id ∈ readset do
14:         (obj, ver) ← GETVERSION(id, ∞)
15:         if ver > start then
16:             return failure
17:     return success
```

```
Thread q on request r from client c (executed on one replica)
18: txDescriptor t ← ⊥                          // type: record (id, start, end, readset, updates, stats)
19: response res ← ⊥
20: upon INIT
21:     wait until LC ≥ r.clock
22:     raise TRANSACTION
23:     return (r.id, LC, res) to client c
24: upon TRANSACTION
25:     mode ← TransactionOracle.query()
26:     if mode = DU then
27:         t ← (a new unique id, 0, 0, ∅, ∅, ∅)
28:         lock { t.start ← LC }
29:         res ← execute r.code with r.args
30:         raise COMMIT()
31:     else                                                          // mode = SM
32:         TO-BROADCAST r
33:         wait for (outcome, res, t)
34:         UPDATEORACLESTATISTICS(t)
35:         if outcome = retry then
36:             raise TRANSACTION
37: upon READ(objectId oid)
38:     obj ← GETOBJECT(t, oid)
39:     if r.code is not read-only then
40:         t.readset ← t.readset ∪ {oid}
41:     return obj
42: upon WRITE(objectId oid, object obj)
43:     t.updates ← {(oid', obj') ∈ t.updates : oid' ≠ oid} ∪ {(oid, obj)}
44: procedure COMMIT                                                  // for DU transactions
45:     if t.updates = ∅ then
46:         return to INIT
47:     if CERTIFY(t.start, t.readset) = failure then
48:         raise RETRY
49:     TO-BROADCAST t
50:     wait for outcome
51:     if outcome = failure then
52:         raise RETRY
53:     else                                                          // outcome = success
54:         UPDATEORACLESTATISTICS(t)
55:         return to INIT
56: upon ROLLBACK                                                     // for DU transactions
57:     UPDATEORACLESTATISTICS(t)
58:     stop executing r.code and return to INIT
59: upon RETRY                                                        // for DU transactions
60:     stop executing r.code
61:     UPDATEORACLESTATISTICS(t)
62:     raise TRANSACTION
63: procedure UPDATEORACLESTATISTICS(txDescriptor t)
64:     TransactionOracle.feed(t.stats)
```

Algorithm 4. Hybrid Transactional Replication for process p_i (part 2)

```
The main thread of HTR
65:  txDescriptor t ← ⊥                                         // type: record (id, start, end, readset, updates, stats)
66:  enum outcome ← ⊥                                           // type: enum {committed, rolledback, retry, success, failure}
67:  response res ← ⊥
68:  upon TO-DELIVER (txDescriptor t)
69:      outcome ← CERTIFY(t.start, t.readset)
70:      if outcome = success then
71:          lock { LC ← LC + 1
72:              for all (oid, obj) ∈ t.updates
73:                  add obj as a new version of object oid with version number LC }
74:      if transaction with t.id executed locally by thread q then
75:          pass outcome to thread q
76:  upon TO-DELIVER (request r)
77:      raise TRANSACTION
78:      if request r handled locally by thread q then
79:          pass (outcome, res, t) to thread q
80:  upon TRANSACTION                                            // for SM transactions
81:      t ← (a new unique id, 0, 0, ∅, ∅, ∅)
82:      lock { t.start ← LC }
83:      res ← execute r.code with r.args
84:      COMMIT()
85:  upon READ(objectId oid)                                    // for SM transactions
86:      return GETOBJECT(t, oid)
87:  upon WRITE(objectId oid, object obj)                       // for SM transactions
88:      t.updates ← t.updates ∪ {(oid, obj)}
89:  procedure COMMIT                                           // for SM transactions
90:      lock { LC ← LC + 1
91:          for all (oid, obj) ∈ p.updates
92:              add obj as a new version of object oid with version number LC }
93:      outcome ← committed
94:      return to TO-DELIVER
95:  upon ROLLBACK                                              // for SM transactions
96:      outcome ← rolledback
97:      stop executing r.code and return to TO-DELIVER
98:  upon RETRY                                                 // for SM transactions
99:      outcome ← retry
100:     stop executing r.code and return to TO-DELIVER
```

8 Postgres-R

In the previous sections we explained that the great strength of the algorithms such as DUR (or MvDUR) is the fact that there is only one communication step for each transaction's run. However, there is no such thing as free lunch. DUR trades low communication latency for a high volume of data to be broadcast and transaction certification which has to be performed independently by each replica. In this section we present Postgres-R [12], an algorithm originally proposed for database replication, which appears similar to DUR but is able to compensate some of its limitations. Postgres-R has also been used in distributed TM [8]. Unlike in DUR, in Postgres-R no *readset* is broadcast after a transaction completes its execution. Also, in total, all processes perform less certification, thus saving resources. Postgres-R, however, requires an additional communication phase—a process that executed the transaction broadcasts to all replicas the final decision on whether to commit or abort the transaction. This additional broadcast is performed after the process broadcasts and delivers the updates produced by the transaction.

Algorithm 5. Postgres-R for process p_i (part 1)

```
 1: integer LC ← 0
 2: set AbortedTx ← ∅, DecidedTx ← ∅
 3: function GETOBJECT(txDescriptor t, objectId oid)
 4:     if (oid, obj) ∈ t.updates then
 5:         value ← obj
 6:     else
 7:         lock { acquire read lock on oid for transaction t.id }
 8:         value ← retrieve object oid
 9:     return value
```

```
Thread q on request r from client c (executed on one replica)
10: txDescriptor t ← ⊥                                           // type: record (process, id, start, end, updates)
11: response res ← ⊥
12: upon INIT
13:     wait until LC ≥ r.clock
14:     raise TRANSACTION
15:     return (r.id, LC, res) to client c
16: upon TRANSACTION
17:     t ← (p_i, a new unique id, 0, 0, ∅)
18:     lock { t.start ← LC }
19:     res ← execute r.code with r.args
20:     COMMIT()
21: upon READ(objectId oid)
22:     return GETOBJECT(t, oid)
23: upon WRITE(objectId oid, object obj)
24:     lock { acquire write lock on oid for transaction t.id }
25:     t.updates ← {(oid', obj') ∈ t.updates : oid' ≠ oid} ∪ {(oid, obj)}
26: procedure COMMIT
27:     if t.updates ≠ ∅ then
28:         TO-BROADCAST t
29:         wait for outcome
30:     lock { release all the locks held by transaction t.id }
31:     return to INIT
32: upon ROLLBACK
33:     lock { release all the locks held by transaction t.id }
34:     stop executing r.code and return to INIT
35: upon RETRY
36:     lock { release all the locks held by transaction t.id }
37:     stop executing r.code
38:     raise TRANSACTION
39: upon ABORT
40:     raise RETRY
```

Algorithm. The pseudocode for Postgres-R is given in Algorithm 5. Similarly to DUR, Postgres-R executes a transaction on copies of shared objects. Unlike DUR, however, Postgres-R does not maintain *readsets* for executed transactions and extensively relies on the read-write locks associated with each shared object (lines 7 and 24). The locks prevent live transactions from reading an inconsistent snapshot. In this sense, the locks fulfill the same function as the local certification procedure performed upon every read operation in DUR.

Once a transaction T finishes execution, the transaction's descriptor containing the process ID, the transaction ID, start timestamp and the updates that T produced, is broadcast to all replicas using TOB (line 28). Since the message does not contain *readset* (as in DUR), replicas cannot independently certify T. In Postgres-R certification happens somewhat indirectly and is driven by TOB. Similarly as in DUR, TOB is used to establish the serialization order on all (updating) transactions in the system.

Algorithm 5. Postgres-R for process p_i (part 2)

The main thread of Postgres-R (executed on all replicas)
41: **upon** TO-DELIVER (txDescriptor t) **lock**
42:      **if** $t.id \in AbortedTx$ **then**
43:          **return**
44:      **if** transaction with $t.id$ executed locally by thread q **then**
45:          $outcome \leftarrow commit$
46:          R-BROADCAST $(t.id, outcome)$
47:          $DecidedTx \leftarrow DecidedTx \cup \{t.id\}$
48:          apply $t.updates$
49:          $LC \leftarrow LC + 1$
50:          pass $outcome$ to thread q
51:      **else**
52:          **for all** $(oid, obj) \in t.updates$ **do**
53:              **if** read or write lock acquired on oid by some transaction $t'.id$ executed locally by thread q **then**
54:                  $AbortedTx \leftarrow AbortedTx \cup \{t'.id\}$
55:                  R-BROADCAST $(t'.id, abort)$
56:                  **raise** ABORT on thread q
57:              enqueue write lock request on oid for transaction $t.id$
58: **upon** R-DELIVER(integer id, decision d) **lock**
59:      **if** $id \in DecidedTx$ **then**   // transaction executed locally
60:          **return**
61:      **if** $d = commit$ **then**
62:          $DecidedTx \leftarrow DecidedTx \cup \{id\}$
63:      **else**   // $d = abort$
64:          $AbortedTx \leftarrow AbortedTx \cup \{id\}$
65:          release all the locks held by transaction id
66: **upon** GRANTED ALL LOCKS ENQUEUED FOR TRANSACTION $t.id$ AND $t.id \in DecidedTx$ **lock**
67:      apply $t.updates$
68:      release all the locks held by transaction $t.id$
69:      $LC \leftarrow LC + 1$
70: **upon** PROCESS p_j CRASH   // reliable information from group membership mechanism
71:      **lock** { release all locks/dequeue all lock requests for transactions $t.id$ such that $t.process = p_j$ }

Transactions in committing state that are TO-Delivered preempt earlier transactions whose updates are not yet TO-Delivered. This is done in the following way: upon delivery of a new transaction descriptor (line 41) a replica tries to acquire write locks for every object in the update set on behalf of the incoming transaction; if the lock is held by a local transaction whose updates were not yet broadcast and delivered, the local transaction is aborted (lines 54–56) and its locks are released (line 36). At this point the replica is the sole process which has the knowledge about the outcome of this local transaction. Because the aborted transaction might have already broadcast its transaction descriptor, which other processes will eventually deliver, the replica needs to inform them of its decision to abort the transaction.[2] For this purpose the *reliable broadcast (RB)* is used (line 55). It is sufficient because decision messages do not need to be ordered.

If a committing transaction is not preempted and it gets to the point where it is TO-Delivered by the replica which initiated it, then the transaction can finally commit (lines 45–50). Similarly as in case of an aborted transaction, only one process knows about the outcome, so it has to inform others of the decision to commit (line 46). The next step is to apply the updates and increment LC. The updates can be applied straight

---

[2] If the aborted transaction was still in the executing phase, i.e. it did not reach the commit phase, then this step can be ignored. However, this optimization is not reflected in the pseudocode.

away, because in case of a local transaction we are sure that it holds the locks for every modified object since its execution phase.

The commitment of a foreign transaction (initiated by a different replica) is more complicated (lines 52–57). As previously stated, first, the transaction needs to acquire write locks for every updated item. If they are held by local (executing or committing) transactions, the local transactions need to be preempted. However, locks may also be held by other foreign committing transactions which wait to be committed. Therefore, the replica enqueues lock requests on behalf of the incoming transaction (line 57). The operation of acquiring locks and enqueuing lock requests for individual objects must be atomic and the lock requests need to respect FIFO order. Note, that three **upon** statements handled by the main Postgres-R thread feature a **lock** in its declaration (lines 41, 58 and 66) meaning the whole statement is guarded by a global lock. Therefore, all accesses to read/write locks in the pseudocode are protected from interleaving with each other. Besides acquiring the locks one more condition needs to be met for a transaction to be able to commit. The replica that initiated it must take the actual decision to commit it and then broadcast this decision. Only when the appropriate decision is R-Delivered (line 58) and all the required locks are granted (line 66) the process of committing can be finished (lines 67–69). Naturally, if the R-Delivered decision is to abort, then the waiting transaction is dropped and all the locks it managed to acquire are released (line 65).

Sometimes the decision message for some transaction T may arrive at some process before the message with T's transaction descriptor. Postgres-R, therefore, maintains two sets *AbortedTx* and *DecidedTx*, so it knows whether to apply or drop the updates once they arrive. Now, consider a scenario in which the decision message for a transaction T never arrives because of a replica crash. In such a case, every replica would indefinitely hold locks for all objects modified by T. It is easy to show that a simple timeout-based mechanism running independently on each replica is not sufficient. Therefore, replicas need to abort such transactions in a coordinated fashion. For this purpose, Postgres-R utilizes *group communication services*. Whenever processes leave (because of failures or shutdowns) or join (recovering processes), the group communication module creates different views in the computation. A view gives an illusion of a stable configuration consisting of only operational processes. All messages sent within a view are confined to that view.

In case of failures, upon a view change, we can identify active transactions originating at the failed site and we can safely abort them (line 71) without compromising consistency of the non-faulty processes. Even if the crashed replica has broadcast a commit decision just before the crash, this message will not be delivered to any of the processes. This is because a new view is established, and all the messages from previous view were already delivered or are discarded.

Discussion. As described above, the process of certification in Postgres-R is somewhat indirect. Incoming transactions, whose order is established with TOB, invalidate live transactions that are local to specific replicas. Therefore, the certification is distributed and replicas need additional synchronization to disseminate the result of certification. Instead of certifying each transaction directly, the processes have to rely on others to broadcast the final decision in a second phase. The additional broadcast greatly increases the latency of a transaction's commit. It means that the concurrent transactions may have to wait significant amount of time on locks held by a transaction waiting for the decision message. In turn, these concurrent transactions are more prone to abort induced by transactions executed by other replicas. One can see, then, that even low contention is problematic to Postgres-R. It seems, therefore, that Postgres-R is not suitable for transactional replication where transactions are usually short and access few objects but may conflict often. One has to remember, though, that Postgres-R was originally designed for database systems, not distributed TM.

So what types of workloads does Postgres-R handle well? Transactions in Postgres-R have to be long and access many objects. Only then the potential gains that stem from not having to broadcast *readset* (as in DUR) are worth the cost of an additional communication phase.

9   Executive Deferred Update Replication

In this section we present yet another DUR-based algorithm, called *Executive Deferred Update Replication (EDUR)* [15]. The key idea behind EDUR lies in an observation regarding some distributed agreement protocols, such as Paxos. These algorithms feature a distinguished process, *the leader*, which is responsible for coordination of message broadcast. It means that a message broadcast by some process is first received by the leader who, essentially, stamps it with a sequence number before sending it to the rest of the processes. This way each process knows the final message delivery order. Since all messages pass through the leader, we can use the leader to perform some additional work before it forwards the messages to the rest of the replicas. In particular, EDUR uses the leader to certify transactions on behalf of all replicas. Streamlining transaction certification with the broadcast protocol has several advantages. Firstly, certification is performed only by one process, not by all process as in DUR. Secondly, the network traffic is greatly reduced which can be explained as follows. Once a transaction is certified successfully, only the set containing the updates resulting from transaction execution has to be forwarded to all replicas. The often large readset required for transaction certification is no longer needed. In case a transaction fails certification, the leader only needs to inform the process that executed the transaction that it has to be restarted. Finally, unlike Postgres-R, EDUR does not increase the number of communication steps for each transaction's run. It means that EDUR can be implemented efficiently.

It is worth to note that the load of the leader in EDUR not only does not increase compared to DUR but even can be lower. Both in DUR and EDUR the leader certifies transactions but in the latter case the certification procedure occurs earlier and the size of messages broadcast is often much smaller, which attribute to lower load.

Let us focus for a while on a broadcast protocol that serves as a base for EDUR. It turns out that it is insufficient to simply extend this protocol so that the leader executes some routine before a message is forwarded to the rest of the processes. It is because the leader, by processing the messages and possibly changing their content, establishes a prefix order on the sequence of messages it sends. In other words, the messages which were concurrently issued by different replicas and pass through the leader are no longer independent with regard to each other. Any message m that appears later in the sequence is logically dependent on any message m' that appears in the sequence prior to m.[3] This would not be problematic if the leader coordinated only one consensus instance at a time. Then, a new transaction did not undergo a certification until the message regarding the previously certified transaction would not be delivered by the leader (in the total order broadcast sense). This way, upon leader change, the new leader would be aware of all transactions certified by the previous one, thus preserving consistency. However, for performance reasons, TOB protocols such as Paxos allow for concurrent processing of several consensus instances. This means that a different solution is required.

In [15], we point out that it would be possible to build EDUR on top of Extended Virtual Synchrony (EVS) [22]. In EVS, processes are organized within groups of processes that maintain dynamic views of processes that are considered to be operational. As noted in Section 8, a process view gives an illusion of a stable group configuration consisting of only correct processes that never crash. Whenever a process is suspected to have crashed or voluntarily joins or leaves the group a new view is formed. Messages sent within a view are confined to that view. It is therefore possible to safely elect some process in each view and make it responsible for transaction certification. However, EVS limits the performance of EDUR in several ways. Most importantly, EVS requires a system to pause computation upon every view installation event. The overhead should not be noticeable if views do not change often. Unfortunately, a new view has to be installed every time any process begins to be suspected of a failure by any other process from the same group. If a group is large such a situation can be a commonplace. For these reasons, EDUR uses a new broadcast protocol called *Executive Order Broadcast (EOB)*.

Below we characterize EOB informally (see [15] for a formal specification). EOB extends TOB in two aspects. Firstly, EOB introduces a number of new primitives that allow the programmer to define actions to be undertaken by the leader before a message is forwarded to the rest of the replicas (see below). Secondly, in EOB the total order property of TOB is substituted by the *executive order*. This property guarantees that not only all messages are delivered by each replica in the same order but also it ensures that the prefix order imposed by the leader is always preserved. The definition of EOB accounts for multiple concurrent leaders, so it is possible to devise an EOB-enabled algorithm similar to Paxos. In fact, the implementation of EOB in [15] is based on Paxos.

Let us review the primitives and events of EOB. EO-BROADCAST(id, mc) and EO-DELIVER(id, mc') correspond to the ones of TOB. In addition they account for the fact that the content mc of the broadcast message can be changed by the leader. Therefore, the unique identifier id is used to distinguish between messages. The next four primitives are characteristic for EOB: EO-LEADERELECT and EO-LEADERRECALL are used by a local failure detector to inform the process that it has to, respectively, take on or relinquish the duties of the leader process (and we say that during the time periods between these events the process *is a leader*). A leader receives EO-LEADERDELIVER(id, mc)

---

[3] Naturally, all messages issued by replicas as a result of processing requests from the same client form a sequence of logically dependent messages. However, a client cannot issue a new request, until the previous one returns.

events, so it can process the incoming messages. To broadcast a (possibly) modified message, the leader invokes the EO-LEADERBROADCAST(id, mc') primitive.

When the leader promptly forwards all messages that it received through the EO-LeaderDeliver events, with no additional action, EOB is reduced to TOB. In fact, EOB is strictly stronger than TOB. One can also show that EOB is strictly weaker than EVS. It is because, unlike EVS, EOB does not feature the group membership service. Most importantly, however, under stable conditions, EOB can operate as efficiently as TOB but, unlike EVS, it requires reconfiguration only when the current leader is suspected to have crashed (groups in EVS are reconfigured each time any process is suspected).

Algorithm. Once we understand how EOB works, we can describe pseudocode for EDUR, given in Algorithm 6. It is based on MvDUR presented in Section 6. The most apparent difference between MvDUR and EDUR lies in the fact that EDUR features a *leader thread* running on each replica (lines 54–78). During the time between the EO-LeaderElect and EO-LeaderRecall events (lines 62 and 68), the thread performs transaction certification on behalf of other replicas (line 72). Note that, the EO-LEADERELECT primitive takes as an argument *initialHistory*. It is an ordered set which represents the initial (unreliable) knowledge of the leader about the EO-Broadcast but not yet EO-Delivered transaction descriptors. The order in *initialHistory* is consistent with the order in which the transaction descriptors were TO-LeaderBroadcast by previous leaders and in which they will most probably be TO-Delivered soon. It allows the leader to start certifying incoming transactions as soon as possible, i.e. without waiting for the appropriate EO-Deliver events. In case the set contains incorrect information, e.g., it does not include a transaction successfully certified by the previous leader, which was agreed on by majority of processes, EOB guarantees to invalidate all decisions made by the new leader, thus preventing any inconsistencies.[4] The leader thread maintains its own tentative logical clock *TLC*, which is incremented every time a new transaction descriptor is EO-LeaderDelivered and the transaction is successfully certified (line 73). The information about successfully certified transactions that are not yet EO-Delivered is stored in the *ProcessedTx* set.

The certification procedure performed by the leader (lines 54–61) is a bit different from the standard one, featured in MvDUR, and also used in EDUR for local transaction certification (lines 14–19). It is because each transaction T needs to be certified by the leader also against all transactions T' which are (a) concurrent with respect to T, (b) have been successfully certified by the leader, and (c) are not yet EO-Delivered (line 57). After the certification, the transaction descriptor is transformed before it is EO-LeaderBroadcast. Since the certification is already performed, *readset* is no longer needed. Moreover, if the transaction failed certification, the *updates* set also need not be broadcast. In such a case, only the transaction identifier is included in the forwarded message, so that the replica that executed the transaction knows to restart it.[5]

---

[4] In this sense, the EOB primitives give a leader an impression of being the sole leader in the system, capable of making authoritative decisions on behalf of the rest of the processes. Obviously, this makes the work of the programmer much easier.

[5] In fact, only a unicast message would suffice in such circumstances. This optimization, however, would require extending EOB with new primitives, thus making the protocol unjustifiably more complicated [15].

Algorithm 6. Executive Deferred Update Replication for process p_i (part 1)

1: integer $LC \leftarrow 0$, $TLC \leftarrow 0$
2: set $ProcessedTx \leftarrow \emptyset$
3: boolean $IsLeader \leftarrow false$
4: **function** GETVERSION(objectId oid, integer $notNewerThan$)
5:     **lock** { **return** (obj, ver) such that obj is a version of object oid whose version number ver
6:                                 is the highest available such that $ver \leq notNewerThan$ }
7: **function** GETOBJECT(txDescriptor t, objectId oid)
8:     **if** $(oid, obj) \in t.updates$ **then**
9:         $value \leftarrow obj$
10:    **else**
11:        $(obj, ver) \leftarrow$ GETVERSION($oid, t.start$)
12:        $value \leftarrow obj$
13:    **return** $value$
14: **function** CERTIFY(integer $start$, set $readset$)
15:    **for all** $id \in readset$ **do**
16:        $(obj, ver) \leftarrow$ GETVERSION(id, ∞)
17:        **if** $ver > start$ **then**
18:            **return** $failure$
19:    **return** $success$

Thread q on request r from client c (executed on one replica)
20: txDescriptor $t \leftarrow \perp$ // type: record $(id, start, end, readset, updates)$
21: response $res \leftarrow \perp$
22: **upon** INIT
23:    **wait until** $LC \geq r.clock$
24:    **raise** TRANSACTION
25:    **return** $(r.id, LC, res)$ to client c
26: **upon** TRANSACTION
27:    $t \leftarrow$ (a new unique $id, 0, 0, \emptyset, \emptyset$)
28:    **lock** { $t.start \leftarrow LC$ }
29:    $res \leftarrow$ execute $r.code$ with $r.args$
30:    COMMIT()
31: **upon** READ(objectId oid)
32:    $obj \leftarrow$ GETOBJECT(t, oid)
33:    **if** $r.readOnly = false$ **then**
34:        $t.readset \leftarrow t.readset \cup \{oid\}$
35:    **return** obj
36: **upon** WRITE(objectId oid, object obj)
37:    $t.updates \leftarrow \{(oid', obj') \in t.updates : oid' \neq oid\} \cup \{(oid, obj)\}$
38: **procedure** COMMIT
39:    **if** $t.updates = \emptyset$ **then**
40:        **return to** INIT
41:    **if** CERTIFY($t.start, t.readset$) $= failure$ **then**
42:        **raise** RETRY
43:    EO-BROADCAST t
44:    **wait for** $outcome$
45:    **if** $outcome = failure$ **then**
46:        **raise** RETRY
47:    **else**   // $outcome = success$
48:        **return to** INIT
49: **upon** ROLLBACK
50:    stop executing $r.code$ and return to INIT
51: **upon** RETRY
52:    stop executing $r.code$
53:    **raise** TRANSACTION

Algorithm 6. Executive Deferred Update Replication for process p_i (part 2)

The **leader thread** of EDUR (executed on all replicas)
54: **function** LEADERCERTIFY(integer *start*, set *readset*)
55:     **if** CERTIFY(*start*, *readset*) $= failure$ **then**
56:         **return** *failure*
57:     **lock** { $conflictingTx \leftarrow \{(id, updates, clock) \in ProcessedTx :$
58:                         $clock > start \wedge \exists(oid, obj) \in updates : oid \in readset\}$ }
59:     **if** $conflictingTx = \emptyset$ **then**
60:         **return** *success*
61:     **return** *failure*
62: **upon** EO-LEADERELECT (ordered set *initialHistory*) **lock**
63:     $TLC \leftarrow LC$
64:     **for all** $t \in initialHistory : t.updates \neq \emptyset$ **do**
65:         $TLC \leftarrow TLC + 1$
66:         $ProcessedTx \leftarrow ProcessedTx \cup \{(t.id, t.updates, TLC)\}$
67:     $IsLeader \leftarrow true$
68: **upon** EO-LEADERRECALL **lock**
69:     $IsLeader \leftarrow false$
70:     $ProcessedTx \leftarrow \emptyset$
71: **upon** EO-LEADERDELIVER(txDescriptor *t*)
72:     **if** LEADERCERTIFY(*t.start*, *t.readset*) $= success$ **then**
73:         $TLC \leftarrow TLC + 1$
74:         **lock** { $ProcessedTx \leftarrow ProcessedTx \cup \{(t.id, t.updates, TLC)\}$ }
75:     **else**
76:         $t.updates \leftarrow \emptyset$
77:     $t.readset \leftarrow \emptyset$
78:     EO-LEADERBROADCAST *t*

The **main thread** of EDUR (executed on all replicas)
79: **upon** EO-DELIVER(txDescriptor *t*)
80:     **if** $updates \neq \emptyset$ **then**
81:         $outcome \leftarrow success$
82:         **lock** { **if** $IsLeader = true$ **then**
83:                     $ProcessedTx \leftarrow \{(id, updates, clock) \in ProcessedTx : id \neq t.id\}$
84:                 $LC \leftarrow LC + 1$
85:                 **for all** $(oid, obj) \in t.updates$
86:                     add *obj* as new version of object *oid* with version number LC }
87:     **else**
88:         $outcome \leftarrow failure$
89:     **if** transaction with $t.id$ executed locally by thread q **then**
90:         pass *outcome* to thread q

The rest of the pseudocode of EDUR is very similar to MvDUR's. In fact, the execution phase of EDUR differs from MvDUR only in using EOB to broadcast messages (line 43). Naturally, in EDUR processes do not perform certification upon delivering the message (line 79). Instead, they only update their state if the transaction successfully passed certification (lines 81–86).

Discussion. It is easy to see why EDUR introduces no inconsistencies during stable periods, i.e., when a leader process does not change. All messages pass through the leader which certifies, transforms and finally forwards them to all processes. The leader does not wait for a transaction it successfully certified to be committed before it certifies other transactions. It means that implicit order on message delivery is introduced. Since the leader does not change, each process EO-Delivers messages in the order the leader sent them. The consistency is therefore preserved. During unstable periods the consistency is preserved as well. It is because EOB makes sure that the prefix order established on the messages EO-LeaderBroadcast by the leader is always respected, even when the leader changes. The system performance during the leader transition periods is comparable to DUR's since in EOB the changes of the leader occur smoothly (thanks to *initialHistory* passed to EO-LEADERELECT and the fact that multiple concurrent leaders are allowed). In fact, the new leader starts just when the old one is suspected to have crashed, and not only after a distributed agreement is reached to elect a new leader or establish a new view.

Having only one process to certify the transactions enables us to devise all kinds of interesting optimizations, not possible with standard DUR/MvDUR [15]. One of the most interesting involves using a multithreaded certification procedure to improve the throughput of the leader.

10   Comparison

In Table 1, we compare replication algorithms discussed in this chapter, looking at their selected features and performance characteristics. We excluded DUR with multiversioning (MvDUR). This powerful optimization technique boosts DUR's performance but does not change the characteristics of DUR in any aspect that we consider in our comparison. Below we discuss and explain our results.

Semantics.   All discussed replication algorithms (except SMR) support full transactional semantics, so the programmer can use additional constructs to manage the flow of control, such as *abort* and *retry* (and possibly also *commit*). In DUR, Postgres-R and EDUR, a transaction is always executed optimistically. Therefore, these algorithms do not support irrevocable operations. Naturally, requests executed with SMR may include irrevocable operations, because SMR always executes all (updating) requests sequentially. Similarly, abort-free execution of irrevocable transactions is guaranteed in HTR for transactions executed in the SM mode. Additionally, DUR, HTR, Postgres-R and EDUR guarantee abort-free execution of read-only transactions if only they support multiversioning.

Complexity.   We consider three aspects in the quantitative evaluation of the algorithms. Firstly, we compare the overhead due to the used concurrency control mechanisms. All replication schemes featuring transactional semantics require some additional computation steps and data structures, which result in some extra overhead during request processing. DUR, HTR, Postgres-R and EDUR do not update the accessed shared objects directly. Instead, the updates are performed on copies of shared objects and stored in the *updates* set. Additionally, DUR, HTR in DU mode and EDUR maintain *readset* containing object IDs of all shared objects read by the transaction.[6] Postgres-R does not maintain *readset* but acquires locks on accessed shared objects. Similarly, all algorithms but SMR feature a transaction certification phase. Depending on the algorithm, certification is performed by all replicas (DUR, HTR in DU mode), by all replicas but the one that executed the transaction (Postgres-R) or by a single replica (EDUR). Transaction certification differs between the algorithms. Its complexity depends either on the size of *readset* (DUR, HTR in DU mode and EDUR) or *updates* (Postgres-R).

---

[6] *Readset* does not need to be maintained for read-only transactions.

Table 1. Comparison of transactional replication schemes

	SMR	DUR	HTR	Postgres-R	EDUR
Semantics:					
- control flow management	no	yes			
- support for irrevocable operations	yes	no	yes	no	no
Overhead due to concurrency control	none	tracking accesses to shared objects, writes performed on object copies [a]			
Commit-time transaction certification:					
- number of times performed	0	n	n or 0 [a]	$n-1$	1
- complexity	n/a	$O(|readset|)$	$O(|readset|)$ or n/a [a]	$O(|updates|)$	$O(|readset|)$
Number of communication steps	$3\,(TOB)$	$3\,(TOB)$	$3\,(TOB)$	$5\,(TOB+RB)$	$3\,(EOB)$
Number of network transmissions:					
- client's request message	n	1	1 or n [a]	1	1
- transaction readset	0	n	n or 0 [a]	0	1
- transaction updates	0	n	n	n	n or 0 [b]
Sensitivity to a workload type:					
- high contention	none	high	medium	very high	medium
- CPU intensive workload	high	low	low	low	low
- many read operations	none	high	medium	low	low

[a] Depends on the transaction execution mode (HTR only).
[b] Depends on the outcome of transaction certification.

Secondly, we compare the number of communication steps per transaction run which are required for replica synchronization. Naturally, the least number of communication steps is two: the processes send data in the first phase and, to ensure reliable communication, exchange acknowledgments in the second phase. Additionally, if the order of messages is important, the message needs to be first forwarded to the leader/sequencer process which then orders and broadcasts it. Thus under stable conditions two broadcast protocols featured in this chapter, i.e. TOB and EOB, require three communication steps, and third one, RB (reliable broadcast), requires only two. Hence, for each transaction's run SMR, DUR, HTR and EDUR need three communication steps while Postgres-R needs five communication steps.

Thirdly, we check the amount of data that replicas need to exchange in order to synchronize. Typically, SMR requires the least data to be transferred. It is because SMR broadcasts only the request's code and data needed for request execution. On the other hand, other algorithms require to broadcast the updates resulting from the local request execution, and usually some metadata that are necessary for transaction certification. Of course, when using the SM execution mode in HTR, the amount of data needed to be broadcast is the same as in SMR. EDUR reduces the network traffic by performing certification only on one process—this reduction is particularly significant in case of transactions that failed certification.

Finally, we compare three different types of workloads and discuss how they influence the performance and scalability of the algorithms. Replication schemes featuring optimistic concurrency control typically do not tolerate high contention well (i.e., when multiple concurrent requests access the same data). It is because under such workloads many transactions are rolled back and restarted, thus wasting resources. This type of workload is particularly troublesome for Postgres-R because it requires two broadcasts to be performed for each transaction's run. In HTR and EDUR, the negative aspects of high contention can be compensated. HTR allows for transaction execution with abort-free guarantees thus reducing the overall contention. In EDUR, conflict detection is streamlined with message broadcast, thus reducing the total amount of computation and the volume of data transferred through the network. Moreover, other processes do not need to bother with processing transactions that failed certification. On the other hand, in SMR, no conflicts can occur, because all (updating) requests are executed sequentially. However, for the same reason, SMR is not suitable for CPU intensive workloads. On the contrary, DUR, HTR, Postgres-R and EDUR perform better under CPU intensive workloads because they allow for the concurrent execution of all requests, not necessarily the read-only ones.

DUR does not handle well requests that execute multiple read operations. It is because DUR gathers the information about read objects in *readset* and later broadcasts it alongside *updates* to all replicas. Large *readsets* put strain on the network stack and so limit the system's scalability. In HTR, a transaction accessing a large number of objects can be executed in the SM mode (thus no *readset* need to be broadcast). Such a workload is also not problematic for EDUR or Postgres-R as well (in EDUR *readset* is only sent to the leader process; in Postgres-R replicas do not exchange any information about objects read by transactions). On the other hand, the type of operations (read/write) executed within a request does not influence the performance of SMR because it does not feature transactional semantics.

11 Conclusion and Further Reading

In this chapter, we studied distributed algorithms for full transactional replication. We defined the properties of transactional replication in terms of the rules that define the replicated process as well as the interaction between the replicated process and external clients. Then we described and discussed several core algorithms. They included basic schemes, such as state machine replication (SMR) and deferred update replication (DUR), as well as optimized variants that use multiversioning (MvDUR), combine SMR and DUR (HTR), optimize broadcast data (Postgres-R), and optimize the broadcast protocol itself (EDUR).

We then compared their main features and complexity, taking into account concurrency control, computation overhead, network communication overhead, and the application workload type. One can see from this comparison that there is no one solution that fits all purposes. The results of experimental evaluation (see e.g., [37,14]) show that a simple scheme such as SMR performs surprisingly well compared to DUR, even though it provides limited parallelism. However, the optimizations of DUR make it a lot more viable, especially given its full transactional semantics which basic SMR lacks.

We only presented selected SMR and DUR-like algorithms whose main feature is that they all rely on the total order broadcast to serialize the execution of transactions or state updates. There exist many other transactional replication methods and algorithms that differ in a number of ways, e.g., they use pessimistic concurrency control or speculative executions, build the replication protocols on top of non-distributed transactional memory, or explore other models of data space and failure. Below we give some example references to the recent work that is close to the work discussed in this chapter, but they are by no means complete.

Romano, Palmieri, Quaglia, Carvalho, and Rodrigues [31] (see also [24]) explore speculative replication protocols for transactional systems. The key idea is to run an *optimistic atomic broadcast (OAB)* algorithm to provide an early, possibly erroneous, guess on transactions' serialization order, in parallel with the algorithm that is used to determine the actual order.

Marandi, Primi, and Pedone [21] optimize the SMR scheme by using speculative execution to reduce the response time and state partitioning to increase the throughput of SMR. In the follow-up paper [19], the authors propose *parallel state-machine replication (P-SMR)*, which optimizes SMR by exploiting service semantics to determine when commands can execute concurrently and when serial execution is needed (see also [20], where a more aggressive speculative strategy is used).

Arun, Hirve, Palmieri, Peluso, and Ravindran [3] observe that in DUR even in case when remote transactions rarely conflict with each other, the conflicts among local transactions (on the same replica) can significantly decrease performance. They explore speculation to optimize this scenario and prevent some local transactions from aborting each other.

Sciascia, Pedone, and Junqueira [36] propose *scalable deferred update (S-DUR)* aimed at increasing scalability of DUR through optimizing the execution of update transactions. The key idea is to divide the state into logical partitions, replicate each one among a group of servers, and orchestrate the execution and termination of transactions across partitions using a 2PC-like protocol. Pacheco *et al.* [23] build on this idea to scale DUR on multicore processors.

In [35], Sciascia and Pedone research the application of DUR to geo-replicated storage systems. The paper discusses two optimizations of DUR for geo-replication which essentially explore delaying and reordering of transactions.

Some researchers investigated transactional replication algorithms considering complex failure models, in which servers mail fail arbitrarily. For example, Pedone and Schiper [28] discuss DUR under Byzantine faults and propose suitable extensions of this replication scheme in this failure model.

Acknowledgements. This work was funded from National Science Centre funds granted by decision No. DEC-2012/06/M/ST6/00463.

References

1. Agrawal, D., Alonso, G., Abbadi, A.E., Stanoi, I.: Exploiting atomic broadcast in replicated databases (extended abstract). In: Lengauer, C., Griebl, M., Gorlatch, S. (eds.) Euro-Par 1997. LNCS, vol. 1300, pp. 496–503. Springer, Heidelberg (1997)
2. Aguilera, M.K., Chen, W., Toueg, S.: Failure detection and consensus in the crash-recovery model. In: Kutten, S. (ed.) DISC 1998. LNCS, vol. 1499, pp. 231–245. Springer, Heidelberg (1998)
3. Arun, B., Hirve, S., Palmieri, R., Peluso, S., Ravindran, B.: Speculative client execution in deferred update replication. In: Proc. of MW4NG 2014: The 9th Middleware for Next Generation Internet Computing Workshop (December 2014)
4. Bernstein, P.A., Goodman, N.: Multiversion concurrency control—theory and algorithms. ACM Transactions on Database Systems (TODS) 8(4), 465–483 (1983)
5. Cachin, C., Guerraoui, R., Rodrigues, L.: Introduction to Reliable and Secure Distributed Programming. Springer (2011)
6. Chandra, T.D., Hadzilacos, V., Toueg, S.: The weakest failure detector for solving consensus. Journal of the ACM (JACM) 43(4), 685–722 (1996)
7. Charron-Bost, B., Pedone, F., Schiper, A. (eds.): Replication - Theory and Practice. LNCS, vol. 5959. Springer, Heidelberg (2010)
8. Couceiro, M., Romano, P., Rodrigues, L.: Polycert: Polymorphic self-optimizing replication for in-memory transactional grids. In: Proc. of Middleware 2011: The 12th ACM/IFIP/USENIX International Conference on Middleware (December 2011)
9. Défago, X., Schiper, A., Urbán, P.: Total order broadcast and multicast algorithms: Taxonomy and survey. ACM Computing Surveys (CSUR) 36(4), 372–421 (2004)
10. Fischer, M.J., Lynch, N.A., Paterson, M.S.: Impossibility of distributed consensus with one faulty process. Journal of the ACM (JACM) 32(2), 374–382 (1985)
11. Gray, J., Helland, P., O'Neil, P., Shasha, D.: The dangers of replication and a solution. In: Proc. of SIGMOD 1996: The ACM SIGMOD International Conference on Management of Data (June 1996)
12. Kemme, B., Alonso, G.: Don't be lazy, be consistent: Postgres-R, a new way to implement database replication. In: Proc. of VLDB 2000: The 26th International Conference on Very Large Data Bases (September 2000)

13. Kemme, B., Pedone, F., Alonso, G., Schiper, A.: Processing transactions over optimistic atomic broadcast protocols. In: Proc. of ICDCS 1999: The 19th IEEE International Conference on Distributed Computing Systems (1999)

14. Kobus, T., Kokociński, M., Wojciechowski, P.T.: Hybrid replication: State-machine-based and deferred-update replication schemes combined. In: Proc. of ICDCS 2013: The 33rd IEEE International Conference on Distributed Computing Systems (July 2013)

15. Kokociński, M., Kobus, T., Wojciechowski, P.T.: Make the leader work: Executive deferred update replication. In: Proc. of SRDS 2014: The 33rd IEEE International Symposium on Reliable Distributed Systems (October 2014)

16. Kończak, J., Santos, N., Żurkowski, T., Wojciechowski, P.T., Schiper, A.: JPaxos: State machine replication based on the Paxos protocol. Tech. Rep. EPFL-REPORT-167765, Faculté Informatique et Communications, EPFL (July 2011)

17. Lamport, L.: Time, clocks, and the ordering of events in a distributed system. Communications of the ACM (CACM) 21(7), 558–565 (1978)

18. Lamport, L.: The part-time parliament. ACM Transactions on Computer Systems (TOCS) 16(2) (May 1998)

19. Marandi, P.J., Bezerra, C.E., Pedone, F.: Rethinking state-machine replication for parallelism. In: Proc. of ICDCS 2014: The 34th IEEE International Conference on Distributed Systems, pp. 368–377 (June 2014)

20. Marandi, P.J., Pedone, F.: Optimistic parallel state-machine replication. In: Proc. of SRDS 2014: The 33rd International Symposium on Reliable Distributed Systems (October 2014)

21. Marandi, P.J., Primi, M., Pedone, F.: High performance state-machine replication. In: Proc. of DSN 2011: The 41st IEEE/IFIP International Conference on Dependable Systems and Networks (June 2011)

22. Moser, L.E., Amir, Y., Melliar-Smith, P.M., Agarwal, D.A.: Extended virtual synchrony. In: Proc. of ICDCS 1994: The 14th International Conference on Distributed Computing Systems (June 1994)

23. Pacheco, L., Sciascia, D., Pedone, F.: Parallel deferred update replication. In: Proc. of NCA 2014: The 13th IEEE International Symposium on Network Computing and Applications (August 2014)

24. Palmieri, R., Quaglia, F., Romano, P.: OSARE: Opportunistic speculation in actively REplicated transactional systems. In: Proc. of SRDS 2011: The 30th IEEE International Symposium on Reliable Distributed Systems (October 2011)

25. Palmieri, R., Quaglia, F., Romano, P., Carvalho, N.: Evaluating database-oriented replication schemes in software transactional memory systems. In: The 15th IEEE Workshop on Dependable Parallel, Distributed and Network-Centric Systems (April 2010)

26. Pedone, F., Guerraoui, R., Schiper, A.: The database state machine approach. Distributed and Parallel Databases 14(1) (July 2003)

27. Pedone, F., Guerraoui, R., Schiper, A.: Exploiting atomic broadcast in replicated databases. In: Pritchard, D., Reeve, J.S. (eds.) Euro-Par 1998. LNCS, vol. 1470, pp. 513–520. Springer, Heidelberg (1998)

28. Pedone, F., Schiper, N.: Byzantine fault-tolerant deferred update replication. Journal of the Brazilian Computer Society 18, 3–18 (2012)

29. van Renesse, R.: Paxos made moderately complex, available electronically (2012)

30. Romano, P., Carvalho, N., Rodrigues, L.: Towards distributed software transactional memory systems. In: Proc. of LADIS 2008: The 2nd Workshop on Large-Scale Distributed Systems and Middleware (September 2008)

31. Romano, P., Palmieri, R., Quaglia, F., Carvalho, N., Rodrigues, L.: On speculative replication of transactional systems. Journal of Computer and System Sciences 80(1), 257–276 (2014)

32. Schiper, A., Raynal, M.: From group communication to transactions in distributed systems. Communications of the ACM (CACM) 39(4) (April 1996)
33. Schneider, F.B.: Implementing fault-tolerant services using the state machine approach: A tutorial. ACM Computing Surveys (CSUR) 22(4), 299–319 (1990)
34. Schneider, F.B.: Replication management using the state-machine approach, pp. 169–197. ACM Press/Addison-Wesley (1993)
35. Sciascia, D., Pedone, F.: Geo-replicated storage with scalable deferred update replication. In: Proc. of DSN 2013: The 43rd Annual IEEE/IFIP International Conference on Dependable Systems and Networks (June 2013)
36. Sciascia, D., Pedone, F., Junqueira, F.: Scalable deferred update replication. In: Proc. of DSN 2012: The 42nd IEEE/IFIP International Conference on Dependable Systems and Networks (June 2012)
37. Wojciechowski, P.T., Kobus, T., Kokociński, M.: Model-driven comparison of state-machine-based and deferred-update replication schemes. In: Proc. of SRDS 2012: The 31st IEEE International Symposium on Reliable Distributed Systems (October 2012)

Transaction Execution Models in Partially Replicated Transactional Memory: The Case for Data-Flow and Control-Flow

Roberto Palmieri[1], Sebastiano Peluso[2], and Binoy Ravindran[3]

[1] Virginia Tech, 453 Durham Hall, Blacksburg, VA 24061, USA
robertop@vt.edu
[2] Virginia Tech, 452 Durham Hall, Blacksburg, VA 24061, USA
peluso@vt.edu
[3] Virginia Tech, 459 Durham Hall, Blacksburg, VA 24061, USA
binoy@vt.edu

Abstract. In this chapter we describe solutions for managing concurrency of distributed transactional memory accesses in partially replicated deployments. A system is classified as partially replicated if, for each shared object, there is more than one node responsible for storing the object, thus resulting in multiple copies available in the system. In contrast to full replication, where all objects are replicated on all nodes, partial replication allows storing a huge amount of data that, by nature, cannot fit in a single node and improving scalability by (significantly) increasing the number of node serving transaction requests. Solutions that assume partially replicated deployments are categorized according to the mobility of shared objects. In the control-flow approach shared objects are pinned to nodes for the entire system's lifetime, whereas in the data-flow objects are allowed to change residence node (also called owner) whenever a transaction commits a new version of the object. Intuitively, adopting the data-flow model, objects follow committing transactions whereas, relying on the control-flow model, transactions' flow is routed towards objects. There is a number of key factors to be evaluated before preferring one transaction execution model to another. This chapter surveys all of them and provides solutions suited for different deployments. The chapter aims for helping designers to understand the execution model that better fits their requirements.

1 Introduction

Replication applied to transactional systems has been already successfully consolidated in the literature as the reference methodology for building available, fault-tolerant and high performance data management systems. These properties become fundamental when the transactional processing is entirely executed in-memory, without relying on any stable storage support. This is the case of Software Transactional Memory (STM) based systems where, if the machine experiences a failure, undesirable events such that loss of data, service interruption and unfinished computations can happen.

In the last decade, several replication protocols have been proposed. They can be categorized into the *full replication* model [18,25,15,27], in which each node (or replica)

R. Guerraoui and P. Romano (Eds.): Transactional Memory, LNCS 8913, pp. 341–366, 2015.
© Springer International Publishing Switzerland 2015

keeps the entire shared data set, and the *partial replication* model [20,23,19], in which each object is replicated on a subset of all the replicas in the system. In this chapter we focus on the latter model, and we provide an overview on the main different design choices that can be adopted in the implementation of transactional partial replication solutions. We underline the challenges posed by that model, by also discussing its benefits and drawbacks, and we give an overview of some state-of-the-art solutions designed for the execution of transactions in partially replicated STMs.

Partial replication is typically adopted for increasing the scale of the system's deployment, as well as for coping with (very-) large data-set. In fact, replicating each shared object on a limited number of machines (also called nodes or replicas) allows the system's administrator to reserve just a small part of the resources available on a single node to store replicated objects, while still having a large amount free space for hosting new objects. In addition, in order to commit a transaction, the partial replication model enables the design of *genuine* protocols [11,23,20], namely schemes that involve only the nodes responsible for storing the objects accessed by the committing transaction, rather than all the nodes in the system, hence increasing the system's parallelism. This can lead to the processing of an ever growing number of client requests and an enhancement of the overall system throughput.

On the other hand, when compared with the full replication model, partial replication has two major downsides: it offers a smaller degree of resilience, limited to the number of replicas maintaining the same shared object; and it is prone to poor performance due to remote communications that can happen during transaction processing for retrieving objects stored on nodes different from the node where the transaction executes.

Designing a protocol for running transactions in partially replicated systems includes deciding whether the protocol adheres the basic scheme of data-flow or control-flow. This decision is affected by a number of factors that we discuss in Section 3. Subsequently we present two protocols implementing the data-flow and control-flow model in Sections 4 and 5, respectively. After that, in Section 6 we show a hybrid protocol that inherits the advantages from both these models. Before the protocols, a common system model is reported in Section 2. Finally Section 7 concludes the chapter.

2   System Model

We consider a classical asynchronous distributed system [10], which consists of a set of nodes $\Pi = \{n_1, n_2, \cdots\}$ that communicate with each other by message-passing links over a communication network. Messages may experience arbitrarily long (but finite) delays, and no bound on relative site speeds or clock skews is assumed. Nodes have neither a globally shared memory nor a global notion of time. We consider the crash-stop failure model [24], where nodes may fail by crashing, but they do not behave maliciously.

A set of distributed transactions $TSet = \{T_1, T_2, \cdots\}$ is assumed. Transactions share a set of objects $OSet = \{O_1, O_2, \ldots\}$, which are assumed to be distributed on the nodes of the system. Objects are subdivided across m partitions, and each partition is replicated across r nodes, i.e., r represents the replication degree for each object. The set $\Gamma = \{g_1, \ldots, g_j, \ldots, g_m\}$ denotes the set of m groups of nodes, where g_j is the group replicating the j-th objects partition. Each group is composed of exactly r nodes (to ensure the target replication degree), of which at least a majority is assumed to be correct. In order to maximize flexibility of the data placement strategy, groups are not required to be disjoint (they can have nodes in common), and a node may participate to multiple groups, as long as $\bigcup_{j=1...m} g_j = \Pi$. In addition $groups(p_i)$ denotes the set of groups which p_i belongs to, and $replicas(S)$ denotes the set of nodes that replicate the objects partitions containing all the objects $O \in S$, called also owners of S.

The replication protocols presented in this chapter rely on Two-Phase Commit-based (2PC) [2] atomic commitment algorithms in order to ensure atomicity on the commit of a transaction. Even though 2PC is well known to be blocking upon failure of the coordinator, the issue of how to ensure high availability of the transaction coordinator state is well understood, and a range of orthogonal solutions have been proposed in literature to deal with such failure scenarios. Therefore, in this chapter we do not explicitly focus on how handling the failure of a node, even if one may use, for instance, protocols such as Paxos Commit [9] or other consensus based abstractions [8,17], to replicate the state of the coordinator of a transaction T across the replicas of any of the data partitions accessed by T. Note that, since a majority of nodes is assumed to be correct for each replica group, failures of transactions' participants (different from transactions' coordinators) will not lead to blocking scenarios during the execution of a remote read operation. Failures of transactions' participants can, instead, lead to aborts during the commit phase, as the coordinator unilaterally aborts the transaction if it times out while waiting for some reply during the prepare phase. To ensure the liveness of the commit phase, the presented protocols rely on an underlying Group Communication System [3] in order to handle the removal of faulty replicas from the system and manage its reconfiguration, which might also imply the re-distribution of data across replicas to guarantee a desirable replication degree.

Transactions are modeled as a set of *begin, read, write, commit* and *abort* operations on transactional data, and they define a total order in which these operations are executed; therefore a transaction is sequential by nature and no multiple operations of a same transaction can be executed simultaneously (i.e. concurrently). Transactions that do not execute any write operation are called read-only transactions, otherwise they are called update (or equivalently write) transactions.

The last operation of a transaction T_i is either a commit operation, which indicates that T_i is completed successfully, or an abort operation, otherwise. There is at most one commit or abort per transaction, and the first operation of a transaction is the begin, which indicates the transaction starts its execution at that point in time. Furthermore, we suppose that a transaction T_i is always associated with an identifier, $T_i.id$, which univocally identifies T_i in the system.

A client requests the execution of a transaction T_i by contacting one node of the system, which is named T_i's originating node (or equivalently T_i's coordinator).

3   Transaction Execution Models: Data-Flow and Control-Flow

Under the partial replication data model, transactions are commonly executed according to two different flow models, named *data-flow* and *control-flow*, which differ depending on the "mobility" of the shared objects. In particular the distinguishing point between them is the capability of an object to move its physical content, as well as its ownership, from one node to another in the system whenever a transaction commits a change on it. For the sake of clarity, hereafter in this chapter we will refer to the action of moving an object from node n_1 to n_2 as transferring both the ownership and the physical content of the object from n_1 to n_2.

The data-flow model has been introduced by Herlihy and Sun in [14]. In this model, transactions are immobile and objects are dynamically migrated to invoking nodes. This way, when a transaction T is performed by some thread executing on a node n, then T is pinned to n and it executes all its transactional operations on n. Clearly, given the partial replication model, T could require to act on objects that are not maintained by n. If so, T first fetches the object from the node that currently is responsible for storing the object, then it uses this local copy for accomplishing those operations that need the object. Finally, if T is committed successfully, the updated objects are moved to n (i.e., n becomes an owner of those objects).

The control-flow model defines a transactional execution where objects are immobile and transactional operations are invoked on the owners of the accessed objects. In this model, the nodes responsible for maintaining an object are fixed since the creation of the object and until its deletion. When a transaction performs an operation on an object stored on a remote node, the operation is invoked as a remote procedure call on that node.

Intuitively, data-flow differs from control-flow because the former allows objects to migrate among nodes. This feature is appealing because it provides the flexibility to exploit application's locality (e.g., moving data closer to the nodes that represent the source of transactions accessing those objects), but it requires a distributed protocol to implement the functionalities of looking-up, publishing (or adding), moving and deleting objects. This entity is commonly named as *distributed cache-coherence* (or DCC) protocol [14,28,1,26]. On the other hand, protocols implementing the control-flow model cannot physically move objects, thus they do not need a distributed component, such as the DCC protocol, for retrieving and managing the location of the accessed objects. They usually determine an owner by simply executing a local, so called "consistent", logic which, given some invariant of the object (e.g., the object identifier), is able to consistently return the node storing that object despite further modifications to its content and without keeping any explicit mapping between the object and its owner nodes. This approach has the advantage to be application independent because objects' invariants are provided by the application itself. There is another approach that solves the problem of biasing the initial placement of objects by defining appropriate objects' invariants given desired destination nodes. This approach can be leveraged in applications where objects can be customized due to the actual deployment.

In the data-flow model, despite the advantages to move objects, the mapping between objects and nodes cannot be implemented entirely local at each node, as the case of control-flow, because it changes over time and all nodes should be aware of this change. As a result, maintaining updated information about this mapping and retrieving them represent a clear performance bottleneck and one of the main reasons of data-flow protocols' limited scalability. A significant research effort has been made in the area of DCC protocols for increasing their performance, spanning from theoretical aspects to practical optimizations. A commonly used implementation of a DCC protocol, also called *directory*, uses a hash function that, given the invariant of an object, it retrieves the node responsible for maintaining the mapping between the object and the actual owner. This way, if the hash function provides a uniform distribution of keys across nodes, also the load for handling object look-up requests is uniformly distributed.

The simple directory implementation just described shows that the process of retrieving an object involves remote interactions that have an inevitable consequence on the transaction critical path, stretching it in time. As a result, deciding an approach such as control-flow or data-flow is a critical design decision that affect significantly the overall system's performance and scalability.

4 TFA: A Data-Flow Based Replication Protocol

The data-flow model [14] is inspired by the usual hardware mechanisms adopted for executing atomic operations (or transactions) in multiprocessor (and multicore) architectures [12,13]. In those systems, when an object is accessed, the object is marked as "monitored" in the cache memory, such that no other operations are allowed to execute on that object. A transaction T can safely commit only if no other transaction attempted to write any object accessed by T during its execution. Modifications are made in place on the cache memory and written back to the main memory only if the transaction is successfully committed. With this approach, the parallelism of executing transactions is limited because two transactions are always prevented to act on the same object if at least one operation is a write. Despite that, there can be identified two main advantages of such a protocol: *i)* leveraging the data-flow model, objects are moved closer to the transactions such that application locality is exploited; *ii)* the commit operation is lightweight because all objects are already and exclusively fetched through the DCC protocol during the transaction's execution, thus no additional coordination phase is needed to finalize the commit.

When we export this model into a distributed system, the distributed DCC protocol has the duty of ensuring that for each object there exists only a single monitored copy. This model applies also in replicated systems because the DCC protocol treats the multiple object copies as a single copy. However, due to the longer delays caused by the network interactions, blocking two transactions from accessing the same object has a (possibly high) negative impact on performance because the time each object is taken away from other concurrent transactions is much higher than in multiprocessor architectures. As an example, if a transaction is doomed and will abort, a protocol directly inspired by the hardware cache coherence mechanism forbids other transactions to access the last committed version of objects already accessed by the transaction, limiting the concurrency. In order to overcome this limitation, in this section we describe a protocol that still implements the data-flow model but allows multiple concurrent transactions to execute optimistically on same objects. Whenever a transaction commits a new object version, all other concurrent transactions that accessed that object recognize the commit and abort accordingly.

4.1 Protocol Overview

The *Transaction Forwarding Algorithm* (TFA) [22] is a data-flow distributed transactions management algorithm. It is inspired by the TL2 algorithm, already proposed for multiprocessor STM [6]. TFA ensures *One-Copy Serializability* [2] by buffering write operations on shared objects until commit time and adopting a distributed atomic commitment protocol (i.e., Two-Phase Commit [2]) for deterministically validating read objects and making new written objects available to other transactions. Also, TFA guarantees that all transactions (including those aborted) always observe consistent states. This property is highly desirable for in-memory processing systems in order to avoid unexpected application crash. In contrast to TL2's unique clock, TFA uses independent, per node transactional clocks and provides a mechanism to establish the *happened-before* relationship [16] among significant events (e.g., read, write, commit) by updating clocks accordingly.

In this section we focus on detailing TFA and we scope out the problem of managing the location of objects because we assume the existence of a directory or a cache coherence protocol, such as Arrow [5], Ballistic [14], or others [28,1,26], which provide the required services. In particular, we assume a Directory Manager module for locating objects. Its interface includes two methods: $publish(O_x, n_c)$ that registers the node n_c, as an owner of object O_x; $locate(O_x)$, which finds the set of owner nodes of object O_x.

Even though TFA provides fault-tolerance by replicating each object on multiple nodes, for the sake of clarity in the description of the protocol, we assume the existence of a single owner node for each object O_x that is responsible for managing the object against transactions' requests. This node is named O_x's *primary owner* in order to distinguish it from all the other nodes that can maintain a copy of O_x, which are named O_x's *secondary owners*.

Secondary owners of object O_x are still updated synchronously at commit time by O_x's *primary owner*, but they are not involved for serving read and write operations. However they become fundamental in case a failure happens and a new primary owner should be elected for avoiding any loss of data.

Each node has a local logical clock, named LC, which is advanced whenever any local transaction commits. LC is piggybacked on all messages, and Lamport's based synchronization mechanism [16] is used to keep the clocks synchronized. When a transaction starts, it records the current LC into a transaction timestamp, called WV, which is used during the transaction execution for determining whether an object can be consistently accessed or not. Each object is associated with a version number (*vid*), which represents the LC value used by the transaction that committed the last version of the object, and a lock, acquired when a transaction is currently committing a new version of the object.

In the classical multiprocessor timestamp-based TM protocols, when a transaction T_i accesses an object with a version number less than or equal to T_i's timestamp, this means that the object has been committed by a transaction T_j serialized before T_i [6,7]. This invariant does not apply in distributed genuine deployments where a node clock (i.e., LC) is advanced independently of other nodes and only whenever a transaction commits on that node. In fact, in this case, the comparison between transaction's WV and object versions becomes meaningless if objects are not stored on the same node where the transaction is executing. To solve this problem and guaranteeing the above invariant in genuine partial replication model, TFA proposes a *forwarding* mechanism, which provides the support for updating LCs values according to dependencies developed by transactions in the system. As a result, TFA can rely on the usual reading rule adopted by timestamp-based protocols [6,7] where a version is visible is its version number not greater than WV. In addition, with the purpose of increasing the set of visible objects, TFA provides also a procedure, similar to the one adopted in [21], which tries to increase WV whenever an accessed object is detected with a version number greater than that.

4.2   Accessing Objects and Committing Transactions

Algorithms 1–6 describe TFA's main procedures. When a transaction begins, it reads the current clock value of the node on which it is executing. Due to the data-flow model, if the primary owner of an accessed object is remote, read and write operations may involve communication steps. Whenever a remote object is accessed, a local object copy is created and cached at the current node till the transaction terminates. This way, a transaction makes only object modifications to a local copy of the object. Every written object obj, identified by oid is buffered into a private per-transaction memory space called write-set (ws) as a couple $\langle oid, obj \rangle$. Equivalently, objects returned from read operations are stored in the read-set, as $\langle oid, vid \rangle$, where vid represents the version number of oid. If a read operation involves an object that appears also in the write-set, the last value written by the current transaction is retrieved. In the following, we detail the two major operations of TFA: fetching an object (denoted as *Open* in the Algorithm 2) and committing a transaction (Algorithm 6).

When a transaction starts (Algorithm 1), it fetches the value of LC and stores it to the transaction's WV.

Algorithm 1. Begin operation (node n_i)

1: *void Begin(Transaction T)*
2:      $T.WV \leftarrow n_i.LC$

A read operation, as well as a write operation, requires to retrieve the object from the current primary owner node before to act on the object. To do so, the *Open* procedure is called (Algorithm 2).

The node executing the transaction n_i sends a request for retrieving an object with ObjectId oid to oid's primary owner. The current node clock value of n_i, called LC, is piggybacked on this message. Upon receiving the message for retrieving an object at receiver node n_j (i.e., the primary oid object owner) (Algorithm 4), a copy of the object is sent back, and the current clock value, namely n_j's LC, is included in the reply. In addition the *Forward* operation is called (see Algorithm 5). This way, the incoming clock value, n_i's LC, is extracted and compared with the current clock value of n_j. If n_j's $LC < n_i$'s LC, then n_j's LC is advanced to the value n_i's LC; otherwise nothing is changed.

Algorithm 2. Open operation (node n_i)

1: *Object Open(Transaction T, ObjectId oid)*
2:     *Node $n_j \leftarrow$ locate(oid)*
3:     $[Object \quad obj, \quad SnapshotId \quad vid, \quad bool \quad locked, \quad SnapshotId \quad n_j.LC] \leftarrow retrieveObject(n_j, oid, n_i.LC)$
4:     *Forward($n_j.LC$)*
5:     **if** *locked* $= \top$ **then**
6:         **throw** ABORT
7:     **if** *vid* $> T.WV \wedge Extend(T, n_j.LC) = \bot$ **then**
8:         **throw** ABORT
9:     **return** *obj*

When n_i receives the reply from n_j and the object is locked, then the transaction is immediately aborted. In case the object is free of lock and the object's version number is not greater than the transaction's *WV*, the object can be returned. If the object's version number is grater than the transaction's *WV*, then the transaction tries to extend its *WV* (Algorithm 3) to n_j's *LC*, in order to read the object. The procedure for extending the transaction's *WV* includes the validation of the entire read-set. For each object read so far by the transaction, the procedure locates that object and checks its current version number. If it is higher than the version number recorded in the read-set but still less than or equal to n_j's *LC* (the target clock value of the transaction), then the transaction's *WV* cannot be extended and this causes its abort. Otherwise *WV* is extended to n_j's *LC*.

Finally, whenever n_i receives a reply for a retrieve object request, it calls the *Forward* operation to forward (if needed) n_i's *LC* to n_j's *LC*.

Algorithm 3. Extend operation (node n_i)

1: *bool Extend(Transaction T, SnapshotId target)*
2:     **for all** $\langle roid, rvid \rangle \in T.rs$ **do**
3:         *Node $n_j \leftarrow$ locate(roid)*
4:         $[Object \quad obj, \quad SnapshotId \quad vid, \quad bool \quad locked, \quad SnapshotId \quad n_j.LC] \leftarrow retrieveObject(n_j, roid, n_i.LC)$
5:         *Forward($n_j.LC$)*
6:         **if** *locked* $= \top$ **then**
7:             **return** $\bot$
8:         **if** *vid* $> rvid \wedge vid \leq target$ **then**
9:             **return** $\bot$
10:    $T.WV \leftarrow target$
11:    **return** $\top$

When a transaction completes all its transactional operations we need to guarantee that the transaction appears as executed at a unique point in time. If the transaction is a read-only one, it appears as executed at the logical time *WV* thanks to the TFA's reading rule, and it can safely commit without any additional step. Otherwise, in case of an update transaction, we have to guarantee that the entire read-set remains unchanged

---

Algorithm 4. Reception of a RETRIEVEOBJECTMSG (node n_i)

1: **upon receive** RETRIEVEOBJECTMSG(*[ObjectId oid, SnapshotId $n_j.LC$]*) **from** n_j
2:      *Forward($n_j.LC$)*
3:      *Object obj $\leftarrow$ getObject(oid)*
4:      *SnapshotId vid $\leftarrow$ getVersionId(oid)*
5:      *bool locked $\leftarrow$ isLocked(oid)*
6:      **send** RETRIEVEOBJECTRETURN(*[obj,vid,locked,$n_i.LC$]*) **to** n_j

---

Algorithm 5. Forward operation (node n_i)

1: *void Forward(SnapshotId target)*
2:      **if** *target* $> n_i.LC$ **then**
3:          $n_i.LC \leftarrow$ *target*

Algorithm 6. Commit phase (node n_i).

1: *void Commit(Transaction T)*
2:      **for all** $\langle oid,obj \rangle \in T.ws$ **do**
3:          *acquireLock(oid)* **on all** $n_j \in replicas(\{oid\})$ ▷ Lock acquisition on n_j.
4:      **for all** $\langle roid,rvid \rangle \in T.rs$ **do**
5:          *bool valid $\leftarrow$ Validate(roid,rvid)* **on all** $n_j \in replicas(\{oid\})$ ▷ Validation on n_j.
6:          **if** *valid* $= \bot$ **then**
7:              **throw** ABORT
8:      $n_i.LC++$
9:      **for all** $\langle oid,obj \rangle \in T.ws$ **do**
10:          *obj.commitValue()*
11:          *setVersionId(oid,$n_i.LC$)*
12:          *releaseLock(oid)* **on all** $n_j \in replicas(\{oid\})$ ▷ Lock release on n_j.
13:          *publish(oid,n_i)*
14:
15: *void Validate(ObjectId roid, SnapshotId rvid)*
16:      *SnapshotId vid $\leftarrow$ getVersionId(roid)*
17:      *bool locked $\leftarrow$ isLocked(roid)*
18:      **if** *locked* $= \top \vee vid > rvid$ **then**
19:          **return** $\bot$
20:      **return** $\top$

---

at the time when the transaction is actually serialized (i.e., when all objects are made available to other transactions). In order to ensure that, TFA accomplishes the following procedure (see Algorithm 6).

TFA acquires locks for objects belonging to the write-set. As some (or all) of these objects may be remote, a lock request is sent to all object owner nodes. If the lock cannot be acquired for any of the objects, the transaction is aborted and restarted.

After the lock acquisition, the whole read-set is validated against the current version of the accessed objects. The validation succeeds if none of the read objects has a current version number greater than the version stored in the read-set and is locked by other transactions. Upon successful completion of this step, a transaction can safely proceed to commit on the node where the transaction is running.

Before publishing the new object versions, the local clock value LC is incremented by 1, and those new versions are tagged with the new value of LC. After that, all new object versions are published through the directory manager. This step includes the update of other object copies maintained by secondary owners. The commitment phase finishes releasing all acquired locks.

The abort of a transaction consists of releasing all acquired locks (if any), clears its read and write sets, and restarts again by assigning the new WV.

4.2.1 Example

Figure 1 illustrates an example of how TFA operates in a network of three nodes, N_1, N_2, and N_3. Initial values of the respective node clocks are 10, 20, and 5. Lines between the nodes represent requests and replies, and stars represent object access. Any changes in the clock values are due to successfully committed transactions. In this example we consider only primary object owners and we skip the updates to other object copies.

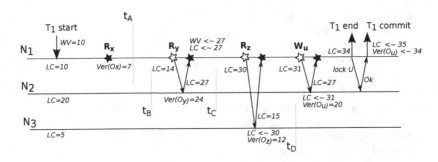

Fig. 1. An execution of a distributed transaction under TFA

Transaction T_1 is invoked at node N_1 with a local clock value, $LC = 10$. Thus, $T_1.WV = 10$. Afterwards, T_1 reads the value of the local object O_x and finds its version number, denoted as $Ver(O_x)$ in the figure, as $7 < T_1.WV$, and adds it to its read-set. The remote object O_y is then accessed for read. N_1 sends an access request to N_2 (O_y's primary object owner) with its current clock value LC. Upon receiving the request at N_2 at time 27 (according to N_2's clock), N_2 replies with the object value and its local clock. N_1 processes the reply and finds that it has to advance its local clock to time 27. In addition, the transaction extension needs to be done. $T_1.WV$ is therefore set to 27. Furthermore, early commit-validation is done on the read-set to ensure that this change will not hide changes happened to any object in the read-set since the transaction started (at any time t_A).

Subsequently, T_1 accesses object O_z located at node N_3, and includes its local clock value to the request. After N_3 replies with a copy of the object and its local time, N_3 detects that its time lags behind N_1's time. Thus, N_3 will advance its time to 30 (the last detected clock value from N_1). Note that in this case, N_1 will not advance its clock, nor will do the transaction extension, as it has a leading clock value.

Now, T_1 requests object O_u at node N_2. Assume that N_2's clock value is still 27 since the last request, while N_1 advances its clock due to other transactions' commit. Now, N_2 will advance its clock to 31 upon receiving object O_u's access request.

Eventually, T_1 completes its execution and does the commit-validation step by acquiring locks on objects in its write-set (i.e., O_u), and validating versions of objects in its read-set (i.e., O_x, O_y, and O_z). Upon successful validation, N_1's local clock is incremented atomically and its old value is written to O_u's versioned-lock. N_1 is published as the new owner of the write-set objects.

5 SCORe: A Control-Flow Based Replication Protocol

In control-flow protocols, shared objects are immobile while transactional flow moves from node to node by following the location of the accessed objects. Therefore in case a transaction T originated by a node n_i issues an operation (either read or write operation) on an object O that is located on a node n_j (different from n_i), the execution flow of T moves from n_i to n_j in order to finalize that operation. This means that, to access a remote object, a transaction makes a remote procedure call (RPC) to the object's owner node, which in turn makes a tentative update (in case of write operation) or returns a result (in case of read operation).

Compared to data-flow based protocols, control-flow based protocols can be more scalable since they do not need to move objects during transactions execution or commit, and they do not rely on expensive distributed protocols for managing (and retrieving) the location of objects. As a result, in case of favorable placement of objects, a transaction is likely executed locally at the originating node without exchanging any additional message in the system for executing remote operations or retrieving objects' location.

However control-flow model has drawbacks in case the distribution of transactional accesses in the system (i.e., the application locality) does not follow the initial distribution of objects, thus generating a significant amount of remote read operations per transaction. Furthermore, since nodes committing a change on an object do not acquire an exclusive ownership on that object, determining the outcome of a transaction after its execution in control-flow based protocols cannot be implemented as a local decision only at the transaction's originating node. In particular, nodes storing the objects accessed by a transaction T need to coordinate in order to determine whether T can be committed or not, and T's commit order against the commits of other concurrent transactions that conflict with T.

Therefore, as soon as a client requests the execution of a transaction to a given node, the node executes the transaction optimistically by returning to the client the values of the read operations and buffering the outcome of write operations in the write-set. The output of a transaction should not be externalized at this stage because its execution advances optimistically without taking into account possible conflicts with concurrent transactions running at other nodes. At commit time, namely whenever the transaction requests the commit, the results of the local processing are replicated on the nodes storing the objects to be updated. The replication does not necessarily entail the application of the updates, which can only happen if all the involved nodes determine a successful completion of the transaction. The decision on whether committing a transaction T or not can be made by relying on an atomic commitment protocol [4,2] in order to execute a deterministic validation procedure of T on the nodes storing the objects in T's read-set, and to apply the changes of T on all the nodes storing the objects in T's write-set. The atomic commitment protocol guarantees that: *i)* for each object O_i in T's read-set, the validation of T produces the same outcome on all the nodes replicating O_i, and *ii)* the updates of T are atomically applied in the same order (with respect to the commits of other concurrent transactions) on all the nodes replicating objects in T's write-set.

In the following, we present SCORe, a multi-version control-flow based partial replication protocol that follows the aforementioned scheme and is able to guarantee One-Copy Serializability on the set of executed transactions (either aborted or committed). This way SCORe ensures that no transaction observes an inconsistent state and therefore read-only transactions are never forcefully aborted without incurring a distributed validation procedure either.

5.1 Protocol Overview

SCORe is a genuine partial replication protocol that implements a One-Copy Serializable distributed multi-version scheme [19]. Unlike data-flow protocols, in control-flow maintaining multiple versions of an object is a common practice to guarantee higher parallelism of transactions execution. This is because a read operation of a transaction T is always able to return the version that is compatible with (i.e., does not violate serializability of) the history of transactions observed by T so far, and read operations do not interfere with the execution of write operations. As a consequence, read-only transactions (i.e., transactions that do not execute any write operation) are never forcefully aborted by the concurrency control scheme.

As in typical non-distributed multi-version algorithms [2], SCORe replicas store multiple versions of the objects that they maintain. Each object o is a sequence of versions $ver = \langle val, vid \rangle$, all associated with an id Oid representing O's identifier, and ordered according to the order of the write operations committed on O. The fields val and vid of a version ver are respectively a value of O and a logical scalar timestamp, i.e., an integer non-negative number, associated with the commit of ver. Given a sequence of versions associated with O and stored on a node n_i, the values of vid are monotonically decreasing going from the most recent committed version to the oldest one. Throughout the description of the protocol, $Oid.last$ identifies the sequence of committed versions associated with the object Oid (i.e., that is identified by Oid), and its value is the last committed one among them. Furthermore, for each version ver of object Oid, $ver.prev$

identifies the version preceding *ver* (e.g., that has been committed before *ver*) in the sequence of versions associated with *Oid*.

SCORe introduces a novel distributed timestamp management scheme that addresses two main issues: (i) establishing the snapshot visible by transactions, i.e., selecting which one, among the multiple versions of an object (replicated across multiple nodes) should be observed by a transaction upon a read operation; (ii) determining the final global serialization order for update transactions via a distributed agreement protocol that takes place during the transactions' commit phase.

To this end SCORe maintains two scalar variables per node, namely *commitId* and *nextId*. The former one maintains the timestamp that was attributed to the last update transaction when committed on that node. *nextId*, on the other hand, keeps track of the next timestamp that the node will propose when it will receive a commit request for a transaction that accessed some of the objects that it maintains. The sequences of values assigned to both variables are guaranteed to be monotonically increasing, since they represent the advancement of logical time on each node.

Snapshot visibility for transactions is determined by associating with each transaction T a scalar timestamp, called *snapshot identifier* or, more succinctly, *sid*. The *sid* of a transaction is established upon its first read operation. In this case the most recent version of the requested object is returned, and the transaction's *sid* is set to the value of *commitId* at the transaction's originating node, if the read can be served locally. Otherwise, if the requested object is not maintained locally, $T.sid$ is set equal to the maximum between *commitId* at the originating node and *commitId* at the remote node from which T reads. From that moment on, any subsequent read operation is allowed to observe the most recent committed version of the requested object having timestamp less than or equal to $T.sid$, as in classical multi-version concurrency control algorithms.

Therefore, unlike the TFA protocol presented in Section 4, SCORe does not advance the observable snapshot on every read operation, and it only ensures that a transaction can observe at least all the writes committed on the transaction's originating node before the transaction began. Note that a procedure for extending the observable snapshot of a read operation in SCORe would follow the one presented for TFA, and however it is not necessary for correctness. In fact, trying to extend the observable snapshot increases the probability of reading the last available version of an object, which in TFA means increasing the probability to commit transactions since no multiple versions are available for each object.

To guarantee that the logical timestamps univocally identify committed snapshots of the transactional state (whether they are *commitId*, *nextId*, *sid* or *vid*), in SCORe they are represented in such a way for any pair of timestamps id_i and id_j, if $id_i \leq id_j \wedge id_j \leq id_i$ then $i = j$, hence they are the same identifier associated to a unique commit. In addition if $i \neq j$, then either $id_i \leq id_j$ or $id_j \leq id_i$, and for any triple id_i, id_j and id_k, if $id_j \leq id_i \wedge id_j \leq id_k$, then $id_i \leq id_k$. Therefore a set of identifiers in SCORe is always totally ordered under the binary relation $\leq$, and this property is ensured by implicitly supposing that a timestamp identifier can be represented as a pair of integer and node identifier (which can be a compact representation of its address that univocally identifies it in the system). In addition, throughout the following description, the notation $id_i < id_j$ is used to indicate that $id_i \leq id_j$ and $id_j \not\leq id_i$, .

Analogously to other control-flow partial replication protocols (e.g., [20]), SCORe relies on a genuine atomic commit protocol that can be seen as the fusion of the Two-Phase Commit algorithm (2PC) [2] and the Skeen's total order multicast [11]. 2PC is used to validate update transactions and to guarantee the atomicity of the application of their post-images. Overlapped with 2PC, SCORe runs a distributed agreement protocol that allows to achieve a twofold goal: (i) totally ordering the commit events of transactions that update any object in a partition j among all the nodes that replicate j (namely, g_j); (ii) tracking the serialization order between *update* transactions that exhibit (potentially transitive) data dependencies by totally ordering them via a scalar *commit timestamp* that is also used as version identifier of the post-images of committed transactions.

A key mechanism used in SCORe to correctly serialize transactions, and in particular to track write-after-read dependencies [2], is to update the *nextId* of a node upon the processing of a read operation. Specifically, if a node receives a read operation from a transaction T having a *sid* larger than its local *nextId*, this is advanced to $T.sid$. This mechanism guarantees that any update transaction T^{up} that requests to commit on node n_i at time t is attributed a commit timestamp larger than the timestamp of any transaction T that read a value from n_i before time t, hence ensuring that T^{up} is serialized after T.

An analogous tracking of dependencies is adopted by TFA as well, because read/write operations executed on a node n_i in TFA may entail an advancement of the logical time on n_i. However, unlike TFA, a read operation in SCORe cannot directly advance the *commitId* of a node (it can only advance *nextId*) because, as it will be clearer in the following, this could result in incorrect behaviors. In fact, if read operations directly changed the value of *commitId*, then in case of concurrent commits of update transactions on n_i, the invariant of monotonically increasing sequence of values assigned to *commmitId* could be violated.

Finally, since a transaction is attributed a snapshot identifier upon its first read, which is used throughout its execution, SCORe guarantees that the snapshot read by a transaction is always consistent with respect to a prefix of the equivalent serial history of committed transactions. As a consequence, in SCORe read-only transactions never abort and do not need to undergo any distributed validation.

The pseudocode of the SCORe protocol is reported in Algorithms 7, 8, 9, 10, 11 and 12, and discussed and analyzed in the following subsections.

5.2   Handling of Read and Write Operations

SCORe buffers write operations of transactions in the write-set (denoted as *ws* in Algorithm 7), which is only made visible upon transaction's commit.

Read operations on an object O first check whether O has already been updated by the transaction, returning in this case the value present in the transaction's write-set (lines 5-6 of Algorithm 7). Otherwise, it is necessary to establish which of the versions of O is visible to the transaction. As already mentioned, transactions establish the *sid* that they use to determine version's visibility upon their first read. If this read operation is local, the transaction's *sid* is simply set equal to the originating node's *commitId* (lines 7-8 of Algorithm 7). Otherwise, it is set equal to the maximum between the *commitId* of the remote node from which the object is read and the *commitId* of the transaction's originating node (lines 17-18 of Algorithm 7 and lines 3-4 of Algorithm 9). Further, if the transaction's *sid* is higher than the node's *nextId*, the latter is set equal to $T.sid$ (line 3 of Algorithm 8). This ensures that update transactions that subsequently issue a commit request on that node are serialized after T.

Algorithm 7. Write and Read operations (node n_i).

1: *void Write(Transaction T, ObjectId oid, Value val)*
2:      $T.ws \leftarrow T.ws \setminus \{\langle oid, - \rangle\} \cup \{\langle oid, val \rangle\}$
3:
4: *Value Read(Transaction T, ObjectId oid)*
5:      **if** $\exists < oid, val > \in T.ws$ **then**
6:          **return** *val*
7:      **if** is first read of T **then**
8:          $T.sid \leftarrow n_i.commitId$
9:      **if** $n_i \in replicas(\{oid\})$ **then**
10:          $[val, last] \leftarrow doRead(T.sid, oid)$
11:     **else**
12:          **if** is first read of T **then**
13:              **send** READREQUEST($[T.id, oid, T.sid, \top]$) **to all** $n_j \in replicas(\{oid\})$
14:          **else**
15:              **send** READREQUEST($[T.id, oid, T.sid, \bot]$) **to all** $n_j \in replicas(\{oid\})$
16:          **wait receive** READRETURN($[tid, val, newRsid, lastCsid, last]$) **from any** $n_h \in$ $replicas(\{oid\})$
17:          **if** is first read of T **then**
18:              $T.sid \leftarrow newRSid$
19:      **if** $last = \bot \wedge T.ws \neq \emptyset$ **then**
20:          **throw** ABORT
21:      $T.rs \leftarrow T.rs \cup \{oid\}$
22:      **return** *val*

Next, the version visible by transaction T is determined, as in conventional MVCC algorithms [2], by selecting the most recent version having commit timestamp less than T's snapshot identifier (lines 6-11 of Algorithm 8). Before doing so, however, T first waits for the completion of the commit phase of any transaction T' that *i)* is updating O, and *ii)* is currently in its commit phase (line 5 of Algorithm 8). In fact, in case T' is committed successfully, as it will be clearer in the following, it might be attributed a timestamp smaller than $T.sid$. Hence, T' would be totally ordered before T and the version of O created by T' would be visible to T. If T' aborted, on the other hand, T should not see its updates. In order to enforce the correct tracking of this read-after-write dependence, SCORe forces any transaction T reading an object O to wait until there are no longer transaction commit events pending on O and with a (either final or temporary) commit timestamp smaller than $T.sid$.

The logic for handling remote read operations is defined by Algorithm 9. It is worthy to highlight that, even though transactions update their own *sid* only upon their first read operation, a node attempts to advance its local timestamps *commitId* and *nextId*

Algorithm 8. Version visibility logic (node n_i).

```
 1: [Value, bool] doRead(SnapshotId readSid, ObjectId oid)
 2:     // Track write-after-read dependence
 3:     n_i.nextId ← max(n_i.nextId, readSid)
 4:     // Enforce read-after-write dependence
 5:     wait until (n_i.commitId ≥ readSid ∨ oid.exclusiveUnlocked())
 6:     Version ver ← oid.last
 7:     bool last ← ⊤
 8:     while ver.vid > sid do
 9:         ver ← ver.prev
10:         last ← ⊥
11:     return [ver.val, last]
```

---

whenever it receives a message (associated with the request or the response of a read operation) from another node in the system informing it that snapshots with higher timestamps have been already committed. This mechanism, which aims for maximizing the freshness of visible snapshots, is encapsulated by the *updateNodeTimestamps* function (lines 12-15 of Algorithm 9). This function advances immediately the *nextId* timestamp, which is used to determine the timestamp proposed for future commit requests. However, additional care needs to be taken before advancing the node's *commitId* timestamp. As this timestamp determines the (minimum) snapshot visible by locally generated transactions, in fact, it can be increased to a new value, say *commitId'*, only if it is found that there are no committing transactions that may be given a timestamp less than or equal to *commitId'* (lines 17-18 of Algorithm 9).

Finally, SCORe includes a simple, yet effective, optimization that consists in immediately aborting update transactions which, based on their snapshot identifier, are forced to observe, upon a read operation, object versions that have been already overwritten by more recently committed transactions (lines 19-20 of Algorithm 7).

5.3   Handling Commits

As already mentioned, in SCORe read-only transactions (lines 2-3 of Algorithm 10) can be committed without undergoing distributed validation phases (unlike, for instance, in [23]).

Update transactions, on the other hand, execute a Two-Phase Commit protocol, which is detailed in the following. To guarantee genuineness, SCORe involves in the commit phase of a transaction T only the nodes that maintain replicas of the objects that T accessed plus the coordinator of T, namely the node originating T. More in detail, when a node n_i requests to commit transaction T, it broadcasts a PREPARE message to all nodes n_j belonging to $replicas(T.rs \cup T.ws) \cup n_i$ (line 6 of Algorithm 10). Upon the receipt of this message, node n_j verifies whether the transaction can be serialized after every transaction that has locally committed so far. To this end, it attempts to acquire exclusive locks for the objects in T's write-set, and shared locks for the objects in T's read-set. This lock acquisition is non-blocking since the node waits for a busy lock only for a certain amount of time, which is determined by means of a configurable timeout

---

Algorithm 9. Handling of remote reads (node n_i).

1: **upon receive** READREQUEST(*[int tid, ObjectId oid, SnapshotId readSid, bool firstRead]*)
      from n_j
2:      *SnapshotId newReadSid* $\leftarrow$ *readSid*
3:      **if** *firstRead* $= \top \wedge n_i.commitId > newReadSid$ **then**
4:          *newReadSid* $\leftarrow$ $n_i.commitId$
5:      $[val, last] \leftarrow doRead(newReadSid, oid)$
6:      **send** READRETURN($[tid, val, newReadSid, n_i.commitId, last]$)
7:      *updateNodeTimestamps(readSid)*
8:
9: **upon receive** READRETURN(*[int tid, Value val, SnapshotId newRsid, SnapshotId lastCsid,*
      bool last]) **from** n_j
10:      *updateNodeTimestamps(lastCsid)*
11:
12: *void updateNodeTimestamps(SnapshotId lastCommittedSid)*
13:      // *Update global snapshot knowledge*
14:      $n_i.nextId \leftarrow max(n_i.nextId, lastCommittedSid)$
15:      $n_i.maxSeenId \leftarrow max(n_i.maxSeenId, lastCommittedSid)$
16:
17: **upon** $(n_i.maxSeenId > n_i.commitId \wedge CommitQueue.isEmpty())$
18:      $n_i.commitId \leftarrow max(n_i.maxSeenId, n_i.commitId)$

---

parameter (lines 2-3 of Algorithm 11). Next, if the acquisition of the locks succeeds, the node validates T's read-set (line 4 of Algorithm 11), verifying that none of the items read by T has been overwritten by a more recently committed transaction (in terms of timestamp identifiers). If any of these operations fails, T is simply rolled back, which will yield to the abort of the whole distributed transaction, as in classic 2PC (lines 6-7 of Algorithm 11).

If the transaction passes the validation phase, however, the VOTE message of 2PC is exploited to overlap a distributed agreement scheme similar in spirit to Skeen's total order multicast algorithm that aims for establishing the final serialization order for the transaction. More in detail, n_j increments the *nextId* timestamp, inserts the triple $\langle T, n_j.nextId, pending \rangle$, defined on the domain *Transaction* $\times$ *SnapshotId* $\times$ {*pending, ready*} in a queue of pending committing transactions (denoted as *CommitQueue*) ordered by *SnapshotId*, and sends back to the transaction coordinator the value of $n_j.nextId$ in piggyback to the VOTE message (lines 8-11 of Algorithm 11). The coordinator gathers the VOTE messages (aborting the transaction in case one of the contacted node does not respond within a predefined timeout), determines the final commit timestamp for T as the maximum among the timestamps proposed by the transaction's participants, and broadcasts back a DECIDE message with the transaction's final commit timestamp (lines 7-15 of Algorithm 10).

Upon the receipt of the DECIDE message (lines 13-25 of Algorithm 11) with a positive outcome, unlike classical 2PC, the transaction is not necessarily immediately committed. In fact, as each object is replicated over more than one node, and since One-Copy Serializability has to be ensured without requiring the validation of

---

Algorithm 10. Commit phase (node n_i).

```
 1:  bool Commit(Transaction T)
 2:      if T.ws = ∅ then
 3:          return ⊤;
 4:      bool outcome ← ⊤;
 5:      Set proposedSn ← ∅;
 6:      send PREPARE([T, T.sid, T.rs, T.ws]) to all n_j ∈ replicas(T.rs ∪ T.ws) ∪ {n_i}
 7:      for all n_j ∈ replicas(T.rs ∪ T.ws) ∪ {n_i} do
 8:          wait receive VOTE([T, sn, res]) from n_j or timeout
 9:          if res = ⊥ ∨ timeout then
10:              outcome ← ⊥
11:              break
12:          else
13:              proposedSn ← proposedSn ∪ sn
14:      T.sid ← max(proposedSn)
15:      send DECIDE([T, T.sid, outcome]) to all n_j ∈ replicas(T.rs ∪ T.ws) ∪ {n_i}
16:      wait until T.completed = ⊤
17:      return T.outcome
18:
19:  bool validate(Set rs, SnapshotId sid)
20:      for all k ∈ rs do
21:          if k.lastFinal.vid > sid then
22:              return ⊥
23:      return ⊤
```

---

read-only transactions, SCORe guarantees that the commit events of all update transactions (even non-conflicting ones) are totally ordered across all the replicas of a same partition. To ensure this result, when a DECIDE message is received on n_j for transaction T with final commit timestamp fsn, T is removed from *CommitQueue* and it is immediately committed (atomically increasing $n_j.nextId$) only if there are no other transactions in *CommitQueue* with snapshot id less than fsn. If this is not the case, the old entry of T is updated in *CommitQueue* with the values $\langle T, fsn, ready \rangle$ and it is ordered accordingly, while the commit of T is delayed till it can be ensured that no other pending transaction will ever receive a final commit snapshot id less than fsn (Algorithm 12).

6   Hybrid-Flow: A Hybrid Approach for Exploiting Application Locality

Hybrid-Flow is a partial replication protocol proposing a hybrid model between dataflow and control-flow, which is optimized for applications with inherent time locality on their objects accesses. On the one hand Hybrid-Flow inherits the advantages of the control-flow model by (i) avoiding to look-up objects remotely in order to serve write requests, thus saving network communication steps; (ii) avoiding to change objects' ownership at commit time when the application locality requirements are met; (iii) resolving objects' position locally in case application exposes locality. On the other hand, it exploits the advantages of data-flow by allowing the possibility to change the object

Algorithm 11. Prepare and Decide messages (node n_i).

```
 1:  upon receive PREPARE([Transaction T]) from n_j
 2:      bool outcome ← getExclLocksWithTimeout(T.id, T.ws)
 3:      outcome ← outcome ∧ getSharedLocksWithTimeout(T.id, T.rs)
 4:      outcome ← outcome ∧ validate(T.rs, T.sid)
 5:      SnapshotIdsn ← NULL_SID
 6:      if outcome = ⊥ then
 7:          releaseLocks(T.id, T.ws, T.rs)
 8:      else
 9:          sn ← n_i.nextId ← n_i.nextId + 1
10:          CommitQueue.put(⟨T, sn, pending⟩)
11:      send VOTE ([T.id, sn, outcome]) to n_j
12:
13:  upon receive DECIDE([Transaction T, SnapshotId fsn, bool outcome]) from n_j
14:      if outcome = ⊤ then
15:          n_i.nextId ← max(n_i.nextId, fsn)
16:          if n_i ∈ replicas(T.ws ∪ T.rs) then
17:              CommitQueue.update(⟨T, fsn, ready⟩)
18:          else
19:              T.outcome ← ⊤
20:              T.completed ← ⊤
21:      else
22:          CommitQueue.remove(T)
23:          releaseLocks(T.id, T.ws, T.rs)
24:          T.outcome ← ⊥
25:          T.completed ← ⊤
```

Algorithm 12. Finalizing the commit phase of transaction T (node n_i).

```
 1:  upon    (∃⟨T, fsn, s⟩ : ⟨T, fsn, s⟩ = CommitQueue.head ∧ s = ready ∧ (∄⟨T̄, s̄n, s̄⟩ ∈
         CommitQueue : s̄n < fsn))
 2:      ∀⟨oid, val⟩ ∈ T.ws : n_i ∈ replicas({oid}) do apply(oid, val, fsn)
 3:      n_i.commitId = fsn
 4:      CommitQueue.remove(T)
 5:      releaseLocks(T.id, T.ws, T.rs)
 6:      T.outcome ← ⊤
 7:      T.completed ← ⊤
```

ownership when a non optimal data placement is detected, according to the application's need.

Hybrid-Flow is *genuine* [11,20,23]: only nodes storing objects accessed by a transaction T during its execution participate in exchanging messages for executing and committing T. The protocol ensures *1-copy-serializability* [2] by acquiring locks on accessed objects at commit time (using two-phase commit) and validating the read objects after lock acquisition. Since Hybrid-Flow does not implement multi-versioning, each shared object only stores the most recent version that was committed on it.

The ownership is transferred, along with object's content, at commit time when objects are locked by a committing transaction and a distributed directory service tracks objects' location. To make the resolution of objects ownership fast, each node is equipped with an own local view of the directory (we assume the directory, or a compact representation of, can be stored in a single node). In case few updates happen on the distributed directory, the local directory is an accurate representation of its distributed version.

Hybrid-Flow uses a locality-aware transactional scheduler, called LTS, for managing concurrent object requests from processing nodes. LTS uses information collected during the transactions dispatching for monitoring the performance of the distributed system and it uses this information for detecting the effectiveness of the current data placement. If the monitoring process does not highlight misplaced objects, transactions take advantage of the local directory, boosting the owner look-up phase whenever they perform an operation on a shared object. Conversely, when the Hybrid-Flow monitoring detects that a considerable number of transactions issue requests for an object from a node different from the current object owner (e.g., due to a fluctuation in the application workload) it enables a change of ownership for that object. This change can actually take place during the commitment of a transaction that is locking that object and it entails transferring the ownership among nodes, along with the content of the object. Therefore objects are not migrated spontaneously or by an external component, instead their ownership changes during the process of committing a transaction that has accessed those objects.

6.1   Protocol Details

Hybrid-Flow is suited for applications that exhibit locality without having any a priori knowledge of data access pattern. When transactions mostly access remote objects instead of local objects, the impact of communication costs on total transaction execution time is significant, resulting in poor performance. Hybrid-Flow addresses this problem by detecting the best location for misplaced objects and moving them closer to their current *requesting nodes*. The requesting node n_r for an object O_i is a node that, according to the current transactions' data access pattern, is mostly performing operations on O_i. Transferring O_i to n_r means avoiding remote communications for those transactions executing on n_r that need O_i. In case O_i is frequently requested by multiple nodes, O_i is replicated and each replica is sent to each requesting node (the object replication degree can be tuned based on the average number of requesting nodes per object).

Objects are transferred exploiting the transactions' commit phase: whenever a transaction commits, it checks whether the current location of the accessed objects is still an appropriate location according to the application locality; in case a change of ownership is needed (see Section 6.2 for details on the policy that decides the trigger of a change), objects are transferred along with their ownership. In this case, the commit phase ends only when the entire transfer is completed.

A local view of current objects location (i.e., distributed directory), called *CurrMap*, is stored at each node. Whenever the transfer of an object takes place, updates on CurrMap are propagated to all nodes. Conversely, when the workload is stable (i.e., most of requests are on local objects), CurrMap is occasionally updated and it is only queried locally for objects localization, thus minimizing the distributed interactions. This architecture is particularly effective in applications having locality properties. Clearly, in the case of highly dynamic applications, where accesses do not comply with specific locality-patterns, Hybrid-Flow is not optimized, thus incurring in the same costs paid by conventional data-flow protocols (e.g., TFA in Section 4).

Each object is associated with a scalar identifier tracking its version, called version number (or *vid*), and that is incremented whenever a transaction commits a modification on that object. Different copies of the same object have the same *vid*. The timestamp of an object O_r is read by a transaction T during a read operation of T on O_r and it is stored with the O_r's read version in the T's *read-set* in order to be used during T's validation in the commit phase: the timestamp of the actual committed version of the object O_r is compared with the timestamp of the version stored in the T's *read-set*. This comparison reveals possible concurrent commits happened during the transaction's execution, which may invalidate the version read.

Hybrid-Flow relies on the two-phase commit protocol [2] at commit time for locking accessed objects and validating read objects. Lock requests are implemented based on predefined timeout, this way there is a maximum waiting time for a busy lock after that the lock is considered as not available. This represents a lightweight mechanism for detecting possible deadlock conditions.

When a transaction T_x on node n_x reads an object O_r, CurrMap is queried for determining the current location of O_r and a read request message is issued to O_r's owner according to n_x's CurrMap. In case the object has been recently moved and the n_x's CurrMap is not yet updated, T_x may receive an *object-not-found* notification to its read request. In this case, T_x simply monitors CurrMap waiting the expected update and re-issuing the read request to the proper node. However, in applications with locality properties, this aforementioned scenario happens a very limited number of times. When O_r's owner receives the read request of T_x and no other transactions are committing O_r concurrently (i.e., O_r is not locked), then an object copy is returned to T_x and the read operation ends successfully. In case O_r is locked by another transaction committing a new version of O_r, an abort is immediately triggered for T_x and T_x restarts its execution. This "early" abort is done only for performance but it is not needed for preserving the correctness of Hybrid-Flow because, otherwise, O_r will be locked and validated by T_x when T_x will enter its commit phase.

When T_x requests a write operation of a value *val* on an object O_w, this is locally executed without interacting with O_w's owner and by inserting the pair $< O_w, val >$ in the T_x's *write-set*.

After completing all its transaction operations, T_x enters its commit phase. Before proceeding further, it must ensure that all the objects in its *read-set* are still consistent and no other transactions are currently committing objects in its *write-set*. This is done in the following four steps:

i) For each object O_{tx} in either T_x's write-set or T_x's read-set, T_x contacts all of O_{tx}'s owners in order to acquire the locks corresponding to O_{tx}.

ii) T_x validates each object O_r in its read-set by comparing O_r's current timestamp with the timestamp associated with O_r at the time T_x read it. This ensures that a committed transaction sees a consistent view of its accessed objects. Upon successful completion of this step, T_x can proceed to commit safely, otherwise an abort is issued.

iii) The timestamp of each written object is incremented. Subsequently, for local objects written by T_x can be safely committed to shared memory, while for remote objects, the updated version is sent using a commit message. During this phase, in case some object needs to be moved to another node, the transfer along with the change of ownership happens. Notice that objects are still locked at this time, thus no other transactions can access them.

iv) Local locks are instantly released and the remote objects are unlocked after receiving the commit message. This message, received by object owners, triggers the operation of LTS (see Sections 6.2).

Hybrid-flow does not guarantee executing transactions to always read consistent snapshots as TFA and SCORe (described in Sections 4 and 5, respectively). In fact, it detects inconsistent executions only at commit time and prevents those transactions to commit by aborting them. A solution like the one SCORe proposes, in which an agreement on a unique timestamp is established at commit time and read operations advance the node timestamp in order to handle write-after-read dependencies, can be integrated for making Hybrid-flow's read operations always consistent.

6.2   Exploiting Locality

In order to exploit locality, we design LTS, a locality-aware transactional scheduler. The key goal of LTS is to help determining when objects are not correctly located in the system. LTS establishes a connection between objects and frequency of accesses classified according to the nodes that are running transactions on those objects.

We define a fixed time window, called *time-frame*, during which each node collects information on the number of accesses observed. Time-frame represents a local time interval. Specifically, each object owner (say *own*) records, for each object (say *obj*), two lists of pairs $< n_i,access\_rate >$, where each pair represents the number of accesses (*access_rate*) in the last time-frame generated by the node n_i. The first list, called *LO*, tracks the access rate of *obj*'s owners. The second list, *LNO*, contains the access rate of all the other nodes (non-owners).

Whenever a transaction commits a new version of an object O_a, its replicas are updated and all transactions that concurrently requested O_a are aborted. Each object owner knows the transactions that have accessed O_a, therefore the *access_rate* is incremented whenever both, a transaction requests O_a and a commit request on O_a is received, for read and write operations, respectively. If the time when the *access_rate* is updated is within the current time-frame, its value is incremented, otherwise it is set to 1.

The list *LO* is maintained in the ascending order of *access_rate*, whereas the list *LNO* is maintained in the descending order. When a new object version is committed and the lists are updated, LTS compares the *access_rate* of *LO* and *LNO*, node-by-node, starting from the first location of *LO*, and generates the subset $\bar{N}$ of nodes in *LNO* that have higher *access_rate* than those in the same positions of *LO* (the size of $\bar{N}$ is less than the object replication degree). $\bar{N}$ represents candidate nodes for becoming new object owners. For each node $n_{ow} \in \bar{N}$, let *y* represent its index in *LNO*. If the difference between N_{ow}'s *access_rate* and the *access_rate* of the node stored at position *y* of *LO* (named *LO*[*y*]) is higher than a threshold, then the ownership is changed from *LO*[*y*] to N_{ow}. When the ownership is moved the object's value is transferred along with its lists *LO* and *LNO*. The threshold represents the maximum difference between number of accesses of a non-owner node and a owner node allowed per time-frame without changing the ownership.

Algorithm 13 shows the procedure for deciding whether to migrate the ownership of an object *O* or not. This procedure is invoked during the commit phase while objects are locked thus preventing any inconsistency on concurrent accesses. This results in an additional overhead on the transaction commit phase which, however, consists of only local computation (i.e., traversing *LO* and *LNO*) without any remote interactions. This additional overhead does not include the cost of moving the object through the network, because it would have still been paid by the data-flow model.

Algorithm 13. LTS - Locality.

1: *void* MovingObject(*LO*, *LNO*)
2:     *candidateList = null*
3:     **for all** *O_node, O_accessRate*} ∈ *LO* **do**
4:         {*node, accessRate*} = *LNO.getFirst*() ▷ getFirst returns the first key and element in the list
5:         **if** *accessRate − O_accessRate > threshold* **then**
6:             *LNO.remove*(*node*)
7:             *candidateList.append*(*node*)
8:     **if** *candidateList.length ≠ 0* **then**
9:         *updateOwnerList*(*candidateList*) ▷ updateOwnerList includes changing the owner-ship

---

This mechanism captures workload changes. When the workload is stable, the number of transactions started on non-object-owner nodes is negligible. Thus, there is no need to change ownership. The protocol manages this scenario using the aforementioned threshold. When the workload changes, a non-trivial number of transactions may request remote objects and, if the workload fluctuation is not temporary, this number will eventually exceed the threshold, triggering a change of ownership.

6.2.1 Example

Figure 2 illustrates an example of how LTS works with four nodes and one object o_A, where n_1 and n_2 are the current owners of o_A. Therefore n_1 and n_2 store the current status of the accesses on o_A in the lists LO and LNO. Let us assume that transactions T_1 and T_2, executed at nodes n_3 and n_4, respectively, both access object o_A by executing a

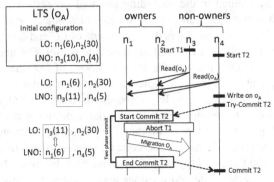

Fig. 2. Example of LTS

read operation followed by a write operation. In particular, after they have both issued a remote read operation on o_A, T_2 executes a write operation on o_A and it commits. On the execution of the read operations, the lists LNO are updated on n_1 and n_2 in order to track the two new accesses on o_A. This increases the number of the accesses associated with nodes n_3 and n_4, by setting them to 11 and 5 respectively. Afterwards the commit of T_2 executed via 2PC on nodes n_1 and n_2 causes the abort of T_1, since it invalidates T_1's read-set. If we assume that the threshold for LTS is 4, the commit of T_2 also triggers a transfer of the object o_A from node n_1 to node n_3. This is because node n_3 has the maximum number of accesses among the nodes in LNO and the difference between that number and the LTS threshold is greater then the minimum number of accesses among the ones in LO (which is associated to n_1). Note that even though that becomes true as soon as T_1 executes the read operation on o_A, the actual migration of object o_A can only be executed whenever o_A is locked by T_2 in order to ensure that no other transactions (except the one locking the object) can concurrently commit an update on o_A during its migration.

7 Conclusion

The transaction execution model is one of the critical choices to be taken while designing a partially replicated transactional system. The data-flow model assumes transactions immobile and objects moving to committing transactions; the control-flow model pins objects to nodes and moves the transaction's flow towards nodes storing accessed objects. On the one hand, the data-flow execution model allows the replication protocol to benefit from application locality and local commit phase, at the cost of maintaining a distributed directory for storing the actual location of objects. Whenever an object is requested or published in the directory, a distributed cache-coherence protocol is needed for querying or updating atomically the directory. On the other hand, the control-flow execution model does not need any directory for retrieving and publishing data because objects cannot move from its original node. Starting from an invariant (e.g., the object Id), the location of an object is computed relying only on a local consistent logic. This way transactions' executions are not burden with additional communication steps. As a disadvantage, the control-flow model is not able to meet application locality, especially if the workload changes over time. Summarizing, the decision of adopting a data-flow or a control-flow transaction execution model is affected by the expected application deployment workload. Both the models expose desirable advantages but their drawbacks could be in unaffordable if the actual deployment does not match the expectation. Hybrid solutions are the way to encompass different requirements and produce effective trade-offs.

Acknowledgements. This work is supported in part by US National Science Foundation under grants CNS-1116190 and CNS-1217385.

References

1. Attiya, H., Gramoli, V., Milani, A.: A Provably Starvation-Free Distributed Directory Protocol. In: Dolev, S., Cobb, J., Fischer, M., Yung, M. (eds.) SSS 2010. LNCS, vol. 6366, pp. 405–419. Springer, Heidelberg (2010)
2. Bernstein, P.A., Hadzilacos, V., Goodman, N.: Concurrency Control and Recovery in Database Systems. Addison-Wesley Longman Publishing Co., Inc. (1987)
3. Chockler, G.V., Keidar, I., Vitenberg, R.: Group Communication Specifications: A Comprehensive Study. ACM Comput. Surv. 33(4), 427–469 (2001)
4. Défago, X., Schiper, A., Urbán, P.: Total Order Broadcast and Multicast Algorithms: Taxonomy and Survey. ACM Comput. Surv. 36(4), 372–421 (2004)
5. Demmer, M.J., Herlihy, M.P.: The Arrow Distributed Directory Protocol. In: Kutten, S. (ed.) DISC 1998. LNCS, vol. 1499, pp. 119–133. Springer, Heidelberg (1998)
6. Dice, D., Shalev, O., Shavit, N.N.: Transactional Locking II. In: Dolev, S. (ed.) DISC 2006. LNCS, vol. 4167, pp. 194–208. Springer, Heidelberg (2006)
7. Fernandes, S.M., Cachopo, J.: Lock-free and Scalable Multi-version Software Transactional Memory. In: Proceedings of the 16th ACM Symposium on Principles and Practice of Parallel Programming, PPoPP 2011, pp. 179–188. ACM (2011)
8. Frølund, S., Guerraoui, R.: Implementing E-Transactions with Asynchronous Replication. IEEE Trans. Parallel Distrib. Syst. 12(2), 133–146 (2001)
9. Gray, J., Lamport, L.: Consensus on Transaction Commit. ACM Trans. Database Syst. 31(1), 133–160 (2006)
10. Guerraoui, R., Rodrigues, L.: Introduction to Reliable Distributed Programming. Springer-Verlag New York, Inc. (2006)
11. Guerraoui, R., Schiper, A.: Genuine Atomic Multicast in Asynchronous Distributed Systems. Theor. Comput. Sci. 254(1-2), 297–316 (2001)
12. Hammond, L., Wong, V., Chen, M., Carlstrom, B.D., Davis, J.D., Hertzberg, B., Prabhu, M.K., Wijaya, H., Kozyrakis, C., Olukotun, K.: Transactional Memory Coherence and Consistency. In: Proceedings of the 31st Annual International Symposium on Computer Architecture, ISCA 2004, pp. 102–113. IEEE Computer Society (2004)
13. Herlihy, M., Luchangco, V., Moir, M.: Obstruction-Free Synchronization: Double-Ended Queues As an Example. In: Proceedings of the 23rd International Conference on Distributed Computing Systems, ICDCS 2003, pp. 522–529. IEEE Computer Society (2003)
14. Herlihy, M., Sun, Y.: Distributed transactional memory for metric-space networks. Distributed Computing 20(3), 195–208 (2007)

15. Kobus, T., Kokocinski, M., Wojciechowski, P.T.: Hybrid Replication: State-Machine-Based and Deferred-Update Replication Schemes Combined. In: Proceedings of the 33rd International Conference on Distributed Computing Systems, ICDCS 2013, pp. 286–296. IEEE Computer Society (2013)

16. Lamport, L.: Time, Clocks, and the Ordering of Events in a Distributed System. Commun. ACM 21(7), 558–565 (1978)

17. Patterson, S., Elmore, A.J., Nawab, F., Agrawal, D., El Abbadi, A.: Serializability, Not Serial: Concurrency Control and Availability in Multi-datacenter Datastores. Proc. VLDB Endow. 5(11), 1459–1470 (2012)

18. Pedone, F., Guerraoui, R., Schiper, A.: The Database State Machine Approach. Distrib. Parallel Databases 14(1), 71–98 (2003)

19. Peluso, S., Romano, P., Quaglia, F.: SCORe: A Scalable One-Copy Serializable Partial Replication Protocol. In: Narasimhan, P., Triantafillou, P. (eds.) Middleware 2012. LNCS, vol. 7662, pp. 456–475. Springer, Heidelberg (2012)

20. Peluso, S., Ruivo, P., Romano, P., Quaglia, F., Rodrigues, L.: When Scalability Meets Consistency: Genuine Multiversion Update-Serializable Partial Data Replication. In: Proceedings of the 32nd International Conference on Distributed Computing Systems, ICDCS 2012, pp. 455–465. IEEE Computer Society (2012)

21. Riegel, T., Felber, P., Fetzer, C.: A Lazy Snapshot Algorithm with Eager Validation. In: Dolev, S. (ed.) DISC 2006. LNCS, vol. 4167, pp. 284–298. Springer, Heidelberg (2006)

22. Saad, M.M., Ravindran, B.: Supporting STM in Distributed Systems: Mechanisms and a Java Framework. In: 6th ACM SIGPLAN Workshop on Transactional Computing, TRANSACT 2011 (2011)

23. Schiper, N., Sutra, P., Pedone, F.: P-Store: Genuine Partial Replication in Wide Area Networks. In: Proceedings of the 29th Symposium on Reliable Distributed Systems, SRDS 2010, pp. 214–224. IEEE Computer Society (2010)

24. Schlichting, R.D., Schneider, F.B.: Fail-stop Processors: An Approach to Designing Fault-tolerant Computing Systems. ACM Trans. Comput. Syst. 1(3), 222–238 (1983)

25. Schneider, F.B.: Replication Management Using the State-machine Approach. In: Distributed systems, 2nd edn., pp. 169–197. ACM Press/Addison-Wesley Publishing Co. (1993)

26. Sharma, G., Busch, C., Srinivasagopalan, S.: Distributed Transactional Memory for General Networks. In: Proceedings of the 26th International Parallel and Distributed Processing Symposium, IPDPS 2012, pp. 1045–1056. IEEE Computer Society (2012)

27. Wojciechowski, P.T., Kobus, T., Kokocinski, M.: Model-Driven Comparison of State-Machine-Based and Deferred-Update Replication Schemes. In: Proceedings of the 31st Symposium on Reliable Distributed Systems, SRDS 2012, pp. 101–110. IEEE Computer Society (2012)

28. Zhang, B., Ravindran, B.: Dynamic Analysis of the Relay Cache-Coherence Protocol for Distributed Transactional Memory. In: Proceedings of the 24th International Parallel and Distributed Processing Symposium, IPDPS 2010, pp. 1–11. IEEE Computer Society (2010)

Directory Protocols
for Distributed Transactional Memory*

Hagit Attiya[1], Vincent Gramoli[2], and Alessia Milani[3]

[1] Technion, Haifa, Israel
hagit@cs.technion.ac.il
[2] NICTA and University of Sydney, Sydney, Australia
vincent.gramoli@sydney.edu.au
[3] Univ. Bordeaux, LaBRI, UMR 5800, F-33400 Talence, France
alessia.milani@labri.fr

Abstract. Distributed directory protocols for shared objects play an important role in providing access to higher level abstractions like transactional memory. They offer primitives to retrieve data and read it, or to move data and allow to write it. This chapter describes directory protocols for large-scale distributed systems and discusses the subtleties of incorporating them in a large-scale distributed transactional memory. We survey existing protocols, their advantages and drawbacks, and detail one protocol, COMBINE, which addresses these drawbacks.

1 Introduction

In large-scale distributed systems, remote accesses require expensive communication, several orders of magnitude slower than local ones. Implementing *transactional memory* (TM) in large-scale distributed systems, abbreviated *DTM*, is challenging due to the cost of communication with objects. Reducing communication costs by accessing nearby data is crucial for achieving good *scalability*, that is, improving performance as the number of nodes increases [2].

In a *data-flow* DTM, a transaction runs at a single node, obtaining copies of the objects it needs from other nodes. Each object has one writable copy, but it may have several read-only copies. A critical part of implementing a DTM is maintaining *coherence* of the transactional objects through a *directory protocol* for locating and moving copies of an object: the writable copy of the object is obtained with a move request, and a read-only copy of the object is obtained with a lookup request. When the writable copy of the object changes, the directory either updates or invalidates the other copies.

Instead of channeling all requests to the current location of the writable copy of the object, some directory protocols implement a *distributed queue* [3], in which a request from node p is enqueued until the object is acquired and released by a *predecessor* node q, which p identifies as having requested the object previously.

---

* The COMBINE directory protocol was presented in the proceedings of SSS 2010 [1]. The new material in this chapter (1) compares the combine directory protocol with four other directory protocols, (2) discusses the role of directory protocols in the implementation of a distributed transactional memory and (3) analyzes the bit complexity of COMBINE.

R. Guerraoui and P. Romano (Eds.): Transactional Memory, LNCS 8913, pp. 367–391, 2015.
© Springer International Publishing Switzerland 2015

When communication is asynchronous and requests are concurrent, it is difficult to ensure *starvation-freedom*, namely, that each request is eventually served. As we show, it is possible that while node p is waiting to get the object from a node q, many other requests are passing over it and being placed ahead of it in the queue, so p's request is never served. This creates a finite, acyclic waiting chain between q and the node owning the object (the head of the queue).

In large-scale distributed systems, communication is often performed over unreliable overlay networks, where *logical links* between nodes is often supported over several physical paths. This increases the possibility of message reordering and requires directory protocols to cope with non-fifo links.

This chapter deals with directory protocols for DTM. We overview several directory-based consistency protocols, which were presented in the context of DTM implementations [1, 4–6], and explain why some of them do not avoid starvation, while others do not accommodate non-FIFO links. Then we present the COMBINE protocol, which addresses these problems, providing a distributed queue protocol, and accommodating asynchrony and concurrent requests.

The rest of this chapter is organized as follows. Section 2 introduces the terminology. Section 3 provides a high level description of some directory protocols that can be used in the context of DTM, and describes some of their limitations. Sections 4 describes and analyzes COMBINE, a directory protocol that copes with these issues. Section 5 studies the difficulties of incorporating a directory protocol into a DTM. We conclude with a discussion, in Section 6.

2 Preliminaries

We consider a set of nodes V, each with a unique identifier, communicating over an asynchronous network. We assume that every pair of nodes can communicate; if two nodes p and q do not have a direct physical link between them, then an underlying routing protocol directs the message from p to q through the physical communication edges. The cost of communication between nodes is symmetric but non-uniform, and each edge (p,q) has a positive weight which represents the cost for sending a message from p to q (or vice versa), denoted $\delta(p,q)$. The cost of communication is a *metric*, that is, $\delta(.,.)$ satisfies the triangle inequality. The *diameter* of the network, denoted Δ, is the maximum of $\delta(p,q)$ over all pairs of nodes.

We assume reliable message delivery, that is, every message sent is eventually received. A node is able to receive a message, compute some local task and send a message in a single atomic step.

An *overlay tree* on the network, T, is a tree whose leaves are all physical nodes and inner nodes are mapped to (a subset of the) physical nodes. Let $d_T(p,q)$ be the number of hops needed to go from a leaf node p up to the lowest common ancestor of p and leaf node q in T, and then down to q (or vice versa); $\delta_T(p,q)$ is the sum of the costs of traversing this path, that is, the sum of $\delta(.,.)$ for the edges along this path. The *depth* of T, denoted D_T, is the number of hops on the longest path from the root of T to a leaf; the *diameter* of T, denoted Δ_T, is the maximum of $\delta_T(p,q)$, over all pairs of nodes.

The *stretch* of a tree is the worst case ratio between the cost of direct communication between two nodes p and q in the network, and the cost of communicating along the shortest tree path between p and q, that is, $\frac{\delta(p,q)}{\delta_T(p,q)}$.

3   Overview of Some Directory Protocols

Our description concentrates on the case where there is a single object in the system. Section 5 discusses the extension to multiple objects, in the context of implementing a DTM.

All directory protocols presented share the same idea: at the beginning, the object is associated to a particular node; as it moves around, the object leaves a trail of pointers to its new location. This idea was originated in ARROW [3], which was not presented in the context of DTM.

The protocols differ on the overlay network used to serve the requests. ARROW and RELAY run on top of a spanning tree, while BALLISTIC, COMBINE and SPIRAL run on a hierarchical overlay network. In particular, BALLISTIC and COMBINE run on top of an overlay tree, while SPIRAL uses a hierarchy of clusters. To decrease communication cost, BALLISTIC and SPIRAL augment their overlay network with shortcuts. In BAL-LISTIC, shortcuts can generate executions where a request by a node p travels far away to be finally served by a neighbour of p. This can be avoided by making BALLISTIC blocking. In SPIRAL, a lookup request can get stuck due to shortcuts, and to ensure it eventually completes, the request backtracks.

In all protocols but RELAY, a request redirects the pointers to the object while travel-ing towards it. This ensures that once the object is reached, the path is already directed to the new owner. In RELAY, pointers are redirected only when the object travels back to the requesting node. This allows several transactions to reach the object location con-currently and then decide on the new owner of the object, according to the priorities of the requesting transactions. However, as we detail later, requests may starve because of this design choice.

Finally, all protocols but COMBINE assume that communication links are FIFO. If links are not FIFO, problems arise when concurrent requests overtake each other, as detailed in this section. As explained in the next section, COMBINE solves these is-sues by letting a request piggybacks a concurrent one, by having lookup requests store information at nodes they travel through.

3.1   ARROW

ARROW [3] is a distributed directory protocol, maintaining a distributed queue, using path reversal. The protocol operates on a *spanning tree*, where all nodes (including inner ones) may request the object. Every node holds a pointer to one of its neighbors in the tree, indicating the direction towards the node owning the object; the path formed by all the pointers indicates the location of a *sink* node either holding the object or that is going to own the object. Figure 1 provides an example.

A move request redirects the pointers as it follows this path to find the sink, so the initiator of the request becomes the new sink. More precisely, a node sends a move

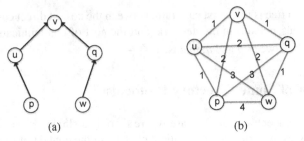

Fig. 1. (a) depicts a spanning tree, in which the object is stored at node v, built on top of the physical overlay in (b)

message towards the object location and sets its *pointer* to itself. If the receiver points to itself, this means it owns the object. In this case, the receiver sends the object directly to the requester as soon as it no longer needs it. Otherwise, the receiver sends a move message to *pointer* in turn and flips its *pointer* setting it to the sender of the message. Hence the path formed by all the pointers indicates the location of a sink node either owning the object or about to own the object. Figure 2 shows a functioning scenario.

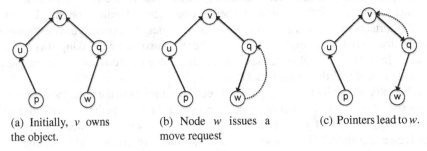

(a) Initially, v owns the object.   (b) Node w issues a move request   (c) Pointers lead to w.

Fig. 2. A move request initialized by node w when the object is located at v

The original paper on ARROW analyzes the protocol under the assumption that requests are sequential. Herlihy, Tirthapura and Wattenhofer [7] analyze ARROW assuming concurrent requests in a *one-shot* situation, where all requests arrive together; starvation-freedom is trivial under this assumption. Kuhn and Wattenhofer [8] allow requests at arbitrary times, but assume that the system is synchronous. They provide a competitive analysis of the distance to the predecessor found by a request (relative to an optimal algorithm aware of all requests, including future ones). The communication cost of ARROW is, at best, proportional to the stretch of the spanning tree used.

3.2 RELAY

RELAY [6] is a directory protocol that also runs on a spanning tree. In RELAY, pointers lead to the node currently holding the object, and they are changed only after the object moves from one node to another. (This is similar to the tree-based mutual exclusion algorithm of Raymond [9].)

In particular, upon receiving a move message, the receiver does not flip its *pointer* towards the sender yet. Instead, the move request piggybacks the path it travels so that when the sink receives the request, it simply sends a message back following the reversed path to flip the pointers of the intermediate nodes. Here the requester does not always wait for the sink to release the object, but may force the sink to release the object. RELAY allows several move requests to be at the sink at the same time, and the sink can decide in which order to serve these requests. The object is then sent to the node p whose request has the highest priority together with the remaining requests. The path piggybacked by the requests is modified accordingly.

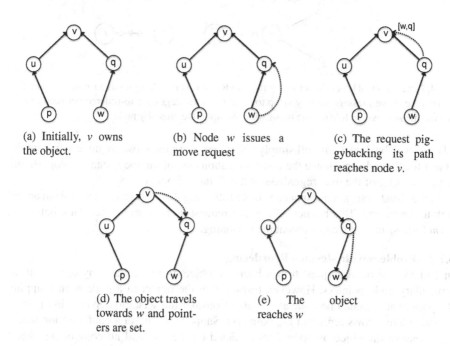

(a) Initially, v owns the object.

(b) Node w issues a move request

(c) The request piggybacking its path reaches node v.

(d) The object travels towards w and pointers are set.

(e) The object reaches w

Fig. 3. A move request initialized by node w when the object is located at v

Ravindran and Zhang [10] present a competitive analysis of RELAY. Given a set of dynamically generated requests, they compare the makespan of RELAY with an optimal clairvoyant offline algorithm, showing that the competitive ratio of RELAY is $O(\log D)$, where D is the diameter of the spanning tree.

3.2.1   Problem with Concurrent Moves

When requests are concurrent, a request can starve, or may travel to a distant node currently holding the object, while it ends up obtaining the object from a nearby node (which receives the object first).

The problems of RELAY with concurrent moves happen because pointers are reversed only on the way back to the requesting node.

Figure 4 shows why concurrent moves cause a problem in RELAY, in a manner similar to BALLISTIC. If two close-by nodes s_1 and s_2 issue concurrent move requests, called m_1 and m_2 respectively, then one move message may follow the other in the tree up to the destination node j. If the second move m_2 reaches node j when m_1 has just

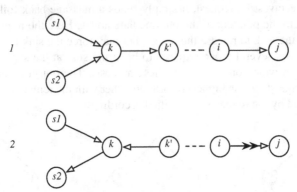

Fig. 4. Long traversal to reach a close-by node in RELAY. (1) Node s_2 sends a move message that follows the move message sent by s_1 up to node i. (2) Messages are re-ordered between i and j and the move message follows the move message up to the close-by node s_2.

taken is way back to s_1, it will simply follow m_1 up to the close-by node s_2 where the object finally ends up. Hence the communication cost of the move can be proportional to the diameter of the tree, regardless of the distance from s_1 to s_2.

In the worst case, a request m can starve following the object as it moves from an old sink to a new one. This happens if another request m' reaches the new sink before m. So m follows m' and we can repeat the reasoning.

3.2.2 Problem with Message Reordering

In RELAY, the move request brings back the object to the initiator by setting all intermediary node pointers. However, transmitting the object to a node p and flipping the pointer at p cannot be done atomically. Consider the scenario depicted in Figure 5 (where white arrows represent the pointers). Suppose we are in a configuration where the owner of the object is node d, as depicted on the top, and no copy of the object is in transit. Suppose that node j issues a move request m. Then, while m leaves node d in its way back to j, a concurrent move m' is issued by node s. When receiving the move message m, node i sets the pointer towards j and sends a message (denoted by a solid black arrow) with the object towards j. When receiving this message, j redirects the pointer that was pointing to i. If the concurrent move message is sent by i to j right after the object was sent to j, it may reach j before the object reaches j and the pointer towards i be redirected. The state in which the system is when m' is received by j is depicted on the bottom. In this scenario, j will simply send back the move message m' to i, because the pointer still points to i at the time this message is received. The lookup message will be sent from i to j following the pointer and eventually m will catch up, so m' will stop looping.

3.3 BALLISTIC

BALLISTIC [4] assumes a hierarchical overlay tree structure, whose leaves are the physical nodes, enriched with some shortcuts. Each node at some level ℓ has a single parent but can also access a *parent set* of nodes at level $\ell + 1$. More precisely, the BALLISTIC

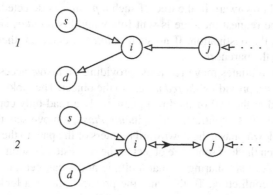

Fig. 5. The loop problem in RELAY. Nodes i and j continuously exchange lookup messages as long as the move message (the black arrow) remains in-transit.

overlay is built starting from the physical connectivity graph at level 0 and by constructing recursively another overlay at level ℓ that is a maximal independent set of the level-$(\ell$-1) overlay where nodes within distance $< 2^{\ell+1}$ are connected. The *lookup parent set* of level-ℓ node x is the set of level-$(\ell+1)$ nodes within distance $10 \times 2^{\ell+1}$ of x. The *move parent set* of level-ℓ node x is the set of level-$(\ell+1)$ nodes within distance $4 \times 2^{\ell+1}$ of x.

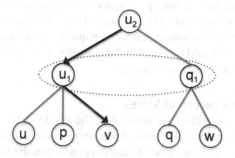

Fig. 6. Ballistic overlay construction resulting from the physical overlay in Figure 1(b)

Figure 6 depicts the BALLISTIC overlay, constructed from the physical overlay in Figure 1(b). In this simplified exemple, for each node the *lookup \ move parent set* at level 1 is $\{u_1, q_1\}$.

Initially, the tree is similar to other protocols', except that no upward *pointers* are set. Only nodes on the path from the root to the object owner have *pointers* directed downward. This downward path is initialized when the object x is created.

Each request proceeds has phases: in the *up phase*, the request message is sent upward in the tree until it reaches a node with a downward pointer set, then, in the *down phase*, the request message follows the downward pointers to the object owner. During the up phase, the node probes all nodes of its parent set to detect if the *pointer* of one of them is oriented downward in the tree. If such a *pointer* is detected, then the down phase starts and the request message is sent following this *pointer*, since it indicates a shortcut towards the destination. If no such *pointer* is detected, then the request is forwarded through the parent p.

BALLISTIC differentiates move requests, providing *exclusive* access to the object, from lookup requests, providing *shared* access to the object. The lookup does not modify any pointer and at the end of its down phase, only a read-only copy of the object is sent to the requester. In contrast, during its *up phase*, a move sets the *pointer* of p downward. In the down phase, the downward pointers of the path to the destination leaf node are unset. Then the leaf sends the object to the requester, as soon as it releases it.

BALLISTIC allows read sharing so that multiple nodes can get a read-only copy of the object without conflicting. To this end, the protocol allows a lookup to return to node i a read-only copy of the object by routing a lookup message to the destination node j, which is one of the next object's owners. The destination node j sends a read-only copy to node i, as soon at it has the object and keeps a link to node i to send potential invalidation. After modifying the object, it invalidates the read-only copy that node i has obtained. If node i has not committed before receiving the invalidation, then it aborts.

Herlihy and Sun [4] estimate the ratio between the communication cost of an operation in BALLISTIC and the cost of communicating directly from the requesting node to its destination, for executions where move requests do not overlap. Their analysis focuses on constant-doubling networks.[1] They show that a lookup that does not overlap a move has constant ratio. Then, they prove a similar result for the case where some move requests can overlap the lookup, but they consider the maximum cost of communicating directly from the requesting node to the source of any overlapping move request. We next show that when there are concurrent move requests, the communication cost of an operation in BALLISTIC could be equal to the diameter of the overlay tree, even when the the direct communication cost is constant.

3.3.1   Problem with Concurrent Moves

The move(x) operation modifies the direction of the tree links by setting pointers indicating the new location of object x, thus, it may impact the performance of concurrent operations targeting x. Since no move(x) can happen before the publish(x) terminates, it can only affect a concurrent lookup(x) or another concurrent move(x).

We present an execution example showing that in BALLISTIC, the communication performance of both operations may degrade if executed concurrently with another move(x). This problem stems from the additional shortcuts of the BALLISTIC tree structure: during the up-phase of an operation, each node at level ℓ probes multiple nodes at level $\ell + 1$, its *parent-set*, using these shortcuts to locate a potential downward link. During this probe, a node probes its father in the tree last, before the node issuing the move sets a downward pointer from its father to itself. There can be two nodes i and j at the same level ℓ, each of their fathers belonging to the *parent-set* of the other. This is illustrated in Figure 7, where the father of i is in the *parent-set* of j and vice-versa,

---

[1] A network is *constant-doubling* if every neighborhood of radius $2r$ can be covered by at most C neighborhoods of radius r, for a fixed constant C.

as depicted by the dashed links. If i is executing the up-phase of a move while j is executing the up-phase of its operation, j may miss the downward pointer to i that is being set. The same scenario may occur at higher levels between the father of i that sets the pointer to itself and the father of j. Consequently, even though i and j have one common ancestor among their respective ancestors at level $\ell + 1$, the operation of j may traverse higher levels before reaching i. Sun's thesis [11] discusses this problem and suggests a variant that integrates a mutual exclusion protocol in each level; however, this version is blocking and introduces further delay.

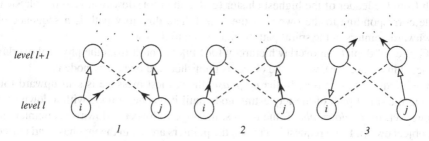

level $l+1$

level l

Fig. 7. The concurrent move problem in BALLISTIC. The lookup issued by j misses the pointer set by i during a concurrent move. Dashed links indicate shortcuts of the BALLISTIC tree structure, solid black arrows indicate in-transit messages while the white arrows are the pointers towards the next object owner.

In BALLISTIC, overtaking can happen when serving concurrent move requests: a move invoked at a later time than another move can be served earlier. This can happen a finite number of times, as proved in [4]. So BALLISTIC ensures starvation-freedom, provided that communication links are FIFO. In the next section, we show that a request can starve if links are not FIFO.

3.3.2 Problem with Message Reordering

Message reordering may cause BALLISTIC to get stuck, as described in the following scenario. Assume a lookup and a move concurrently follow the downward pointers towards the node that owns the object. Assume that node i sends first the lookup message to j before sending the move message to j. If the move message reaches j before the lookup message, then the move will discard the pointer from j towards the destination before j can send a lookup message to the destination. The result is that the lookup gets stuck and will not terminate because j has become a sink node without outgoing pointers when the lookup reaches it.

3.4 SPIRAL

SPIRAL [5] also operates on a hierarchical overlay of clusters: at level 0, each physical node constitutes a cluster, at the highest level of the hierarchy, all the nodes form a single cluster, and for each level i, several clusters exist such that each physical node u belongs to $O(\log n)$ clusters and at least one of these clusters contains all the neighbors of u within distance 2^{i-1}. Each cluster has a leader, chosen arbitrarily. At each level, clusters are labeled, so that no two clusters containing the same node have the same label.

The request of a node u go through the hierarchy following the *spiral path of u*. This path is built by visiting all designated leaders of all the clusters u belongs to, starting from level 0 up to the highest level, and according to the total ordering of the labels at each level.

SPIRAL supports three operations: publish, lookup and move. A publish operation is used by the creator of the object to introduce it into the network and create the directory path from the leader of the highest cluster (called the root) downwards to the physical node corresponding to the owner of the object. The directory path is a sequence of downward pointers in the spiral path from the root to the owner.

Figure 3.4 depicts an overlay hierarchy for SPIRAL, built from the physical overlay depicted in Figure 1(b), where the object is published and owned by node v.

Each request has phases: In the *up phase*, the request message is sent upward following the spiral path of the requesting node until it reaches a node with a downward pointer set. In the *down phase*, the request message follows the downward pointers to the object owner. If the request is a move, the pointers are set in the up phase and erased in the down phase, to update the directory path in a way similar to BALLISTIC. Once the request of a node u reaches the owner of the object, the object or a read-only copy of it is sent to u, depending on whether the request is a move or a lookup. The object is sent via a shortest path.

Figure 8 depicts the execution of SPIRAL, where node v publishes the object and then node w issues a move request. For each cluster the corresponding leader is pointed out. For clarity, we do not show the spiral path of each node and only show the spiral path of node v, which is the directory path to the object at the beginning.

As pointed out in [5], to avoid the problem suffered by BALLISTIC when concurrent moves occur, the leaders of clusters have to be contacted one after the other, and the protocol has to use shortcuts. Because of these shortcuts (not depicted in Figure 8), however, a lookup request that is concurrent with move may reach a node u without a downward link. In this case, to avoid that the lookup is stuck, node u sends the lookup request back to the sending node. Finally, like BALLISTIC and RELAY, SPIRAL requires FIFO links to work correctly.

Spiral guarantees starvation freedom. The corresponding proof as well as the complexity analysis of SPIRAL are provided in [5].

4 COMBINE **Directory Protocol**

In this section, we describe a protocol that avoids the problems caused by concurrent moves, message reordering and non-FIFO overlay links. COMBINE [1] is particularly suited for systems in which the cost of communication is not uniform, that is, some nodes are "closer" than others. Scalability in COMBINE is achieved by communicating on an *overlay tree* and ensuring that the cost of performing a lookup or a move is proportional to the cost of the shortest path between the requesting node and the serving node (its predecessor), in the overlay tree. The simplicity of the overlay tree, and in

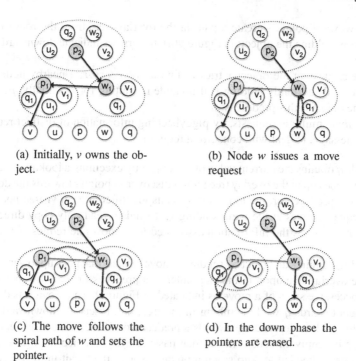

(a) Initially, v owns the object.

(b) Node w issues a move request

(c) The move follows the spiral path of w and sets the pointer.

(d) In the down phase the pointers are erased.

Fig. 8. A move request invoked by node w when the object is located at v

particular, the fact that the object is held only by leaf nodes, greatly facilitates the proof that a node finds a previous node holding the object.

The communication cost of COMBINE is proportional to the cost of the shortest path between the requesting node and the serving node, *times the stretch of the overlay tree*. Thus, the communication cost improves as the stretch of the overlay tree decreases. Specifically, the cost of a lookup request by node q that is served by node p is proportional to the cost of the shortest tree path between p and q, that is, to $\delta(p,q)$ times the stretch of the tree. The cost of a move request by node p is the same, with q being the node that will pass the object to p.

COMBINE does not require FIFO communication links; ensuring this property through a link-layer protocol can significantly increase message delay. Instead, as its name suggests, COMBINE handles requests that overtake each other by *combining* multiple requests that pass through the same node. Originally used to reduce contention in multistage interconnection networks [12,13], combining means piggybacking information of distinct requests in the same message.

4.1 Overview

The protocol works on an overlay tree. When the algorithm starts, each node knows its parent in the overlay tree. Some nodes, in particular, the root of the overlay tree, also have a *downward* pointer towards one neighbor.

The downward pointers create a path in the overlay tree, from the root to the leaf node initially holding the object; in Figure 9(a), the arrows indicate downward pointers towards p.

A node requesting the object x tries to find a *predecessor*: a nearby node waiting for x or the node currently holding x, if no node is waiting for x. Initially, p, the node holding the object is this predecessor.

We *combine* multiple requests, by piggybacking information of distinct requests in the same message, to deal with concurrent requests.

- A node q obtains the current value of the object by executing a lookup request. This request goes up in the overlay tree until it discovers a pointer towards the downward path to a predecessor; the lookup records its identifier at each visited node. When the request arrives at the node holding x, it sends a read-only copy directly to q. Each node stores the information associated to at most one request for any other node.

- A node q acquires an object by sending a move request that goes up towards the root of the overlay tree upon it finds a pointer to a predecessor. This is represented by the successive steps of a move as indicated in Figure 9. The move sets downward pointers towards q while climbing in the tree, and resets the downward pointers it follows while descending towards a predecessor. If the move discovers a stored lookup it simply embeds it rather than passing over it. When the move and (possibly) its embedded lookup reach a predecessor p, they wait until p receives the object. After having received the object and released it, p sends the object to q and a read-only copy of the object to the node that issued the lookup.

Since the downward path to the object may be changing while a lookup (or a move) is trying to locate the object, the lookup may remain blocked at some intermediate node u on the path towards the object. Without combining, a move request could overtake a lookup request and remove the path of pointers, thus, preventing it from terminating. However, the identifier stored in all the nodes a lookup visits on its path to the predecessor allows an overtaking move to embed the lookup. This guarantees termination of concurrent requests, even when messages are reordered. Information stored at the nodes ensures that a lookup is not processed multiple times.

4.2 Details of COMBINE

The state of a node appears in Algorithm 1. Each node knows its *parent* in the overlay tree and may have a *pointer* towards one of its children. It maintains a variable *lookups* where it can store information useful for combining.

A lookup request r issued by a node q carries a unique identifier including its sequence number ts and its initiator q. Its pseudocode appears in Algorithm 2. A lookup can be in three distinct states: it is either running and no move overtook it (not_served), it is running and a move request overtook and embedded it (passed), or it is over (served).

The lookup request proceeds in two subsequent phases. First, its initiator node sends a message that traverses its ancestors up to the first ancestor whose *pointer* indicates the

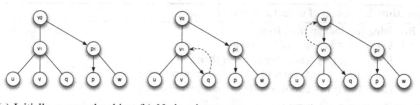

(a) Initially, p owns the object
(b) Node q issues a move request
(c) Pointers from the root lead to q

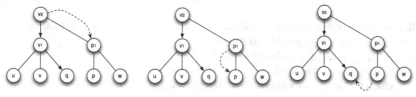

(d) Previous pointers are discarded
(e) The request reaches p
(f) Object is moved from p to q

Fig. 9. A move request initialized by node q when the object is located at p

---

Algorithm 1. State

1: **State of a node u at level ℓ:**
2:    *parent* $\in \mathbb{N} \cup \{\bot\}$, representing the parent node in the tree
3:    *pointer* $\in \mathbb{N} \cup \{\bot\}$, the direction towards the known predecessor, initially $\bot$
4:    *lookups* a record with fields:
5:       $q \in \mathbb{N}$, the identifier of the node initiating the request, initially $\bot$
6:       $ts \in \mathbb{N}$, the version number of the request, initially 0
7:       *status* $\in \{\text{not\_served}, \text{served}, \text{passed}\}$, the request status, initially not_served
8:    *moves* a record with fields:
9:       $q \in \mathbb{N}$, the identifier of the node initiating the request, initially $\bot$
10:      $ts \in \mathbb{N}$, the version number of the request, initially 0
11:   *message* a record with fields:
12:      *type* $\in \{\text{move}, \text{lookup}\}$
13:      *phase* $\in \{\text{up}, \text{down}\}$
14:      $ts \in \mathbb{N}$
15:      $id \in \mathbb{N} \times \mathbb{N}$
16:      *lookups*

---

direction towards a predecessor—this is the *up phase* (Lines 1–8). Second, the lookup message follows successively all the downward pointers down to a predecessor—this is the *down phase* (Lines 9–16). The protocol guarantees that there is a downward path of pointers from the root to a predecessor, hence, the lookup finds it (see Lemma 2).

A node keeps track of the lookups that visited it by recording their identifier in the field *lookups*, containing some lookup identifiers (i.e., their initiator identifier q and their sequence number ts) and their status. The information stored by the lookup at

---

Algorithm 2. Lookup of object x at node u

1: **Receiving** $\langle \text{up}, \text{lookup}, q, ts \rangle$ **from** v: ▷ *Lookup up phase*
2:   **if** $\nexists \langle q, ts', * \rangle \in lookups : ts' \geq ts$ **then**
3:     **if** $\exists r_q = \langle q, \tau, * \rangle \in u.lookups : \tau < ts$ **then**
4:       $u.lookups \leftarrow u.lookups \setminus \{s_q\} \cup \{\langle q, ts, \text{not\_served} \rangle\}$
5:     **else** $u.lookups \leftarrow u.lookups \cup \{\langle q, ts, \text{not\_served} \rangle\}$
6:     **if** $u.pointer = \bot$ **then**
7:       $send(u, \langle \text{up}, \text{lookup}, q, ts \rangle)$ to $u.father$
8:     **else** $send(u, \langle \text{down}, \text{lookup}, q, ts \rangle)$ to $u.pointer$

9: **Receiving** $r = \langle \text{down}, \text{lookup}, q, ts \rangle$ **from** v: ▷ *Lookup down phase*
10:   **if** $\nexists \langle q, ts', * \rangle \in u.lookups : ts' \geq ts$ **then**
11:     **if** $\exists r_q = \langle q, \tau, * \rangle \in u.lookups : \tau < ts$ **then**
12:       $u.lookups \leftarrow u.lookups \setminus \{r_q\} \cup \{\langle q, ts, \text{not\_served} \rangle\}$
13:     **else** $u.lookups \leftarrow u.lookups \cup \{\langle q, ts, \text{not\_served} \rangle\}$
14:   **if** u is a leaf **then**
15:     $send(u, x_{read\_only})$ to q ▷ *Blocking send, executes as soon as u releases x*
16:   **else** $send(u, \langle \text{down}, \text{lookup}, q, ts \rangle)$ to $u.pointer$

---

each visited node ensures that a lookup is embedded at most once by a move. When a new lookup is received by a node u, u records the request identifier of this freshly discovered lookup. If u had already stored a previous lookup from the same initiator, then it overwrites it by the more recent lookup (Lines 3–4).

Due to combining, the lookup may reach its predecessor either by itself or embedded in a move request. If the lookup request r arrives at its predecessor by itself, then the lookup sends a read-only copy of the object directly to the requesting node q (Line 15 of Algorithm 2).

The move request, described in Algorithm 3, proceeds in two phases to find its predecessor, as for the lookup. In the up phase (Lines 1–16), the message goes up in the tree up to the first node whose downward pointer is set. In the down phase (Lines 17–36), it follows the pointers down to its predecessor. The difference in the up phase of a move request is that an intermediate node u receiving the move message from its child v sets its $u.pointer$ down to v (Line 13). The difference in the down phase of a move request is that each intermediary node u receiving the message from its parent v resets its $u.pointer$ to $\bot$ (Line 26).

For each visited node u, the move request embeds all the lookups stored at u that need to be served and stores at u those lookups as served (Lines 8–11, 27–30 of Algorithm 3).

Along its path, the move may discover that either some lookup r it embeds has been already served or that it overtakes some embedded lookup r' (Line 39 or Line 41, respectively, of Algorithm 3). In the first case, the move just erases r from the lookups it embeds, while in the second case the move marks, both in the tuple it carries and locally at the node, that the lookup r' has been passed (Line 40 or Lines 42–43, respectively, of Algorithm 3).

As shown in Algorithm 3, once obtaining the object at its predecessor, the move request first serves all the lookups that it embeds (Lines 33, 34), then sends the object to the node that issued the move (Line 35) and finally deletes the object at the current node (Line 36). Sending reliably at Lines 34 and 35 ensures that the object is received remotely before being locally deleted.

If the object is not at its predecessor when the request arrives, the request is enqueued and its initiator node will receive the object as soon as the predecessor releases the object (after having obtained it).

4.3 Handling Concurrent Requests

Note that a lookup may not arrive at its predecessor because a concurrent move request overtook it and embeds it, that is, the lookup r found at a node u that $u.pointer$ equals v, later, a move m follows the same downward pointer to v, but arrives at v before r. The lookup detects the overtaking by m and stops once at node v (Line 23 of Algorithm 3, and Line 10 of Algorithm 2). Finally, the move m embeds the lookup r and serves it once it reaches its predecessor (Lines 33, 34 of Algorithm 3 and Lines 41, 42 of Algorithm 3).

Additionally, note that no multiple move requests can arrive at the same predecessor node, as a move follows a path of pointers that it immediately removes. Similarly, no lookup arrives at a node where a move already arrived, unless embedded. Finally, observe that no move is issued from a node that is waiting for the object or that stores the object.

4.4 Constructing an Overlay Tree

Constructing an overlay tree with good stretch is the key to obtaining good performance in COMBINE. We discuss two approaches for doing so.

The first approach is a direct construction of an overlay tree, in a manner similar to [4]. At level 0 we consider all the nodes, denoted Π_0. Then, for each level $\ell > 0$, the set of nodes that belong to ℓ, denoted Π_ℓ, are nodes that constitute a maximal independent set of the graph $G_{\ell-1} = (\Pi_{\ell-1}, E_{\ell-1})$, where $(u, u') \in E_{\ell-1}$ iff $\delta(u, u') < 2^\ell$. Finally, we create a link between each node $u \in \Pi_{\ell-1}$ and one of its closest nodes $u' \in \Pi_\ell$, that is, $\delta(u, u') \leq \delta(u, u'')$ for any $u'' \in \Pi_\ell$. Observe that a node may be linked to itself at several levels of the construction; we abuse notation and write $\delta(u, u) = 0$, because there is no cost to traverse this virtual link.

There are distributed algorithms to compute maximal independent sets in constant-doubling metric networks in $O(\log \Delta \log^* n)$ time, where Δ is the diameter of the graph (e.g., [14]). Using these constructions yields lookup and move with communication cost that is only a constant times the optimal.

Another approach is to derive an overlay tree T from any spanning tree $ST = (V_{ST}, E_{ST})$, without deteriorating the stretch, as follows:

Pick a *center* v of ST as the root of the overlay tree. (I.e., a node minimizing the longest hop distance to a leaf node.)

Let k be the level of u in the resulting rooted tree.

By backwards induction, we augment ST with virtual nodes and virtual links to obtain an overlay tree T where all nodes of ST are leaf nodes, without increasing the stretch of the tree. (See Figure 10.) The depth of T, D_T, is k. At level $k - 1$ we add to T a duplicate of the root u and create a virtual link between this duplicate and u itself.

Algorithm 3. Move of object x at node u

1: **Receiving** $m = \langle \mathsf{up}, \mathsf{move}, q, ts \rangle$ **from** v: ▷ *Move up phase*
2:    send(ack) to v
3:    **if** $\nexists \langle q, ts' \rangle \in u.moves : ts' \geq ts$ **then**
4:       **if** $\exists \langle q, \tau \rangle \in u.moves : \tau < ts$ **then**
5:          $u.moves \leftarrow u.moves \setminus \{\langle q, \tau \rangle\} \cup \{\langle q, ts \rangle\}$
6:       **else** $u.moves \leftarrow u.moves \cup \{\langle q, ts \rangle\}$
7:    clean(m)
8:    **for all** $\tau_a = \langle a, ts, \mathsf{not\_served} \rangle \in u.lookups$ **do**
9:       **if** $\nexists \langle a, ts', * \rangle \in m.lookups : ts' \geq ts$ **then**
10:         $m.lookups \leftarrow m.lookups \cup \{\tau_a\}$
11:      $u.lookups \leftarrow u.lookups \setminus \{\tau_a\} \cup \langle a, ts, \mathsf{served} \rangle$
12:   $oldpointer \leftarrow u.pointer$
13:   $u.pointer \leftarrow v$
14:   **if** $oldpointer = \perp$ **then**
15:      send$(u, \langle \mathsf{up}, \mathsf{move}, q, ts, m.lookups \rangle)$ to $u.father$
16:   **else** send$(u, \langle \mathsf{down}, \mathsf{move}, q, ts, m.lookups \rangle)$ to $u.oldpointer$

17: **Receiving** $m = \langle \mathsf{down}, \mathsf{move}, q, ts, lookups \rangle$ **from** v: ▷ *Move down phase*
18:    send(ack, move, q, ts) to v
19:    **if** $\nexists \langle q, ts' \rangle \in u.moves : ts' \geq ts$ **then**
20:       **if** $\exists \langle q, \tau \rangle \in u.moves : \tau < ts$ **then**
21:          $u.moves \leftarrow u.moves \setminus \{\langle q, \tau \rangle\} \cup \{\langle q, ts \rangle\}$
22:       **else** $u.moves \leftarrow u.moves \cup \{\langle q, ts \rangle\}$
23:    clean(m)
24:    **if** u not a leaf **then**
25:       $oldpointer \leftarrow u.pointer$
26:       $u.pointer \leftarrow \perp$
27:       **for all** $\tau_a = \langle a, ts, \mathsf{not\_served} \rangle \in u.lookups$ **do**
28:          **if** $\nexists \langle a, ts', * \rangle \in m.lookups : ts' \geq ts$ **then**
29:             $m.lookups \leftarrow m.lookups \cup \{\tau_a\}$
30:          $u.lookups \leftarrow u.lookups \setminus \{\tau_a\} \cup \{\langle a, ts, \mathsf{served} \rangle\}$
31:       send(u, m) to $u.oldpointer$
32:    **else**
33:       **for** $(\langle a, ts, status \rangle \in m.lookups : \nexists \langle a, ts', * \rangle \in u.lookups$ with $ts' \geq ts)$ **do**
34:          send$(v, \langle ts, x_{read\_only} \rangle)$ to a ▷ *Blocking send, executes as soon as u releases x*
35:       send$(v, \langle ts, x \rangle)$ to q ▷ *Blocking send, executes as soon as u releases x*
36:       delete(x)

37: clean(m):   ▷ *Clean-up the unused information*
38:    **for all** $\langle a, ts, \mathsf{not\_served} \rangle \in m.lookups$ **do**
39:       **if** $\exists \tau_a = \langle a, ts', status \rangle \in u.lookups : (status = \mathsf{served} \wedge ts' = ts) \vee (ts' > ts)$ **then**
40:          $m.lookups \leftarrow m.lookups \setminus \{\langle a, ts, \mathsf{not\_served} \rangle\}$
41:       **if** $\langle a, ts, * \rangle \notin u.lookups$ **then**
42:          $m.lookups \leftarrow m.lookups \setminus \{\langle a, ts, \mathsf{not\_served} \rangle\} \cup \{\langle a, ts, \mathsf{passed} \rangle\}$
43:          $u.lookups \leftarrow u.lookups \cup \{\langle a, ts, \mathsf{passed} \rangle\}$

Then, for every level $\ell < k - 1$, we augment level ℓ of the spanning tree with a virtual node for each (virtual or physical) node at level $\ell + 1$ and create a virtual link between a node at level ℓ and its duplicate at level $\ell + 1$.

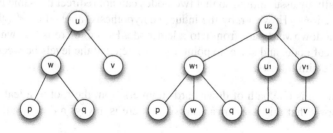

Fig. 10. Deriving an overlay tree from a spanning tree

To see why the stretch of the overlay tree T is equal to the stretch of the underlying spanning tree ST, note that we do not change the structure of the spanning tree, but augment it with virtual paths consisting of the same node, so that each becomes a leaf. Since the cost of sending a message from a node u to itself is negligible compared with the cost of sending a message from u to any other node in the system, the cost of these virtual paths (which have at most k hops) is also negligible.

There are constructions of a spanning tree with low stretch, e.g., [15], which can be used to derive an overlay tree with the same stretch.

4.5 Complexity Analysis of COMBINE

A request initiated by node p is *served* when p receives a copy of the object, which is read-only in case of a lookup request. This section shows that every request is eventually served, and analyzes the communication cost. We start by considering only move requests, and then extend the analysis to lookup requests.

Inspecting the pseudocode of the up phase shows that, for every $\ell > 1$, a move request m sets a downward pointer from a node u at level ℓ to a node u' at level $\ell - 1$ only if it has previously set a downward pointer from u' to a node at level $\ell - 2$. Thus, *assuming no other move request modifies these links*, there is a downward path from u to a leaf node. The proof of the next lemma shows that this path from u to a leaf exists even if another move request redirects a pointer set by m at some level $\ell' \leq \ell$.

Lemma 1. *If there is a downward pointer at a node u, then there is a downward path from u to a leaf node.*

Proof. We prove that if there is a downward pointer at node u at level ℓ, then there is a path from u to a leaf node. We prove that this path exists even when move requests may redirect links on this path from u to a leaf node.

The proof is by induction on the highest level ℓ' such that no pointer is redirected between levels ℓ' and ℓ. The base case, $\ell' = 1$, is obvious.

For the inductive step, $\ell' > 1$, assume that there is always a path from u to a leaf node, even if move requests change any of the pointers set by m at some level below $\ell' - 1$. Let m' be a move request that redirects the downward pointer at level ℓ', that is, m' redirects the link at node u' to a node v at level $\ell' - 1$. (Note that the link redirection is done atomically by assumption, so that two nodes can not redirect the same link in two different directions.) However, by the inductive hypothesis (applied to m'), this means that there is a downward path from v to a leaf node. Hence, there is a downward path from u' to a leaf node, and since no pointer is redirected at the levels between ℓ' and ℓ, the inductive claim follows.   □

Initially, there is one path of downwards pointers from the root to a leaf node, and Lemma 1 shows that this is an invariant, since there is always a downward pointer at the root.

Lemma 2. *At any configuration, there is a path of downward pointers from the root to a leaf node.*

We next argue that a request never backtracks its path towards the object.

Lemma 3. *A* move *request m does not visit the same node twice.*

Proof. Assume, by way of contradiction, that m visits some node twice. Inspecting the pseudocode shows that during the up / down phase, a request always moves to a higher / lower (resp.) level, relative to its previous one. Thus, the only way for a move request m to visit a node twice is that m visits this node first in its up phase and then in its down phase.

Let u be the first node that m visits twice. By the tree structure, this means that during its up phase, m visits node u and later visits the parent u' of u, where m finds a downward pointer to u. By Lemma 1, this means that also at u there is a downward pointer.

The downward pointer from u' to u does not exist immediately before m visited u. Otherwise, by Lemma 1, a downward pointer exists at u at the same time and m starts its down phase at u.

Observe that the reception of a move request and the creation of a link happens in an atomic step. Thus, any move request that visits u at some time between the time at which m visits u and the time at which m visits u', will start its down phase at u. This is because a move erases a downward link only in the second step of its down phase. Hence, the downward pointer from u' to u does not exist when m visits u', which is a contradiction.   □

A node p is the *predecessor* of node q if the move message sent by node p has reached node q and p is waiting for q to send the object.

Lemma 4. *A* move *request m by node p reaches its predecessor q within $d_T(p,q)$ hops and $\delta_T(p,q)$ total cost.*

Proof. Since there is always a downward pointer at the root, Lemma 1 implies that the request m eventually reaches its predecessor q. Moreover, by Lemma 3 and the tree structure, the up-phase eventually completes by reaching the lowest common ancestor of p and q. Then m follows the path towards q using only downward pointers. Observe that a move request is not passed by another move request, since setting of the link and sending the same request in the next step of the path (upon receiving a move request) happen in an atomic step. Thus, the total number of hops traversed by m during both phases is $d_T(i, j)$ and the total cost is $\delta_T(p, q)$. ☐

This means that D_T is an upper bound on the number of hops for a request to find its predecessor.

Lemma 4 already allows to bound the *communication cost* of a request issued by node q, that is, the cost of reaching the node p from which a copy of the object is sent to q. Observe that once the request reaches p, the object is sent directly from p to q without traversing the overlay tree.

Theorem 1. *The communication cost of a request issued by node q and served by node p is $O(\delta_T(p, q))$.*

Note that finding a predecessor does not immediately imply that the request of p does not starve, and must be eventually served. It is possible that although the request reaches the predecessor q, q's request itself is still on the path to its own predecessor. During this time, other requests may constantly take over p's request and be inserted into the queue ahead of it. We next limit the effect of this to ensure that a request is eventually served.

For a given configuration, we define a *chain of requests* starting with the initiator of the request m. Let u_0 be the node that initiated m; the node before u_0 is its predecessor, u_1. The node before u_1 is u_1's predecessor, *if u_1 has reached it*. The chain ends at a node that does not have a predecessor (yet), or at the node that holds the object.

The *length* of the chain is the number of nodes in it. So, the chain ends at a node whose request is still on its way to its predecessor, or when the node holds the object. In the last case, where the end of the chain holds the object, we say that the chain is *complete*.

Observe that at a configuration, a node appears at most once in a chain, since a node cannot have two outstanding requests at the same time.

For the rest of the proof, we assume that each message takes *at most* one time unit, that is, d hops take at most d time units.

Lemma 5. *A chain is complete within at most $n \cdot D_T$ time units after m is issued.*

Proof. We show, by induction on k, that after $k \cdot D_T$ time units, the length of the chain is either at least k, *or the chain is complete*. Base case, $k = 0$, is obvious. For the induction step, consider the head of the chain. If it holds the object, then the chain is complete and we are done. Otherwise, as it has already issued a request, by Lemma 4, within at most D_T hops, and hence, time units, it finds its predecessor, implying that the length of the chain grows by one.

Since a node appears at most once in a chain, its length, k, can be at most n, and hence, the chain is complete within $n \cdot D_T$ time units. ☐

Once a chain is complete, the position of r in the queue is fixed, and the requests start waiting.

Assume that the time to execute a request at a node is negligible, and that the object is sent from one node in the chain to its successor within one hop. Thus, within n hops the object arrives at i_0, implying the next theorem.

Theorem 2 (No starvation). *A request is served within* $n \cdot \Delta_T + n$ *time.*

We now discuss how to modify the proof to accommodate a lookup request r. Lemma 1 (and hence, Lemma 2) does not change since only move requests change the downward paths. For Lemma 3, the path can be changed only if r is passed by m, so r stops once at u'. The move request m that embeds r will not visit u twice, as argued above. Hence, the claim follows. For Lemma 4, if a lookup request is passed at a node u, then a move request m embeds the lookup at a node u', that is, the parent or the child of u, respectively, if m passed the lookup in the up or down phase. Thus, the move request will reach its predecessor, which is also the predecessor of the lookup. A read-only copy of the object will be sent to the lookup before the object is sent to the node that issued the move request that embeds the lookup.

COMBINE may embed many lookup request in a single move request. This does not increase the message complexity, but could lead to long messages consuming large communication bandwidth. We evaluate the total number of bits sent on behalf of a request (possibly, weighted by distances), and show that combining does not increase the number of bits transmitted due to a lookup request. (The argument is straightforward for move requests, which are never embedded.)

This is done by proving that the information about a lookup request issued by a node q and served by p, travels at most twice (once embedded in a move) the links in the shortest path from q to p (this node exists by Theorem 2). Moreover, we prove that the information about the lookup travels only through the above links. In other words, the bit complexity due to a lookup is at most twice the bit complexity if combining is avoided.

Lemma 6. *A* lookup *request r by a node q visits only a single leaf node* $p \neq q$ *(either by itself or embedded in a* move *request).*

Proof. Consider a lookup request r and assume, by way of contradiction, that r visits two different leaf nodes p and p', either by itself or embedded in a move request.

First, assume r reaches by itself a leaf node p'. To visit another leaf node p, r has to be embedded in a move request m, issued by a node u. Since m embeds r when it arrives at p, there is a node v in the shortest path from u to p, such that r visited v before m and no other move request visited v after r and before m. Let S be the sequence of nodes visited by r after v on its path towards the object. If m visits the same sequence of nodes as r, then m arrives at the same leaf node, which is a contradiction. Otherwise, another move request m' redirected the path of m at some node $v' \in S$ (i.e., m' either creates a downward pointer at v' or redirects the existing one), after r visited v' and before m visited v'. Hence, r is stored as *served* at v' when m arrives, and m does not embed the lookup r after v', which is a contradiction.

Otherwise, assume that r does not arrive at a leaf by itself. Let v be the node where r stops because it is overtaken by a move request m. For r to be overtaken at v, we have that r visited a node v' before m, but it arrived at v after m; v' is either an ancestor of

v or vice versa, depending on whether r was in its down or up phase when it visits v. Every other move request m' that embeds r should visit some node visited by r before reaching v. But then m' will either visit v' or there is a node v'' in the path of r to v', where m' will be redirected either because of a new downward pointer or because of the redirection of an existing pointer. In both nodes v' and v'', r is stored as *served*. Hence, m stops embedding r when visiting one of these nodes. Thus, the lookup does not arrive at two different leaf nodes, and the lemma follows. □

Lemma 7. *Consider a* lookup *request* r *issued by a node* q, *which is served by node* p. *Then* r *visits (either by itself or embedded in a* move *request) only nodes in the shortest path from* q *to* p *in* T.

Proof. Because of the tree structure, r looks for a downward pointer at the parent of q. Once a downward pointer is found, the request follows the downward path to a leaf node p. By Lemma 3, the first downward pointer is found at u, the lowest common ancestor of node p and q.

Assume that r is embedded in a move request m. By Lemma 6, m either stops to embed r at some point, or eventually reaches the same leaf node p. But for m to embed r, it has to be the first move request to visit some node v visited by r. If r visits v during its up phase, then m finds its first downward pointer at u, the lowest common ancestor of p and q. Otherwise, another move request redirected the path at some node between v and u. This means that, at this node, r is stored as *served* and m stops embedding it.

Therefore, in the worst case, m embeds the lookup at each node in the shortest path from v to p, which is a subset of the nodes in the shortest path from q to p, which proves the lemma. □

Lemma 8. *Consider a* lookup *request* r *by node* q, *which is served by node* p. *Let* $q = u_0, \ldots, u_g = p$ *be the shortest path from* q *to* p, *in the overlay tree. For every node* u_i, $0 \le i \le g - 1$, *at most one* move *request embeds* r *when traveling from* u_i *to* u_{i+1}.

Proof. The proof is by induction on i. For $i = 0$, observe that $u_0 = q$, the node that issued r, and thus it does not store the information about r, so no successive move request can embed r at u_0. Hence, no move embeds r when traveling from u_0 to u_1.

For the inductive step, assume that at most one move request embeds r when traveling from u_{k-1} to u_k for any $k = 1, \ldots, i$. We prove that at most one move request embeds r when traveling from node u_i to u_{i+1}.

By the inductive hypothesis, only a move request m reaches u_i embedding r. Observe that the first move request that visits node u_i immediately after r, records at u_i that the lookup r has been served. Thus, if m is not the first move request to reach u_i after r, m will stop to embed r at u_i. Any other move request that reaches u_i will not embed r at u_i because m stored r as served, implying the lemma. □

5 Using a Directory Protocol in DTM

Directory protocols were suggested as a way to manage objects, when implementing DTM in large-scale distributed systems [4]: The lookup and move requests support read and write operations of transactional objects, respectively: Before reading or writing a transactional object, a transactional memory proxy module checks whether the object is in the local cache, and calls the directory protocol to fetch it, if it is not. A lookup request is issued to obtain a read-only copy of the object, while a move request is issued to obtain the writable copy of the object.

It can be shown that each object is linearizable [16]. However, the DTM has to ensure that an entire transaction, accessing several objects, is *atomic*. This is often done by handling *conflicts* between concurrent transactions accessing the same object (at least one of them for a write) with a a *contention manager* (CM). The CM decides which transaction is delayed or aborted in case of a conflict, and when to restart an aborted transaction. The CM should ensure progress: at any time, at least one running transaction eventually commits (if it executes in isolation for long enough).

ARROW was not designed in the context of DTM, so no description is provided on how to incorporate it with a CM. In BALLISTIC, when a request arrives at the node having the object, if there is a running transaction the CM decides whether to surrender the object by aborting the local transaction or to give the local transaction a chance to commit, by postponing the response for a fixed duration. SPIRAL also considers the possibility of aborting the requesting transaction. A similar policy can be implemented in COMBINE.

Transactions must have globally-consistent priorities for arbitration. If transactions can have different priorities for different objects, then it is simple to see that we can have either a deadlock or a livelock. Moreover, as we show next, regardless of the policy applied by the CM to arbitrate conflicts, transactions accessing several objects may deadlock when executing on top of BALLISTIC, SPIRAL and COMBINE.

Consider two transactions T_1 and T_2 issued by two different nodes i and j, respectively, such that T_1 has higher priority than T_2 in some globally-consistent scheme. Transaction T_1 first requests and obtains object o_1 and then requests object o_2 to complete. Similarly, transaction T_2 first requests and obtains object o_2 and then requests object o_1 to complete. A third transaction T_3 with lower priority than T_2 is concurrently issued by node k and requests object o_2. Different objects have different directory paths, so it is possible that T_3 reaches node j first, so T_1 is redirected to node k. This means that T_3 is the immediate predecessor of T_1 in the distributed queue for o_2. Transaction T_2 reaches node i where T_1 is executing.

If the transaction with lower priority waits for the local transaction to complete, then a deadlock is possible. Specifically, we have a deadlock if T_3 waits for T_2 to commit and release o_2 while T_2 waits for T_1 to commit and release o_1. The other option, where the transaction with a lower priority aborts the transaction with higher priority, may cause a livelock where transactions continuously abort each other. For instance, consider two transactions T_1 and T_2 trying to acquire a single object o. Suppose that initially o is owned by the node i where T_1 is executing, and that T_2 reaches node i following the directory path. Suppose that T_2 can abort T_1 independently of their priority. Then T_1 will abort, the object will be sent to the node j that issued T_2 and T_1 will restart its execution. Since the next directory path finishes at node j where T_2 is executing, T_1 will reach node j and abort T_2. This can be repeated infinitely many times.

SPIRAL sends the object o_1 to node j regardless of whether T_2 is aborted or not. Thus, while waiting for the object at node j, transaction cannot know whether T_2 was aborted or not at node i.

Intuitively, the problem arises because these directory protocols order requests in FIFO order, while a CM orders requests according to the priority of the transaction they belong to. Priority inversion happens when transactions with higher priority are enqueued behind transactions with lower priority.

RELAY avoids this problem, since when a transaction reaches its predecessor in the queue, the predecessor owns the object. This is guaranteed because a request redirects the link when the object travels back to the requesting node. So when the directory path is redirected, it points to the node owning the object. To avoid deadlock and livelocks RELAY has to use a CM with a globally-consistent priority assignment. The authors suggest to use the greedy contention manager, because it guarantees that the transaction with the highest priority is executed without interruption. Originally devised for the shared memory model, the greedy contention manager relies on a global clock, which is not always available in a distributed system. Furthermore, as explained in section 3.2.1, RELAY does not avoid starvation of individual requests.

Finally, BALLISTIC, SPIRAL and COMBINE support read sharing. After modifying the object, the owner of the object has to invalidate the read-only copies of it, in order to guarantee consistency. If a node using a read-only copy has not committed before receiving the invalidation, then it aborts its transaction regardless of the priority policy. As a result, there might be an infinite execution where a transaction T_1 that successively writes x and reads y, and another transaction T_2 that successively writes y and reads x, repeatedly invalidate the read-only copy of each other.

To the best of our knowledge, no existing CM can be integrated with an existing directory protocol, to ensure that eventually some transaction will complete. More generally, it is not clear if it is possible to integrate a CM with an independently-designed directory protocol. It seems that to ensure the progress of a DTM, the directory protocol must incorporate contention management.

6 Discussion

Table 1 summarizes the protocols discussed in this chapter, and compares the communication cost of a request by node p, served by node q. In the table, $\delta_{ST}(p,q)$ denotes the (weighted) distance between p and q on a *spanning tree*; while Δ_{ST} is the diameter of the spanning tree. As implied by the construction of Section 4.4, these are not better

Table 1. Comparison of directory protocols presented in this chapter

Protocol	Communication cost	Assumes FIFO	Runs on
ARROW	$O(\delta_{ST}(p,q))$	Yes	Spanning tree
BALLISTIC	$O(\Delta_T)$	Yes	Hierarchical overlay
RELAY	$O(\Delta_{ST})$	Yes	Spanning tree
SPIRAL	$O(\delta(p,q)log^4 n)$	Yes	Hierarchical overlay
COMBINE	$O(\delta_T(p,q))$	No	Overlay tree

(asymptotically) than the distance and diameter of the overlay tree ($\delta_T(p,q)$ and Δ_T). Competitive analysis of the protocols in sequential, concurrent, one-shot and dynamic executions, appears in [5].

Existing data-flow DTMs [17–20] incorporate a component similar to a directory protocol. Some of these DTMs follow a lazy conflict detection strategy, e.g., by acquiring a global lock [17]. TM^{2}C [20] has both lazy and eager conflict detection. It encapsulates a specialized distributed contention manager, FairCM, which ensures progress. Each object has a unique owner and the directory protocol does not move objects. Processes access objects remotely without moving them, and concurrent reading is allowed.

Smaller-scale cluster-based systems offer some form of *broadcasting*, whose cost is uniform across all pairs of nodes. Broadcasting can be used at commit-time to maintain consistency of objects [18, 19]. DTM is also different than TM implementations on hardware shared-memory systems. These systems provide fast access to local and remote objects, and the critical factor in TM implementations is the *single-processor* overhead of bookkeeping [21].

Directory protocols were originally presented in the context of hardware cache-coherent systems, as a mechanism for storing the memory addresses of all data in the cache of each node, and for maintaining coherence by allowing cache hits or by (re)reading a block of data from the memory [22–24]. A block can be in one of three states: shared, exclusive or invalid [22]. A block is invalidated either when some specific action may violate coherence or when receiving an invalidation broadcast message [25]. In addition, the directory can maintain information to restrict the broadcast to affected nodes [26].

The size of the directory can be reduced by linking the nodes that hold a copy of a block [27]. Upon invalidation of the block, a message successively invalidates the caches of all linked nodes. This method is similar to the distributed queue, where it is used for passing exclusive accesses and not for invalidating read-only copies. Hardware directory protocols are space constraints, which may suffer from *false conflicts* when a whole block is invalidated due to the modification of only one of its data. A recent directory protocol that avoids this constraint by detecting conflicts at the byte level was used in a transactional memory that does not need cache coherence [20].

References

1. Attiya, H., Gramoli, V., Milani, A.: A provably starvation-free distributed directory protocol. In: Dolev, S., Cobb, J., Fischer, M., Yung, M. (eds.) SSS 2010. LNCS, vol. 6366, pp. 405–419. Springer, Heidelberg (2010)
2. Nussbaum, D., Agarwal, A.: Scalability of parallel machines. Communications of the ACM (March 1991)
3. Demmer, M.J., Herlihy, M.P.: The arrow distributed directory protocol. In: Kutten, S. (ed.) DISC 1998. LNCS, vol. 1499, pp. 119–133. Springer, Heidelberg (1998)
4. Herlihy, M., Sun, Y.: Distributed transactional memory for metric-space networks. Distributed Computing 20(3), 195–208 (2007)
5. Sharma, G., Busch, C.: Distributed transactional memory for general networks. Distributed Computing, 1–34 (2014)
6. Zhang, B., Ravindran, B.: Relay: A cache-coherence protocol for distributed transactional memory. In: OPODIS, pp. 48–53 (2009)

7. Herlihy, M., Tirthapura, S., Wattenhofer, R.: Competitive concurrent distributed queuing. In: PODC, pp. 127–133 (2001)

8. Kuhn, F., Wattenhofer, R.: Dynamic analysis of the arrow distributed protocol. In: SPAA, pp. 294–301 (2004)

9. Raymond, K.: A tree-based algorithm for distributed mutual exclusion. TOCS 7(1), 61–77 (1989)

10. Zhang, B., Ravindran, B.: Dynamic analysis of the relay cache-coherence protocol for distributed transactional memory. In: IPDPS, pp. 1–11 (2010)

11. Sun, Y.: The Ballistic Protocol: Location-aware Distributed Cache Coherence in Metric-Space Networks. PhD thesis, Brown University (May 2006)

12. Kruskal, C.P., Rudolph, L., Snir, M.: Efficient synchronization of multiprocessors with shared memory. In: PODC, pp. 218–228 (1986)

13. Pfister, G.F., Norton, V.A.: "hot spot" contention and combining in multistage interconnection networks. IEEE Trans. on Comp. 34(10), 943–948 (1985)

14. Kuhn, F., Moscibroda, T., Nieberg, T., Wattenhofer, R.: Fast deterministic distributed maximal independent set computation on growth-bounded graphs. In: Fraigniaud, P. (ed.) DISC 2005. LNCS, vol. 3724, pp. 273–287. Springer, Heidelberg (2005)

15. Emek, Y., Peleg, D.: Approximating minimum max-stretch spanning trees on unweighted graphs. SIAM Journal on Computing 38(5), 1761–1781 (2008)

16. Herlihy, M., Wing, J.M.: Linearizability: A correctness condition for concurrent objects. ACM Transactions on Programming Languages and Systems 12(3), 463–492 (1990)

17. Manassiev, K., Mihailescu, M., Amza, C.: Exploiting distributed version concurrency in a transactional memory cluster. In: PPoPP, pp. 198–208 (2006)

18. Bocchino, R.L., Adve, V.S., Chamberlain, B.L.: Software transactional memory for large scale clusters. In: PPoPP, pp. 247–258 (2008)

19. Couceiro, M., Romano, P., Carvalho, N., Rodrigues, L.: D2STM: Dependable distributed software transactional memory. In: PRDC, pp. 307–313 (2009)

20. Gramoli, V., Guerraoui, R., Trigonakis, V.: TM2C: A software transactional memory for many-cores. In: EuroSys, pp. 351–364 (2012)

21. Dice, D., Shavit, N.: Understanding tradeoffs in software transactional memory. In: Proceedings of the International Symposium on Code Generation and Optimization, pp. 21–33 (2007)

22. Censier, L.M., Feautrier, P.: A new solution to coherence problems in multicache systems. IEEE Trans. on Comp. C-27(12), 1112–1118 (1978)

23. Chaiken, D., Fields, C., Kurihara, K., Agarwal, A.: Directory-based cache coherence in large-scale multiprocessors. Computer 23(6), 49–58 (1990)

24. Agarwal, A., Chaiken, D., Kranz, D., Kubiatowicz, J., Kurihara, K., Maa, G., Nussbaum, D., Parkin, M., Yeung, D.: The MIT Alewife machine: A large-scale distributed-memory multiprocessor. In: Proceedings of Workshop on Scalable Shared Memory Multiprocessors (1991)

25. Archibald, J.K., Baer, J.L.: An economical solution to the cache coherence problem. In: ISCA, pp. 355–362 (1984)

26. Agarwal, A., Simoni, R., Hennessy, J.L., Horowitz, M.: An evaluation of directory schemes for cache coherence. In: ISCA, pp. 280–289 (1988)

27. James, D.V., Laundrie, A.T., Gjessing, S., Sohi, G.: Scalable coherent interface. Computer 23(6), 74–77 (1990)

Applications and Self-tuning

Tuning the Level of Concurrency in Software Transactional Memory: An Overview of Recent Analytical, Machine Learning and Mixed Approaches

Diego Rughetti, Pierangelo Di Sanzo, Alessandro Pellegrini,
Bruno Ciciani, and Francesco Quaglia

DIAG — Sapienza, University of Rome, Rome, Italy
{rughetti,disanzo,pellegrini,ciciani,quaglia}@dis.uniroma1.it

Abstract. Synchronization transparency offered by Software Transactional Memory (STM) must not come at the expense of run-time efficiency, thus demanding from the STM-designer the inclusion of mechanisms properly oriented to performance and other quality indexes. Particularly, one core issue to cope with in STM is related to exploiting parallelism while also avoiding thrashing phenomena due to excessive transaction rollbacks, caused by excessively high levels of contention on logical resources, namely concurrently accessed data portions. A means to address run-time efficiency consists in dynamically determining the best-suited level of concurrency (number of threads) to be employed for running the application (or specific application phases) on top of the STM layer. For too low levels of concurrency, parallelism can be hampered. Conversely, over-dimensioning the concurrency level may give rise to the aforementioned thrashing phenomena caused by excessive data contention—an aspect which has reflections also on the side of reduced energy-efficiency. In this chapter we overview a set of recent techniques aimed at building "application-specific" performance models that can be exploited to dynamically tune the level of concurrency to the best-suited value. Although they share some base concepts while modeling the system performance vs the degree of concurrency, these techniques rely on disparate methods, such as machine learning or analytic methods (or combinations of the two), and achieve different tradeoffs in terms of the relation between the precision of the performance model and the latency for model instantiation. Implications of the different tradeoffs in real-life scenarios are also discussed.

1   Introduction

As mentioned earlier in this book, the TM paradigm has been conceived to ease the burden of developing concurrent applications, which is a major achievement when considering that, nowadays, even entry-level computing platforms rely on hardware parallelism, in the form of, e.g., multi-core chips. By simply encapsulating code that is known to access shared data within transactions, the programmer can produce a parallel application which is guaranteed to be correct, without incurring the complexities related to, e.g., lock-based programming.

The achievement of optimized run-time efficiency is clearly another core objective, given that the TM paradigm is not meant to achieve synchronization transparency while

R. Guerraoui and P. Romano (Eds.): Transactional Memory, LNCS 8913, pp. 395–417, 2015.
© Springer International Publishing Switzerland 2015

(excessively) sacrificing, e.g., performance. For STM systems, synchronization is demanded to an STM-library whose (run-time) configuration is crucial to achieve efficient runs of the overlying applications. This requires proper techniques to be put in place in order to effectively exploit the computing power offered by modern parallel architectures. Particularly, the central problem to be addressed by these techniques is related to exploiting parallelism while also avoiding thrashing phenomena due to excessive transaction rollbacks, caused by excessive contention on logical resources, namely concurrently-accessed data portions. We note that this aspect has reflections also on the side of resource provisioning in the Cloud, and associated costs, since thrashing leads to suboptimal usage of resources (including energy) by, e.g., PaaS providers offering STM based platforms to customers (see, e.g., [1]).

In order to cope with this issue, a plethora of solutions have been proposed, which can be framed into two different sets of orthogonal approaches. On one side, we find optimized schemes for transaction conflict detection and management [7,11,15,16,24]. These include proposals aimed at dynamically determining which threads need to execute specific transactions, so as to allow transactions that are expected to access the same data to run along a same thread in order to sequentialize and spare them from incurring the risk of being aborted with high probability. Other proposals rely instead on pro-active transaction scheduling [2,25] where the reduction of performance degradation due to transaction aborts is achieved by avoiding to schedule (hence delaying the scheduling of) transactions whose associated conflict probability is estimated to be high.

On the other side we find solutions aimed at supporting performance optimization via the determination of the best-suited level of concurrency (i.e., number of threads) to be exploited for running the application on top of the STM layer (see, e.g., [5,8,14]). These solutions are clearly orthogonal to the aforementioned ones, being potentially usable in combination with them. We can further distinguish these approaches depending on whether they cope with dynamic or static application execution profiles, and on the type of methodology that is used to predict the well-suited level of concurrency for a specific application (or application phase). Approaches coping with static workload profiles are not able to predict the optimal level of concurrency for applications where typical parameters expressing proper dynamics of the applications (such as the average number of data objects touched by a transactional code block) can vary over time.

The focus of this chapter is exactly on approaches for the (dynamic) tuning of the level of concurrency. Particularly, we will overview the STM-suited solutions we recently provided in [6,20,21]. The reason for selecting and focusing on these works in this comparative overview is twofold:

- They share the same basic model describing the level of performance as a function of the level of concurrency, which leads them to exhibit some kind of homogeneity; this will help drawing reliable conclusions while comparing them, which are likely to generalize. Also, the exploited basic model is able to capture scenarios where the application profile can vary over time, hence they appear as solutions whose usage is not limited to contexts with static profiles.
- They rely on alternative techniques to instantiate "application-specific" performance models, which range from analytical approaches to machine learning to a mix of

the two. However, all of them are based on model-instantiation schemes exploiting training samples coming from the observation of the real application behavior during an (early) phase of deploy, which do not require stringent assumptions to be met by the real STM application in order for its dynamics to be reliably captured by the model. This further widens their usability in real life contexts.

Nonetheless, we will also provide a comparative discussion with literature approaches that stand as valuable alternatives for predicting the level of performance vs the degree of concurrency and/or for dynamically regulating the concurrency level to suited values.

We will initially start by discussing common points to all the overseen approaches, then we will enter details of each of them. Successively, we will provide hints on the organization of associated concurrency regulation architectures and present experimental data for an assessment of the different alternatives. A comparative discussion with literature alternatives ends the chapter.

2 The Common Base-Ground

We overview concurrency-regulation approaches targeted at STM systems where the execution flow of each thread is characterized by the interleaving of transactional and non-transactional code blocks. During the execution of a transaction, the thread can perform read/write operations on a set of shared data objects and can run code blocks where it does not access shared data objects (e.g. it accesses variables within its own stack). Read (written) data objects by a transaction are included in its read-set (write-set). If a data conflict between concurrent transactions occurs, one of the conflicting transactions is aborted and is subsequently re-started. A non-transactional code block starts right after the thread executes the commit operation of a transaction, and ends right before the execution of the begin operation of the subsequent transaction along the same thread.

Typical STM-oriented concurrency-control algorithms [7] rely on approaches where the execution flow of a transaction never traps into operating system blocking services. Rather, spin-locks are exploited to support synchronization activities across the threads. In such a scenario, the primary index having an impact on the throughput achievable by the STM system (which also impacts how energy is used for productive work) is the so called *transaction wasted time*, namely the amount of CPU time spent by a thread for executing transaction instances that are eventually aborted. The ability to predict the transaction wasted time for a given application profile (namely for a specific data access profile) while varying the degree of parallelism in the execution is the fulcrum of the concurrency regulation techniques presented in [6,20,21], which we are overseeing in this chapter.

In more details, these proposals aim at computing pairs of values $\langle w_{time,i}, i \rangle$ where i indicates the level of concurrency, namely the number of threads which are supposed to be used for executing the application, and $w_{time,i}$ is the expected transaction wasted time (when running with degree of concurrency equal to the value i). Denoting with t the average transaction execution time (namely the expected CPU time required for running an instance of transaction that is not eventually aborted) and with ntc the average time required for running a non-transactional code block (which is interleaved between two subsequent transactional code blocks in the target system model), the system throughput when running with i threads can be computed as

$$thr_i = \frac{i}{w_{time,i} + t + ntc} \tag{1}$$

By exploiting Equation (1), the objective of the concurrency regulation proposals in [6,20,21] is to identify the value of i, in the reference interval $[1, max\_threads]$, such that thr_i is maximized[1].

As we will see, $w_{time,i}$ is expressed in the different considered approaches as a function of t and ntc. However, these quantities may depend, in their turn, on the value of i due to different thread-contention dynamics on system-level resources when changing the number of threads. As an example, per-thread cache efficiency may change depending on the number of STM threads operating on a given shared cache level, thus impacting the CPU time required for a specific code block, either transactional or non-transactional. To cope with this issue, once the value of t (or ntc) when running with k threads—which we denote as t_k and ntc_k respectively—is known, analytic correction functions are typically employed to predict the corresponding values when supposing a different number of threads. This yields the final throughput prediction (vs the concurrency level) to be expressed as:

$$thr_i = \frac{i}{w_{time,i}(t_i, ntc_i) + t_i + ntc_i} \tag{2}$$

where for $w_{time,i}$ we only point out the dependence on t_i and ntc_i, while we intentionally delay to the next sections the presentation of the other parameters playing a role in its expression. Overall, the finally achieved performance model in Equation (2) has the ability to determine the expected transaction wasted time when also considering contention on system-level resources (not only logical resources, namely shared data) while varying the number of threads in the system.

As already pointed out, one core objective of the concurrency-regulation proposals that we are overseeing consists in modeling the system performance so as to capture the effects of variations of the application execution profile. This has been achieved by relying on a model of $w_{time,i}$ that has the ability to capture changes in the transaction wasted time not only in relation to variations of the number of threads running the application, but also in relation to changes in the run-time behavior of transactional code blocks (such as variations of the amount of shared-data accessed in read/write mode by the transaction). In fact, the latter type of variation may require changing the number of threads to be used in a given phase of the application execution (exhibiting a specific execution profile) in order to re-optimize performance. The proposals in [6,20,21]

---

[1] Approaches to regulate concurrency typically rely on setting $max\_threads$ to the maximum number of CPU-cores available for hosting the STM application. This choice is motivated by the fact that using more threads than the available CPU-cores is typically unfavorable since the overhead caused by context-switches among the threads may become predominant [10]. Also, thread-reschedule latencies may further unfavor performance due to secondary effects related to increasing the so-called transaction vulnerability-window, namely the interval of time along which actions by concurrent transactions can ultimately lead to the abort of some ongoing transaction [17].

all share the common view that capturing the combined effects of concurrency degree and execution profile on the transaction wasted time can be achieved in case $w_{time,i}$ is expressed as a function f depending on a proper set of input parameters, namely

$$w_{time,i} = f(rs, ws, rw, ww, t, ntc, i) \tag{3}$$

where t, ntc and i have the meaning explained above, while the other input parameters are explained in what follows:

- rs is the average read-set size of transactions;
- ws is the average write-set size of transactions;
- rw (read-write conflict affinity) is an index providing an estimation of the likelihood for an object read by some transaction to be also written by some other transaction;
- ww (write-write conflict affinity) is an index providing an estimation of the likelihood for an object written by some transaction to be also written by another transaction.

We note that the above parameters cover the set of workload-characterizing parameters that have been typically accounted for by performance studies of concurrency control protocols for traditional transactional systems, such as database systems (see, e.g., [23,26]). In other words, the idea behind the above model is to exploit a knowledge base (provided by the literature) related to workload aspects that can, more or less relevantly, impact the performance provided by concurrency-control protocols.

The objective of the modeling approaches in [6,20,21] is to provide approximations of the function f via proper estimators. The first estimator we discuss, which we refer to as f_A, has been presented in [6] and is based on an analytic approach. The second one, which we refer to as f_{ML}, has been presented in [20] and relies on a pure Machine Learning (ML) approach. Finally, the third estimator, which we refer to as f_{AML}, has been presented in [21] and is based on a mixed approach combining analytic and ML techniques.

We refer the reader to the technical articles in [6,20,21] for all the details related to the derivation of these estimators, so that the following presentation is intended as an overview of each of the approaches, and as a means to discuss virtues and limitations of each individual solution. The discussion will be then backed by experimental data we shall report later on in this chapter.

3   The f_A Estimator

The solution presented in [6] tackles the issue of predicting the optimal concurrency level (and hence regulating concurrency) in STM via an analytic approach that differentiates from classical ones. Particularly, it relies on a *parametric analytic expression* capturing the expected trend in the transaction abort probability (versus the degree of concurrency) as a function of a set of features associated with the actual workload profile. The parameters appearing in the model exactly aim at capturing execution dynamics and effects that are hard to be expressed through classical (non-parametric) analytic modeling approaches (such as [5]), which typically make the latter reliable only in case the modeled system conforms the specific assumptions that underlie the analytic expressions.

Further, the parametric analytic model is thought to be easily customizable for a specific STM system by calculating the values to be assigned to the parameters (hence by instantiating the parameters) via regression analysis. One relevant virtue of this kind of solution is that the actual sampling phase, needed to provide the knowledge base for regression, can be very lightweight. Specifically, a very limited number of profiling samples, related to few different concurrency levels for the STM system, likely suffices for successful instantiation of the model parameters via regression.

The core analytical expression provided by the study in [6] is the one encapsulating the probability for a transaction to be aborted, namely p_a, which is built as a function of the parameters appearing in input to Equation (3). Particularly, the abort probability is expressed as:

$$p_a = \beta(rs, ws, rw, ww, t, ntc, i) \tag{4}$$

More precisely:

$$p_a = 1 - e^{-\rho \cdot \omega \cdot \phi} \tag{5}$$

where the function ρ is assumed to depend on the input parameters rs, ws, rw and ww, the function ω is assumed to depend on the parameter i (number of concurrent threads), and the function ϕ is assumed to depend on the parameters t and ntc. For the reader's convenience, we report below the final shape of each of these functions as determined in [6]:

$$\rho = [c \cdot (\ln(b \cdot ws + 1)) \cdot \ln(a \cdot ww + 1)]^d$$
$$+ [e \cdot (\ln(f \cdot rw + 1)) \cdot \ln(g \cdot rs + 1) \cdot ws]^z \tag{6}$$

$$\omega = h \cdot (\ln(l \cdot (k - 1) + 1)) \tag{7}$$

$$\phi = m \cdot \ln(n \cdot \frac{t}{t + ntc} + 1) \tag{8}$$

where m, n, h, l, e, f, g, z, c, b, a, d are all fitting parameters to be instantiated via regression. In more details, regression analysis is performed by exploiting a set of sampling data gathered through run-time observations of the STM application. Each sample includes the average values of all the input parameters (independent variables) and of the abort probability (dependent variable) in Equation (4), measured over different time slices. Hence, Equation (5) is used as regression function, whose fitting parameters' values are estimated to be the ones that minimize the sum of squared residuals [3].

The abort probability expression, as provided by relying on Equations (4)–(8), has been exploited in order to analytically express the expected transaction wasted time (when running with i threads), namely to instantiate the function f_A, as

$$w_{time,i} = f_A = \frac{p_a}{1 - p_a} \cdot tr \tag{9}$$

where tr is the average CPU time for a single aborted run of the transaction, and $p_a/(1 - p_a)$ is the expected number of aborted transaction runs (per successful transaction commit).

4 The f_{ML} Estimator

The solution presented in [20] addresses the issue of concurrency regulation by a perspective that stands as different from the one in [6]. Particularly, this solution is based on a *pure* ML approach, whose general virtue is to provide an extremely precise representation of the target system behavior, provided that the training process is based on a sufficiently wide set of configurations, spanning many of the parameters potentially impacting this behavior. Generally speaking, good coverage of the domain typically guarantees higher accuracy of ML based models when compared to their analytic counterpart [19].

The exploited ML method in [20] is a Neural Network (NN) [19], which provides the ability to approximate various kinds of functions, including real-valued ones. Inspired by the neural structure of the human brain, a NN consists of a set of interconnected processing elements which cooperate to compute a specific function, so that, provided a given input, the NN can be used to calculate the output of the function. By relying on a learning algorithm, the NN can be trained to approximate an unknown function f exploiting a data set $\{(\mathbf{i}, \mathbf{o})\}$ (training set), which is assumed to be a statistical representation of the function f such that, for each element $(\mathbf{i}, \mathbf{o})$, $\mathbf{o} = f\{\mathbf{i}\} + \delta$, where δ is a random variable (also said *noise*). In [20], the training set is formed by samples $(\mathbf{input}, \mathbf{output})$, with $\mathbf{input} = \{rs, ws, rw, ww, t, ntc, i\}$ and $\mathbf{output} = w_{time,i}$, which are collected during real executions of the STM application.

On the other hand, significant coverage of the domain of values for the above $\mathbf{input}$ parameters may require long training phases, imposing a delay in the optimization of the actual run-time behavior of the STM application. Overall, this ML based scheme might not fully fit scenarios where fast construction of application-specific performance models needs to be actuated in order to promptly optimize performance and resource usage (including energy). An example case is the one of dynamic deploy of applications in Cloud Computing environments.

5 The f_{AML} Estimator

The proposal in [21] is based on mixing analytic and ML techniques (hence AML) according to a scheme aimed at providing a performance prediction model f_{AML} showing the same capabilities (in terms of precision) as the ones offered by the ML approach, namely f_{ML}, but offering a reduced training latency, comparable to the one allowed by the pure parametric-analytic based approach f_A. In other words, the attempt in this proposal is to get the best of the two worlds, which is operatively achieved by a sequence of algorithmic steps performing the combination of f_A and f_{ML}.

A core aspect in this combination is the introduction of a new type of training set for the machine learning component f_{ML}, which has been referred to as Virtual Training Set (denoted as VTS). Particularly, VTS is a set of virtual $(\mathbf{input^v}, \mathbf{output^v})$ training samples where:

- $\mathbf{input^v}$ is the set $\{rs^v, rs^v, rw^v, ww^v, t^v, ntc^v, i^v\}$ formed by stochastically selecting the value of each individual parameter belonging to the set;
- $\mathbf{output^v}$ is the output value computed as $f_A(\mathbf{input^v})$, namely the estimation of w_{time,i^v} actuated by f_A on the basis of the stochastically selected input values.

In other word, VTS becomes a representation of how the STM system behaves, in terms of the relation between the expected transaction wasted time and the value of configuration or behavioral parameters (such as the degree of concurrency), which is built without the need for actually sampling the real system behavior. Rather, the representation provided by VTS is built by sampling Equation (9), namely f_A. We note that the latency of such sampling process is independent of the actual speed of execution of the STM application, which determines in its turn the speed according to which individual (**input**, **output**) samples, referring to real executions of the application, would be taken. Particularly, the sampling process of f_A is expected to be much faster, especially because the stochastic computation (e.g. the random computation) of any of its input parameters, which needs to be actuated at each sampling-step of f_A, is a trivial operation with negligible CPU requirements. On the other hand, the building the VTS requires the previous instantiation of the f_A model. However, as said before, this can be achieved via a very short profiling phase, requiring the collection of a few samples of the actual behavior of the STM application. Overall, we list below the algorithmic steps required for building the application specific VTS, to be used for finalizing the construction of the f_{AML} model:

(**A**) A number Z of different values of i are randomly selected in the domain $[1, max\_threads]$, and for each selected value of i, the application run-time behavior is observed by taking δ real-samples, each one including the set of parameters $\{rs, ws, rw, ww, t, ntc, i\} \cup \{tr\}$.

(**B**) Via regression all the fitting parameters requested by Equations (6)–(8) are instantiated. Hence, at this stage an instantiation of Equation (5), namely the model instance for p_a, has been achieved.

(**C**) The instantiated model for p_a is filled in input to Equation (9), together with the average value of tr sampled in step **A**, and then the VTS is generated. This is done by generating δ' virtual samples (**input^v**, **output^v**) where, for each of these samples, **input^v** $= \{rs^v, ws^v, rw^v, ww^v, t^v, ntc^v, i^v\}$ and **output^v** $= w_{time,i^v}$ as computed by the model in Equation (9). Each **input^v** sample is instantiated by randomly selecting the values of the parameters that compose it[2]. For the parameter i the random selection is in the interval $[1, max\_threads]$, while for the other parameters the randomization needs to take into account a plausible domain, as determined by observing the actual application behavior in step **A** (recall that all these parameters have anyhow non-negative values). Particularly, for each of these parameters, its randomization domain is defined by setting the lower extreme of the domain to the minimum value that was observed while sampling that same parameter in step **A**. On the other hand, the upper extreme for the randomization domain is calculated as the value guaranteeing the 90-percentile coverage of the whole set of values sampled for that parameter in step **A**, which is done in order to reduce the effects due to spikes.

After having generated the VTS, the proposal in [21] uses it in order to train the machine learning component f_{ML} of the modelling approach. However, training f_{ML} by

---

[2] Generally speaking, this step could take advantage of a selection algorithm providing minimal chances of collision.

only relying on VTS would give rise to the scenario where the curve learned by f_{ML} would correspond to the one modelled by f_A. Hence, in order to improve the quality of the machine learning based estimator, the actual combination of the analytical and machine learning methods presented in [6,20] relies on additional algorithmic steps where VTS is used as the base for the construction of an additional training set called Virtual-Real Mixed Training Set (denoted as VRMTS). This set represents a variation of VTS where some virtual samples are replaced with real samples taken by observing the real behavior of the STM application (according to proper rules aimed at avoiding clustering phenomena leading the final VRMTS image to contain training samples whose distribution within the whole domain significantly differs from the original distribution determined by the random selection process used for the construction of VTS). The rationale behind the construction of VRMTS is to improve the quality of the final training set to be used to build the machine learning model by complementing the virtual samples originally appearing in VTS with real data related to the execution of the application.

Once achieved the final VRMTS image, it is used to train f_{ML} in order to determine the final AML estimator. Overall, f_{AML} is defined in [21] as the instance of f_{ML} trained via VRMTS.

6   Correcting Functions

As pointed out, the instantiation of the different estimators of the function f in Equation (3), which are ultimately aimed at predicting $w_{time,i}$, needs to be complemented with a predictor of how t and ntc are expected to vary vs the degree of parallelism i. In fact, $w_{time,i}$ is expressed in the various modeling approaches as a function of t and ntc. Further, the final equation establishing the system throughput, namely Equation (2), which is used for evaluating the optimal concurrency level by all the overseen proposals, also relies on the ability to determine how t and ntc change when changing the level of parallelism (due to contention on hardware resources). To cope with this issue, one can rely on correcting functions aimed at determining (predicting) the values t_i and ntc_i once known the values of these same parameters when running with parallelism level $k \neq i$. To achieve this goal, the early samples taken in all the approaches for instantiating the performance models can be used to build, via regression, the function expressing the variation of the number of clock-cycles the CPU-core spends waiting for data or instructions to come-in from the RAM storage system. The expectation is that the number of clock-cycles spent in waiting phases scales (almost) linearly vs the number of concurrent threads used for running the application. Hence, even if applied on a very limited number of samples, regression should suffice for reliable instantiation of the correction functions. To support this claim, we report in Figure 1 and in Figure 2 the variation of the clock-cycles spent while waiting for data to come from RAM for two different STM applications of the STAMP benchmark suite [18], namely intruder and vacation[3], while varying the number of threads running the benchmarks between 1 and 16. These data have been gathered on top of a 16-core HP ProLiant machine,

---

[3] The description of these (and other) STAMP benchmarks exploited in this chapter is postponed to Section 8.

equipped with 2 AMD Opteron^{TM}6128 Series Processor, each one having eight hardware cores, and 32 GB RAM, running a Linux Debian distribution with kernel version 2.6.32-5-amd64. By the curves, the close-to-linear scaling is fairly evident, hence, once determined the scaling curve via regression, which we denote as sc, we let:

$$t_i = t_k \cdot \frac{sc(i)}{sc(k)} \qquad ntc_i = ntc_k \cdot \frac{sc(i)}{sc(k)} \tag{10}$$

where:

- t_i is the estimated expected CPU time (once known/estimated t_k) for a committed transaction in case the application runs with level of concurrency i;
- ntc_i is the estimated expected CPU time (once known/estimated ntc_k) for a non-transactional code block in case the application runs with level of concurrency i;
- $sc(i)$ (resp. $sc(k)$) is the value of the correction function for level of concurrency i (resp. k).

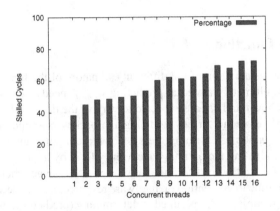

Fig. 1. Stalled cycles for the intruder benchmark

7 The Concurrency Regulation Architecture

Beyond providing the performance models and the concurrency regulation schemes, the works in [6,20,21] also provide guidelines for integrating concurrency regulation capabilities within operating STM environments. In this section we provide an overview of how the concurrency regulation architecture based on f_{AML}, selected as a reference instance, has been integrated with a native STM layer. Given that f_{AML} is the combination of the other two approaches, the architectures relying on the corresponding two estimators f_A and f_{ML} can be simply derived by removing functional blocks from the one presented here.

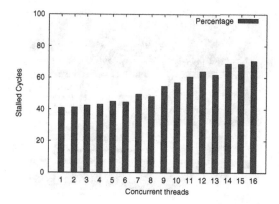

Fig. 2. Stalled cycles for the **vacation** benchmark

The organization of the reference instance[4], which we name AML-STM, is shown in Figure 3. AML-STM is composed of the following three building blocks:

- A Statistics Collector (SC);
- A Model Instantiation Component (MIC);
- A Concurrency Regulator (CR).

The MIC module initially interacts with CR in order to induce variations of the number of running-threads i so that the SC module is allowed to perform the sampling process requested to support the instantiation of the AML model[5]. After the initial sampling phase, the MIC module instantiates f_A (and the correction function sc) and computes VTS. It then interacts again with CR in order to induce variations of the concurrency level i that are requested to support the sampling process (still actuated via SC) used for building VRMTS. It then instantiates f_{AML} by relying on a neural network implementation of the f_{ML} predictor, which is trained via VRMTS. Once the f_{AML} model is built, MIC continues to gather statistical data from SC, and depending on the values of $w_{time,i}$ that are predicted by f_{AML} (as a function of the average values of the sampled parameters rs, ws, rw, ww, t_i, and ntc_i), it determines the value of i providing the optimal throughput by relying on Equation (2). This value is filled in input to CR (via queries by CR to MIC), which in its turn switches off or activates threads depending on whether the level of concurrency needs to be decreased or increased for the next observation period.

As noted above, in case the concurrency regulation architecture would have been based on f_A or f_{ML}, then the initial training set TS would have been directly used

---

[4] The source code of the actual implementation is freely available at
http://www.dis.uniroma1.it/~hpdcs/AML-STM.zip. It exploits TinySTM [12] as the core STM layer.

[5] As for the parameters to be monitored via SC, rw can be calculated as the dot product between the distribution of read operations and the distribution of write operations (both expressed in terms of relative frequency of accesses to shared data objects). Similarly, ww can be calculated as the dot product between the distribution of write operations and itself. This can be achieved by relying on histograms of relative read/write access frequencies.

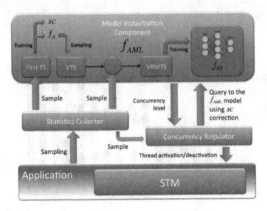

Fig. 3. System architecture

to instantiate f_A (as already shown in the picture), or f_{ML} (which could be achieved by simply collapsing VRMTS onto TS in the architectural organization). On the other hand, the training phase, namely the phase along which real samples of the application behavior are collected in order to instantiate the different estimators, would be of different length. We will provide data for a quantitative assessment of this aspect in the next section. We recall again that the shorter such a length, the more promptly the final performance model (based on a given estimator) to be used for concurrency regulation is available. Hence, a reduction in the length of this phase, while still guaranteing accuracy of the finally built performance model, will allow more prompt optimization of the run-time behavior of the STM-based application.

8 Experimental Assessment

In this section we provide experimental data for a comparative assessment of the concurrency regulation techniques (and of the associated performance prediction models) we have overseen in this chapter. The experimentation has been based on applications belonging to the STAMP benchmark suite [18], which have been run on top of the aforementioned 16-cores HP ProLiant machine. Particularly, we focus the discussion on the results achieved with kmeans, yada, vacation, and intruder, which have been selected from the STAMP suite as representatives of a mix of applications with very different transactional profiles, as we shall describe below.

kmeans is a transactional implementation of a partition-based clustering algorithm [4]. A cluster is represented by the mean value of all the objects it contains, and during the execution of this benchmark the mean points are updated by assigning each object to its nearest cluster center, based on Euclidean distance. This benchmark relies on threads working on separate subsets of the data and uses transactions in order to assign portions of the workload and to store final results concerning the new centroid updates. The peculiarity of this benchmark lies in a very reduced amount of shared data structures being updated by transactions.

yada implements Ruppert's algorithm for Delaunay mesh refinement [22], which is a key step used for rendering graphics or to solve partial differential equations using the finite-element method. This benchmark discretizes a given domain of interest using triangles or thetraedra, by iteratively refining a coarse initial mesh. In particular, elements not satisfying quality constraints are identified, and replaced with new ones, which in turn might not satisfy the constraints as well, so that a new replacement phase must be undertaken. This benchmark shows a high level of intrinsic parallelism, due to the fact that elements which are distant in the mesh do not interfere with each other, and operations enclosed by transactions involve only updates of the shared mesh representation and cavity expansion. Also, transactions are relatively long.

intruder is an application which implements a signature-based network intrusion detection systems (NIDS) that scans network packets for matches against a known set of intrusion signatures. In particular, it emulates Design 5 of the NIDS described in [13]. Three analysis phases are carried on in parallel: *capture*, *reassembly*, and *detection*. The capture and reassembly phases are both enclosed by transactions, which are relatively short and show a contention level which is either moderate or high, depending on how often the reassembly phase re-balances its tree.

vacation implements a travel reservation system supported by a single-instance database, where tables are implemented as red-black trees. In the database, there are four different tables, each one representing cars, rooms, flights, and customers, respectively. The customers' table is used to keep track of the reservations made by each customer, along with the total price of the reservations they made. The other tables have relations with fields representing, e.g., reserved quantity, total available quantity, and price. In this benchmark several clients (concurrently) interact with the database, making actual reservations. Each client session is enclosed in a coarse-grain transaction to ensure validity of the database. Additionally, the amount of shared data touched by transactions is (on average) non-negligible.

Fixed the above applications as the test-bed, we initially focus on assessing the quality of the different performance prediction models we have overseen, hence of the different estimators of the function f in Equation (3). This is done by reporting how the error in predicting $w_{time,i}$ changes for the different estimators (f_A, f_{ML} and f_{AML}) with respect to the length of the sampling phase used to gather training data to instantiate each individual performance model. In other words, the focus is initially on determining how fast we can build a "reliable" model for performance estimation vs the level of concurrency in STM systems when considering the three different target methodologies (analytical, machine learning and mixed) in comparison with each other. To this end, we have performed the following experiments. We have profiled STAMP applications by running them with different levels of concurrency, which have been varied between 1 and the maximum amount of available CPU-cores in the underlying computing platform, namely 16. All the samples collected up to a point in time have been used either to instantiate f_A via regression, or to train f_{ML} in the pure machine learning approach. On the other hand, for the case of f_{AML} they have been used according to the following rule. The 10% of the initially taken samples in the observation interval are used to instantiate f_A (see steps **A** and **B** in Section 5), which is then used to build VTS, while the remaining 90% are used to derive VRMTS. Each real sample taken during the execution of the application aggregates the statistics related to 4000 committed transactions, and the samples are taken in all the scenarios along a single thread, thus leading to similar rate of production of profiling data independently of the actual level of concurrency while running the application. Hence, the knowledge base on top of which the models are instantiated is populated with similar rates in all the scenarios.

Table 1. Comparison of error by different predictors/sampling times

		A	ML	AML
1 min	intruder	15.79%	80.04%	15.91%
	kmeans	5.82%	9.63%	2.66%
	vacation	6.08%	99.43%	6.19%
	yada	41.25%	99,82%	41.48%
5 mins	intruder	15.79%	80.04%	15.85%
	kmeans	5.90%	2.66%	2.59%
	vacation	4.93%	71.58%	5.01%
	yada	4.20%	13.24%	1.15%
10 mins	intruder	12.57%	45.01%	12.45%
	vacation	3.77%	3.31%	3.26%
	yada	4.20%	1.15%	1.16%
15 mins	intruder	11.46%	14.13%	8.84%
25 mins	intruder	10.00%	5.36%	5.35%

Then, for different lengths of the initial sampling phase (namely for different amounts of samples coming from the real execution of the application), we instantiated the three different performance models and compared the errors they provide in predicting $w_{time,i}$. These error values are reported in Table 1, and refer to the average error while comparing predicted values with real execution values achieved while varying the number of threads running the applications between 1 and the maximum value 16. Hence, they are average values over the different possible configurations of the concurrency degree for which predictions are carried out.

By the data we can draw the following main conclusions. We cannot avoid relying on machine learning if extremely precise predictions of the level of performance vs the degree of concurrency are required. In fact, considering the asymptotic variation of the prediction error of $w_{time,i}$ (while increasing the length of the sampling phase used to build the knowledge base for instantiating the performance prediction models), the f_A estimator gives rise to an error which is on the order of 100% (or more) greater than the one provided by the other two estimators f_{ML} and f_{AML}. The machine learning technique would therefore look adequate for scenarios where the error in predicting the level of performance may have a severe impact on, e.g., some business process built on top of the STM system, such as when the need for guaranteeing predetermined Quality-of-Service levels by the transactional applications arises. However, we note that the sampling times reported in Table 1 for instantiating performance models offering specific levels of reliability have all been achieved for the case of pre-specified transactional profiles (e.g. a pre-specified mix of transactional operations), for which the domain of values for the parameters characterizing the actual workload are essentially known (or easily determinable). This has led to building adequate training sets allowing, e.g., good coverage of the whole domain along the sampling period, which would lead to kinds of best-case latencies for instantiating machine learning based schemes. On the other hand, in case the transactional profile of the application is not predetermined (as it may occur when deploying new applications, whose actual profile can be determined a-posteriori of the real usage by its clients), the length of the sampling phase for building the reliable machine learning based model can be significantly stretched, which may also negatively impact the overlying business process (e.g. because the application can be forced to run with sub-optimal concurrency levels for longer time due to the need for longer latencies for materializing good approximation and coverage of the actual domain during some on-line operated sampling phase). The role of the analytical component in coping with the reduction of the number of samples (hence the reduction of the coverage of the domain of values for the parameters determining the actual application workload) for the achievement of reliable predictions is clearly evident by the reported data. In particular, the f_{AML} estimator provides non-asymptotic results which outperform both the analytic approach and the pure machine learning approach (see, e.g., kmeans—5 minutes, yada–5 minutes, vacation–10 minutes, or intruder–15 minutes). This is exactly related to the fact that f_{AML} is able to get benefits from both prediction methods, and is therefore able to provide a faster convergence to the "optimal" estimator.

As a second assessment, we provide experimental data related to the runtime performance that can be achieved when relying on concurrency regulation architectures based on the different performance models we are comparing (which we refer to as A-STM, ML-STM and AML-STM). As a matter of fact, this part of the assessment provides hints on whether (and to what extent) concurrency regulation, operated according to each of the discussed approaches, can be effective. Also, we study the actual performance delivered by the different solutions while again varying the length of the sampling phase along which the knowledge base for instantiating the different performance models is built, which we refer to as *model instantiation time* in the reported graphs. The concurrency regulation architectures here considered adhere to the architectural organization depicted in Section 7 and all rely on TinySTM as their core STM layer. The experimental data we provide refer again to the four STAMP benchmark applications as before, namely intruder, kmeans, vacation, and yada. In Figures 4–7 we report plots showing how the throughput provided by the different solutions (which is expressed in terms of committed transactions/second, on the average run) varies vs the model instantiation time. We also report the throughput values obtained when running with plain TinySTM (i.e. with no concurrency regulation scheme) or sequentially, which will be used as baselines in the discussion. Clearly, these data appear as flat curves, given that they do not depend on any performance model to be instantiated along time via application sampling.

By the data we can draw the following main conclusions. First, (dynamically) controlling the level of concurrency is a first class approach to achieve speedup as compared to the case where all the operations are processed sequentially along a single thread. In fact, settings where the level of concurrency is simply determined by the number of available CPU-cores (namely by deploying a single thread per CPU-core), as for the case of plain TinySTM, do not provide significant speedup, and may even give rise to significant slow down in the execution speed (of committed work), as for the case of yada (see Figure 7). Further, a machine learning based performance model gives rise to the asymptotically optimal approach for concurrency regulation, while analytical techniques provide the orthogonal advantage of allowing faster instantiation of an "adequate" performance model to be employed for concurrency regulation purposes. However, the additional information convoyed by the reported plots is the quantification of the final (asymptotic) performance gain achievable thanks to the increased precision by machine learning based approaches (such as ML-STM or AML-STM), which is on the order of up to 30% as compared to the analytical approach (say A-STM).

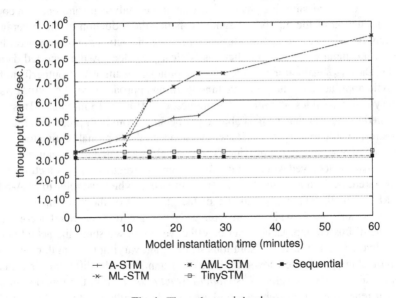

Fig. 4. Throughput – intruder

The last aspect we would like to point in this experimental assessment relates to energy efficiency, and its improvement thanks to concurrency regulation. As for this aspect, we focus on kmeans given that it is more likely to incur logical contention (hence transaction aborts and unfruitful usage of energy for rolled back work) when a larger number of threads is used. Hence, the energy saving via concurrency regulation (e.g. vs the TinySTM baseline) with this benchmark likely represents a kind of lower bound on the saving that we may expect with the other benchmarks.

In Figure 8 we report measurements related to per-transaction energy consumption (in Joule/Transaction)—which is an index of how much power is required by the

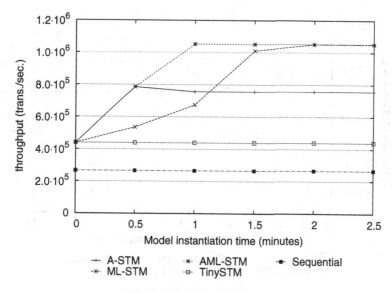

Fig. 5. Throughput – kmeans

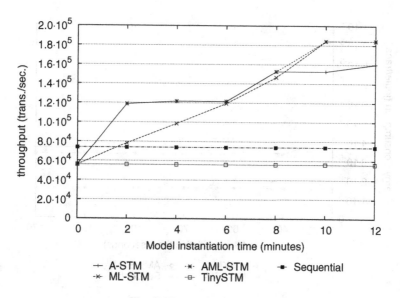

Fig. 6. Throughput – vacation

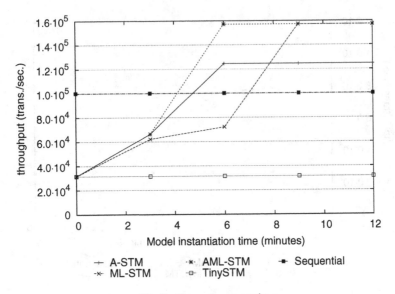

Fig. 7. Throughput – yada

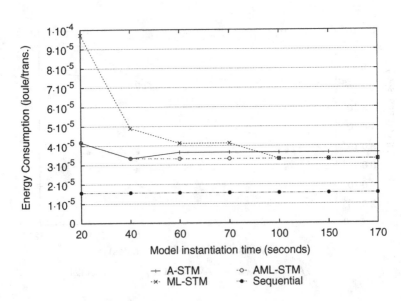

Fig. 8. Energy consumption per committed transaction – kmeans

application to successfully complete the execution of a single transaction—again while varying the model instantiation time. By the results we note first of all that the configuration exhibiting the lowest energy consumption is the sequential one. This is clearly due to the fact that in a sequential execution no operation is aborted, and therefore the amount of energy used on average per each operation is exactly the one strictly required for carrying on the associated work. Nevertheless, this configuration exploits no parallelism at all. On the other hand, AML-STM and ML-STM asymptotically show the same energy consumption. At the same time, we note that AML-STM and A-STM give rise to comparable (but non-minimal) energy consumption in case of very reduced model instantiation times (say on the order of 20 secs).

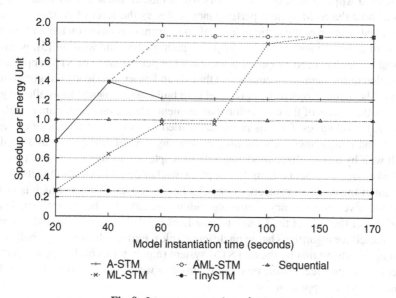

Fig. 9. Iso-energy speedup – kmeans

To provide more insights into the relation between speed and usage of energy, we report in Figure 9 the curves showing the variation of the ratio between the speedup provided by any specific configuration (again while varying the performance model instantiation time) and the energy scaling per committed transaction (namely the ratio between the energy used in a given configuration and the one used in the sequential run of the application). Essentially, the curves in Figure 9 express the speedup per unit of energy, when considering that the unit of energy for committing a transaction is the one employed by the sequential run. Hence they express a kind of iso-energy speedup. Clearly, for the sequential run this curve has constant value equal to 1. By the data we see how AML-STM achieves the peak observed iso-energy speedup for a significant reduction of the performance model instantiation time. On the other hand, the pure analytical approach does not achieve such a peak value even in case of significantly stretched application sampling phases, used to build the model knowledge-base.

Also, the configuration with concurrency degree set to 16, namely TinySTM, further shows how not relying on smart (and promptly optimized) concurrency regulation may degrade both performance and energy efficiency.

9   A Look at Literature Alternatives

Other studies exist in literature coping with predicting/identifying the optimal level of concurrency in STM systems and (possibly) dynamically regulating this level while the application is in progress. We can classify them in two categories, for each of which recent achievements are described in what follows.

Model-Based Approaches. In this category we include all the solutions where the prediction of how the STM system performance scales vs the level of concurrency (and thus the identification of the optimal level of concurrency) is based on the a-priori construction of a performance model. Along this path we find the work in [5], where an analytical model has been proposed to evaluate the performance of STM applications as a function of the number of concurrent threads and other workload configuration parameters. The actual target of this proposal is to build mathematical tools allowing the analysis of the effects of the contention management scheme on performance while the concurrency level varies. For this reason a detailed knowledge of the specific conflict detection and management scheme used by the target STM is required, and needs to be dealt with by a specialized modeling scheme capturing its dynamics. The proposed analytical model is in fact build up by coupling two building block sub-models: one independent of the actual concurrency control scheme, and another one which is instead specific to a given concurrency control algorithm. The latter has been instantiated in the work in [5] for the case of the Commit-Time-Locking (CTL) algorithm, and cannot be directly reused for algorithms based on different rules. Further, the model globally relies on assumptions to be met by the real STM system (e.g. in terms of data access pattern) in order for it to provide reliable predictions. In other words, this solution stands as kind of *scenario specific* approach.

The work in [14] presents an analytical model taking in input a workload characterization of the application expressed in terms of transaction profiles, contention probability and hardware resources consumption. This model is able to predict the application execution time as function of the number of concurrent threads sustaining the application. However the prediction only accounts for the average system behavior over the whole lifetime of the application (as expressed by the workload characterization). In other words, given an application, a unique "optimal" concurrency level can be identified via this approach, the most suited one for coping with situations where the application would behave according to expected values of the parameters determining the actual workload. In case of employment of this model in a real concurrency regulation architecture, the binding to the average system behavior would reduce the ability to capture the need for readapting the concurrency level on the basis of run-time variations of the application transactional profile in the different phases of its execution.

The proposal in [9] is targeted at evaluating scalability aspects of STM systems. It relies on the usage of different types of functions (e.g. polynomial and logarithmic functions) to approximate the application performance when considering different numbers

Table 2. Comparison of the different approaches

Approach	Suitable for any conflict manager	Bound to a given Tx profile	Explicitly captures variations of Tx profiles	Initial training required	Reduced training latency
f_A / A-STM	✓	✗	✓	✓	✓
f_{ML} / ML-STM	✓	✗	✓	✓	✗
f_{AML} / AML-STM	✓	✗	✓	✓	✓
[5]	✗	✓	✗	✓	✗
[14]	✓	✗	✗	✓	✓
[9]	✓	✗	✗	✓	✓
[2]	✓	✗	✗	✗	–
[8]	✓	✗	✗	✗	–

of concurrent threads. The approximation process is based on measuring the speed-up of the application over a set of runs, each one executed with a different number of concurrent threads, and then on calculating the proper function parameters by interpolating the measurements, so as to generate the final function (namely the performance model) used to predict the speed-up of the application vs the number of threads. In this approach the workload profile of the application is not taken into account, hence the prediction may prove unreliable when the profile changes wrt the one characterizing the behavior of the application during measurement and interpolation phases. Variance, or shifts, in the profile due to changes in the data-set content (possibly giving rise to, e.g., changes in the read/write set size) are therefore not captured by this kind of approach, and hence cannot be dealt with in terms of dynamic re-tuning of the level of concurrency in case of their materialization.

Heuristic Methods. In this category we find solutions that do not rely on a-priori constructing any model expressing the variation of performance vs the level of concurrency. The idea underlying these proposals is to try to push the system to its "optimal" performance level without building/relying on any knowledge base on how the level of performance would actually vary when chancing the number of threads. In this category we find the proposal in [2], which presents a control algorithm that dynamically changes the number of threads concurrently executing transactions on the basis of the observed transaction conflict rate. It is decreased when the rate exceeds some threshold value while it is increased when the rate is lower than another threshold. Another proposal along this direction can be found in [8], where a concurrency regulation approach is provided, based on the hill-climbing heuristic scheme. The approach determines whether the trend of increasing/decresing the concurrency level has positive effects on the STM throughput, in which case the trend is maintained. These works do not directly attempt to capture the relation between the actual transaction profile and the achievable performance (depending on the level of parallelism). This leads them to be mostly suited for static application profiles.

We also report in Table 2 a summary comparison of the approaches we have overseen in this chapter with literature alternatives. It is based on five indexes we identify as relevant, which are related to either the extent to which each approach is widely applicable, or its operating mode.

References

1. Cloud-TM: A Novel Programming Paradigm for the Cloud, http://www.cloudtm.eu/
2. Ansari, M., Kotselidis, C., Jarvis, K., Luján, M., Kirkham, C., Watson, I.: Advanced concurrency control for transactional memory using transaction commit rate. In: Luque, E., Margalef, T., Benítez, D. (eds.) Euro-Par 2008. LNCS, vol. 5168, pp. 719–728. Springer, Heidelberg (2008)
3. Bates, D., Watts, D.: Nonlinear regression analysis and its applications. Wiley series in probability and mathematical statistics. Wiley, New York [u.a.] (1988)
4. Bezdek, J.C.: Pattern Recognition with Fuzzy Objective Function Algorithms. Kluwer Academic Publishers, Norwell (1981)
5. Di Sanzo, P., Ciciani, B., Palmieri, R., Quaglia, F., Romano, P.: On the analytical modeling of concurrency control algorithms for software transactional memories: The case of commit-time-locking. Performance Evaluation 69(5), 187–205 (2012)
6. Di Sanzo, P., Del Re, F., Rughetti, D., Ciciani, B., Quaglia, F.: Regulating concurrency in software transactional memory: An effective model-based approach. In: Proceedings of the Seventh IEEE International Conference on Self-Adaptive and Self-Organizing Systems. SASO, IEEE Computer Society (September 2013)
7. Dice, D., Shalev, O., Shavit, N.: Transactional Locking II. In: Proceedings of the 20th International Symposium on Distributed Computing, pp. 194–208. ACM, New York (2006)
8. Didona, D., Felber, P., Harmanci, D., Romano, P., Schenker, J.: Identifying the optimal level of parallelism in transactional memory applications. In: Gramoli, V., Guerraoui, R. (eds.) NETYS 2013. LNCS, vol. 7853, pp. 233–247. Springer, Heidelberg (2013)
9. Dragojević, A., Guerraoui, R.: Predicting the scalability of an STM: A pragmatic approach. Presented at: 5th ACM SIGPLAN Workshop on Transactional Computing (2010)
10. Ennals, R.: Software transactional memory should not be obstruction-free. Tech. rep., Intel Research Cambridge Tech Report (January 2006)
11. Felber, P., Fetzer, C., Riegel, T.: Dynamic performance tuning of word-based software transactional memory. In: Proceedings of the 13th ACM SIGPLAN Symposium on Principles and Practice of Parallel Programming PPoPP, pp. 237–246. ACM (2008)
12. Felber, P., Fetzer, C., Riegel, T.: Dynamic performance tuning of word-based software transactional memory. In: Proceedings of the 13th ACM Symposium on Principles and Practice of Parallel Programming, pp. 237–246. ACM, New York (2008)
13. Haagdorens, B., Vermeiren, T., Goossens, M.: Improving the performance of signature-based network intrusion detection sensors by multi-threading. In: Lim, C.H., Yung, M. (eds.) WISA 2004. LNCS, vol. 3325, pp. 188–203. Springer, Heidelberg (2005)
14. He, Z., Hong, B.: Modeling the run-time behavior of transactional memory. In: Proceedings of the 2010 IEEE International Symposium on Modeling, Analysis and Simulation of Computer and Telecommunication Systems, pp. 307–315. IEEE Computer Society, Washington, DC (2010)
15. Herlihy, M.P., Moss, J.E.B.: Transactional memory: architectural support for lock-free data structures. ACM SIGARCH Computer Architecture News 21(2), 289–300 (1993)
16. Lev, Y., Luchangco, V., Marathe, V.J., Moir, M., Nussbaum, D., Olszewski, M.: Anatomy of a scalable software transactional memory. In: Proceedings of the 4th ACM SIGPLAN Workshop on Transactional Computing, TRANSACT. ACM (2009)

17. Maldonado, W., Marlier, P., Felber, P., Suissa, A., Hendler, D., Fedorova, A., Lawall, J.L., Muller, G.: Scheduling support for transactional memory contention management. In: Proceedings of the 15th ACM SIGPLAN Symposium on Principles and Practice of Parallel Programming, PPOPP, pp. 79–90 (2010)

18. Minh, C.C., Chung, J., Kozyrakis, C., Olukotun, K.: STAMP: Stanford Transactional Applications for Multi-Processing. In: Proceedings of the IEEE International Symposium on Workload Characterization, pp. 35–46. IEEE Computer Society, Washington, DC (2008)

19. Mitchell, T.M.: Machine Learning, 1st edn. McGraw-Hill (1997)

20. Rughetti, D., Di Sanzo, P., Ciciani, B., Quaglia, F.: Machine learning-based self-adjusting concurrency in software transactional memory systems. In: Proceedings of the 20th IEEE International Symposium On Modeling, Analysis and Simulation of Computer and Telecommunication Systems, MASCOTS, pp. 278–285. IEEE Comp. Soc. (August 2012)

21. Rughetti, D., Di Sanzo, P., Ciciani, B., Quaglia, F.: Analytical/ML mixed approach for concurrency regulation in software transactional memory. In: Proceedings of the 14th IEEE/ACM International Symposium on Cluster, Cloud and Grid Computing, CCGrid. IEEE Comp. Soc. (August 2014)

22. Ruppert, J.: A delaunay refinement algorithm for quality 2-dimensional mesh generation. Journal of Algorithms 18(3), 548–585 (1995)

23. Di Sanzo, P., Ciciani, B., Quaglia, F., Romano, P.: A performance model of multi-version concurrency control. In: Proceedings of the 16th IEEE/ACM International Symposium on Modeling, Analysis, and Simulation of Computer and Telecommunication Systems, MASCOTS, pp. 41–50 (2008)

24. Spear, M.F., Dalessandro, L., Marathe, V.J., Scott, M.L.: A comprehensive strategy for contention management in software transactional memory. In: Proceedings of the 14th ACM Symposium on Principles and Practice of Parallel Programming, pp. 141–150. ACM, New York (2009)

25. Yoo, R.M., Lee, H.H.S.: Adaptive transaction scheduling for transactional memory systems. In: Proceedings of the Twentieth Annual Symposium on Parallelism in Algorithms and Architectures, SPAA, pp. 169–178. ACM (2008)

26. Yu, P.S., Dias, D.M., Lavenberg, S.S.: On the analytical modeling of database concurrency control. Journal of the ACM, 831–872 (1993)

Self-tuning in Distributed
Transactional Memory

Maria Couceiro, Diego Didona, Luís Rodrigues, and Paolo Romano

INESC-ID, Instituto Superior Técnico, Universidade de Lisboa,
Lisbon, Portugal

Abstract. Many different mechanisms have been developed to implement Distributed Transactional Memory (DTM). Unfortunately, there is
no "one-size-fits-all" design that offers the desirable performance across
all possible workloads and scales. In fact, the performance of these mechanisms is affected by a number of intertwined factors that make it hard,
or even impossible, to statically configure a DTM platform for optimal
performance. These observations have motivated the emergence of self-
tuning schemes for automatically adapting the algorithms and parameters used by the main building blocks of DTM systems. This chapter
surveys existing research in the area of autonomic DTM design, with a
focus on the approaches aimed at answering the following two fundamental questions: how many resources (number of nodes, etc.) should a
DTM platform be provisioned with, and which protocols should be used
to ensure data consistency.

1 Introduction

After more than a decade of research, implementations of the Transactional
Memory (TM) abstraction have matured and are now ripe to enter the realm of
mainstream commodity computing. Over the last couple of years, TM support
has been integrated in the most popular open-source compiler, GCC, and also
in the CPUs produced by industry-leading manufacturers such as Intel [1] and
IBM [2]. Distributed Transactional Memory (DTM) [3,4,5] represents a natural
evolution of this technology, in which transactions are no longer confined within
the boundaries of a single multi-core machine but, instead, may be used as a synchronization mechanism to coordinate concurrent executions taking place across
a set of distributed machines. Just like TM have drawn their fundamental motivation in the advent of multi-core computing, the need for identifying simple,
yet powerful and general programming models for the cloud is probably one of
the key factors that have garnered growing research interest in the area of DTM
over the last years [6]. Another major driver underlying existing research efforts
in the area of DTM is fault-tolerance: as TM-based applications are expected
to turn mainstream in the short term, it becomes imperative to devise efficient
mechanisms capable of replicating the state of a TM system across a set of distributed nodes in order to ensure their consistency and high-availability despite
the failures of individual nodes [7,8].

R. Guerraoui and P. Romano (Eds.): Transactional Memory, LNCS 8913, pp. 418–448, 2015.

From the existing literature in the area of DTM, it can be observed that the design space of DTM platforms is very large and encompasses many complex issues, such as data placement and caching policies, replication protocols, concurrency control mechanisms, and group communication support, just to name a few. The performance of these fundamental building blocks of a DTM is affected by multiple intertwined factors. This has motivated the development of a wide range of alternative implementations, each exploring a different trade-off in the design space and optimized for different workload types, platform's scales, and deployment scenarios. As a result, the body of literature on DTM encompasses solutions tailored for read-intensive [7] vs conflict-prone [9,10] workloads, replication mechanisms optimized for small clusters [11], large scale data centers [12,13], as well as approaches specifically targeting geographically distributed DTM platforms [3].

One of the key conclusions that can be easily drawn by analyzing the results above is that there is no "one-size-fits-all" solution that can provide optimal performance across all possible workloads and scales of the platform. This represents a major obstacle for the adoption of DTM systems in the cloud, which bases its success precisely in its ability to adapt the type and amount of provisioned resources in an elastic fashion depending on the current applications' needs. Besides, a DTM encompasses an ecosystem of complex subcomponents whose performances are governed by a plethora of parameters: manually identifying the optimal tuning of these parameters can be a daunting task even when applications are faced with static workloads and fixed deployments. Guaranteeing optimal efficiency in presence of a time varying operational envelope, as typically occurs in cloud computing environments, requires to adjust these parameters in a dynamic fashion — a task that is arguably extremely onerous, if not impossible, without the aid of dedicated self-tuning mechanisms.

This is precisely the focus of this chapter, in which we dissect the problem of architecting self-tuning mechanisms for DTM platforms, with a special emphasis on solutions that tackle the following two fundamental issues:

- *elastic scaling:* DTM systems can be deployed over platforms of different scales, encompassing machines with different computational capacities interconnected via communication networks exhibiting diverse performances. Hence, a fundamental question that needs to be addressed when architecting a DTM-based application is how many and what types of resources (number of nodes, their configuration, etc.) should be employed (e.g., acquired from an underlying IaaS (Infrastructure as a Service) cloud provider) in order to ensure predetermined performance and reliability levels. In cloud computing environments, where resources can be dispensed elastically, this is not a one-off problem, but rather a real-time optimization problem. Its optimal solution requires not only to estimate the performance of applications when deployed over infrastructures of different scale and types, but also to encompass economical aspects (e.g., by comparing the cost of a DTM deployment over a large number of relatively slow nodes against a deployment on a smaller number of more powerful machines) as well as issues related to the on-line reconfiguration of the platform (namely, how to rearrange data after scaling);

- *adapting the data consistency protocol:* the literature on data consistency protocols for distributed and replicated transactional systems is a quite prolific one. Existing approaches explore a number of different design choices, concerning aspects such as whether to execute transactions on all nodes (as in active replication [14]) or executing in just one replica and only propagating the transaction's updates (a.k.a. deferred update schemes [15]), how to implement transaction validation [16], and whether to use distributed locking [17] vs total order communication protocols [18] to serialize transactions. This has motivated research aimed at supporting the automatic switching between multiple data consistency protocols, and, in some cases even the simultaneous coexistence of different protocols. The key challenges addressed in these works are related to how to preserve consistency despite the (possibly concurrent) employment of alternative consistency protocols, as well as to the identification of the best strategy to adopt given the current workload and system's characteristics.

The remainder of this chapter is structured as follows. We first provide, in Section 2, an overview of the main building blocks encompassing typical DTM architectures, and illustrate some of the key choices at the basis of their design. Next, in Section 3, we identify the DTM components that would benefit the most from the employment of adaptive, self-tuning designs. In Section 4, we provide background on the main methodologies employed in the literature to decide when to trigger an adaptation and to predict which among the available strategies to adopt. In Section 5 we focus on elastic scaling, and in Section 6 we discuss adaptation of the consistency protocols. Finally, Section 7 concludes the paper.

2   Background on DTM

This section is devoted to overview on the key mechanisms that are encompassed by typical DTM architectures. It should be noted that the discussion that follows does not aim at providing a thorough and exhaustive survey of existing DTM designs, but rather to facilitate the description of the self-tuning DTM systems described in the remainder of this chapter.

The diagram in Figure 1 depicts the high level architecture of a typical DTM platform, illustrating the key building blocks that compose the software stack of this type of system.

DTM API. At their top most layer, existing DTM platforms expose APIs analogous to those provided by non-distributed TMs that allow to define a set of accesses to in-memory data to be performed within an atomic transaction. The actual API exposed by a DTM is ultimately influenced by the data model that it adopts; the range of data models explored in the DTM literature includes, besides the object-based [7] and word-based [5] ones (typically employed

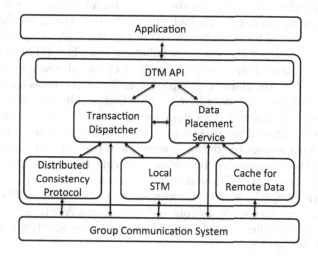

Fig. 1. High level architecture of typical DTM platforms (single node)

in non-distributed TMs), also popular alternatives in the NoSQL domain, like the key-value [13,19] model. Certain DTM platforms [20,21] that support partial replication schemes (i.e., which do not replicate data at *every* replica of the system) provide also dedicated API support to influence the policies employed to determine the placement of data (and its replicas) across the nodes of the system, with the goal of enhancing the data locality achieved by DTM applications. These include programmatic mechanisms to ensure the co-location of data items [21] or to provide the data placement service with semantic information (like the data item's type and the relations in which it is involved) concerning the data access patterns generated by the nodes of the platform [20].

Data Placement Service. The data placement service, as the name suggests, is responsible for locating the nodes that maintain (replicas of) the data items accessed during the transaction execution. This module is required exclusively in case the DTM platform adopts a partial replication scheme (as in fully replicated systems each node maintain a replica of every data item), although certain DTM platforms may rely on analogous abstractions to establish ownership privileges of nodes on data items [21]. The actual implementation of this service is strongly affected by the transaction execution model embraced by the DTM, which can be either *control-flow* or *data-flow*. In *control-flow* systems data items are statically assigned (unless the platform is subject to elastic scaling) to the nodes of the platform, which retrieve non-local data items via RPC. In *data-flow* systems, conversely, transactions are immobile and objects are dynamically migrated to invoking transactional nodes. As in the control-flow model the placement of data is static, several control-flow DTM systems [21,22,12] adopt simple policies based on consistent hashing [23]. This technique, which essentially maps data items to nodes of the platform randomly via the use of a hash function, has the desirable properties of executing data items look ups locally (i.e., the nodes that replicate a given data item can be identified by computing the hash of its identifier) and achieving a good balance in the data distribution. Data-flow DTMs, on the other hand, rely on ad-hoc (distributed) directory or cache coherence protocols, such as the Arrow [24] or the Ballistic [25] protocols. These protocols require that, in order for a node to access a data item, it must first acquire its ownership (which implies locating the current data item owner). As a result, data-flow models can introduce additional network hops along the critical path of execution of transactions with respect to control-flow solutions (that do not allow migration of data). On the pro-side, by dynamically moving the ownership of items to the nodes that access them, data-flow systems can spontaneously lead to data placement strategies achieving better locality than static policies, like consistent hashing, supported exclusively by control-flow systems. A detailed discussion on control-flow and data-flow models, as well as on systems adopting these models, can be found in Chapter 16.

Transaction Dispatcher. The transaction dispatcher is a component present in several DTM platforms [10,5,26], and is in charge of determining whether the execution of a transaction should take place on the node that generated it, on a different one, or even by all nodes in the platform. This decision can be driven by different rationales, such as reducing data contention [26] or enhancing data locality [10,5,21]. In order to support the migration and execution of entire transactions at remote nodes, the transaction dispatching mechanism typically requires ad-hoc support at the DTM API layer in order to ensure proper encapsulation of the transaction logic, i.e., a function/procedure encoded in a programming language, and of its input parameters (using classic RPI mechanisms).

Local STM. As for the local data stores, existing DTM platforms typically leverage on state of the art local STMs, which implement efficient concurrency control algorithms optimized for modern multi-core architectures [7,11,9,27].

Cache for Remote Data. Some partially replicated DTM platforms [28,21] cache frequently accessed remote data items, and update them using lazy/asynchronous invalidation strategies. Clearly, it must be possible to manipulate also cached data without breaking consistency: therefore they are maintained in memory and their manipulation is subdued to some form of concurrency control. However, cached data need typically to be associated with different meta-data and managed with different rules than the data stored in the local STM (whose ownership can be established via the data placement service). As a consequence, cached data are normally maintained in separate in-memory structures.

Distributed Consistency Protocol. Clearly, the data accesses performed by local transactions need to be synchronized with those issued by transactions

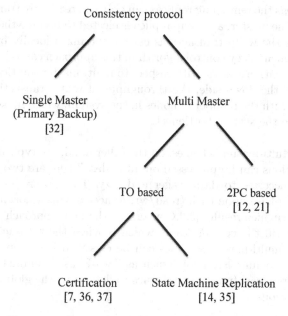

Fig. 2. Taxonomy for consistency protocols in transactional systems

executing at different nodes. The responsibility of this task is delegated to a distributed consistency protocol, which is ultimately responsible for enforcing the consistency guarantees ensured by the DTM platform. The literature on DTM (and more in general on distributed transactional platforms, e.g., distributed DBMS) has explored a number of alternative consistency levels, like 1-copy serializability [13], virtual world consistency [9], extended update serializability [12] and parallel SI [29]. Clearly, the choice of the consistency criterion has a strong impact on the design of the underlying distributed consistency protocol. Another factor that has a key impact on the distributed consistency protocol is whether the system employs full or partial replication. In fully replicated DTM platforms, in fact, once the transaction serialization order is established (typically by means of a consensus or atomic broadcast service [7]), the nodes can determine the outcome of committing transactions locally (by validating their read-set with respect to the most recent committed version). Conversely, in partially replicated DTM systems, some sort of 2PC-like agreement is unavoidable, as the snapshot accessed by a committing transaction needs to be validated, in general, by multiple nodes, which must certify the freshness of the transaction's snapshot with respect to the locally stored authoritative copies of data. Over the last decades, a vast literature on distributed consistency protocols for transactional systems has emerged [15,30,31]. A possible taxonomy of existing solutions is reported in Figure 2.

Single-master. In single master schemes, also known as primary backup, write transactions are executed exclusively at a single node (also called master or primary), whereas the remaining replicas can only run read-only transactions [32]. Upon failure of the master, a backup replica is elected to become the new master.

Note that, as the write transactions can be serialized locally by the master using its local concurrency control algorithm, this approach can rely on a simpler replica synchronization scheme with respect to multi-master solutions (as we will see shortly). On the down side, the throughput of write transactions does not clearly scale up with the number of nodes in the system, which makes the master prone to become the system bottleneck.

Multi-master. Multi-master schemes, on the other hand, are typically more scalable as transactions can be processed on all nodes. There are two types of synchronizing the accesses to data: eager and lazy. The first relies on a remote synchronization phase upon each (read/write) access, which normally results in very poor performance results [33].Conversely, the lazy approach defers replica synchronization till the commit time, which is when the transaction is finally validated. Lazy multi-master schemes can be classified based on whether they rely on Atomic Commit Protocols (such as Two-Phase Commit) or Total Order (TO) [34] broadcast/multicast schemes to determine the global serialization order of transactions.

Two-Phase Commit. In solutions based on Two-Phase Commit (2PC), transactions attempt to atomically acquire locks at all nodes that maintain data accessed by the transaction. Even though these schemes normally incur in minor communication overheads with respect to those relying on TO, these solutions are well known to suffer of scalability problems due to the rapid growth of the distributed deadlock rate as the number of replicas in the system grows [17].

Total Order based schemes. Conversely, TO-based replication is a family of (distributed) deadlock-free algorithms that serializes transactions according to the total order established by a TO service [34]. These solutions can be distinguished into two further classes: state machine replication and certification.

State Machine Replication. In the state machine replication [14,35], all replicas[1] execute the same set of transactions in the same order. The transactions are shipped to all replicas using total order broadcast and, consequently, all replicas receive transactions in the same order and execute them in that order. However, both transactions and validation scheme must be fully deterministic so that all replicas begin and finish transactions in the same state.

Certification. Unlike State Machine Replication, certification based techniques undertake a *speculative* approach, which can achieve higher scalability, in low conflict workloads, by fully executing the transaction only at one node. This means that different transactions may be executed on different replicas concurrently. If the transaction aborts during its execution, no further coordination is

---

[1] This technique has been proposed for fully replicated systems.

required. However, if the transaction is ready to commit, a transaction validation phase is triggered in order to certify that it has not accessed stale items. The information exchanged to certify transactions varies depending on the considered certification protocol (e.g., non-voting [36], voting [37] or bloom-filter based [7]), but the certification request is disseminated by means of a TO broadcast service that targets all the nodes that maintain replicas of the data items accessed by the transaction. In case of partial replication, as already mentioned, this certification phase may have to involve a voting phase to gather positive acknowledgements from at least one replica of each data item accessed within the transaction; in this case the message pattern of the distributed consistency protocols coincides with the one of the 2PC scheme, in which the prepare messages are disseminated using a TO service.

3   What Should Be Self-tuned in a DTM?

As it clearly emerges from the discussion in the previous section, the design and configuration space of DTM is quite vast, and there are several components in the DTM stack whose setting and parametrization has a strong impact on DTM performance. Indeed, performance of a DTM application are driven by complex non-linear dynamics stemming from the intertwined effects of workload's resource utilization (e.g., in terms of CPU and network bandwidth), data access pattern (e.g., data contention and locality), inter-nodes communication (e.g., for remote read operations) and distributed synchronization (e.g., for committing transactions).

Typical Key Performance Indicators (KPIs) of a DTM are general purpose metrics like transactions response time and achievable throughput. DTM-specific KPIs include also metrics like transactions abort probability, execution time of the distributed commit phase, number of remote accesses during the execution phase, and number of nodes involved in the transaction processing. While Quality of Service specifications are typically expressed in terms of throughput and response time, DTM-specific KPIs are fundamental metrics in many DTM self-tuning schemes, as they allow for pinpointing bottlenecks and for identifying sub-optimal configurations. For example, a high abort rate may imply an excessive concurrency level in the platform and may lead to the decrease of the number of concurrently active transactions in the platform.

Recent research [26,38,39,40] has shown that transactional workloads are very heterogeneous and affected by so many variables that no-one-size-fits-all solution exists for the DTM configuration that guarantees optimal performance across all possible applications' workloads. To address this issue, a number of alternative solutions have been proposed to tackle the problem of self-tuning DTMs. Such solutions draw from different fields of performance modeling and forecasting and aim to optimize several major building blocks/configuration parameters of DTMs, focusing in particular on the following five aspects: elastic scaling, choice of the consistency protocol, data placement and replication degree, communication layer and local TM implementation.

In the following, we analyze the main trade-offs that emerge in the self-tuning of these DTM building blocks. In Section 5 and Section 6 we will return to investigate in greater detail the problems of automating the elastic scaling process and the choice of consistency protocol, by surveying existing research in these areas.

Scale. The scale of a DTM consists in the number of nodes composing the platform and, possibly, the maximum number of active threads allowed on each node, namely, the multiprogramming level (MPL). Accordingly, the elastic scaling, i.e., dynamic resizing, of a DTM can take place horizontally, by altering number of nodes in the platform, or vertically, by adapting the MPL.

Different scales in the DTM not only result in a different physical resources utilization, but also into different data access patterns. In fact, increasing the number of active transactions in the system, either by scaling horizontally or vertically the platform, other than requiring more processing power, also results into a higher concurrency in accessing and modifying shared data, with a possible commensurate increase of conflicts and, hence, abort rate. This poses a major challenge when devising elastic scaling schemes for DTMs as the bottleneck of a DTM application may lie in data contention. Hence, scalability trends of DTM applications are far from being easily predictable, as increasing the processing power, i.e., number of nodes, or processing units, i.e., number of threads, does not always entail better performance.

Scaling out a DTM poses additional challenges than altering its MPL level: changing the number of nodes composing a DTM, in fact, results not only into an increased processing power, but also into a modification of the placement of data, which can get redistributed across the nodes of the platform (as it is case, for instance, when using consistent hashing-based placement policies). Such modification can imply a shift in data locality, and affect the probability that a transaction accesses data maintained by its originating node. For write transactions this results also in a change in the number of nodes to be contacted at commit time to propagate updates and, hence, in the duration of the corresponding phase.

The aforementioned DTM dynamics are not encompassed by the vast majority of available state-of-the-art solutions for automatic resource provisioning, as they mainly target stateless applications or neglect the impact of elastic scaling on data distribution and contention [41,42,43,44,45,46]. Devising an optimal autonomic elastic scaling schemes for DTM is, thus, a very challenging task, which needs to be tackled by means of *ad hoc* solutions.

Distributed Consistency Protocol. Like for the scale, the choice of the distributed consistency protocol has a huge impact on both logical and physical resource utilization. Single master approaches deal with the concurrency control of update transactions on the master node: on one side this tends to mitigate data contention, as conflicts can be resolved more efficiently, i.e., in a fully local fashion and without the need to run a distributed consensus algorithm to determine the outcome of a transaction; on the other hand, the master node may become a bottleneck in case the arrival rate of update transactions exceeds its processing capacity.

Multi-master schemes, instead, allow for a better load balancing among nodes even in write dominated workloads (by distributing update transactions across all the nodes of the DTM platform), but generally require onerous inter-node synchronization mechanisms for detecting and resolving conflicts among transactions. As mentioned in Section 2, consistency protocols based on 2PC require only two round-trip between a transaction's initiator and other involved nodes to agree on the outcome of the transaction, but are liable to distributed deadlocks; TO-based protocols, conversely, achieve deadlock freedom, but the latency induced by the TO primitive may lead to higher synchronization costs at commit time [39].

Data Placement and Replication Degree. Data locality plays a role of paramount importance in DTMs, as it determines the frequency of access to remote data present in the critical path of execution of transactions [20]. The tuning of the data placement and of the replication degree is aimed at enhancing the quality of the data layout, so as to increase data locality and reduce the execution time of transactions.

Two fundamental challenges that need to be tackled for implementing effective self-tuning data placement schemes are i) how to identify the optimal data layout (i.e., the data layout that maximizes the performance of the platform), and ii) how to keep track of the new mapping between data item replicas and nodes in the DTM platform. The former is in fact a distributed optimization problem, which has been addressed both in its on-line [20,47] and off-line [48,49] formulation, considering different objective functions and constraints (e.g., maximizing locality [20,48] vs balancing load [47]) and both centralized [48] and decentralized [20] solutions. As for the tracking of the mapping between data items and nodes of the DTM platform, there are two main trade-offs that need to be taken into account. Approaches relying on external (and properly dimensioned) directory services [48,47] can typically support fine-grained mapping strategies also for large data sets, but impose non-negligible additional latency in the transaction's critical path. Approaches that explicitly store the mapping of the entire data set at each node either rely on random hash functions [21] or on coarse grained mapping strategies — as the overhead for storing and keeping synchronized a fine-grained mapping would be unbearable with large data sets. This has motivated the usage of probabilistic techniques [20,49] that sacrifice accuracy of data items lookups in order to reduce the memory footprint of the meta-data used to encode the data-to-nodes mapping.

The tuning of the replication degree in a DTM [50,38] is another closely related problem, which encompasses a subtle trade-off between the probability of accessing locally stored data and the cost of the synchronization phase necessary to validate committing transactions. On one hand, in fact, increasing the replication degree generally results into a higher probability that a transaction accesses a data item that is maintained by the local node; on the other hand, for update transactions, it also typically leads to an increase in the number of nodes to be contacted at commit time for validating the transaction and propagating its updates [38].

Group Communication System. Inter-nodes communication represents a major source of overhead in DTM, as it can introduce relatively large latencies in the critical path of execution of transactions, both for the retrieval of remote data items and to support the distributed commit phase [4,51]. Other than increasing transactions' completion time (and hence reducing the achievable throughput), these latencies can have a great impact also on the conflict rate of transactions: in fact, the longer a transaction takes to execute, the higher is the chance that another transaction will try to concurrently access and/or modify a common datum.

A typical trade-off that arises in the design of coordination services, like consensus or total order multicast primitives, is that configurations/protocols that exhibit minimum latencies at low message arrival rate tend also to support relatively low throughputs. Conversely, protocols/configurations optimized for supporting high throughputs normally introduce much higher latencies when operating at low throughput levels. These trade-offs have motivated the development of self-tuning mechanisms supporting both the dynamic switching between alternative implementations of communication primitives (e.g., variants of TO) [52,53], as well as automatic configuration of internal parameters of these protocols (e.g., message batching) [54,55].

Local TM. As discussed in Section 4.2, the typical architecture stack of DTM systems includes a non-distributed (S)TM, which is used to regulate concurrent access to locally stored data. The problem of self-tuning TM has also been largely explored in literature, as TM and DTM, unsurprisingly, exhibit similar trade-offs, e.g., the workload characteristics can strongly affect the performance of the concurrency control algorithm, as well as the optimal MPL. Examples of self-tuning solutions that dynamically adjust these TM mechanisms/parameters can be found in [56,57,58,59].

Another TM parameter that has been object of self-tuning techniques is the lock granularity [60]. Lock granularity expresses what is the atomic portion of the data set (or of the memory space, for centralized TMs) that the concurrency control scheme deals with. The finer is the granularity, the higher is the concurrency that the concurrency control scheme allows for, but also the overhead incurred to maintain and manage meta-data. For example, in a per-item locking scheme, every data item is guarded by a lock and conflicts can be detected at the granularity of the single item. A coarser scheme, instead, reduces the number of employed locks at the cost of inducing false conflicts, i.e., conflicts among transactions that access different data items, which, nonetheless, insist on the same lock.

Finally, self-tuning techniques have been proposed to optimize the thread mapping strategy [61] and efficiently exploit the memory hierarchy of modern multiprocessors. In these architectures, just like we just described for the distributed case, data locality plays a fundamental role in determining the performance of an application. Thread mapping consists in placing threads on cores so as to amortize memory access latency and/or to reduce memory contention, i.e., it tries to allocate a thread that frequently accesses a given memory region on the core that incurs the minimal latency when accessing that portion of the memory space.

4   When and Which Adaptation to Trigger?

In this section, we provide background on the main methodologies that are commonly employed in the literature of self-tuning systems to tackle two key issues: when to trigger an adaptation, and how to predict which among the available reconfigurations to enact.

4.1   When to Trigger Adaptations?

An important aspect to consider when dealing with self-tuning of systems is determining *when* to trigger an adaptation. This aspect gains a paramount importance in DTMs, in particular when performing elastic scaling, replication switching or change in the replication degree. In fact, global reconfigurations and data migration can pose significant overhead on transactions processing, which may severely hinder performance during a non-negligible time window [62].

In this context, a key classification of existing self-tuning techniques is whether they react to workload changes, or they try to anticipate them. Another fundamental problem is related to the issue of distinguishing in a robust way actual workload changes from transient noise, which frequently affect workload metrics measurements in large scale systems. Finally, another relevant issue, which is at the basis of proactive schemes, is how to predict future workload trends. In the following we provide an overview of the key methodologies/building blocks that are used to address these issues. It should be noted that the techniques described below can be employed in a broad range of self-tuning systems, and their applicability is not restricted to adaptive DTM platforms.

Before describing each of these techniques, it is worth noting that in a DTM environment a workload can be characterized using a multitude of metrics. Besides classical/general-purpose metrics, like transactions arrival rate and CPU/bandwidth demand to perform operations, the workload of a DTM can be characterized also using DTM-specific metrics, such as the ratio of read-only vs update transactions, the number of accessed data items per transaction, and the transaction conflict probability.

Reacting to vs Predicting Workload Changes. A key characteristic that allows for coarsely classifying existing self-tuning mechanisms is whether they rely on *reactive* vs *proactive* approaches. Reactive schemes evaluate the need for reconfiguration based on the current workload, whereas proactive self-tuning strategies attempt to anticipate the need for changing system's configuration by predicting future workload trends.

Since reactive schemes track variations of the workload based on recent observations,they typically allow the system to react promptly even to abrupt workload changes due to exogenous factors (like flash crowds [63]), which would be very hard, if not impossible, to predict using proactive schemes. However, given that the reconfiguration is carried out against the current workload, reactive schemes can yield sub-optimal performance during transitory phases, especially in case the adaptation phase incurs a non-negligible latency.

On the other hand, the pros of proactive strategies coincide with the cons of reactive ones. By anticipating the need for changing system's configuration, adaptations can be enacted before the occurrence of workload changes. As a result, proactive approaches can reduce the period of time during which suboptimal configurations are used. On the other hand, the effectiveness of proactive approaches is strongly dependent on the accuracy of the mechanisms that they adopt to predict future workload trends (which we will overview shortly). For this reason, proactive and reactive schemes are sometimes combined into hybrid schemes [63,64,45].

Robust Change Detection. Workload measurement, especially in complex distributed platforms like DTMs, are typically subject to non-negligible noises. Hence, the robustness of any self-tuning scheme is strongly affected by its ability to distinguish small workload fluctuations, e.g., due to short transitory phases or transient spikes, from actual workload shifts, i.e., transitions from one workload to a different, stable one. This is a fundamental requisite to enforce the system's stability, i.e., to avoid its continuous oscillation among different states, namely configurations, due to frequent re-adaptations triggered by unavoidable, fleeting workload's fluctuations.

A principled approach to tackle this issue is based on the idea of considering the workload as a generic signal. Filtering techniques [65] can, then, be applied in order to reduce/remove noise and extract statistically meaningful information. One of the simplest examples of a filter is the Moving Average (MA), in which, given a time window composed by t intervals, the value v at observation j is given by $v_j = \sum_{i=j-t+1}^{j} \frac{v_i}{t}$; in the Exponential Moving Average (EMA), elements in the summation are given a weight that decreases as the measurement becomes older, in order to give more importance to recent measurements.

A more advanced filter employed to perform measurements in presence of noise is the Kalman Filter [66], which computes the value of the target metric as a weighted sum of the last prediction and the latest measurement. The weights reflect the confidence of such estimate and measurement and it is inversely proportional to the variance associated with those two values. The Kalman Filter represents a reference technique to track systems' parameters [67] and have been successfully applied in a wide range of applications, from CPU provisioning in virtualized environments [68] to performance optimization with energy constraints [69].

Another prominent related technique, originally introduced in the literature on statistical process control [70] to verify whether a process complies to its behavioral expectations, is the CUSUM (Cumulative Sum Control Chart) [71]. CUSUM involves the computation of a cumulative sum: noting x_n the n-th measurement for the target metric and w_n the corresponding weight, the cumulative sum at the n-th step, namely S_n, is expressed as $S_n = max\{0, S_{n-1} + w_n x_n\}$, with $S_0 = 0$. When S_n grows over a predefined threshold, a change in the metric is identified.

The CUSUM technique, whose employment has been borrowed from the manufacturing field, has been applied not only to workload monitoring and characterization for distributed transactional platforms [72], but also to tackle other issues like tracking faults in distributed systems [73] and detecting divergence from a desired QoS [74].

Workload Forecasting. As already mentioned, workload forecasting is a key problem at the basis of proactive self-tuning techniques. The techniques used to this purpose are typically borrowed from the literature on time-series analysis and forecasting, and can be classified depending on whether they operate in the time or in the frequency domain [75].

Time-domain methods. Techniques belonging to this category forecast the value for a metric in the next time window based on the raw measurements of such metric in the past. Auto Regression and Moving Averages methods are at the basis of a broad family of time-domain solutions: ARMA (Auto-Regressive Moving Average), which combines the two; ARIMA (AR Integrated MA), which generalizes the previous one to the case of non-stationary time series (i.e., time series whose shape changes over time); SARIMA (Seasonal ARIMA), which allows the ARIMA technique to incorporate preexistent knowledge about seasonal, namely recurring, behaviors [76]. Other popular solutions are based on the use of filtering techniques, such as the aforementioned Kalman Filter. In fact, due to its recursive nature, once instantiated, the Kalman Filter can be queried not only to filter out noisy components from the current measurements, but also to predict future values of the tracked workload metrics.

Frequency-domain methods. Techniques belonging to this category are aimed at extracting from time series information about seasonality and recurrence. Frequency-domain methods rely either on spectral analysis or on wavelet analysis. They are both based on the idea of decomposing a time series into a summation in the frequency domain: the former uses sinusoids as basis, the latter uses wavelets [76].

4.2 Which Adaptation to Trigger?

Once workload changes are detected, self-tuning systems need to decide which adaptation to trigger, if any, to react to such change. The identification of the optimal configuration is typically performed by means of performance models,

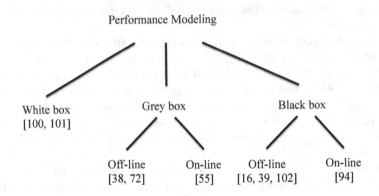

Fig. 3. Taxonomy of performance modeling techniques

which allow for the estimation/prediction of the system's performance in the various available configurations. The literature on performance modeling of computing systems is very prolific, and the models used in self-tuning system differ significantly in their nature and complexity. In Figure 3, we classify them into white, black and gray (an hybrid of black and white) box techniques, according to whether (and how) they exploit knowledge on the internal dynamics of the system. Moreover, we further classify black box, and hence grey box, approaches into off-line and on-line, depending on whether the model is built before putting the application in execution or at runtime.

White Box Modeling. This approach leverages on available expertise on the internal dynamics of systems and/or applications, and uses such knowledge to build an Analytical Model (AM) (e.g., based on queueing theory) or simulators, aimed at capturing how system's configuration and workload's parameters map onto performance [77]. Once defined, analytical models typically require no training (or a minimal profiling to obtain the value for some basic parameters) for being instantiated. In order to ensure their mathematical tractability, however, analytical models typically rely on approximations and simplifying assumptions on how the modeled system and/or its workload behave. Their accuracy can hence be challenged in scenarios (i.e., areas of the configurations' space or specific workload conditions) in which such approximations are too coarse, or are simply not matched. In addition, aside from possible re-evaluations of internal parameters, analytical models' inaccuracies are not amendable, as the mathematical characterization of the system's dynamics in encoded by means of immutable equations.

Black Box Modeling. This approach lies on the opposite side of the spectrum with respect to the white box solutions. Black box modeling does not require any knowledge about the target system/application's internal behavior. Conversely, it relies on a *training phase*, namely on observing the system's actual behavior under different configurations and while subject to different workloads, in order to infer a statistical performance model via different Machine Learning (ML) techniques [78]. Over the last years, these approaches have become more and more popular as tools for performance prediction of modern systems and applications, whose ever growing complexity challenges the viability of developing sufficiently detailed, and hence accurate, analytical models.

In practice, the accuracy achievable by black box models strongly depends on the representativeness of configurations and workloads that the ML has witnessed with during its training phase. This results in the ability of black box models to achieve a very good accuracy for scenarios sufficiently close to the ones observed during the training phase; on the other hand, predictions' accuracy of ML techniques is typically poor in regions of the parameters' space that were not sufficiently sampled during the training (in which case the model is often said to be used in extrapolation).

Unfortunately, the space of all possible configurations for a target system/application grows exponentially with the number of variables (a.k.a. features in the ML terminology) that can affect its performance — the so called curse of dimensionality [79]. Hence, in complex systems, like DTMs, the cost of conducting an exhaustive training process, spanning all possible configurations of the design and configuration's space and experimenting with all possible workloads, can typically be prohibitive.

Grey Box Modeling. Grey box approaches, as the name suggests, employ white and black model methodologies in hybrid fashions, so as to inherit the best features of the two worlds: the good accuracy in extrapolation (i.e., for unseen configuration/workloads) and minimal training time typical of white box models, and the robustness and possibility to incrementally enhance accuracy, via periodic retraining, of black box models.

Grey box techniques can, in their turn, be grouped into three categories.

- *Parameter fitting*: this solution relies on fitting techniques [80] to identify the values of (a subset of) the input parameters of a white box model, whose direct measurement is undesirable or infeasible. This is the case, for instance, of models that require detailed workload characterization [42] or service demand times [41], and whose measurement from an operational system may introduce prohibitive overheads. This technique is used also in case some parameters of white-box models do not map directly to any physical aspect of the system, and are instead used to encapsulate complex systems' dynamics that would be otherwise hard to capture explicitly via analytical techniques [58]. In these situations, fitting techniques can be used to determine the values of the unknown parameters that minimize the model's prediction errors over a given training set.
- *Divide et impera*: this technique consists in building performance models of individual parts of the entire system, which are either based on AM or on ML. The sub-models are then combined in order to obtain a prediction of the system as a whole [72,38]. This approach is particularly suited for

scenarios in which the internals dynamics of certain sub-components of the system are not known and/or are not easy to model using white-box analytical models, e.g., the networking infrastructure in a cloud-based distributed platform. The performance of these sub-components can then be predicted using black-box ML-based techniques, whereas white-box modeling can be used for the remainder of the system. By narrowing the domain over which ML techniques are used, their learning time is normally significantly reduced; also, the joint usage of white box models allows for achieving better accuracy in extrapolation when compared with pure black-box approaches.

- *Bootstrapping*: this methodology relies on an AM predictor to generate an initial synthetic training set for the ML, with the purpose of avoiding the initial, long profiling phase of the target application under different settings. Then, the ML is retrained over time in order to incorporate the knowledge coming from samples collected from the operational system [59,55].

While white box modeling is an inherently off-line technique, ML solutions, at the basis of purely black or grey box models, can be instantiated either off-line or on-line.

Off-line Learning. Off-line black box performance models are typically built by means of *Supervised Learning (SL)*, in which the ML algorithm is trained on labeled features, i.e., input for which the output is known.

In SL, the training algorithm, noted γ, is a function defined over the *training set* $D_{tr} = \{< \mathbf{x}, y >\}$, where $\mathbf{x} =< x_1, \ldots, x_n >$ is a point in a $n-$dimensional features' space, noted F, and y is the value of some unknown function $\phi : F \to C$. The co-domain C of the function may be a discrete set, whose elements are called *classes*, or a continuous space. The problem of learning the mapping of elements of F to C is called *classification* in the first case, and *regression* in the second one.

The output of γ is a function, also called model, noted Γ, which represents an approximation of ϕ over the features' space F. More precisely, a model $\Gamma : F \to C$ takes as input a point $\mathbf{x} \in F$, possibly not observed in D_{tr}, and returns a value $\hat{y} \in C$.

In off-line SL, the training set D_{tr} is assumed fully available to the learning algorithm. When new data is available, e.g. by gathering new sample from a running application, a new model can be built from scratch, considering the whole available training data set. Note that this palingenesis of the statistical model does not qualify as an instance of on-line learning, as we shall discuss briefly, as the model is built *ex novo* over an ever-increasing training set. Examples of off-line SL algorithms are Decision Trees, Support Vector Machines and Artificial Neural Networks [78].

On-line Learning. We distinguish three main approaches to on-line black box learning. The first one consists in on-line SL, according to which the model is built incrementally over a stream of training samples, i.e., only a subset of D_{tr} (possibly of cardinality 1) is available at the time, and it has to be incorporated in the model without being stored for further consideration [81]. Approaches in this domain typically assume that the learning algorithm can access each sample only once during the training phase. As a consequence, they normally require considerably less computational resources than off-line techniques, but may also achieve lower prediction accuracy.

A second on-line ML technique is *Reinforcement Learning (RL)*. RL aims at inferring the best way of performing actions in an environment (characterized in DTM context by a set of workload and performance indicators) given a state (i.e., a workload), so as to maximize some notion of cumulative reward (e.g., throughput). The main challenge tackled by RL techniques [82,83] is finding a balance between exploration (of untested actions for a given state) and exploitation (of available, and typically incomplete, knowledge), while minimizing the, so called, *regret*, that is the cumulative error with respect to the optimal strategy. Frequent explorations allow for acquiring a good knowledge of the rewards corresponding to different actions in a given state, but also causes the system to oscillate among several sub-optimal configurations, yielding to instability and hindering performance. On the other hand, an overly conservative policy, which does not test the available options sufficiently often, may get stuck in local maxima, especially in scenarios in which the reward distribution is subject to large variance (and may hence require a relatively large number of samples to be accurately estimated).

Finally, on-line black box self-tuning schemes can be based on optimization techniques like Gradient Descent or Genetic algorithms [84]. These approaches seek to minimize/maximize a given application's performance indicator: similarly to RL approaches, they combine exploration and exploitation; however, they do not encompass the notion of cumulative reward, thus differing from RL in the way the search of the optimal configuration is carried out and in the amount of information maintained about the system/application's state and previously performed explorations.

5   Elastic Scaling in DTM Systems

In this section we review solutions aimed at self-tuning the scale of DTMs. Though we focus on this kind of platform, we also include in the analysis solutions that have been proposed and evaluated in the broader field of elastic scaling of distributed data platforms and which could be applied also to the case of DTMs.

In our analysis we will focus on three main technical challenges, which need to be tackled in order to implement effective elastic scaling solutions for DTM, namely: how to preserve consistency during elastic scaling, when to trigger elastic scaling, how to determine the new scale of the DTM.

How Is Elastic Scaling Supported? DTM can either scale vertically, namely, by changing the number of concurrent threads active in each of the platform's nodes, or horizontally, namely, changing the number of nodes in the platform. In the first case, the scaling procedure does not encompass inter-node synchronization or state transfer, as it simply consists of activating/deactivating the desired number of threads [57].

Scaling out a DTM is, conversely, a much more challenging task given the stateful nature of the platform that implies the need for a state transfer phase and the constraint of preserving the consistent and atomic access to data items during the reconfiguration. In this paragraph we survey some state transfer techniques that have been proposed to elastically scale databases but that are applicable also to the case of DTMs.

The simplest solution to scale out a distributed transactional platform is the *stop and go* technique, which naively consists in blocking transactions execution during the state transfer and restoring it when it is over. Of course, the major drawback of this solution is that it implies service unavailability during the scaling phase, and it is, thus, employed only when there is no other option available [21].

For this reason, a number of solutions have been proposed to perform the state transfer at the application level, i.e., relying only on the transactional middleware of the platform.

A first one represents an improvement over the *stop and go*: while a new node is being initiated it cannot serve requests, but other nodes can, thus maintaining the service available. This technique basically consists of three phases. In the first one, a new node is spawned and starts receiving data from the source nodes designated by the data placement component. In the second one, it receives newer versions of data that it has already received during the first phase, but which have been updated in the meanwhile. In the last phase, the new node receives the last stream of data and starts processing transactions; in order to allow the new node to catch up with the state of running nodes without breaking atomicity and consistency, this phase may require all the nodes in the system to stop processing transactions, thus resulting into a short service unavailability window. This technique has been applied to the context of live migrations of databases in multi-tenant [85] and single instance [86,46] environments. Optimized variants for partially replicated systems also exist, in which the amount of data sent by live nodes to the joining one(s) is evenly split, thus resulting into an optimal load balancing [87].

A further optimization of the aforementioned scheme consists in allowing the new node to start serving transactions as soon as it gets data. In order to maintain atomic and consistent access to data, schemes relying on this optimization integrate the state transfer with the distribution and concurrency control protocol employed by the platform [88].

Another technique employed for elastic scaling of distributed databases, especially in the case of multi-tenant infrastructures, consists in transferring a snapshot of the database, i.e., an image of the database state at a given point in time. This can be achieved by means of VM migration [89] and backup tools [90,91] or by relying on the presence of a Network Attached Storage [85].

Finally, Barker et al. [92] show that no-one-size-fits-all solutions exists in the landscape of the described techniques for databases migration and state transfer.

Therefore, they introduce a hybrid scheme that automatically selects the best elastic scaling scheme to employ, choosing between a black-box VM migration and a database-aware, application-level state transfer.

When to Trigger Elastic Scaling? As introduced in Section 4, the literature on elastic scaling of distributed data platforms includes proposals based on the reactive and proactive approaches.

Among the solutions based on reactive schemes, Exponential Moving Average (EMA) is employed in the provisioning of a one-copy serializable database by Soundararajan et Amza [46] and of an eventually consistent data store by Trushkowsky et al. [93]: given a current raw measurement v_r and the output of last EMA computation v_l, the current value for target metric v_c (average response time of queries in the first case and arrival rate to a dataset partition in the second one) is obtained as $v_c = \alpha v_r + (1 - \alpha)v_l$. Here, α is a weighting factor: the higher, the faster older observation are discounted.

Scaling the size of a DTM, however, is a very onerous operation, as it triggers a state transfer phase that can induce significant additional load on the system for a potentially long time [62,92,89]. Thus, as a result of relying on a reactive scheme to trigger the elastic scaling, during the whole reconfiguration phase, the platform can suffer from severe performance degradation due to a sub-optimal configuration with respect to the incoming workload. To avoid such a shortcoming, the majority of recent research works on automatic resource provisioning rely on proactive schemes to trigger the elastic scaling of data platforms.

Approaches operating in the time domain, based on simple linear extrapolation [94] and filtering [62], have been applied to drive the elastic scaling of distributed databases. Solutions relying on time series analysis, namely ARMA and ARIMA, have also been frequently applied to drive automatic elastic scaling policies for Cloud applications [43,95,44].

Likewise, works based on time series analysis in the frequency domain find application in automatic resource provisioning scheme for Cloud infrastructures. They are either used alone, as in the case of the Agile system [96], or in conjunction with ANN in a recent work by Napoli et al. [97].

Approaches [45,64] combining reactive and proactive techniques, especially in QoS-oriented and SLA-based Cloud platforms, typically favor a more aggressive scheme in adding nodes and more conservative ones in scaling down removing nodes from a platform. The rationale behind this choice is that the cost, both monetary and in terms of performance, for maintaining resources that are not strictly necessary to guarantee a desired QoS is lower than the one resulting from an unfortunate scaling down choice, both because of the overhead due to a new scaling up phase and to the penalties stemming from possible SLA violations.

In the Cloud-TM data platform [40,98], Kalman filter and polynomial regression are employed to predict future workloads; however, they are complemented by a reactive scheme based on a filter that detects variations of average values over two consecutive time-windows, and the CUSUM algorithm. Different trade-offs between pro and reactiveness can be achieved depending on the parametrization of such algorithms. A similar approaches is undertaken also in ShuttleDB [92], where a threshold-based reactive scheme is complemented by times series forecasting by means of an ARIMA model. Iqbal et al. [45] propose a hybrid scheme which is reactive in acquiring resources, while it employs a second order regression to detect over-provisioning with respect to the incoming workload and, accordingly, release resources. In MeT [64], resources are greedily acquired in a non-linear and iterative fashion, i.e., if the system is under-provisioned, the number of acquired nodes at iteration i is twice as much as at last iteration; nodes in the system are, instead, released linearly, namely, one by one. Ali-Eldin et al. [63] provide a thorough analysis of controllers for elastic Cloud-based application relying on nine different schemes combining reactive and proactive approaches. Their work suggest that, indeed, hybrid schemes do perform better than pure ones.

With the exception of the techniques integrated in the Cloud-TM platform, the aforementioned solutions typically target either stateless/non-transactional platforms or transactional ones with external storage systems (e.g., Network Attached Storages) or backup services.

Their application to DTMs without those specific supports or in typical, commercial Cloud deployment is, hence, not straightforward. Moreover, such proposals do not account for other potential concurrent reconfigurations of the platforms at other levels, e.g., at the consistency protocol one. Challenging research problems in this direction that demand further investigation are the estimation of the duration of the reconfiguration phase and of SLA violations incurred during that time.

Which Scale to Choose? A plethora of analytical and simulative models for distributed transactional data platforms exist [99,100] that are aimed at computing the performance of the platform when deployed over different number of nodes. However, they mainly target relational databases and do not encompass complex dynamics that stem from elastically scaling the platform at runtime, like the variation in data locality. For this reason, in recent years, performance modeling and forecasting specifically aimed at supporting elastic scaling of DTM has garnered much attention, resulting into solutions that cover the whole spectrum of the techniques introduced in Section 4.2.

A pure white box model, relying on Parallel Discrete Event Simulation, has been proposed by Di Sanzo et al. [101]. It allows for the definition of trace based workloads in order to forecast the effect of elastically scaling, both vertically and horizontally, a DTM, encompassing generic data placement schemes and arbitrary data access patterns exhibited by the hosted application.

Pure black box approaches, instead, have been undertaken in [50,102], where ANN are employed to predict transactions' throughput and response time while varying the number of nodes composing a DTM. In particular, the work in [102] allows for supporting what-if analysis at the granularity of individual transactional classes, and not only on the overall average performance of the entire transactional workload.

A *divide et impera* grey box modeling approach is proposed by Didona et al., which targets performance prediction of fully [72] and partially replicated [38] DTMs when varying its scale over Cloud infrastructures. In such approach, analytical modeling is employed to model resource contention over the CPU and to capture transactions' conflict probability on data. Conversely, ML, and specifically decision tree based regression, is employed to predict the latency of network-bound operations, e.g., the retrieval of remote data and the execution of the distributed commit phase.

A variant of the *bootstrapping* grey box methodology is proposed in [57], and extended in [103], with the aim of determining the scale for a DTM application that results in the higher throughput. This approach combines analytical modeling, supervised learning and pure exploration in order to build a performance model that incrementally enhances its accuracy. A DT regressor is employed to learn at runtime a corrective function to be applied to the output of the base performance predictor (based on [72]) so as to progressively reduce its prediction error. The DT is incrementally trained over the base model's mis-predictions for workloads and scales that the DTM has experienced with. In order to widen the training set of the DT without incurring the cost of state transfer, different levels of MPL are explored for a given workload and number of nodes in the DTM.

6 Adaptation of the Data Consistency Protocol

In this section we review the most relevant solutions that focus on the adaptation of the protocol used to enforce data consistency in DTM platforms. Each system is described according to the three major concerns for supporting automatic protocol switching in DTM platforms: how is consistency ensured despite the on-line switching between different data consistency protocols, when the system should switch the protocol, and which is the most suitable consistency protocol according to the current conditions.

How Is Protocol Switching Supported? There are two main architectural approaches for protocol switching in DTM platforms, ad-hoc and generic, which explore different trade-offs between simplicity, efficiency and generality.

In the ad-hoc approach, the system is designed to accommodate specific and predetermined protocols and it is highly tailored to provide seamless switching mechanisms between protocols, i.e., to minimize the impact on performance during the switching phase. By exploiting the knowledge on the internal dynamics of the origin and target consistency protocols (for instance, how they are implemented), one can indeed design specialized switching mechanisms that exploit possible compatibilities with the purpose of reducing the overhead and/or duration of the switching phase. Typically, it is not possible to support the switching from/to additional protocols without making profound changes in the system.

Examples of these systems include PolyCert [16] and HTR [26]. PolyCert is a DTM that relies on three certification-based consistency protocols: non-voting certification, which sends the read-set of transactions as is; Bloom filter certification, which encodes the transaction's read-set in a Bloom filter, minimizing the size of the messages exchanged by nodes but increasing the complexity of processing the received message; and voting certification, in which only the write-set of transactions is disseminated but replicas must wait for a commit decision from the node where the transaction originally executed. As transactions finish their local execution, the protocol that minimizes the commit phase is selected from the three available (using techniques described further ahead in the section), improving therefore the throughput of the system. HTR also determines the optimal protocol on a per transaction basis: based on the abort rate on the moment each transaction is issued, either the deferred update model, which takes advantage of multicore hardware to process transactions in parallel, is chosen or the state machine approach, which guarantees an abort free execution. Both systems are tailored for those specific protocols and do not contemplate the addition of others.

Ideally, developers should be allowed to choose the most suitable replication protocols for their systems and workloads. Also, these protocols should be easy to plug into the system, and oblivious of other protocols (i.e., there should be no dependencies between protocols neither while the system is in normal operation nor when during the switching phase).

Recently, a new approach was proposed that offers both flexibility and performance. MorphR [39] is a framework that supports multiple replication protocols by only requiring their adherence to a specified API. It provides two mechanisms for the switching phase: stop and go and fast switching. The first approach relies on a blocking scheme to guarantee that there is no transaction from the old protocol running in the system when the new protocol starts executing, ensuring isolation between the switching protocols and avoiding the need to implement interactions between protocols. The second approach leverages on the knowledge of developers to implement specialized switching algorithms between pairs of protocols enabling their co-existence so that the performance of the system is not affected by this adaptation. MorphR's prototype was tested with three very different protocols representing distinct classes of replication approaches: 2PC, PB and a TOB-based scheme.

When to Switch? The most common approach to trigger switching in these systems is employing reactive schemes, that detect changes in the workload and react to those changes. Most adaptive DTM systems [39,72] rely on this approach, especially systems like HTR and PolyCert, which determine the best protocol on a per-transaction basis and transactions' operations are not known prior to their actual execution.

On the opposite side of the spectrum, CloudTM platform [40] integrates workload and resource demand prediction schemes, by including algorithms for time-series forecasting which allow predicting future workload's trends and allow the system to enact proactive self-tuning schemes. This functionality represents a fundamental building block for any proactive adaptation scheme, i.e., schemes triggering reconfigurations of the platform anticipating imminent workload's changes, which are particularly desirable in case the platform's reconfiguration (as in the case of elastic scaling) can have non-negligible latencies.

Which Protocol to Choose? The most straightforward way to approach the problem of determining the most suitable protocol is to set thresholds that, using one or more metrics, define the scenarios in which each protocol delivers (or is expected to deliver) the best performance. HTR follows this approach: it monitors the abort rate of the system before each transaction and if it exceeds a certain threshold, the transaction is executed in the state machine mode, which guarantees abort free execution. When the abort rate is lower than the set threshold, transactions will revert to executing in the deferred update mode.

However, threshold-based approaches become very hard to properly tune when the complexity of the replication schemes and workloads increases, as the increasing number of metrics and thresholds will eventually become unmanageable by an administrator. Let aside, the lack of flexibility imposed by the usage of fixed values for the thresholds. Both PolyCert and MorphR rely on the black box approach, namely machine learning techniques which were previously presented in Section 4, to cope with a larger number of protocols, with potentially complex algorithms, system configurations and workloads. While PolyCert assesses protocol suitability on a per transaction basis (i.e., each transaction issued will be certified with the protocol that minimizes its total execution time), MorphR evaluates the state of the system periodically (at a frequency tuned by the administrator) to verify whether the protocol in use is the optimal one and, if not, changes the protocol used by the entire system to match the most suitable option for the observed conditions.

However, a pure black box approach will not be able to cope with workloads and system configurations that were not included in the data used as its training set. The grey box approach, used in TAS [72,38], relies on analytical models designed to predict the behavior of 2PC and PB regardless of the workload and system configuration (number of machines, hardware used, etc.). This method is especially well tailored for systems in which administrators do not have prior knowledge of workloads and deployment configurations or when these two aspects are constantly varying. On the other hand, taking advantage of this approach entails possessing a very deep knowledge of the system's internals to be able to design a complete and accurate model.

7   Conclusions and Open Research Questions

In this chapter we have investigated the problem of designing self-tuning DTM platforms. Along the way, we have exposed some of the key trade-offs in the design of the main components of DTM systems, and recalled some of the base methodologies that are commonly employed in self-tuning systems. We have then focused our attention on two specific self-tuning problems, elastic scaling and adaptation of the distributed consistency protocol, and critically analyzed existing literature in these areas.

The analysis that we have conducted in this chapter shows that, despite being a relatively young research area, the existing literature encompasses already a number of self-tuning solutions that target the key building blocks of DTM platforms. On the other hand, our analysis suggests also that there are still a number of unexplored areas and open research problems, which represent interesting opportunities for future research.

In the elastic scaling area, for instance, we are not aware of solutions for estimating the impact on performance due to the occurrence of the state transfer activities that are necessary to redistribute data across nodes of the DTM platform. Another aspect that has not been satisfactorily addressed, to the best of our knowledge, by existing solutions in the area of elastic scaling of DTM is the prediction of the locality shifts (i.e., the change in the probability of incurring in remote accesses) due to the redistribution of data among the nodes caused by the elastic scaling process.

As for the dynamic switching of the DTM consistency protocol, existing solutions only take into account adaptations of the distributed consistency mechanisms, and do not seek integration with the self-tuning mechanisms for non-distributed TMs (e.g., targeting the local concurrency control or the thread mapping).

A related, albeit more fundamental open question, is how to effectively integrate the various self-tuning mechanisms proposed in literature and targeting different modules/parameters of DTM platforms. These systems are constituted by a complex ecosystem of components, each one associated with specific key performance indicators, utility functions and monitorable/tunable parameters. These components exhibit non-trivial mutual interdependencies; hence, in general, it is not possible to optimize separately different modules of a DTM, as the effect on performance of tuning different parameters are often intertwined. The complexity of this type of system is simply too high for monolithic self-tuning approaches, i.e., approaches that try to optimize the system as a whole by trying to identify all possible relations among the feasible adaptation alternatives of the entire ecosystem of components. Alternative, modular approaches would be highly desirable, as they would allow for unifying the large set of existing self-tuning mechanisms that target different aspects of DTMs. To the best of our knowledge, this problem is still unexplored by existing research.

References

1. Yoo, R.M., Hughes, C.J., Lai, K., Rajwar, R.: Performance evaluation of Intel® transactional synchronization extensions for high-performance computing. In: International Conference for High Performance Computing, Networking, Storage and Analysis, pp. 1–19. ACM (2013)
2. Jacobi, C., Slegel, T., Greiner, D.: Transactional memory architecture and implementation for ibm system z. In: Proceedings of the Annual nternational Symposium on Microarchitecture (MICRO), pp. 25–36. IEEE Computer Society (2012)
3. Herlihy, M.P., Sun, Y.: Distributed transactional memory for metric-space networks. In: Fraigniaud, P. (ed.) DISC 2005. LNCS, vol. 3724, pp. 324–338. Springer, Heidelberg (2005)
4. Romano, P., Carvalho, N., Rodrigues, L.: Towards distributed software transactional memory systems. In: Proceedings of the Workshop on Large-Scale Distributed Systems and Middleware (LADIS), pp. 1–4. ACM (2008)
5. Bocchino, R.L., Adve, V.S., Chamberlain, B.L.: Software transactional memory for large scale clusters. In: Proceedings of the Symposium on Principles and Practice of Parallel Programming (PPoPP), pp. 247–258. ACM (2008)

6. Romano, P., Rodrigues, L., Carvalho, N., Cachopo, J.: Cloud-tm: harnessing the cloud with distributed transactional memories. SIGOPS Operating Systems Review 44, 1–6 (2010)
7. Couceiro, M., Romano, P., Carvalho, N., Rodrigues, L.: D2STM: Dependable distributed software transactional memory. In: Proceedings of the Pacific Rim International Symposium on Dependable Computing (PRDC), pp. 307–313. IEEE Computer Society (2009)
8. Palmieri, R., Quaglia, F., Romano, P.: Aggro: Boosting stm replication via aggressively optimistic transaction processing. In: Proceedings of the International Symposium on Network Computing and Applications (NCA), pp. 20–27. IEEE Computer Society (2010)
9. Carvalho, N., Romano, P., Rodrigues, L.: Asynchronous lease-based replication of software transactional memory. In: Gupta, I., Mascolo, C. (eds.) Middleware 2010. LNCS, vol. 6452, pp. 376–396. Springer, Heidelberg (2010)
10. Hendler, D., Naiman, A., Peluso, S., Quaglia, F., Romano, P., Suissa, A.: Exploiting locality in lease-based replicated transactional memory via task migration. In: Afek, Y. (ed.) DISC 2013. LNCS, vol. 8205, pp. 121–133. Springer, Heidelberg (2013)
11. Fernandes, S.M., Cachopo, J.A.: Strict serializability is harmless: A new architecture for enterprise applications. In: Proceedings of International Conference Companion on Object Oriented Programming Systems Languages and Applications Companion (SPLASH), pp. 257–276. ACM (2011)
12. Peluso, S., Ruivo, P., Romano, P., Quaglia, F., Rodrigues, L.: When scalability meets consistency: Genuine multiversion update-serializable partial data replication. In: International Conference on Distributed Computing Systems (ICDCS), pp. 455–465. IEEE (2012)
13. Peluso, S., Romano, P., Quaglia, F.: SCORe: A scalable one-copy serializable partial replication protocol. In: Narasimhan, P., Triantafillou, P. (eds.) Middleware 2012. LNCS, vol. 7662, pp. 456–475. Springer, Heidelberg (2012)
14. Schneider, F.B.: Replication management using the state-machine approach. ACM Press/Addison-Wesley Publishing Co. (1993)
15. Pedone, F., Guerraoui, R., Schiper, A.: The database state machine approach. Distributed Parallel Databases 14(1), 71–98 (2003)
16. Couceiro, M., Romano, P., Rodrigues, L.: PolyCert: Polymorphic self-optimizing replication for in-memory transactional grids. In: Kon, F., Kermarrec, A.-M. (eds.) Middleware 2011. LNCS, vol. 7049, pp. 309–328. Springer, Heidelberg (2011)
17. Gray, J., Helland, P., O'Neil, P., Shasha, D.: The dangers of replication and a solution. In: Proceedings of the SIGMOD International Conference on Management of Data, pp. 173–182. ACM (1996)
18. Kemme, B., Pedone, F., Alonso, G., Schiper, A., Wiesmann, M.: Using optimistic atomic broadcast in transaction processing systems. IEEE Transactions on Knowledge and Data Engineering (TKDE) 15(4), 1018–1032 (2003)
19. Ruivo, P., Couceiro, M., Romano, P., Rodrigues, L.: Exploiting total order multicast in weakly consistent transactional caches. In: Proceedings of the Pacific Rim International Symposium on Dependable Computing (PRDC), pp. 99–108. IEEE Computer Society (2011)
20. Paiva, J., Ruivo, P., Romano, P., Rodrigues, L.: Autoplacer: Scalable self-tuning data placement in distributed key-value stores. In: Proceedings of the International Conference on Autonomic Computing (ICAC), pp. 119–131. USENIX, San Jose (2013)
21. Marchioni, F., Surtani, M.: Infinispan Data Grid Platform. Packt Publishing (2012)
22. Dash, A., Demsky, B.: Integrating caching and prefetching mechanisms in a distributed transactional memory. IEEE Transactions on Parallel and Distributed Systems (TPDS) 22(8), 1284–1298 (2011)

23. Karger, D., Lehman, E., Leighton, T., Panigrahy, R., Levine, M., Lewin, D.: Consistent hashing and random trees: Distributed caching protocols for relieving hot spots on the world wide web. In: Proceedings of the Symposium on Theory of Computing (STOC), pp. 654–663. ACM (1997)

24. Demmer, M.J., Herlihy, M.P.: The arrow distributed directory protocol. In: Kutten, S. (ed.) DISC 1998. LNCS, vol. 1499, pp. 119–133. Springer, Heidelberg (1998)

25. Herlihy, M.P., Sun, Y.: Distributed transactional memory for metric-space networks. In: Fraigniaud, P. (ed.) DISC 2005. LNCS, vol. 3724, pp. 324–338. Springer, Heidelberg (2005)

26. Kobus, T., Kokocinski, M., Wojciechowski, P.T.: Hybrid replication: State-machine-based and deferred-update replication schemes combined. In: Proceedings of the International Conference on Distributed Computing Systems (ICDCS), pp. 286–296. IEEE (2013)

27. Carvalho, N., Romano, P., Rodrigues, L.: A generic framework for replicated software transactional memories. In: Proceedings of the International Symposium on Networking Computing and Applications (NCA), pp. 271–274. IEEE Computer Society (2011)

28. Pimentel, H., Romano, P., Peluso, S., Ruivo, P.: Enhancing locality via caching in the gmu protocol. In: Proceedings of the International Symposium on Cluster, Cloud and Grid Computing (CCGRID). IEEE Computer Society (2014)

29. Sovran, Y., Power, R., Aguilera, M.K., Li, J.: Transactional storage for geo-replicated systems. In: Proceedings of the Symposium on Operating Systems Principles (SOSP), pp. 385–400. ACM (2011)

30. Kemme, B., Alonso, G.: A suite of database replication protocols based on group communication primitives. In: Proceedings of the International Conference on Distributed Computing Systems (ICDCS), pp. 156–163. IEEE Computer Society (1998)

31. Patiño-Martínez, M., Jiménez-Peris, R., Kemme, B., Alonso, G.: Scalable replication in database clusters. In: Herlihy, M.P. (ed.) DISC 2000. LNCS, vol. 1914, pp. 315–329. Springer, Heidelberg (2000)

32. Manassiev, K., Mihailescu, M., Amza, C.: Exploiting distributed version concurrency in a transactional memory cluster. In: Proceedings of the Symposium on Principles and Practice of Parallel Programming (PPoPP), pp. 198–208. ACM (2006)

33. Franklin, M.J., Carey, M.J., Livny, M.: Transactional client-server cache consistency: Alternatives and performance. ACM Transactions on Database Systems (TODS) 22(3), 315–363 (1997)

34. Défago, X., Schiper, A., Urbán, P.: Total order broadcast and multicast algorithms: Taxonomy and survey. ACM Computing Surveys (CSUR) 36(4), 372–421 (2004)

35. Lamport, L.: The part-time parliament. ACM Transactions on Computing Systems (TOCS) 16(2), 133–169 (1998)

36. Agrawal, D., Alonso, G., El Abbadi, A., Stanoi, I.: Exploiting atomic broadcast in replicated databases (extended abstract). In: Lengauer, C., Griebl, M., Gorlatch, S. (eds.) Euro-Par 1997. LNCS, vol. 1300, pp. 496–503. Springer, Heidelberg (1997)

37. Muñoz-Escoí, F.D., Irún-Briz, L., Galdámez, P., Decker, H., Bernabéu, J., Bataller, J., del Carmen Bañuls, M.: Globdata: A platform for supporting multiple consistency modes. In: Proceedings of the International Conference on Information Systems and Databases (ISDB), pp. 104–109. Acta Press (2002)

38. Didona, D., Romano, P.: Performance modelling of partially replicated in-memory transactional stores. In: Proceedings of the International Symposium on Modeling, Analysis and Simulation of Computer and Telecommunication Systems (MASCOTS). IEEE (2014)

39. Couceiro, M., Ruivo, P., Romano, P., Rodrigues, L.: Chasing the optimum in replicated in-memory transactional platforms via protocol adaptation. In: Proceedings of the International Conference on Dependable Systems and Networks (DSN), pp. 1–12. IEEE Computer Society (2013)
40. Didona, D., Romano, P.: Self-tuning transactional data grids: The cloud-tm approach. In: Proceedings of the Symposium on Network Cloud Computing and Applications (NCCA), pp. 113–120. IEEE (2014)
41. Singh, R., Sharma, U., Cecchet, E., Shenoy, P.J.: Autonomic mix-aware provisioning for non-stationary data center workloads. In: Proceedings of the International Conference on Autonomic Computing (ICAC), pp. 21–30. ACM (2010)
42. Zhang, Q., Cherkasova, L., Mi, N., Smirni, E.: A regression-based analytic model for capacity planning of multi-tier applications. Cluster Computing 11(3), 197–211 (2008)
43. Roy, N., Dubey, A., Gokhale, A.S.: Efficient autoscaling in the cloud using predictive models for workload forecasting. In: Proceedings of the International Conference on Cloud Computing (CLOUD), pp. 500–507. IEEE (2011)
44. Chen, G., He, W., Liu, J., Nath, S., Rigas, L., Xiao, L., Zhao, F.: Energy-aware server provisioning and load dispatching for connection-intensive internet services. In: Symposium on Networked Systems Design & Implementation (NSDI), pp. 337–350. USENIX Association (2008)
45. Iqbal, W., Dailey, M.N., Carrera, D., Janecek, P.: Adaptive resource provisioning for read intensive multi-tier applications in the cloud. Future Generation Computing Systems 27(6), 871–879 (2011)
46. Soundararajan, G., Amza, C.: Reactive provisioning of backend databases in shared dynamic content server clusters. ACM Transactions on Adaptive and Autonomous Systems (TAAS) 1(2), 151–188 (2006)
47. You, G.-w., Hwang, S.-w., Jain, N.: Scalable load balancing in cluster storage systems. In: Kon, F., Kermarrec, A.-M. (eds.) Middleware 2011. LNCS, vol. 7049, pp. 101–122. Springer, Heidelberg (2011)
48. Curino, C., Jones, E., Zhang, Y., Madden, S.: Schism: A workload-driven approach to database replication and partitioning. Proceedings of the VLDB Endowment 3(1-2), 48–57 (2010)
49. Turcu, A., Palmieri, R., Ravindran, B.: Automated data partitioning for highly scalable and strongly consistent transactions. In: Proceedings of the International Systems and Storage Conference (SYSTOR), pp. 1–11. ACM (2014)
50. di Sanzo, P., Rughetti, D., Ciciani, B., Quaglia, F.: Auto-tuning of cloud-based in-memory transactional data grids via machine learning. In: Proceedings of the Symposium on Network Cloud Computing and Applications (NCCA), pp. 9–16. IEEE (2012)
51. Vale, T.M., Dias, R.J., Lourenço, J.M.: On the relevance of total-order broadcast implementations in replicated software transactional memories. In: Lourenço, J.M., Farchi, E. (eds.) MUSEPAT 2013 2013. LNCS, vol. 8063, pp. 49–60. Springer, Heidelberg (2013)
52. Mocito, J., Rodrigues, L.: Run-time switching between total order algorithms. In: Nagel, W.E., Walter, W.V., Lehner, W. (eds.) Euro-Par 2006. LNCS, vol. 4128, pp. 582–591. Springer, Heidelberg (2006)
53. Mocito, J., Rosa, L., Almeida, N., Miranda, H., Rodrigues, L., Lopes, A.: Context adaptation of the communication stack. International Journal of Parallel, Emergent and Distributed Systems 21(3), 169–181 (2006)
54. Didona, D., Carnevale, D., Galeani, S., Romano, P.: An extremum seeking algorithm for message batching in total order protocols. In: Proceedings of the International Conference on Self-Adaptive and Self-Organizing Systems (SASO), pp. 89–98. IEEE (2012)

55. Romano, P., Leonetti, M.: Self-tuning batching in total order broadcast protocols via analytical modelling and reinforcement learning. In: Proceedings of the International Conference on Computing, Networking and Communications, ICNC, pp. 786–792. IEEE (2011)
56. Wang, Q., Kulkarni, S., Cavazos, J., Spear, M.F.: A transactional memory with automatic performance tuning. ACM Transactions on Architecture and Code Optimization (TACO) 8(4), 1–54 (2012)
57. Didona, D., Felber, P., Harmanci, D., Romano, P., Schenker, J.: Identifying the optimal level of parallelism in transactional memory applications. Computing (2013)
58. di Sanzo, P., Re, F.D., Rughetti, D., Ciciani, B., Quaglia, F.: Regulating concurrency in software transactional memory: An effective model-based approach. In: Proceedings of the International Conference on Self-Adaptive and Self-Organizing Systems (SASO), pp. 31–40. IEEE (2013)
59. Rughetti, D., Di Sanzo, P., Ciciani, B., Quaglia, F.: Analytical/ml mixed approach for concurrency regulation in software transactional memory. In: Proceedings of the International Symposium on Cluster, Cloud and Grid Computing (CCGRID), pp. 81–91. IEEE (2014)
60. Felber, P., Fetzer, C., Riegel, T.: Dynamic performance tuning of word-based software transactional memory. In: Proceedings of the Symposium on Principles and Practice of Parallel Programming, pp. 237–246. ACM (2008)
61. Castro, M.B., Góes, L.F.W., Méhaut, J.F.: Adaptive thread mapping strategies for transactional memory applications. Journal of Parallel and Distributed Computing (JPDC) 74(8), 2845–2859 (2014)
62. Chen, J., Soundararajan, G., Amza, C.: Autonomic provisioning of backend databases in dynamic content web servers. In: Proceedings of the International Conference on Autonomic Computing (ICAC), pp. 231–242. IEEE (2006)
63. Ali-Eldin, A., Tordsson, J., Elmroth, E.: An adaptive hybrid elasticity controller for cloud infrastructures. In: Proceedings of the Network Operations and Management Symposium (NOMS), pp. 204–212. IEEE (2012)
64. Cruz, F., Maia, F., Matos, M., Oliveira, R., Paulo, J., Pereira, J., Vilaça, R.: Met: workload aware elasticity for nosql. In: Proceedings of EuroSys, pp. 183–196. ACM (2013)
65. Shenoi, B.A.: Introduction to Digital Signal Processing and Filter Design. John Wiley & Sons (2005)
66. Kalman, R.: A new approach to linear filtering and prediction problems. Journal of Basic Engineering 82, 35–45 (1960)
67. Zheng, T., Woodside, C.M., Litoiu, M.: Performance model estimation and tracking using optimal filters. IEEE Transactions on Software Engineering (TOSE) 34(3), 391–406 (2008)
68. Kalyvianaki, E., Charalambous, T., Hand, S.: Self-adaptive and self-configured cpu resource provisioning for virtualized servers using kalman filters. In: Proceedings of the International Conference on Autonomic Computing (ICAC), pp. 117–126. IEEE (2009)
69. Hoffmann, H., Maggio, M.: Pcp: A generalized approach to optimizing performance under power constraints through resource management. In: Proceedings of the International Conference on Autonomic Computing (ICAC), pp. 241–247. USENIX Association (2014)
70. Wheeler, D.J.: Understanding Statistical Process Control, 3rd edn. SPC Press & Statistical Process Control, Inc. (2010)
71. Page, E.S.: Continuous inspection schemes. Biometrika 41(1), 100–115 (1954)
72. Didona, D., Romano, P., Peluso, S., Quaglia, F.: Transactional auto scaler: elastic scaling of replicated in-memory transactional data grids. ACM Transactions on Adaptive and Autonomous Systems (TAAS) 9(2) (July 2014)

73. Nguyen, H., Tan, Y., Gu, X.: Pal: Propagation-aware anomaly localization for cloud hosted distributed applications. In: Proceedings of Managing Large-scale Systems via the Analysis of System Logs and the Application of Machine Learning Techniques (SLAML), pp. 1–8. ACM (2011)

74. Amin, A., Colman, A., Grunske, L.: Statistical detection of qos violations based on cusum control charts. In: Proceedings of the International Conference on Performance Engineering (ICPE), pp. 97–108. ACM (2012)

75. Chatfield, C.: The analysis of time series: An introduction, 6th edn. CRC Press (2004)

76. Shumway, R.H., Stoffe, D.S.: Time Series Analysis and Its Applications, 3rd edn. Springer Texts in Statistics (2011)

77. Tay, Y.C.: Analytical Performance Modeling for Computer Systems, 2nd edn. Synthesis Lectures on Computer Science. Morgan & Claypool Publishers (2013)

78. Bishop, C.M.: Pattern Recognition and Machine Learning. Springer (2006)

79. Bellman, R.: Dynamic Programming. Princeton University Press (1957)

80. Marquardt, D.W.: An algorithm for least-squares estimation of nonlinear parameters. SIAM Journal on Applied Mathematics 11(2), 431–441 (1963)

81. Domingos, P., Hulten, G.: Mining high-speed data streams. In: Proceedings of the International Conference on Knowledge Discovery and Data Mining (KDD), pp. 71–80. ACM (2000)

82. Auer, P.: Using upper confidence bounds for online learning. In: Proceedings of the Annual Symposium on Foundations of Computer Science (FOCS), pp. 270–279. IEEE Computer Society (2000)

83. Watkins, C.J.C.H., Dayan, P.: Technical note q-learning. Machine Learning 8, 279–292 (1992)

84. Russell, S.J., Norvig, P.: Artificial Intelligence - A Modern Approach, 2nd edn. Pearson Education (2010)

85. Das, S., Nishimura, S., Agrawal, D., El Abbadi, A.: Albatross: Lightweight elasticity in shared storage databases for the cloud using live data migration. PVLDB 4(8), 494–505 (2011)

86. Minhas, U.F., Liu, R., Aboulnaga, A., Salem, K., Ng, J., Robertson, S.: Elastic scale-out for partition-based database systems. In: ICDE Workshops, pp. 281–288 (2012)

87. Raghavan, N., Vitenberg, R.: Balancing the communication load of state transfer in replicated systems. In: International Symposium on Resliable Distributed Systems (SRDS), pp. 41–50. IEEE (2011)

88. Elmore, A.J., Das, S., Agrawal, D., El Abbadi, A.: Zephyr: live migration in shared nothing databases for elastic cloud platforms. In: Proceedings of the SIGMOD International Conference on Management of Data, pp. 301–312. ACM (2011)

89. Cecchet, E., Singh, R., Sharma, U., Shenoy, P.J.: Dolly: virtualization-driven database provisioning for the cloud. In: Proceedings of the International Conference on Virtual Execution Environments (VEE), pp. 51–62. ACM (2011)

90. Barker, S.K., Chi, Y., Moon, H.J., Hacigümüs, H., Shenoy, P.J.: "cut me some slack": latency-aware live migration for databases. In: International Conference on Extending Database Technology (EDBT), pp. 432–443. ACM (2012)

91. Sousa, F.R.C., Machado, J.C.: Towards elastic multi-tenant database replication with quality of service. In: Proceedings of the International Conference on Utility and Cloud Computing, pp. 168–175. IEEE (2012)

92. Barker, S., Chi, Y., Hacigümüs, H., Shenoy, P., Cecchet, E.: Shuttledb: Database-aware elasticity in the cloud. In: Proceedings of the International Conference on Autonomic Computing (ICAC), pp. 33–43. USENIX Association (2014)

93. Trushkowsky, B., Bodík, P., Fox, A., Franklin, M.J., Jordan, M.I., Patterson, D.A.: The scads director: Scaling a distributed storage system under stringent performance requirements. In: Proceedings of the Conference on File and Storage Technologies (FAST), pp. 163–176. USENIX Association (2011)

94. Ghanbari, S., Soundararajan, G., Chen, J., Amza, C.: Adaptive learning of metric correlations for temperature-aware database provisioning. In: Proceedings of the International Conference on Autonomic Computing (ICAC), pp. 1–26. IEEE (2007)

95. Chandra, A., Gong, W., Shenoy, P.J.: Dynamic resource allocation for shared data centers using online measurements. In: Proceedings of the International Conference on Measurements and Modeling of Computer Systems, pp. 300–301. ACM (2003)

96. Nguyen, H., Shen, Z., Gu, X., Subbiah, S., Wilkes, J.: Agile: Elastic distributed resource scaling for infrastructure-as-a-service. In: Proceedings of the International Conference on Autonomic Computing (ICAC), pp. 69–82. USENIX (2013)

97. Napoli, C., Pappalardo, G., Tramontana, E.: A hybrid neuro–wavelet predictor for qoS control and stability. In: Baldoni, M., Baroglio, C., Boella, G., Micalizio, R. (eds.) AI*IA 2013. LNCS, vol. 8249, pp. 527–538. Springer, Heidelberg (2013)

98. Cloud-TM: Cloud-tm, d4.6: Final architecture (2013),
    `http://cloudtm.ist.utl.pt/cloudtm/final-deliverables/`
    `D4.6-ArchitectureReport.pdf`

99. Elnikety, S., Dropsho, S.G., Cecchet, E., Zwaenepoel, W.: Predicting replicated database scalability from standalone database profiling. In: Proceedings of EuroSys, pp. 303–316. ACM (2009)

100. Nicola, M., Jarke, M.: Performance modeling of distributed and replicated databases. IEEE Transactions on Knowledge and Data Engineering 12(4), 645–672 (2000)

101. di Sanzo, P., Antonacci, F., Ciciani, B., Palmieri, R., Pellegrini, A., Peluso, S., Quaglia, F., Rughetti, D., Vitali, R.: A framework for high performance simulation of transactional data grid platforms. In: Proceedings of the International Conference on Simulation Tools and Techniques (SimuTools), pp. 63–72. ACM (2013)

102. di Sanzo, P., Molfese, F., Rughetti, D., Ciciani, B.: Providing transaction class-based qos in in-memory data grids via machine learning. In: Proceedings of the Symposium on Network Cloud Computing and Applications (NCCA), pp. 46–53. IEEE (2014)

103. Didona, D., Quaglia, F., Romano, P., Torre, E.: Enhancing Performance Prediction Robustness by Combining Analytical Modeling and Machine Learning. In: Proceedings of the International Conference on Performance Engineering (ICPE). ACM (2015)

Case Study: Using Transactions in Memcached

Michael Spear, Wenjia Ruan, Yujie Liu, and Trilok Vyas

Lehigh University, Bethlehem PA
spear@cse.lehigh.edu

Abstract. To synthesize the topics in previous chapters of this book, we now turn to the question of how to use transactions in real-world code. We use a concrete example, transactionalization of the memcached application, as a vehicle for exploring the challenges and benefits that arise from using transactions instead of locks. Specific topics that receive attention in this chapter include irrevocability, contention management, language-level semantics and privatization, write-through and write-back algorithms, and condition synchronization.

1 Introduction

Prior to 2007, software transactional memory implementations were distributed as libraries, and programmers were required to manually annotate their code to achieve transactional behavior. This entailed both (a) using macros to indicate the beginning and ending points of the transactions, and (b) instrumenting the individual shared memory accesses within the transaction, and within all functions called by that transaction. In order to ensure that rollback of transactions ran smoothly, it was also necessary to perform some manner of manual checkpoint and recovery of thread-local variables that could be modified within transactions that aborted and then retried.

Needless to say, this situation did not encourage the creation of large or realistic benchmarks. Library interfaces encouraged excessive optimization of programs (i.e., based on complex reasoning about which locations were or were not shared between threads). Worse, the absence of transaction-safe standard libraries resulted in programmers re-implementing basic data structures and functions in ad-hoc ways. Frequently, the resulting code did not behave in the same manner as the original standard library codes. By 2008, there were a number of small transactional benchmarks, and even one large benchmark suite [29]. All relied on hand-instrumentation of individual shared memory accesses.

The Draft C++ TM Specification released in 2009 helped to change this situation, by introducing platform-independent TM extensions for C++ [3]. Existing compiler support for TM rapidly converged upon this draft standard, resulting in GCC [4], ICC, and xlC all supporting transactions in C and C++ programs. Based on experience using the specification [32], the mechanisms for self-abort and error handling were refined [2]. While the draft specification is still under review and revision, at the time this chapter was written, the specification was relatively stable and feature-complete, and the implementations in modern compilers fairly mature. Consequently, it was at last possible to use transactions in complex programs, without requiring manual (and mostlikely incomplete) instrumentation of every single access to shared memory.

R. Guerraoui and P. Romano (Eds.): Transactional Memory, LNCS 8913, pp. 449–467, 2015.

The use of transactions in large software systems allows an exploration of many questions pondered by researchers. Among them are questions of whether transactions can be used "in the small" (i.e., only in limited portions of a program) [26], how to perform condition synchronization [18], whether privatization is a significant issue in practice [49, 27], how choices of algorithm affect performance [14, 41, 40], and the need for irrevocability and I/O within transactions [46, 44].

In this chapter, we first review the Draft C++ TM Specification. We then motivate our decision to transactionalize the open-source memcached application. With that background in place, we discuss the steps necessary to transform memcached into an application in which transactions provide value. The value is not strictly in terms of performance; after all, memcached employs fine-grained locks to avoid contention in most cases. However, transactions both (a) offer good performance without requiring a complex locking protocol, and (b) enable interesting simplifications and optimizations that are not obvious with locks.

2   The Draft C++ TM Specification

The Draft C++ TM Specification [2] serves two roles: it defines an interface that programmers can use to employ TM in their programs, and it also defines the transformations and analyses that a compiler must perform in order to guarantee the correctness of a program that uses the specification.

The specification is careful to describe how transactions must behave, but not how they must be implemented. In particular, the specification does not require any specific TM algorithm: transactions can be implemented in either hardware or software, with the software TM using eager [14] or lazy [41] acquisition of ownership records, reader/writer locks [10], or other mechanisms [9, 43]. The specification does, however, require TM to be compatible with the C++ memory model. At the time this chapter was written, this requirement roughly equated to single global lock atomicity [27].

2.1   Types of Transactions

The specification is broad, supporting many use cases for TM. In particular, there is support both for transactions that can perform I/O, and transactions that can explicitly self-abort. To distinguish between these two uses, there are two keywords: `__transaction_relaxed` and `__transaction_atomic`. Both precede a statement or lexically scoped block of code that ought to run as a transaction. A relaxed transaction is allowed to perform I/O and system calls, acquire and release locks, access volatile and atomic variables, execute in-line assembly code, and generally call code whose effects cannot be rolled back ("unsafe code"). However, such transactions must be run in a "serial irrevocable" mode [35, 31]. That is, relaxed transactions that execute unsafe code run non-speculatively, and to ensure that these transactions never abort, the system forbids concurrent execution of other transactions [46, 44]. In contrast, atomic transactions can abort and roll back at any time, and may even do so at the request of the programmer (via the `__transaction_cancel` statement). However, atomic transactions must only call code whose effects can be undone by the run-time system ("safe code").

When the body of a transaction is visible to the compiler, and that body is free of unsafe code, relaxed and atomic transactions behave identically. However, if an atomic transaction is to call a function from a separate compilation unit, then it is necessary to somehow convey to the compiler that the function can be rolled back. To this end, the draft specification includes the transaction_safe keyword. When compiling a function marked as transaction_safe, the compiler statically verifies the absence of unsafe code, and then generates two versions of the function, where the second is instrumented such that its reads and writes can be rolled back. Every function called from an atomic transaction must be annotated as transaction_safe, and every such call will be directed to the instrumented version of the function.

When a relaxed transaction calls a function that is not annotated, it must serialize. However, there are cases in which a function is not safe, but there exist flows of control through the function that do not entail calls to unsafe code. The transaction-_callable annotation instructs the compiler to generate two versions of a function that is unsafe, such that a relaxed transaction can avoid serializing when a specific call to that function only results in instructions that can be rolled back. Note that transaction_callable is a performance optimization, whereas transaction_safe is required for correctness.

2.2 Exceptions and Self-abort

When a transaction encounters an exception that cannot be handled within the transaction scope, there are two possibilities: that the transaction should commit its intermediate state and continue to throw the exception, or that it should discard its effects and act as if it never executed. Both options have their merits [1]. To support the latter behavior, the __transaction_cancel statement indicates that a transaction ought to undo its effects and jump to the first statement after the end of the transaction body.

It is forbidden to call __transaction_cancel from an relaxed transaction, since that transaction might be irrevocable. Unfortunately, when there is separate compilation, the compiler may not be able to tell whether a transaction_safe function called by a relaxed transaction calls __transaction_cancel. To assist in this analysis, the draft specification also provides a may_cancel_outer annotation. Like transaction_safe, this is required for correctness.

2.3 Extensions to the Draft Specification

There are three additional features in the GCC TM implementation that warrant discussion. The first is an annotation, transaction_pure, which indicates that a function is safe to call from atomic transactions, but does not require the compiler to create a separate instrumented version (e.g., a function with no side effects). This annotation is intended for the case where the safety of a function can be checked by the compiler, but that safety needs to be communicated between compilation units. However, in practice this annotation is interpreted as an un-checked contract between the programmer and the compiler: if the function is not, indeed, safe, then the behavior of the transaction is undefined. This means, for example, that it is possible to call printf from a transaction_pure function.

Secondly, within the TM implementation, GCC provides a mechanism for registering actions to run after a transaction commits or aborts. These onCommit and onAbort handlers [7] take a single untyped parameter. Strictly speaking, registration of handlers is not part of the public API. However, the symbols for the registration functions are visible, and can be accessed via code. The GCC implementation does not allow the code registered with these handlers to use transactions, and if the code accesses memory that can be concurrently accessed by transactions, the behavior is undefined.

Finally, GCC provides a transaction_wrap attribute. Using this attribute, one can associate a safe function s() with an unsafe function u(). In this manner, when the compiler encounters a call to u() from within a transaction, it will replace the call with a call to the safe variant of s() instead. within

3   Why Memcached?

There are many C/C++ transactional benchmarks in existence, covering a broad design space. STAMP [29] consists of eight applications written in C. Its components capture some common use cases for TM, such as multi-word compare and swap (SSCA2), explicit speculation (Labyrinth), and shared transactional data structures (Vacation). EigenBench [20] is a synthetic workload generator that can produce access patterns and behaviors similar to STAMP. STMBench7 [17] models the data structures and operations of a Computer Aided Design (CAD) workload. Lee-TM [5], SynQuake [24], and RMS-TM [21] demonstrate the use of TM in realistic settings (circuit routing, gaming, and data mining). Atomic Quake [50] employs TM within the Quake game engine itself. Though not benchmarks *per se*, studies by Rossbach et al. [36] and Pankratius and Adl-Tabatabai [32] produced transactional C and C++ code.

These benchmarks and programs vary along many dimensions. Among the most important are whether a library or compiler API is used to achieve transactional behavior; whether I/O within transactions is acceptable; whether fundamental data structures and libraries were rewritten to be usable within transactions, and whether the API to the TM allows escape actions [30]. A host of other issues also differentiate the efforts, such as whether read-only transactions abound, and whether transactions access scalars of varying sizes. Unfortunately, we are not aware of any large-scale use of these programs in a production environment. Such an outcome is not surprising, since these programs were either written by TM researchers, or are transactional versions of *older* versions of existing programs. Nonetheless, the question arises as to whether TM works well for the latest version of widely-used programs.

To answer this question, we will transactionalize memcached. Memcached possesses many of the quirks and peculiarities researchers should expect of high-performance production-grade code [37, 34]: there is a lock hierarchy that is sometimes violated; reference counting with volatile variables (analogous to C++11 atomics) and in-line assembly is on the critical path; high-performance external libraries (i.e., libevent [25]) and internal libraries (i.e., the C standard library) are used frequently; and locks are used for both mutual exclusion and condition synchronization. The experience of transactionalizing such an application, using the C++ TM implementation present in GCC, should be instructive both when designing new applications, and when transactionalizing existing code.

4 Preparing to Transactionalize

The primary data structure in memcached is an in-memory key-value store, implemented as a hash table. The individual key/value pairs are protected by item locks, which serve as the top of the lock hierarchy. When the hash table needs to be resized, a cache lock is used to ensure only one resize occurs at a time; this lock comes second in the lock hierarchy. A slab subsystem (protected by the slabs_lock) simplifies memory management when a key's value changes in size. Program-level statistics are protected by a global stats_lock, and each thread has a single-writer, many-reader set of statistics, protected by a per-thread lock. Statistics locks are the bottom of the lock hierarchy.

By profiling a workload for 5 minutes using mutrace [33], we found that the cache-_lock and stats_lock were the only locks that exhibited contention. However, it is difficult to replace only those critical sections guarded by these locks with transactions. First, consider lock hierarchies: in the case of cache_lock and slabs_lock, when a cache_lock critical section acquires slabs_lock, then the corresponding transaction must acquire slabs_lock. Lock acquisition forces a transaction to become serial, so unless slabs_lock is replaced with transactions, slabs_lock acquisitions will cause cache_lock transactions to serialize. Likewise, critical sections related to per-thread statistics locks must be transformed into transactions, or else statistics updates would cause transactions to serialize.

Second, under certain circumstances, an item lock is acquired after cache_lock. To prevent serialization, one must either (a) replace all item lock critical sections with transactions, or (b) implement the item lock with a transaction. While option (a) ultimately performed better, option (b) merits further discussion. Consider the examples in Figure 1: In func1, a cache_lock transaction must perform a simple operation on an item. In func2, there is no running transaction when the thread performs a complex operation on an item. To avoid races, func1 cannot access the item concurrently with func2.

The left side uses privatization [27, 42]: func2 uses a transaction only to acquire and release the item lock, not to access the item. This is advantageous when use_item_complex performs an operation that cannot be undone (e.g., I/O). However, when func2 is holding the lock, func1 must explicitly deal with the fact that a lock it needs is currently held. This necessitates a mechanism (save_for_later) for deferring the work, or else the transaction must explicitly self-abort. In contrast, on the right side, all accesses to items use transactions. There is no longer the need for an item lock, and if func1 and func2 conflict, the underlying TM system will chose which transaction to abort. Put another way, when privatization is used, the programmer is effectively circumventing the TM system's contention manager. Contention managers play several roles, to include ensuring progress guarantees [39, 19] and maximizing throughput [48, 6]. In general, using privatization in place of contention management should be discouraged.

Third, cache_lock and slabs_lock are used both for mutual exclusion and condition synchronization via pthread_cond_t objects. Condition synchronization is not currently supported by the Draft C++ TM Specification, though it is a well-known problem [47, 13, 49, 18, 8, 23]. Recently, an OS and hardware-neutral solution to the

```
func1a:                             func1b:
  __transaction_atomic {             __transaction_atomic {
    ... // cache_lock work             ... // cache_lock work
    if ¬i.lock                         use_item_simple(i)
      use_item_simple(i)             }
    else
      save_for_later(i)
  }


func2a:                             func2b:
  transaction_acquire(i.lock)        __transaction_atomic {
  use_item_complex(i)                  use_item_complex(i)
  transaction_release(i.lock)        }
```

Fig. 1. On the left, func2 privatizes i, and func1 must check the lock guarding i. On the right, there is no privatization, but all accesses to i must be made from within transactions.

problem was proposed [45]. However, a simpler but less general approach is possible: In both cases, the condition variable is used to wake a dedicated maintainer thread only when a data structure (the hash table or the slab table) becomes unbalanced, and waiting is the last operation within a critical section. That being the case, it is possible to replace each condition variable with a semaphore, replace calls to cond_signal with semaphore increments (made within the critical section), and replace calls to cond_wait with semaphore decrements (made immediately after the critical section). This change, which is valid even prior to transactionalizing the program, had no noticeable impact on performance.

5   Naive Transactionalization

With condition variables removed and a set of possibly-contended locks identified, it is now possible to replace critical sections with transactions. The easiest approach is to remove the declarations of the locks from the program, and then use compiler errors to guide the placement of transactions. In order to get a program executing as quickly as possible, the programmer can use *relaxed* transactions throughout the program, and omit annotations. Since relaxed transactions serialize whenever calling code that cannot be shown to be transaction-safe, it is useful to annotate every function called by a transaction, using the transaction_callable attribute. In memcached 1.4.15, this results in 51 relaxed transactions, and 49 annotations.

The performance of this naive transactionalization, both with and without the use of callable annotations, appears in Figure 2. The figure also shows performance of the baseline memcached versus the performance when condition variables are replaced with semaphores. The experimental platform consisted of a dual-chip Intel Xeon 5650 system with 12 GB of RAM, running Ubuntu Linux 13.04, kernel version 3.8.0-21. Each chip has 6 cores, each two-way multithreaded, for a total of 24 hardware threads. Code was compiled for 64-bit execution using GCC 4.9.0. Results are the average of 5 trials, and error bars show one standard deviation.

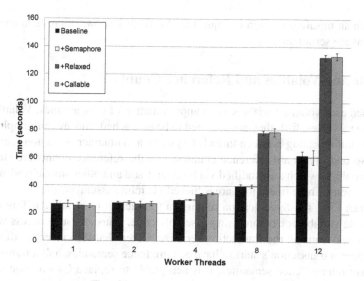

Fig. 2. Performance of baseline transactional memcached

Table 1. Frequency and cause of serialization for a 4-thread execution from Fig. 2

Branch	Transactions	In-Flight Switch	Start Serial	Abort Serial
Relaxed	3.46M	625K (18%)	1.25M (36%)	0
Callable	3.46M	625K (18%)	1.25M (36%)	0

The workload for this experiment was generated using memslap v1.0. Both memslap and memcached ran on the same machine, so that network latencies did not hide any change in latency for transactions versus locks. The experiment used parameters `--concurrency=x --execute-number=625000 --binary`. By varying the memslap concurrency parameter (x) from 1 to 12, we assessed performance with up to 12 concurrent requests to memcached. It is important to note that each memslap thread performs 625K operations; perfect scaling should correspond to the execution time remaining unchanged as the thread count increases.

Figure 2 shows that the switch from condition variables to semaphores has a negligible impact on performance, but that for 4 or more threads, the use of transactions in place of locks results in increased latency. Furthermore, the application of the `transaction_callable` attribute has no impact on performance. To gain further insight into why performance degraded, we instrumented GCC to report the frequency of serialization. GCC relies on serialization in two cases: First, if a transaction aborts too many times, then serialization is used as a form of contention management [39] to ensure that the aborting transaction runs in isolation and completes. Second, when a relaxed transaction wishes to perform an unsafe operation (e.g., one that cannot be rolled back), the transaction must run in isolation, so that it does not encounter inconsistencies that require it to abort. When GCC determines that all paths through a relaxed transaction require serialization, it starts the transaction in serial mode on the first attempt. Otherwise, it starts the transaction in non-serial mode, and aborts and restarts in serial mode when an unsafe operation is requested. As Table 1 shows, more than half of all transactions are serializing.

6   Replacing Volatiles and Reference Counts

Memcached uses volatile variables as an approximation of C++ atomics. Volatile variables serve two roles: first, they are assumed to be un-cached, and are thus employed as flags for communicating between threads (typically a maintainer and a non-maintainer thread). Second, items are reference counted, and the reference counts are stored as volatile variables, which are modified via fetch-and-add and other atomic read-modify-write operations. These operations are achieved via inline assembly.

The Draft C++ TM Specification requires a transaction to serialize before accessing a volatile variable, or before using assembly code. Thus any such access within a transaction was causing the transaction serialize. Given that the current draft specification defines a transaction's start to have acquire fence semantics, and a transaction's end to have release fence semantics, it is acceptable to replace C++ atomic variable accesses with transactions that access non-atomic variables. The easiest way to achieve this transformation was to rename volatile variables and then use compilation errors as a guide for fixing the code. There were only three such variables in memcached.

This change introduced the capacity for an unbounded increase in the number of executed transactions, since a loop waiting on a volatile condition became a loop executing a read-only transaction repeatedly. This is particularly concerning since single-location transactions are not currently optimized in GCC. It also required manual inspection to ensure that there was never bi-directional communication between critical sections via volatile variables; such communication is not possible with transactions. We used the same technique, with the same caveats, to replace reference count operations with transactions.

The net effect of these changes was to introduce a large number of new transactions, when the corresponding access was performed outside of a transaction, in order to allow accesses to these variables from within a transaction to proceed without serialization. Figure 3 depicts the impact on performance. Surprisingly, performance decreased. As Table 2 shows, we only removed a handful of cases where transactions serialized during execution. In return, more transactions required serialization in order to ensure progress. This is an unfortunate, but expected, consequence of the interleaving of almost 3M single-location transactions alongside of the original 3.46M transactions of memcached. Furthermore, these transactions aborted *more frequently*, in order to reach the point where they requested serialization. Since the underlying TM algorithm in GCC uses eager locking and undo logs [14, 38], these aborts are expensive.

7   Handling Standard Library Calls

At this point, a large number of transactions still encounter mandatory serialization. In most cases, this serialization is due to calls to standard libraries. While Miletic et al. have shown that creating a transaction-safe standard library interface is a complex research problem [28], it is possible to employ ad-hoc solutions.

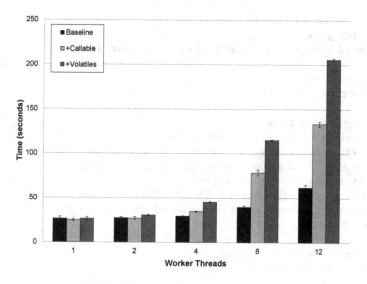

Fig. 3. Performance without volatile variables

Table 2. Frequency and cause of serialization for a 4-thread execution from Fig. 3

Branch	Transactions	In-Flight Switch	Start Serial	Abort Serial
Callable	3.46M	625K (18%)	1.25M (36%)	0
Volatiles	6.37M	559K (9%)	1.25M (20%)	66K

We observed three categories of unsafe code. First, there were calls to functions that take variable arguments. Variable argument functions are not currently supported, but we were able to create multiple versions of each variable-argument function, to match all possible parameter combinations that occurred in the program. Though tedious, it was sufficient to avoid serialization.

Secondly, there were functions that are not currently safe, but that are easy to implement in a safe manner. These include memcmp, memcpy, strlen, strncmp, strncpy, and strchr. By using the transaction_wrap attribute, it was possible to provide our own "safe but slow" versions of these functions (i.e., no inline assembly). Similarly, we provided our own realloc, which employed application-specific knowledge to know the size of the initial object without having to access allocator metadata.

Lastly, there were unsafe string functions. Instead of reimplementing these functions, at considerable developer cost, we combined transaction_pure with a lightweight marshaling scheme: First, we would write any input parameters to a stack object. Second, we would pass the address of the stack object to the original (unsafe) function, which we annotated as being pure. We could then marshal the return value back from the stack to the heap.

Figure 4 demonstrates the technique. We assume there exists a function called copy_mutate, which takes as input a constant string, and returns a new string. We also assume that transaction_wrap has been used to provide a safe version of

```
// Allow calls to unsafe copy_mutate()
transaction_pure
extern void copy_mutate(const char *in, char *out);

void example() {
  _transaction_atomic {
    ...
    // prepare buffers
    int size = strlen(shared_in_string);
    char *in = malloc(size), *out = malloc(size);
    // marshal data onto stack, using transactional reads
    for (int i = 0; i < size; ++i)
      in[i] = shared_in_string[i];
    // invoke function with non-shared parameters
    copy_mutate(in, out);
    // marshal data off of stack, using transactional writes
    for (int i = 0; i < size; ++i)
      shared_out_string[i] = out[i];
    ...
  }
}
```

Fig. 4. Example of marshaling shared memory onto the stack to invoke an unsafe library function

strlen. We begin by indicating that the function is pure, so that the compiler will allow its use from within a transaction.

Now that we have coaxed the compiler into calling the *un-instrumented* function from within a transaction, we must make sure that such calls both (a) have access to the correct data, even if there are speculative writes to that data by the current transaction, and (b) do not result in the function modifying the heap without proper instrumentation, or else a transaction rollback will result in partially-visible state.

For simplicity of presentation, we assume in Figure 4 that the output string is the same length as the input string. This being the case, the process is as follows: first, two temporary buffers are created, named in and out. Then, the input parameter to copy_mutate is copied to in, using transactional reads. GCC optimizes accesses to the stack [35] and captured memory [12], and thus while reads of shared_in_string will be instrumented, writes to in will not. When copy_mutate is called, it will see the input values via in, and it will write its output to out. Lastly, we copy out back to shared_out_string. This will use regular reads to the captured memory of out, but transactional writes, thereby ensuring that the final result can be rolled back.

This technique must be used with care. In addition to manually inspecting the compiler-generated code to ensure that accesses to in and out do not use compiler instrumentation, we must also be sure that the implementation of copy_mutate does not use transactions, access static variables, or in any other way risk introducing races if it is not instrumented.

While these techniques do not generalize, they succeeded in reducing the incidence of serialization: Table 3 shows that half of the transactions that previously started in serial mode were now able to run concurrently, and all transactions that previously

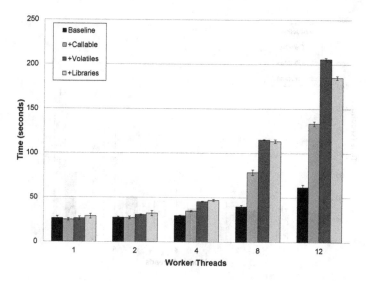

Fig. 5. Performance with safe library functions

Table 3. Frequency and cause of serialization for a 4-thread execution from Fig. 5

Branch	Transactions	In-Flight Switch	Start Serial	Abort Serial
Callable	3.46M	625K (18%)	1.25M (36%)	0
Volatiles	6.37M	559K (9%)	1.25M (20%)	66K
Safe Libs	8.21M	0	625K (8%)	10K

switched to serial mode during execution now could run to completion. Furthermore, the use of serialization for contention management decreased, largely because there were fewer cascading aborts to cause serialization. However, Figure 5 shows that performance increases only slightly: serialization is still hurting performance with 4 or more threads.

8 Delaying Transactional I/O

The remaining serialization in memcached can be traced to six functions: `event-_get_version`, `assert`, `sem_post`, `fprintf`, `perror`, and `abort`. Of these, `event_get_version` returns the version of libevent being used. We assumed that the version would not change during execution, and moved this code to a program initialization routine, so that the function was called once and the value cached.

Since the Draft C++ TM Specification implies that the underlying TM algorithm must be opaque [16], any call to `assert` or `abort` that ought to result in program termination is free to simply terminate the program, even if the call was made from within an active transaction: since all reads performed up to the point of the error are valid, it must be the case that in an equivalent non-transactional execution, the program would have also requested termination. To prevent the compiler from serializing, we

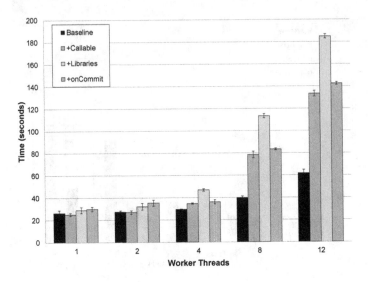

Fig. 6. Performance with delayed I/O via onCommit

Table 4. Frequency and cause of serialization for a 4-thread execution from Fig. 6

Branch	Transactions	In-Flight Switch	Start Serial	Abort Serial
Callable	3.46M	625K (18%)	1.25M (36%)	0
Safe Libs	8.21M	0	625K (8%)	10K
onCommit	8.13M	0	0	8K

marked these functions as pure. Any I/O they might induce (which would only involve string constants) is not a concern.

Of the remaining functions, none requires atomicity with respect to its critical section: the many-to-one communication with maintainer threads allows for the sem_post to run after the calling transaction commits; similarly, any non-fatal error messages can be printed after the corresponding transaction commits (especially since the I/O only involved constants). Consequently, we were able to delay these calls, by using GCC onCommit handlers.

Table 4 shows that with these changes, all mandatory serialization in memcached is eliminated. Only a small number of transactions serialize, and only for the sake of contention management. Furthermore, performance improves notably, though still only to the level seen in the original naive transactionalization.

9   Removing Bottlenecks in GCC

Even without any mandatory serialization, our transactional memcached performs much worse than locks, particularly at higher thread counts. Though we initially thought that contention management for the handful of serializing transactions might be to blame, ultimately we discovered that bottlenecks within GCC itself were causing the slowdown.

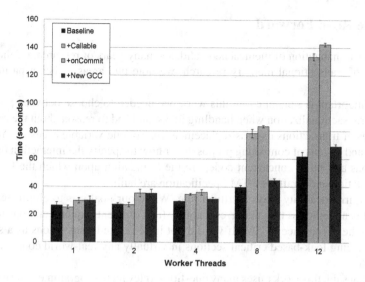

Fig. 7. Performance with a modified GCC TM implementation

GCC's TM implementation is complex, with support for dynamically changing the underlying TM algorithm, arbitrary arrival and departure of threads, and both relaxed and atomic transactions. It also assumes that serialization is unavoidable. To keep serialization fast, and to avoid complex coordination between serializing and non-serializing transactions, GCC uses a global readers/writer lock to coordinate transaction begin. Regular (abortable) transactions serve as readers, and serialized transactions are writers.

Our efforts move memcached outside of the common case: there are no transactions that require serialization, and during a long-running execution, the workload is expected to be sufficiently homogeneous that changing the TM algorithm would be unnecessary. By specializing GCC's TM to this case we were able to substantially improve performance.

Making this change necessitated an explicit contention manager. We experimented with various forms of exponential backoff [19], and also a modified form of serialization called "hourglass" [15, 22]. We also ran with no contention management whatsoever. We found backoff to be sensitive to its parameters, resulting in occasional steep performance drops. Otherwise, the various options all performed roughly on par with each other. Figure 7 shows performance with no contention manager.

In Figure 7, we see that removing support for serialization from GCC brings performance to within 10% of the original memcached performance. Unfortunately, our modifications to GCC could not be applied until after all serialization was eliminated; thus it is not possible to evaluate the impact of our changes to GCC on variants of memcached other than our last, which used onCommit handlers. Still, the result is impressive: TM performs almost as well as the original, well-tuned code. It does so without the benefit of a complex lock hierarchy for preventing non-conflicting operations from contending over locks, and without much TM-specific optimization.

10   The Road Forward

Our transactionalization of memcached validates many years of research. Of the many sub-areas of transactional memory research, we note two areas as being particularly relevant.

Most important is semantics: In this work, we needed to choose between privatization and transactionalization when handling locks, and had to reason about the ordering guarantees of transactions used as replacement for volatile variable accesses. Years of research, and dozens of competing proposals for how to specify the interaction between transactions and other concurrent code, are the foundation upon which the GCC TM implementation and Draft C++ TM Specification are built.

Second, irrevocability plays a critical role. While our goal was to eliminate serialization, it is nonetheless true that irrevocability (and efficient implementations thereof) is vital to the acceptance of TM. If we did not have relaxed transactions as a starting point, replacing lock-based critical sections in virtually any real-world code would be impossible.

With that said, this work raises many questions, relevant to programmers, researchers, and system designers. The most pressing is how a programmer ought to identify and eliminate sources of serialization. In this work, we took the position that since mandatory serialization of atomic transactions (e.g., due to unsafe code) is forbidden, that there was an implicit performance model offered by the specification. Our two-step approach was to first transactionalize the program with relaxed transactions, and then to replace relaxed transactions with atomic transactions. Whenever a transaction could not be made atomic, we used compiler errors to identify what line(s) of code were unsafe. We then categorized unsafe code, and systematically removed it. But is this appropriate? Should programmers think of relaxed transactions as a "last resort", and favor atomic transactions due to their static guarantee that they need not serialize? Would it be better to think of relaxed transactions as the default, reserve atomic transactions for situations in which explicit self-abort is desired, and build new tools to help identify causes of serialization?

A second question for programmers is when, and how, to optimize based on transactional features. There are two interesting examples in memcached. First, as reported by Yoo et al. [47], performance can improve through transaction coarsening. Coarsening can also remove bugs. Consider the code segments in Figure 8 and Figure 9. Both approximate code appear in memcached. In the first case, we see two tiny critical sections, one of which runs infrequently. While lock re-acquisition is usually cheap, the process of starting a transaction (especially a software transaction) is orders of magnitude more expensive. Thus coarsening to a single transaction that includes a condition should decrease latency. In the second case, the lack of atomicity between the first and second reads of volatile_var seems like a bug. Coarsening the two single-statement transactions into a larger transaction will both (a) reduce latency when the first condition is not true, and (b) prevent erroneous calls to action3.

Third, programmers may need to re-consider the use of techniques like reference counting, access a datum, and then decrement the reference count. With transactions, it might be possible to replace the modifications of the reference count with a simple read [11].

```
stats_lock.lock()
counter1.increment()
stats_lock.unlock()
if (unlikely_condition()) {
  stats_lock.lock()
  counter2.increment()
  stats_lock.unlock()
}
```

```
volatile int v
...
if (1 == transaction_read(v))
  action1()
else if (2 == transaction_read(v))
  action2()
else
  action3()
```

Fig. 8. Rapid re-locking

Fig. 9. Re-reading a volatile within a conditional

Lastly, maintainers of legacy code will need to decide when the benefits of simpler transactional program become compelling enough to accept a small performance penalty. In addition to removing a complex locking protocol, transactional memcached admits a simpler protocol for accepting new connections. Currently, every new connection must first query the `cache_lock` to determine whether a hash table resize is in-flight or not. In the transactional version, this small constant overhead on every transaction can be removed, eliminating a handshake that adds latency to every operation. Reference counts could also be simplified, as in [11]. When coupled with increased maintainability (handshaking spans two files and involves a libevent callback; the comments in the code suggest that some reference counts may not be right), this becomes yet another incentive to transactionalize.

For implementers of transactional systems, we also see many opportunities. If we take memcached as a proxy for real-world applications, then flag-based communication (like that in Figure 9) will be common, so adding optimizations for single-location transactions could have significant impact: it is likely that a thread checkpoint will not be needed. Furthermore, since the code in Figure 9 could easily be called from a transactional context, it would be worth evaluating heuristics for when and how to flatten nested transactions. It would certainly be a waste of cycles to use closed nesting to execute the individual accesses of `volatile_var`.

We also encourage implementers to begin the long and painful process of making standard libraries transaction-safe. While it is easy to dismiss this task as being relevant only to "legacy code", the truth is that no real-world application starts from scratch; every program is built upon a huge body of run-time libraries and data structures. To prevent programmers from using the unsafe techniques we used in Section 7, it will be necessary to transactionalize as much of the C++ standard template library and C standard library as possible. We are encouraged by recent work by Miletic et al. [28].

For researchers and language designers, we suggest a focus on providing simple syntax for advanced features. Allowing programmers to fine-tune contention management policies is an obvious first step, and our experience also suggests that some form of `onCommit` and `transaction_wrap` support will be useful, so long as the implementation can ensure safety. Inventing new mechanisms to allow relaxed transactions to serialize *without introducing bottlenecks*, and to permit condition synchronization as a language-level feature of TM, are also critical steps.

11   Conclusions

In this chapter, we applied transactional memory to replace locks with transactions in the memcached in-memory web cache. Our focus was analyzing the effectiveness of the Draft C++ TM Specification, and on providing recommendations to programmers and researchers.

Among our most significant findings is that the core research in transactional memory that has taken place over the last decade has, indeed, been fruitful. From semantics to compiler optimizations to irrevocability mechanisms, the contributions of researchers have had a profound impact on both the Draft C++ TM Specification, and its implementation in GCC. Without these contributions, this work would not have been possible. The performance of transactional memcached, and the opportunities to optimize and simplify that are afforded by TM, confirm that TM is poised to begin delivering on its promises.

Acknowledgments. We thank the TRANSACT 2013 and ASPLOS 2014 communities, for their feedback on previous versions of this work. We also thank Justin Gottschlich, Victor Luchangco, Jens Maurer, and Torvald Riegel for many helpful conversations about the Draft C++ TM Specification. This work was supported in part by the National Science Foundation under grants CNS-1016828, CCF-1218530, and CAREER-1253362.

Source Code

The source code for our transactional version of memcached is available at `https://github.com/mfs409/tm_memcached`.

References

[1] Adl-Tabatabai, A.R., Luchangco, V., Marathe, V.J., Moir, M., Narayanaswamy, R., Ni, Y., Nussbaum, D., Tian, X., Welc, A., Wu, P.: Exceptions and Transactions in C++. In: Proceedings of the First USENIX Workshop on Hot Topics in Parallelism, Berkeley, CA (March 2009)

[2] Adl-Tabatabai, A.R., Shpeisman, T., Gottschlich, J.: Draft Specification of Transactional Language Constructs for C++, version 1.1 (February 2012), http://justingottschlich.com/tm-specification-for-c-v-1-1/

[3] Adl-Tabatabai, A.R.: Shpeisman (Eds.), T.: Draft Specification of Transactional Language Constructs for C++, version 1.0 (August 2009), http://software.intel.com/file/21569

[4] Afek, Y., Drepper, U., Felber, P., Fetzer, C., Gramoli, V., Hohmuth, M., Riviere, E., Stenstrom, P., Unsal, O., Maldonado, W., Harmanci, D., Marlier, P., Diestelhorst, S., Pohlack, M., Cristal, A., Hur, I., Dragojevic, A., Guerraoui, R., Kapalka, M., Tomic, S., Korland, G., Shavit, N., Nowack, M., Riegel, T.: The velox transactional memory stack. In: Proceedings of the 43rd IEEE/ACM International Symposium on Microarchitecture, Atlanta, GA (December 2010)

[5] Ansari, M., Kotselidis, C., Jarvis, K., Lujan, M., Kirkham, C., Watson, I.: Lee-TM: A Non-trivial Benchmark for Transactional Memory. In: Proceedings of the International Conference on Algorithms and Architectures for Parallel Processing, Ayia Napa, Cyprus (June 2008)

[6] Attiya, H., Epstein, L., Shachnai, H., Tamir, T.: Transactional contention management as a non-clairvoyant scheduling problem. In: Proceedings of the 25th ACM Symposium on Principles of Distributed Computing, Denver, CO (August 2006)

[7] Carlstrom, B.D., McDonald, A., Chafi, H., Chung, J., Minh, C.C., Kozyrakis, C., Olukotun, K.: The Atomos Transactional Programming Language. In: Proceedings of the 27th ACM Conference on Programming Language Design and Implementation, Ottawa, ON (June 2006)

[8] Charles, P., Donawa, C., Ebcioglu, K., Grothoff, C., Kielstra, A., von Praun, C., Saraswat, V., Sarkar, V.: X10: An Object-Oriented Approach to Non-Uniform Cluster Computing. In: Proceedings of the 20th ACM Conference on Object-Oriented Programming, Systems, Languages, and Applications, San Diego, CA (October 2005)

[9] Dalessandro, L., Spear, M., Scott, M.L.: NOrec: Streamlining STM by Abolishing Ownership Records. In: Proceedings of the 15th ACM Symposium on Principles and Practice of Parallel Programming, Bangalore, India (January 2010)

[10] Dice, D., Shavit, N.: TLRW: Return of the Read-Write Lock. In: Proceedings of the 22nd ACM Symposium on Parallelism in Algorithms and Architectures, Santorini, Greece (June 2010)

[11] Dragojevic, A., Herlihy, M., Lev, Y., Moir, M.: On The Power of Hardware Transactional Memory to Simplify Memory Management. In: Proceedings of the 30th ACM Symposium on Principles of Distributed Computing, San Jose, CA (June 2011)

[12] Dragojevic, A., Ni, Y., Adl-Tabatabai, A.R.: Optimizing Transactions for Captured Memory. In: Proceedings of the 21st ACM Symposium on Parallelism in Algorithms and Architectures, Calgary, AB, Canada (August 2009)

[13] Dudnik, P., Swift, M.M.: Condition Variables and Transactional Memory: Problem or Opportunity? In: Proceedings of the 4th ACM SIGPLAN Workshop on Transactional Computing, Raleigh, NC (February 2009)

[14] Felber, P., Fetzer, C., Riegel, T.: Dynamic Performance Tuning of Word-Based Software Transactional Memory. In: Proceedings of the 13th ACM Symposium on Principles and Practice of Parallel Programming, Salt Lake City, UT (February 2008)

[15] Fich, F.E., Luchangco, V., Moir, M., Shavit, N.: Obstruction-free Algorithms Can Be Practically Wait-free. In: Proceedings of the 19th International Symposium on Distributed Computing, Cracow, Poland (September 2005)

[16] Guerraoui, R., Kapalka, M.: On the Correctness of Transactional Memory. In: Proceedings of the 13th ACM Symposium on Principles and Practice of Parallel Programming, Salt Lake City, UT (February 2008)

[17] Guerraoui, R., Kapalka, M., Vitek, J.: STMBench7: A Benchmark for Software Transactional Memory. In: Proceedings of the EuroSys 2007 Conference, Lisbon, Portugal (March 2007)

[18] Harris, T., Marlow, S., Peyton Jones, S., Herlihy, M.: Composable Memory Transactions. In: Proceedings of the 10th ACM Symposium on Principles and Practice of Parallel Programming, Chicago, IL (June 2005)

[19] Herlihy, M.P., Luchangco, V., Moir, M., Scherer III, W.N.: Software Transactional Memory for Dynamic-sized Data Structures. In: Proceedings of the 22nd ACM Symposium on Principles of Distributed Computing, Boston, MA (July 2003)

[20] Hong, S., Oguntebi, T., Casper, J., Bronson, N., Kozyrakis, C., Olukotun, K.: Eigenbench: A Simple Exploration Tool for Orthogonal TM Characteristics. In: Proceedings of the IEEE International Symposium on Workload Characterization, Atlanta, GA (December 2010)

[21] Kestor, G., Stipic, S., Unsal, O., Cristal, A., Valero, M.: RMS-TM: A Transactional Memory Benchmark for Recognition, Mining and Synthesis Applications. In: Proceedings of the 4th ACM SIGPLAN Workshop on Transactional Computing, Raleigh, NC (February 2009)

[22] Liu, Y., Spear, M.: Toxic Transactions. In: Proceedings of the 6th ACM SIGPLAN Workshop on Transactional Computing, San Jose, CA (June 2011)

[23] Luchangco, V., Marathe, V.: Transaction Communicators: Enabling Cooperation Among Concurrent Transactions. In: Proceedings of the 16th ACM Symposium on Principles and Practice of Parallel Programming, San Antonio, TX (February 2011)

[24] Lupei, D., Simion, B., Pinto, D., Misler, M., Burcea, M., Krick, W., Amza, C.: Transactional Memory Support for Scalable and Transparent Parallelization of Multiplayer Games. In: Proceedings of the EuroSys2010 Conference, Paris, France (April 2010)

[25] Mathewson, N., Provos, N.: Libevent – An Event Notification Library (2011–2013), http://libevent.org/

[26] McKenney, P.E., Michael, M.M., Walpole, J.: Why The Grass Not Be Greener On The Other Side: A Comparison of Locking vs. Transactional Memory. In: Proceedings of the 4th ACM SIGOPS Workshop on Programming Languages and Operating Systems, Stevenson, WA (October 2007)

[27] Menon, V., Balensiefer, S., Shpeisman, T., Adl-Tabatabai, A.R., Hudson, R., Saha, B., Welc, A.: Practical Weak-Atomicity Semantics for Java STM. In: Proceedings of the 20th ACM Symposium on Parallelism in Algorithms and Architectures, Munich, Germany (June 2008)

[28] Miletic, N., Smiljkovic, V., Perfumo, C., Harris, T., Cristal, A., Hur, I., Unsal, O., Valero, M.: Transactification of a Real-World System Library. In: Proceedings of the 5th ACM SIGPLAN Workshop on Transactional Computing, Paris, France (April 2010)

[29] Minh, C.C., Chung, J., Kozyrakis, C., Olukotun, K.: STAMP: Stanford Transactional Applications for Multi-processing. In: Proceedings of the IEEE International Symposium on Workload Characterization, Seattle, WA (September 2008)

[30] Moravan, M., Bobba, J., Moore, K., Yen, L., Hill, M., Liblit, B., Swift, M., Wood, D.: Supporting Nested Transactional Memory in LogTM. In: Proceedings of the 12th International Conference on Architectural Support for Programming Languages and Operating Systems, San Jose, CA (October 2006)

[31] Ni, Y., Welc, A., Adl-Tabatabai, A.R., Bach, M., Berkowits, S., Cownie, J., Geva, R., Kozhukow, S., Narayanaswamy, R., Olivier, J., Preis, S., Saha, B., Tal, A., Tian, X.: Design and Implementation of Transactional Constructs for C/C++. In: Proceedings of the 23rd ACM Conference on Object Oriented Programming, Systems, Languages, and Applications, Nashville, TN (October 2008)

[32] Pankratius, V., Adl-Tabatabai, A.R.: A Study of Transactional Memory vs. Locks in Practice. In: Proceedings of the 23rd ACM Symposium on Parallelism in Algorithms and Architectures, San Jose, CA (June 2011)

[33] Poettering, L.: Measuring Lock Contention (2009–2013), http://0pointer.de/blog/projects/mutrace.html

[34] Pohlack, M., Diestelhorst, S.: From Lightweight Hardware Transactional Memory to Lightweight Lock Elision. In: Proceedings of the 6th ACM SIGPLAN Workshop on Transactional Computing, San Jose, CA (June 2011)

[35] Riegel, T., Fetzer, C., Felber, P.: Automatic Data Partitioning in Software Transactional Memories. In: Proceedings of the 20th ACM Symposium on Parallelism in Algorithms and Architectures, Munich, Germany (June 2008)

[36] Rossbach, C., Hofmann, O., Witchel, E.: Is Transactional Programming Really Easier? In: Proceedings of the 15th ACM Symposium on Principles and Practice of Parallel Programming, Bangalore, India (January 2010)

[37] Ruan, W., Vyas, T., Liu, Y., Spear, M.: Transactionalizing Legacy Code: An Experience Report Using GCC and Memcached. In: Proceedings of the 19th International Conference on Architectural Support for Programming Languages and Operating Systems, Salt Lake City, UT (March 2014)

[38] Saha, B., Adl-Tabatabai, A.R., Hudson, R.L., Minh, C.C., Hertzberg, B.: McRT-STM: A High Performance Software Transactional Memory System For A Multi-Core Runtime. In: Proceedings of the 11th ACM Symposium on Principles and Practice of Parallel Programming, New York, NY (March 2006)

[39] Scherer III, W.N., Scott, M.L.: Advanced Contention Management for Dynamic Software Transactional Memory. In: Proceedings of the 24th ACM Symposium on Principles of Distributed Computing, Las Vegas, NV (July 2005)

[40] Spear, M.: Lightweight, Robust Adaptivity for Software Transactional Memory. In: Proceedings of the 22nd ACM Symposium on Parallelism in Algorithms and Architectures, Santorini, Greece (June 2010)

[41] Spear, M., Dalessandro, L., Marathe, V.J., Scott, M.L.: A Comprehensive Strategy for Contention Management in Software Transactional Memory. In: Proceedings of the 14th ACM Symposium on Principles and Practice of Parallel Programming, Raleigh, NC (February 2009)

[42] Spear, M., Marathe, V., Dalessandro, L., Scott, M.: Privatization Techniques for Software Transactional Memory (POSTER). In: Proceedings of the 26th ACM Symposium on Principles of Distributed Computing, Portland, OR (August 2007)

[43] Spear, M., Michael, M.M., von Praun, C.: RingSTM: Scalable Transactions with a Single Atomic Instruction. In: Proceedings of the 20th ACM Symposium on Parallelism in Algorithms and Architectures, Munich, Germany (June 2008)

[44] Spear, M., Silverman, M., Dalessandro, L., Michael, M.M., Scott, M.L.: Implementing and Exploiting Inevitability in Software Transactional Memory. In: Proceedings of the 37th International Conference on Parallel Processing, Portland, OR (September 2008)

[45] Wang, C., Liu, Y., Spear, M.: Transaction-Friendly Condition Variables. In: Proceedings of the 26th ACM Symposium on Parallelism in Algorithms and Architectures, Prague, Czech Republic (June 2014)

[46] Welc, A., Saha, B., Adl-Tabatabai, A.R.: Irrevocable Transactions and their Applications. In: Proceedings of the 20th ACM Symposium on Parallelism in Algorithms and Architectures, Munich, Germany (June 2008)

[47] Yoo, R., Hughes, C., Lai, K., Rajwar, R.: Performance Evaluation of Intel Transactional Synchronization Extensions for High Performance Computing. In: Proceedings of the International Conference for High Performance Computing, Networking, Storage and Analysis, Denver, CO (November 2013)

[48] Yoo, R., Lee, H.H.: Adaptive Transaction Scheduling for Transactional Memory Systems. In: Proceedings of the 20th ACM Symposium on Parallelism in Algorithms and Architectures, Munich, Germany (June 2008)

[49] Yoo, R., Ni, Y., Welc, A., Saha, B., Adl-Tabatabai, A.R., Lee, H.H.: Kicking the Tires of Software Transactional Memory: Why the Going Gets Tough. In: Proceedings of the 20th ACM Symposium on Parallelism in Algorithms and Architectures, Munich, Germany (June 2008)

[50] Zyulkyarov, F., Gajinov, V., Unsal, O., Cristal, A., Ayguade, E., Harris, T., Valero, M.: Atomic Quake: Using Transactional Memory in an Interactive Multiplayer Game Server. In: Proceedings of the 14th ACM Symposium on Principles and Practice of Parallel Programming, Raleigh, NC (February 2009)

Author Index

Attiya, Hagit   50, 72, 367
Avni, Hillel   228

Barreto, João   192
Bushkov, Victor   32

Ciciani, Bruno   395
Cohen, Ernie   283
Couceiro, Maria   418
Cristal, Adrian   283

Dias, Ricardo J.   166
Didona, Diego   418
Di Sanzo, Pierangelo   395
Dolev, Shlomi   228
Dziuma, Dmytro   3

Elmas, Tayfun   283

Fatourou, Panagiota   3, 72, 101
Felber, Pascal   245
Fetzer, Christof   245
Filipe, Ricardo   192

Gramoli, Vincent   245, 367
Guerraoui, Rachid   32
Gutierrez, Eladio   127

Hans, Sandeep   50
Harmanci, Derin   245
Hendler, Danny   213

Iaremko, Mykhailo   101

Kanellou, Eleni   3, 101
Keidar, Idit   150
Kestor, Gokcen   283
Kobus, Tadeusz   309
Kokociński, Maciej   309
Kosmas, Eleftherios   101, 228
Kuru, Ismail   283
Kuznetsov, Petr   50

Liu, Yujie   449
Lourenço, João M.   166

Milani, Alessia   367
Mutluergil, Suha Orhun   283

Nowack, Martin   245

Ozkan, Burcu Kulahcioglu   283

Palmieri, Roberto   341
Pellegrini, Alessandro   395
Peluso, Sebastiano   341
Perelman, Dmitri   150
Plata, Oscar   127

Quaglia, Francesco   395
Quislant, Ricardo   127

Ravi, Srivatsan   50
Ravindran, Binoy   341
Rodrigues, Luís   418
Romano, Paolo   418
Ruan, Wenjia   449
Rughetti, Diego   395

Spear, Michael   449
Suissa-Peleg, Adi   213

Tasiran, Serdar   283

Unsal, Osman   268, 283

Vale, Tiago M.   166
Vyas, Trilok   449

Wojciechowski, Paweł T.   309

Yalcin, Gulay   268

Zapata, Emilio L.   127

Author Index